ERISA
FACTS

Frank J. Bitzer, J.D., CEBS and Nicholas W. Ferrigno, Jr., J.D., CLU, ChFC

2002

The
NATIONAL
UNDERWRITER
Company
PROFESSIONAL PUBLISHING GROUP

P.O. Box 14367 · Cincinnati, Ohio 45250-0367 · 1-800-543-0874 · www.nationalunderwriter.com

2002 Edition

ISBN: 0-87218-610-5

Printed in U.S.A.

DEDICATION

Together we dedicate this book to the Glory of God for His goodness and grace.

Frank dedicates this edition to the memory of his friend, classmate and teammate — Douglas MacMillan Cherry (April 2, 1963 - September 11, 2001) — and to the other innocent victims of the terrorist attacks on that terrible day.

He also dedicates this edition to Doug's children Emma, Isabel and Jack. To them, I humbly offer the following advice:

> The best way to honor your father is to live a life that is filled with faith, love, joy and wonder.

May God's blessings be upon all of you.

Frank also dedicates this edition to his family for being the joy in his life.

Nick dedicates this book to the blessings in his life, Rhonda, Brittany, and Alexis, for their continued love, patience, support, and understanding.

ACKNOWLEDGMENT

We would like to thank our editor, Deborah A. Miner, J.D., CLU, ChFC, associate editors, April K. Caudill, J.D., CLU, ChFC, Deborah Price Rambo, J.D., assistant editors, Joseph F. Stenken, J.D., CLU, ChFC, Sonya E. King, J.D., LL.M., and all the staff at The National Underwriter Company for their assistance, without whose efforts *ERISA Facts* would not be a reality.

We also would like to acknowledge, and extend our sincere gratitude to, the following people:

Bill Mauch for providing Frank the opportunity to expand and build upon his career in employee benefits, and Guy J. Settipane, Esq. for inspiring Nick to enter the practice of law.

FOREWORD

As with any other year, 2001 brought forth a great deal of change in the employee benefits field. We've seen an entirely new tax act, new regulations and countless court opinions, exemptions and private rulings, all of which have impacted the industry. These issues have been exhaustively researched and our analysis of changes pertinent to this text are discussed in this edition (current through early February, 2002).

It is our intention that the analysis and practical information detailed in this text will become a valuable resource for plan sponsors and service providers who have assumed the obligation to manage plans and assets appropriately in this ever-changing environment. This includes practical insight into recently stepped up DOL enforcement activities based upon our experience within the DOL. We have attempted to put together a clear, concise "soup to nuts" resource on ERISA that is easy to read and comprehend.

This year promises sweeping changes in the industry as a result of the collapse of the Enron 401(k) plan. We anticipate major activity with respect to fiduciary obligations, plan accounting rules, account portability and other items being brought to the forefront as this situation unfolds. We will work hard to update this text annually for our subscribers so that they will have the most current, accurate and practical analysis of ERISA, and the rulings and regulations which affect them.

Frank J. Bitzer, Esq., CEBS
Nicholas W. Ferrigno, Jr., Esq.

ABOUT THE AUTHORS

FRANK J. BITZER, ESQ., CEBS is Manager of Operations for Phoenix Research, Inc. (www.hrliability.com). He also offers his services as an ERISA Advisor with Quantilex, LLP of Brookfield, Wisconsin (www.Quantilex.com), an internet-based business consulting consortium. He has thirteen years of experience in the field of employee benefits. Frank has also served as the Manager of Pension Compliance Services for one of the nation's top 25 mutual life insurance companies.

Mr. Bitzer is a featured speaker of The National Underwriter Company Speakers Bureau and has made presentations on ERISA fiduciary matters to organizations across the United States. He is also a contributor of articles to the *Journal of Pension and Benefits*, *Spencer's Research Reports*, *The Pension Actuary*, *Pension Plan Administrator* and other publications. He is a member of the American Society of Pension Actuaries, Government Affairs Committee, Sub-Committee on Department of Labor Enforcement; the International Foundation of Employee Benefit Plans and the Cincinnati Bar Association-Employee Benefits Committee.

In addition to this text, Frank is also a co-author of *Benefits Facts*, and *The Insider's Guide to DOL Plan Audits*, both published by The National Underwriter Financial Services Publishing Company (www.nuco.com).

NICHOLAS W. FERRIGNO, JR., ESQ, is Member of the law firm of Greenebaum Doll & McDonald PLLC with offices in Covington, Frankfort, Lexington, and Louisville, Kentucky; Nashville, Tennessee; Cincinnati, Ohio; and Washington, D.C. Mr. Ferrigno received his B.S. (Finance) from the University of Rhode Island and Juris Doctorate (cum laude) from the Salmon P. Chase College of Law, Northern Kentucky University. Mr. Ferrigno has particular experience in ERISA fiduciary and compliance matters, having previously served with the U.S. Department of Labor - Pension and Welfare Benefits Administration. He is a member of the American Society of Pension Actuaries, Government Affairs Committee, Sub-Committee on Department of Labor Enforcement. Mr. Ferrigno also is a featured speaker with The National Underwriter Company Speakers Bureau and contributor of articles to the *Journal of Pension and Benefits*, *The Pension Actuary*, *Pension Plan Administrator*, and other publications. Mr. Ferrigno is resident in the Covington, Kentucky office of Greenebaum Doll & McDonald PLLC.

TABLE OF CONTENTS

Appendices and Tables

ABBREVIATIONS

BNA	Bureau of National Affairs
CA or — Cir.	United States Court of Appeals
CB	Cumulative Bulletin of Internal Revenue Service
COBRA	Consolidated Omnibus Budget Reconciliation Act of 1985
DC	District Court
DOL	Department of Labor
DOL Adv. Op.	Department of Labor Advisory Opinion
EGTRRA 2001	Economic Growth and Tax Relief Reconciliation Act of 2001
ERISA	Employee Retirement Income Security Act of 1974
Fed. Reg.	Federal Register
FERSA	Federal Employees' Retirement System Act of 1986
F.2d	Federal Reporter, second series (later decisions of U.S. Court of Appeals to Mid-1993)
F.3rd	Federal Reporter, third series (decisions of U.S. Court of Appeals since Mid-1993)
F. Supp.	Federal Supplement (decisions of U.S. District Courts)
FERSA	Federal Employees Retirement System Act
FMLA	Family and Medical Leave Act of 1993
GCM	General Counsel Memorandum (IRS)
HIPAA '96	Health Insurance Portability and Accountability Act
IB	Interpretive Bulletin
IRB	Internal Revenue Bulletin of Internal Revenue Service
IRC	Internal Revenue Code
IRS	Internal Revenue Service
Let. Rul.	Letter Ruling (issued by IRS)
NMHPA	Newborns' and Mothers' Health Protection Act of 1996
PBGC	Pension Benefit Guaranty Corporation
PBGC Adv. Op.	Pension Benefit Guaranty Corporation Advisory Opinion
PHS Act	Public Health Service Act
P.L.	Public Law
PTE	Prohibited Transaction Exemption
Prop. Reg.	Proposed Regulation
PWBA	Pension and Welfare Benefits Administration
Reg.	Labor Regulation
Rev. Proc.	Revenue Procedure (issued by IRS)
SBJPA '96	Small Business Job Protection Act of 1996
TC	Tax Court (official reports)
TRA	Tax Reform Act of (year of enactment)
TRA '97	Taxpayer Relief Act of 1997
Treas. Reg.	Regulation (final)
US	United States Supreme Court decisions
USDL	United States Department of Labor News Release
USERRA	Uniformed Services Employment and Reemployment Rights Act of 1994
WPPDA	Welfare and Pension Plans Disclosure Act

CHAPTER I

ESTABLISHMENT AND ADMINISTRATION

BASIC ERISA REQUIREMENTS

1. What employee benefit plans are subject to ERISA?

ERISA Sections 3(1), 3(2) and 3(3) provide that for purposes of ERISA coverage, an "employee benefit plan" means an employee welfare benefit plan or an employee pension plan which is established or maintained by an employer or an employee organization for the purpose of providing benefits to participants and their beneficiaries.

An "employee welfare benefit plan" is one which has been established for the provision of:

1.   Medical, surgical, or hospital care or benefits;

2.   Benefits in the event of sickness, accident, disability, death or unemployment;

3.   Vacation benefits, apprenticeship, or other training programs;

4.   Day care centers, scholarship funds, or prepaid legal services; or

5.   Any benefit described under Section 302(c) of the Labor Management Relations Act of 1947 (excluding pensions on retirement or death, and insurance to provide for such pensions).

An "employee pension benefit plan" is any plan, fund or program established for the provision of retirement income to employees or that results in the deferral of income by employees for periods extending to the termination of covered employment and beyond, regardless of the method of calculating the contribution made to the plan, the method of calculating the benefits under the plan, or the method of distributing benefits from the plan.

An "employer" is any person acting directly as an employer, or indirectly in the interest of an employer, in relation to an employee benefit plan, and includes a group or association of employers acting for an employer in such capacity. ERISA Sec. 3(5). An "employee organization" is any labor union or any organization of any kind, or any agency or employee representation committee, association, group, or plan, in which employees participate and which exists for the purpose, in whole or part, of dealing with employers concerning an employee benefit plan. ERISA Sec. 3(4).

2002 ERISA Facts

All plans that satisfy the definition of an ERISA covered plan are subject to the fiduciary rules set forth in ERISA. ERISA Section 402(a)(1) requires that all plans subject to ERISA provide for one or more named fiduciaries who jointly and severally have authority to control and manage the administration and operation of the plan.

2. Must a plan be in writing in order to be subject to ERISA?

Yes and no. ERISA requires that every employee benefit plan be established and maintained pursuant to a written instrument that provides for the identification of named fiduciaries with authority to manage and control plan operations, and must provide procedures for funding, amending, allocating responsibilities for administration and establishing a basis on which payments will be made from the plan. ERISA Secs. 402(a), 402(b). However, the courts have ruled that certain unwritten policies of employers that provide for pension benefits or welfare benefits have been established plans subject to ERISA.

Court decisions have held that an employee benefit plan will be subject to ERISA if, from the surrounding circumstances, it is reasonable for a person to ascertain the intended benefits, the procedures for obtaining those benefits, the source of funding and the intended beneficiaries. *Scott v. Gulf Oil Corp.*, 754 F.2d 1499 (9th Cir. 1985); *Donovan v. Dillingham*, 688 F.2d 1367 (11th Cir. 1982); *Elmore v. Cone Mills Corp.*, 23 F.3d 855 (4th Cir. 1994). Although a failure to establish a plan in writing is a violation of ERISA, it will not prevent the plan from being subject to the provisions of ERISA. *Adams v. Avondale Indus., Inc.*, 905 F.2d 943 (6th Cir. 1990). The mere decision to offer an extension of benefits will subject a plan to ERISA. *Donovan v. Dillingham*, 688 F.2d 1367 (11th Cir. 1982); *James v. National Business Sys.*, 924 F.2d 718 (7th Cir. 1991).

3. What are the additional requirements for establishing ERISA covered plans?

In addition to the requirement that the plan be in writing and provide for the identification of named fiduciaries, ERISA Section 402(b) requires every employee benefit plan to:

1. Provide a procedure for establishing and carrying out a funding policy and method consistent with the objectives of the plan and the requirements of ERISA;

2. Describe any procedure under the plan for the allocation of responsibilities for the operation and administration of the plan;

3. Provide for a procedure for amending such plan, and for identifying persons who have authority to amend the plan; and

4. Specify the basis on which payments are made to and from the plan.

ERISA Section 405(c)(1) also provides that the plan may expressly provide for procedures for allocating fiduciary responsibilities (other than trustee responsibilities) among named fiduciaries, and for named fiduciaries to designate persons other than named fiduciaries to carry out fiduciary responsibilities (other than trustee responsibilities) under the plan. "Trustee responsibility" means any responsibility provided in the plan's trust instrument (see Q 4) to manage or control the assets of the plan, other than a power under the trust instrument of a named fiduciary to appoint an investment manager in accordance with the provisions of ERISA Section 402(c)(3). ERISA Sec. 405(c)(3). See Q 317 through Q 330 for details of investment manager issues.

The employee benefit plan may provide that any person or group of persons may serve in more than one fiduciary capacity. It may also provide that a named fiduciary may employ one or more persons to render advice with regard to any responsibility such fiduciary has under the plan; or that a person who is a named fiduciary may appoint an investment manager or more than one person to manage (including the power to acquire and dispose of) any assets of the plan. ERISA Secs. 402(c)(1), 402(c)(2), 402(c)(3).

4. What are the trust requirements in establishing an ERISA covered plan?

ERISA Section 403 provides that all assets of an employee benefit plan must be held in trust by one or more trustees. Such trustees must either be named in the trust instrument or in the plan's governing documents or appointed by a named fiduciary. Upon acceptance of being named or appointed, the trustee or trustees must have exclusive authority and discretion to manage and control the assets of the plan, except to the extent that:

1.   The plan expressly provides that such trustees are subject to the direction of a named fiduciary who is not a trustee, in which case the trustees must be subject to proper directions of such fiduciary that are made in accordance with the terms of the plan and are in accordance with the provisions of ERISA; or

2.   Authority to manage, acquire, or dispose of assets of the plan is delegated to one or more investment managers (in accordance with the provisions of ERISA Section 402(c)(3)).

The Conference Committee Reports to ERISA (P.L. 93-406) state that a plan may provide for an investment committee to manage the plan's investments, so long as all members of the investment committee are named fiduciaries. The Committee Reports also provide that a trustee is not liable for the acts of a properly appointed investment manager. H.R. Conf. Rep. No. 93-1280, 93rd Cong., 2nd Sess., 323 (1974) (ERISA Conference Report). See Chapter IV for details of the fiduciary responsibility of investment managers.

ERISA Section 403(b) holds that the trust requirements do not apply:

1. To any assets of a plan that consist of insurance contracts or policies issued by an insurance company qualified to do business in a state;

2. To any assets of such an insurance company or any assets of a plan that are held by such an insurance company;

3. To a plan in which some or all of the participants are self-employed (within the definition of IRC Section 401(c)(1)), or which consists of one or more individual retirement accounts (as described under IRC Section 408), to the extent that such plan's assets are held in one or more custodial accounts which are qualified under the Code;

4. To a plan which the Secretary of Labor has exempted from the trust requirements and which is not subject to the participation, vesting, funding and plan termination insurance provisions of ERISA; or

5. To a tax sheltered annuity contract established under the provisions of IRC Section 403(b) to the extent the assets are held in one or more custodial accounts.

5. What are the rules that govern trusts?

Generally, all assets of an employee benefit plan must be held in trust by one or more trustees pursuant to a written trust instrument. Labor Reg. §2550.403a-1. Trustees must either be named in the trust instrument or in the plan documents, or appointed by a named fiduciary. Upon acceptance of being named or appointed, such trustees must have exclusive authority and discretion to manage and control the assets of the plan, except to the extent that:

1. The plan instrument or the trust instrument expressly provides that the trustees are subject to the direction of a named fiduciary who is not a trustee, in which case the trustees shall be subject to the proper instructions of the named fiduciary; or

2. Authority to manage, acquire or dispose of plan assets is delegated to one or more investment managers. Labor Reg. §2550.403a-1(c).

The written trust requirement will not be violated merely because securities of a plan are held in the name of a nominee or in street name, provided such securities are held on behalf of the plan by:

1. A bank or trust company that is subject to the supervision of the United States or of any state, or nominee of such bank or trust company;

2.   A broker-dealer registered under the Securities Exchange Act of 1934, or a nominee of such broker-dealer; or

3.   A "clearing agency" as defined in Section 3(a)(23) of the Securities Exchange Act of 1934, or its nominee. Labor Reg. §2550.403a-1(b).

The trust requirement will also be satisfied if a corporation described under IRC Section 501(c)(3) holds real property on behalf of the plan if all stock of the corporation is held in trust on behalf of the plan. Labor Reg. §2550.403a-1(b)(2).

Where plan assets are invested in an entity such as a corporation or a partnership, the trust requirement is satisfied if the indicia of ownership (certificate or contract) of the plan's interest in the entity are held in trust on behalf of the plan. Labor Reg. §2550.403a-1(b)(3).

6. Are plans which are not established by an employer or employee organization subject to ERISA?

No. ERISA Section 4(a) states that ERISA will not apply to any employee benefit plan which is not established or maintained by any employer engaged in commerce or any industry or activity affecting commerce, or by an employee organization or organizations representing employees engaged in commerce or any industry or activity affecting commerce, or both.

7. Which employee benefit plans does ERISA expressly exclude from coverage?

ERISA Section 4(b) establishes that the provisions of ERISA do not apply to any employee benefit plan if:

1.   The plan is a governmental plan (as defined under ERISA Section 3(32));

2.   It is a church plan (as defined in ERISA Section 3(33)) which has not made an IRC Section 410(d) election to have participation, funding and vesting provisions apply;

3.   It is maintained solely for the purpose of complying with applicable workmen's compensation laws or unemployment compensation laws or disability insurance laws;

4.   It is maintained outside of the United States primarily for the benefit of persons substantially all of whom are nonresident aliens; or

5. The plan is an unfunded excess benefit plan (as described under ERISA Section 3(36), which provides benefits for certain employees in excess of the limitations on contributions and benefits imposed by IRC Section 415).

8. What welfare benefit plans are not subject to ERISA?

The following welfare benefit arrangements are not subject to the general fiduciary provisions of ERISA:

1. Payroll practices which are established by an employer and which provide for payment by an employer to employees on account of overtime pay, shift premiums, holiday premiums or weekend premiums, sick pay, vacation pay, jury duty pay and pay while on leave for military service (Labor Reg. §2510.3-1(b));

2. The maintenance of on-premises facilities such as recreation, dining, or medical/first aid for the treatment of work-related injuries or illness occurring during normal work hours, or other facilities (excluding day care centers) for use by employees (Labor Reg. §2510.3-1(c));

3. Programs for the provision of holiday gifts such as turkeys or hams (Labor Reg. §2510.3-1(d));

4. Sales to employees of articles or commodities (whether or not they are offered at below market prices) of the kind the employer offers for sale in the regular course of business (Labor Reg. §2510.3-1(e));

5. Hiring halls maintained by one or more employers, employee organizations or both (Labor Reg. §2510.3-1(f));

6. Remembrance funds under which contributions are made to provide remembrances such as flowers, small gifts or obituary notices on occasion of the illness, hospitalization or death of an employee (Labor Reg. §2510.3-1(g));

7. Strike funds maintained by an employee organization to provide payment to its members during strikes and for related purposes (Labor Reg. §2510.3-1(h));

8. Industry advancement programs which have no employee participants and do not provide benefits, regardless of whether the program serves as a conduit through which funds or other assets are

channeled to employee benefit plans subject to ERISA (Labor Reg. §2510.3-1(i)); and

9.   Unfunded scholarship programs, including tuition and education reimbursement programs, under which payments are made solely from the general assets of an employer or employee organization (Labor Reg. §2510.3-1(k)).

9. What type of group or group type insurance programs are expressly excluded from ERISA coverage?

For purposes of ERISA coverage, the term "employee welfare benefit plan" does not include a group or group type employee pay-all insurance program offered by an insurer to employees or members of an employee organization, under which:

1.   No contributions are made by the employer or employee organization;

2.   Participation in the program is completely voluntary for employees or members;

3.   The sole functions of the employer or employee organization with respect to the program are, without endorsing the program, to permit the insurer to publicize the program to employees or members, to collect premiums through payroll deductions or dues checkoffs and to remit them to the insurer; and

4.   The employer or employee organization receives no consideration in the form of cash or otherwise in connection with the program, other than reasonable compensation, excluding any profit, for administrative services actually rendered in connection with payroll deductions or dues checkoffs. Labor Reg. §2510.3-1(j).

PRACTITIONER'S POINTER

Such employers who pay all of an insurance program may, unintentionally, find themselves subject to ERISA where the employer or employee organization that has offered the program inadvertently endorses it (e.g., advising employees that the program offers a "valuable" extension of existing insurance coverage, or the marketing pamphlets for the program contain the employer or employee organization's logos). *Hansen v. Continental Ins. Co.*, 940 F.2d 971 (5th Cir. 1991).

10. Which employee benefit pension plans are expressly excluded from ERISA coverage?

The regulations provide that the following employer sponsored plans will not be deemed employee benefit pension plans for purposes of ERISA coverage:

1. Severance pay plans that provide for the payment of severance benefits on account of termination of an employee's service so long as:

    a) such payments are not contingent, directly or indirectly, upon the employee's retiring,

    b) the total amount of such payments does not exceed the equivalent of twice the employee's annual compensation during the year immediately preceding the termination of his service, and

    c) all such payments to any employee are completed (Labor Reg. §2510.3-2(b));

2. Bonus programs that provide payments made by an employer to some or all of its employees as bonuses for work performed (unless such payments are systematically deferred to the termination of covered employment or beyond, so as to provide retirement income to employees)(Labor Reg. §2510.3-2(c)); and

3. Individual retirement accounts established under IRC Section 408(a) and individual retirement annuities established under IRC Section 408(b) provided that there are no employer contributions, employee participation is voluntary and the sole involvement of the employer or employee organization is without endorsement to permit the sponsor to publicize the availability of the program, to collect contributions through payroll deduction or dues checkoffs and for which the employer or employee organization receives no consideration from the sponsor other than reimbursement for services rendered in connection with payroll deductions or dues checkoffs (Labor Reg. §2510.3-2(d)).

11. What is the safe harbor that permits an employer to establish an IRA payroll deduction program that is not subject to ERISA?

The DOL has issued an Interpretive Bulletin that sets forth a safe harbor under which an employer may establish a payroll deduction program to fund employee IRAs without the program being subject to the employee benefit provisions of ERISA. The safe harbor will exempt a payroll deduction IRA program from ERISA if the program satisfies the following requirements:

1. In all communications to employees regarding the program, the employer must be neutral. The employer must make clear that it is

involved in the program only to the extent that it is collecting the payroll deductions and remitting them to the IRA sponsor.

2. The employer may limit the number of IRA options it makes available to employees (to as few as one), if it fully discloses any costs or limitations on the employees' ability to roll over the contributions to another IRA. The Interpretive Bulletin cautions that the employer will fall outside of the safe harbor if it negotiates special fees, terms or conditions with the IRA sponsor which are not available to other IRA participants.

3. The employer may pay fees connected with the establishment and maintenance of the payroll deduction procedure for the program. However, the employer is not permitted to pay any administrative, investment management or other fee that the IRA sponsor would charge employees for establishing and maintaining the IRA.

4. The employer may be paid "reasonable compensation for services rendered in connection with payroll deductions and dues check-offs." Payments from the IRA sponsor may not include any profit to the employer such as a payment based on a percentage of assets contributed by the employees or an extension of credit to the employer in exchange for making the program available. IB 99-1, 64 Fed. Reg. 32999 (June 18, 1999).

12. Does ERISA expressly exclude tax sheltered annuities from ERISA coverage?

For purposes of ERISA, a program for the purchase of an annuity contract or the establishment of a custodial account as described under IRC Section 403(b), pursuant to salary reduction agreements or agreements to forego an increase in salary and which satisfies the requirements of treasury regulations under Section 403(b) will not be considered "established or maintained by an employer" as that term is used in the definition of the terms "employee pension benefit plan" and "pension plan" if:

1. Participation is completely voluntary for employees;

2. All rights under the annuity contract or custodial account are enforceable solely by the employee, by a beneficiary of such employee, or any authorized representative of such employee or beneficiary;

3. The sole involvement of the employer is limited to any of the following:

a) permitting annuity contractors to publicize their products to employees,

b) requesting information concerning proposed funding media, products or annuity contractors,

c) summarizing or otherwise compiling the information provided with respect to the proposed funding media or products which are made available, or the annuity contractors whose services are provided, in order to facilitate review and analysis by the employees,

d) collecting annuity or custodial account considerations as required by salary reduction agreements or by agreements to forego salary increases, remitting such considerations to annuity contractors and maintaining records of such considerations,

e) holding in the employer's name one or more group annuity contracts covering its employees, and

f) limiting the funding media or products available to employees, or the annuity contractors who may approach employees, to a number and selection which is designed to afford employees a reasonable choice in light of all relevant circumstances; and

4. The employer receives no direct or indirect consideration or compensation in cash or otherwise other than reasonable compensation to cover expenses properly and actually incurred by the employer. Labor Reg. §2510.3-2(f).

13. What ERISA covered plans are exempt from ERISA's fiduciary provisions?

The fiduciary responsibility provisions of ERISA Part IV do not apply to any employee benefit plan that is an unfunded plan maintained by an employer primarily for the purpose of providing deferred compensation for a select group of management or highly compensated employees (commonly referred to as "top hat" plans). ERISA Sec. 401(a)(1).

The fiduciary provisions of ERISA will also not apply to any agreement described in IRC Section 736 that provides payments to a retired partner or deceased partner or a deceased partner's successor in interest. ERISA Sec. 401(a)(2).

14. What are "settlor functions" under ERISA?

Settlor functions are those decisions and services that relate to the formation, design and termination of an employee benefit plan and that relate to the business activities of an employer. DOL Information Letter to Kirk Maldonado (3/2/87). The decision of whether or not to even offer an employee benefit plan would be a settlor function.

Fiduciaries are permitted to implement settlor functions in a non-fiduciary capacity, as an agent of the plan sponsor, on behalf of an employee benefit plan. *NLRB v. Amax Coal Co.*, 453 U.S. 322 (1981); *Siskind v. Sperry Retirement Program*, 47 F.3d 498 (2nd Cir. 1995). In general, settlor functions are not subject to the fiduciary provisions of ERISA where the fiduciaries who carry them out do so without the exercise of any discretion. *Akers v. Palmer*, 71 F.3d 226 (6th Cir. 1995), *cert. denied*, (1996); *Trenton v. Scott Paper Co.*, 832 F.2d 806 (3rd Cir. 1987), *cert. denied*, 485 U.S. 1022 (1988). Even where the fiduciary has exercised some discretion in the carrying out of settlor functions, fiduciary obligations will not normally be attached if the settlor functions have been properly documented and exercised as they relate to the general business activities of the employer.

15. Are expenses incurred in the execution of settlor functions payable out of plan assets?

In a Department of Labor (DOL) Information Letter to Kirk Maldonado (dated 3/2/87), the DOL advised that "the use of plan assets to pay fees and expenses incurred in connection with the provision of services would not be a reasonable expense of administering a plan if the payments are made for the employer's benefit or involve services for which an employer could reasonably be expected to bear the cost in the normal course of such business or operations. In this regard, certain services provided in conjunction with the establishment, termination and design of plans, so called 'settlor' functions, relate to the business activities of an employer and, therefore, generally would not be the proper subject of payment by an employee benefit plan."

The letter goes on to provide that the prohibited transaction provisions of ERISA come into play in connection with payments for administrative services. ERISA Section 408(b)(2) exempts from the prohibited transaction provisions of ERISA Section 406(a) any contract or reasonable arrangement with a party in interest for office space, or legal or accounting or other services necessary for the establishment or operation of a plan. Such expenditures are to be reviewed on a case by case basis by taking into consideration all relevant facts and circumstances. "Thus, the fiduciaries of a plan should review all services provided to determine whether such services are 'necessary services' for which payment would be lawful."

The DOL later reiterated the position set forth in the Maldonado letter. In discussing its long-standing position forbidding plans from reimbursing settlor expenses to the plan sponsor, the DOL advises that "Expenses incurred in the connection with the performance of settlor functions would not be reasonable expenses of a plan as they would be incurred for the benefit of the employer and would involve services for which an employer could reasonably be expected to bear the cost in the normal course of its business operations." DOL Adv. Op. 2001-01A. Although start-up expenses may not be paid out of plan expenses, the Economic Growth and Tax Relief Reconciliation Act of 2001 (EGTRRA) provides a nonrefundable tax credit of 50% of certain administrative and retirement-education expenses of a small employer (100 employees or less) that adopts a new qualified defined benefit or defined contribution plan, SIMPLE plan, SEP or payroll deduction IRA program. The credit applies to the first $1,000.00 of such expenses for the plan for each of the first three plan years. The credit is effective for plans adopted after December 31, 2001. IRC Sec. 45E, as added by EGTRRA 2001. For a discussion of the reimbursement to the plan sponsor of expenses incurred in the ongoing maintenance of the tax-qualified status of a plan, see Q 16.

16. What plan expenses may be paid out of plan assets?

Plan documents must expressly provide for the payment of plan expenses out of plan assets in order for the plan to be allowed to pay them. ERISA Section 402(b)(4) requires plans to specify the basis upon which payments will be made from the plan. ERISA Section 403(c)(1) provides that the assets of a plan shall never inure to the benefit of any employer and shall be held for the exclusive purposes of providing benefits to participants in the plan and their beneficiaries and defraying reasonable expenses of administering the plan. This is mirrored in ERISA Section 404(a)(1)(A), which requires fiduciaries to discharge their duties for the exclusive purpose of providing benefits to participants and beneficiaries and defraying reasonable expenses of administering the plan.

Reimbursable expenses include those which are reasonable and are for services rendered to the plan by a fiduciary. ERISA Sec. 408(c). Whether or not compensation paid to a party in interest by the plan is reasonable under ERISA Section 408(b)(2) and ERISA Section 408(c)(2) depends on the particular facts and circumstances of each case. Labor Reg. §2550.408c-2. Reasonable compensation does not include any compensation to a fiduciary who is already receiving full-time pay from an employer or association of employers or from an employee organization, except for the reimbursement of direct expenses properly and actually incurred and not otherwise reimbursed. Labor Reg. §2550.408c-2(b)(2).

An expense is not a direct expense to the extent that it would have been sustained had the service not been provided or if it represents an allocable portion of overhead costs. Labor Reg. §2550.408c-2(b)(3).

The reimbursement of reasonable compensation to service provider arrangements where plan sponsor employees act in a fiduciary capacity may be a properly reimbursable direct expense if:

1.   The expense would not have been sustained had the service not been provided;

2.   The expense can be properly allocated to the services provided;

3.   The expense does not represent an allocable portion of overhead costs; and

4.   The service is a necessary service. DOL Adv. Op. 93-06A.

The general fiduciary requirements of prudence will apply to these arrangements. Therefore, a proper evaluation of the arrangement which includes employees of the plan sponsor will be necessary, as well as the obligation to properly monitor the ongoing activities of such employees under the arrangement.

The DOL has issued guidance to assist plan sponsors in determining the extent to which an employee benefit plan may pay the costs attendant to maintaining tax-qualified status, without regard to the fact that tax qualification confers a benefit on the plan sponsor. Implementation of a tax-qualified plan is, the DOL advises, a settlor function for which a plan may not pay (See Q 15). However, the ongoing maintenance of a plan's tax-qualified status may require fiduciaries to undertake certain activities for which a plan may pay reasonable expenses. The Advisory Opinion offers six hypothetical situations to provide clarification and facilitate compliance on this issue. DOL Adv. Op. 2001-01A, clarifying DOL Adv. Op. 97-03A.

17. For purposes of ERISA, who is a participant and who is a beneficiary?

ERISA Section 3(7) defines a "participant" as an employee or former employee of an employer, or any member or former member of an employee organization, who is or may become eligible to receive a benefit of any type from an employee benefit plan which covers employees of such employer or members of such organization, or whose beneficiaries may be eligible to receive any such benefit.

The Supreme Court has applied the term "may become eligible" to include employees in, or reasonably expected to be in, covered employment, or former employees who have a reasonable expectation of returning to covered employment or those who have a colorable claim to vested benefits. *Firestone Tire & Rubber Co. v. Bruch*, 489 U.S. 101 (1989). A claim that a participant may become eligible for benefits is established if the claimant can establish a "colorable claim" that they will prevail in a suit for benefits, or that they will fulfill eligibility requirements in the future. *Firestone Tire & Rubber Co. v. Bruch*, above.

A "beneficiary" means a person designated by the participant, or by the terms of an employee benefit plan, who is or may become entitled to a benefit under the plan. ERISA Sec. 3(8). ERISA preempts state laws invalidating beneficiary designations pursuant to divorce. *Egelhoff v. Egelhoff*, 532 U.S. ___, 25 EBC 2089 (2001); rev'g 989 P.2d 80 (Wash. 1999).

18. What are the basic requirements for vesting under ERISA?

ERISA Section 203 establishes the minimum vesting standards for an ERISA covered pension plan. Under that section, each pension plan must provide that an employee's right to his normal retirement benefit is nonforfeitable upon the attainment of normal retirement age. ERISA Section 203(a)(1) states that an employee's accrued benefit derived from his own contributions must, at all times, be nonforfeitable.

With respect to employer contributions, the minimum vesting standards are satisfied if an employee who has completed at least five years of service has a nonforfeitable right to 100% of his accrued benefit. ERISA Sec. 203(a)(2)(A); IRC Sec. 411(a)(2)(A). This is often referred to as "cliff vesting" because participants have no right to employer contributions until they have completed five years of credited service, after which they have a 100% nonforfeitable right.

In the alternative, graduated vesting is permissible if it is established on a schedule which vests benefits at least as rapidly as the following (ERISA Sec. 203(a)(2)(B); IRC Sec. 411(a)(2)(B)):

| | The nonforfeitable |
Year of service:	percentage is:
3	20
4	40
5	60
6	80
7 or more	100

Most qualified retirement plans provide for a graduated vesting schedule on a "2/20" basis. That is a vesting schedule that provides for 20% vesting after two years of credited service and then increases the vesting percentage by 20% for each additional year of credited service until the participant becomes 100% vested. For contributions made after December 31, 2001, employer-matching contributions (as defined under IRC Section 401(m)(4)(A)) must be vested on a 3-year cliff or 6-year graded vesting schedule. ERISA Sections 203(a)(2)(A) and (B), as amended by Title VI, Subtitle C, EGTRRA (H.R. 1836).

For defined contribution plans, the "accrued benefit" is the balance of assets allocated to the participant's individual account. IRC Sec. 411(a)(7)(A)(ii). For purposes of a defined benefit plan, "accrued benefit" is defined as the employee's accrued benefit as determined under the plan and expressed in the form of an annual benefit commencing at normal retirement age. IRC Sec. 411(a)(7)(A)(I).

Both ERISA and the Internal Revenue Code generally prohibit any plan amendment that has the effect of decreasing accrued benefits under a plan. ERISA Sec. 204(g)(1); IRC Sec. 411(d)(6). This would include any amendment increasing the vesting schedule. The IRS takes this provision very seriously and has disqualified plans for violations of this prohibition. Such violations are often referred to as the "death penalty" for qualified plans. See Q 26.

19. What kinds of service may a plan disregard for purposes of vesting?

In computing the period of service under a qualified plan for purposes of determining the nonforfeitable percentage of an employee's accrued benefit, all of an employee's years of service with the employer maintaining the plan must be taken into account, except that the following may be disregarded:

1. All years of service prior to age 18;

2. All years of service during a period for which the employee declined to contribute to a plan requiring employee contributions;

3. All years of service with an employer during any period for which the employer did not maintain the plan or a predecessor plan;

4. All years of service before January 1, 1971, unless the participant has had at least three years of service after December 31, 1970;

5. In general, all years of service accrued prior to a 5-year break in service (see Q 35 to Q 37 for details); and

6. In the case of a multiemployer plan, years of service—

    a) with an employer after a complete withdrawal of such employer from the plan or a partial withdrawal in connection with the decertification of the collective bargaining representative, and

    b) with any employer under the plan after the termination date of the plan. ERISA Sec. 203(b)(1); IRC Sec. 411(a)(4).

20. What plans are subject to ERISA's vesting rules?

A plan will not be a "qualified" plan under IRC Section 401 unless it satisfies the minimum vesting standards established under IRC Section 411 (which are mirrored under ERISA Section 203(a) — see Q 18). IRC Sec. 401(a)(7). Under ERISA, these vesting rules apply to all pension plans that are established or maintained by any employer engaged in commerce or in any industry or activity affecting commerce, or by any employee organization or organizations representing employees engaged in commerce or in any industry or activity affecting commerce, or both. ERISA Secs. 4(a), 203(a). As such, both qualified and nonqualified plans that provide for retirement income or result in the deferral of income to termination or retirement are generally subject to the vesting requirements of ERISA. See Q 21 for plans that are exempt from the general vesting rules.

21. What plans are exempt from ERISA's vesting rules?

The following types of plans are exempt from the general vesting rules of ERISA:

1. A governmental plan established or maintained by the government of the United States, any state or political subdivision, or agency or instrumentality thereof (including any plan to which the Railroad Retirement Act of 1935 or 1937 applies) (ERISA Sec. 3(32); IRC Sec. 411(e)(1)(A));

2. Church plans (those plans established and maintained for its employees by a church or a convention of churches which is tax exempt under IRC Section 501) that have not made an irrevocable election to be subject to the participation, vesting and funding rules of ERISA (ERISA Sec. 4(b)(2); IRC Sections 410(d), 411(e)(1)(B));

3. Plans which are adopted by fraternal beneficiary societies and voluntary employee beneficiary associations that are tax exempt under IRC Section 501(c)(8) or IRC Section 501(c)(9) if no contributions are made by employers (ERISA Sec. 201(3)(A); IRC Sec. 411(e)(1)(D));

4. Workmen's compensation plans and plans established to comply with unemployment compensation or disability insurance laws (ERISA Sec. 4(b)(3));

5. Plans maintained outside of the United States primarily for persons substantially all of whom are nonresident aliens (ERISA Sec. 4(b)(4));

6. Welfare benefit plans (ERISA Sec. 201(1));

7. A plan which is unfunded and maintained by an employer primarily for the purpose of providing deferred compensation for a select group of management or highly compensated employees (i.e., "top hat" plans) (ERISA Sec. 201(2));

8. Excess benefit plans which are maintained solely for the purpose of providing benefits for certain employees in excess of the accrual limits under IRC Section 415 (ERISA Sec. 201(7));

9.   Any agreement described under IRC Section 736 which provides payments to a retired partner or deceased partner or a deceased partner's successor in interest (ERISA Sec. 201(5));

10.   Individual retirement accounts and individual retirement annuities (ERISA Sec. 201(6)); and

11.   A Keogh plan that covers only self-employed individuals and does not extend coverage to common-law employees (Labor Regs. §§2510.3-3(b), 2510.3-3(c)).

22. How are the vesting rules affected by the presence of a controlled group?

All employees of all corporations that are members of a controlled group of corporations, and all employees of trades or businesses (whether or not incorporated) that are under common control, must be treated as employed by a single employer. ERISA Secs. 210(c), 210(d). For credited service under an applicable vesting schedule, participants will be credited for all years of service with members of the controlled group of corporations or employers under common control, as defined under the terms of the plan's governing documents.

A "controlled group of corporations" can be one of three types: parent-subsidiary, brother-sister, and combined. All three types are defined under IRC Section 1563(a) as follows:

(1)   PARENT-SUBSIDIARY CONTROLLED GROUP. One or more chains of corporations connected through stock ownership with a common parent corporation if—

    (A) stock possessing at least 80% of the total combined voting power of all classes of stock entitled to vote or at least 80% of the total value of shares of all classes of stock of each of the corporations, except the common parent corporation, is owned ... by one or more of the other corporations, and

    (B) the common parent corporation owns ... stock possessing at least 80% of the total combined voting power of all classes of stock entitled to vote or at least 80% of the total value of shares of all classes of stock of at least one of the other corporations, excluding, in computing such voting power or value, stock owned directly by such other corporations.

(2)   BROTHER-SISTER CONTROLLED GROUP. Two or more corporations if five or fewer persons who are individuals, estates, or trusts own stock ... possessing—

(A) at least 80% of the total combined voting power of all classes of stock entitled to vote or at least 80% of the total value of shares of all classes of the stock of each corporation, and

(B) more than 50% of the total combined voting power of all classes of stock entitled to vote or more than 50% of the total value of shares of all classes of stock of each corporation, taking into account the stock ownership of each such person only to the extent such stock ownership is identical with respect to each such corporation.

(3)　COMBINED GROUP. Three or more corporations each of which is a member of a group of corporations described in paragraphs (1) or (2), and one of which—

(A) is a common parent corporation included in a group of corporations described in paragraph (1), and also,

(B) is included in a group of corporations described in paragraph (2).

A combined group of trades or businesses under common control "means any group of three or more organizations, if (1) each such organization is a member of either a parent-subsidiary group of trades or businesses under common control or a brother-sister group of trades or businesses under common control, and (2) at least one such organization is the common parent organization of a parent-subsidiary group of trades or businesses under common control and is also a member of a brother-sister group of trades or businesses under common control." Treas. Reg. §1.414(c)-2(d).

23. How are the vesting rules affected by the presence of an affiliated service group?

As with a controlled group of corporations and trades or businesses under common control, all employees of employers who are members of an affiliated service group are treated as employed by a single employer. IRC Sec. 414(m)(1). This is for purposes of the vesting provisions of IRC Section 411 and ERISA Section 203(a).

An affiliated service group is defined as a group consisting of a service organization (i.e., the "first organization") and one or more of the following:

(A)　Any service organization which—

(i) is a shareholder or partner in the first organization, and

(ii) regularly performs services for the first organization or is regularly associated with the first organization in performing services for third persons, and

(B)   Any other organization if—

(i) a significant portion of the business of such organization is the performance of services (for the first organization, for organizations described in subparagraph (A), or for both) of a type historically performed in such service field by employees, and

(ii) 10% or more of the interests in such organization is held by persons who are highly compensated employees (within the meaning of [IRC] [S]ection 414(q)) of the first organization or an organization described in subparagraph (A). IRC Sec. 414(m)(2).

A "service organization" is any organization the principal business of which is the performance of services. IRC Sec. 414(m)(3).

24. What are the vesting rules for multiemployer plans?

Multiemployer plans are generally subject to the same vesting schedules that are applied to single employer plans (i.e., either a 5-year cliff vesting schedule or a graduated schedule of no more than seven years with a minimum vesting percentage of 20% after three years — see Q 18). SBJPA '96, Sec. 1442(b) repealing ERISA Sec. 203(a)(2)(C); SBJPA '96, Secs. 1442(a)(1), 1442(a)(2) repealing IRC Sec. 411(a)(2)(C). Different rules applied for plan years beginning prior to 1997.

The change in vesting schedules could be delayed (but no later than for plan years beginning after 1998) until the date on which the last of the collective bargaining agreements under which the multiemployer plan is maintained terminate (without regard to any extensions after August 5, 1996) if such termination occurs after January 1, 1997. SBJPA '96, Sec. 1442(c).

The change in vesting schedules does not apply to employees who do not have more than one hour of credited service under the multiemployer plan on or after the first day of the first plan year to which the change in vesting schedules applies. SBJPA '96, Sec. 1442(c).

25. May plan fiduciaries amend plan vesting schedules?

Plans are permitted to change their vesting schedules through appropriate plan amendment processes. However, a plan amendment that changes a vesting schedule will not be treated as satisfying the vesting requirements of ERISA and the Code if the nonforfeitable percentage of the accrued benefit derived from employer contributions (determined as of the later of the date such amendment is adopted or becomes effective) of any employee who is a participant in the plan is less than such nonforfeitable percentage computed under the plan without regard to such amendment. ERISA Sec. 203(c)(1)(A); IRC Sec. 411(a)(10)(A).

A plan amendment that changes a vesting schedule also will not be treated as satisfying the vesting requirements unless each participant having three or more years of service is permitted to elect, within a reasonable period after the adoption of such amendment, to have his nonforfeitable percentage computed under the plan without regard to such amendment. IRC Sec. 411(a)(10)(B). An election is not required where the amended vesting schedule would not result in a lesser vesting percentage. Treas. Temp. Reg. §1.411(a)-8T(b)(1).

The period during which a participant may make such an election must begin no later than the date the plan amendment is adopted and must end no later than the following:

1.　Sixty days after the date the amendment is adopted;

2.　Sixty days after the date the amendment becomes effective; or

3.　Sixty days after the date the participant is given written notice of the amendment by the employer or the plan administrator. Treas. Temp. Reg. §1.411(a)-8T(b)(2).

26. Will a plan amendment that establishes surrender charges under an annuity contract violate ERISA's minimum vesting and benefit accrual standards?

A violation of ERISA's minimum vesting and benefit accrual standards was found to occur where a plan amendment established surrender charges that had the effect of reducing participants' accrued benefits. *Arakelian v. National Western Life Ins. Co.*, 724 F. Supp. 1033 (DC D.C. 1989). Generally, any plan amendment that has the effect of reducing a participant's accrued benefit under the plan is prohibited. ERISA Sec. 204(g)(1); IRC Sec. 411(d)(6).

In *Arakelian v. National Western Life Ins. Co.*, National Western argued that the amendment at issue merely reallocated front end administrative costs. This position was unpersuasive to the court. The court explained that the plan documents may have allowed surrender charges to be considered in establishing the accrued benefits under the plan; however, the original plan document did not impose any surrender charges. Therefore, the amendment establishing surrender charges decreased the accrued benefits of the plan participants.

BENEFIT ACCRUAL AND FORFEITURE

27. What are the general benefit accrual rules under ERISA?

In the case of a defined benefit plan, the term "accrued benefit" means the employee's accrued benefit as determined under the plan and expressed in the form of an annual benefit commencing at normal retirement age. IRC Sec. 411(a)(7)(A)(i). In the case of an individual account defined contribution plan, the term "accrued benefit" means the balance of the employee's account (whether vested or not). IRC Sec. 411(a)(7)(A)(ii).

Generally, the accrued benefits of participants may not be decreased by a plan amendment (commonly referred to as the "anti-cutback" rule). ERISA Sec. 204(g)(1); IRC Sec. 411(d)(6). For purposes of this rule, a plan amendment that has the effect, with respect to benefits attributable to service before the amendment, of eliminating or reducing an early retirement benefit or a retirement-type subsidy, or eliminating an optional form of benefit, will be treated as reducing accrued benefits. ERISA Sec. 204(g)(2); IRC Sec. 411(d)(6)(B). A pension plan's cost-of-living adjustment has been deemed an accrued benefit that cannot be decreased by a plan amendment. *Hickey v. Chicago Truck Drivers, Helpers & Warehouse Workers*, 980 F.2d 465 (7th Cir. 1992).

An optional form of benefit is defined as a distribution form with respect to an employee's benefit that is available under the plan and is identical with respect to all features relating to the distribution form, including the payment schedule, timing, commencement, medium of distribution, the portion of the benefit to which such distribution features apply and the election rights with respect to such optional forms. Treas. Reg. §1.411(d)-4(b).

28. May a retirement plan reduce the rate of future benefit accruals?

Yes. However, a defined benefit or money purchase pension plan may not be amended to provide for a significant reduction in the rate of future benefit accruals, unless the plan administrator provides written notice setting forth the plan amendment and its effective date to the following:

1.   Each plan participant;

2.   Each beneficiary who is an alternate payee under an applicable qualified domestic relations order; and

3.   Each employee organization representing participants in the plan.

This notice must be provided after the adoption of the plan amendment and not less than 15 days before the effective date of the plan amendment. ERISA Sec. 204(h). The Court of Appeals for the Third Circuit has ruled that failure to provide the required notice under ERISA Section 204(h) invalidated an amendment to convert a money purchase pension plan into a discretionary profit sharing plan. *Brothers v. Miller Oral Surgery, Inc. Retirement Plan*, 25 EBC 1369, 230 F.3d 1348 (3rd Cir. 2000).

29. What service must be taken into account for purposes of benefit accrual?

Participants will be credited with service for purposes of benefit accruals from the earliest date on which they become a participant in the plan. See ERISA Sec. 204(b)(4); IRC Sec. 411(b)(4). The following service need not be considered for purposes of benefit accrual:

1. Service prior to the participant becoming a participant in the plan;

2. Service that is not required to be taken into account under ERISA Section 202(b) and IRC Section 410(a)(5) as a result of a 1-year break in service;

3. Service that is not required to be taken into account under ERISA Section 204(b)(4)(C) and IRC Section 411(b)(4)(C) because it is less than 1,000 hours during a 12-consecutive-month period; and

4. Service before the conclusion of a series of consecutive 1-year breaks in service that permit the plan to disregard service which need not be counted for vesting on account of the rule of parity provided for under ERISA Section 203(b)(3)(D) and IRC Section 411(a)(6)(D). See Labor Reg. §2530.204-1(b).

30. Are age-related reductions in accruals permissible?

A defined contribution plan will be deemed to have satisfied the basic accrual requirements of ERISA and the Code if allocations to the participant's account under the plan do not cease and the rate at which amounts are allocated to the participant's account is not reduced because of the attainment of any age. ERISA Sec. 204(b)(2)(A); IRC Sec. 411(b)(2).

A defined benefit plan will be deemed to have failed to satisfy the basic accrual requirements of ERISA and the Code if an employee's benefit accrual under the plan does cease or the rate of an employee's benefit accrual is reduced because of the attainment of any age. ERISA Sec. 204(b)(1)(H); IRC Sec. 411(b)(1)(H).

However, certain reductions in accruals are permissible. Defined benefit plans will not violate the basic accrual requirements where the plan (without regard to the participant's age) imposes a limitation on the amount of benefits that the plan provides or a limitation on the number of years of service or years of participation which are taken into account for purposes of determining benefit accruals under the plan. ERISA Sec. 204(b)(1)(H)(ii); IRC Sec. 411(b)(1)(H)(ii). Where a participant in a defined benefit plan continues to be actively employed by the plan sponsor beyond his attainment of the plan's normal retirement age, and the participant has commenced distribution of benefits, the rate of accrual may be reduced by the value of the actuarial equivalent of an in-service distribution of benefits to that participant. Further, where an actively employed participant works beyond normal retirement age and has not commenced distribution of his benefits, the plan may make an adjustment in the benefit payable due to the delay in the distribution of benefits after the attainment of normal retirement age. ERISA Sec. 204(b)(1)(H)(iii); IRC Sec. 411(b)(1)(H)(iii).

31. What are the benefit accrual rules specific to defined contribution plans?

As noted in Q 27, under a defined contribution plan, the participant's accrued benefit is the balance of assets in his individual account under the plan. IRC Sec. 411(a)(7)(A)(ii). As such, separate accounting is required for each participant's accrued benefit. ERISA Sec. 204(b)(3)(B); IRC Sec. 411(b)(3)(B).

In general, defined contribution assets accrue when they are actually allocated to the participants' accounts. However, the Internal Revenue Service has ruled that accrual occurs when a participant is entitled to an allocation of assets under the terms of the plan, even where there has not been an actual crediting of the benefits to the participant's account. Let. Rul. 9735001. Thus, the plan sponsor's determination of a discretionary annual profit sharing contribution which was committed to, but which was not yet allocated to the participants' accounts, was part of the accrued benefit.

The position taken by the IRS is in contradiction to a prior Fifth Circuit Court ruling, which held that the employer's contribution of employer stock did not accrue under the plan until actually allocated. *Izzarelli v. Rexene Products Co.*, 24 F.3d 1506 (5th Cir. 1994). In that case, the court permitted the plan sponsor to amend the plan's provisions and revalue the stock before the contribution had actually accrued to the participants, without violating ERISA's restrictions on reductions in accrued benefits.

PRACTITIONER'S POINTER

It is always best to make a thorough evaluation of any contemplated amendment to a plan that may have an effect on the accrual of benefits. Given the seriousness with which the IRS considers the "anti-cutback" rules, the best service a trustee or fiduciary can offer the plan is to seek the professional opinion of qualified legal counsel before carrying out the considered amendment.

Voluntary Employee Contributions

The accrued benefit derived from contributions made by an employee is the balance of the employee's separate account consisting of his contributions and income, expenses, gains and losses attributable thereto. If a separate account is not maintained for an employee's contributions, the accrued benefit derived from such contributions is the amount which bears the same ratio to the participant's total accrued benefit as the total amount of the employee's contributions (less withdrawals) bears to the sum of such contributions and the contributions made on his behalf by the employer (less withdrawals). ERISA Sec. 204(c)(2)(A); IRC Sec. 411(c)(2)(A).

For vesting purposes, voluntary employee contributions are always 100% vested. ERISA Sec. 203(a)(1); IRC Sec. 411(a)(1).

32. What are the benefit accrual rules specific to defined benefit plans?

As stated in Q 27, accrued pension or retirement benefits under a defined benefit plan are determined under the plan and expressed in the form of an annual benefit commencing at normal retirement age. IRC Sec. 411(a)(7); Treas. Reg. §1.411(a)-7(a)(1).

Normal retirement age is defined as the earlier of:

1.   The time a plan participant attains normal retirement age under the plan; or

2.   The later of (a) the time a plan participant attains age 65 or (b) the fifth anniversary of the time a plan participant commenced participation in the plan. ERISA Sec. 3(24); IRC Sec. 411(a)(8).

Defined benefit plan participants are required to have their accrued benefit provided by an annual benefit in the form of a single life annuity. If an employee's accrued benefit is to be determined as an amount other than an annual benefit commencing at normal retirement age, or if the accrued benefit derived from contributions made by an employee is to be determined with respect to a benefit other than an annual benefit in the form of a single life annuity commencing at normal retirement age, the employee's accrued benefit, or the accrued benefits derived from contributions made by an employee, must be actuarially adjusted. ERISA Sec. 204(c)(3); IRC Sec. 411(c)(3).

ERISA and the Code provide for three optional methods in calculating accruals under a defined benefit plan. In general, the three methods apply as follows:

1.   The "3% method" entitles a participant to a benefit at normal retirement age of not less than 3% of the normal retirement benefit to which he would be entitled if he began participation at the earliest possible entry age under the plan and served continuously until the earlier of age 65 or the plan's normal retirement age, multiplied by the number of years (not in excess of 33⅓%) of his participation in the plan;

2.   The "133⅓% rule" entitles a participant to a benefit at normal retirement age which is equal to the normal retirement benefit and the annual rate at which any individual who is or could be a participant can accrue the retirement benefits payable at normal retirement age under the plan for any later plan year is not more

than 133⅓% of the annual rate at which he can accrue benefits for any plan year beginning on or after such particular plan year and before such later plan year; or

3.   The "fractional rule" provides that the accrued benefit to which a participant is entitled upon his separation from service is not less than a fraction of the annual benefit commencing at normal retirement age to which he would be entitled under the plan as in effect on the date of his separation if he continued to earn annually until normal retirement age the same rate of compensation upon which his normal retirement benefit would be computed under the plan, determined as if he had attained normal retirement age on the date on which any such determination is made (but taking into account no more than 10 years of service immediately preceding his separation from service). Such fraction must be a fraction, not exceeding one, the numerator of which is the total number of years of participation in the plan (as of the date of his separation from service) and the denominator of which is the total number of years he would have participated in the plan if he separated from the service at the normal retirement age. ERISA Sec. 204(b)(1); IRC Sec. 411(b)(1).

These rules apply for an accrual of a defined benefit in an even manner that does not result in the acceleration of accruals for older participants or participants with extensive years of service over the rate of accrual for younger participants or participants who have attained fewer years of credited service.

Insurance Contract Plans

Defined benefit plans that are funded exclusively through the purchase of individual insurance contracts purchased on behalf of participants are not required to satisfy any of the three accrual methods detailed above. ERISA Secs. 204(b)(1)(F), 301(a)(2); IRC Secs. 411(b)(1)(F), 412(h)(2).

In order to satisfy this exemption from the defined benefit accrual rules, the insurance contracts must provide for level annual premium payments to be paid extending not later than the retirement age for each individual participating in the plan, and commencing with the date the individual became a participant in the plan (or in the case of an increase in benefits, commencing at the time such increase becomes effective). Also, the benefits provided by the plan must be equal to the benefits provided under each contract at normal retirement age under the plan and must be guaranteed by an insurance carrier to the extent the premiums have been paid.

Finally, all premiums must be paid for the plan year before the contract lapses (or there is reinstatement of the policy), no rights under the contracts have been subject to a security interest at any time during the plan year, and no policy loans may be outstanding at any time during the plan year. ERISA Sec. 301(b); IRC Sec. 412(i). In order for the exemption from the defined benefit accrual standards to apply, the insurance contract plan must provide that the employee's accrued benefit as of any applicable date is not less than the cash surrender value the employee's insurance contracts would have on that date. ERISA Sec. 204(b)(1)(F); IRC Sec. 411(b)(1)(F); Treas. Reg. §1.411(b)-1(d)(2).

33. For purposes of vesting and accrual, how is a participant's service computed?

An employee's statutory entitlement with regard to participation, vesting and benefit accrual is generally determined by reference to years of service and years of participation completed by the employee and 1-year breaks in service incurred by the employee. The units used for determining an employee's credit towards statutory participation, vesting and benefit accrual entitlements are in turn defined in terms of the number of hours of service credited to the employee during a specified period — in general, a 12-consecutive-month period referred to under ERISA as a "computation period." Labor Reg. §2530.200b-1(a).

An employee who is credited with 1,000 hours of service during an eligibility computation period must generally be credited with a year of service for purposes of participation and vesting standards under ERISA and the Code. Labor Reg. §2530.200b-1a. A "year of service" is defined as a calendar year, plan year, or other 12-consecutive-month period designated by the plan (and not prohibited under ERISA regulations) during which the participant has completed 1,000 hours of service. ERISA Sec. 203(b)(2)(A); IRC Sec. 411(a)(5).

An "hour of service" must be counted for purposes of determining a year of service, a year of participation for benefit accrual and breaks in service. Labor Reg. §2530.200b-2(a). An "hour of service" is determined under ERISA regulations. ERISA Sec. 202(a)(3)(C); IRC Sec. 410(a)(3)(C). Three definitions are provided under ERISA regulations.

Under the first definition, an hour of service is each hour for which an employee is paid, or entitled to payment, for the performance of duties for the employer during the applicable computation period. Labor Reg. §2530.200b-2(a)(1).

The second definition of hour of service is each hour for which an employee is paid, or entitled to payment, by the employer on account of a period of time during which no duties are performed (irrespective of whether the employment relationship has terminated), due to vacation, holiday, illness, incapacity (including disability), layoff, jury duty, military duty or leave of absence. However, no more than 501 hours of service are required to be credited to an employee on account of any single continuous period during which the employee performs no duties (whether or not such period occurs in a single computation period). Labor Reg. §2530.200b-2(a)(2).

Finally, an hour of service includes each hour for which back pay, irrespective of mitigation of damages, is either awarded or agreed to by the employer (however, there will be no credit for hours of service awarded under this provision if the same hours have already been granted to the participant by reason of the preceding two paragraphs). Labor Reg. §2530.200b-2(a)(3).

Hours of service need not be credited to a participant if payment is made or due under a plan maintained solely for the purpose of complying with applicable workmen's compensation or disability insurance laws, nor for payments which solely reimburse an employee for medical and medically related expenses incurred by the employee. Labor Regs. §§2530.200b-2(a)(2)(ii), 2530.200b-2(a)(2)(iii).

Alternative Methods for Crediting Hours of Service

Plans are permitted to adopt one of the following three alternative methods for crediting "hours of service":

1. Counting hours of service: these are detailed above (Labor Reg. §2530.200b-2(a));

2. Use of equivalencies: a plan may adopt an equivalency of hours of service to be credited based upon:

    a) periods of employment: days — 10 hours, weeks — 45 hours, semi-monthly — 95 hours, or monthly — 190 hours (Labor Reg. §2530.200-3(e));

    b) earnings: for hourly rate employees, a plan must divide the employee's total earnings during a computation period by one of three hourly rates to establish the hours of service to be credited (actual hourly rates; employee's lowest hourly rate during the computation period; and lowest hourly rate paid to employees in the same or similar job classification) and 870 hours must be credited as equivalent to 1,000 hours and 435 hours must be credited as equivalent to 500 hours. For non-hourly employees, hours of service to be credited under this equivalency method are determined by dividing the employee's total earnings by the lowest hourly rate and 750 hours must be credited as equivalent to 1,000 hours and 375 hours must be credited as equivalent to 500 hours (Labor Reg. §2530.200-3(d)); or

    c) hours of working time: this is divided into two types — (i) in the case of those based on hours worked (i.e., those hours for which an employee is paid or is entitled to payment for the performance of duties, including back pay awards), 870 hours must be treated as equivalent to 1,000 hours and 375 hours must be credited as equivalent to 500 hours; and (ii) in the case of those based on regular time (i.e., the same as the hours worked equivalency excluding overtime hours), 750 regular time hours must be treated as equivalent to 1,000 hours and 375 regular time hours must be treated as equivalent to 500 hours (Labor Reg. §2530.200-3(f)).

Elapsed Time Calculation Method

In addition to the methods of crediting hours of service detailed above, a plan may determine hours of service to be credited for participation, vesting and accrual purposes on an elapsed time method. Under this method, service is credited by reference to the total period of time which elapses while the employee is employed with the employer or the employer maintains the plan (regardless of the actual number of hours worked). Such service must be taken into account from the date the employee first performs an "hour of service" to the date of severance. The regulation states that the elapsed time method is designed to enable a plan to lessen the administrative burdens associated with maintenance of records by permitting each employee to be credited with his total period of service with the employer. Treas. Reg. §1.410(a)-7(a).

Under the elapsed time method, the employer may not require as a condition of participation that an employee complete a period of service beyond the later of the employee attaining:

1.　　Age 21; or

2.　　The completion of a 1-year period of service (based upon the 1-year anniversary of employment commencement date). Treas. Reg. §1.410(a)-7(c).

If the eligibility under the elapsed time method is satisfied, the participant must commence participation in the plan no later than the first day of the first plan year beginning after the date on which the employee satisfied the minimum requirements for eligibility to participate, or the date six months after the date on which the employee satisfied the minimum requirements. Treas. Reg. §1.410(a)-7(c)(3).

Excludable Service under the Elapsed Time Method

Plans that utilize the elapsed time method of calculating credited service may disregard the following forms of employee service:

1.　　The period of service completed by the employee prior to the attainment of age 18;

2.　　In the case of a plan that requires mandatory employee contributions, the period of service that falls within the period of time to which a particular employee contribution relates, if the employee had the opportunity to make a contribution for such period of time and failed to do so;

3.   The period of service during any period for which the employer did not maintain the plan or a predecessor plan;

4.   The period of service which is not required to be taken into account by reason of the break in service rules of IRC Section 410(d)(4);

5.   The period of service completed by an employee prior to January 1, 1971, unless the employee completes at least three years of service at any time after December 31, 1970; and

6.   The period of service completed before the first plan year for which IRC Section 410 applies to the plan, if such service would have been disregarded under the plan rules relating to breaks in service in effect at that time. Treas. Reg. §1.410(a)-7(d)(2).

Break in Service

A 1-year break in service is a 12-consecutive month period beginning on the employee's severance from employment and ending on the first anniversary of that date, provided that the employee fails to perform an "hour of service" (as defined under ERISA regulations, see above) during that 12-consecutive month period for the employer maintaining the plan. Under the elapsed time method, the term "one-year break in service" will be substituted with the term "one-year period of severance" Treas. Reg. §1.410(a)-7(d)(4).

Service completed prior to a 1-year break in service or a 1-year period of severance is not required to be taken into account for the determination of eligibility and vesting until the employee has completed one year of service upon his return to active employment. Treas. Reg. §1.410(a)-7(d)(5).

34. What are the basic "break in service" rules?

A 1-year break in service is defined as a calendar year, plan year or other 12-consecutive-month period designated by the plan during which the participant has not completed 500 or more hours of service. ERISA Sec. 203(b)(3)(A); IRC Sec. 411(a)(6)(A). The computation period to be used in applying the break in service rules is the computation period established under the plan for purposes of calculating eligibility, benefit accruals and vesting.

One-Year Break in Service

In the case of an employee who has had any 1-year break in service, years of service completed before such break are not required to be taken into account until the participant has completed a year of service after his return to employment. ERISA Sec. 203(b)(3)(B); IRC Sec. 411(a)(6)(B).

Where an employee has performed one year of service upon re-employment (after a 1-year break in service), he must receive credit for all pre-break and post-break service (including the re-employment waiting year) for purposes of benefit accrual and vesting.

Five Consecutive One-Year Breaks in Service

In the case of a participant in an individual account plan or an insured defined benefit plan who has five consecutive 1-year breaks in service, years of service after such five consecutive 1-year breaks in service will not be required to be taken into account for purposes of determining the nonforfeitable percentage of his accrued benefit derived from employer contributions that accrued prior to the 5-year period. ERISA Sec. 203(b)(3)(C); IRC Sec. 411(a)(6)(C).

Rule of Parity

In the case of an employee who has no vested benefits, years of service with the employer maintaining the plan before any period of consecutive 1-year breaks in service need not be taken into account if the number of consecutive 1-year breaks in service within such period equals or exceeds the greater of five, or the aggregate number of years of service before such period. ERISA Sec. 203(b)(3)(D); IRC Sec. 411(a)(6)(D). If the participant returns to work within five years, he must be given credit for his pre-break years of service for purposes of vesting. ERISA Sec. 203(b)(3)(D)(iii); IRC Sec. 411(a)(6)(D)(iii).

35. How is the 5-year break in service rule applied to a re-employed participant who had previously terminated with a vested percentage under the plan?

In a defined contribution plan, where a participant has accumulated five or more consecutive 1-year breaks in service, all service of the participant must be taken into account upon his re-employment (including all service credited prior to his re-employment) if the participant was partially vested in employer contributions at the time of his separation from service. IRS Alert Guidelines No. 2, III.

36. How is a participant's credited service accrued prior to five consecutive 1-year breaks in service treated where the number of years of service before the break exceeds the number of consecutive 1-year breaks in service?

Upon re-employment, if a participant has five or more consecutive 1-year breaks in service, he must be given full credit for all pre-termination breaks in service, for purposes of vesting and benefit accrual, if the number of years of service prior to termination exceeds the number of consecutive 1-year breaks in service. IRS Alert Guidelines Number 2, III.

For plans that utilize the elapsed time method in determining years of service, the plan is also required to provide full credit for all service completed for vesting purposes if the period of consecutive 1-year periods of severance does not exceed the number of years of pre-termination service.

37. What are the rights of veterans upon re-employment after a severance from service for military service?

The Uniformed Services Employment and Reemployment Rights Act of 1994 (USERRA) establishes that upon reemployment after a period of military service, participants are entitled to all rights and benefits which are based upon seniority that they would have accrued with reasonable certainty had they maintained continuous employment without the separation from service for military service (including basic seniority). IRC Sec. 414(u).

With respect to qualified retirement plans, reemployed veterans are given an opportunity to make up elective deferrals that they would have made had it not been for the separation from service for military service. The compensation considered in making up salary deferrals will be the amount of compensation the reemployed veteran would have made from the employer had he not separated from service for military service. Where it would be difficult to establish the compensation the reemployed veteran would have been paid had he not incurred a separation from service, the plan must use the reemployed veteran's average compensation from the 12-month period preceding the break in service for military service. Any make-up of employee salary deferrals and matching contributions will not result in the plan violating the limits on contributions, and minimum participation rules. IRC Sec. 414(u)(2).

Additionally, reemployed veterans will not be treated as having incurred any breaks in service for the period of time spent on active military duty. That period of time is to be considered service with the employer even though the veteran was actually in active military status. This rules applies to the plan's rules regarding nonforfeitability of accrued benefits and for determining accruals under the plan. IRC Sec. 414(u)(8).

Finally, the suspension by the plan of participant loan repayment requirements is permitted for the period the participant was in active military service. IRC Sec. 414(u)(4).

Plan amendments required for purposes of adopting the mandatory veterans reemployment rights established under USERRA generally had to be adopted by the first day of the first plan year beginning after 1997. Rev. Proc. 96-49, 1996-2 CB 369.

38. How are the break in service rules affected by parental leaves?

For participation and vesting purposes, a participant will be deemed to have completed all hours of service for which he or she was absent (not to exceed 501 hours) if the leave of service was for the purpose of parental leave taken for the following purposes:

1. The participant's pregnancy;

2. The birth of the participant's child;

3. The placement of a child as a result of adoption by the participant; or

4. The care of a child during that period immediately following the birth or placement of the child through adoption. ERISA Sec. 203(b)(3)(E); IRC Sec. 411(a)(6)(E).

Hours of service are to be based upon the actual hours the participant would have completed, or eight hours for each day the participant was absent if the actual number of hours cannot be reasonably calculated. ERISA Sec. 203(b)(3)(E)(ii); IRC Sec. 411(a)(6)(E)(ii).

Hours credited under these circumstances are not required to be credited for purposes of benefit accruals under the plan; they are required to be credited only for participation and vesting. ERISA Sec. 203(b)(3)(E)(i), flush language; IRC Sec. 411(a)(6)(E)(i), flush language.

39. What are the general rules regarding plan forfeitures?

Any accrued benefit that has vested in the participant may not be forfeitable. ERISA Sec. 203(a); IRC Sec. 411(a). In general, an accrued benefit is considered to be nonforfeitable at any given time if it is an unconditional right. Where there is a conditional right to a benefit, such as a right to a benefit which is conditioned upon the occurrence of a subsequent event, performance or forbearance, the plan may be amended to provide for the reduction or elimination of that benefit. See Treas. Reg. §1.411(a)-4.

Rights that are conditioned upon the sufficiency of plan assets in the event of plan termination or partial termination are considered to be forfeitable. Treas. Reg. §1.411(a)-4.

If a participant retires and begins the receipt of retirement benefits under the plan, it is not considered a forfeiture of monthly benefits where such payments attributable to employer contributions are suspended upon the reemployment of the participant. ERISA Sec. 203(a)(3)(B); IRC Sec. 411(a)(3)(B). Benefit payments that are attributable to employee contributions may not be suspended once they have commenced.

Retirement plans generally may not be amended to retroactively reduce benefits that have already accrued to a participant. ERISA Sec. 204(g)(1); IRC

Sec. 411(d)(6). However, a pension plan is permitted to reduce benefits accrued in the current plan year if an amendment specifying the reduction is adopted within 2½ months after the close of the affected plan year. The amendment may not retroactively reduce benefits accrued in prior plan years. Further, such amendment must be approved by the Department of Labor following a determination that such amendment is necessary due to a substantial business hardship incurred by the plan sponsor. ERISA Sec. 302(c)(8); IRC Sec. 412(c)(8).

Also, participants in contributory pension plans who withdraw mandatory employee contributions may have their vested portion of employer contributions forfeited if, at the time of the withdrawal of mandatory employee contributions, they were less than 50% vested in such employer contributions. ERISA Sec. 203(a)(3)(D); IRC Sec. 411(a)(3)(D). However, a pension plan that contains such a forfeiture provision must permit the participant an opportunity to "buy back" the forfeited employer contributions upon the repayment by the participant of the full amount of the withdrawal and, in the case of a defined benefit plan, interest. ERISA Sec. 203(a)(3)(D)(ii); IRC Sec. 411(a)(3)(D)(ii).

Once a forfeiture has occurred (where there is a terminated non-vested participant), such amounts in a pension plan must be applied to reduce future employer contributions. In a profit sharing or 401(k) plan, the plan document may provide that such forfeitures may be used to reduce future employer contributions or reallocated to the accounts of remaining participants.

40. May a plan forfeit a participant's benefits in the event of his death prior to retirement?

A plan generally may forfeit a participant's vested benefits that are attributable to employer contributions in the event of the participant's death prior to retirement. ERISA Sec. 203(a)(3)(A); IRC Sec. 411(a)(3)(A). However, in the event a vested participant dies before retirement and the participant has a surviving spouse, the plan must provide for the issuance of a qualified preretirement survivor annuity to the surviving spouse. ERISA Sec. 205(a)(2); IRC Sec. 401(a)(11); Treas. Reg. §1.401(a)-11.

41. Are non-competition and "bad boy" clauses that result in the forfeiture of benefits enforceable?

A non-competition agreement that authorizes the plan to deny or defer benefits provided by the plan sponsor in the event that a participant terminated employment with the plan sponsor and began employment with one of the plan sponsor's competitors may, generally, be enforced. However, such a forfeiture may never be applied to employee contributions. *Brower v. Comark Merchandising, Inc.*, 949 F. Supp. 1183 (DC NJ 1996).

"Bad boy" clauses traditionally are plan provisions that call for the forfeiture of plan benefits in the event, during the period of employment with the plan sponsor, of any act of dishonesty, fraud, theft or a felony conviction by a participant.

ERISA Section 206(d)(4) provides that the anti-alienation provisions of ERISA will not apply to any offset of a participant's benefits provided under an employee pension plan against an amount that the participant is ordered or required to pay to the plan if the order or requirement to pay arises under a judgment of conviction for a crime involving such plan; under a civil judgment entered by a court in an action brought in connection with a violation of the fiduciary provisions of ERISA; or pursuant to a settlement agreement between the DOL and the participant or the PBGC and the participant in connection with a violation (or alleged violation) of the fiduciary provisions of ERISA by a fiduciary or any other person. Further, the judgment, decree, order or settlement agreement must expressly provide for the offset.

Courts have denied forfeiture of benefits under "bad boy" clauses that are related to acts of fraud committed by the participant. *Crausman v. Curtiss-Wright Corp.*, 676 F. Supp. 1302 (DC NJ 1988); *Vink v. SVH North American Holding Corp.*, 549 F. Supp. 268 (S.D. NY 1982). The courts reasoned that a fraud exception to the nonforfeitability provisions of ERISA Section 203(a) and IRC Section 411(a) would be improper. However, courts have upheld forfeiture provisions as a result of fraudulent acts as they applied to non-vested benefit accruals and benefits in excess of minimum vesting standards under the plan. *Clark v. Lauren Young Tire Center Profit Sharing Tr.*, 816 F.2d 480 (9th Cir. 1987); *Montgomery v. Lowe*, 507 F. Supp. 618 (S.D. Tex. 1981); *Noell v. American Design, Inc. Profit Sharing Plan*, 764 F.2d 827 (11th Cir. 1985).

A forfeiture of benefits under a "bad boy" clause in a plan provision that applied in the event of a participant's conviction of a criminal act in connection with his employment with the plan sponsor (outside of any actions involving the plan) was enforceable in that it did not violate the participant's rights to equal protection under the U.S. Constitution. *Parente v. Town of West Warwick*, 685 F. Supp. 873 (DC R.I. 1988), *aff'd*, 868 F.2d 522 (1st Cir. 1989).

42. May a participant's assets in an ERISA covered plan be accessed by his creditors when the participant files bankruptcy?

No, a participant's assets generally may not be accessed by his creditors in bankruptcy proceedings filed by the participant. See 11 U.S.C. 541(c)(2). This is one of two exceptions (referred to as "applicable nonbankruptcy law") to the United States Bankruptcy Code provision which generally holds that an individual's bankruptcy estate includes all property in which the debtor has a legal or equitable interest at the time of the bankruptcy proceedings. 11 U.S.C. 541(a).

In 1992, the U.S. Supreme Court settled the issue of whether or not the anti-alienation provisions of ERISA Section 206(d)(1) qualified as "applicable nonbankruptcy law" that would exclude the applicant's plan assets from his individual bankruptcy estate. *Patterson v. Shumate*, 504 U.S. 753 (1992). ERISA Section 206(d)(1) states that "each pension plan shall provide that benefits provided under the plan may not be assigned or alienated." The Supreme Court ruled this plain language to be the "applicable nonbankruptcy law," which constitutes a restriction on the transfer of assets in bankruptcy proceedings. However, the Ninth Circuit Court of Appeals has ruled that ERISA's exclusion of qualified plan benefits from a debtor's bankruptcy estate does not extend to an individual who is the owner of the sponsor and sole participant in the plan, because such a plan is not covered by ERISA. *In re Lowenschuss*, 171 F.3d 673 (9th Cir. 1999).

Participants in retirement plans that are not covered by the anti-alienation provisions of ERISA (e.g., IRAs, plans covered by the Railroad Retirement Act, church plans, etc.) may have their plan assets protected from alienation in bankruptcy proceedings by the second major exception to the general holding of the Bankruptcy Code, which is referred to as the "federal pension exemption." Under this exemption, an individual debtor may exempt from his bankruptcy estate his right to receive a payment under a stock bonus, pension, profit sharing, annuity, or similar plan or contract on account of illness, disability, death, age, or length of service, to the extent reasonably necessary for the support of the debtor and any dependent of the debtor. 11 U.S.C. 522(d)(10). In order for this exemption to apply, the plan must be qualified under IRC Section 401(a), 403(a), 403(b), or 408. 11 U.S.C. 522(d)(10)(E).

The Ninth Circuit has ruled that liability for breach of fiduciary duty under ERISA is dischargeable in bankruptcy if it does not involve the misappropriation of funds or failure to provide a proper accounting of funds. *Corse v. Hemmeter*, 2001 U.S. App. LEXIS 4559 (9th Cir).

43. Are retiree pension and health benefits protected when their former employer files bankruptcy?

Under the federal bankruptcy code, companies that have filed bankruptcy under Chapter 11 of the Bankruptcy Code are required to continue paying retiree benefits until a modification of those benefits is agreed to by the parties or is ordered by the court. 11 U.S.C. 1114. These benefits include medical, surgical, or hospital care benefits or those benefits payable in the event of sickness, disability, or death under any plan established or maintained by the company prior to the bankruptcy filing.

These rules are not applicable to retirees with gross income in excess of $250,000 per year, unless comparable coverage cannot be obtained.

The court will allow these retiree benefits the status of an allowed administrative expense under the Bankruptcy Code. These benefits may be modified in the bankruptcy proceedings if it is necessary to permit the reorganization of the employer, it is clearly favored by a balance of the equities, and it is fair and equitable to all affected parties.

Retirees are protected where there are attempts to reverse claims for which they had received payments.

44. What procedures must a plan have in place regarding participant claims?

Every employee benefit plan must provide adequate notice, in writing, to any participant or beneficiary whose claim for benefits under a plan has been denied. That notice must also set forth the specific reasons for the denial in a "manner calculated to be understood by the participant." ERISA Sec. 503(1).

Every employee benefit plan must also establish and maintain reasonable claims procedures. These procedures must be set forth in the plan's Summary Plan Description and they may not contain any provisions or be administered in such a way as to unduly inhibit or hamper the processing of a participant claim. Labor Reg. §2560.503-1(b).

A claim is a request for a plan benefit that has been submitted by a participant or beneficiary. Where a plan has failed to establish a reasonable procedure for filing claims, a claim shall be deemed filed when a written or oral request is made by the claimant which is reasonably calculated to bring such claim to the attention of the persons or business unit which customarily handles employee benefits matters of the plan sponsor. Labor Reg. §2560.503-1(d). Under the "federal mailbox rule" as applied in benefits dispute cases, a participant can document the timing of his application for benefits through the mail by the date on the postmark or certified mail return receipt . See *Schikore v Bankamerica Supp. Ret. Plan*, 2001 US App LEXIS 22384 (9th Cir).

If a participant's or beneficiary's claim for benefits is partially or wholly denied, notice of the decision must be furnished to the claimant within a reasonable period of time, not to exceed 90 days, after receipt of the claim by the plan. Labor Reg. §2560.503-1(e).

The written notice to be provided in the event of a denial of a claim for benefits must contain the following information:

1. The specific reason or reasons for the denial;

2. Specific reference to pertinent plan provisions on which the denial is based;

3. A description of any additional material or information necessary for the claimant to perfect the claim and an explanation of why such material or information is necessary; and

4. Appropriate information as to the steps to be taken if the participant or beneficiary wishes to submit his or her claim for review. Labor Reg. §2560.503-1(f).

If the notice is not provided in a reasonable period of time, the claim is deemed to have been denied and the participant may proceed to the claims review stage. Labor Reg. §2560.5031(e)(2). Numerous federal court cases have required claimants to "exhaust their remedies" before they may file an action in federal court under a claim of denial of benefits. This means that participants are required to follow through on a plan's claims procedures, including the review procedures.

45. What recent steps has the DOL taken to strengthen participant health benefit claims procedures?

In November, 2000, the Department of Labor (DOL) issued a notice of final regulations designed to speed up the time health plans would have to respond to urgent health care claims. These regulations are a streamlined version of the proposed regulations issued in September, 1998. They were modified in response to hundreds of comment letters and subsequent hearings on the subject, held by the DOL with industry leaders. For pension and welfare benefit plans, the new procedures are applicable as of the first day of the second plan year beginning on or after January 20, 2001. The final regulations provide that benefit claims involving urgent care must be resolved within 72 hours of submission, and participants must be notified of incomplete benefit claims within 24 hours of submission. Labor Regs. §§2560.503-1(o), 2560.503-1(f).

Further, the regulations contain provisions that require pre-service claims to be decided within a maximum of 15 days after the receipt of the claim by the plan. This period can be extended by an additional 15 days if the plan administrator determines it is necessary due to matters beyond the control of the plan and the claimant is notified prior to the close of the initial 15 days. Labor Reg. §2560.503-1(f)(iii)(A). Adverse benefit determinations for post-service claims must be provided within 30 days of receipt of the claim by the plan. As with pre-service claims, the plan administrator may extend the deadline by an additional 15 days if it is necessary due to matters beyond the control of the plan and the claimant is notified prior to the close of the initial 30 day period. Labor Reg. §2560.503-1(f)(iii)(B).

In notifying a participant of an adverse benefit determination, the plan is required to provide a written or electronic notification. Such notification must disclose to the participant the specific reason for the adverse determination as well as the specific provisions of the plan upon which such determination was made. Participants must also be advised of any material or information necessary to perfect the claim, along with an explanation as to why the material or information is necessary. The notice of adverse determination must disclose the plan's review procedures and the time limits for undertaking such procedures. Finally, the notice of adverse determination must notify the participant of his right to file a civil action under ERISA section 502(a), should he believe there is a cause of action due to the adverse benefit determination. Labor Reg. §2560.503-1(g).

The new claims procedure regulations will begin to apply to group health plans on the first day of the first plan year beginning on or after July 1, 2002, but not later than January 1, 2003. Labor Regs. §§2560.503-1(o)(1), 2560.503-1(o)(2); 66 Fed. Reg. 35886. The Department of Labor has provided detailed guidance on the new claims procedure regulations in the form of frequently asked questions and answers. That information is available on the internet at http://askpwba.dol.gov/faq-claims-proc-reg.html.

46. What are a participant's rights with respect to appealing a denial of a claim for benefits?

Every employee benefit plan must provide a reasonable opportunity to a participant who has had a claim for benefits denied to have a "full and fair review" of the denial. ERISA Sec. 503(2).

The review procedure must allow the participant a reasonable opportunity to appeal a denied claim to an appropriate named fiduciary (or a person designated by such fiduciary) under which a full and fair review of the claim and its denial may be obtained. Such procedures must include provisions that permit claimants to:

1.   Request a review upon written application to the plan;

2.   Review pertinent documents; and

3.   Submit issues and comments in writing. Labor Reg. §2560.503-1(g).

Employee benefit plans may establish a limited period within which a participant must file a request for review of a denial. This period may not be less than 60 days from the date of the receipt of the written denial by the participant. Labor Reg. §2560.503-1(g)(3). A decision on the review by an appropriate named fiduciary shall not ordinarily be made more than 60 days after the receipt of the request for a review by the plan. The 60-day limit may be extended to no more than 120 days under special circumstances that require an extension of time for processing the claimant's appeal for review. Written notice of such an extension must be provided to the claimant. Labor Reg. §2560.503-1(h). If the plan provides for the review of appeals by an appointed board or committee which meets at least quarterly, the 60-day limit will not apply. The board must review the matter at its first meeting after the request is filed (unless the request is filed within 30 days of a scheduled meeting, in which case it can be delayed until the next scheduled meeting). Labor Reg. §2560.503-1(h)(1)(ii).

The decision on review must be furnished to the claimant in writing and must include specific reasons for the decision, as well as specific references to the pertinent plan provisions on which the decision is based. Labor Reg. §2560.503-1(h)(3).

A failure to have a formal, written claims procedure is a procedural violation of ERISA. See *Harris v. Pullman Standard, Inc.*, 809 F.2d 1495 (11th Cir. 1987). Where a plan provides for compulsory arbitration to settle an employee benefits dispute under its claims procedure, any requirement that the claimant bear an equal share of the expenses of arbitration (with the plan bearing an equal share) is a violation of ERISA. DOL Adv. Op. 82-46A.

47. What plans are covered by ERISA's funding standards?

ERISA Section 302 establishes minimum funding standards that are applicable to every employee pension benefit plan subject to the coverage provisions of ERISA (see Q 6, Q 7, Q 10, Q 12). Thus, ERISA's minimum funding standards apply to defined benefit plans, money purchase plans and target benefit arrangements, as well as those pension plans that do not satisfy the qualification requirements of the Internal Revenue Code.

48. What plans are specifically exempted from ERISA's funding standards?

The following plans are expressly exempted from ERISA's funding requirements:

1. An employee welfare benefit plan;

2. A plan that is unfunded and is maintained for the provision of benefits to a select group of management or highly compensated employees;

3. An insurance contract plan funded exclusively by individual annuity contracts;

4. A plan that has not required employer contributions after January 1, 1975;

5. Individual retirement accounts or annuities;

6. Agreements providing payments to retired or deceased partners;

7. Excess benefit plans;

8. Individual account plans (other than money purchase and target benefit plans); or

9. Any plan in which an employer, all of whose stock is owned by employees, former employees or beneficiaries, who proposes through an unfunded arrangement to compensate retired employees for benefits which were forfeited under a plan maintained by a former employer prior to the date that such plan became subject to ERISA. ERISA Sec. 301(a).

Additionally, plans designed to comply with worker's compensation, unemployment compensation or disability insurance laws and plans maintained outside of the United States for the primary benefit of nonresident aliens are exempted. ERISA Secs. 4(b)(3), 4(b)(4).

49. What are the minimum funding standards under ERISA?

For those plans subject to the funding requirements, ERISA requires plan sponsors to make sufficient contributions to the plan to ensure that the plan will have enough money to pay for those benefits promised to employees when they retire. Every employee pension plan subject to the minimum funding standards must establish and maintain a minimum funding standard account to be charged with the sum of:

1. The normal cost of benefits earned by participants of the plan for the plan year;

2. The amount necessary to amortize in equal annual installments:

   a) the unfunded past service liability of plans in existence on January 1, 1974, on the first day of the first plan year to which ERISA applies to the plan, over a period of 40 plan years;

   b) in the case of plans that came into existence after January 1, 1974, the unfunded past service liability on the first day of the first plan year to which ERISA applies, over a period of 30 plan years;

   c) separately, with respect to each plan year, the net increase (if any) in unfunded past service liability under the plan arising from plan amendments adopted in such year, over a period of 30 years;

   d) separately, with respect to each plan year, the net experience loss (if any) under the plan, over a period of five plan years (15 plan years in the event of a multiemployer plan); and

   e) separately, with respect to each plan year, the net loss (if any) resulting from changes in actuarial assumptions used under the plan, over a period of 10 plan years (30 plan years in the event of a multiemployer plan);

3. The amount necessary to amortize each waived funding deficiency (within the meaning of ERISA Section 303(c)) for each prior plan year in equal annual installments over a period of five plan years, and

4. The amount necessary to amortize in equal annual installments (until fully amortized) over a period of five plan years any amount

credited to the funding standard account under the alternative minimum funding standard (see Q 51). ERISA Secs. 302(a)(1), 302(b)(1); IRC Sec. 412(b).

For money purchase plans, the minimum funding requirement is that amount established under the plan's contribution formula. For target benefit plans, the minimum funding requirement is that amount based upon the participant's compensation, age and assumed interest rate detailed under the plan.

50. What funding requirements must be determined using actuarial assumptions?

Normal retirement benefit costs, accrued liability, past service liabilities, and experience gains and losses must be determined under the funding method used to determine costs under the plan. ERISA Sec. 302(c)(1); IRC Sec. 412(c)(1). The costs, liabilities, rates of interest, and other factors under the plan must be determined on the basis of actuarial assumptions and methods. ERISA Sec. 302(c)(3); IRC Sec. 412(c)(3).

The actuarial assumptions and methods utilized must be reasonable (taking into account the experience of the plan and reasonable expectations) or, when aggregated, result in a total contribution equivalent to that which would be determined if each such assumption and method were reasonable. ERISA Sec. 302(c)(3)(A); IRC Sec. 412(c)(3)(A). In addition, when taken together, such actuarial assumptions and methods must offer the actuary's best estimate of anticipated experiences under the plan. ERISA Sec. 302(c)(3)(B); IRC Sec. 412(c)(3)(B).

51. What is the alternative minimum funding standard?

A plan that uses a funding method requiring contributions in all years not less than those required under the entry age normal funding method may maintain an alternative minimum funding standard account for any plan year. ERISA Sec. 305(a)(1); IRC Sec. 412(g)(1).

Such minimum funding standard accounts for a plan year must be charged with the sum of:

1.   The lesser of normal cost under the funding method used under the plan or normal cost determined under the unit credit method;

2.   The excess, if any, of the present value of accrued benefits under the plan over the fair market value of the assets; and

3.   An amount equal to the excess, if any, of credits to the alternative minimum funding standard account for all prior plan years over

charges to such account for all such years. ERISA Sec. 305(b)(1); IRC Sec. 412(g)(2)(A).

Further, alternative minimum funding standard accounts must be credited with the amount considered contributed by the employer to or under the plan for the plan year. ERISA Sec. 305(b)(2); IRC Sec. 412(g)(2)(B).

Alternative minimum funding standard accounts must be charged or credited with interest in the same manner as interest charged or credited to the funding standard account. ERISA Sec. 305(c); IRC Sec. 412(g)(3).

52. What are the employer deduction limits for minimum required funding contributions?

Generally, contributions paid by an employer to a pension plan are deductible in the taxable year when paid. IRC Sec. 404(a). The amount that is deductible is based on:

1.   The amount necessary to provide the remaining unfunded cost of past and current service credits over the remaining future service of each such employee; or

2.   The amount equal to the normal cost of the plan, plus the amount necessary to amortize the unfunded past service costs attributable to such credits in equal annual payments over 10 years. IRC Sec. 404(a)(1)(A).

Where the plan is subject to the full funding limitation in a given year, the maximum deduction may not exceed the full funding limit. IRC Sec. 404(a)(1)(A)(i). However, any amount paid in a taxable year in excess of the deductible amount for such year will be deductible in the succeeding taxable years (in order of time) to the extent of the difference between the amount paid and deductible in each such succeeding year and the maximum amount deductible for such year. IRC Sec. 404(a)(1)(E).

For non-multiemployer defined benefit plans with more than 100 participants, the maximum amount deductible will not be less than the unfunded current liability as determined under IRC Section 412(l). For purposes of determining whether a plan has 100 participants, all defined benefit plans maintained by the same employer (or any member of the employer's controlled group) are treated as one plan, but only employees of such controlled group member or employer are taken into account. IRC Sec. 404(a)(1)(D).

If a collectively bargained plan has satisfied the full funding limitation in a plan year and, as a result of an amendment applying to such year, the current liability of the plan exceeds the full funding limitation, the plan may elect the maximum amount of the deduction for such plan year to be equal to the lesser of:

1.   The full funding limitation for such year, taking into account any decrease in the present value of unamortized liability as a result of the amendment; or

2.   The normal cost under the plan reduced by the amount necessary to amortize in equal annual installments over 10 years (until fully amortized) the amount of the decrease in the present value of unamortized liability as a result of the amendment. IRC Sec. 404(a)(1)(B).

If the election is taken, the amount deductible with respect to any of the plan years following the plan year for which the election was made must be reduced by the amount required to amortize the benefit reduction.

53. How are the terms "full-funding limitation," "current liability" and "interest rate" defined?

"Full-funding limitation" is defined as the excess (if any) of:

1.   The lesser of 150% (155% for plan years beginning in 1999 or 2000) of current liability (including the expected increase in current liability due to benefits accruing during the plan year) or the accrued liability (including normal cost) under the plan; over

2.   The lesser of the fair market value of the plan's assets, or the value of such assets determined on the basis of any reasonable actuarial method of valuation that takes into account fair market value and is permitted under Treasury regulations. ERISA Sec. 302(c)(7); IRC Sec. 412(c)(7).

"Current liability" is defined as all liabilities to participants and beneficiaries under the plan. ERISA Sec. 302(d)(7); IRC Sec. 412(l)(7). Any calculation of current liability must utilize a rate of interest within the "permissible range" established under ERISA and the Code. The "permissible range" means a rate of interest that is not more than 10% above, nor more than 10% below, the weighted average of the rates of interest on 30-year Treasury securities during the 4-year period ending on the last day before the beginning of the plan year. ERISA Sec. 302(b)(5)(B); IRC Sec. 412(b)(5)(B). If the Secretary finds that the lowest rate of interest permissible under the range is unreasonably high, the Secretary may prescribe a lower rate of interest which may not be less than 80% of the average rate determined under the "permissible range" rules. ERISA Sec. 302(b)(5)(B)(ii)(II); IRC Sec. 412(b)(5)(B)(ii)(II).

The interest rate used under the plan must be determined without taking into account the experience of the plan and reasonable expectations, but consistent with the assumptions which reflect the purchase rates that would be used by insurance companies to satisfy the liabilities under the plan. ERISA Sec. 302(b)(5)(B)(iii); IRC Sec. 412(b)(5)(B)(iii).

54. May a pension plan subject to the minimum funding standards be converted to an insurance contract plan?

A defined benefit pension plan is permitted to convert to an insurance contract plan wherein premium payments would replace minimum funding requirements. Rev. Rul. 94-75, 1994-2 CB 59. The conversion to an insurance contract plan will result in premium payments starting after the date that employees began participating in the plan, in apparent violation of IRC Section 412(i) (see Q 32). However, an existing defined benefit plan that is converted in accordance with the requirements listed below will not be considered to fail to meet the requirements of IRC Section 412(i) merely because of participation in the plan before level annual premiums commence.

Such conversion will be effective on the first day of the plan year in which the following conditions have been satisfied:

1. The plan is funded by level premium annuity contracts under which all benefits accruing for each participant on or after the date of conversion are funded by level annual premium contracts;

2. All benefits accrued for each participant prior to the date of the conversion are guaranteed through insurance or annuity contracts, the purchase price of which equals the minimum amount required by the life insurance company for a contract which guarantees the provision of accrued benefits to participants; and

3. There are "meaningful continuing benefit accruals" under the plan after the conversion (for at least three plan years after conversion date).

The following actions must occur prior to, or on, the effective date of the conversion:

1. Insurance contracts which guarantee benefits that have accrued prior to the conversion date are purchased (this includes contracts purchased within one month after the first day of the plan year);

2. The remaining plan assets are applied to the payment of premiums for the level annual premium contracts; and

3. All necessary amendments to satisfy the requirements of IRC Section 403(a), IRC Section 404(a)(2) and IRC Section 412(i) have been adopted.

Where a plan has failed to satisfy the necessary requirements prior to the effective date of the conversion, the prior minimum funding requirements will continue to apply to the plan. Where a plan terminates prior to providing meaningful continuing benefit accruals for at least three plan years after the conversion date, the plan will be subject to the minimum funding requirements for the period of time after the effective date of the conversion.

55. What is the employer's deduction limit for converted insurance contract plans?

For plan years beginning after the effective date of the conversion from a defined benefit plan to an insurance contract plan, the employer's deductible limit in the conversion year and subsequent plan years will equal the sum of:

1.   An amount equal to the normal cost of the insurance contract plan established on the conversion date for post-conversion benefit accruals;

2.   The limit adjustments for any 10-year amortization base created because the plan was treated as if terminated on the last day of the plan year immediately preceding the conversion year; and

3.   The limit adjustments for any 10-year amortization bases remaining unamortized as of the conversion date that are maintained for purposes of IRC Section 404(a)(1)(A)(iii). Rev. Rul. 94-75, 1994-2 CB 59.

Normal cost will be based upon the annual premiums for level annual premium contracts providing for the post-conversion benefit accruals (including increases in benefits), that are reasonable in view of the funding mechanism and reasonable expectations regarding the effects of mortality, interest and other relevant factors.

56. What are the general rules regarding the amortization of pension costs?

The minimum funding standards of ERISA Section 302 mandate that the annual contributions to a defined benefit plan must be enough to satisfy the normal costs of retirement benefits accrued during that plan year and be sufficient to satisfy the amortization of unfunded past service liability and changes in past service liability due to plan amendments, assumption changes and experience gains and losses. For a review of the specific rules regarding the amortization of normal costs, initial past service costs and experience gains and losses, see Q 49 and Q 50.

The interest rate charged in calculating the amount of amortization is the same rate that is applied to initial past service liabilities for a new plan, as found under ERISA Section 302(b)(5)(B) — see Q 53 for details.

Experience Gains and Losses

A change in benefits under the Social Security Act or in other retirement benefits created under federal or state law, a change in the definition of the term "wages" under IRC Section 3121, or a change in the amount of such wages taken into account under applicable Treasury regulations that results in an increase or decrease in the accrued liability of a plan will be treated as an experience gain or loss. ERISA Sec. 302(c)(4); IRC Sec. 412(c)(4). A determination of experience gains and losses and a valuation of the plan's liability is required to be completed at least once every plan year. ERISA Sec. 302(c)(9); IRC Sec. 412(c)(9). Such adjustments to experience gains or losses will result in an adjustment to the plan sponsor's deduction for plan contributions. IRC Sec. 404(a)(1)(A).

Extensions in Amortization Periods

The period of years required to amortize any unfunded liability of a plan may be extended for a period of time not to exceed 10 years if the Secretary of Labor determines that such an extension would provide adequate protection for participants and beneficiaries, and if the Secretary determines that the failure to permit such an extension would:

1. Result in a substantial risk to the voluntary continuation of the plan;

2. Result in a substantial curtailment of pension benefit levels or employee compensation; and

3. Be adverse to the interests of plan participants in the aggregate. ERISA Sec. 304(a); IRC Sec. 412(e).

When an application for an extension of the amortization period is going to be filed, the plan administrator is required to provide notice of such application to the participants, beneficiaries, alternate payees and any employee organization representing employees, which details the extent to which the plan is funded for benefits guaranteed by the PBGC and for benefit liabilities. IRC Sec. 412(f)(4)(A).

The following facts generally must be furnished when an application for the extension of an amortization period is requested:

1. The unfunded liability for which the extension is being requested (i.e., past service costs, etc.);

2. The reasons which detail the necessity for the extension;

3. The period of time for which the extension is being requested (not to exceed 10 years); and

4. A numerical illustration that details how the annual plan costs will be affected by the extension. Rev. Proc. 79-61, 1979-2 CB 575, as amplified by Rev. Proc. 94-8, 1994-1 CB 544; Rev. Proc. 79-408, 1979-2 CB 191.

Applications must also be accompanied by the annual financial statements of the plan sponsor for the previous five years, the most recent Annual Report Form 5500 and the most recent actuarial valuation report. Rev. Proc. 79-61, supra.

The application for an extension of the amortization period should be sent to the following address:

Internal Revenue Service
Attention: CP:E:EP:R
P.O. Box 14073, Ben Franklin Station
Washington, DC 20044

A user fee will also be required. See Rev. Proc. 94-8, 1994-1 CB 544, 550.

Where an application for an extension of the amortization period has been granted, a copy of the letter granting the approval must be attached to the plan's Annual Report Form 5500, Schedule B for the applicable plan year.

57. What are the financial accounting standards applicable to pension plans?

The Financial Accounting Standards Board ("FASB") is the body that is charged with the development of generally accepted accounting principles. Generally, employee benefit plans are required to file a financial statement based upon an examination of the books and records of the plan presented fairly in conformity with generally accepted accounting principles applied on a basis consistent with that report prepared and filed for the previous plan year. ERISA Sec. 103(a)(3)(A).

Regarding those principles to be applied in review of the accounting practices of pension plans, FASB has issued three pertinent statements to offer guidance to accountants who are charged with preparing annual financial statements for pension plans.

FASB Statement No. 35, titled "Accounting and Reporting by Defined Benefit Pension Plans," stipulates that defined benefit, multiemployer, governmental and church pension plans' financial statements be prepared on an accrual basis. The financial statement is required to detail the actuarial value of accumulated benefits (at the start or end of the plan year) based upon earnings and services provided by participants prior to the measurement date. Significant changes that affect the accumulated benefits must also be disclosed. The financial statements are required to provide information on net assets available for benefits and any changes affecting those net assets available for the payment of benefits.

FASB Statement No. 87, titled "Employer's Accounting for Pensions," stipulates the reporting required for employers who offer pension plans. Under FASB Statement No. 87, employers are required to report pension liabilities on an accrual basis. The statement also requires employers to provide information on the delayed recognition of retroactive plan amendments and changes in pension liabilities, offsetting assets and liabilities, and the reporting of net periodic pension costs that are in accordance with the standards detailed under FASB Statement No. 87.

FASB Statement No. 88, titled "Employer's Accounting for Settlements and Curtailments of Defined Benefit Pension Plans and Termination Benefits," stipulates that employers detail the settlement of defined benefit pension obligations, curtailments of defined benefit plans, and any special termination benefits offered by plans in accordance with the separate accounting standards spelled out under FASB Statement No. 88.

58. What are the financial accounting standards applicable to post-employment and postretirement benefits other than pension plans?

The Financial Accounting Standards Board (FASB) has issued *FASB Statement No. 112*, titled "Employer's Accounting for Post-Employment Benefits." FASB Statement No. 112 requires employers to account for severance benefits, termination benefits, supplemental unemployment benefits, disability benefits, health care continuation benefits, survivor benefits and all other post-employment benefits that are not pension retirement benefits on an accrual basis, in advance (just as they are required to do for pension benefits).

FASB Statement No. 112 requires employers to accrue liabilities for post-employment benefits other than pensions where:

1.   The obligation is attributable to services previously provided;

2.   Employee rights to the benefits accumulate or vest;

3.   Payment of the benefits is probable; and

4.   The amount of benefits can be reasonably estimated.

FASB Statement No. 106, titled "Employer's Accounting for Post-Retirement Benefits other than Pensions," stipulates that employers charge the cost of postretirement benefits other than pensions against income during the years an employee provides services to the employer.

The DOL has issued a Notice advising that Form 5500s filed by multiemployer welfare plans will be rejected if the accountant's opinion accompanying the Form is "qualified" or "adverse" due to a failure to comply with the financial statement disclosure provisions of the AICPA Statement of Position 92-6, which is mirrored in FASB Statement No. 106. This notice is a rejection by the DOL of its previously proposed policy of non-enforcement, issued in 1997, wherein the DOL advised that it would not reject Form 5500 filings of multiemployer welfare plans for any funds that did not comply with the reporting standards. FASB Statement No. 106, 62 Fed. Reg. 11929 (3-13-97). The DOL advises that under their new policy, Form 5500s of multiemployer welfare benefit plans filed for plan years commencing on or after January 1, 2000, will be subject to rejection if there is any material qualification in the accountant's opinion due to failure to comply with FASB Statement No. 106. Notice of Annual Reporting Enforcement Policy, 63 Fed. Reg. 65505 (11-25-98).

59. What are the financial accounting standards applicable to employer disclosures about pensions and other postretirement benefits?

The Financial Accounting Standards Board (FASB) has issued *FASB Statement No. 132* entitled "Employer's Disclosures about Pensions and other Postretirement Benefits." That statement provides that, effective for fiscal years starting on or after December 15, 1997, FASB Statements No. 87 (Employer's Accounting for Pensions), No. 88 (Employer's Accounting for Settlements and Curtailments of Defined Benefit Pension Plans and Termination Benefits), and No. 106 (Employer's Accounting for Postretirement Benefits other than Pensions) have been amended to provide standardized disclosure requirements for pension and postretirement benefits. The statement also requires additional information on changes in the benefit obligations and the fair values of plan assets that will improve financial analysis and eliminate certain disclosure requirements.

The disclosure requirements eliminated under FASB Statement 132 include:

1. The requirement to provide a description of the plan including employee groups covered, types of assets held and benefit formulas, funding policy, significant nonbenefit liabilities, and the effect of significant matters affecting comparability of information for all periods presented; and

2. Alternative measures of the benefit obligation, including vested benefit obligations, accumulated benefit obligations for pension plans with assets in excess of the accumulated benefit obligation, and various portions of postretirement benefit obligations for retirees, other active participants and other fully eligible participants.

Plan sponsors with two or more plans are permitted under FASB Statement 132 to aggregate required disclosures for their defined benefit pension plans and defined benefit postretirement benefit plans. FASB Statement 132 also eliminates the requirement to disaggregate disclosures for plans with accumulated pension benefit obligations that exceed plan assets. FASB Statement 132 permits the aggregation of these disclosures with other disclosures about plans with accumulated benefit obligations in excess of assets.

Defined contribution plan sponsors are required under FASB Statement 132 to disclose the amount of cost recognized for the plan or other postretirement benefit plan during the period separately from the amount of cost recognized for a defined benefit plan. Defined contribution plan sponsors are also required to include in disclosures a description of any significant changes that would affect comparability (i.e., changes in the rate of sponsor contributions).

FASB Statement 132 requires defined benefit pension plan sponsors and defined benefit postretirement plan sponsors to provide the following information:

1.   A reconciliation of the beginning and ending balances of the benefit obligation for the period;

2.   A reconciliation of the beginning and ending balances of the fair value of plan assets;

3.   The funding status of the plans;

4.   All amounts not recognized in the statement of financial position;

5.   All amounts recognized in the statement of financial position;

6.   The amount of net periodic benefit costs recognized in net income and the amount recognized in other comprehensive income;

7.   The following assumptions used in the accounting for the plans (on a weighted basis):

a) assumed discount rate,

b) rate of compensation increase (pay-related plans),

c) health care cost trend rate, and

d) the expected long-term rate of return on plan assets;

8.   The effect of a one percentage point increase and decrease in the weighted average of the assumed health care cost trend rates on:

a) the aggregate of the service and interest cost components of net periodic postretirement health care benefit costs, and

b) the accumulated postretirement benefit obligation for health care benefits, and

c) an explanation of any significant change in the benefit obligations or plan assets not otherwise apparent in the other disclosure required by the statement.

FASB Statement 132 requires employers to disclose the amount of contributions to multiemployer plans.

RECORDKEEPING

60. What employee recordkeeping is required to be maintained under ERISA?

In administering a qualified plan, plan sponsors must maintain certain records in order to assure that they are maintaining and operating the plan in accordance with the participation, accrual, vesting and distribution requirements of ERISA and the Code. ERISA Section 209 says that every employer must maintain records, with respect to each employee, which are sufficient to determine the benefits that are due or may become due to such employees. That section goes on to require that the employer furnish the plan administrator with the information necessary to prepare mandated reports for participants. These reports include statements of account balances and vested percentages, as well as summary annual reports. Records necessary for the preparation of required reports include those pertaining to employment history, birth, pay and marital status.

Employment History Records

In addition to the necessity of maintaining employment history records for non-retirement benefit reasons, these records will be necessary for determining:

(1) Eligibility to participate (in general, ERISA Section 202(a)(1) and IRC Section 410(a)(1)(A) mandate participation in a qualified plan upon the completion of one year of service and the attainment of age 21);

(2) Benefit accrual (ERISA Section 202(a)(3)(A) and IRC Section 410(a)(3)(A) define a "year of service" for purposes of qualifying for a benefit accrual and ERISA Section 203(b)(2) and IRC Section 411(a)(5) define a year of service for vesting purposes as 1,000 hours of service — excluding seasonal or part-time employees who have alternative rules);

(3) Vesting (see the discussion of vesting requirements in Q 18); and,

(4) In certain cases, eligibility for early retirement benefit incentives.

Employment records must also be maintained for purposes of determining whether an employee has experienced a "break in service." "Break in service" rules state that any participant who has not completed 500 hours of service in a plan year has experienced a break in service. A break in service will have an impact upon a participant's accrual of vesting percentages and may require the participant, upon re-attainment of full-time status (1,000 hours of service), to satisfy the plan's active service requirements before returning to active participation in the underlying plan. ERISA Sec. 202(b)(1); IRC Sec. 410(a)(5).

Birth Records

Employee birth records are required to be maintained for purposes of determining eligibility to participate in the plan (see ERISA Section 202(a)(1) and IRC Section 410(a)(1)(A) — referred to above); vesting (ERISA Section 203(b) and IRC Section 411(a)(4) mandate that all years of service with a plan sponsor after the attainment of age 18 must be taken into consideration when calculating a participant's vesting percentage); and to receive distributions from the plan, either through early retirement benefits or upon the attainment of normal retirement age. A qualified plan must commence the payment of benefits — unless the participant elects otherwise — not later than the 60th day after the latest of the close of the plan year:

(1)   In which the participant attains the earlier of age 65 or the normal retirement age specified under the plan,

(2)   The tenth anniversary occurs of the year in which the participant began to participate in the plan, or

(3)   The participant terminates his service with the employer. IRC Section 401(a)(14).

Pay Records

IRC Section 415 details the limitations on benefits and contributions under qualified plans. These limitations are typically based upon the compensation paid to participants, and govern annual contributions under individual account plans (the lesser of $40,000 (in 2002) or 100% of compensation) and annual benefit limits for participants under defined benefit plans. Plan administrators must pay particular attention to these records and their accuracy because the IRS considers violations under IRC Section 415 limits to be very serious. Indeed, plans that violate the Section 415 limits face the very real possibility of disqualification.

Marital Status Records

Records of the marital status of plan participants are necessary in order to determine eligibility for mandated spousal benefits under ERISA and the Internal Revenue Code. Where a participant with vested benefits under a plan dies prior to attaining the earliest retirement age under the plan (i.e., generally the time when benefits under a plan are payable in the form of an annuity), the surviving spouse, if any, is entitled to a qualified pre-retirement survivor annuity (QPSA) (with certain exceptions). ERISA Sec. 205(e)(1); IRC Sec. 417(c).

The surviving spouse of a participant who dies after reaching the earliest retirement age under the plan generally must be provided a qualified joint and survivor annuity (QJSA) (again, with certain exceptions). A QJSA is defined as an annuity for the life of the spouse which is not less than 50% of (and not greater than 100% of) the amount of the annuity which is payable during the joint lives of the participant and the spouse and which is the actuarial equivalent of a single annuity for the life of the participant. ERISA Sec. 205(d)(1); IRC Sec. 417(b). Qualified plans subject to the spousal annuity rules must also provide written explanations to participants of their QPSA and QJSA rights. ERISA Sec. 205(c)(3); IRC Sec. 417(a)(3). Spouses must consent in writing to any waiver of their pre-retirement survivor annuity and joint and survivor annuity rights. ERISA Sec. 205(c)(2); IRC Sec. 417(a)(2).

Where a participant has experienced a divorce, the former spouse may be eligible to receive benefits under a qualified domestic relations order (QDRO). The plan administrator will need to maintain accurate participant benefit records in this situation in order to ascertain the exact amount of accrued benefits the participant must provide to his ex-spouse under a court-ordered QDRO. A QDRO is defined as any judgment, decree, or order that relates to the provision of child support, alimony payments or marital property rights (including accrued retirement benefits) to a spouse, former spouse, child or other dependent of a participant, and that is made pursuant to a state domestic relations law (including community property law). ERISA Sec. 206(d)(3)(B)(ii); IRC Sec. 414(p)(1)(B).

Marital records are also necessary when a plan permits participants to access their accrued benefits through participant loans. If the plan is subject to the spousal annuity rules, the plan must obtain the written consent of the participant's spouse, within 90 days of issuance, for any participant loan under the plan in excess of $5,000. Treas. Reg. §1.401(a)-20, A-24.

61. What are the rules regarding the use of electronic media for the maintenance and retention of employee benefit plan records?

The DOL has issued proposed regulations concerning the use of electronic media for the maintenance and retention of employee benefit plan records in electronic form. The proposal provides standards for the use of electronic media, including electronic storage and automatic data processing systems, for the maintenance and retention of records required by ERISA Sections 107 and 209. The record maintenance and retention requirements of ERISA will be satisfied when using electronic media if:

1.   The electronic recordkeeping system has reasonable controls to ensure the integrity, accuracy, authenticity and reliability of the records in electronic form;

2. The electronic records are maintained in reasonable order and in a safe and accessible place, and in such manner as they may be readily inspected or examined (for example, the recordkeeping system should be capable of indexing, retaining, preserving, retrieving and reproducing the electronic records);

3. The electronic records are readily convertible into legible and readable paper copy as may be needed to satisfy reporting and disclosure requirements or any other obligation under Title I of ERISA;

4. The electronic recordkeeping system is not subject, in whole or in part, to any agreement or restriction that would, directly or indirectly, compromise or limit a person's ability to comply with any reporting and disclosure requirement or any other obligation under Title I of ERISA; and

5. Adequate records management practices are established and implemented (for example, following procedures for labeling of electronically maintained or retained records, providing a secure storage environment, creating back-up electronic copies and selecting an off-site storage location, observing a quality assurance program evidenced by regular evaluations of the electronic recordkeeping system including periodic checks of electronically maintained or retained records; and retaining paper copies of records that cannot be clearly, accurately or completely transferred to an electronic recordkeeping system). Labor Prop. Reg. §2520.107-1(b).

All electronic records must exhibit a high degree of legibility and readability when displayed on a video display terminal and when reproduced in paper form. The term "legibility" means the observer must be able to identify all letters and numerals positively and quickly to the exclusion of all other letters or numerals. The term "readability" means that the observer must be able to recognize a group of letters or numerals as words or complete numbers. Labor Prop. Reg. §2520.107-1(c).

Original paper records may be disposed of any time after they are transferred to an electronic recordkeeping system that complies with the requirements of the proposed regulations, except that original records may not be discarded if they have legal significance or inherent value as original records, so that an electronic reproduction would not constitute a duplicate record (for example, notarized documents, insurance contracts, stock certificates, and documents executed under seal). Labor Prop. Reg. §2520.107-1(d).

62. What type of forms must a plan maintain regarding disability retirement benefits?

Where a qualified plan permits the distribution of accrued benefits in the case of the disability of a participant, the plan will need to maintain a basic disability application to be completed by the participant, and a separate form for the certification of disability to be completed by the participant's physician.

The basic application for disability benefits will provide for the standard information all participants will be required to provide when they apply for benefits. In addition, this form will allow sufficient space for the participant to detail the disability and provide the identification of attending physicians who have identified and treated the disability.

The certification form will be completed, and attested, by the attending physician who satisfies the plan or plan sponsor's requirements for competency in determining the nature and extent of the participant's disability. Most plan sponsors have established written procedures to designate a physician of their choosing for the completion of this form. Multiemployer plans will often provide for a medical board to review these determinations and will often provide for a union-appointed physician to review the disability claims of a participant.

REPORTING AND DISCLOSURE

63. What plans are subject to reporting rules?

The ERISA provisions governing reporting and disclosure are applicable to an employee benefit plan established or maintained by an employer engaged in commerce or in an industry affecting commerce. In addition, these provisions are applicable to employee organizations representing employees engaged in commerce or in an industry affecting commerce. *Baucom v. Pilot Life Ins. Co.*, 674 F. Supp. 1175 (M.D. NC 1987).

64. What plans are exempt from the reporting rules?

The provisions of Title I of ERISA do not apply to an employee benefit plan if the plan is:

1. A governmental plan (as defined in ERISA Section 3(32));

2. A church plan (as defined in ERISA Section 3(33)) with respect to which no election has been made under IRC Section 410(d);

3. Maintained solely for the purpose of complying with applicable workmen's compensation, unemployment compensation, or disability insurance laws;

4. Maintained outside of the United States primarily for the benefit of persons substantially all of whom are nonresident aliens; or

5.   An excess benefit plan (as defined in ERISA Section 3(36)), and is unfunded. ERISA Sec. 4(b).

In addition, individual retirement accounts and individual retirement annuities (IRAs, as defined in IRC Section 408), and Keogh plans that cover a single self-employed individual are also exempt from ERISA's reporting rules.

65. What reports are required to be provided to the Internal Revenue Service?

ERISA covered plans must comply with certain duties of disclosure and reporting, set forth in ERISA Section 101.

Annual Report, Schedules and Supplemental Information

The reporting obligations include the furnishing of an annual report that satisfies the requirements of ERISA Section 103. ERISA Sec. 101(b)(4). ERISA Section 103 details the information on the characteristics and financial operations of the plan for which the annual report has been filed.

The Annual Report Form 5500 (5500) is required to be filed with the Pension and Welfare Benefits Administration by the last day of the seventh month after the close of the plan year. The DOL will process these reports after receipt and provide a copy of the 5500 to the IRS (thereby eliminating the need for the plan administrator to file two copies of the same report). As detailed in Chapter XII, the DOL utilizes the 5500s it receives in enforcement and other program activities.

The IRS and DOL issued the "final" version of the dramatically revised Form 5500 on February 3, 1999. The three different types of 5500s were consolidated into a three page form. The prior Form 5500-C/R filed by small plans (those with fewer than 100 participants) was eliminated, and the Form 5500-EZ was retained. Under the revised format, there are 13 schedules that accompany the new Form 5500. A plan will complete and file only those schedules that apply. The 13 schedules include the prior eight schedules (A, B, C, E, F, G, P and SSA) and five additional schedules (D, H, I, R and T). Schedules A, C and G have undergone substantial revisions. See Q 66 for details on these new schedules.

Plans with 100 or more participants are required to file a supplemental report prepared by an independent qualified public accountant that provides for the accountant's opinion (unqualified or qualified) on the financial statements and schedules contained in the 5500, the accounting principles and practices utilized in the preparation of the 5500, and any changes in the accounting principles that may have affected the information in the financial statements. This requirement is also subject to final rules issued by the DOL that require some plans with fewer than 100 participants to file supplemental reports prepared by independent qualified public accountants. See Q 113 for details of these small plan audit requirements.

Notice of Plan Changes

A plan administrator who is required to file an annual registration statement (known as Schedule SSA, see Q 66) is also required to notify the IRS of:

1. A change in the name of the plan;

2. A change in the name or address of the plan administrator;

3. The termination of the plan; or

4. The merger or consolidation of the plan with any other plan, or its division into two or more plans (on Form 5310-A). IRC Sec. 6057(b).

Furthermore, plan administrators are required to notify the IRS in the event of a plan termination. This notification may be made by checking the "Final Return" box at the top of the Form 5500 filed by the plan. Plan administrators may file Form 5310 with the IRS to seek a favorable opinion on the plan's qualification; however, such a filing is not required. It is recommended that terminating plans seek a favorable IRS determination to assure that funds distributed from the terminating plan and transferred to other qualified plans or individual retirement accounts will retain their tax deferred status.

Electronic Filing of Form 5500

Plan administrators may file the 5500 and related schedules via magnetic media (e.g., magnetic tapes, computer discs, etc.) or electronically. If the plan administrator files the 5500 electronically or on magnetic media, he must also file Form 8453-E, Employee Benefit Plan Declaration and Signature for Electronic/Magnetic Media Filing. This is the declaration and signature media return.

The DOL has posted computer scannable copies of the paper and electronic versions of the revised Form 5500 on its website as a part of the DOL's new computerized system for processing the revised Form 5500. It is a priority of the DOL to increase the number of plans filing electronically through the new computerized system, known as "EFAST" (ERISA Filing Acceptance System). The proposed Form 5500 can be accessed on the internet at http://www.dol.gov/dol/pwba/public/pubs/forms/fm99inx.htm. EFAST was developed in conjunction with the revisions to the Form 5500 for the 1999 reporting year. Under EFAST, Forms 5500 are required to be filed in one of two computer scannable formats: "machine print" and "hand print." The EFAST system is designed to accept 5500 filings only on one of these two approved forms. Although 1999 reports could have been filed on non-approved forms (such as photocopies), beginning with the 2000 reporting year, all 5500 submissions were required to be in one of the two approved formats. The EFAST system may not properly process forms that do not meet the new specifications. This could result in non-standard form filings being rejected as deficient. For information on both EFAST approved forms, as well as a list of approved EFAST software providers, see the official DOL EFAST website at http://www.efast.dol.gov.

The DOL has announced that effective March 1, 2001, employee benefit plan professionals can receive help in completing their Annual Report Form 5500 returns by calling the DOL's Pension and Welfare Benefits Administration at (866) 463-3278. This is a toll-free number. "This new toll-free number will provide plan filers with easy access to technical assistance the PWBA, the Internal Revenue Service and the Pension Benefit Guaranty Corporation" according to Acting Assistant Secretary of Labor, Alan Lebowitz, as quoted in the PWBA press release announcing the new toll-free assistance line.

66. What are the schedules that are filed with the Annual Report Form 5500?

A filed Form 5500 must be accompanied by the appropriate schedules that are designed to provide detailed information supporting the basic facts and figures reported on Form 5500. The following is a brief review of the schedules, the information they must contain, and which plans are required to file each schedule. For 1999 and subsequent reporting years, the DOL and IRS issued revisions to the preexisting schedules and issued five additional schedules (detailed below). These revised schedules are available for electronic and paper filing. They are available for downloading on the DOL's website at http://www.dol.gov/dol/pwba/public/pubs/forms/fm99inx.htm.

Schedule A

Schedule A is filed by those plans that provide benefits through an insurance company. It provides a statement from the insurance company that details the premium rate for subscription charge, the total subscription charges paid to each insurance carrier, and the number of individuals covered by each class of benefits. Schedule A also reports the total amount of premiums received by the insurance carrier, the number of individuals covered in each class of benefits, and the total amount of claims paid. The information provided in Schedule A is required by ERISA Section 103(e). Schedule A was revised for 1999 and subsequent reporting years. The revised form was designed to better collect information on the types of insurance products, the types of coverage and insured benefits being reported. It is also designed to conform required reporting to various accounting industry changes (Generally Accepted Accounting Principles) on current value financial reporting of investment-type contracts with insurance companies.

Schedule A is not required from plans that file a Form 5500-EZ.

Schedule B

Schedule B is filed by defined benefit plans to provide details on the actuarial information for those plans to which the minimum funding standards of IRC Section 412 apply. It is prepared and signed by an enrolled actuary. Schedule B contains a description of the funding method and actuarial assumptions used to determine the costs of the plan and a certification of the contribution necessary to reduce the accumulated funding deficiency (if any) to zero.

Schedule C

Schedule C details the service provider and trustee information. It is used to report those service providers receiving, directly or indirectly, $5,000 or more in compensation for services provided to the plan during the plan year being reported. Schedule C also details information regarding service providers who have terminated (or were terminated from) services to the plan during the reporting year. Schedule C was revised for 1999 and subsequent reporting years. The most dramatic revisions limited the report to the 40 top paid service providers and eliminated the requirement of separately identifying plan trustees. Terminated service provider reporting requirements were reduced to require only the reporting of terminating accountants and enrolled actuaries.

Schedule D

Schedule D serves two purposes:

1.   Part I provides a standardized reporting format for any Direct Filing Entity (DFE) (the primary plan reporting); and

2.   Part II provides a standardized reporting form for plans participating in the primary plan reporting (including Master Trust Investment Accounts, or MTIAs).

Schedule E

Schedule E details employee stock ownership information for the reporting year and is completed by the plan sponsor or plan administrator of a qualified plan that provides benefits through an employee stock ownership program. Schedule E is required to be filed with Forms 5500 and 5500-EZ.

Schedule F

Schedule F is required to be filed by cafeteria plans and educational assistance programs.

Schedule G

This schedule is required to be filed by all large plans (100 or more participants) and DFEs and MTIAs. The financial schedules provided in Schedule G are designed to provide a uniform method for the reporting of investment and asset information, including loans and fixed income obligations in default or determined to be uncollectible and non-exempt prohibited transactions (see Q 67 for details).

Schedule H

Schedule H contains required reporting of financial information for larger plans and DFEs. It reports detailed financial information about the plan by incorporating asset and liability, and income and expense questions from the pre-1999 version of the basic Form 5500.

Schedule I

Schedule I serves the same function as Schedule H, however, it is required filing for smaller plans. The new Schedule I closely resembles the simplified financial statements contained in the old Form 5500-R.

Schedule P

Schedule P is the Annual Return of Fiduciary of Employee Benefit Trust. It is filed by a trustee or custodian with either Form 5500 or 5500-EZ.

Schedule R

Schedule R is required for both tax qualified and nonqualified pension benefit plans (large and small) that are required to file Form 5500 (except for Section 403(b) plans). Schedule R reports certain information about the plan's participants, asset distribution and funding. It also requires the reporting of any plan amendments that have the effect of increasing the value of benefits in a defined benefit plan.

Schedule SSA

The plan administrator of a plan to which the vesting standards of the Code and ERISA apply for the plan year must file a registration statement (Schedule SSA) that sets forth:

1. The name of the plan;

2. The name and address of the plan administrator;

3. The name and taxpayer identifying number of each participant in the plan:

   a) who, during the plan year, separated from service covered by the plan,

   b) who is entitled to a deferred vested benefit under the plan as of the end of the plan year, and

   c) with respect to whom retirement benefits were not paid under the plan during the plan year;

4.   The nature, amount, and form of the deferred vested benefit to which the participant is entitled; and

5.   Any other information the Secretary of Treasury may require. IRC Sec. 6057(a).

Schedule T

Schedule T is required to be filed by all qualified plans in order to demonstrate whether the plan satisfies the coverage requirements of IRC Section 410(b). Plans that test on a qualified separate line of business basis would reflect this election on Schedule T. Participating employers in multiple employer plans are not required to file separate 5500s. Rather, a separate Schedule T is attached from each participating employer to a single Form 5500 filed on behalf of the entire multiple employer plan.

67. What are the required contents of the financial statements filed with Form 5500?

Schedule G to the Annual Report Form 5500 is used for the reporting of financial statements. Schedule G is used to report the following:

1.   A statement of assets and liabilities;

2.   A statement of changes in the fund balance;

3.   A statement of changes in financial position; and

4.   A statement of changes in net assets available for plan benefits.

The financial statement with respect to an employee welfare benefit plan provides a statement of assets and liabilities, changes in the fund balance, and changes in the financial position of the plan. In the notes to the financial statements, disclosures concerning the following items must be considered by the accountant:

1.   A description of the plan, including any significant changes in the plan made during the period and the impact of such changes on benefits;

2.   A description of material lease commitments, other commitments, and contingent liabilities;

3.   A description of agreements and transactions with people known to be parties in interest;

4.   A general description of priorities upon termination of the plan;

5. Information concerning whether or not a tax ruling or determination letter has been obtained; and

6. Any other matters necessary to fully and fairly present the financial statements of the plan. ERISA Sec. 103(b)(1).

The financial statement with respect to an employee retirement benefit plan will contain a statement of assets and liabilities and a statement of changes in net assets available for plan benefits that must include details of revenues and expenses and other charges aggregated by general source and application. In the notes to financial statements, disclosures concerning the following items must be considered by the accountant:

1. A description of the plan, including any significant changes in the plan made during the period and the impact of those changes on benefits;

2. The funding policy (including the policy with respect to prior service cost), and any changes with respect to those policies during the year;

3. A description of any significant changes in plan benefits made during the period;

4. A description of material lease commitments, other commitments and contingent liabilities;

5. A description of agreements and transactions with people known to be parties in interest;

6. A general description of priorities upon termination of the plan;

7. Information concerning whether or not a tax ruling or determination letter has been obtained; and

8. Any other matters necessary to fully and fairly present the financial statements of the retirement benefits plan. ERISA Sec. 103(b)(2).

All employee benefit plans must have attached the following information in separate schedules:

1. A statement of the assets and liabilities of the plan aggregated by categories and valued at their current value, and the same data displayed in comparative form for the end of the previous fiscal year of the plan;

2. A statement of receipts and disbursements during the preceding 12-month period aggregated by general sources and applications;

3. A schedule of all assets held for investment purposes aggregated and identified by issuer, borrower, lessor, or similar party to the transaction (including a notation as to whether the party is known to be a party in interest), maturity date, rate of interest, collateral, par or maturity value, cost, and current value;

4. A schedule of each transaction involving a person known to be a party in interest and each nonexempt transaction he is involved in;

5. A list of all leases that were in default or were classified as uncollectible;

6. A list of all loans or fixed income obligations that were in default as of the close of the plan year;

7. If some or all of the assets of a plan or plans are held in a common or collective investment trust maintained by a bank or similar institution or in a separate account maintained by an insurance carrier or a separate trust maintained by a bank as trustee, the report must include the most recent annual statement of assets and liabilities of the common or collective trust; and

8. A schedule of each reportable transaction (see Q 68 for details on reportable events). ERISA Sec. 103(b)(3).

68. What is a reportable transaction for purposes of filing Form 5500?

A reportable transaction required to be detailed in Form 5500 for a reporting year is a transaction, or series of transactions, with or in conjunction with the same person which, when aggregated, regardless of the category of the asset and the gain or loss on any transaction, involves an amount in excess of 5% of the current value of plan assets. Labor Reg. §2520.103-6(c).

The schedule of reportable transactions will apply to any series of transactions (other than transactions with respect to securities) within the plan year or with or in conjunction with the same person which, when aggregated (regardless of the category of asset and the gain or loss on any transaction), involves an amount in excess of 5% of the current value of plan assets. It also includes any transaction within the plan year involving securities of the same issue if within the plan year any series of transactions with respect to the securities, when aggregated, involves an amount in excess of 5% of the current value of plan assets. Labor Reg. §2520.103-6(c).

Plans whose assets are held in whole or in part in a common or collective trust or a pooled separate account (as provided under Labor Regulation Section 2520.203-3 and Labor Regulation Section 2520.103-4 and that satisfy the requirements of those sections) are not required to prepare schedules of reportable transactions with respect to the individual transactions of the common or collective trust or pooled separate account. Labor Reg. §2520.103-6(c)(3).

The schedule of reportable transactions requires the following information as to each transaction or series of transactions:

1. The name of each party, except that in the case of a transaction or series of transactions involving a purchase or sale of a security on the market, the schedule need not include the person from whom it was purchased or to whom it was sold (a purchase or sale on the market is a purchase or sale of a security through a registered broker-dealer acting as a broker under the Securities Exchange Act of 1934);

2. A brief description of each asset;

3. The purchase or selling price in the case of a purchase or sale, the rental cost in the case of a lease, and the amount of principal, interest rate, payment schedule (e.g., fully amortized, partly amortized with balloon), and maturity date in the case of a loan;

4. Expenses incurred, including, but not limited to, any fees or commissions;

5. The cost of any asset;

6. The current value of any asset acquired or disposed of at the time of acquisition or disposition; and

7. The net gain or loss. Labor Reg. §2520.103-6(d)(1).

The term "current value" is defined as the fair market value where available, and otherwise the fair value as determined in good faith by a trustee or a named fiduciary pursuant to the terms of the plan and in accordance with the ERISA's regulations, assuming an orderly liquidation at the time of the determination. ERISA Sec. 3(26).

There is an exemption from the 5% reportable transaction requirements for any plan assets held in common or collective trusts maintained by a bank, trust company, or similar institution, or assets held in an insurance company pooled separate account. The plan is not required to include in the annual report any information concerning the individual transaction of the common or collective trust or pooled separate account. Labor Regs. §§2520.103-3, 2520.103-4.

69. What actuarial information is required to be provided in Schedule B of Form 5500?

Schedule B of Form 5500 is required to be filed on an annual basis by a defined benefit plan that is subject to the minimum funding standards of ERISA. The completed Schedule B must be signed by an enrolled actuary and based upon an actuarial valuation of the plan, which must be made at least once every three years. The information reported on Schedule B includes:

1.   A description of the funding method and actuarial assumptions used to determine the plan costs;

2.   A certification of the contribution necessary to fully fund the plan;

3.   A statement that the report is complete and accurate and that the actuarial assumptions are reasonable and represent the actuary's best estimate of anticipated experience under the plan; and

4.   Any other information necessary to fully and fairly disclose the actuarial position of the plan.

70. What is the due date for filing Form 5500?

Form 5500 is required to be filed (with its accompanying schedules) on or before the last day of the seventh month following the close of the plan year. For plans operating on a calendar year basis, that date is July 31. Form 5500 is filed with the IRS. A plan being absorbed in a merger has a short plan year ending on the date of the merger, for which the accountant's report is required to be filed with Annual Report Form 5500. *PWBA v USAirways, Inc.*, 24 EBC 2604 (Office of Admin. Law Judges 2000).

Where the plan requires an extension of time beyond the filing date, the plan sponsor may receive an automatic extension if the plan year is the same as the plan sponsor's tax year, and the plan sponsor has been granted an extension to file its federal income tax return. In order to receive the automatic extension, a copy of the extension to file the federal income tax return must be attached to Form 5500 when it is filed.

An extension for filing may also be requested by filing Form 5558 prior to the initial due date for filing. This form requires a detailed statement that explains why the extension is necessary. If granted, the extension may be for up to two and one-half months beyond the original filing deadline. If refused, the plan will receive a 10-day grace period beyond the original filing deadline in order to timely file the annual report.

PRACTITIONER'S POINTER

The extension of time for filing Form 5500 that has been granted through an automatic extension or through a Form 5558 filing does not provide the employer with an extension of time for the filing of PBGC Form 1. The DOL, IRS and PBGC have extended certain filing deadline for plans affected by the September 11, 2001 terrorist attacks. The extension applies to plan administrators, employers and other entities who file the Form 5500 and Form 5500-EZ that are located in the areas designated as federal disaster areas because of the terrorist attacks.

The extension also applies to filers located outside the designated disaster areas who are unable to obtain the information necessary for filing from service providers, banks or insurance companies whose operations are directly affected by the disasters.

The DOL, IRS and PBGC extended certain filing deadlines for plans affected by the September 11, 2001 terrorist attacks. The extension applied to plan administrators, employers and other entities who file the Form 5500 and Form 5500-EZ that are located in the areas designated as federal disaster areas because of the terrorist attacks. The extension also applied to filers located outside the designated disaster areas who were unable to obtain the information necessary for filing from service providers, banks or insurance companies whose operations were directly affected by the disasters.

In a September 14, 2001 Press Release, the DOL advised that "under the extension, those with filings originally due between September 11, 2001, and November 30, 2001 will be allowed an additional six months plus 120 days to file." Filers on an extension that expired between September 11, 2001, and November 30, 2001, were allowed an additional 120 days to file.

Filers entitled to the extension relief described above should check Part 1, Box D, on the Form 5500, or Part 1, Box B on the Form 5500-EZ, and attach a statement labeled "SEPTEMBER 11, 2001 TERRORIST ATTACK" that explains the basis for the extension being claimed under this release. Filers who have additional questions may contact the PWBA Help Desk at 1-866-463-3278. PWBA Press Release 01-36, September 14, 2001.

71. What is the Delinquent Filer Voluntary Compliance Program (DFVC)?

The Department of Labor describes the program as follows: "In an effort to encourage pension and welfare plan administrators to file overdue annual reports (commonly referred to as the Form 5500), the Department of Labor's Pension and Welfare Benefits Administration is providing plan administrators with the opportunity to pay reduced civil penalties for voluntarily complying with the annual reporting requirements." DOL Procedure: PWBA's Delinquent Filer Voluntary Compliance Program; Office of Chief Accountant Frequently Asked Questions

About The Delinquent Filer Voluntary Compliance Program, http://www.dol.gov/dol/pwba/public/programs/oca/ocafaqs.htm.

From the time of its inception in 1995, the DFVC Program has been designed to afford eligible plan administrators the opportunity to avoid the assessment of civil penalties otherwise applicable to administrators who fail to file timely annual reports. Eligible administrators may avail themselves of the DFVC Program by complying with the filing requirements and paying the civil penalties specified in the DFVC Program. See DOL Procedure: PWBA's Delinquent Filer Voluntary Compliance Program, 60 Fed. Reg. 20874 (4-27-95).

72. Who is eligible to take advantage of the DFVC Program?

The DOL has stated that "Plan administrators are eligible to pay reduced civil penalties under the program if the required filings under the DFVC Program are made prior to the date on which the administrator is notified in writing by the department of a failure to file a timely annual report under Title I of the Employee Retirement Security Act of 1974 (ERISA).

Participation under the DFVC Program is not available to all Form 5500 Series filers. The relief under the DFVC Program is available only to the extent that a Form 5500 is required to be filed under Title I of ERISA. For example, Form 5500-EZ filers and Form 5500 filers for plans without employees (as described in 29 CFR §2510.3-3(b) and (c)) are not eligible to participate in the DFVC Program because such plans are not subject to Title I of ERISA. Plan administrators may call (202) 693-8360 if they have questions about whether the program applies to their filings." DOL Procedure: PWBA's Delinquent Filer Voluntary Compliance Program; Office of Chief Accountant Frequently Asked Questions About The Delinquent Filer Voluntary Compliance Program, http://askpwba.dol.gov/faq-dfvc.html.

73. What civil penalties may be assessed by the DOL against plan administrators who fail to file a timely annual report and do not participate in the DFVC Program?

The DOL has the authority, under ERISA Section 502(c)(2) to assess civil penalties of up to $1,100 a day against plan administrators who fail or refuse to file complete and timely annual reports (Form 5500 Series Annual Return/Reports) as required under ERISA Section 101(b)(4), and the DOL regulations (see 29 CFR Part 2520). Labor Reg. §2570.502c-2, redesignated as Labor Reg. §2575.502c-2, 64 Fed. Reg. 2246 (8-3-99). Pursuant to the regulations, PWBA has maintained a program for the assessment of civil penalties for noncompliance with the annual reporting requirements. See Labor Regs. §§2560.502c-2, 2570.60, et seq. Under this program, plan administrators filing annual reports after the date on which the report was required to be filed may be assessed $50 per day for each day an annual report is filed after the date on which the annual report(s) was required to be filed, without regard to any extensions for filing. Plan administrators who fail to file an annual report may be assessed a penalty of $300 per day, up to $30,000 per year, until a complete annual report is filed. Penalties are applicable to each annual report required to be filed under Title I of ERISA. The DOL may, in its discretion, waive all or part of a civil penalty assessed under ERISA Section 502(c)(2) upon a showing by the administrator that there was reasonable cause for the failure to file a complete and timely annual report.

The DOL states that "the following penalties may be assessed by the DOL against plan administrators:

- *Late filers.* Plan administrators filing a late annual report (i.e., after the date the report was required to be filed, including extensions) may be assessed $50 per day, with no limit, for the period they failed to file, determined without regard to any extensions for filing.

- *Non-filers.* Plan administrators who fail to file an annual report may be assessed a penalty of $300 per day, up to $30,000 per year, until a complete annual report is filed.

For example, assume an administrator for a plan with a calendar plan year files the annual report for the 2001 plan year on October 31, 2002, and does not participate in the DFVC Program. The administrator would receive a written notice indicating the department's intent to assess a penalty of $4,600 ($50 x 92 days delinquent). If there are other annual reports that either have not been filed or have been filed late, the plan administrator may be subject to the assessment of additional penalties because the penalties are separately calculated for each filing.

Pursuant to the department's regulations, upon issuance by the department of a notice of intent to assess a penalty, the plan administrator may file a statement of reasonable cause why the penalty, as calculated, should not be assessed. A showing of reasonable cause must be in the form of a written statement setting forth all the facts alleged as reasonable cause and must contain a declaration by the administrator that the statement is made under penalty of perjury."

DOL Procedure: PWBA's Delinquent Filer Voluntary Compliance Program; Office of Chief Accountant Frequently Asked Questions About The Delinquent Filer Voluntary Compliance Program, http://askpwba.dol.gov/faq-dfvc.html.

74. How does a plan administrator file a delinquent Form 5500 under the DFVC Program?

The DOL has published guidance stating that "participation in the DFVC Program is a two part process:

1.   File a complete Form 5500 Annual Return/Report, including all schedules and attachments, for each year the plan administrator is requesting relief. See Q 75. This filing should be sent to PWBA at the appropriate ERISA Filing Acceptance System (EFAST) address listed in the instructions for the most current Form 5500 Annual Return/Report, or electronically in accordance with the EFAST electronic filing requirements. The EFAST addresses in the 2001 Form 5500 instructions are as follows:

   Paper
   Pension and Welfare Benefits Administration
   P.O. Box 7043
   Lawrence, Kansas 66044-7043

   Floppy Disc, CD-Rom or Tape
   Pension and Welfare Benefits Administration
   P.O. Box 7041
   Lawrence, Kansas 66044-7041

   Private Delivery Service
   PWBA/NCS
   Attn: EFAST
   3833 Greenway Drive
   Lawrence, Kansas 66046-1290

2.   Submit to the DFVC Program, P.O. Box 530292, Atlanta, GA 30353-0292:

   • A paper copy of the completed Form 5500, without schedules or attachments, for any filings using a 1999 or later version of the Form (or a paper copy of the first page of the Form 5500 or Form 5500-C, as applicable, for filings submitted on pre-1999 versions of the Form).

   • A check for the applicable penalty amount, made payable to the U.S. Department of Labor. See Q 76.

   • If the submission is for a small plan sponsored by an Internal Revenue Code (Code) Section 501(c)(3) organization (including a Code section 403(b) small plan), the notation "501(c)(3) Plan" must be in the upper-right corner of the paper copy of the first page of the Form 5500 submitted to the DFVC Program in Atlanta, Georgia. This notation should not be included in the filing made with PWBA in Lawrence, Kansas. See Q 78.

It is recommended that all filings for a plan be submitted to the DFVC Program in the same envelope or package in order to ensure that those filings count towards the "per-plan" capped penalty amount." See Q 76, Q 77. DOL Procedure: PWBA's Delinquent Filer Voluntary Compliance Program; Office of Chief Accountant Frequently Asked Questions About The Delinquent Filer Voluntary Compliance Program, http://askpwba.dol.gov/faq-dfvc.html.

If a joint employer-union board of trustees or committee is the administrator, at least one employer representative and one union representative must sign the form.

75. Which version of the Form 5500 should be filed?

According to guidance published by the DOL, "The plan administrator shall file either:

- The most current Form 5500 Annual Return/Report form issued (and, if necessary, indicate in the appropriate space on the first page of the Form 5500 the plan year for which the annual return/report is being filed), or

- The Form 5500 Series Annual Return/Report form issued for the plan year for which the relief is sought (but not a Form 5500-R if the filing is for a 1998 plan year or a prior year)."

DOL Procedure: PWBA's Delinquent Filer Voluntary Compliance Program; Office of Chief Accountant Frequently Asked Questions About The Delinquent Filer Voluntary Compliance Program, http://askpwba.dol.gov/faq-dfvc.html.

76. What is the applicable penalty amount under the DFVC program?

Guidance from the DOL states as follows:

"Small Plan Filers: In the case of a plan with fewer than 100 participants at the beginning of the plan year (i.e. "small plan"), the applicable penalty amount is $10 per day for each day the annual report is filed after the date on which the annual report was due (without regard to any extensions), not to exceed $750. In the case of a DFVC submission relating to more than one delinquent annual report filing for the same plan, the maximum penalty amount is $750 for each annual report, not to exceed $1,500 per plan.

Note: The "80/120" participant rule described in 29 CFR [Sec.] 2520.103-1(d) is applicable in determining whether a plan is a small or large plan.

Large Plan Filers: In the case of a plan with 100 or more participants at the beginning of the plan year and which is not eligible for the "80/120" participant rule (hereinafter "large plan"), the applicable penalty amount is $10 per day for each day the annual report is filed after the date on which the annual report was due (without regard to any extensions), not to exceed $2,000. In the case of a DFVC submission relating to more than one delinquent filing for the same plan, the maximum penalty amount is $2,000 for each annual report, not to exceed $4,000 per plan.

It is recommended that all filings for a plan be submitted to the DFVC Program in the same envelope or package in order to ensure that those filings count towards the "per-plan" capped penalty amount.

Example 1. An administrator of a large plan with a calendar year plan year files the annual report for the 2001 plan year on August 6, 2002. The administrator failed to properly extend the filing due date of July 31, 2002. Under the DFVC Program, the applicable penalty amount would be $60 (6 days x $10).

Example 2. Assume the same facts as in Example 1, except that the filer filed the annual report on March 31, 2003. Under the DFVC Program, the applicable penalty amount is $2,000 (though the penalty amount calculated at $10 per day would be $2,430 for 243 days, the "per-filing" cap of $2000 applies).

Example 3. Assume the same facts as in Example 2, except that the filer filed annual reports for the same plan for the 1999, 2000 and 2001 plan years on March 31, 2003. Under the DFVC Program, the applicable penalty amount is $4,000, which is the "per-plan" filing cap for large plans.

Example 4. Assume the same facts as in Example 3, except that the filer is also submitting an additional plan year 2001 filing under the DFVC Program for another plan. Under the DFVC Program, the penalty amount is $6,000 ($4,000 applicable to the three filings discussed in Example 3, plus $2,000 for the Form 5500 filed for the other plan)."

DOL Procedure: PWBA's Delinquent Filer Voluntary Compliance Program; Office of Chief Accountant Frequently Asked Questions About The Delinquent Filer Voluntary Compliance Program, http://askpwba.dol.gov/faq-dfvc.html.

77. A plan administrator for a plan is delinquent on Form 5500 filings for multiple years. If during that period, the plan's classification has shifted between being a "large" and "small plan," which penalty cap applies to the plan's DFVC Program submission?

DOL guidance explains that "If, during the years of non-filing, there is at least one year where the plan is a large plan, for purposes of the DFVC Program the plan must use the large plan penalty amounts of $10 per day up to a maximum of $2,000 per filing, not to exceed $4,000 per plan." DOL Procedure: PWBA's Delinquent Filer Voluntary Compliance Program; Office of Chief Accountant Frequently Asked Questions About The Delinquent Filer Voluntary Compliance Program, http://askpwba.dol.gov/faq-dfvc.html.

78. Is there a different "per-plan" penalty cap that applies to administrators of small plans sponsored by Internal Revenue Code section 501(c)(3) organizations (including Code section 403(b) small plans)?

Guidance from the DOL states that "Yes. In the case of a small plan sponsored by a Code section 501(c)(3) organization (including a Code section 403(b) small plan), the applicable penalty amount is $10 per day for each day the annual report is filed after the date on which the annual report was due (without regard to any extensions), not to exceed $750 regardless of the number of delinquent annual reports for the plan submitted as part of the same DFVC submission.

This "per-plan" penalty cap, however, will not be available if, as of the date the plan files under the DFVC Program, there is a delinquent or late annual report due for a plan year during which the plan was a large plan. See Q 76, Q 77.

Small plan filings that are eligible for this special "per-plan" penalty cap must bear the notation "501(c)(3) Plan" in the upper-right corner of the first page of the Form 5500 that is submitted to the DFVC Program in Atlanta, Georgia. This notation should not be included in the filing made with PWBA in Lawrence, Kansas." DOL Procedure: PWBA's Delinquent Filer Voluntary Compliance Program; Office of Chief Accountant Frequently Asked Questions About The Delinquent Filer Voluntary Compliance Program, http://askpwba.dol.gov/faq-dfvc.html.

79. Are extensions considered when calculating penalties under the DFVC Program?

The DOL states that "No. All penalties under the DFVC Program are calculated at $10 per day, beginning on the day after the date the filing was due, without regard to any extensions." DOL Procedure: PWBA's Delinquent Filer Voluntary Compliance Program; Office of Chief Accountant Frequently Asked Questions About The Delinquent Filer Voluntary Compliance Program, http://askpwba.dol.gov/faq-dfvc.html.

80. Does a plan administrator waive any rights upon filing under the DFVC Program?

The DOL has answered this question as follows:

> "Yes. Payment of the penalty amount under the terms of the DFVC Program constitutes, with regard to the filings submitted under the Program, a waiver of the right both to receive notice of the assessment from the department and to contest the department's assessment of the DFVC Program penalty amount."

DOL Procedure: PWBA's Delinquent Filer Voluntary Compliance Program; Office of Chief Accountant Frequently Asked Questions About The Delinquent Filer Voluntary Compliance Program, http://askpwba.dol.gov/faq-dfvc.html.

81. If a filing has been made under the DFVC Program, will the plan administrator be liable for any other Department of Labor annual reporting civil penalties?

The DOL answers this question as follows:

"Annual reports that are filed under the DFVC Program are subject to the usual edit checks. Plan administrators will have an opportunity to correct deficiencies in accordance with the procedures described in 29 CFR §2560.502c-2. The failure to correct deficiencies in accordance with these procedures may result in the assessment of further deficient filer penalties."

DOL Procedure: PWBA's Delinquent Filer Voluntary Compliance Program; Office of Chief Accountant Frequently Asked Questions About The Delinquent Filer Voluntary Compliance Program, http://askpwba.dol.gov/faq-dfvc.html.

82. Can plan assets be used to pay the civil penalties assessed under ERISA Section 502(c)(2)?

Guidance on this question from the DOL says:

"No. The plan administrator is personally liable for the payment of civil penalties assessed under ERISA Section 502(c)(2). Therefore, civil penalties, including penalties paid under the DFVC Program, may not be paid from the assets of an employee benefit plan."

DOL Procedure: PWBA's Delinquent Filer Voluntary Compliance Program; Office of Chief Accountant Frequently Asked Questions About The Delinquent Filer Voluntary Compliance Program, http://askpwba.dol.gov/faq-dfvc.html.

83. May an administrator of an apprenticeship and training plan, as described in 29 CFR Section 2520.104-22, or an administrator of a "top hat" plan, as described in 29 CFR Section 2520.104-23, participate in the DFVC Program?

DOL guidance states: "Yes. Administrators of apprenticeship and training plans and administrators of pension plans for a select group of management or highly compensated employees ("top hat plans"), may file the applicable notice and statement described in regulation Sections 2520.104-22 and 2520.104-23, respectively, under the DFVC Program in lieu of filing any past due annual reports. By properly filing these statements and meeting the other applicable DFVC Program requirements (see Q 84, 85), administrators will be considered as having elected compliance with the exemption and/or alternative method of compliance prescribed in Sections 2520.104-22 or 2520.104-23, as appropriate, for all subsequent plan years." See DOL Procedure: PWBA's Delinquent Filer Voluntary Compliance Program; Office of Chief Accountant Frequently Asked Questions About The Delinquent Filer Voluntary Compliance Program, http://askpwba.dol.gov/faq-dfvc.html.

84. How does an administrator of an apprenticeship and training plan participate in the DFVC Program?

In this situation, guidance from the DOL states that "the plan administrator must prepare the statement described in ... 29 CFR Section 2520.104-22 and file it at the following address:

> Apprenticeship and Training Plan Exemption
> Pension and Welfare Benefits Administration
> Room N-1513
> U.S. DOL of Labor
> 200 Constitution Avenue N.W.
> Washington, DC 20210

The plan administrator must also complete the most current Form 5500 Annual Return/Report (without schedules or attachments), items 1a-1b, 2a-2c, 3a-3c, and use plan number 999 for all apprenticeship and training plans. The paper copy of the form must be signed and dated, and be accompanied by a check for $750 made payable to the U.S. Department of Labor, and sent to:

> DFVC Program
> Pension and Welfare Benefits Administration
> P.O. Box 530292
> Atlanta, Georgia 30353-0292

The applicable $750 penalty amount is for each DFVC submission, without regard to the number of plans maintained by the same plan sponsor for which the notices and statements are being filed or the number of participants covered by the plan or plans."

DOL Procedure: PWBA's Delinquent Filer Voluntary Compliance Program; Office of Chief Accountant Frequently Asked Questions About The Delinquent Filer Voluntary Compliance Program, http://askpwba.dol.gov/faq-dfvc.html.

85. How does an administrator of a "top-hat" plan participate in the DFVC Program?

The DOL has stated that "the plan administrator must prepare the statement described in regulation section 29 CFR §2520.104-23 and file it at the following address:

> Top Hat Plan Exemption
> Pension and Welfare Benefits Administration Room N-1513
> U.S. DOL of Labor
> 200 Constitution Avenue N.W.
> Washington, DC 20210

Note: A plan sponsor maintaining more than one "top hat" plan is not required to file a separate statement for each such plan. See 29 CFR §2520.104-23.

The plan administrator must also complete the most current Form 5500 Annual Return/Report (without schedules or attachments), items 1a-1b, 2a-2c, 3a-3c, and use plan number 888 for all "top hat" plans. The paper copy of the form must be signed and dated, and be accompanied by a check for $750 made payable to the U.S. Department of Labor, and sent to:

> DFVC Program
> Pension and Welfare Benefits Administration
> P.O. Box 530292
> Atlanta, Georgia 30353-0292

The applicable $750 penalty amount is for each DFVC submission, without regard to the number of plans maintained by the same plan sponsor for which the notices and statements are being filed or the number of participants covered by the plan or plans." DOL Procedure: PWBA's Delinquent Filer Voluntary Compliance Program; Office of Chief Accountant Frequently Asked Questions About The Delinquent Filer Voluntary Compliance Program, http://askpwba.dol.gov/faq-dfvc.html.

86. Is there a requirement to write "DFVC Program" in red ink on the top of the Form 5500 being filed?

The DOL says "No. Unlike the 1995 DFVC Program, the forms and penalty payment no longer have to be annotated in bold red print identifying the filing as a DFVC filing. In fact, notations inserted in the margins or borders of 1999 or later year Form 5500s may adversely affect the processing of the form and require a substitute filing. Filers using the 2001 or subsequent version of the Form 5500 to participate in the DFVC Program should check box D of the Form 5500 and attach the required statement to the Form 5500 filed with EFAST (see the Form 5500 instructions).

Filers of Forms 5500 under the DFVC Program for small plans sponsored by 501(c)(3) organizations (including Code section 403(b) plans) must make the notation "501(c)(3) Plan" in the upper right-hand corner of the first page of the Form 5500 that is being submitted to the DFVC Program in Atlanta, Georgia. See Q 78. The notation is not required to be in red ink." DOL Procedure: PWBA's Delinquent Filer Voluntary Compliance Program; Office of Chief Accountant Frequently Asked Questions About The Delinquent Filer Voluntary Compliance Program, http://askpwba.dol.gov/faq-dfvc.html.

87. Does the DFVC Program only apply to plan years beginning on or after January 1, 1988?

Guidance from the DOL says that "a plan administrator is required to file an annual report for an employee benefit plan beginning with the 1975 plan year. However, during the DFVC Program, the department is targeting all plan years beginning on or after January 1, 1988 — the effective date of ERISA Section 502(c)(2)." DOL Procedure: PWBA's Delinquent Filer Voluntary Compliance Program; Office of Chief Accountant Frequently Asked Questions About The Delinquent Filer Voluntary Compliance Program, http://askpwba.dol.gov/faq-dfvc.html.

88. Is the DFVC Program applicable to filings made by direct filing entities (DFEs) (i.e., master trusts, pooled separate accounts, common/collective trusts, 103-12 IEs, and group insurance arrangements)?

The DOL answers this question as follows:

"The DFVC Program is not applicable to DFE filings made for master trusts, pooled separate accounts, common/collective trusts and 103-12 IEs. The Form 5500 filed by these DFEs is an integral part of the annual report of the participating employee benefit plans. If a Form 5500 was timely filed for the participating employee benefit plans, a failure to timely file a DFE Form 5500 for these entities may cause the plan's annual report to be incomplete or inaccurate, but it does not result in the plan being a late or non-filer. The plan's Form 5500, however, may be subject to rejection for being incomplete or inaccurate, and, if rejected, a plan administrator who failed to correct the problem would be subject to penalty assessments by the department.

A Form 5500 filed for a group insurance arrangement (GIA) under the department's regulations relieves the plan administrators of the individual plans participating in the GIA from the requirement to file a separate Form 5500 for each plan. The department will allow a GIA that failed to file a GIA Form 5500 on time to use the DFVC Program to correct the late filing. GIAs participating in the DFVC Program are subject to the conditions applicable to large plan filers." See Q 76.

DOL Procedure: PWBA's Delinquent Filer Voluntary Compliance Program; Office of Chief Accountant Frequently Asked Questions About The Delinquent Filer Voluntary Compliance Program, http://askpwba.dol.gov/faq-dfvc.html.

89. If a plan administrator participated in the DFVC Program prior to the effective date of the revised Program, and paid the then applicable program penalties, may the administrator obtain a refund for the difference between the previous and the current penalty applicable amounts?

This question is answered by DOL guidance as follows:

> "No. By filing under the prior DFVC Program, the plan administrator paid the reduced penalties and received the relief with respect to which the paid penalty related. The primary protection the plan administrator received was, and continues to be, relief from possible assessment of higher late filer or non-filer penalties. While the DFVC penalty amounts have changed, the plan administrator continues to have the relief that was originally provided under the DFVC Program."

DOL Procedure: PWBA's Delinquent Filer Voluntary Compliance Program; Office of Chief Accountant Frequently Asked Questions About The Delinquent Filer Voluntary Compliance Program, http://askpwba.dol.gov/faq-dfvc.html.

90. Prior to participating in the DFVC Program, a plan administrator was notified in writing by the department that its plan's filings are delinquent. Can the plan administrator participate in the DFVC Program?

The DOL has stated that "No. The DFVC Program is only available to a plan administrator that complies with the requirements of the Program before the date on which the administrator is notified in writing by the department of a failure to file a timely annual report under Title I of ERISA." DOL Procedure: PWBA's Delinquent Filer Voluntary Compliance Program; Office of Chief Accountant Frequently Asked Questions About The Delinquent Filer Voluntary Compliance Program, http://askpwba.dol.gov/faq-dfvc.html.

91. Is it possible to obtain a waiver from the applicable penalty amount under the DFVC Program if the plan administrator can demonstrate that there is reasonable cause why the penalty should not be assessed?

The DOL answers this question in its DOL Procedure: PWBA's Delinquent Filer Voluntary Compliance Program; Office of Chief Accountant Frequently Asked Questions About The Delinquent Filer Voluntary Compliance Program, http://askpwba.dol.gov/faq-dfvc.html.

"No. Payment of a penalty under the terms of the DFVC Program constitutes a waiver of an administrator's right both to receive a notice of assessment from the department and to contest the department's assessment of the penalty amount. If the plan administrator chooses not to waive these rights, the plan administrator must file with EFAST in Lawrence, Kansas in the regular manner and not pursuant to the DFVC Program. See Q 73 regarding possible civil penalties that may be assessed by the department under ERISA section 502(c)(2), and the department's regulations which provide the plan administrator with the opportunity to file a statement of reasonable cause."

92. Does participation in the DFVC Program protect the plan administrator from other civil penalties that may be assessed by the Internal Revenue Service (IRS) or the Pension Benefit Guaranty Corporation (PBGC) for failing to timely file a Form 5500 Annual Return/Report?

The DOL answers this question as follows: "Both the IRS and PBGC have agreed to provide certain penalty relief under the Code and Title IV of ERISA for delinquent Form 5500s filed for Title I plans where the conditions of the DFVC Program have been satisfied. See sections 5.02 and 5.03 of the DFVC Program Federal Register Notice and IRS Notice 2002-23." DOL Procedure: PWBA's Delinquent Filer Voluntary Compliance Program; Office of Chief Accountant Frequently Asked Questions About The Delinquent Filer Voluntary Compliance Program, can be found at http://askpwba.dol.gov/faq-dfvc.html.

93. What reports and disclosures are plans required to submit to the Department of Labor?

Employee benefit plan administrators are required to file the following documents with the Department of Labor:

1. Summary Plan Description (only upon request of the DOL) (see Q 94);

2. Annual Reports (actual filing is made to the IRS) (see Q 65 through Q 70);

3. Notice of Material Modifications (only upon request of DOL) (see Q 95);

4. Terminal Reports (see Q 96); and

5. Notice of Plan Amendments (see Q 97).

The DOL has issued proposed rules that would implement certain amendments to ERISA made under the Taxpayer Relief Act of 1997 that impact the responsibility of third party administrators to comply with DOL requests for disclosure of plan records. The proposed rule details the procedures for the DOL to follow in requesting documents and assessing penalties for which third party administrators can be held personally liable for non-compliance.

The DOL may request copies of SPDs and other relevant plan documents from third party administrators only on behalf of requesting participants, fiduciaries, alternate payees under a QDRO (or prospective alternate payees under a QDRO), qualified COBRA beneficiaries, alternative recipients under a qualified medical child support order (or prospective alternate payees under a qualified child medical support order), or a duly authorized representative of any of the foregoing. Failure to comply with a DOL request may result in the imposition of penalties for each such failure up to $100 per day from the date of such failure (not to exceed $1,000).

The DOL can waive all or a part of the penalty if the third party administrator can show that the failure or refusal to comply was due to matters reasonably beyond the control of the third party administrator. The third party administrator has 30 days from receipt of a notice of intent to assess the penalty to provide an explanation as to why it should not be assessed. RIN 1210-AA67 and RIN 1210-AA68, 64 Fed. Reg. 42797 (8-5-99).

94. What are the Summary Plan Description (SPD) filing requirements?

ERISA Section 104(a)(6) provides that a plan administrator must file a copy of the plan's SPD with the Department of Labor (DOL) only if it is requested by the DOL.

For a detailed review of the format and content requirements of an SPD, as well as the obligations to provide them to participants and beneficiaries, see Q 101.

95. What are the filing requirements regarding the Summary of Material Modifications (SMM)?

A plan administrator is required to provide an SMM to the DOL only upon the request of the DOL. ERISA Sec. 104(a)(6). The DOL may impose a civil penalty of up to $100 per day (up to a maximum of $1,000) against a plan administrator for failure to respond within 30 days to a DOL request for an SMM. ERISA Sec. 502(c)(6).

96. What are the filing requirements regarding terminal reports?

Each administrator of a defined benefit plan that is winding up its affairs and terminating must file "such terminal reports as the Secretary [of Labor] may consider necessary." A copy of the terminal report is also required to be filed with the Pension Benefit Guaranty Corporation. ERISA Sec. 101(c). The terminal report is required to be filed regardless of the number of people actively participating in the plan.

The Department of Labor may also require a terminal report to be filed on behalf of a welfare benefit plan that is terminating.

97. What are the filing requirements regarding a notice of plan amendments?

Any amendment applying to a plan year that reduces the accrued benefits of a participant may not take effect unless the plan administrator files a notice with the Department of Labor. ERISA Sec. 302(c)(8)(C).

98. What reports and disclosures are required to be submitted to the Pension Benefit Guaranty Corporation?

The Pension Benefit Guaranty Corporation (PBGC) is a corporation wholly owned by the federal government. It is charged with the administration of the defined benefit plan termination rules detailed in Title IV of ERISA. The PBGC is also charged with establishing and maintaining the defined benefit plan benefit insurance program. See Chapter XII for a detailed review of the PBGC and its operations regarding defined benefit plans.

Defined benefit plans subject to PBGC jurisdiction are required to file the following forms with the PBGC:

1. PBGC Form 1, Annual Premium Payment;

2. PBGC Form 1-ES (Annual Premium Payment Form for plans with 500 or more participants that must pay an estimated premium by the last day of the second full calendar month after the close of the prior plan year);

3. Notice of Reportable Events (see Q 704 for a detailed review of the contents of a Notice of Reportable Events);

4. Notice of Intent to Terminate (see Q 706 for a detailed review of the contents of a Notice of Intent to Terminate);

5. Notice of the Withdrawal of a Substantial Employer;

6. Annual Reports (Form 5500); and

7. Terminal Reports.

99. What reports and disclosures are required to be furnished under the Multiemployer Pension Plan Amendments Act of 1980?

The Multiemployer Pension Plan Amendments Act of 1980 provides that a multiemployer plan in reorganization may be amended to reduce or eliminate accrued benefits in accordance with ERISA Section 4244A where the contributions are not eligible for the Pension Benefit Guaranty Corporation's (PBGC's) guarantee. Accrued benefits may not be reduced unless a notice has been given to the following at least six months before the first day of the plan year in which the amendment reducing benefits is adopted:

1. Plan participants and beneficiaries;

2. Each employer who has an obligation to contribute under the plan; and

3. Each employee organization that, for purposes of collective bargaining, represents plan participants employed by the employer. ERISA Sec. 4244A(b)(1)(A).

The notice must advise recipients that the plan is in reorganization and that if contributions under the plan are not increased, accrued benefits under the plan will be reduced or an excise tax will be imposed on the employers.

The plan sponsors should include in any notice issued to plan participants and beneficiaries information as to the rights and remedies of plan participants and beneficiaries, as well as how to contact the Department of Labor for further information and assistance where appropriate.

If the plan sponsor of a plan in reorganization determines that the plan may become insolvent, the plan sponsor must notify the following that if the insolvency occurs, certain benefit payments will be suspended but basic benefits will continue to be paid:

1. The Secretary of the Treasury;

2. The PBGC;

3. Each employer who has an obligation to contribute under the plan;

4. Each employee organization that represents plan participants employed by that employer; and

5. The plan participants and beneficiaries. ERISA Sec. 4245(e)(1).

100. What are the reports and disclosures that plans must provide to participants?

2002 ERISA Facts

In the ongoing operation of an ERISA covered employee benefit plan, the plan administrator is required to provide participants certain reports and disclosures. At various points in time and upon the occurrence of specific events, the plan administrator is required to provide participants the following documents:

1.   Summary Plan Description (see Q 101);

2.   Notice of Material Plan Changes (see Q 107);

3.   Summary of Annual Reports (see Q 108);

4.   Written Explanation of Joint and Survivor Annuity Option (see Q 109) and the Preretirement Survivor Annuity Option (see Q 110);

5.   Rollover Distribution Notice (see Q 111);

6.   Statement of Participant's Rights (see Q 112);

7.   Statement of Participant's Accrued and Vested Benefits (see Q 114);

8.   Notice to Participants in Underfunded Plans (see Q 117);

9.   Notice of Failure to Fund (see Q 118);

10. Notice to Missing Participants (see Q 119); and

11. COBRA Notices (see Q 173).

ERISA Section 104(b) requires the plan to produce only the "latest" annual report and summary plan description. It does not require plans to produce documents that simply do not exist. *Staib v. Vaughn Industries*, 2001 U.S. Dist. LEXIS 17838 (N.D. Ohio).

PRACTITIONER'S POINTER:

The ruling in *Staib v. Vaughn Industries* is important in that it minimizes the ability of attorneys and participants to conduct legal "fishing expeditions" in which they request "any and all documents" in an effort to discover any potential issue for litigation.

Federal courts have been increasingly active in ruling when plan fiduciaries must disclose plan amendments and other actions that may affect benefit levels within a plan (under the concept of "serious consideration"). In one such ruling, the Second Circuit ruled that the fiduciary duty to deal fairly and honestly with beneficiaries prohibits fiduciaries from making false or misrepresentative statements regarding future benefit enhancements wherein an inquiry seeking relevant, accurate information has been presented. *Caputo v Pfizer, Inc.*, 2001 US App LEXIS 21707 (2nd Cir. 2001).

The Ninth Circuit opined that there is no affirmative duty to provide considered changes in benefits after an amendment is under serious consideration, *but* where the employer has agreed to follow up with an inquiring employee, it must provide affirmative disclosure when the consideration later comes under serious consideration. *Bins v Exxon Co. USA*, 24 EBC 2377 (9th Cir. 2000).

101. What information must be contained in the Summary Plan Description (SPD)?

The requirement that a plan administrator file a copy of the SPD with the Department of Labor (DOL) has been eliminated, unless he is specifically requested by the DOL to do so. ERISA Sec. 104(a)(6). The SPD must accurately reflect the contents of the plan as of a date not earlier than 120 days prior to the date that the SPD is disclosed. Labor Reg. §2520.102-3.

The following information must be included in the SPD of both employee welfare benefit plans and employee pension benefit plans:

1. The name of the plan, and, if different, the name by which the plan is commonly known by its participants and beneficiaries;

2. The name and address of:

   a) in the case of a single employer plan, the employer whose employees are covered by the plan;

   b) in the case of a plan maintained by an employee organization, the employee organization that maintains the plan;

   c) in the case of a collectively bargained plan established or maintained by one or more employee organizations, the representative organization of the parties that established or maintain the plan, as well as: (i) a statement that a complete list of the employer and employee organizations sponsoring the plan may be obtained by participants and beneficiaries upon written request, and the list is available for examination by participants and beneficiaries in accordance with the appropriate regulations, or (ii) a statement that participants and beneficiaries may receive from the plan administrator, upon written request, information as to whether a particular employer or employee organization is a sponsor of the plan, and, if the employer or employee organization is a plan sponsor, the sponsor's address;

   d) in the case of a plan established or maintained by two or more employers, the representative organization of the parties who established or maintain the plan, as well as: (i) a statement that a complete list of the employers sponsoring the plan may be obtained by participants and beneficiaries upon written request to the plan administrator, and the list is available for examination by participants and beneficiaries, as required by applicable regulations, or (ii) a statement that participants and beneficiaries may receive from the plan administrator, upon written request, information as to whether a particular employer is a sponsor of the plan, and if the employer is a plan sponsor, the sponsor's address;

3. The employer identification number assigned by the Internal Revenue Service to the plan sponsor and the plan number assigned by the plan sponsor;

4. The type of pension or welfare plan (e.g., for pension plans — defined benefit, money purchase, profit sharing, ERISA Section 404(c), etc., and for welfare plans — hospitalization, disability, prepaid legal service, etc.);

5. The type of administration of the plan, (e.g., contract administration, insurer administration, etc.);

6. The name, business address, and business telephone number of the plan administrator (as defined in ERISA Section 3(16));

7. The name of the person designated as agent for service of legal process, the address at which process may be served on that person, and a statement that service of legal process may be made upon a plan trustee or the plan administrator;

8. The name, title, and address of the principal place of business of each trustee of the plan;

9. If a plan is maintained pursuant to one or more collective bargaining agreements, a statement that the plan is so maintained and that a copy of the collective bargaining agreement may be obtained by participants and beneficiaries upon written request to the plan administrator, and that it is available for examination by participants and beneficiaries, as required by applicable regulations;

10. The plan's requirements respecting eligibility for participation and for benefits; the SPD must describe the plan's provisions relating to eligibility to participate in the plan, such as the age or years of service requirements, and the following items (as appropriate):

    a) for employee pension benefit plans, it must also include a statement describing the plan's normal retirement age (as defined in ERISA

Section 3(24)), and a statement describing any other conditions that must be met before a participant will be eligible to receive benefits; the benefits must be described or summarized; and

b) for employee welfare benefit plans, it must also include a statement of the conditions pertaining to eligibility to receive benefits, and a description or summary of the benefits;

11.   In the case of an employee pension benefit plan, a statement describing any joint and survivor benefits provided under the plan, including any requirement that an election be made as a condition to select or reject the joint and survivor annuity;

12.   For both pension and welfare benefit plans, a statement clearly identifying circumstances that may result in disqualification, ineligibility, denial, loss, forfeiture, or suspension of any benefits that a participant or beneficiary might otherwise reasonably expect the plan to provide on the basis of the benefits required by (10) and (11), above;

13.   For an employee pension benefit plan the following information:

a) if the benefits of the plan are not insured by the Pension Benefit Guaranty Corporation (PBGC), a statement of this fact, and the reason for the lack of insurance; and

b) if the benefits of the plan are insured by the PBGC, a statement of this fact, a summary of the Pension Benefit Guaranty Corporation provisions of Title IV of ERISA, and a statement indicating that further information on the provisions of Title IV can be obtained from the plan administrator or the PBGC; the address of the PBGC must be provided;

14.   In the case of an employee pension benefit plan, a description and explanation of the plan provisions for determining years of service for eligibility to participate, vesting, breaks in service, and years of participation for benefit accrual; the description must state the service required to accrue full benefits and the manner in which accrual of benefits is prorated for employees failing to complete full service for a year;

15.   In the case of an employee pension benefit plan that will use the "cutback" rule of Revenue Ruling 76-378, 1976-2 CB 112, to make retroactive changes in the vesting or accrual provisions described in the SPD, a statement that certain provisions of the plan are subject

to amendment that directly or indirectly modifies certain plan rights and benefits, the nature of those modifications, and the identification by reference of the portions of the SPD where those provisions are described; the statement may be either printed within the text of the SPD or it may be printed in a separate sheet and disclosed together with the SPD;

16. The sources of contributions to the plan — for example, employer, employee organization, employees — and the method by which the amount of contributions is calculated; defined benefit pension plans may state without further explanation that the contribution is actuarially determined;

17. The identity of any funding medium used for the accumulation of assets through which benefits are provided; the SPD must identify the insurance company, trust fund, or any other institution, organization, or entity that maintains a fund on behalf of the plan or through which the plan is funded or benefits are provided;

18. The date of the end of the year for purposes of maintaining the plan's fiscal records; and

19. The procedures to be followed in presenting claims for benefits under the plan and the remedies available under the plan for the redress of claims that are denied in whole or in part. Labor Reg. §2520.102-3.

Final rules, recently issued, also require the SPD for welfare benefit plans to include a description or summary of the benefits and service providers available under the plan. If the schedule of benefits and/or service providers is extensive, the plan sponsor may provide the lists under separate documents if such documents are referenced in the SPD and participants are advised in the SPD that such lists are available without cost to any participant or beneficiary who requests one. Labor Reg. §§2520.102-3(j)(2) and (3). Such welfare benefit plans are also required to disclose to participants and beneficiaries such cost-sharing measures as the plan may have in place with insurance providers (premiums, deductibles, coinsurance, etc.), as well as any annual or lifetime caps, which preventative services are offered, whether, and under what circumstances existing and new drugs are covered, and any other conditions or limits on the type and availability of coverage offered. Labor Reg. §2520.102-3(j)(3). These final rules are effective as of the first day of the second plan year beginning on or after January 22, 2001.

Other provisions of the final rules include a requirement that plans include a description of the procedures governing QDROs, or a statement that participants and beneficiaries can obtain, without charge, a copy of such procedures.

Labor Reg. §2520.102-3(j)(1). A description of the procedures governing qualified medical child support orders is also required to be disclosed in the SPD of welfare benefit plans. Labor Reg. §2520.102-3(j)(2). In addition, welfare plans are required to disclose COBRA rights and any model language required as a result of the Newborns' and Mothers' Health Protection Act. Labor Regs. §§2520.102-3(t)(2) and (u)(1).

SPDs must be written in a manner calculated to be understood by the average plan participant, and must be sufficiently accurate and comprehensive to reasonably apprise participants and beneficiaries of their rights and obligations under the plan. ERISA Sec. 102(a).

102. What are the Summary Plan Description (SPD) requirements in a successor plan situation?

The ERISA regulations establish an alternative method of SPD compliance for certain successor pension plans. Labor Reg. §2520.104-4. Where a portion of plan participants and beneficiaries have rights established under a successor plan, while continuing to be eligible for benefits under the former plan which has been merged into the successor plan, the plan administrator is not required to describe the relevant provisions of the old plan in the SPD of the successor plan.

The provisions of this alternative compliance method are applicable only to plan mergers that occur after the issuance by the successor plan of the initial SPD under ERISA.

The alternative method of compliance is available only if the plan administrator of the successor plan furnishes to the participants covered under the merged plan and beneficiaries receiving pension benefits under the merged plan, within 90 days after the effective date of the merger, the following:

1.   A copy of the most recent SPD of the successor plan;

2.   A copy of any summaries of material modifications to the successor plan not incorporated in the most recent SPD; and

3.   A separate statement containing a brief description of the merger; a description of the provisions of, and benefits provided by, the merged and successor plans which are applicable to the participants and beneficiaries of the merged plan; and a notice that copies of the merged and successor plan documents, as well as the plan merger documents (including the portions of any corporate merger documents which describe or control the plan merger), are available for inspection and that copies may be obtained upon written request for a duplication charge (in accordance with the provisions of Labor Regulation Section 2520.104b-2(a)).

After the merger, the plan administrator in all subsequent summary plan descriptions must clearly and conspicuously identify the class of participants and beneficiaries affected by the provisions of the merged plans, and state that the documents above are available for inspections and that copies may be obtained upon written request for a duplication charge.

103. What are the distribution requirements for the Summary Plan Description?

A plan administrator is required to furnish to each plan participant and beneficiary receiving benefits under the plan a copy of the Summary Plan Description as well as a statement of ERISA rights. These documents must be provided within 90 days after a person becomes a participant, or (in the case of a beneficiary) within 90 days after he first receives benefits, or if later, within 120 days after the plan becomes subject to the reporting and disclosure provisions of ERISA. ERISA Sec. 104(b)(1); Labor Reg. §2520.104b-2(a).

Where a plan is made prospectively effective to take effect after a certain date or after a condition is satisfied, the date upon which the plan becomes subject to the reporting and disclosure provisions of ERISA is the day after the date or condition is satisfied. Where a plan is adopted with a retroactive effective date, the 120-day period begins on the day after the plan is adopted. Where a plan is made retroactively effective dependent on a condition, the day on which the plan becomes subject to the reporting and disclosure provisions of ERISA is the day after the day on which the condition is satisfied. Where a plan is made retroactively effective subject to a contingency which may or may not occur in the future, the day on which the plan becomes subject to the reporting and disclosure provisions of ERISA is the day after the day on which the contingency occurs. Labor Reg. §2520.104b-2(a)(3).

ERISA also requires a plan administrator to provide a copy of the latest Summary Plan Description upon the *written request* of a participant or beneficiary. ERISA Sec. 104(b)(4) (emphasis added). The penalty for failure to comply with such a written request is $110 per day. ERISA Sec. 502(c)(1); Labor Reg. §2570.502c-1. The Ninth Circuit Court of Appeals has held that a participant's request for a Summary Plan Description under this provision (ERISA Section 104(b)(4)) did not have to be in writing for this penalty to apply, because the Summary Plan Description was something the participant is entitled to receive automatically, without any request. *Crotty v. Cook*, 121 F.3d 541 (9th Cir. 1997).

104. What are the rules regarding the use of electronic media to provide Summary Plan Descriptions (SPDs) and other required disclosures?

On January 28, 1999, the DOL issued proposed regulations on the use of electronic media to provide SPDs and other required disclosures to plan participants as well as the standards for the maintenance and retention of employee benefit plan records in electronic form (see Q 61). The proposal would establish a safe harbor pursuant to which all pension and welfare benefit plans covered by Title I of ERISA may satisfy their obligations to furnish summary plan descriptions, summaries of material modifications, updated summary plan descriptions, and summary annual reports using electronic media. The administrator of an employee benefit plan furnishing documents described in ERISA Section 104(b)(1) (SPDs and SMMs) or ERISA Section 104(b)(3) (updated SPDs and SMMs) through electronic media will be deemed to satisfy its disclosure requirements under ERISA if:

1. The administrator takes appropriate and necessary measures to ensure that the system for furnishing documents results in actual receipt by participants of transmitted information and documents (e.g., uses return-receipt electronic mail feature or conducts periodic reviews or surveys to confirm receipt of transmitted information);

2. Electronically delivered documents are prepared and furnished in a manner consistent with the applicable style, format and content requirements (see Q 101 and Q 105);

3. Each participant is provided notice, through electronic means or in writing, apprising the participant of the document(s) to be furnished electronically, the significance of the document (e.g., the document describes the changes in the benefits provided by the plan) and the participant's right to request and receive, free of charge, a paper copy of each such document; and

4. Upon request of any participant, the administrator furnishes, free of charge, a paper copy of any document delivered to the participant through electronic media. Labor Prop. Reg. §2520.104b-1(c)(1).

The furnishing of documents through electronic media will satisfy the safe harbor only with respect to participants who have the ability at their worksite to effectively access documents furnished in electronic form, and who have the opportunity at their worksite to readily convert furnished documents from electronic form to paper form free of charge. Labor Prop. Reg. §2520.104b-1(c)(2).

105. What information regarding plan termination must be contained in the Summary Plan Description?

A Summary Plan Description (SPD) is required to include information regarding the provisions of the plan that relate to the termination of the plan. It is the position of the Department of Labor that since a plan termination may result in the denial or loss of benefits to participants and beneficiaries, the SPD must include the following:

1.   A summary of any plan provisions on the rights of the plan sponsor, or other entity, to terminate the plan, and the circumstances, if any, under which the plan may be terminated;

2.   A summary of plan provisions that govern the benefits, rights, and obligations of participants and beneficiaries, including provisions on the accrual and vesting of benefits under the plan upon termination; and

3.   A summary of those provisions of the plan that deal with the allocation and disposition of plan assets upon termination. Technical Release 84-1, 5A Pension Plan Guide (CCH) 22,475.

106. What are the plan's obligations regarding the updating of the Summary Plan Description?

The administrator must furnish to each participant, and to each beneficiary receiving benefits under the plan, an updated Summary Plan Description (SPD) that integrates all plan amendments made within a 5-year period. The updated SPD must be distributed every fifth year after the plan becomes subject to the reporting and disclosure provisions of ERISA. If no amendments have been made during the 5-year period, this requirement does not apply. The administrator must furnish to each participant, and to each beneficiary receiving benefits under the plan, the SPD every tenth year after the plan becomes subject to the reporting and disclosure provisions of ERISA. ERISA Sec. 104(b)(1).

Updated SPDs must be provided to each participant and beneficiary receiving benefits under the plan no later than 210 days following the end of the plan year in which a 5-year or 10-year period (described above) ends. Labor Reg. §2520.104b-2(b).

107. What information regarding material plan changes must be provided to participants?

A Summary of Material Modifications (SMM) in plan provisions is required to be provided to participants and beneficiaries. The SMM must be provided within 210 days after the close of the plan year in which the modification was adopted (even for the adoption of amendments that take effect on a date in the future), and must be written in a manner calculated to be understood by the average participant. ERISA Secs. 102(a)(1), 104(b)(1); Labor Reg. §2520.104b-3(a).

The disclosure date is not affected by retroactive applications to a prior plan year of an amendment that makes a material modification to the plan; a modification does not occur before it is adopted. Labor Reg. §2520.104b-3(a).

The SMM is not required where it has been rescinded or otherwise does not take effect. Labor Reg. §2520.104b-3(a). Also, an SMM is not required if the changes or modifications are described in a timely summary plan description. Labor Reg. §2520.104b-3(b).

Where an SPD has been provided to participants in accordance with ERISA, it must be accompanied by all SMMs or changes in information required to be included in the SPD that have not been incorporated into that SPD.

Any change in the name of a plan trustee is a modification or change that must be disclosed to participants and beneficiaries through an SMM. DOL Adv. Op. 80-32A.

For plan changes in a group health plan that is subject to the provisions of HIPAA '96, changes must be disclosed to participants and beneficiaries no later than 60 days after the first day of the first plan year. Labor Reg. §2520.102-3(v)(1).

Plan changes to maternity and newborn infant hospital coverage in a group health plan that is subject to the provisions of the Newborns' and Mothers' Health Protection Act of 1996 (NMHPA) must be disclosed to participants and beneficiaries no later than 60 days after the first day of the first plan year. ERISA Sec. 711(d); Labor Reg. §2520.1023(v)(2).

108. What are the Summary Annual Report requirements?

The plan administrator is required to furnish annually to each participant and beneficiary receiving benefits a Summary Annual Report (SAR). ERISA Sec. 104(b)(3); Labor Reg. §2520.104b-10. Regulations dictate the content, style and format requirements for SARs and even provide prototype formats to be reproduced for pension and welfare benefit plans. Plan administrators may not vary the format of the SAR; however, information that is not applicable to the plan may be omitted. Also, plan administrators may elaborate upon information contained within the SAR. The information used to complete the forms must be based upon information contained in the most recent annual report of the plan. Labor Regs. §§2520.104b-10(d)(3), 2520.104b-10(d)(4).

The SAR is required to be provided to participants and beneficiaries receiving benefits under the plan no later than nine months after the close of the plan year. In the case of welfare benefit plans that use group health insurance arrangements, the SAR is required to be provided within nine months of the close of the fiscal year of the trust or other entity that files the report. Labor Reg. §2520.104b-10(c).

A plan that covers fewer than 100 participants at the beginning of a plan year in which 25% or more of the plan participants are literate only in the same non-English language, or a plan that covers 100 or more participants in which 500 or more participants or 10% or more of all plan participants, whichever is less, are literate only in the same non-English language must provide to these non-English language participants an English language SAR that prominently displays a notice, in the non-English language common to these participants, offering them assistance. The actual assistance provided need not be in writing. The notice must clearly set forth any procedures participants must follow to obtain the assistance. Further, plans that provide an explanatory notice accompanying Form 5500-R or the notice of the availability of Form 5500-R must also provide a notice, in the non-English language common to these participants, offering assistance. Labor Reg. §2520.104b-10(e).

The following plans are exempted from the SAR provisions of ERISA:

1.   Totally unfunded welfare benefit plans;

2.   Small unfunded or insured welfare benefit plans (that satisfy these definitions in Labor Regulation Section 2520.104b-20(b));

3.   An apprenticeship or other training plan;

4.   A pension or welfare plan for selected employees;

5.   A day care center; and

6.   A dues financed pension or welfare plan. Labor Reg. §2520.104b-10(g).

It is the opinion of the Department of Labor that ERISA and its attendant regulations require SARs to be distributed to affected participants and beneficiaries for the plan year in which the plan terminates. This information is necessary to assist participants and beneficiaries in evaluating the financial information relating to the distribution of residual assets of the plan. DOL Adv. Op. 79-64A.

For defined benefit plans, if the current value of the assets of the plan is less than 70% of the current liability under the plan, this must be disclosed in a statement in the annual report that indicates the level to which the plan is underfunded (see Q 119 for further details). ERISA Sec. 103(d)(11). A similar notice of underfunding is required to be placed in the SAR. ERISA Sec. 104(b)(3).

109. What are the plan disclosure obligations regarding the joint and survivor annuity option?

A plan that provides a qualified joint and survivor annuity must provide to each participant, within a reasonable period of time before the annuity starting date, a written explanation of:

1.   The terms and conditions of the qualified joint and survivor annuity;

2.   The participant's right to make, and the effect of, an election to waive the joint and survivor annuity form of benefits;

3.   The rights of the participant's spouse; and

4.   The right to make, and the effect of, a revocation of an election. ERISA Sec. 205(c)(3); IRC Sec. 417(a)(3)(A).

The provision of a written notice is not required if the plan fully subsidized the cost of the benefit and the plan does not permit a participant to waive the benefit or designate another beneficiary. ERISA Sec. 205(c)(5)(A); IRC Sec. 417(a)(5)(A).

110. What is the plan disclosure obligation regarding the qualified pre-retirement survivor annuity?

A plan must provide a written explanation of the qualified pre-retirement survivor annuity to each participant that details:

1.   The terms and conditions of the qualified pre-retirement survivor annuity;

2.   The participant's right to make, and the effect of, an election to waive the qualified pre-retirement survivor annuity;

3.   The rights of the participant's spouse; and

4.   The right to make, and the effect of making, a revocation of an election. ERISA Sec. 205(c)(3)(B); IRC Sec. 417(a)(3)(B)(i).

This information must be provided no later than whichever of the following periods ends last:

1.   The period beginning with the first day of the plan year in which the participant attains age 32 and ending with the close of the plan year preceding the plan year in which the participant attains age 35;

2.   A reasonable period after the individual becomes a participant;

3.   A reasonable period of time after the end of the subsidization by the plan of a survivor benefit with respect to a participant;

4.   A reasonable period of time after the survivor benefit provisions of ERISA Section 205 become applicable to a participant; or

5.   A reasonable period of time after separation from service in the case of a participant who separates from service before the age of 35. ERISA Sec. 205(c)(3)(B); IRC Sec. 417(a)(3)(B)(ii).

The provision of a written notice is not required if the plan fully subsidized the cost of the benefit and the plan does not permit a participant to waive the benefit or designate another beneficiary. ERISA Sec. 205(c)(5)(A); IRC Sec. 417(a)(5)(A).

111. What is the plan obligation regarding the rollover distribution notice?

The plan administrator of a plan must, within a reasonable period of time before making an eligible rollover distribution from an eligible retirement plan, provide a written explanation to the recipient of:

1.   The provisions under which the recipient may have the distribution directly transferred to another eligible retirement plan, and that the automatic distribution by direct transfer applies to certain distributions;

2.   The provisions that require the withholding of tax on the distribution if it is not directly transferred to another eligible retirement plan;

3.   The provisions under which the distribution will not be subject to tax if transferred to an eligible retirement plan within 60 days after the date on which the recipient received the distribution; and

4.   If applicable, the tax on lump sum distributions (of IRC Section 402(d)) or related taxability rules (of IRC Section 402(e)). IRC Sec. 402(f), as amended by EGTRRA 2001.

112. What information is required to be contained in the statement of ERISA rights?

A plan administrator is required to furnish, in the Summary Plan Description (SPD), to each participant and beneficiary receiving benefits under the plan, a statement of ERISA rights of participants and beneficiaries. The statement of rights must appear as one consolidated statement. ERISA Sec. 104(c). A model statement of ERISA rights is contained in the regulations. See Labor Reg. §2520.102-3(t)(2). An SPD will be deemed to comply with the statement of rights requirements if it includes the model statement (excluding inapplicable material). The statement of rights must disclose that participants and beneficiaries are entitled to certain rights, including the rights to:

1. Examine, without charge, all plan documents, supporting documents, and documents filed with the Department of Labor (DOL);

2. Obtain copies of the plan documents upon written request to the plan administrator (who may make a reasonable charge for these copies);

3. Receive the plan's Summary Annual Report;

4. Obtain a statement of any right to receive a pension upon the attainment of normal retirement age, and what that pension would be at normal retirement age should the employee terminate employment now;

5. Obtain a statement, upon written request, of how many more years an employee must work to obtain a pension benefit upon the attainment of normal retirement age;

6. An explanation of the fiduciary duties imposed upon plan fiduciaries (including the prohibition against discriminating against participants and beneficiaries for seeking to enforce their rights under ERISA);

7. A written explanation of any reason for the denial of a claim for benefits under the plan;

8. Appeal the denial of a claim for benefits; and

9. Enforce their rights by taking certain specified steps (i.e., civil action or seeking DOL assistance). Labor Reg. §2520.102-3(t)(2).

The style and format of the statement must not have the effect of misleading, misinforming, or failing to inform participants and beneficiaries. All information contained in the statement of rights must be written in a manner calculated to be understood by the average plan participant, taking into account factors such as the level of comprehension and education of typical participants in the plan and the complexity of the items required in the statement of rights. Inaccurate, incomprehensible, or misleading explanatory material will fail to meet the requirements of the statement of rights. If the plan administrator finds it desirable to make additional mention of certain rights elsewhere in the SPD, it may do so. The SPD may state that the statement of ERISA rights is required by federal law and regulations. Labor Reg. §2520.102-3(t)(1).

For group health plans, the model statement of ERISA rights may be modified under the regulations to require group health plans to instruct participants and beneficiaries to contact the nearest DOL field office, or the DOL

Division of Technical Assistance and Inquiries, with questions regarding their rights. Labor Reg. §2520.102-3(t)(2).

113. Does ERISA provide additional protection to small business retirement plans?

ERISA Section 103(a)(3)(A) requires qualified plans to engage an independent qualified public accountant and to file the opinion of the accountant with the plan's Annual Report Form 5500. Regulations provide a waiver of the annual examination and report of an independent qualified public accountant for plans with fewer than 100 participants as of the beginning of the plan year. Labor Reg. §2520.104-46. The Department of Labor (DOL) has issued final regulations which are designed to increase the security of assets in small business retirement plans. The regulations apply to retirement plans covering less than 100 participants and impose additional requirements in order to remain exempt from having an annual audit of the plan.

The regulations provide that the administrator of a qualified plan with fewer than 100 participants is not required to comply with the annual audit requirement if, with respect to each plan year, the following conditions are satisfied:

1. At least 95% of the assets of the plan constitute "qualifying plan assets," as defined below; or

2. Any person who handles assets of the plan that do not constitute qualifying plan assets is bonded under ERISA Section 412 with the amount of the bond being not less than the value of the non-qualifying assets. Labor Reg. §2520.104-46(b)(1)(i)(A)(1) and (2).

"Qualifying plan assets" are defined under the final regulations as:

1. Qualifying employer securities as defined in ERISA Section 407(d)(1);

2. Participant loans meeting the requirements of ERISA Section 408(b)(1);

3. Shares issued by a registered investment company (mutual fund);

4. Investment and annuity contracts issued by an insurance company; and

5. Any assets held by the following institutions: (a) a bank or similar financial institution as defined in Labor Regulation Section 2550.408b-4(c); (b) an insurance company; (c) a broker-dealer

registered under the Security and Exchange Act of 1934; or (d) any other organization authorized to act as a trustee for individual retirement accounts under Internal Revenue Code Section 408. Labor Reg. §2520.104-46(b)(1)(i)(C)(ii).

The summary annual report for the plan must also include the following enhanced disclosures:

1.   The name of each institution holding qualifying plan assets and the amount of such assets held by each institution as of the end of the plan year (excluding employer securities, participant loans that satisfy ERISA Section 408(b)(1) and participant-directed individual accounts);

2.   The name of the surety company issuing any bond required under the regulation;

3.   A notice indicating that participants and beneficiaries may, upon request and without charge, examine or receive copies of evidence of any bond required under the regulation and copies of the statements received from each institution holding qualified assets which describe the assets held by the institution as of the end of the plan year; and

4.   A notice stating that participants and beneficiaries should contact the Pension and Welfare Benefits Administration of the DOL if they are unable to examine or obtain copies of the statements or evidence of the bond. Labor Reg. §2520.104-46(b)(1)(i)(B).

Further, the plan administrator must, upon the request of a participant or beneficiary, make available for inspection, or provide copies of (at no charge), the evidence of any bond required by the regulation and the statement of assets from the financial institutions holding qualifying assets. Labor Reg. §2520.104-46(b)(1)(i)(C).

The changes under the final regulations are effective for plan years beginning after April 17, 2001. For calendar year plans, these final regulations are effective for the 2002 plan year.

114. What is the Statement of Participant's Accrued and Vested Benefits?

Each plan administrator of an employee pension benefit plan must furnish to any plan participant or beneficiary who so requests in writing, a statement indicating, on the basis of the latest available information, the total benefits accrued, and the nonforfeitable pension benefits, if any, that have accrued, or the earliest date on which benefits will become nonforfeitable. ERISA Sec. 105(a).

Plan sponsors must maintain records with respect to each of their employees sufficient to determine the benefits due or that may become due to those employees. The plan administrator must make a report, in such a form as required by regulations, to each employee who is a participant under the plan and who:

1. Requests the report, in the manner and at the time as is provided in the regulations;

2. Terminates his service with the employer; or

3. Has a 1-year break in service. ERISA Sec. 209(a).

No more than one statement need be provided to any participant within a 12-month period. However, the report required to be furnished must be sufficient to inform the employee of his accrued benefits under the plan and the percentage of benefits that are nonforfeitable. ERISA Sec. 209(a).

115. What guidance has the DOL provided participants who wish to learn more about the fees and expenses of their 401(k) plan?

In 1998, the DOL released the results of its study on 401(k) plan fees and expenses. The study was undertaken on behalf of the DOL by an independent firm, in an effort to develop information allowing participants to understand the ways service providers charge for different services. The study also pointed out that many plan sponsors are not fully aware of how fees are calculated and where they may be charged against participant accounts.

Although the report makes no recommendations, it does provide a checklist for plan sponsors and participants to use in reviewing their 401(k) plan fees and expenses. This checklist helps the user to see how fees and expenses affect investment returns and impact retirement income. The checklist provides the following 10 questions for readers to ask in evaluating the fees and expenses of their 401(k) plan:

1. What investment options are offered under your company's 401(k) plan?

2. Do you have all available documentation about the investment choices under your plan and the fees charged to your plan?

3. What types of investment education are available to you under your plan?

4. What arrangement is used to provide services under your plan?

5. Do you and other participants use most or all of the optional services offered under your 401(k) plan, such as participant loan programs and insurance coverages?

6.   If administrative services are paid separately from investment management fees, are they paid for by the plan, your employer, or are they shared?

7.   Are the investment options tracking an established market index or is there a higher level of investment management services being provided?

8.   Do any of the investment options under your plan include sales charges (such as loads or commissions)?

9.   Do any of the investment options under your plan include any fees related to specific investments, such as 12b-1 fees, insurance charges or surrender fees, and what do they cover?

10. Does your plan offer any special funds or special classes of stock (which are generally sold to larger group investors)?

The full text of the DOL's release, titled "Study of 401(k) Plan Fees and Expenses," as well as its participant handbook entitled "A Look at 401(k) Plan Fees" are available on the DOL's website at: www.dol.gov/dol/pwba.

116. How can a plan sponsor understand and evaluate the fees and expenses related to its 401(k) plan?

Plan sponsors, or their assigned representatives, when establishing a 401(k) plan, are responsible for the selection of investment options from which participants will choose. They are also responsible for the selection of service providers to the plan, as well as the monitoring of the services provided and of the performance of the investment options. It is the stated view of the DOL that all of these duties require a fiduciary of the plan sponsor to consider the costs to the plan while complying with the fiduciary standards under ERISA.

In addition, the DOL advises in its pamphlet *A Look at 401(k) Plan Fees for Employers* that "understanding fees and expenses is important in providing for the services necessary for" a plan's operation. The DOL also says that "after careful evaluation during the initial selection, the plan's fees and expenses should be monitored to determine whether they continue to be reasonable."

As part of the evaluation process, the DOL offers 10 questions to assist in the evaluation and consideration of fees and expenses:

1.   Have you given each of your prospective service providers complete and identical information with regard to your plan?

2.   Do you know what features you want to provide (e.g., loans, number of investment options, types of investments, internet trading)?

3. Have you decided which fees and expenses you, as plan sponsor, will pay, which your employees will pay, and/or which you will share?

4. Do you know which fees and expenses are charged directly to the plan and which are deducted from investment returns?

5. Do you know what services are covered under the base fee and what services incur an extra charge? Do you know what the fees are for extra or customized services?

6. Do you understand that some investment options have higher fees than others because of the nature of the investment?

7. Does the prospective service arrangement have any restrictions, such as charges for early termination of your relationship with the provider?

8. Does the prospective arrangement assist your employees in making informed investment decisions for their individual accounts (e.g., providing investment education, information on fees, and the like) and how are you charged for this service?

9. Have you considered asking potential providers to present uniform fee information that includes all fees charged?

10. What information will you receive on a regular basis from the prospective provider so that you can monitor the provision of services and the investments that you select and make changes, if necessary?

The DOL recommends, in its 401(k) pamphlet described above, that the plan sponsor provide all prospective service providers "with complete and identical information about the plan" and to consider the specific services desired for the plan. The DOL cites as examples, "the types and frequency of reports to the employer, communications to participants, educational materials and meetings for participants and the availability and frequency of participant investment transfers, the level of responsibility you (the plan sponsor) want the prospective service provider to assume, what services must be included and what are possible extras or customized services, and optional features such as loans, Internet trading and telephone transfers."

To assist in gathering this information and in making equivalent comparisons, the DOL has developed a *401(k) Plan Fee Disclosure Form* to help plan sponsors make informed cost-benefit decisions with a plan and compare investment product fees and plan administration expenses charged by competing service providers, regardless of how each service provider structures its fees. A copy of the DOL pamphlet on 401(k) plan fee disclosure is available on the internet at http://www.dol.gov/dol/pwba/.

117. What is the Notice to Participants in Underfunded Plans?

The plan administrator of a plan that is less than 90% funded must provide, in a form and manner and at such time as prescribed in Pension Benefits Guaranty Corporation (PBGC) regulations, notice to plan participants and beneficiaries of the plan's funding status and the limits on the PBGC's guarantee should the plan terminate while underfunded. This notice must be written in a manner calculated to be understood by the average plan participant. ERISA Sec. 4011.

The notice for a plan year must be issued no later than two months after the deadline for filing the plan's Form 5500. PBGC Reg. §4011.8.

The notice must explain the employer's obligation to fund the plan and indicate the percentage at which the plan is actually funded. The notice is also required to disclose the dollar amount the employer must pay in satisfaction of the minimum funding standards. PBGC Reg. §4011.10.

The PBGC has established a model notice that plan administrators may use in providing notice to participants in underfunded plans. PBGC Reg. §4011, App. A. See Appendix A.

118. What is the Notice of Failure to Fund?

If an employer maintaining a plan (other than a multiemployer plan) fails to make a required payment, it must notify each participant and beneficiary (including alternate payees) of the failure to make a required installment or other payment required to meet the minimum funding standard to a plan. The notice must be made before the sixtieth day following the due date for the installment or other payment. ERISA Sec. 101(d).

A plan administrator who fails to meet this notice requirement may be held liable to participants and beneficiaries in the amount of up to $110 a day from the date of the failure to provide notice. ERISA Sec. 502(c)(1).

119. How can a plan distribute notices to missing participants?

The Department of Labor has advised that plan administrators must attempt to locate missing participants to satisfy their fiduciary obligations. DOL Adv. Op. 11-86. Where a plan administrator, after a diligent good faith effort, is having difficulty locating missing plan participants, he may seek the assistance of the Internal Revenue Service (IRS). The IRS will forward correspondence of a "humane nature" to taxpayers who have proven difficult to locate. The IRS considers information regarding participant retirement benefits to be of a humane nature. Rev. Proc. 94-22, 1994-1 CB 608.

To seek the assistance of the IRS through their letter forwarding program, the plan administrator must forward a written request to the IRS that briefly explains the need for assistance in forwarding the letter. The request must provide the participant's Social Security number and identify the letter to be forwarded.

The IRS will make an attempt to forward the plan administrator's letter to the participant's last known address in its files. They will not, however, make any attempt to verify that the letter was successfully delivered. They also will not provide the plan administrator with any information they have on file regarding the missing participant. The request for assistance in locating fewer than 50 missing participants should be forwarded to the Disclosure Officer at the IRS district office that services the plan.

The IRS does not charge a fee for the letter forwarding assistance if the plan administrator is attempting to forward information to fewer than 50 participants. If the plan administrator is attempting to locate 50 or more missing participants, a request must be made through IRS Project 753, Computerized Mailout Program. Under this program, the plan administrator must submit a request that:

1.   Briefly explains the need for forwarding the letters;

2.   Contains the approximate number of recipients the plan is trying to locate;

3.   Contains a statement that the plan administrator has a Social Security number for each missing participant (provided on magnetic tape) and that the administrator is aware that a fee will be charged for the service; and

4.   Provides one copy of the letter to be forwarded.

The letter must contain a required disclosure, situated in a conspicuous place, that advises the participant of the IRS's limited role in forwarding the letter. Requests to locate 50 or more missing participants must be submitted to:

IRS Director of the Office of Disclosure, CP:EX:D
Room 1603, 1111 Constitution Avenue, NW
Washington, DC 20224

Under IRS Project 753, the plan administrator is required to submit a flat fee of $1,750 per request, along with $.50 for each letter to be forwarded and $.01 per address search. Rev. Proc. 94-22, 1994-1 CB 608.

For defined benefit plans subject to Pension Benefit Guaranty Corporation (PBGC) coverage that are terminating, the PBGC advises that the plan must purchase an irrevocable commitment from an insurance company for the provision of benefits to any missing participant who is entitled to $5,000 or more in benefits. Missing participants who were married as of their separation from service must have a joint and survivor annuity purchased on their behalf. PBGC Adv. Op. 91-8.

For further details on the PBGC's role in locating missing participants, see Q 718.

QUALIFIED DOMESTIC RELATIONS ORDERS

120. What is a qualified domestic relations order?

ERISA and the Internal Revenue Code do not permit a participant to assign or alienate his interest in a qualified plan to another person. These "anti-assignment and alienation" rules are intended to ensure that a participant's retirement benefits are actually available to provide financial support during the participant's retirement years. A limited exception to the anti-assignment and alienation rules permits the assignment of pension benefits through a qualified domestic relations order ("QDRO"). ERISA Sec. 206(d)(3)(A); IRC Sec. 414(p).

Under the QDRO exception, a domestic relations order may assign some or all of a participant's pension benefits to a spouse, former spouse, child, or other dependent to satisfy family support or marital property obligations, but only if the order is a "qualified domestic relations order." ERISA and the Code require that qualified plans pay benefits in accordance with the applicable requirements of any "qualified domestic relations order" that has been submitted to the plan administrator. The plan administrator's determination of whether a domestic relations order is a QDRO, therefore, has significant implications both for the parties to a domestic relations proceeding and for the plan.

A *qualified* domestic relations order is defined as a domestic relations order (see Q 121):

1.   That creates or recognizes the existence of an "alternate payee's" right to receive, or assigns to an alternate payee the right to receive (see Q 122) benefits under the plan;

2.   Under which all or a portion of the benefits are payable with respect to a participant under a pension plan; and

3.   That includes certain information (see Q 123) and meets certain other requirements. (For details, see Q 124 to Q 139.) ERISA Sec. 206(d)(3)(B); IRC Sec. 414(p)(1)(A).

121. What is a domestic relations order?

To be recognized as a QDRO, an order must be a "domestic relations order." A domestic relations order is defined as a judgment, decree, or order (including the approval of a property settlement);

1. That is made pursuant to state domestic relations law (including community property law); and

2. That relates to the provision of child support, alimony payments, or marital property rights for the benefit of a spouse, former spouse, child, or other dependent of a participant. ERISA Sec. 206(d)(3)(B)(ii); IRC Sec. 414(p)(1)(B).

The DOL has stated that "[a] state authority, generally a court, must actually issue a judgment, order, or decree or otherwise formally approve a property settlement agreement before it can be considered a 'domestic relations order' under ERISA and the Code." ERISA Sec. 206(d)(3)(B)(ii); IRC Sec. 414(p)(1)(B). "The mere fact that a property settlement has been agreed to and signed by the parties will not, in and of itself, cause the agreement to be a domestic relations order."

"There is no requirement that both parties to a marital proceeding sign or otherwise endorse or approve an order. It is also not necessary that the pension plan be brought into state court or made a party to a domestic relations proceeding for an order issued in that proceeding to be considered a 'domestic relations order' or a 'qualified domestic relations order.' Indeed, because state law is generally preempted to the extent that it relates to pension plans, the Department takes the position that pension plans cannot be joined as a party in a domestic relations proceeding pursuant to state law. Moreover, pension plans are neither permitted nor required to follow the terms of domestic relations orders purporting to assign pension benefits unless they are QDROs." *QDROs, The Division of Pensions Through Qualified Domestic Relations Orders*, Questions 1-2 and 1-3, DOL-PWBA (1997).

122. Who can be an "alternate payee" under a QDRO?

According to the DOL, "a domestic relations order can be a QDRO only if it creates or recognizes the existence of an alternate payee's right to receive, or assigns to an alternate payee the right to receive, all or part of a participant's benefits. For purposes of the QDRO provisions, an alternate payee cannot be anyone other than a spouse, former spouse, child, or other dependent of a participant." *QDROs The Division of Pensions Through Qualified Domestic Relations Orders*, Question 1-4, DOL-PWBA (1997); see ERISA Sec. 206(d)(3)(K); IRC Sec. 414(p)(8).

The Court of Appeals for the Ninth Circuit held that an alternate payee could perfect a domestic relations order into a QDRO after the participant's death where the plan was on notice of the domestic order before the death of the participant. *Trustees of the Directors Guild of America - Producer Pension Benefit Plans v. Tise*, 2000 US App. Lexis 31161 (9th Cir. 2000).

123. What information must a domestic relations order contain in order to be considered a QDRO?

The DOL has stated that QDROs must contain the following information:

1. The name and last known mailing address of the participant and each alternate payee;

2. The name of each plan to which the order applies;

3. The dollar amount or percentage (or the method of determining either) of the benefit to be paid to the alternate payee; and

4. The number of payments or the time period to which the order applies. *QDROs The Division of Pensions Through Qualified Domestic Relations Orders*, Question 1-5, DOL-PWBA (1997); see ERISA Sec. 206(d)(3)(C); IRC Sec. 414(p)(2).

124. What is a QDRO prohibited from containing?

DOL guidance states that there are certain provisions that a QDRO must not contain. The order *must not*:

1. Require a plan to provide an alternate payee or participant with any type or form of benefit, or any option, not otherwise provided under the plan;

2. Require a plan to provide for increased benefits (determined on the basis of actuarial value);

3. Require a plan to pay benefits to an alternate payee that are required to be paid to another alternate payee under another order previously determined to be a QDRO; and

4. Require a plan to pay benefits to an alternate payee in the form of a qualified joint and survivor annuity for the lives of the alternate payee and his or her subsequent spouse. *QDROs The Division of Pensions Through Qualified Domestic Relations Orders*, Question 1-6, PWBA-DOL (1997); see ERISA Secs. 206(d)(3)(D), 206(d)(3)(E)(i)(III); IRC Secs. 414(p)(3), 414(p)(4)(A)(iii).

125. May a QDRO provide for payment to the guardian of an alternate payee?

Yes. "If an alternate payee is a minor or is legally incompetent, the order can require payment to someone with legal responsibility for the alternate payee (such as a guardian or a party acting *in loco parentis* in the case of a child, or a trustee acting as an agent for the alternate payee)." *QDROs, The Division of Pensions Through Qualified Domestic Relations Orders*, Question 1-9, DOL-PWBA (1997). (See also General Explanation of the Tax Reform Act of 1984, 100th Cong., 1st Sess., p. 222.)

126. Can a QDRO cover more than one plan?

Yes. According to the Department of Labor, "[a] QDRO can assign rights to pension benefits under more than one pension plan of the same or different employers as long as each plan and the assignment of benefit rights under each plan are clearly specified." *QDROs The Division of Pensions Through Qualified Domestic Relations Orders*, Question 1-10, PWBA-DOL (1997). ERISA Sec. 206(d)(3)(C)(iv); IRC Sec. 414(p)(2)(D).

127. Who determines whether a domestic relations order is "qualified"?

The DOL has addressed this question as follows:

> Under Federal law, the administrator of the pension plan that provides the benefits affected by an order is the individual (or entity) initially responsible for determining whether a domestic relations order is a QDRO. Plan administrators have specific responsibilities and duties with respect to determining whether a domestic relations order is a QDRO. Plan administrators, as plan fiduciaries, are required to discharge their duties prudently and solely in the interest of plan participants and beneficiaries. Among other things, plans must establish reasonable procedures to determine the qualified status of domestic relations orders and to administer distributions pursuant to qualified orders. Administrators are required to follow the plan's procedures for making QDRO determinations. Administrators also are required to furnish notice to participants and alternate payees of the receipt of a domestic relations order and to furnish a copy of the plan's procedures for determining the qualified status of such orders.
>
> It is the view of the DOL that a state court (or other state agency or instrumentality with the authority to issue domestic relations orders) does not have jurisdiction to determine whether an issued domestic relations order constitutes a "qualified domestic relations order." In the view of the Department, jurisdiction to challenge a plan administrator's decision about the qualified status of an order lies exclusively in Federal court.

QDROs, The Division of Pensions Through Qualified Domestic Relations Orders, Question 1-12, DOL-PWBA (1997). See ERISA Sec. 206(d)(3)(G)(i)(II); IRC Sec. 414(p)(6)(A)(ii).

In a 1999 Advisory Opinion, the DOL stated that when a plan administrator is made aware of evidence indicating that a domestic relations order was fraudulently obtained, he must take reasonable steps to determine the credibility of the evidence.

If the administrator determines that the evidence is credible, the administrator must decide how best to resolve the question of the validity of the order without inappropriately spending plan assets or inappropriately involving the plan in the State domestic relations proceeding. The appropriate course of action will depend on the facts and circumstances of the particular case and may vary depending on the fiduciary's exercise of discretion. However, in these circumstances, we note that appropriate action could include relaying the evidence of invalidity to the State court or agency that issued the order and informing the court or agency that its resolution of the matter may affect the administrator's determination of whether the order is a QDRO under ERISA. ... If, however, the administrator is unable to obtain a response from the court or agency within a reasonable time, the administrator may not independently determine that the order is not valid under State law and therefore is not a "domestic relations order" [under ERISA], but should rather proceed with the determination of whether the order is a QDRO. DOL Adv. Opinion 99-13A.

The California Supreme Court, in contrast, has rejected the argument that the federal courts have exclusive jurisdiction over the question whether a state domestic relations order is qualified under ERISA. *In re Marriage of Odino*, 939 P.2d 1266 (Cal. 1997), *cert. den.*, 118 S. Ct. 1302 (1998). Instead, the court concluded that state courts have subject matter jurisdiction, concurrent with that of the federal courts, over whether a domestic relations order is a QDRO. According to the court, the determining factor in deciding whether there is state jurisdiction to decide whether a superior court's order was a QDRO under ERISA, is whether the action is one by a beneficiary to recover, enforce rights to, or clarify future benefits under the terms of a plan, within the meaning of 29 USC Sec. 1132(a)(1)(B).

Since "Congress extended concurrent state jurisdiction to any action by a participant or beneficiary to obtain or clarify benefits under the terms of a plan," the court agreed that "[A]n action to qualify a domestic relations order and obtain benefits pursuant to it is an action to obtain or clarify benefits claimed under the terms of a plan. While Congress clearly intended that actions to enforce rights created by ERISA's title I would be limited to federal courts, rights to benefits awarded in a QDRO are not derived from ERISA, but from state law and plan terms." Thus, a former spouse, who seeks enforcement of a state court order giving the former spouse a right to a portion of the participant's plan benefits, is not seeking to enforce ERISA, but to obtain benefits the former spouse claims are due the former spouse under the terms of the plan and the state court order. Accordingly, a state has concurrent subject matter jurisdiction if a former spouse is seeking payment of benefits the alternate payee claims are due him or her under the plan and a superior court's division of marital property. *In re Marriage of Odino*, above.

128. What are the requirements of a plan's QDRO procedures?

According to the DOL, a qualified plan's "QDRO procedures must:

- be in writing;

- be reasonable;

- provide that each person specified in a domestic relations order as entitled to payment of benefits under the plan will be notified (at the address specified in the domestic relations order) of the plan's procedures for making QDRO determinations upon receipt of a domestic relations order; and

- permit an alternate payee to designate a representative for receipt of copies of notices and plan information that are sent to the alternate payee with respect to domestic relations orders.

It is the view of the Department that a plan's QDRO procedures would not be considered 'reasonable' if they unduly inhibited or hampered the obtaining of a QDRO determination or the making of distributions under a QDRO." *QDROs The Division of Pensions Through Qualified Domestic Relations Orders*, Question 2-4, PWBA-DOL (1997); see ERISA Sec. 206(d)(3)(G)(ii); IRC Sec. 414(p)(6); DOL Adv. Op. 94-32A.

129. May a plan administrator charge a participant or alternate payee for determining the qualified status of a domestic relations order?

No. According to the DOL, imposing a separate fee or cost on a participant or alternate payee (either directly or as a charge against a plan account) in connection with a determination of the status of a domestic relations order or administration of a QDRO would constitute an impermissible encumbrance on the exercise of the right of an alternate payee, under Title I of ERISA, to receive benefits under a QDRO. DOL Adv. Op. 94-32A. Thus, it is the DOL's position that "pension plans may not impose a fee or charge a participant or alternate payee (either directly or as a charge against a plan account) in connection with a determination of the status of a domestic relations order or the administration of a QDRO." *QDROs, The Division of Pensions Through Qualified Domestic Relations Orders*, Question 2-6, DOL-PWBA (1997).

In addition, because Title I of ERISA imposes specific statutory duties on plan administrators regarding QDRO determinations and the administration of QDROs, reasonable administrative expenses thus incurred by the plan may not appropriately be allocated to the individual participants and beneficiaries affected by the QDRO. ERISA Secs. 206(d)(3), 404(a); DOL Adv. Op. 94-32A.

130. Is a plan administrator required to reject a domestic relations order as defective if the order fails to specify factual identifying information that is easily obtainable by the plan administrator?

No. According to the DOL, a domestic relations order that is submitted to a plan that clearly describes the identity and rights of the parties, but is "incomplete only with respect to factual identifying information within the plan administrator's knowledge or easily obtained through a simple communication with the alternate payee or the participant" should not be rejected on that basis. "For example, an order may misstate the plan's name or the names of participants or alternate payees, and the plan administrator can clearly determine the correct names, or an order may omit the addresses of participants or alternate payees, and the plan administrator's records include this information. In such a case, the plan administrator should supplement the order with the appropriate identifying information, rather than rejecting the order as not qualified." *QDROs, The Division of Pensions Through Qualified Domestic Relations Orders*, Question 2-9, DOL-PWBA (1997); see ERISA Secs. 206(d)(3)(C), 206(d)(3)(I); IRC Sec. 414(p)(2); see also S. Rep. No. 98-575, 98th Cong., 2nd Sess. 20 (1984).

131. What is the time limit within which an administrator must determine the qualification of a domestic relations order?

The DOL has stated that "[p]lan administrators must determine whether a domestic relations order is a QDRO within a reasonable period of time after receiving the order. What is a reasonable period of time will depend on the specific circumstances.... Plans are required to adopt reasonable procedures for determining the qualified status of domestic relations orders. Compliance with such procedures should ensure that determinations of the qualified status of an order take place within a reasonable period of time. Procedures that unduly inhibit or hamper the QDRO determination process will not be considered reasonable procedures." *QDROs, The Division of Pensions Through Qualified Domestic Relations Orders*, Question 2-10, DOL-PWBA (1997); see ERISA Sec. 206(d)(3)(G)(i)(II); IRC Sec. 414(p)(6)(A)(ii).

132. How can a plan protect against wrongly paying benefits to the participant (instead of the alternate payee) during the determination process?

The DOL addresses this issue as follows:

> During any period in which the qualification of a domestic relations order is being determined (by a plan administrator, by a court of competent jurisdiction, or otherwise), ERISA requires that the plan administrator separately account for the amounts that would be payable to an alternate payee under the terms of the order during such period if the order had been determined to be qualified. These amounts are referred to as "segregated amounts."

During the period in which the status of a domestic relations order is being determined, the plan administrator must take steps to ensure that amounts that would have been payable to the alternate payee, if the order were a QDRO, are not distributed to the participant or any other person.

The plan administrator's duty to separately account for and to preserve the segregated amounts is limited in time. ERISA provides that the plan administrator must preserve the segregated amounts for not longer than the end of an "18-month period." This "18-month period" does not begin until the first date (after the plan receives the order) that the order would require payment to the alternate payee. ...

... [D]uring the determination period, the administrator, as a plan fiduciary, may not permit distributions to the participant or any other person of any amounts that would be payable to the alternate payee if the domestic relations order were determined to be a QDRO. If the domestic relations order is determined to be a QDRO before the first date on which benefits are payable to the alternate payee, the plan administrator has a continuing duty to account for and to protect the alternate payee's interest in the plan to the same extent that the plan administrator is obliged to account for and to protect the interests of the plan's participants. The plan administrator also has a fiduciary duty to pay out benefits in accordance with the terms of the QDRO. *QDROs The Division of Pensions Through Qualified Domestic Relations Orders,* Questions 2-11, 2-12, DOL-PWBA (1997); see ERISA Sec. 206(d)(3)(H); IRC Sec. 414(p)(7).

The Fifth Circuit Court of Appeals has held that a QDRO may not be issued after the death of a participant in order to establish a former spouse's interest in a qualified joint and survivor annuity under applicable state community property law when the survivor annuity is payable to the participant's current spouse. *Rivers v. Central and South West Corp.,* 186 F.3d 681 (5th Cir., 1999).

133. What type of notice is required to be provided by a plan administrator following a qualification determination?

According to the Department of Labor:

The plan administrator is required to notify the participant and each alternate payee of the administrator's determination as to whether the order constitutes a QDRO. This notice should be in writing and furnished promptly following a determination.

In the case of a determination that an order is not qualified, the notice should include the reasons for the rejection. ...[I]n most instances where there has been a reasonable good faith effort to prepare a qualified domestic relations order, the parties will attempt to correct any deficiencies in the order and resubmit a corrected order for the plan administrator to review. The Department believes that where a reasonable good faith effort has been made to draft a QDRO, prudent plan administration requires the plan administrator to furnish to the parties the information, advice, and guidance that is reasonably required to understand the reasons for a rejection, either as part of the notification process or otherwise, if such information, advice, and guidance could serve to reduce multiple submissions of deficient orders and, therefore, the burdens and costs to plans attendant on review of such orders. *QDROs, The Division of Pensions Through Qualified Domestic Relations Orders*, Question 2-14, DOL-PWBA (1997); see ERISA Sec. 206(d)(3)(G); IRC Sec. 414(p)(6).

Where a plan administrator, comprised of a committee of plan trustees and officers of the plan sponsor, failed to inform the former spouse of a plan participant and committee member of its decision that a domestic relations order the former spouse presented to the plan was not qualified, the Ninth Circuit ruled that the committee violated its fiduciary duties. Specifically, the participant spouse on the committee violated his duty to carry out the plan's written QDRO procedures and the other committee members violated their duties as co-fiduciaries in failing to exercise their affirmative duty to prevent the spouse committee member from breaching his fiduciary duties. The failure to inform the former spouse of the plan's QDRO procedures and of the decision that the domestic relations order she presented was not qualified denied her the opportunity to obtain a valid QDRO. The fiduciary violations gave the former spouse standing to sue the committee members in order to protect her rights and interests as an alternate payee. *Stewart v. Thorpe Holding Company Profit Sharing Plan*, 207 F.3d 1143 (9th Cir. 2000).

134. What must be disclosed to an alternate payee under a QDRO?

Guidance issued by the Department of Labor states that:

[A] person who is an alternate payee under a QDRO generally shall be considered a beneficiary under the plan for purposes of ERISA. Accordingly, the alternate payee must be furnished, upon written request, copies of a variety of documents, including the latest summary plan description, the latest annual report, any final annual report, and the bargaining agreement, trust agreement, contract, or other instrument under which the plan is established or operated. The administrator may impose a reasonable charge to cover the cost of furnishing such copies. It is the view of the Department that, at such time as benefit payments to the alternate payee commence under the QDRO, the alternate payee must be treated as a "beneficiary receiving benefits under the plan" and automatically furnished with the summary plan description, summaries of material plan changes, and the plan's summary annual report. *QDROs The Division of Pensions Through Qualified Domestic Relations Orders*, Question 2-16, DOL-PWBA (1997); see ERISA Secs. 203(d)(3)(J), 104(b); Labor Regs. §§2520.104b-1, et seq.

135. What happens to rights created under a QDRO if the underlying plan is amended, merged or maintained by a successor employer?

According to the DOL, "[t]he rights of an alternate payee under a QDRO are protected in the event of plan amendments, a plan merger, or a change in the sponsor of the plan to the same extent that rights of participants or beneficiaries are protected with respect to benefits accrued as of the date of the event." *QDROs The Division of Pensions Through Qualified Domestic Relations Orders*, Question 2-17, DOL-PWBA (1997); see ERISA Secs. 204(g), 206(d)(3)(A), 403(c)(1); IRC Secs. 401(a)(13)(B), 411(d)(6). See also General Explanation of the Tax Reform Act of 1984, 100th Cong., 1st Sess., p. 224.

136. What happens to the rights created by a QDRO if a plan is terminated?

The DOL has stated that "[i]n the view of the Department, the rights granted by a QDRO must be taken into account in the termination of a plan as if the terms of the QDRO were part of the plan. To the extent that the QDRO grants the alternate payee part of the participant's benefits, the plan administrator, in terminating the plan, must provide the alternate payee with the notification, consent, payment, or other rights that it would have provided to the participant with respect to that portion of the participant's benefits." *QDROs, The Division of Pensions Through Qualified Domestic Relations Orders*, Question 2-18 DOL-PWBA (1997); see ERISA Secs. 206(d)(3)(A), 403(d).

137. What happens to the rights created by a QDRO if a defined benefit plan is terminated and the PBGC becomes trustee of the plan?

Guidance issued by the Department of Labor states that:

When [a Pension Benefit Guaranty Corporation ("PBGC") insured defined benefit] ... plan terminates without enough money to pay all guaranteed benefits, PBGC becomes trustee of the terminating plan and pays the plan benefits, subject to certain limits on amount and form. For instance, PBGC does not pay certain death and supplemental benefits. In addition, benefit amounts paid by PBGC are limited by ERISA, and the forms of benefit PBGC pays are also limited.

PBGC has special rules that apply to the payment of benefits under QDROs. For example, if a QDRO is issued prior to plan termination, PBGC will not modify the form of benefit payable to an alternate payee specified in the QDRO. If, in contrast, a QDRO is issued after plan termination, PBGC will generally limit the form of benefit that PBGC will pay under the QDRO to the form permitted by PBGC in other circumstances (generally a single life annuity). There are other special rules that apply to the administration by PBGC of QDROs. These rules are explained in PBGC's booklet, *Divorce Orders & PBGC. QDROs The Division of Pensions Through Qualified Domestic Relations Orders*, Question 2-19, DOL-PWBA (1997).

138. How much can be provided to an alternate payee through a QDRO?

In guidance addressing this issue, the DOL has stated that

A QDRO can give an alternate payee any part or all of the pension benefits payable with respect to a participant under a pension plan. However, the QDRO cannot require the plan to provide increased benefits (determined on the basis of actuarial value); nor can a QDRO require a plan to provide a type or form of benefit, or any option, not otherwise provided under the plan (with one exception ... for an alternate payee's right to receive payment at the participant's "earliest retirement age"). The QDRO also cannot require the payment of benefits to an alternate payee that are required to be paid to another alternate payee under another QDRO already recognized by the plan. *QDROs The Division of Pensions Through Qualified Domestic Relations Orders*, Question 3-2, DOL-PWBA (1997). See ERISA Secs. 206(d)(3)(D), 206(d)(3)(E); IRC Secs. 414(p)(3); 414(p)(4). See Q 139.

Although ERISA provides that a QDRO cannot require a plan to pay a type or form of benefit not otherwise available under the plan, the DOL has issued an Advisory Opinion which holds that any interest a participant has in a plan (for example, incidental death benefits) is subject to being paid to an alternate payee under a QDRO. DOL Adv. Op. 2000-09A. In the fact pattern subject to the Advisory Opinion, a former spouse sought a ruling that the QDRO received in the divorce from the plan participant covered the incidental company-paid survivor benefits provided under the plan, even though the plan provisions specifically limited potential recipients of these incidental benefits to surviving current spouses, minor children or surviving parents of the participant.

139. What is the significance of "earliest retirement age" in regard to a QDRO?

According to the DOL:

> For QDROs, Federal law provides a very specific definition of "earliest retirement age," which is the earliest date as of which a QDRO can order payment to an alternate payee (unless the plan permits payments at an earlier date). The "earliest retirement age" applicable to a QDRO depends on the terms of the pension plan and the participant's age. "Earliest retirement age" is the *earlier* of two dates:

- the date on which the participant is entitled to receive a distribution under the plan; or

- the *later* of either:

  • the date the participant reaches age 50, or

  • the earliest date on which the participant could begin receiving benefits under the plan if the participant separated from service with the employer.

QDROs The Division of Pensions Through Qualified Domestic Relations Orders, Question 3-10, DOL-PWBA (1997); see ERISA Sec. 206(d)(3)(E)(ii); IRC Sec. 414(p)(4)(B).

140. What are the proposed DOL rules regarding Qualified Medical Child Support Order Notices?

ERISA Section 609(a) provides that each group health plan shall provide benefits in accordance with applicable requirements of any qualified medical child support order (QMCSO). ERISA Section 609(a)(2) defines a QMCSO as a medical child support order issued under any state law that creates or recognizes the existence of an "alternate recipient's" right to receive benefits for which a participant or beneficiary is eligible under a group health plan. Upon receipt of a medical child support order, the plan administrator of a group health plan is required to determine, within a reasonable period of time, whether a medical child support order received by the plan is qualified. ERISA Sec. 609(a)(5).

Congress enacted Section 401 of the Child Support Performance and Incentive Act of 1998 to amend both ERISA and the Social Security Act to require State agencies to enforce the medical child support obligations of noncustodial parents by issuing to their employers a National Medical Support Notice (NMSN). ERISA requires plan administrators, upon receipt of the notice from the employer, to accept an appropriately completed notice that also complies with the requirements of ERISA Section 609(a) as a QMCSO. The DOL and the Department of Health and Human Services have issued final rules that grant states the authority to serve NMSNs upon employers of noncustodial parents. 29 CFR Part 2590, 65 Fed. Reg. 82128 (12-27-2000). Accompanying these final rules was the release of a model "National Medical Support Notice" which included model Part A "Notice to Withhold for Health Care Coverage" and model Part B "Medical Support Notice to Plan Administrator." These model forms are included in Appendix A.

Under the final rules, the 2-part NMSN would be issued to an employer of a non-custodial parent. Part A, the employer withholding notice, advises employers of an identified employee's obligation to provide medical coverage for a child (or children) to whom the QMCSO applies. Within 20 business days, the employer is then required to forward Part B of the NMSN, the "Medical Support Notice to Plan Administrator" to its group health plan administrator. Under Part A, the employer is also required to withhold from the earnings of the employee any participant contributions required under the plan for coverage of the identified child and to transmit those amounts to the plan.

The plan administrator, after receipt of Part B, would determine whether group health coverage of the child is available under plan provisions, whether the child has been enrolled in the plan, and, if not, what steps must be taken to provide coverage under the plan. The plan administrator is required to provide a report back to the state issuing the NMSM within 40 days of receipt of the Notice. 29 CFR Part 2590, 65 Fed. Reg. 82128 (12-27-2000).

Under the final rules, an employer must provide covered benefits to a child under its group health plan even if:

1.   The child is born out of wedlock;

2.   The child does not reside within the plan's service area;

3.   The employee does not claim the child as a dependent; or

4.   The child would have to be added outside of the plan's open enrollment period.

Part A of the NMSN contained in the proposed rules includes a draft "employer response" form, which an employer would complete and file with a state if health coverage does not exist or if state or federal withholding limitations preclude the employer from withholding. The employer response also contains general instructions that identify the various types of health coverage that may be required by the QMCSO, and a warning that penalties may apply if the employer fails to withhold pursuant to the NMSN.

The final rules were originally scheduled to take effect January 26, 2001, but The DOL delayed the effective date until March 27, 2001. See Memorandum for the Heads and Acting Heads of Executive Departments and Agencies, 66 Fed. Reg. 7701 (1-24-2001).

141. Does the DOL offer guidance in understanding COBRA, HIPAA and NMHPA?

The Department of Labor has made available at its internet web site (www.dol.gov/dol/pwba) three brochures designed to familiarize participants in employer sponsored health plans with the provisions of COBRA (see Q 173 to Q 185), HIPAA (see Q 142 to Q 164) and NMHPA, as well as how these protections and rights apply to life changes and health benefits.

The brochure "Top 10 Ways to Make Your Health Benefits Work for You" sets forth guidance for participants who are selecting a health plan or are changing their benefits under existing health coverage. The brochure advises individuals of the right to change benefits under HIPAA and the right to continuation of health coverage under COBRA when changing jobs.

"Life Changes Require Health Choices" provides readers with guidance on what an employee may do when they experience a life changing event, such as the birth of a child. It also explains how COBRA, HIPAA and NMHPA provide health care rights under certain life changing events.

The final brochure "Work Changes Require Health Choices" details the effect of retirement, lay-off, termination, or job changes on the provision of health benefits. It provides details on employee rights under COBRA and HIPAA where certain health benefits are protected when a work change occurs.

In late 1999, the DOL announced, as a result of its increasing role in the health field, that it has formed the Office of Health Plan Standards and Compliance Assistance. The new office will succeed the DOL's Health Care Task Force and will develop regulations, interpretive bulletins, opinions, forms and rulings relating to health care portability, nondiscrimination requirements and other health-related provisions. PWBA Office Press Release: 00-05 (Dec. 7, 1999).

CHAPTER II

HEALTH BENEFIT ISSUES

HIPAA Requirements

142. What is the Health Insurance Portability and Accountability Act of 1996?

The Health Insurance Portability and Accountability Act of 1996 (HIPAA) includes protections for employees and their families who have pre-existing medical conditions or might suffer discrimination in health coverage based on a factor that relates to an individual's health. HIPAA's provisions amend Title I of ERISA (Protection of Employee Benefit Rights) as well as the Internal Revenue Code and the Public Health Service Act. Additionally, HIPAA places requirements on employer-sponsored group health plans, insurance companies, and health maintenance organizations (HMOs). HIPAA includes changes that:

1. Limit exclusions for pre-existing conditions;

2. Prohibit discrimination against employees and dependents based upon their health status;

3. Guarantee renewability and availability of health coverage to certain employers and individuals; and

4. Protect many workers who lose health coverage by providing better access to individual health insurance coverage.

The DOL, the IRS, and the Department of Health and Human Services jointly issued interim final regulations and new proposed regulations on January 8, 2001, which were designed to provide guidance on the nondiscrimination provisions of HIPAA. 66 Fed. Reg. 1378 and 1421 (1-8-2001).

The interim final rule includes the following provisions:

1. Plans may not prohibit eligibility or enrollment in health plans for individuals who engage in inherently dangerous activities, such as bungee jumping and skiing. However, plans may deny coverage for injuries sustained while undertaking such inherently dangerous leisure time activities (Labor Regs. §§2590.702(b)(2)(iii)(A), 2590.702(b)(2)(iii)(B) Ex. 2);

2. Plans may not deny benefits for injuries resulting from acts of domestic violence or a physical or mental condition. The rules

provide the example of injuries sustained in a failed suicide attempt where the actions were the result of the mental condition of depression (Labor Regs. §§2590.702(b)(2)(iii)(A), 2590.702(b)(2)(iii)(B) Ex. 1);

3. Plans may not implement non-confinement clauses that deny eligibility to individuals confined to a hospital or who are unable to engage in normal life activities (Labor Reg. §2590.702(e)(1));

4. Plans may not implement an "actively at work" clause that restricts eligibility to people who are on the job when a new benefit program takes effect, unless the plan defines "on the job" to include employees who are absent from work due to health factors (Labor Reg. §2590.702(e)(2));

5. Plans may provide differing levels of benefits and services, as long as they are applied uniformly to people covered by the plan (even though differing levels may affect individuals with health problems more severely than others). This does not mean, however, that individuals with health problems may be subject to less favorable eligibility or enrollment standards (Labor Regs. §§2590.702(b)(2)(i)(A), 2590.702(b)(2)(i)(B)); and

6. Plans may not be amended to reduce benefits for a specific treatment or service as a result of a specific individual's claim for those benefits. There is a presumption, however, that a plan amendment reducing or eliminating such benefits as of the first day of the next plan year is not directed at a specific individual (Labor Regs. §§2590.702(b)(2)(i)(B), 2590.702(b)(2)(i)(C)).

Under the proposed rules, wellness programs must meet a 4-part test. The benefit of satisfying the criteria of a bona fide wellness program is that the plan may offer participants who satisfy objective criteria a reward, such as reduced premiums, or low-cost benefits such as health club memberships, without violating ERISA. The criteria of a bona fide wellness program include:

1. The reward for the wellness program must not exceed a percentage of the cost of employee only coverage under the plan. The final regulations will specify a percentage of either 10%, 15%, or 20%;

2. The program must be reasonably designed to promote good health or prevent disease;

3. The reward under the program must be available to all similarly situated individuals, unless a reasonable alternative standard for

attaining the reward is offered to participants for whom a medical condition makes it medically inadvisable or unreasonably difficult to satisfy; and

4.   The plan must disclose, in all plan materials describing the terms of the program, the availability of a reasonable alternative standard for those who attempt, but fail to meet the wellness goals. Prop. Labor Regs. §§2590.702(f)(1)(i) through 2590.702(f)(1)(iv).

The Department of Health and Human Services has issued guidance on the administrative simplification guidelines that must be in place by October 16, 2002. Specifically, the simplification guidelines are designed to improve the efficiency and effectiveness of the health care system through the adoption of national standards for electronic health care transactions, privacy, and security. Detailed guidance on the administrative simplification guidelines can be found on the internet at http://www.aspe.hhs.gov/admnsimp/.

143. What are the pre-existing condition exclusions under HIPAA?

Under HIPAA, a group health plan or a health insurance issuer offering group health insurance coverage may impose a pre-existing condition exclusion with respect to a participant or beneficiary only if the following requirements are satisfied:

1.   The pre-existing condition exclusion must relate to a condition for which medical advice, diagnosis, care, or treatment was recommended or received during the 6-month period prior to an individual's enrollment date. IRC Sec. 9801(a); Labor Reg. §2590.701-3(a)(1); Temp. Treas. Reg. §54.9801-3T(a)(1);

2.   The pre-existing condition exclusion may not last for more than 12 months (18 months for late enrollees) after an individual's enrollment date. IRC Sec. 9801(a); Labor Reg. §2590.701-3(a)(2); Temp. Treas. Reg. §54.9801-3T(a)(1); and

3.   This 12-month (or 18-month) period must be reduced by the number of days of the individual's prior creditable coverage, excluding coverage before any break in coverage of 63 days or more. IRC Sec. 9801(a); Labor Reg. §2590.701-4; Temp. Treas. Reg. §54.9801-4T.

144. How does HIPAA define a "pre-existing condition"?

HIPAA states that a "pre-existing condition" is a condition present before an individual's enrollment date in any new health plan. Under HIPAA, the only pre-existing conditions that may be excluded under a pre-existing condition exclusion are those for which medical advice, diagnosis, care, or treatment were recommended or received within the 6-month period ending on the individual's enrollment date. IRC Sec. 9801(a)(1).

If an employee has had a medical condition in the past, but has not received any medical advice, diagnosis, care, or treatment within the 6-month period prior to his enrollment date in the plan, the employee's prior condition is not a "pre-existing condition" for which an exclusion can be applied. Labor Regs. §§2590.701-2, 2590.701-3; Temp. Treas. Reg. §54.9801-3T.

145. What pre-existing conditions cannot be excluded from coverage under HIPAA?

Pre-existing condition exclusions cannot be applied to pregnancy, regardless of whether the woman had previous coverage. IRC Sec. 9801(d)(3). In addition, a pre-existing condition exclusion cannot be applied to a newborn, adopted child under age 18, or a child under 18 placed for adoption, as long as the child became covered under the health plan within 30 days of birth, adoption, or placement for adoption, and provided that the child does not incur a subsequent 63-day (or longer) break in coverage. IRC Sec. 9801(d); Labor Reg. §2590.701-3(b); Temp. Treas. Reg. §54.9801-3T(b).

146. May states modify HIPAA's portability requirements?

Yes, in certain circumstances. States may impose stricter obligations on health insurance issuers in the seven areas listed below. If certain requirements are met, states may:

1.   Shorten the 6-month "look-back" period prior to the enrollment date to determine what is a pre-existing condition;

2.   Shorten the 12-month and 18-month maximum pre-existing condition exclusion periods;

3.   Increase the 63-day significant break in coverage period;

4.   Increase the 30-day period for newborns, adopted children, and children placed for adoption to enroll in the plan so that no pre-existing condition exclusion period may be applied thereafter;

5.   Expand the prohibitions on conditions and people to whom a pre-existing condition exclusion period may be applied beyond the "exceptions" described in federal law (see Q 145);

6.   Require additional special enrollment periods; and

7.   Reduce the maximum HMO affiliation period to less than two months (three months for late enrollees). Labor Regs. §§2590.701-

1(b), 2590.701-4(b)(2); Temp. Treas. Regs. §§54.9801-1T(b), 54.9801-4T(b)(2).

Therefore, if employee health coverage is offered through an HMO or an insurance policy issued by an insurance company, the employee should check with the state insurance commissioner's office regarding the rules in his state.

147. How do subsequent group health plans determine the length of a newly hired employee's pre-existing condition exclusion period?

A plan can exclude coverage for a pre-existing condition only if it relates to a condition (whether physical or mental, and regardless of the cause of the condition) for which medical advice, diagnosis, care, or treatment was recommended or received within the 6-month "look-back" period ending on an individual's "enrollment date." The *enrollment date* is the first day of coverage, or, if there is a waiting period, the first day of the waiting period (typically, the date of hire). Labor Regs. §§2590.701-2, 2590.701-3; Temp. Treas. Reg. §54.9801-3T(a)(2).

The maximum length of a pre-existing condition exclusion period is 12 months after the enrollment date, or 18 months in the case of a "late enrollee." A *late enrollee* is an individual who enrolls in a plan on a date other than: (1) the earliest date on which coverage can become effective under the terms of the plan; or (2) a special enrollment date. Labor Reg. §2590.701-3(a)(2); Temp. Treas. Reg. §54.9801-3T(a)(2).

A plan must reduce an individual's pre-existing condition exclusion period by the number of days of an individual's "creditable coverage" (see Q 149). However, a plan is not required to take into account any days of creditable coverage that precede a break in coverage of 63 days or more, known as a "significant break in coverage." IRC Sec. 9801(c)(2)(A); Labor Reg. §2590.701-4; Temp. Treas. Reg. §54.9801-4T. A plan generally receives information about an individual's creditable coverage from a certificate furnished by a prior plan or issuer (e.g., an insurance company or HMO).

148. Does HIPAA prohibit an employer from establishing a waiting period for enrollment in the plan?

HIPAA does not prohibit a plan or issuer from establishing a waiting period. However, if a plan has a waiting period and a pre-existing condition exclusion period, the pre-existing condition exclusion period must begin when the waiting period begins. Labor Reg. §2590.701-2; Temp. Treas. Reg. §54.9801-2T.

For group health plans, a waiting period is the period that must pass before an employee or a dependent is eligible to enroll under the terms of a group health plan. However, if the employee or dependent is a late enrollee or a special enrollee, any period before such late or special enrollment is not a waiting period. Labor Reg. §2590.701-3(a)(2); Temp. Treas. Reg. §54.9801-3T(a)(2).

If an individual seeks and obtains coverage by purchasing an individual insurance policy, the period between the date when the individual files a substantially complete application for coverage and the first day of coverage is a waiting period. Labor Reg. §2590.701-2.

149. What is creditable coverage?

Most health coverage is creditable coverage. It is defined as coverage of an individual under many types of health plans, including a group health plan, health insurance coverage, HMO, individual health insurance policy, Part A or Part B of Title XVIII of the Social Security Act (Medicare), a state health benefits risk pool, and a public health plan. IRC Sec. 9801(c)(1).

Creditable coverage does not include coverage consisting solely of "excepted benefits," such as coverage solely for dental or vision benefits. Days in a waiting period during which an individual has no other coverage are not creditable coverage under the plan, nor are these days taken into account when determining a significant break in coverage (i.e., a break of 63 days or more). Labor Reg. §2590.701-4(a); Temp. Treas. Reg. §54.9801-4T(a).

A pre-existing condition exclusion period is not permitted to extend for more than 12 months, or 18 months for late enrollees, after an individual's enrollment date in the plan. The period of any pre-existing condition exclusion that would apply under a group health plan is generally reduced by the number of days of creditable coverage.

150. How does crediting for prior coverage work under HIPAA?

Most plans use the "standard method" of crediting coverage. Under the standard method, an employee receives credit for his previous coverage that occurred without a break in coverage of 63 days or more. Any coverage occurring prior to a break in coverage of 63 days or more is not credited against a pre-existing condition exclusion period. Labor Reg. §2590.701-4(b)(2)(iv); Temp. Treas. Reg. §54.9801-4T(b)(2)(iv).

It is also important to remember that, during any pre-existing condition exclusion period under a new plan, an employee may be entitled to COBRA continuation coverage under his former plan. "COBRA" is the name for a federal law that provides workers and their families with the opportunity to purchase group health coverage through their employer's health plan for a limited period of time (generally 18, 29, or 36 months) if they lose coverage due to specified events, including termination of employment, divorce, or death. Workers in companies with 20 or more employees generally qualify for COBRA. Some states have laws similar to COBRA that may apply to smaller companies. See Q 173 to Q 185.

151. Can an employee receive credit for previous COBRA continuation coverage?

Yes. Under HIPAA, any period of time during which an employee was receiving COBRA continuation coverage is counted as previous health coverage, as long as the coverage occurred without a break in coverage of 63 days or more. Labor Reg. §2590.701-6; Temp. Treas. Reg. §54.9801-6T.

For example, if an employee was covered continuously for five months by a previous health plan, and then received seven months of COBRA continuation coverage, the employee would be entitled to receive credit for 12 months of coverage under the new group health plan.

152. Is there an alternative method to credit coverage under HIPAA?

Yes, a plan or issuer may elect the "alternative method" for crediting coverage for all employees. Under the alternative method of counting creditable coverage, the plan or issuer determines the amount of an individual's creditable coverage for any of the five specified categories of benefits. These categories are: (1) mental health; (2) substance abuse treatment; (3) prescription drugs; (4) dental care; and (5) vision care. Labor Reg. §2590.701-4(c); Temp. Treas. Reg. §54.9801-4T(c). The standard method (see Q 150) is used to determine an individual's creditable coverage for benefits that are not within any of the five categories that a plan or issuer may use. (The plan or issuer may use some or all of these categories.)

When using the alternative method, the plan or issuer looks to see if an individual has coverage within a category of benefits, regardless of the specific level of benefits provided within that category.

If an employer's plan requests information from a new employee's former plan regarding any of the five categories of benefits under the alternative method, the former plan must provide the information regarding coverage under the categories of benefits. Labor Reg. §2590.701-5; Temp. Treas. Reg. §54.9801-5T(b).

153. What is involved in the certification of creditable coverage?

Group health plans and health insurance issuers are required to furnish a certificate of coverage to an individual to provide documentation of the individual's prior creditable coverage. A certificate of creditable coverage:

1. Must be provided automatically by the plan or issuer when an individual either loses coverage under the plan or becomes entitled to elect COBRA continuation coverage, and when an individual's COBRA continuation coverage ceases;

2. Must be provided, if requested, before the individual loses coverage or within 24 months of losing coverage; and

3.   May be provided through the use of the model certificate. Labor Reg. §2590.701-5; Temp. Treas. Reg. §54.9801-5T.

154. Who is responsible for providing information on a newly hired employee's prior health coverage?

Under HIPAA, providing information about an employee's prior health coverage is the responsibility of an employee's former group health plan and/or the insurance company providing such coverage. Labor Reg. §2590.701-5(a); Treas. Temp. Reg. §54.9801-5T(a). HIPAA sets specific disclosure and certification requirements for group health plans, insurance companies, and HMOs.

A certificate stating when an employee was covered under the plan must be provided automatically to the employee when he loses coverage under the plan, or otherwise becomes entitled to elect COBRA continuation coverage, as well as when COBRA continuation coverage ceases. Labor Reg. §2590.701-5(a)(2)(ii).

Employees may also request a certificate, free of charge, until 24 months after the time when their coverage ended. An employee may request a certificate even before his coverage ends. Labor Reg. §2590.701-5(a)(2)(iii).

155. When must group health plans and issuers provide certificates of creditable coverage?

Plans and issuers must furnish a certificate of creditable coverage automatically to:

1.   An individual who is entitled to elect COBRA continuation coverage at a time no later than when a notice is required to be provided for a qualifying event under COBRA;

2.   An individual who loses coverage under a group health plan and who is not entitled to elect COBRA continuation coverage, within a reasonable time after coverage ceases; and

3.   An individual who has elected COBRA continuation coverage, either within a reasonable time after the plan learns that COBRA continuation coverage ceased, or, if applicable, within a reasonable time after the individual's grace period for the payment of COBRA premiums ends.

Plans and issuers must also generally provide a certificate to an employee if he requests one, or if someone requests one on his behalf (with the employee's permission), at the earliest time that a plan or issuer, acting in a reasonable and prompt fashion, can provide the certificate. Labor Reg. §2590.701-5(a)(2); Temp. Treas. Reg. §54.9801-5T(a)(2).

156. What is the minimum period of time that should be covered by the certificate of creditable coverage?

The minimum period of time that should be covered by the certificate depends on whether the certificate is issued automatically or upon request. A certificate that is issued automatically should reflect the most recent period of continuous coverage ending on the date when the coverage ceased. A certificate that is issued upon request should reflect each period of continuous coverage ending within the 24-month period ending (or continuing) on the date of the request. Separate certificates may be provided for each such period of continuous coverage. Labor Reg. §2590.701-5(a)(3)(iii); Temp. Treas. Reg. §54.9801-5T(a)(3)(iii).

At no time must the certificate reflect more than 18 months of creditable coverage that is not interrupted by a break in coverage of 63 days or more.

157. What are the basic nondiscrimination requirements under HIPAA?

Individuals may not be excluded from coverage under the terms of the plan, or charged more for benefits offered by a plan or issuer, based upon specified factors related to health status. IRC Secs. 9802(a)(1), 9802(b)(1).

Group health plans and issuers may not establish rules for eligibility (including continued eligibility) of any individual to enroll under the terms of the plan based on "health status-related factors." IRC Sec. 9802(a)(1). These factors are:

1. Health status;

2. Medical condition (physical or mental);

3. Claims experience;

4. Receipt of health care;

5. Medical history;

6. Genetic information;

7. Evidence of insurability; and

8. Disability.

An employee cannot be excluded or dropped from coverage under his health plan just because he has a particular illness. Labor Reg. §2590.702; Treas. Reg. §54.9802-1.

Plans may establish limits or restrictions on benefits or coverage for similarly situated individuals. Treas. Reg. §54.9802-1. In addition, a plan may change covered services or benefits if it gives participants notice of such "material reductions" within 60 days after the change is adopted.

Also, plans may not require an individual to pay a premium or contribution greater than that for a similarly situated individual based on a health status-related factor. IRC Sec. 9802(b)(1); Labor Reg. §2590.702(b); Treas. Reg. §54.9802-1(c).

158. What are the special enrollment rules under HIPAA?

Group health plans and health insurance issuers are required to permit special enrollment rights for certain employees and their dependents. These rights are provided to:

1. Employees who were eligible but declined enrollment in the plan when first offered because they were covered under another plan; and

2. Individuals upon marriage, birth, adoption, or placement for adoption of a new dependent.

These special enrollment rights permit these individuals to enroll without having to wait until the plan's next regular enrollment period. Labor Regs. §§2590.701-6(a), 2590.701-6(b).

A special enrollment occurs if an individual with other health insurance coverage loses that coverage, or if a person becomes a dependent through marriage, birth, adoption, or placement for adoption. A special enrollee is not treated as a late enrollee. Therefore, the maximum pre-existing condition exclusion period that may be applied to a special enrollee is 12 months, and that 12-month period is reduced by the special enrollee's creditable coverage. A newborn, adopted child, or child placed for adoption cannot be subject to a pre-existing condition exclusion period if the child is enrolled within 30 days of birth, adoption, or placement for adoption. IRC Sec. 9801(d); Labor Regs. §§2590.701-6(a), 2590.701-6(b).

A plan must provide a description of the plan's special enrollment rights to an employee on or before the time when he is offered the opportunity to enroll in group health coverage. Labor Reg. §2590.701-6(c).

159. Does HIPAA require employers to offer health coverage or require plans to provide specific benefits?

No. The provision of health coverage by an employer is voluntary. HIPAA does not require specific benefits, nor does it prohibit a plan from restricting the amount or nature of benefits for similarly situated individuals. Treas. Reg. §54.9802-1(b)(2).

There is no requirement for any employer to offer health insurance coverage. If a subsequent employer does not offer health insurance, the individual may be able to continue coverage under his previous employer's plan through COBRA continuation coverage. See Q 173 et seq.

160. May an individual obtain guaranteed individual insurance coverage under HIPAA?

Yes. Individuals may be able to obtain coverage under an individual insurance policy issued by an insurance company. Health and Human Services Regs. §§148.102, 148.103. HIPAA guarantees access to individual insurance for "eligible individuals." Eligible individuals are individuals who:

1. Have had coverage for at least 18 months, and the most recent period of coverage was under a group health plan;

2. Did not have their group coverage terminated because of fraud or nonpayment of premiums;

3. Are ineligible for COBRA continuation coverage or have exhausted their COBRA benefits (or continuation coverage under a similar state provision); and

4. Are not eligible for coverage under another group health plan, Medicare, Medicaid, or any other health insurance coverage.

The opportunity to buy an individual insurance policy is the same whether the individual is laid off or is voluntarily or involuntarily terminated.

HIPAA does not set premium rates, but it does prohibit plans and issuers from charging an individual more than similarly situated individuals in the same plan because of health status. Plans may offer premium discounts or rebates for participation in wellness programs. Treas. Reg. §54.9802-1(c).

In addition, many states limit insurance premiums. HIPAA does not preempt such current or future state laws regulating the cost of insurance.

161. Does HIPAA extend COBRA continuation coverage?

Generally, no. HIPAA makes two changes to the length of the COBRA continuation coverage period. Qualified beneficiaries who are determined to be disabled under the Social Security Act within the first 60 days of COBRA continuation coverage will be able to purchase an additional 11 months of coverage beyond the usual 18-month coverage period. IRC Sec.

4980B(f)(2)(B)(i); DOL Technical Release 96-1. This is a change from the old law, which required that a qualified beneficiary be determined to be disabled at the time of the qualifying event in order to receive 29 months of COBRA continuation coverage.

This extension of coverage is also available to nondisabled family members who are entitled to COBRA continuation coverage. Treas. Reg. §54.4980B-7, A-5. See Q 180.

COBRA rules are also modified and clarified to ensure that children who are born or adopted during the continuation coverage period are treated as "qualified beneficiaries." Treas. Reg. §54.4980B-3, A-1. A model notice discussing these changes appears in Appendix A. See Q 175.

162. What information must group health plans disclose to participants?

HIPAA and other legislation made important changes in ERISA's disclosure requirements for group health plans. Group health plans must ensure that their summary plan descriptions (SPDs) and summaries of material modifications (SMMs):

1. Notify participants and beneficiaries of "material reductions in covered services or benefits" (for example, reductions in benefits and increases in deductibles and co-payments), generally within 60 days of adoption of the change (see Q 163);

2. Disclose to participants and beneficiaries information about the role of issuers (e.g., insurance companies and HMOs) with respect to their group health plan. In particular, the name and address of the issuer, whether and to what extent benefits under the plan are guaranteed under a contract or policy of insurance issued by the issuer, and the nature of any administrative services (e.g., payment of claims) provided by the issuer;

3. Tell participants and beneficiaries which DOL office they should contact for assistance or information on their rights under ERISA and HIPAA; and

4. Tell participants and beneficiaries that federal law generally prohibits the plan and health insurance issuers from limiting hospital stays for childbirth to under 48 hours for normal deliveries and 96 hours for delivery by caesarean section. Labor Regs. §§2520.102-3, 2520.104b-3.

In addition, the SPD must describe:

1.   Any cost-sharing provisions (including premiums, deductibles, coin-surance, and co-payment amounts), any annual or lifetime caps or other limits on benefits, the extent to which preventive services are covered under the plan, which existing and new drugs are covered under the plan (this may be done by reference to a schedule), and the coverage provided for medical tests, devices and procedures;

2.   Any provisions governing the use of network providers, the composition of the provider network (this may be provided in a separate document, if referenced in the SPD and provided without charge), and whether coverage is provided for out-of-network services (and, if so, under what circumstances); and

3.   Any conditions or limits on the selection of primary care providers or specialists, any conditions or limits applicable to emergency medical care; and any provisions requiring pre-authorizations or utilization review as a condition to obtaining a benefit or service under the plan. Labor Reg. §2520.102-3(j)(3).

Group health plans subject to the COBRA continuation coverage rules (see Q 173) must include information concerning the rights and obligations of participants and beneficiaries under COBRA. The regulations also provide that the initial COBRA notice obligation (see Q 177) will be satisfied by furnishing the covered employee and spouse with an SPD that includes the COBRA continuation coverage notice information at the time when their plan coverage commences. Labor Reg. §2520.102-3(o).

The SPD of a group health plan must set forth the claims procedure (see Q 182), including any plan procedures for pre-authorization, approval, or utilization review. A plan may furnish the claims procedures as a separate document, so long as (1) that separate document satisfies the style and format requirements of Labor Regulation §2520.102-2; (2) such claims procedures set forth in a separate document are provided (a) automatically with the SPD, and (b) without charge; and (3) the SPD contains a statement indicating that the claims procedures are furnished automatically, without charge, as a separate document. Labor Reg. §2520.102-3(s).

Beginning in 2001, funded health plans with 100 or more participants are subject to new disclosure rules under revised standards issued by the American Institute of Certified Public Accountants (AICPA). These changes will affect annual report filings (Form 5500 series) for the 2001 plan year. Plans providing benefits entirely through insurance contracts, and plans with fewer than 100 participants are exempt from the new standards. AICPA SOP 01-2 (*Accounting and Reporting by Health and Welfare Plans*).

163. What is a material reduction in covered services or benefits subject to the 60-day notice requirement?

2002 ERISA Facts

A "material reduction in covered services or benefits" means any modification to a group health plan or change in the information required to be included in the summary plan description that, independently or in conjunction with other contemporaneous modifications or changes, would be considered by the average plan participant to be an important reduction in covered services or benefits under the group health plan. Labor Reg. §2520.104b-3(d)(3).

The regulations cite examples of "reductions in covered services or benefits" as generally including any plan modification or change that:

1. Eliminates benefits payable under the plan;

2. Reduces benefits payable under the plan, including a reduction that occurs as a result of a change in the formulas, methodologies, or schedules that serve as the basis for benefit determinations;

3. Increases deductibles, co-payments, or other amounts to be paid by a participant or beneficiary;

4. Reduces the service area covered by a health maintenance organization; or

5. Establishes new conditions or requirements (e.g., pre-authorization requirements) to obtain services or benefits under the plan. Labor Reg. §2520.104b-3(d)(3)(ii).

164. Who has the authority to enforce HIPAA?

The Secretary of Labor enforces the health care portability provisions of HIPAA under ERISA, including self-insured health care arrangements. In addition, participants and beneficiaries can file suit to enforce their rights under ERISA, as amended by HIPAA.

The Secretary of the Treasury enforces the health care portability provisions of HIPAA under the Internal Revenue Code, including self-insured health care arrangements. A taxpayer that fails to comply with these provisions may be subject to an excise tax.

States also have enforcement responsibility for group and individual requirements imposed on health insurance issuers, including available sanctions under state law. If a state does not act in the areas of its responsibility, the Secretary of Health and Human Services may make a determination that the state has failed "to substantially enforce" the law, assert federal authority to enforce the law, and impose sanctions on health insurance issuers as specified in the statute, including civil money penalties.

The DOL has initiated a field level HIPAA compliance enforcement program aimed at service providers in the health care industry. See Q 657 for a detailed analysis of the field audit checklist utilized by the DOL in executing individual HIPAA compliance investigations.

The Department of the Treasury, the Department of Labor, and the Department of Health and Human Services entered into a Memorandum of Understanding, effective April 21, 1999, which formally establishes an inter-agency agreement among the Secretary of the Treasury, the Secretary of Labor, and the Secretary of Health and Human Services. This agreement is intended to ensure the coordination of the regulations, rulings, and interpretations relating to changes made by HIPAA and to coordinate policies relating to HIPAA enforce-ment, in order to avoid duplication of enforcement efforts and to assign priorities in enforcement. 64 Fed. Reg. 70163 (See also http://www.dol.gov/dol/pwba/public/regs/fedreg/notices/99032500.htm).

Women's Health and Cancer Rights

165. What is the Women's Health and Cancer Rights Act of 1998?

The Women's Health and Cancer Rights Act (Women's Health Act), signed into law on October 21, 1998, added Section 713 to ERISA and Sections 2706 and 2752 to the Public Health Service Act (PHS Act). Under the Women's Health Act, insured and self-insured group health plans of private and govern-mental employers, collectively bargained health plans, insurance companies, and health maintenance organizations (HMOs) that provide coverage for medical and surgical benefits with respect to a mastectomy must also provide coverage for reconstructive surgery, in a manner determined in consultation between the attending physician and the patient. Coverage includes reconstruction of the breast on which the mastectomy was performed, surgery and reconstruction of the other breast to produce a symmetrical appearance, and prostheses and treatment of physical complications at all stages of the mastectomy, including lymphedemas. These requirements are effective for plan years beginning on or after October 21, 1998, and also apply to individual health insurance policies offered, sold, issued, renewed, in effect, or operated on or after October 21, 1998. The requirements for individual health insurance policies were placed in the PHS Act within the jurisdiction of the Department of Health and Human Services (HHS).

The Women's Health Act permits the imposition of deductibles or coinsur-ance requirements for reconstructive surgery in connection with a mastectomy, but only if the deductibles and coinsurance are consistent with those established for other benefits under the plan or coverage. However, the Women's Health Act prohibits a patient from being denied eligibility, or continued eligibility, to enroll or to renew coverage under the terms of the plan, in order to avoid the requirements of the Women's Health Act. In addition, a plan may not penalize or otherwise reduce or limit the reimbursement of an attending provider, or provide incentives (monetary or otherwise) to an attending provider, to induce the provider to provide care to an individual participant or beneficiary in a manner inconsistent with the Women's Health Act. However, the Women's Health Act does not prevent a group health plan or a health insurance issuer offering group health insurance coverage from negotiating the level and type of reimbursement with a provider for the coverage prescribed by the Women's Health Act. The Women's Health and Cancer Rights Act of 1998, P.L. 105-277. See http://www.dol.gov/dol/pwba/public/pubs/womhlth.htm for Questions & Answers from the DOL about the Women's Health Act.

166. What are the notice requirements of the Women's Health Act?

The Women's Health Act requires that group health plans, insurance companies, and HMOs that offer coverage for medical and surgical benefits with respect to a mastectomy provide two separate notices regarding the coverage required under the Women's Health Act. The first notice is a one-time requirement, under which group health plans, and their insurance companies or HMOs, must furnish a written description of the benefits that the Women's Health Act requires. The second notice must also describe the required benefits, but it must be provided upon enrollment in the plan and it must be furnished annually thereafter. In addition, the Women's Health Act requires that the notices be in writing and prominently positioned in any literature or correspondence made available or distributed by the plan or issuer. The Women's Health and Cancer Rights Act of 1998, P.L. 105-277. See http://www.dol.gov/dol/pwba/public/pubs/womhlth.htm for Questions & Answers from the DOL.

In October, 1999, the DOL issued a Model Annual Notice and a series of questions and answers designed to provide additional guidance on frequently asked questions about the enrollment and annual notice requirements under the provisions of ERISA. See http://www.dol.gov/dol/pwba/public/pubs/finalq&a.htm.

167. What information must be included in the Women's Health Act notices?

The notices must describe the benefits required under the Women's Health Act. According to the DOL, the notice must indicate that coverage will be provided in a manner determined in consultation between the attending physician and the patient, for:

1.   Reconstruction of the breast on which the mastectomy was performed;

2.   Surgery and reconstruction of the other breast to produce a symmetrical appearance; and

3.   Prostheses and treatment of physical complications at all stages of the mastectomy, including lymphedemas.

The notice must also describe any deductibles and coinsurance limitations applicable to such coverage. The Women's Health and Cancer Rights Act of 1998, P.L. 105-277. See http://www.dol.gov/dol/pwba/public/pubs/womhlth.htm for Questions & Answers from the DOL.

168. When must the initial one-time notice under the Women's Health Act be furnished to participants and beneficiaries?

The initial one-time notice must have been furnished as part of the next general mailing (made after October 21, 1998) by the group health plan and its insurance companies or HMOs, or in the yearly informational packet sent out regarding the plan. In no event can the one-time notice have been furnished later than January 1, 1999. The Women's Health and Cancer Act of 1998, P.L. 105-277. See http://www.dol.gov/dol/pwba/public/pubs/womhlth.htm for Questions & Answers from the DOL about the Women's Health Act.

169. How must the notices required by the Women's Health Act be delivered to participants and beneficiaries?

These notices must be delivered in accordance with the regulations applicable to summary plan descriptions (SPDs). See Q 103, et seq.; see also Labor Reg. §2520.104b-1. The notices may be provided, for example, by first class mail or by any other means of delivery prescribed in the regulations. In addition, a separate notice must be furnished to a group health plan beneficiary, where the last known address of the beneficiary is different from the last known address of the covered participant.

170. Must group health plans that have already provided the coverage required by the Women's Health Act provide the initial one-time notice?

A group health plan that, prior to the date of enactment (October 21, 1998), had already provided the coverage required under the Women's Health Act (and continues to provide such coverage) will have satisfied the initial one-time notice requirement if the information that must be provided in the initial notice was previously furnished to participants and beneficiaries in accordance with the regulations on disclosure of information to participants and beneficiaries. See Q 103, et seq. The Women's Health and Cancer Act of 1998, P.L. 105-277. See http://www.dol.gov/dol/pwba/public/pubs/womhlth.htm for Questions & Answers from the DOL.

171. Must a group health plan, and its insurance companies or HMOs, furnish separate notices under the Women's Health Act?

No. In order to avoid duplication of notices, the DOL allows a group health plan or its insurance companies or HMOs to satisfy the notice requirements of the Women's Health Act by contracting with another party to provide the required notice. For example, in the case of a group health plan funded through an insurance policy, the group health plan satisfies the notice requirements with respect to a participant or beneficiary if the insurance company or HMO actually provides the notice that includes the information required by the Women's Health Act. The Women's Health and Cancer Act of 1998, P.L. 105-277. See http://www.dol.gov/dol/pwba/public/pubs/womhlth.htm for Questions & Answers from the DOL.

172. Does the Women's Health Act preempt state laws requiring similar coverage for breast reconstruction?

It depends. The federal Women's Health Act permits state law protections to apply to certain health coverage. State law protections apply if the state law was in effect on October 21, 1998 (the date of enactment of the Women's Health Act), and the state law requires at least the level of coverage for reconstructive breast surgery required under the federal Women's Health Act.

According to the DOL, if a state law meets these requirements, then the state law applies to coverage provided by an insurance company or HMO ("insured" coverage). If, however, coverage is not provided by an insurance company or HMO (e.g., coverage is provided under a self-funded health plan), then state law does not apply. The Women's Health and Cancer Act of 1998, P.L. 105-277. See http://www.dol.gov/dol/pwba/public/pubs/womhlth.htm for Questions & Answers from the DOL.

COBRA Requirements

173. What is COBRA?

Health insurance programs allow workers and their families to take care of essential medical needs. These programs can be one of the most important benefits provided by an employer. Prior to the enactment of the Consolidated Omnibus Budget Reconciliation Act of 1985 (COBRA), there was a time when group health coverage may have been terminated when a worker lost his job or changed employment. That changed in 1986 with the passage of the health benefit provisions in COBRA, which amended ERISA, the Internal Revenue Code, and the Public Health Service Act to provide continuation of group health coverage that otherwise would be terminated. Under COBRA, employees and beneficiaries who lose coverage because of certain "qualifying events" may be able to buy group coverage for limited periods of time. ERISA Secs. 601, 607(1); IRC Secs. 4980B(f), 4980B(g)(2); Treas. Reg. §54.4980B-5, A-1.

If a participant or beneficiary is entitled to COBRA benefits, the health plan must provide such individual with a notice stating his right to choose to continue benefits provided by the plan (see Q 177). Participants and beneficiaries have 60 days to elect COBRA coverage or lose all rights to benefits. Once COBRA coverage is chosen, terminated participants may be required to pay for the coverage.

COBRA provides certain former employees, retirees, spouses, and dependent children with the right to temporary continuation of health coverage at group rates. This coverage is only available if such an individual has lost coverage as a result of a "qualifying event" (see Q 175). Group health coverage for COBRA participants is usually more expensive than health coverage for active employees, because the employer usually pays a part of the premium for active employees, while COBRA participants generally pay the entire premium themselves. COBRA coverage is ordinarily less expensive than individual health coverage.

COBRA applies to plans in the private sector and those sponsored by state and local governments that are administered by the Department of Health and Human Services. The law does not, however, apply to plans sponsored by the federal government, certain church-related organizations, or small employer plans. A small employer plan is defined as a group health plan maintained by an employer that normally employed fewer than 20 employees during the preceding calendar year (except in the case of a multiemployer plan--see Chapter 10). Treas. Regs. §§54.4980B-2, A-4, 54.49808-2, A-5.

Under COBRA, a group health plan ordinarily is defined as a plan that provides health care for the individuals who have an employment-related connection to the employer or employee organization or to their families through insurance or another mechanism, such as a trust, health maintenance organization, self-funded pay-as-you-go basis, reimbursement, or combination of these. ERISA Sec. 607(1); IRC Sec. 4980B(g)(2); Treas. Reg. §54.4980B-2, A-1. (See Q 178.) Medical benefits provided under the terms of the plan and available to COBRA beneficiaries may include:

1. Inpatient and outpatient hospital care;

2. Physician care;

3. Surgery and other major medical benefits;

4. Prescription drugs; and

5. Any other medical benefits, such as dental and vision care.

Life insurance, however, is not covered under COBRA.

174. Who has the obligation to make COBRA coverage available to qualified beneficiaries where there has been a business reorganization or employer withdrawal from a multiemployer plan?

Since the introduction of COBRA coverage, the IRS has been concerned with cases of coverage being dropped or denied in the context of certain corporate transactions. In many cases, as it turns out, both the buyer and the seller have told qualified beneficiaries that the other party is responsible for the provision of COBRA coverage.

The regulations make clear that the parties to a transaction are free to allocate the responsibility for the provision of COBRA coverage by contract, even if the contract imposes responsibility on a different party than would the regulations. As long as the party who has assumed this responsibility under the contract performs its obligations, the other party will have no responsibility for providing COBRA coverage. If, however, the party assuming the contractual obligation to provide COBRA coverage defaults on its obligation, and if, under the regulations, the other party would have the obligation to provide COBRA coverage in the absence of the contractual agreement, then that other party would retain that obligation. The party with the underlying obligation under the regulations may insist on appropriate security and may pursue contractual remedies against the defaulting party. Treas. Reg. §54.4980B-9, A-7.

For both sales of stock and sales of substantial assets, the seller retains the obligation to keep COBRA coverage available to existing qualified beneficiaries. In addition, where the seller ceases to provide any group health plan to any employees in connection with the sale and therefore is not responsible for providing COBRA continuation coverage (which will be determined on the facts and circumstances of each case), the buyer is responsible for providing COBRA continuation coverage to existing qualified beneficiaries. This secondary liability for buyers applies in all stock sales, and in all sales of substantial assets in which the buyer continues the business operations associated with the assets without interruption or substantial change. Treas. Reg. §54.4980B-9, A-8.

Where an employer ceases contributions to a multiemployer group health plan, the multiemployer plan generally continues to have the obligation to make COBRA coverage available to all qualified beneficiaries associated with that employer. Treas. Reg. §54.4980B-9, A-10. However, there is no obligation on the part of the multiemployer plan to make COBRA coverage available to continuing employees of the withdrawing employer, as cessation of contributions is not a qualifying event. Treas. Reg. §54.4980B-9, A-9. Once the withdrawing employer makes group health coverage available to a class of its employees who were formerly covered under the multiemployer group health plan, or starts contributing to another multiemployer group health plan on their behalf, the employer's plan (or the new multiemployer group health plan) would then assume the obligation to make COBRA coverage available to the existing qualified beneficiaries. Treas. Reg. §54.4980B-9, A-10.

175. Who is entitled to COBRA benefits?

There are three elements to qualifying for COBRA benefits. COBRA establishes specific criteria for plans, beneficiaries, and events that initiate the coverage.

All group health plans are subject to COBRA, except small employer plans (see Q 173), church plans (within the meaning of IRC Section 414(e)), and governmental plans (within the meaning of IRC Section 414(d)). Treas. Reg. §54.4980B-2, A-4. The term "employees" includes all full-time and part-time employees, as well as self-employed individuals. ERISA Sec. 607(2); IRC Sec. 4980B(f)(7). For this purpose, the term "employees" also includes agents, independent contractors, and directors, but only if they are eligible to participate in a group health plan. IRC Sec. 4980B(f)(7).

A qualified beneficiary generally is any individual covered by a group health plan on the day before a qualifying event. A qualified beneficiary may be an employee, the employee's spouse, or the employee's dependent children; and, in certain cases, a retired employee, the retired employee's spouse, and his dependent children. A qualified beneficiary may also be any child who is born to or placed for adoption with a covered employee during the period of COBRA continuation coverage. ERISA Sec. 607(3)(A); IRC Sec. 4980B(g)(1)(A); Treas. Reg. §54.4980B-3, A-1.

A qualified beneficiary who does not elect COBRA continuation coverage in connection with a qualifying event ceases to be a qualified beneficiary at the end of the election period. Treas. Reg. §54.4980B-3, A-1(f).

Leased employees, for the purposes of COBRA coverage requirements, are to be treated as employees of the recipient of the employee's services. IRC Secs. 414(n)(1), 414(n)(3)(C).

A nonresident alien with no U.S. source of income from the employer during his period as a covered employee is not a qualified beneficiary. Under this rule, the nonresident alien's spouse or dependent children would also not be considered "qualified beneficiaries." IRC Sec. 4980B(g)(1)(C); Treas. Reg. §54.4980B-3, A-1(e).

"Qualifying events" are certain types of events that, but for COBRA continuation coverage, would cause an individual to lose health coverage. The type of qualifying event will determine who the qualified beneficiaries are and the required amount of time that a plan must offer COBRA coverage to them. A plan, at its discretion, may provide longer periods of continuation coverage. The types of qualifying events for employees are:

1.   Voluntary or involuntary termination of employment, for reasons other than "gross misconduct";

2.   Reduction in the number of hours of employment; and

3.   A proceeding in bankruptcy under Title 11 of the U.S. Code with respect to an employer from whose employment a covered employee retired at any time.

The types of qualifying events for spouses are:

1.   The death of the covered employee;

2.   Divorce or legal separation from the covered employee;

3.   The covered employee's becoming entitled to Medicare;

4.   Reduction in the hours worked by the covered employee; and

5.   Termination of the covered employee's employment, for any reason other than "gross misconduct."

ERISA Sec. 603; IRC Sec. 4980B(f)(3); Treas. Reg. §54.4980B-4, A-1.

The types of qualifying events for dependent children are the same as for the spouse with one addition: the loss of "dependent child" status under the rules of the plan.

Final COBRA regulations introduce the term, "similarly situated non-COBRA beneficiaries," which is defined as the group of covered employees, their spouses, or dependent children receiving coverage under a group health plan maintained by the employer or employee organization who are receiving that coverage for a reason other than the rights provided under COBRA, and who are most similarly situated to the situation of the qualified beneficiary just before the qualifying event, based on all the facts and circumstances. Treas. Reg. §54.4980B-3, A-3.

176. For purposes of COBRA, how is the number of group health plans that an employer or employee organization maintains determined?

Proposed regulations permit employers and employee organizations broad discretion in determining the number of group health plans that they maintain. This reduces burdens on employers and employee organizations by permitting them to structure their group health plans in an efficient and cost-effective manner, and to satisfy their COBRA obligations based upon that structure. The number of group health plans pursuant to which those benefits are provided is determined by the instruments governing the arrangement or arrangements. However, a multiemployer plan and a non-multiemployer plan are always separate arrangements. Treas. Regs. §§54.4980B-2, A-6(b). Where it is not clear from the governing instruments how many group health plans provide benefits, or if there are no governing instruments, then all health care benefits will be deemed to be provided under a single plan. Treas. Regs. §§54.4980B-2, A-6(a).

However, if the principal purpose of establishing separate plans is to evade any requirement of law, then separate plans will be considered to be a single plan to the extent necessary to prevent this evasion. Treas. Reg. §54.4980B-2, A-6(c).

177. What are the notice and election procedures under COBRA?

An initial general notice must be furnished to employees covered under the group health plan, their covered spouses, and newly hired employees informing them of their rights under COBRA and describing provisions of the law. ERISA Sec. 606(a)(1); IRC Sec. 4980B(f)(6)(A).

In addition, specific notice requirements are triggered for employers, qualified beneficiaries, and plan administrators when a qualifying event occurs. Employers must notify plan administrators within 30 days after an employee's death, termination, reduction in hours of employment, or entitlement to Medicare. Multiemployer plans may provide for a longer period of time. ERISA Sec. 606(a)(2); IRC Sec. 4980B(f)(6)(B).

A qualified beneficiary must notify the plan administrator within 60 days after events such as divorce, legal separation, or a child's ceasing to be covered as a dependent under plan rules. ERISA Sec. 606(a)(3); IRC Sec. 4980B(f)(6)(C).

Disabled beneficiaries must notify plan administrators of Social Security disability determinations. A notice must be provided within 60 days of a disability determination and prior to the expiration of the 18-month period of COBRA coverage. These beneficiaries must also notify the plan administrator within 30 days of a final determination that they are no longer disabled. ERISA Sec. 606(a)(3); IRC Sec. 4980B(f)(6)(C).

Plan administrators, upon notification of a qualifying event, must automatically provide employees and family members with a notice of their right to elect COBRA coverage. The notice must be provided in person or by first class mail within 14 days of receiving information that a qualifying event has occurred, and must be provided to each qualified beneficiary. ERISA Sec. 606(a)(4). The DOL has advised that this requirement may, in some cases, be met by mailing one election notice where more than one qualified beneficiary resides at the same address. Where, at the time of the notification, the last known addresses of the covered employee, the covered employee's spouse, and dependent children (if any) are the same, the DOL will consider a single first-class mailing addressed to the covered employee, the covered employee's spouse, and dependent children (if any) to be good faith compliance with the election notice requirements of ERISA Section 606(a)(4). DOL Adv. Op. 99-14A.

The mere posting of the election notice at the place of employment is not considered adequate. COBRA Conf. Rep. No. 453, 99th Cong., 1st Sess., 563 (1985).

There are two special exceptions to the notice requirements for multiemployer plans. First, the time frame for providing notices may be extended beyond the 14-day and 30-day requirements if allowed by plan rules. IRC Sec. 4980B(f)(6)(D). Second, employers are relieved of the obligation to notify plan administrators when employees terminate or reduce their work hours. IRC Sec. 4980B(f)(6)(B). Plan administrators are responsible for determining whether these qualifying events have occurred. IRC Sec. 4980B(f)(6)(D).

The election period is the period of time during which each qualified beneficiary may choose whether to continue health care coverage under an employer's group health plan. Qualified beneficiaries have a 60-day period to elect whether to continue coverage. This period is measured from the later of the coverage loss date or the date when the notice to elect COBRA coverage is sent. COBRA coverage is retroactive to the loss of coverage if the qualified beneficiary elects and pays for the coverage retroactively. ERISA Sec. 605(1); IRC Sec. 4980B(f)(5)(A). An election is considered to be made on the date it is sent to the plan administrator. The election period must begin not later than the date when the qualified beneficiary would lose coverage on account of the qualifying event. Treas. Reg. §54.4980B-6, A-1.

A covered employee or the covered employee's spouse may elect COBRA coverage on behalf of any other qualified beneficiary. Each qualified beneficiary, however, may independently elect COBRA coverage. A parent or legal guardian may make the election on behalf of a minor child. Treas. Reg. §54.4980B-6, A-6.

A waiver of coverage may be revoked by or on behalf of a qualified beneficiary before the end of the election period. The waiver, or revocation of waiver, is considered to have been made on the date that it has been sent to the plan or plan administrator. A beneficiary may then reinstate coverage, in which case, the plan need only provide continuation coverage beginning on the date when the waiver is revoked. Treas. Reg. §54.4980B-6, A-4. Coerced waivers that are obtained through the withholding of benefits are invalid. *Meadows v. Cagle's, Inc.*, 954 F.2d 686 (11th Cir. 1992).

Due to COBRA and ERISA being vague on the issue of a statute of limitations for the filing of claims, the trial court looked to the most analogous state statute for determining whatever a COBRA claim filed four years after termination was time barred (it wasn't—a six year limitation was applied). *Mattson v. Farrell Distributing Corp.*, 2001 US Dist LEXIS 16159.

178. What benefits are covered by COBRA?

The original COBRA proposed regulations, issued in 1987, required group health plans to offer qualified beneficiaries the option to elect only core (health) coverage under a group health plan that provides both core and non-core (e.g., vision and dental) coverage or core coverage plus non-core coverage. Final regulations issued in 1999 eliminate this distinction.

Effective for plan years beginning after December 31, 1999, each qualified beneficiary must be offered the opportunity to make an independent election to receive COBRA coverage. If the plan allows similarly situated active employees, with respect to whom a qualifying event has not occurred, to choose among several options during an open enrollment period, then each qualified beneficiary must also be offered an independent election to choose, during an open enrollment period, among the options made available to similarly situated active employees with respect to whom a qualifying event has not occurred. Treas. Reg. §54.4980B-6, A-6.

A change in the benefits under the plan for active employees may apply to qualified beneficiaries. ERISA Sec. 602(1); IRC Sec. 4980B(f)(2)(A). Beneficiaries may also change coverage during periods of open enrollment. The coverage may not be conditioned upon, or discriminate on the basis of, the insurability of a designated beneficiary. ERISA Sec. 602(4); IRC Sec. 4980B(f)(2).

179. How do the COBRA continuation coverage requirements apply to cafeteria plans and other flexible benefit arrangements?

In the case of a cafeteria plan or other flexible benefit arrangement, the COBRA coverage requirements apply only to the health care benefits thereunder that an employee has actually chosen to receive (and is actually receiving on the day before the qualifying event). Treas. Reg. §54.4980B-2, A-8.

180. What is the duration of COBRA coverage?

COBRA establishes required periods of coverage for continuation health benefits. A plan, may, however, provide longer periods of coverage than those required by COBRA. COBRA beneficiaries generally are eligible to purchase group coverage for a maximum of 18 months in the case of qualifying events due to employment termination or reduction in work hours. Certain qualifying events, or a second qualifying event during the initial period of coverage, may permit a beneficiary to purchase a maximum of 36 months of coverage. ERISA Secs. 602(2)(A)(i), 602(2)(A)(ii); IRC Secs. 4980B(f)(2)(B)(i), 4980B(f)(2)(B)(ii); Treas. Reg. §54.5980B-7, A-6.

Special rules for disabled individuals may extend the maximum periods of coverage. If a qualified beneficiary is determined, under Title II or XVI of the Social Security Act, to have been disabled at any time during the first 60 days of continuation coverage, and the beneficiary properly notifies the plan administrator of the disability determination before the expiration of the 18-month period, then the 18-month period is expanded to 29 months (see Q 161). ERISA Sec. 602(2)(A)(iv); IRC Sec. 4980B(f)(2)(B)(i).

Regulations clarify that this extension of coverage to 29 months due to disability is available if three conditions are satisfied: (1) a termination or reduction of hours of a covered employee's employment occurs; (2) an individual (whether or not the covered employee) who is a qualified beneficiary in connection with the qualifying event described in (1) is determined to have been disabled at any time during the first 60 days of COBRA coverage; and (3) any of the qualified beneficiaries affected by the qualifying event described in (1) provides notice to the plan administrator of the disability determination on a date that is both within 60 days after the date the determination is issued and before the end of the original 18-month period. This extension due to disability applies independently to each qualified beneficiary, whether or not the beneficiary is disabled. Treas. Reg. §54.4980B-7, A-5.

Coverage begins on the date when coverage would otherwise end because of a qualifying event, and can end when:

1. The last day of the maximum coverage period is reached;

2. Premiums are not paid on a timely basis;

3. The employer ceases to maintain any group health plan;

4. The individual "becomes covered" under another employer group health plan that does not contain any exclusion or limitation with respect to any pre-existing condition of such beneficiary; and

5. A beneficiary is entitled to Medicare benefits.

ERISA Sec. 602(2); IRC Sec. 4980B(f)(2).

If a determination is made that a qualified beneficiary is no longer disabled, then a plan may terminate the COBRA coverage prior to the end of the disability extension (however, not before the end of the maximum coverage period that would apply without regard to the disability extension). Treas. Reg. §54.4980B-7, A-4(c).

A group health plan can terminate for cause the coverage of a qualified beneficiary receiving COBRA coverage on the same basis that the plan terminates for cause the coverage of similarly situated non-COBRA beneficiaries (i.e., the submission of a fraudulent claim). Treas. Reg. §54.4980B-7, A-1(b). However, the coverage of a qualified beneficiary can be terminated for failure to make timely payment to the plan only if the payment is not "timely" under the regulations (see Q 181). Treas. Reg. §54.4980B-8, A-5.

When a qualified beneficiary first becomes covered under another group health plan after the date on which COBRA continuation coverage is elected for the qualified beneficiary, the plan may terminate the qualified beneficiary's COBRA coverage as of the date on which the qualified beneficiary first becomes covered under the other group health plan. Treas. Reg. §54.4980B-7, A-2. By contrast, if a qualified beneficiary first becomes covered under another group health plan on or before the date on which COBRA coverage is elected, then that other coverage cannot be a basis for terminating the qualified beneficiary's COBRA coverage. *Geissal v. Moore Medical Corp.*, 524 U.S. 74 (1998), 118 S. Ct. 1869, (1998); Treas. Reg. §54.4980B-7, A-2(a).

Although COBRA specifies certain maximum required periods of time that continued health coverage must be offered to qualified beneficiaries, COBRA does not prohibit plans from offering continuation health coverage beyond the COBRA periods. Treas. Reg. §54.4980B-7, A-6.

Some plans allow beneficiaries to convert group health coverage to an individual policy. If this conversion option is available under the plan, it must be offered to qualified beneficiaries. In this case, the beneficiary must have the option to enroll in a conversion health plan within 180 days before COBRA coverage ends. The premium is generally not at a group rate. The conversion option, however, need not be available if the beneficiary ends COBRA coverage before reaching the maximum period of entitlement. Treas. Reg. §54.4980B-7, A-8.

181. What rules govern the payment for COBRA coverage?

Beneficiaries may be required to pay the entire premium for coverage. The premium cannot exceed 102% of the cost to the plan for similarly situated individuals who have not incurred a qualifying event. ERISA Sec. 602(3); IRC Sec. 4980B(f)(2)(C). Premiums reflect the total cost of group health coverage, including both the portion paid by active employees and any portion paid by the employer before the qualifying event, plus 2% for administrative costs. ERISA Sec. 602(3); IRC Sec. 4980B(f)(2)(C).

In the case of disabled beneficiaries receiving an additional 11 months of coverage after the initial 18 months, the premium for those additional months may be increased to 150% of the plan's total cost of coverage. ERISA Sec. 602(3); IRC Sec. 4980B(f)(2)(C). If a qualified beneficiary entitled to a disability extension experiences a second qualifying event within the original 18-month maximum coverage period, then the plan is not permitted to require the payment of an amount that exceeds 102% of the applicable premium for any period of COBRA coverage. By contrast, if a qualified beneficiary entitled to a disability extension experiences a second qualifying event after the end of the original 18-month maximum coverage period, the plan may require the payment of an amount up to 150% of the applicable premium for the remainder of the period of COBRA continuation coverage, as long as the disabled qualified beneficiary is included in that coverage. Treas. Reg. §54.4980B-8, A-1(b).

Premiums may be increased if the costs to the plan increase, but generally must be fixed in advance of each 12-month premium cycle. IRC Sec. 4980B(f)(4)(C). The plan must allow terminated participants to pay premiums on a monthly basis if they ask to do so. ERISA Sec. 602(3); IRC Sec. 4980B(f)(2)(C).

The initial premium payment must be made within 45 days after the date of the qualified beneficiary's COBRA election. ERISA Sec. 602(3); IRC Sec. 4980B(f)(2)(C). Payment generally must cover the period of coverage from the date of COBRA election retroactive to the date of the loss of coverage due to the qualifying event. Premiums for successive periods of coverage are due on the date stated in the plan, with a minimum 30-day grace period. ERISA Sec. 602(2)(C); IRC Sec. 4980B(f)(2)(B)(iii). The due date may not be prior to the first day of the period of coverage. A group health plan must allow payment for COBRA coverage to be made in monthly installments. The plan may also allow alternative payment intervals such as weekly, quarterly, or semiannually. Treas. Reg. §54.4980B-8, A-3.

An employer cannot require a beneficiary to pay premiums for a period of continuation coverage exceeding the length of coverage requested by the beneficiary. *Popovits v. Circuit City Stores Inc.*, 185 F.3d 726 (7th Cir. 1999).

Premiums for the rest of the COBRA period must be made within 30 days after the due date for each such premium or longer period as provided by the plan. The plan, however, is not obligated to send monthly premium notices.

A plan must treat a timely payment that is not significantly less than the amount required as full payment, unless the plan notifies the qualified beneficiary of the amount of the deficiency and grants a reasonable period for payment. A reasonable period of time for this purpose is 30 days after the date when notice is provided. An amount will be considered as "not significantly less" if the shortfall is no greater than the lesser of $50 or 10% of the amount the plan requires to be paid. Treas. Reg. §54.4980B-8, A-5(b).

COBRA beneficiaries remain subject to the rules of the plan, and therefore must satisfy all costs related to deductibles, catastrophic events, and other benefit limits.

182. What are the claims procedures for COBRA?

Health plan rules must explain how to obtain benefits and must include written procedures for processing claims. Claims procedures are to be included in the SPD booklet. See Q 101.

Terminated participants should submit a written claim for benefits to whomever is designated to operate the health plan (e.g., employer, plan administrator). If the claim is denied, notice of denial must be in writing and furnished generally within 90 days after the claim is filed. The notice should state the reasons for the denial, as well as any additional information needed to support the claim and procedures for appealing the denial.

Participants have 60 days after a claim is denied in which to appeal the denial. Such participants must receive a decision on the appeal within 60 days after appealing, unless the plan:

1.   Provides for a special hearing; or

2.   Requires that the decision be made by a group that meets only on a periodic basis.

183. How does COBRA coverage coordinate with other benefits?

The Family and Medical Leave Act of 1993 (FMLA) requires an employer to maintain coverage under any "group health plan" for an employee on FMLA leave, under the same conditions that coverage would have been provided if the employee had continued working. Coverage provided under the FMLA is not COBRA coverage, and FMLA leave is not a qualifying event under COBRA. Treas. Reg. §54.4980B-10, A-1. A COBRA qualifying event may occur, however, when an employer's obligation to maintain health benefits under FMLA ceases, such as when an employee notifies an employer of his intent not to return to work following FMLA leave. The qualifying event occurs on the last day of FMLA leave. The employer must notify the plan administrator within 30 days of the last day of FMLA leave. Notice 94-103, 1994-2 CB 569; Treas. Reg. §54.4980B-10, A-2.

The Uniformed Services Employment and Reemployment Rights Act of 1994 (USERRA) gives certain members of the military reserves the right to purchase up to 18 months of COBRA coverage when they are called to active duty. The final regulations clarify that USERRA coverage is alternative coverage, and, therefore, the USERRA and COBRA periods of continuation coverage run concurrently. Treas. Reg. §54.4980B-7, A-7.

184. Who is responsible for administering the continuation coverage laws under COBRA?

Continuation coverage laws are administered by several agencies. The Department of Labor (DOL) and the Department of Treasury have jurisdiction over private sector health plans. The United States Public Health Service administers the continuation coverage law as it affects public sector health plans.

The DOL's interpretative and regulatory responsibility is limited to the disclosure and notification requirements.

The Internal Revenue Service (IRS), which is under the Department of the Treasury, is responsible for publishing regulations relating to eligibility and premiums. Both the DOL and the Treasury share jurisdiction for enforcement.

185. What are the applicable sanctions and penalties under COBRA?

Any administrator who fails to meet the notice requirements of COBRA may be subject to: (1) a civil penalty; and/or (2) personal liability. Further, plan administrators who fail to provide timely notice may be subject to a fine of up to $100 per day, "and the court may in its discretion order such other relief as it deems proper." ERISA Sec. 502(c)(1). In *Phillips v. Riverside*, 796 F. Supp. 403, (E.D. Ark. 1992), the court deemed proper and awarded relief in the amount that would place the beneficiary in the same position he would have been in had full continuation coverage under COBRA been provided. The penalty is $110 per day for failures or refusals occurring after July 29, 1997. Labor Reg. §2575.502c-1. ERISA statutory penalties awarded for COBRA notice violation extend only to the participant. *Wright v. Hanna Steel Corp.*, 2001 US App. LEXIS 22878 (11th circuit).

No statutory penalty of $110 per day is permitted under COBRA where an employer allows a participant to elect COBRA coverage retroactive to the date of termination. *Gigliotti v. Sprint Spectrum, L.P.*, 2001 US Dist. LEXIS 20221 (NDNY).

ERISA Section 502(a)(1) authorizes participants or beneficiaries to bring a civil action to enforce their rights under COBRA, clarify their rights to future benefits, or recover benefits due to them under the terms of the plan.

The court, in its discretion, may allow reasonable attorney's fees and costs of action incurred under a civil suit to enforce COBRA rights, and such other legal or equitable relief as the court deems appropriate. ERISA Sec. 502(g)(1). Various court cases have established the following factors for the courts to consider in determining an award of attorney's fees:

1. The degree of the opposing party's culpability or bad faith;

2. The ability of the opposing party to personally satisfy an award of fees;

3. Whether the award would deter other parties from acting in a similar way under similar circumstances;

4. Whether the party requesting the fees sought to benefit all plan participants and beneficiaries or to resolve a significant legal question; and

5.   The relative merits of the opposing party's position.

Eaves v. Penn, 587 F.2d 453 (10th Cir. 1978); *Gordon v. United States Steel Corp.*, 724 F.2d 106 (10th Cir. 1983); *Krogh v. Chamberlain*, 708 F. Supp. 1235 (DC Utah 1989).

Internal Revenue Code Section 4980B(a) provides for the imposition of an excise tax against any group health plan that fails to meet the requirements of COBRA continuation coverage. The excise tax is $100 for each day that a group health plan fails to meet the continuation coverage requirements, which is doubled to $200 per day where there is more than one beneficiary with respect to the same qualifying event. IRC Secs. 4980B(b), 4980B(c)(3)(B). The employer or the plan itself (in the case of a multiemployer plan) will be held liable for the excise tax (unless the plan is exempt from the COBRA rules). IRC Sec. 4980B(e)(1)(A); Treas. Reg. § 54.4980B-2, A-10.

There is a 30-day grace period to correct a failure due to reasonable cause and not willful neglect. If the failure is corrected within the grace period, the excise tax will not be imposed. IRC Sec. 4980B(c)(2).

Where there has been an inadvertent compliance failure during any period in which the persons who would be liable for the tax did not know, or could not know through the exercise of reasonable diligence, of the failure, the excise tax will not be imposed. IRC Sec. 4980B(c)(1).

The annual limit on the liability for the excise tax that must be paid during an employer's tax year is the lesser of 10% of the total amount paid or incurred by the employer or predecessor employer (or trust, in the case of a multiemployer plan) during the preceding tax year for the employer's group health plans, or $500,000. IRC Sec. 4980B(c)(4)(A)(i).

CHAPTER III

FIDUCIARIES

186. Who is an ERISA fiduciary?

The term "fiduciary" is broadly defined to include any *person* (see Q 187) who: (1) exercises any discretionary authority or discretionary control respecting management of the plan; (2) exercises any authority or control respecting management or disposition of its assets; (3) renders investment advice for a fee or other compensation, direct or indirect, with respect to any moneys or other property of the plan, or has any authority or responsibility to do so; or (4) has any discretionary authority or discretionary responsibility in the administration of the plan. ERISA Secs. 3(21)(A) and 3(9).

It is important to determine who the fiduciaries are of any employee benefit plan covered by ERISA, because parties who are considered fiduciaries with respect to the plan have specified duties and responsibilities, must conduct plan business under established standards of care, and are prohibited from engaging or causing the plan to engage in certain transactions under ERISA. Fiduciaries who breach these requirements are often held liable for actions taken with respect to the plan.

187. What types of "persons" can be fiduciaries?

The term "person" means any individual, partnership, joint venture, corporation, mutual company, joint-stock company, trust, estate, unincorporated organization, association, or employee organization. ERISA Sec. 3(9).

188. How is fiduciary status determined under ERISA?

A person can be deemed a fiduciary by performing certain specified acts (see Q 186) with or without authority to do so, by holding certain positions with duties and responsibilities that require by their very nature, performance of those acts, or by being expressly designated or named as a fiduciary in the plan document. ERISA Sec. 3(21)(A).

189. How is a person deemed a fiduciary?

Any person who performs one or more of the fiduciary functions described in ERISA Section 3(21)(A) (see Q 186) performs activities that confer fiduciary status. "The term fiduciary is to be broadly construed and a person's title does not necessarily determine if one is a fiduciary." *Consolidated Beef Indus., Inc. v. New York Life Ins. Co.*, 949 F.2d 960 (8th Cir. 1991) cert. denied, 503 U.S. 985 (1992). "ERISA defines 'fiduciary' not in terms of formal trusteeship, but in functional terms of control and authority over the plan, thus expanding the universe of persons subject to fiduciary duties." *Mertens v. Hewitt Assocs.*, 508 U.S. 248 (1993).

Status as a fiduciary is determined by a person's functions with respect to the plan, rather than by his or her title, office or formal designation. Under this functional test, fiduciary status is determined with reference to an individual's activities with respect to a plan and does not depend upon a formal undertaking or agreement. H.R. Conf. Rep. No. 93-1280, 93rd Cong., 2nd Sess., 323 (1974) (ERISA Conference Report). Additionally, it is the nature and extent of a person's duties and responsibilities with respect to the plan that determines a person's status as a fiduciary. *Swint v. Protective Life Ins. Co.*, 779 F. Supp. 532 (S.D. Ala. 1991). A person becomes a fiduciary under ERISA Section 3(21)(A), "only when fulfilling certain defined functions, including the exercise of discretionary authority or control over plan management or administration." *Lockheed Corp. v. Spink*, 116 S.Ct. 1783 (1996), quoting *Siskind v. Sperry Retirement Program*, 47 F.3d 498 (2nd Cir. 1995). A party is considered a fiduciary to the extent it actually exercises control over the disposition of plan assets, even if it did not possess any discretionary authority. *Slyman v. Equitable Life Assurance Soc'y*, 1987 US Dist. LEXIS 8652 (N.D. NY 1987). The absence of any grant of authority does not automatically preclude a finding of fiduciary status. *Olson v. E.F. Hutton & Co., Inc.*, 957 F.2d 622 (8th Cir. 1992). "[T]he linchpin of fiduciary status under ERISA is discretion." *Curcio v. John Hancock Mut. Life Ins. Co.*, 33 F.3d 226 (3rd Cir. 1994). Thus, whether an individual is a fiduciary within the meaning of ERISA Section 3(21)(A) is inherently factual and will depend on the particular discretionary actions or functions that a person performs on behalf of a plan. Labor Regs. §§2509.75-5, 2509.75-8.

190. What is an automatic fiduciary?

According to the Department of Labor, some offices or positions of an employee benefit plan by their very nature require persons who hold them to perform one or more of the functions described in Section 3(21)(A)(iii) of ERISA. Labor Reg. §2509.75-8, D-3. Thus, with certain exceptions, fiduciary status will automatically be conferred upon the persons who hold these positions. For instance, a plan administrator or a trustee of a plan is, per se, a fiduciary because he must have "discretionary authority or discretionary responsibility in the administration" of the plan within the meaning of ERISA Section 3(21)(A)(iii). *U.S. Steel Mining Co. v. District 17, United Mine Workers of America*, 897 F.2d 149 (4th Cir. 1990). "As the administrator of the employee benefit plan, [the entity] is a fiduciary for ERISA purposes." *Reilly v. Blue Cross & Blue Shield United of Wis.*, 846 F.2d 416 (7th Cir. 1988), cert. denied, 488 U.S. 856 (1988). "[T]he statute, regulations and case law lead to the conclusion that trustees are fiduciaries by virtue of their position." *Reich v. Hosking*, 94-CV-10363-BC, 20 EBC 1090 (E.D. Mich. 1996).

On the other hand, a plan administrator who does not possess discretionary authority with respect to a plan is not a fiduciary for purposes of ERISA. *Pohl v.*

National Benefits Consultants, Inc., 956 F.2d 126 (7th Cir. 1992). Similarly, trustees may not be considered fiduciaries where the plan instrument "does not accord the trustees any discretionary authority over investment decisions" of the plan and the plan does not name the trustees as fiduciaries. *Arakelian v. National Western Life Ins. Co.*, 748 F. Supp. 17 (DC D.C. 1990). Thus, whether automatic fiduciary status exists with respect to a particular office or position is dependent upon the facts and circumstances and whether the office or position performs any of the functions described in ERISA Section 3(21)(A). See Labor Reg. §2509.75-8, D-3.

191. What is a named fiduciary?

Every employee benefit plan must provide for one or more named fiduciaries. ERISA Sec. 402(a)(1). A "named fiduciary" is a fiduciary who is named in the plan document or who is identified as a fiduciary, pursuant to a procedure specified in the plan, (A) by a person who is an employer or employee organization with respect to the plan, or (B) by such an employer and such an employee organization acting jointly. ERISA Sec. 402(a)(2). The named fiduciaries have joint or several authority to control and manage the operation and administration of the plan. Since the "named fiduciary" is a fiduciary who is named in the plan document or who is identified as a fiduciary, it is the only person who is a fiduciary by title.

192. What is the purpose of having a named fiduciary?

The purpose of naming a fiduciary in the plan document is to enable employees and other interested persons to ascertain who is responsible for operating the plan. A plan must designate a named fiduciary "so that responsibility for managing and operating the plan and liability for mismanagement are focused with a degree of certainty." *Birmingham v. Sogen-Swiss Int'l Corp. Retirement Plan*, 718 F.2d 515 (2nd Cir. 1983), citing H.R. Conf. Rep. No. 93-1280, 93rd Cong., 2nd Sess. (1974) (ERISA Conference Report).

193. Who may be a named fiduciary?

A named fiduciary may be any "person" meeting the definition of fiduciary set forth in ERISA Section 3(21)(A). A named fiduciary may be a person whose name actually appears in the document, or may be a person who holds an office specified in the document, such as the company president. A named fiduciary also may be a person who is identified by the employer or union, under a procedure set out in the document. For example, the plan may provide that the employer's board of directors is to choose the person who manages or controls the plan. In addition, a named fiduciary may be a person identified by the employers and union acting jointly. Further, the members of a joint board of trustees of a Taft-Hartley plan would usually be named fiduciaries (see Q 556). H.R. Conf. Rep. No. 93-1280, 93rd Cong., 2nd Sess., 297 (1974) (ERISA Conference Report).

194. How should named fiduciaries be designated in the plan document?

2002 ERISA Facts

According to DOL guidance, the preferred practice is to explicitly designate the plan's named fiduciaries in the plan document. Labor Reg. §2509.75-5, FR-1. However, the "named fiduciary" requirement of ERISA Section 402(a) is fulfilled by clearly identifying one or more persons, by name or title, combined with a statement that such person or persons have authority to control and manage the operation and administration of the plan. For example, a plan document that provides that "the plan committee shall control and manage the operation and administration of the plan," and specifies, by name or position, who will constitute the committee, fulfills this latter requirement. Likewise, a plan document of a union negotiated employee benefit plan which provides that a clearly identified joint board on which employees and employers are equally represented will control and manage the operation and administration of the plan adequately satisfies the "named fiduciary" requirement in ERISA Section 402(a). In the latter case, the persons designated to be members of such joint board would be named fiduciaries under ERISA Section 402(a). See Labor Reg. §2509.75-5, FR-1.

195. May an employee benefit plan covering employees of a corporation designate the corporation as the "named fiduciary?"

Yes. The DOL has stated that under ERISA Section 402(a)(2), "a 'named fiduciary' is a fiduciary either named in the plan instrument or designated according to a procedure set forth in the plan instrument. A fiduciary is a 'person' falling within the definition of fiduciary set forth in ERISA Section 3(21)(A). A 'person' may be a corporation under the definition of person contained in ERISA Section 3(9). While such a designation satisfies the requirement of enabling employees and other interested persons to ascertain the person or persons responsible for operating the plan, a plan instrument which designates a corporation or other entity as 'named fiduciary' should provide for designation by the corporation of specified individuals or other persons to carry out specified fiduciary responsibilities under the plan...." Labor Reg. §2509.75-5, FR-3 (ERISA Interpretive Bulletin 75-5).

196. Are persons who perform administrative functions fiduciaries?

A person who performs purely ministerial functions for an employee benefit plan within a framework of policies, interpretations, rules, practices and procedures made by other persons is not a fiduciary because such a person does not perform the discretionary functions within ERISA Section 3(21)(A), nor have the power to make such decisions. These persons are not fiduciaries because they do not exercise any discretionary authority or discretionary control respecting management of the plan or the disposition of its assets.

The DOL has provided guidance concerning what types of functions will make a person a fiduciary with respect to a plan. Specifically, the following types of administrative activities are *not* considered to be fiduciary functions (Labor Reg. §2509.75-8, D-2):

1. Application of rules determining eligibility for participation or benefits;

2. Calculation of services and compensation credits for benefits;

3. Preparation of employee communications material;

4. Maintenance of participants' service and employment records;

5. Preparation of reports required by government agencies;

6. Calculation of benefits;

7. Orientation of new participants and advising participants of their rights and options under the plan;

8. Collection of contributions and application of contributions as provided in the plan;

9. Preparation of reports concerning participant's benefits;

10. Processing claims; and

11. Making recommendations to others for decisions with respect to plan administration.

Pursuant to these provisions, the determination of whether a person is a fiduciary with respect to a plan, or is one who merely performs ministerial duties, requires an analysis of the types of functions performed and actions taken by the person on behalf of the plan, to determine whether particular functions or actions are fiduciary in nature and, therefore, subject to ERISA's fiduciary responsibility provisions. The Fourth Circuit has ruled that plan administrators are not liable as fiduciaries for the miscalculation of benefits because the calculation of benefits is not a fiduciary function. *Cunningham Pension Plan v. Mathieu*, 153 F.3d 720 (4th Cir. 1998).

For example, a plan might designate as a "benefit supervisor" a plan employee whose sole function is to calculate the amount of benefits to which each plan participant is entitled in accordance with a mathematical formula contained in the written instrument pursuant to which the plan is maintained. The benefit supervisor, after calculating the benefits, would then inform the plan administrator of the results of his calculations, and the plan administrator would authorize the payment of benefits to a particular plan participant. The benefit supervisor does not perform any of the functions described in ERISA Section 3(21)(A) and, therefore, is not a plan fiduciary. See Labor Reg. §2509.75-8, D-3.

On the other hand, the plan might designate as a "benefit supervisor" a plan employee who has the final authority to authorize or disallow benefit payments in cases where a dispute exists as to the interpretation of plan provisions relating to eligibility for benefits. Under these circumstances, the benefit supervisor would be a fiduciary within the meaning of ERISA Section 3(21)(A). See Labor Reg. §2509.75-8, D-3.

Whether a person is a fiduciary with respect to a plan or one who merely performs ministerial duties is often determined in the courts. For example, a party who performs only clerical or ministerial tasks is not a fiduciary. *Pohl v. National Benefits Consultants, Inc.*, 956 F.2d 126 (7th Cir. 1992). "It is well established that one who performs only ministerial tasks is not cloaked with fiduciary status." *Olson v. E.F. Hutton & Co., Inc.*, 957 F.2d 622 (8th Cir. 1992), citing *Anoka Orthopaedic Assoc. v. Lechner*, 910 F.2d 514 (8th Cir. 1990). Similarly, performing administrative actions within a framework of policies established by others is not considered the exercise of fiduciary responsibility. *Gelardi v. Pertec Computer Corp.*, 761 F.2d 1323 (9th Cir. 1985) (per curiam). A claims processor is not a fiduciary if he has not been granted the authority to review benefits denials and make the ultimate decisions regarding eligibility. *Howard v. Parisian, Inc.*, 807 F.2d 1560 (11th Cir. 1987). Nor is a plan supervisor who merely calculates claims according to the plan document a fiduciary. *Confer v. Custom Engineering Co.*, 952 F.2d 34 (3rd Cir. 1991). See also *Baxter v. C.A. Muer Corp.*, 941 F.2d 451 (6th Cir. 1991) (affirming that a plan administrator was not an ERISA plan fiduciary but simply a claims processor). However, a claims processor who acts beyond a purely ministerial capacity risks being deemed a fiduciary. *IT Corp. v. General American Life Ins. Co.*, 107 F.3d 1415 (9th Cir. 1997).

Although a person who performs only functions listed above may not be a plan fiduciary, he may be subject to the bonding requirements contained in ERISA Section 412 if he handles funds or other property of the plan. Labor Reg. §2509.75-8, D-2.

197. Are professional services providers such as an attorney, accountant, consultant, or actuary fiduciaries?

Many courts have held that professional service providers such as attorneys, accountants, actuaries or consultants who render legal, accounting, actuarial or consulting services to employee benefit plans (other than an investment advisor to the plan) are not fiduciaries to a plan solely by virtue of the rendering of such services. See *Anoka Orthopaedic Assoc. v. Lechner*, 910 F.2d 514 (8th Cir. 1990) (lawyers and financial consultants); *Painters of Philadelphia Dist. Council v. Price Waterhouse*, 879 F.2d 1146 (3rd Cir. 1989) (accountants); *Yeseta v. Baima*, 837 F.2d 380 (9th Cir. 1988) (neither attorney who reviewed plan's compliance with law nor accountant who prepared tax returns and financial statements were fiduciaries); and *Chapman v. Klemick*, 3 F.3d 1508 (11th Cir. 1993), cert. denied, 510 U.S. 1165 (1994) (attorney for plan beneficiary). See also *Nieto v. Ecker*, 845 F.2d 868 (9th Cir. 1988) (attorney who gave professional advice to a plan not a fiduciary). The courts support this position by reading the terms "discretionary authority," "discretionary control," and "discretionary responsibility" in ERISA Section 3(21)(A) as speaking to actual decision-making power, rather than to the influence that a professional may have over the decisions made by the plan trustees "that the professional advises." *Pappas v. Buck Consultants, Inc.*, 923 F.2d 531 (7th Cir. 1991) (actuaries performing ordinary professional functions).

According to the courts, the power to act for the plan is essential to status as a fiduciary under ERISA. Thus, without the ability to exercise any decision-making authority over the plan or plan assets, lawyers, accountants, actuaries and consultants may render services to employers, plan trustees, and plan beneficiaries without becoming a fiduciary of the plan. The mere provision of professional services to employers, plan trustees, and plan beneficiaries "does not give lawyers, accountants, and actuaries decision-making authority over the plan or plan assets, since the power to act for the plan is essential to status as ERISA fiduciary." *Associates In Adolescent Psychiatry v. Home Life Ins. Co.*, 941 F.2d 561 (7th Cir. 1991), cert. denied 502 U.S. 1099 (1992). Further, attorneys do not become fiduciaries even when legal advice is commingled with incidental business observation and investment-related observations, especially in the case of giving advice to sophisticated business persons. *Useden v. Acker*, 947 F.2d 1563 (11th Cir. 1991), cert. denied, 508 U.S. 959 (1993).

While attorneys, accountants, actuaries and consultants performing their usual professional functions will ordinarily not be considered fiduciaries, if the fact situation in a particular case indicates that such a person exercises discretionary authority or discretionary control over the management or administration of the plan, or exercises authority or control respecting management or disposition of the plan's assets, such professionals would be regarded as fiduciaries. Labor Reg. §2509.75-5, D-1. Fiduciary status could also encompass consultants and advisors whose special expertise leads them to formulate and act on discretionary judgments while performing administrative functions not otherwise contemplated as those of a fiduciary. *Eaton v. D'Amato*, 581 F. Supp. 743 (DC D.C. 1980), citing H.R. Conf. Rep. No. 93-1280, 93rd Cong., 2nd Sess., 323 (1974) (ERISA Conference Report). In addition, fiduciary status was imposed on accountants when they provided far more than ministerial professional accounting services and instead, "recommended transactions, structured deals, and provided investment advice to such an extent that they exercised effective control over the ESOP's assets, since none of the other corporate insiders had the expertise in accounting and employee benefits law needed to spin the tangled web of transactions at issue." *Martin v. Feilen*, 965 F.2d 660 (8th Cir. 1992), cert. denied sub. nom. *Henss v. Martin*, 506 U.S. 1054 (1993).

198. Are officers, members of the board of directors, or employees of a plan sponsor fiduciaries?

According to the DOL, members of the board of directors, officers and employees of an employer or employee organization that maintains an employee benefit plan are not fiduciaries solely by reason of holding such office or employment. Labor Regs. §§2509.75-8, D-4, D-5; see also *Confer v. Custom Engineering Co.*, 952 F.2d 34 (3rd Cir. 1991) (holding that individual officers of an ERISA plan's fiduciary are not fiduciaries by virtue of their offices). In comparison, the court in *Kayes v. Pacific Lumber Co.*, 51 F.3d 1449 (9th Cir. 1995) rejected the Third Circuit's interpretation in *Confer* that an officer who acts on behalf of a named fiduciary corporation cannot be a fiduciary if he acts within his official capacity, and if no fiduciary duties are delegated to him individually. See also *Thomas v. Peacock*, 39 F.3d 493 (4th Cir. 1994), in which the court determined that a corporate officer was a fiduciary.

Members of the board of directors, officers and employees will be fiduciaries to the extent that they have responsibility for the functions described in ERISA Section 3(21)(A). If an employer has no power with respect to a plan other than to appoint the plan administrator and the trustees, then its fiduciary duty extends only to those functions. *Gelardi v. Pertec Computer Corp.*, 761 F.2d 1323 (9th Cir. 1985). Additionally, "plan officers, directors and members of the investment or administrative committees are fiduciaries, in that they exercise discretionary authority or control over plan management and asset disposition. Similarly, an officer and director of a plan sponsor are fiduciaries if they exercise control through the selection of the investment committee, administrative committee or plan officers or directors." *Eaves v. Penn*, 587 F.2d 453 (10th Cir. 1978), citing S. Rep. No. 93-383, 93rd Cong., 1st Sess., 3. Additionally, "officers and directors of an employer who sponsors a pension plan may be fiduciaries to the extent they maintain authority for the selection, oversight, or retention of plan administrators." *Martin v. Schwab*, 15 EBC 2135 (W.D. Mo. 1992); see also *Leigh v. Engle*, 727 F.2d 113 (7th Cir. 1984) remanded, 669 F. Supp. 1390 (N.D. Ill. 1985), aff'd 858 F.2d 361 (7th Cir. 1988), cert denied, 489 U.S. 1078 (1989); *Newton v. Van Otterloo*, 756 F. Supp. 1121 (N.D. Ind. 1991); *Sandoval v. Simmons*, 622 F. Supp. 1174 (C.D. Ill. 1985); *Shaw v. Int'l Ass'n of Machinists & Aerospace Workers Pension Plan*, 563 F. Supp. 653 (C.D. Cal. 1983), aff'd, 750 F.2d 1458 (9th Cir. 1985), cert. denied, 471 U.S. 1137 (1985).

If the members of the board of directors are responsible for the selection and retention of plan fiduciaries and exercise "discretionary authority or discretionary control respecting management of such plan" they are fiduciaries with respect to the plan. However, their responsibility, and, consequently, their liability, is limited to the selection and retention of fiduciaries (apart from co-fiduciary liability arising under circumstances described in ERISA Section 405(a)). In addition, if the directors are made named fiduciaries of the plan, their liability may be limited pursuant to a procedure provided for in the plan instrument for the allocation of fiduciary responsibilities among named fiduciaries or for the designation of persons other than named fiduciaries to carry out fiduciary responsibilities, as provided in ERISA Section 405(c)(2). Labor Regs. §§2509.75-8, D-4, D-5.

199. Are insurance companies and insurance agents fiduciaries?

An insurance company may be a fiduciary of a plan, depending upon the degree to which it exercises discretionary control over the assets or administration of the plan. An insurance company does *not* become an ERISA "fiduciary" simply by performing administrative functions and claims processing within a framework of rules established by an employer. *Gelardi v. Pertec Computer Corp.*, 761 F.2d 1323 (9th Cir. 1985). Where an insurance company provides only administrative claims processing services to a plan within a framework established by the employer, and is not granted authority to review benefit denials, nor to make ultimate decisions regarding eligibility, it is not a fiduciary. *Baker v. Big Star Div. of Grand Union Co.*, 893 F.2d 288 (11th Cir. 1989). See also *DeGeare v. Alpha Portland Indus., Inc.*, 652 F. Supp. 946 (E.D. Mo. 1986) (payment of claims pursuant to provisions of benefits plan does not clothe administrator with discretionary authority to such an extent as to make administrator's role that of a fiduciary).

However, fiduciary status may be invoked if an insurance company has the ability to make policy decisions outside of a pre-existing or separate framework of policies, practices and procedures. *Munoz v. Prudential Ins. Co. of America*, 633 F. Supp. 564 (DC Colo. 1986). Similarly, an insurance company may be a fiduciary if it has the discretionary authority to grant or deny claims in the administration of the plan. *Confer v. Custom Engineering Co.*, 952 F.2d 41 (3rd Cir. 1991), citing *McLaughlin v. Connecticut Gen. Life Ins. Co.*, 565 F. Supp. 434 (N.D. Cal. 1983). In addition, an insurance company can become a fiduciary where it makes payments of claims using the money of the plan and it makes final dispositions of denied claims. See, *Sixty-Five Security Plan v. Blue Cross & Blue Shield*, 583 F. Supp. 380 (S.D. NY 1984); *Blue Cross v. Peacock's Apothecary, Inc.*, 567 F. Supp. 1258 (N.D. Ala. 1983); *McLaughlin v. Connecticut Gen. Life Ins. Co.*, 565 F. Supp. 434 (N.D. Cal. 1983). An insurance company that processes claims may be a fiduciary if it exceeds its purely ministerial capacity by exercising discretionary authority in deciding doubtful or disputed claims for referral back to the plan sponsor and it controls the plan's bank account for the payment of claims. *IT Corp. v. General American Life Ins. Co.*, 107 F.3d 1415 (9th Cir. 1997).

In addition, an insurance company was held to be a plan fiduciary where it retained the power to amend certain terms of an annuity without the consent of the plan's trustees. *Associates In Adolescent Psychiatry v. Home Life Ins. Co.*, 941 F.2d 561 (7th Cir. 1991), cert. denied, 502 U.S. 1099 (1992). An insurance company also was held to be a fiduciary where it had the power to unilaterally amend an annuity contract covering employee benefit plan assets in a guaranteed rate account, to the extent of its obligations connected with the amendment. The policy itself, as an asset of the plan, and the insurance company's ability to amend it and thereby alter its value, was not qualitatively different from the insurance company's ability to choose investments for the plan in its exercise of control over the assets of the plan. *Chicago Bd. of Options v. Connecticut Gen. Life Ins. Co.*, 713 F.2d 256 (7th Cir. 1983). The Supreme Court has held that an insurance company has a fiduciary responsibility for management of "free funds" or the non-guaranteed portion of group annuity contracts issued to a pension plan, to the extent that the insurance company engages in the discretionary management of assets attributable to that phase of the contract which provides no guarantee of benefit payments, no fixed rates of return, and where the investment risk was borne primarily by the contract holder. *Harris Tr. & Sav. Bank v. John Hancock Mut. Life Ins. Co.*, 510 U.S. 86 (1993).

However, simply urging "the purchase of its products does not make an insurance company an ERISA fiduciary with respect to those products."*American Fed'n of Unions, Local 102 v. Equitable Life Assurance Soc'y*, 841 F.2d 658 (5th Cir. 1988). In addition, simply issuing insurance policies to a covered plan does not render an insurance company a fiduciary. *Austin v. General American Life Ins. Co.*, 498 F. Supp. 844, (N.D. Ala. 1980); *Cate v. Blue Cross & Blue Shield of Ala.*, 434 F. Supp. 1187 (E.D. Tenn. 1977). See also, *Lederman v. Pacific Mut. Life Ins. Co.*, 494 F. Supp. 1020 (C.D. Cal. 1980) (dicta). An insurance company is not a fiduciary if it develops a retirement plan in conjunction with the plan fiduciaries, does not control the plan assets, and does not recommend specific investments beyond selling its own annuities to the plan. *Consolidated Beef Indus., Inc. v. New York Life Ins. Co.*, 949 F.2d 960 (8th Cir. 1991). An insurance company's suggestion that a health and welfare plan self-insure did not make it a fiduciary, because its suggestion did not fit within the definition of investment advice under ERISA where the advice was not given on a regular basis, pursuant to a mutual agreement for a fee. *American Fed'n of Unions, Local 102 v. Equitable Life Assurance Soc'y*, 841 F.2d 658 (5th Cir. 1988).

An insurance agent who markets and sells his insurance company's Section 401(k) plan and financial products, does not provide investment advice to the plan, and acts merely as a salesperson earning commissions, is not a plan fiduciary. *Consolidated Beef Indus., Inc. v. New York Life Ins. Co.*, 949 F.2d 960 (8th Cir. 1991). However, an agent who works on amendments to a plan, informs employees about the plan, meets with the company's independent accountant to discuss key issues affecting the plan, consults on plan investments and has the authority to make press releases concerning the plan, may be exercising discretionary authority with respect to the administration or management of a plan and considered a fiduciary. *Monson v. Century Mfg. Co.*, 739 F.2d 1293 (8th Cir. 1984).

An insurance agent who sold life and health policies to a health and welfare fund, then later became a fund administrator, was held to be a fiduciary. Even though his compensation arrangement was agreed on prior to his becoming an administrator, the court noted that his compensation was directly linked to his discretionary activities in determining which claims would be paid. As a result, he was a fiduciary with respect to the commissions and administrative expenses paid to him, and to the extent those amounts were paid to ineligible persons, he was liable to the fund. *American Fed'n of Unions, Local 102 v. Equitable Life Assurance Soc'y*, 841 F.2d 658 (5th Cir. 1988).

200. Can a person be a fiduciary for a limited purpose?

Yes, a person can be a fiduciary only *to the extent* that he has responsibility for the functions described in ERISA Section 3(21)(A). Labor Reg. §2509.75-8, D-4. The phrase "to the extent" indicates that a person is a fiduciary only with respect to those aspects of the plan over which he exercises authority or control.

Sommers Drug Stores Co. Profit Sharing Tr. v. Corrigan Enter., Inc., 793 F.2d 1456 (5th Cir. 1986), cert. denied, 479 U.S. 1034 (1987), citing *Brandt v. Grounds*, 687 F.2d 895 (7th Cir. 1982). See also *Arakelian v. National Western Life Ins. Co.*, 748 F. Supp. 17 (DC D.C. 1990) (trustees were not liable for certain fiduciary breaches involving surrender charges and investment decisions because of a lack of discretionary authority over the investment of plan assets). "It is a well established principle that under ERISA, fiduciary status is not an all or nothing proposition." *Demaio v. Cigna Corp.*, 16 EBC 1627 (E.D. Pa. 1993). "ERISA recognizes that a person may be a fiduciary for some purposes and not others." *Leigh v. Engle*, 727 F.2d 113 (7th Cir. 1984).

201. How many fiduciaries must an employee benefit plan have?

Although a plan is not required to have a specified number of fiduciaries, each plan must have at least one named fiduciary who serves as plan administrator. Labor Reg. §2509.75-8, FR-12. Additionally, if the plan assets are held in trust, the plan must have at least one trustee. There is no limit on the number of fiduciaries a plan may have. A plan may have as few or as many fiduciaries as are necessary for its operation and administration. Furthermore, if the plan so provides, any person or group of persons may serve in more than one fiduciary capacity, including serving both as trustee and administrator. ERISA Sec. 402(c)(1).

202. Is person's state of mind or title a prerequisite to fiduciary status?

No. A person's belief or formal title is irrelevant in determining his or her fiduciary status under ERISA. See, e.g., *Freund v. Marshall & Ilsley Bank*, 485 F. Supp. 629 (W.D. Wis. 1979); *Donovan v. Mercer*, 747 F.2d 304 (5th Cir. 1984); *McNeese v. Health Plan Marketing, Inc.*, 647 F. Supp. 981 (N.D. Ala. 1986). Congress intended the term to be broadly construed. "The definition includes persons who have authority and responsibility with respect to the matter in question, regardless of their formal title." H.R. Rep. No. 93-1280, 93rd Cong., 2nd Sess. (1974) (ERISA Conference Report). *Blatt v. Marshall & Lassman*, 812 F.2d 810 (2nd Cir. 1987). Thus, whether or not an individual or entity is an ERISA fiduciary rests on an objective evaluation of functions performed, and not on an individual's state of mind, or the title held.

203. Who is a plan administrator?

The term "administrator" means: (1) the person specifically so designated by the terms of the instrument under which the plan is operated; (2) if an administrator is not so designated, the plan sponsor; *or* (3) in the case of a plan for which an administrator is not designated and a plan sponsor cannot be identified, such other person as the Department of Labor may by regulation prescribe. ERISA Sec. 3(16)(A). Plan documents generally designate the person or entity who is assigned the role of the plan administrator. If the document is silent as to this position, the plan sponsor is designated in accordance with the statute.

204. Is a plan administrator a fiduciary?

Although nothing in ERISA specifically states that a plan administrator is a fiduciary, both the courts and the Department of Labor are in accord that the holder of this position automatically has fiduciary status solely on the basis of his role as plan administrator because, by the very nature of the position, plan administrators have "discretionary authority or discretionary responsibility in the administration" of the plan. Thus, a plan administrator who has discretionary authority or discretionary responsibility in the administration of the plan is a fiduciary within under the terms of ERISA Section 3(21)(A)(iii) and has a duty to act in accordance with the rules of fiduciary conduct under ERISA. Labor Reg. §2509.75-8 D-3; see *Hozier v. Midwest Fasteners, Inc.*, 908 F.2d 1155 (3rd Cir. 1990); *U.S. Steel Mining Co. v. District 17, United Mine Workers of America*, 897 F.2d 149 (4th Cir. 1990). A plan administrator who does not possess discretionary authority over the plan or its assets but merely performs "ministerial" functions is not a fiduciary. For an explanation of what actions constitute "ministerial" functions, see Q 196.

The DOL has stated that the determination of whether a third party administrator (TPA) is a fiduciary is a *functional test*. Sherwin Kaplan, Deputy Solicitor General for the Plan Benefit Security Division of the DOL, speaking at the meeting of Workers in Employee Benefits, February 18, 1998. Furthermore, if a TPA exercises discretionary control he is probably a fiduciary. Kaplan added that courts have been expanding the definition of fiduciary, and that contracts disclaiming fiduciary responsibility do not provide the protection they once did.

The Ninth Circuit has ruled that a TPA was not a fiduciary under ERISA and did not have a duty to disclose to participants its suspicion of asset embezzlement by the plan sponsor CEO/plan co-trustee because the TPA's primary duty was the preparation of financial reports on behalf of the plan. The Court ruled that since the TPA lacked discretionary control over the plan, and control remained with the CEO/co-trustee, the TPA could not be deemed a fiduciary under ERISA. *CSA 401(k) Plan v. Pension Professionals, Inc.*, 195 F.3d 1135 (9th Cir. 1999).

205. Who is a plan sponsor?

A plan sponsor is (1) the employer, in the case of an employee benefit plan established or maintained by a single employer, (2) the employee organization, in the case of a plan established or maintained by an employee organization, or (3) in the case of a plan established or maintained by two or more employers or jointly by one or more employers and one or more employee organizations, the association, committee, joint board of trustees, or other similar group of representatives of the parties who establish or maintain the plan. ERISA Sec. 3(16)(B).

206. When does a plan sponsor act as a fiduciary?

"ERISA allows employers to wear 'two hats,' and they act as a fiduciary 'only when and to the extent' that they function in their capacity as plan administrators, not when they conduct business that is not regulated by ERISA." *Amato v. Western Union Int'l, Inc.*, 773 F.2d 1402 (2nd Cir. 1985), cert. dismissed, 474 U.S. 1113 (1986). Since the roles of plan administrator and plan sponsor are distinct, a plan sponsor who does not serve in the capacity of a trustee, named fiduciary or plan administrator is not deemed to be a fiduciary. Thus, a plan sponsor steps into the role of a fiduciary under ERISA Section 3(21)(A) only when exercising discretionary authority or control over the plan management or administration. *Siskind v. Sperry Retirement Program*, 47 F.3d 498 (2nd Cir. 1995). For example, if an employer has no power with respect to a plan other than to appoint the plan administrator and the trustees, then its fiduciary duty extends only to those functions. See *Gelardi v. Pertec Computer Corp.*, 761 F.2d 1323 (9th Cir. 1985); *Leigh v. Engle*, 727 F.2d 113 (7th Cir. 1984); see Labor Reg. §2509.75-8 D-4. However, a plan sponsor may be found to be a fiduciary if it controls the trustee's investment decisions (either through the use of its position or otherwise) by causing the trustees to relinquish their independent discretion in making investment decisions for the plan and to follow an investment course prescribed by the plan sponsor. *Sommers Drug Stores Co. Profit Sharing Tr. v. Corrigan Enter., Inc.*, 793 F.2d 1456 (5th Cir. 1986), cert. denied, 479 U.S. 1034 (1987).

Fiduciary status may also attach in the situation where a plan sponsor serves in the dual capacity as both a plan sponsor and plan administrator. Although not all of a plan sponsor's business activities involve plan management or administration, a plan sponsor may act in the capacity of a plan fiduciary and not as an employer in communicating to plan participants about "business decisions" that may affect plan benefits. In communicating to employees, a plan sponsor may wear its "fiduciary," as well as its "employer," hat. In communicating business decisions with respect to a plan and their effect on the plan benefits, reasonable employees may not be able to distinguish consciously between the plan sponsor's roles as employer and as plan administrator. Thus, an employer may be exercising "discretionary authority" respecting the plan's "management" or "administration" in communicating the business decision, combined with a plan-related nature of the decision, if a reasonable employee would believe that the plan sponsor is communicating to him in the capacity of plan administrator. *Varity Corp. v. Howe*, 514 U.S. 1082 (1996). See Q 207.

A plan sponsor acts as a fiduciary of a plan with respect to retaining the authority in the selection and retention of plan fiduciaries. For example, plan sponsors often have the responsibility for the appointment of and removal of the plan's trustees, administrators, or members of an administrative committee that administers the plan. By virtue of this responsibility, and by virtue of the plan sponsor's exercise of the appointment power, the plan sponsor is a fiduciary of the plan within the meaning of ERISA. ERISA Sec. 3(21)(A); see *Eaves v. Penn.*, 587 F.2d 453 (10th Cir. 1978); *Batchelor v. Oak Hill Medical Group*, 870 F.2d 1446 (9th Cir. 1989) (consortium of physicians operating medical clinics held liable for breach of fiduciary duty in selection of a third party as fund administrator); *Hickman v. Tosco Corp.*, 840 F.2d 564 (8th Cir. 1988) (company was a fiduciary within the meaning of ERISA because it appointed and removed the members of the administrative committee that administered the pension plan);

Whitfield v. Tomasso, 682 F. Supp. 1287 (E.D. NY 1988) (union that had authority to appoint and remove trustees had exercised discretionary control over the management of the welfare fund and was, therefore, a fiduciary to the fund); *McKinnon v. Cairns*, 698 F. Supp. 852 (W.D. Okla. 1988); *Moehle v. NL Indus., Inc.*, 646 F. Supp. 769 (E.D. Mo. 1986) (employer which appointed and removed plan committee members was a fiduciary).

207. What is the settlor doctrine? May an employer rely on the settlor doctrine to avoid fiduciary status?

Relying on the distinction between an employer's role as a plan fiduciary and an employer's role conducting business, the settlor doctrine sets forth the theory that certain actions of an employer in the course of the design, establishment and termination of a plan are settlor functions (see Q 227) which are not governed by the fiduciary standards of ERISA. However, as explained below, an employer cannot necessarily rely on this doctrine under all circumstances.

It is well established that decisions involving the design, establishment, and termination of a plan are employer tasks, and not within the purview of the fiduciary provisions of ERISA. These settlor functions are discretionary activities that relate to the formation, rather than the management of a plan, and thus, are allowed to be made without considering the interests of plan participants and beneficiaries. Moreover, Congress made it clear that "ERISA does not require that day-to-day corporate business transactions, which may have a collateral effect on prospective, contingent employee benefits, be performed solely in the interest of plan participants." *Adams v. Avondale Indus., Inc.*, 905 F.2d 943 (6th Cir. 1990), cert. denied, 498 U.S. 984 (1990).

In effect, "ERISA permits employers to wear 'two hats,' and they assume fiduciary status 'only when and to the extent' that they function in their capacity as plan administrators, not when they conduct business that is not regulated by ERISA." Thus, under the settlor doctrine, ordinary business decisions that directly affect the plan and plan participants, such as the decision to modify or terminate welfare benefits, are not governed by ERISA's fiduciary obligations because they do not involve discretionary administration of the plan. See *Curtiss-Wright Corp. v. Schoonejongen*, 514 U.S. 73 (1995).

The ability of an employer to rely on this settlor doctrine, however, is limited. The Supreme Court has held that an employer serving in the dual capacity as both a plan sponsor and plan administrator may invoke fiduciary status upon itself in communicating to plan participants about "business decisions" that may affect plan benefits, thus subjecting it to the fiduciary standards of ERISA. *Varity Corp. v. Howe*, 514 U.S. 1082 (1996).

The employer in *Varity* intentionally misled employees about the financial health of a subsidiary it had created, leading them to forfeit benefits in a financially sound plan in exchange for benefits backed by a subsidiary that the employer knew was insolvent. In the lawsuit that later ensued, the employer argued that its deceptive statements about the subsidiary's financial health were made in its capacity as an employer, not as a plan fiduciary.

The Court rejected the employer's argument, stating that "reasonable employees ... could have thought that Varity was communicating with them *both* in its capacity as employer *and* in its capacity as plan administrator. Reasonable employees might not have distinguished consciously between the two roles. But they would have known that the employer was their plan's administrator and had expert knowledge about how their plan worked." The Court noted further that the employees' conclusion that their benefits with the subsidiary would be secure "could well have drawn strength from their awareness of that expertise," and, in fact, that such a perception was the employer's intention.

The Court concluded that while the employer in *Varity* had made an employer business decision with respect to the plan (i.e., splitting off unprofitable divisions into a subsidiary, as well as transferring a number of employees and debts—including the liability for their benefits—to that subsidiary), it acted in a fiduciary capacity when it discussed the decision and its impact on the plan benefits to employees. Indeed, its intentional misleading of employees as to the future of plan benefits in that context was an act of plan administration and the employer was found liable for its actions.

Thus, under *Varity*, although a business decision relating to the plan should not, in itself, trigger the fiduciary standards, an employer's communications to employees about the effect of the business decision on the plan's benefits may likely be considered a fiduciary act, thereby subjecting it to scrutiny under the fiduciary provisions of ERISA.

208. Is a trustee a fiduciary?

Yes, under most circumstances. With certain exceptions, ERISA generally mandates that all assets of an employee benefit plan must be held in trust by one or more trustees. ERISA Sec. 403(a). The trustees must either be named in the plan document, named in the trust agreement, or appointed by a named fiduciary. The trustees have exclusive authority and discretion to acquire, manage, control, and dispose of the assets of the plan, except to the extent that trustees are subject to the direction of a named fiduciary (non-trustee), or where these functions are delegated to an investment manager. Thus, trustees who have the authority and discretion to acquire, manage, control, and dispose of the assets of the plan by, definition, are fiduciaries. ERISA Sec. 3(21)(A)(I).

209. May an officer of the plan sponsor serve as a plan fiduciary?

Yes. ERISA specifically allows an officer, employee, agent, or other representative of a union or plan sponsor to also serve as a fiduciary of the plan sponsor's employee benefit plan. ERISA Section 408(c) states that "nothing in... this title shall be construed to prohibit any fiduciary from ... serving as a fiduciary in addition to being an officer, employee, agent, or other representative of a party in interest."

In addition, the courts have held that there is no inherent conflict of interest where an officer of a corporation is also a fiduciary of the corporation's benefit plan. In fact, ERISA contemplates such a situation where an officer of a corporation wears two hats; when acting in the capacity of an employee of the corporation, the officer owes a duty to act on behalf of the corporation. See *Amato v. Western Union Int'l, Inc.*, 773 F.2d 1402 (2nd Cir. 1985), cert. dismissed, 474 U.S. 1113 (1986). For example, a trustee of an employee benefit plan does not violate ERISA merely by also serving in a position with an employee organization, or employer, that requires him to represent the entity in the collective bargaining negotiations that determine the funding of the plan. In those negotiations, the bargaining representative represents either the employer or the employees. *Evans v. Bexley*, 750 F.2d 1498 (11th Cir. 1985).

On the other hand, an officer of the plan sponsor also owes a duty to the plan as plan fiduciary to avoid placing himself in a position where his role as an officer of the plan sponsor prevents him from functioning with complete loyalty to the participants of the plan. *Donovan v. Bierwirth*, 680 F.2d 263 (2nd Cir. 1982), cert. denied, 459 U.S. 1069 (1982). Thus, when an officer of a plan sponsor acts in the capacity of a plan fiduciary, the officer owes a duty to act in the best interest of the plan's participants and beneficiaries.

An officer of a plan sponsor was held to be a fiduciary with respect to his obligation to timely deposit withheld employee contributions, in spite of the fact that he was not the plan administrator, nor otherwise designated as a fiduciary. See *LoPresti v. Terwilliger*, 126 F.3d 34 (1997).

210. When does a person render investment advice?

A person renders "investment advice" (within the meaning of ERISA Section 3(21)(A)) only if:

1. The person renders advice to the plan as to the value of securities or other property, or makes recommendations as to the advisability of investing in, purchasing, or selling securities or other property; and

2. The person either directly or indirectly (e.g., through or together with any affiliate): (a) has discretionary authority or control, whether or not pursuant to agreement, arrangement or understanding, with respect to purchasing or selling securities or other property for the plan; or (b) renders any advice described in paragraph (1), above, on a regular basis to the plan pursuant to a mutual agreement, arrangement or understanding, written or otherwise, between such person and the plan or a fiduciary with respect to the plan, that the services will serve as a primary basis for investment decisions with respect to plan assets, and that such person will render individualized investment advice to the plan

based on the particular needs of the plan regarding such matters as, among other things, investment policies or strategy, overall portfolio composition, or diversification of plan investments. Labor Reg. §2510.3-21(c).

211. Is a person who renders investment advice a fiduciary?

A person is considered a fiduciary with respect to an employee benefit plan to the extent that he "renders investment advice for a fee or other compensation, direct or indirect, with respect to any moneys or other property of such plan, or has any authority to do so." Accordingly, the definition of fiduciary is a 2-part test requiring both the provision of "investment advice" and the receipt of a "fee or other compensation" for such advice. ERISA Sec. 3(21)(A)(ii).

212. What is a "fee or other compensation" for the rendering of investment advice?

According to the Department of Labor, "a fee or other compensation," direct or indirect, for the rendering of investment advice to a plan by a fiduciary, is deemed to include all fees or other compensation incident to the transaction in which the investment advice to the plan has been rendered or will be rendered. This may include, for example, brokerage commissions, mutual fund sales commissions, and insurance sales commissions. DOL Adv. Op. 83-60A, DOL Adv. Op. 84-36A.

213. Does the provision of research or recommendations by a broker-dealer constitute the rendering of "investment advice?"

Generally, no. According to the Department of Labor, the provision by broker-dealers of research, information and advice concerning securities to a plan in the ordinary course of their business as broker-dealers would not, in and of itself, constitute the rendering of "investment advice" unless the services are rendered pursuant to a mutual agreement (written or otherwise) to provide individualized advice to a plan on a regular basis, which will serve as the primary basis for plan investment decisions. Thus, for example, the provision of general research materials to a broker-dealer's customers, including employee benefit plans, would not fall into that category. In other instances, a determination of whether the provision of research or recommendations by a broker-dealer constitutes the rendering of "investment advice" within the meaning of ERISA Section 3(21)(A)(ii) will depend on the particular facts and circumstances. DOL Adv. Op. 83-60A.

214. Does the provision of investment-related information to participants and beneficiaries in participant-directed individual account plans constitute the rendering of "investment advice"?

Not necessarily. In 1996 the Department of Labor issued guidance identifying categories of investment-related information and related materials that an employer may make available to participants without the provision of such items constituting "investment advice" for purposes of the definition of "fiduciary" under ERISA. See Labor Reg. §2509.96-1 (IB 96-1), 61 Fed. Reg. 29586 (June 11, 1996). For an explanation of the regulations under ERISA Section 3(21)(A)(ii), with respect to what constitutes the rendering of "investment advice" see Q 324.

The "safe harbor" treatment of these items applies regardless of who provides the information, how often it is shared, the form in which it is provided (e.g., in writing, via video or software, on an individual or group basis), or whether an identified category of information and materials is furnished alone or in combination with other identified categories of information and materials. The materials identified by the DOL include:

1. Information and materials that inform participants about the benefits of plan participation, the benefits of increasing plan contributions, the impact of preretirement withdrawals, the operation and terms of the plan, and investment alternatives available under the plan (including their investment objectives and philosophies, risk and return characteristics, and historical return information), see Q 522;

2. General financial and investment concepts, such as risk and return, diversification, dollar cost averaging, compounded return and tax deferred investing, historical differences in rates of return between different asset classes based on standard market indices, effects of inflation, estimating future retirement needs, determining investment time horizons, and assessing risk tolerance, provided that the information has no direct relationship to investment alternatives available under the plan, see Q 523;

3. Asset allocation information (e.g., pie charts, case studies or graphs) made available to all participants and beneficiaries, that provide participants with models of asset allocation portfolios of hypothetical individuals with different time horizons and risk profiles (however, the models must be based on accepted investment theories and all material facts and assumptions on which the models are based must be specified, and the models must include certain other disclosures), see Q 524; and

4. Interactive investment materials, such as questionnaires, worksheets, software and similar materials that provide participants a means of estimating future retirement income needs, provided that requirements similar to those for asset allocation information in (3), above, are met; see Q 525. Labor Reg. §2509.96-1(d), above.

215. Must a person who renders investment advice, but who does not exercise or have the right to exercise discretionary authority with respect to the assets of the plan, be bonded solely by reason of the provision of such investment advice?

No. A person who renders investment advice, but who does not exercise or have the right to exercise discretionary authority with respect to plan assets, is not required to be bonded solely by reason of the provision of such investment advice. Such a person is not considered to be "handling" funds within the meaning of the temporary bonding regulations. Labor Reg. §2509.75-5, FR-7. See Chapter VIII for a discussion of the bonding requirements.

216. Is a broker-dealer a fiduciary?

Generally, no. A broker or dealer registered under the Securities Exchange Act of 1934, a reporting dealer in United States Government or agency securities, or a supervised bank (federal or state), will not be considered a fiduciary merely because the person executes transactions for the purchase or sale of securities on behalf of an employee benefit plan if the following requirements are met:

1. The transactions are executed (a) in the ordinary course of the business of the broker, dealer, or bank; and (b) pursuant to the instructions of a plan fiduciary;

2. The fiduciary or its affiliates are not affiliated with the broker, dealer, or bank; and

3. The fiduciary's instructions specify (a) the security to be purchased or sold, (b) a price range within which such security is to be purchased or sold, (c) a time span during which the security may be purchased or sold (not to exceed five business days), and (d) the minimum or maximum quantity of the security which may be purchased or sold within the price range. Labor Reg. §2510.3-21(d)(1).

However, subject to the provisions governing co-fiduciary liability and the rules governing prohibited transactions as a party-in-interest (see ERISA Secs. 405(a), 3(14)(B)) a broker-dealer, reporting dealer or bank is not considered a fiduciary regarding any plan assets with respect to which it:

1. Does not have any discretionary authority, discretionary control or discretionary responsibility;

2. Does not exercise any authority or control;

3. Does not render investment advice for a fee or other compensation; *and*

4.   Does not have any authority or responsibility to render such investment advice. Labor Reg. §2510.3-21(d)(2).

The foregoing regulations have been interpreted as requiring all of the following five elements in order to support a finding of fiduciary status of a broker-dealer: (1) individualized investment advice was provided; (2) the advice was given pursuant to a mutual understanding; (3) the advice was provided on a regular basis; (4) the advice pertained to the value of the property or consisted of recommendations as to the advisability of investing in certain property; and (5) the advice was rendered for a fee. See *Thomas, Head & Greisen Employees Tr. v. Buster*, 24 F.3d 1114 (9th Cir. 1994).

A broker-dealer who recommended securities for a plan to purchase was held to be merely a broker and not a fiduciary, because the broker-dealer had no discretionary authority over the plan, he had no discretion to dispose of any of the plan's assets, and there was no mutual understanding that the broker-dealer would provide to the plan individualized investment advice that would be the primary basis for the plan's investment decisions. Thus, the broker-dealer did not rise to the status of a fiduciary by merely selling suggested securities to the plan in a sales pitch, which the court described as "the very cornerstone of a typical broker-client relationship." *Farm King Supply, Inc. v. Edward D. Jones & Co.*, 884 F.2d 288 (7th Cir. 1989). In addition, a finding that the investment advisor rendered advice on a "regular basis" is essential to a determination that a fiduciary relationship existed. *American Fed'n of Unions, Local 102 v. Equitable Life Assurance Soc'y*, 841 F.2d 658 (5th Cir. 1988).

217. Who is an investment manager?

An "investment manager" is a fiduciary (other than a trustee or named fiduciary) who has the power to manage, acquire, or dispose of any asset of a plan. This power is delegated by a named fiduciary for the purpose of managing the assets of a plan. The investment manager must be either registered as an investment advisor under the Investment Advisors Act of 1940, a bank (as defined in that Act), or an insurance company with the power to manage, acquire, or dispose of any asset of a plan under the laws of more than one state. In addition, an investment manager is required to acknowledge in writing that it is a fiduciary with respect to the plan. ERISA Secs. 3(38), 402(c)(3).

218. May an investment adviser who is neither a bank nor an insurance company, and who is not registered under the Investment Advisors Act of 1940, in reliance upon an exemption from registration provided in that act, be appointed an investment manager under ERISA Section 402(c)(3)?

No. The only persons who may be appointed as an investment manager under ERISA Section 402(c)(3) are persons who meet the requirements of ERISA Section 3(38)—namely, banks (as defined in the Investment Advisors Act of 1940), insurance companies qualified under the laws of more than one state to manage, acquire and dispose of plan assets, or persons registered as investment advisors under the Investment Advisors Act of 1940. Labor Reg. §2509.75-5, FR-6.

219. May an investment advisor who has a registration application pending under the Investment Advisors Act of 1940 function as an investment manager under the act prior to the effective date of registration under the Investment Advisors Act?

No, for the same reasons as stated in Q 218. Labor Reg. §2509.75-5, FR-7.

220. What is the procedure for state-registered investment advisors to obtain investment manager status under ERISA?

Under temporary procedures instituted by the Department of Labor, state registered investment advisors seeking investment manager status under ERISA must file with the Department of Labor a copy of their most recently filed state registration form and any subsequent filings. Generally, this filing requirement applies to investment advisors who manage less than $25 million and who are required to register under state law. Advisors who are required to register in multiple states need only provide the department a copy of the registration form filed in the state where they maintain their principal office and place of business.

Investment advisors could initially file their registration forms with the DOL anytime prior to November 10, 1998, to satisfy the requirement for ERISA investment manager status. Any subsequent filings with the state should be filed with the DOL at the same time. Copies of these filings should be mailed to the DOL at the following address:

Investment Advisor Filings, Room N-5638
U.S. Department of Labor, PWBA
Office of Program Services
200 Constitution Avenue, NW
Washington, DC 20210

As a temporary filing requirement, the procedures are scheduled to remain in effect only until a centralized database containing the registration forms (or substantially similar information) is available through the Securities and Exchange Commission (SEC) or other organization. At that time the DOL intends to provide notice that filing with the DOL is no longer necessary. ERISA Sec. 3(38)(B), as amended by P.L. 105-72, effective November 10, 1997.

221. What persons are barred from serving as fiduciaries?

Any person who has been convicted of any of a broad range of crimes is barred from serving as a fiduciary or service provider of an employee benefit plan. ERISA Sec. 411. The statute automatically disqualifies individuals by its terms and subjects these persons to prosecution for violating its provisions. Anyone who has been convicted of, or imprisoned as a result of the following offenses is prohibited from serving as a fiduciary: (1) Robbery, bribery, extortion, embezzlement, fraud, grand larceny, burglary, arson, murder; (2) Rape, kidnaping, perjury, assault with intent to kill; (3) A felony violation of Federal or State law involving "controlled substances" defined in section 802(6) of Title 21 of the U.S. Code (Comprehensive Drug Abuse Prevention and Control Act of 1970); (4) Any crime described in Section 80a-9(a)(1) of Title 15, U.S. Code (Investment Company Act of 1940); (5) A violation of any crime in ERISA (411, 501 and 511); (6) A violation of section 186 of Title 29, U.S. Code (prohibited payments to labor unions, labor union officials, and employee representatives); (7) A violation of Chapter 63 of Title 18, U.S. Code (e.g., mail fraud, wire fraud, etc.); (8) A violation of section 874, 1027, 1503, 1505, 1506, 1510, 1951, or 1954 of Title 18, U.S. Code; (9) A violation of the Labor-Management Reporting and Disclosure Act of 1959 (29 U.S.C. 401); (10) Any felony involving abuse or misuse of such person's position or employment in a labor organization or employee benefit plan to seek or obtain an illegal gain at the expense of the members of the labor organization or the beneficiaries of the employee benefit plan; (11) A conspiracy or attempt to commit any of the foregoing crimes; and (12) Any crime in which any of crimes described in ERISA Section 411 is an element.

See Chapter XIII, Criminal Enforcement for further discussion.

222. May an employee pension or welfare benefit plan trustee be appointed for "life" subject to removal for "cause"?

In Advisory Opinion 85-41A (December 5, 1985), the DOL expressed the view that a lifetime term of appointment for a pension plan trustee would generally be inconsistent with ERISA's fiduciary responsibility provisions. In addition, applicable regulations state, in part, that a contract or arrangement to provide trustee or other services to the plan is reasonable only if it permits termination of the contract or arrangement by the plan on reasonably short notice without penalty to the plan. Labor Reg. §2550.408b-2c.

The principles articulated in Advisory Opinion 85-41A apply equally to the terms of the appointment of trustees of funded welfare plans according to the DOL in Advisory Opinion 99-17A. Accordingly, an arrangement whereby trustees are to serve for unlimited terms subject to removal only upon proof of malfeasance, misconduct or incapacity, or upon their own voluntary resignation or death, would not be reasonable within the meaning of the regulation.

CHAPTER IV

FIDUCIARY DUTIES

223. What standards of conduct does ERISA impose on fiduciaries?

Borrowing from trust law, ERISA imposes high standards of fiduciary duty upon those responsible for administering an ERISA plan and investing and disposing of its assets. The general standards governing fiduciary conduct require, among other things, that fiduciaries discharge their duties solely in the interest of plan participants and beneficiaries, for the exclusive purpose of providing them benefits "with the care, skill, prudence, and diligence" of a "prudent man acting in a like capacity and familiar with such matters," and in accordance with the documents and instruments governing the plan. ERISA Sec. 404. This chapter explains these duties and the standards of care governing the conduct of employee benefit plan fiduciaries.

224. What are the fiduciary duties prescribed by ERISA?

In addition to making certain actions by fiduciaries illegal per se, ERISA also codified the common law duties of loyalty and prudence for ERISA trustees. The central and fundamental obligations imposed on fiduciaries by ERISA are contained in Title I of ERISA (at Subtitle B, Part 4), titled *Fiduciary Responsibility*. This section sets forth the standards of conduct applicable to fiduciaries of employee benefit plans. In relevant part, the fiduciary provisions of ERISA Section 404(a) require that a plan fiduciary discharge his duties with respect to an employee benefit plan solely in the interest of the participants and beneficiaries, and:

1. For the exclusive purpose of: (a) providing benefits to participants and their beneficiaries; and (b) defraying reasonable expenses of administering the plan;

2. With the care, skill, prudence, and diligence under the circumstances then prevailing that a prudent man acting in a like capacity and familiar with such matters would use in the conduct of an enterprise of a like character and with like aims;

3. By diversifying the investments of the plan so as to minimize the risk of large losses, unless under the circumstances it is clearly prudent not to do so; and

4. In accordance with the documents and instruments governing the plan insofar as such documents and instruments are consistent with the provisions of ERISA.

2002 ERISA Facts

The fiduciary provisions of ERISA Section 404 embody the "central and fundamental obligation imposed on fiduciaries by ERISA," containing a carefully tailored law of trusts, including the requirements of undivided loyalty to beneficiaries, the prudent man rule, the rule requiring diversification of investments and the requirement that fiduciaries comply with the provisions of plan documents to the extent that they are not inconsistent with ERISA. *Eaves v. Penn*, 587 F.2d 453 (10th Cir. 1978). These rules are supplemented by ERISA Section 403(c)(1), which provides that "the assets of a plan shall never inure to the benefit of any employer and shall be held for the exclusive purposes of providing benefits to participants in the plan and their beneficiaries and defraying reasonable expenses of administering the plan."

In addition to these fiduciary standards, other sections of ERISA supplement these duties by expressly prohibiting numerous specific transactions between the plans and their affiliated "parties in interest" and by placing limits on the acquisition and holding of employer securities and real property by plans. See ERISA Secs. 406, 407. Counterbalancing these duties and prohibitions are certain statutory and administrative exemptions. See ERISA Sec. 408.

ERISA Section 404(a) establishes uniform fiduciary standards to prevent transactions that dissipate or endanger plan assets. Much of the content of these provisions was drawn from the common law of trusts, which was the law governing most benefit plans before ERISA's enactment. In constructing the provisions of ERISA, Congress invoked the common law of trusts to define the general scope of fiduciaries' authority and responsibility, rather than explicitly enumerating all of the powers and duties of trustees and other fiduciaries. See *Varity Corp. v. Howe*, 514 U.S. 1082 (1996). Still, while ERISA imposes trust-like fiduciary standards, Congress expected that the courts would interpret these various fiduciary standards, bearing in mind the special nature and purpose of modern employee benefit plans. See *Varity Corp. v. Howe*, above.

225. What plans are covered by the fiduciary rules?

The fiduciary rules of ERISA generally apply to employee welfare and pension benefit plans maintained by employers and employee organizations, or both, that are engaged in commerce, industry or activity that affects commerce. ERISA Secs. 401(a), 3(3), 4, 5.

226. What plans are exempted from the fiduciary rules?

Not all employee benefit plans are subject to the fiduciary duty requirements of ERISA Section 404(a). The fiduciary rules do not apply to the following types of employee benefit plans (See ERISA Secs. 4(b), 401(a)):

1. Governmental plans (as defined in ERISA Section 3(32));

2. Church plans (as defined in ERISA Section 3(33)) for which no election has been made to apply the participation, vesting and funding provisions of IRC Section 410(d);

3.   Plans that are maintained solely for the purpose of complying with applicable workmen's compensation laws or unemployment compensation or disability insurance laws;

4.   Plans that are maintained outside of the United States primarily for the benefit of persons substantially all of whom are nonresident aliens;

5.   Plans that are unfunded excess benefit plans (as defined in ERISA Section 3(36));

6.   Plans that are unfunded and are maintained by an employer primarily for the purpose of providing deferred compensation for a select group of management or highly compensated employees; and

7.   Any agreement described in IRC Section 736 which provides payments to a retired partner or deceased partner or a deceased partner's successor in interest.

In order to fit within exemption (6) above, a plan must satisfy two prerequisites: it must be unfunded, and it must be maintained by an employer primarily for the purpose of providing deferred income for select employees. An unfunded plan is one in which only the employer provides the necessary funding for the benefits under the plan. See *Bruch v. Firestone Tire & Rubber Co.*, 828 F.2d 134 (3rd Cir. 1987) (an unfunded plan is one where "every dollar provided in benefits is a dollar spent by ... the employer"), aff'd in part, rev'd in part, 489 U.S. 101 (1989); *Miller v. Eichleay Engineers, Inc.*, 886 F.2d 30 (3rd Cir. 1989) (same). If the employer itself is the source of all the benefits and payments under the plan, and no contributions are made by the employee or any other third party, the plan is unfunded for purposes of exemption (6), above. Thus, the plan is exempt from the fiduciary duty requirements of ERISA. *Crumley v. Stonhard, Inc.*, 920 F. Supp. 589 (DC N.J. 1996), aff'd 106 F.3d 384 (3rd Cir. 1996) ("phantom stock" plan).

227. What is a "settlor" function?

A "settlor" function is a discretionary activity made by a plan sponsor which relates to the formation, rather than the administration or management, of a plan. These so-called "settlor" functions include decisions made by the plan sponsor (or the employers and labor representatives in the case of a collectively bargained plan) relating to the establishment, termination and design of plans.

Both the Department of Labor and a number of courts have agreed that these "settlor" functions, or business activities, as distinguished from administrative functions, are not fiduciary activities, and therefore not subject to ERISA's fiduciary duty requirements in light of the voluntary nature of the private pension system and ERISA's overall statutory scheme. Therefore, in undertaking "settlor" functions, an employer does not act in the capacity of a fiduciary because it is not exercising any discretionary authority or discretionary control respecting management of a plan under the definition of a fiduciary in ERISA Section 3(21)(A). Instead, these activities are analogous to those of the settlor of a trust, and when an employer acts in its capacity as a settlor, it is not regulated by the fiduciary duties set forth in ERISA Section 404(a). Thus, employers or other plan sponsors generally have the complete discretion to adopt, modify, or terminate employee benefit plans without acting in the capacity of a fiduciary. See DOL Opinion Letter to John N. Erlenborn, 13 Pens. Rep. (BNA) 472 (March 13, 1986). See, e.g., *Lockheed Corp. v. Spink*, 517 U.S. 882 (1996); *Adams v. Avondale Indus., Inc.*, 905 F.2d 943 (6th Cir. 1990), cert. denied, 498 U.S. 984 (1990).

The ability of an employer to avoid the fiduciary standards of ERISA by relying on the argument that it was performing purely settlor functions may be limited when, in fact, reasonable persons would conclude that it was acting in a dual capacity as both employer and plan fiduciary. See Q 207.

228. Are business decisions of an employer fiduciary acts?

No. Under ERISA, purely business decisions by an employer are not governed by the fiduciary standards set forth in ERISA Section 404. "ERISA ... envisions that employers will act in a dual capacity as both fiduciary to the plan and as employer. ERISA does not prohibit an employer from acting in accordance with its interests as employer when not administering the plan or investing its assets." *Hickman v. Tosco Corp.*, 840 F.2d 564 (8th Cir. 1988), quoting *Phillips v. Amoco Oil Co.*, 799 F.2d 1464 (11th Cir. 1986). See also, *Trenton v. Scott Paper Co.*, 832 F.2d 806 (3rd Cir. 1987), cert. denied, 485 U.S. 1022 (1988).

However, the DOL has determined that the selection of health care services for an employer sponsored health care plan is a fiduciary function as an exercise of authority and control, due to the disposition of plan assets in paying for such services. The DOL has advised that since this selection is a fiduciary function, employers have a fiduciary duty to consider the quality of service to be rendered under the plan when making the selection, and failure to do so will constitute a breach thereof. DOL Information Letter to Service Employees' International Union (February 19, 1998).

"ERISA does not require that day-to-day corporate business transactions, which may have a collateral effect on prospective, contingent employee benefits, be performed solely in the interest of plan participants." *Hickman v. Tosco Corp.*, above; see also *Adams v. Avondale Indus., Inc.*, 905 F.2d 943 (6th Cir. 1990), cert. denied, 498 U.S. 984 (1990). Thus, ordinary business decisions, such as whether to pay a dividend or whether to incur debt, may be made without fear of liability for a breach of fiduciary duty under ERISA, even though they may turn out to have negative consequences for plan participants. Even business decisions that directly affect the plan and plan participants, such as the decision to modify or terminate welfare benefits, are not governed by ERISA's fiduciary obligations because they do not involve discretionary administration of the plan. See *Curtiss-Wright Corp. v. Schoonejongen*, 514 U.S. 73 (1995). (The Supreme Court in *Curtiss-Wright* also quoted *Adams v. Avondale Indus., Inc.*, above, for the proposition that "a company does not act in a fiduciary capacity when deciding to amend or terminate a welfare benefits plan.") For example, under the exclusion from fiduciary standards for business decisions, corporate actions by plan administrators seeking to reduce the amount of unaccrued plan benefits, terminating a pension plan, and deciding whether or not to establish a plan, have all been found nonfiduciary in nature. *West v. Greyhound Corp.*, 813 F.2d 951 (9th Cir. 1987); *Cunha v. Ward Foods, Inc.*, 804 F.2d 1418 (9th Cir. 1986); *Moore v. Reynolds Metals Co.*, 740 F.2d 454 (6th Cir. 1984), cert. denied, 469 U.S. 1109 (1985).

229. Do employers owe a fiduciary duty to participants?

Generally, employers owe no fiduciary duty towards plan beneficiaries under ERISA. However, when employers choose to "wear two hats" (i.e., act as both employer and plan administrator), they become subject to ERISA fiduciary duties regarding plan administration. See *Payonk v. HMW Indus., Inc.*, 883 F.2d 221 (3rd Cir. 1989); see also Q 207. Employers who act as plan administrators "assume fiduciary status only when and to the extent that they function in their capacity as plan administrators, not when they conduct business that is not regulated by ERISA." *Payonk v. HMW Indus., Inc.*, above, quoting *Amato v. Western Union Int'l, Inc.*, 773 F.2d 1402 (2nd Cir. 1985), cert. dismissed, 474 U.S. 1113 (1986).

230. Are employers' communications to plan participants about business decisions that may affect pension benefits subject to the fiduciary standards?

They can be. In 1996, the Supreme Court articulated a new standard for determining the existence of fiduciary status, when it held that conveying information about the likely future of plan benefits, in the context of communicating about a business decision, is a fiduciary act, and that an employer breached its fiduciary duties by lying to the plan participants. *Varity Corp. v. Howe*, 514 U.S. 1082 (1996).

In *Varity* (see Q 207), the employer made intentional misrepresentations for the purpose of inducing employees to make a choice about continued participation in an employee benefit plan. The Supreme Court emphasized the importance of that factual context in its conclusions that the employer's acts were acts of "plan administration" and, therefore, were subject to fiduciary review. Abandoning the statutory definition of what constitutes fiduciary conduct, and replacing it with a rule that turns on the subjective perceptions of plan participants, the Court held that an employer who sponsors an ERISA covered plan, and who communicates to participants about a business decision, may rise to the status of a fiduciary if the communications pertain to or bear on the "likely future of plan benefits."

The Sixth Circuit has ruled that an employer has a fiduciary duty to avoid making material misrepresentations concerning benefit entitlements as soon as any plan enhancements are subject to "serious consideration" by the plan sponsor. The case arose because the plan sponsor offered certain employees an early retirement incentive plan while, unbeknownst to the employees offered early retirement, developing an enhanced retirement plan that became effective soon after the employees retired. The retired employees sued, claiming that the plan sponsor used material misrepresentations and deliberate nondisclosure to fraudulently induce them to opt for early retirement rather than using a leave of absence option that would have made them eligible for the enhanced benefit plan. In the ruling, the court relied on a Third Circuit ruling (*Fischer v. Philadelphia Electric Co.*, 96 F.3d 1533, 3rd Cir. 1996) applying a three-part "serious consideration" test. Under the test, "serious consideration" occurs "when (1) a specified proposal (2) is being discussed for purposes of implementation (3) by senior management with the authority to implement the change." *McAuley v. IBM Corp.*, 165 F.3d 1038 (6th Cir. 1999).

231. What is the exclusive purpose rule?

The "exclusive purpose" rule of ERISA Section 404(a)(1)(A) requires a fiduciary to discharge his duties with respect to a plan solely in the interest of the plan participants and beneficiaries and for the exclusive purpose of providing benefits to participants and beneficiaries and defraying reasonable expenses of administering the plan. Federal courts have described this responsibility as the "duty to act with complete and undivided loyalty to the beneficiaries," (see *Freund v. Marshall & Ilsley Bank*, 485 F. Supp. 629 (W.D. Wis. 1979)) and with an "eye single to the interests of the participants and beneficiaries." (see *Donovan v. Bierwirth*, 680 F.2d 263 (2nd Cir. 1982), cert. denied, 459 U.S. 1069 (1982)).

Under this duty of loyalty, a trustee bears an unwavering duty of complete loyalty to the beneficiary of the trust, to the exclusion of the interests of all other parties. *NLRB v. Amax Coal Co.*, 453 U.S. 322 (1981), citing *Restatement (Second) of Trusts*, §170(1); *Scott on Trusts*, §170. This includes the trustee's own interests, as well as the interests of the trust's creditors. See *General American Life Ins. Co. v. Castonguay*, 984 F.2d 1518 (9th Cir. 1993). A fiduciary must not subordinate the interests of participants and beneficiaries to unrelated objectives; thus, in deciding whether and to what extent to enter into a course of action with respect to a plan, a fiduciary must ordinarily consider only factors relating to the interests of plan participants and beneficiaries. He may not be influenced by factors unrelated to these interests. Although nothing in ERISA Section 404(a)(1) expressly prohibits or limits the exercise of any particular method of decision-making by plan fiduciaries, any decision by a fiduciary that subordinates the interests of the plan's participants and beneficiaries may contravene the exclusive purpose rule.

232. What kinds of actions will result in a breach of the exclusive purpose rule?

The exclusive purpose requirement is violated if plan assets have been removed or diverted for the benefit of anyone other than plan participants. This was illustrated when plan fiduciaries caused or permitted virtually all of a plan's assets to be loaned back to the sponsoring companies in exchange for unsecured promissory notes. The complete lack of security on the notes presented significant risks for the plan and the interest rates paid on the notes did not adequately compensate for the risks involved. The court compared the exclusive benefit rule to the duty of loyalty under the common law of trusts, stating that the trustees had the duty to act with "complete and undivided loyalty to the beneficiaries of the trust" and with an "eye single to the interests of the participants and beneficiaries." *Freund v. Marshall & Ilsley Bank*, 485 F. Supp. 629 (W.D. Wis. 1979).

The DOL ruled that transferring the accumulated surplus from a union-sponsored vacation and holiday fund to the local union would violate the exclusive purpose rule, in that it would not be for the exclusive purpose of providing benefits to participants and their beneficiaries and defraying reasonable expenses of administering the fund. DOL Adv. Op. 77-56A.

An employer acting as a trustee of a parent plan and a spin-off plan (thus owing obligations of loyalty to the members of both plans) violated the exclusive purpose rule to participants in the spun-off plan in its allocation of investment gains realized on the parent plan assets to the spin-off plan. The employer failed to allocate the investment gains realized on the parent plan assets to the spin-off plan during the interim period after the closing date of the spin-off but before the transfers of the plan assets, despite the fact that 90% of those parent plan assets were attributable to members of the spun-off plan. The court noted that the employer's duty of loyalty to its parent plan members did not extend to giving them a windfall at the expense of the spin-off plan participants. Because its conduct was inconsistent with the strict duty owed to the spun-off plan participants, it violated its fiduciary duties. *The John Blair Communications, Inc. Profit Sharing Plan v. Telemundo Group, Inc.*, 26 F.3d 360 (2nd Cir. 1994).

Similarly, the trustees of a union-sponsored pension plan violated their duty of loyalty when they acted in the interest of the plan sponsor rather than "with an eye single to the interests of the participants and beneficiaries of the plan" and thereby violated the exclusive purpose and prudence requirements by authorizing loan transactions with an association that was closely related to the union. The evidence indicated that trustees were on both sides of negotiations that resulted in the association's purchase of a loan note from plan for well below the note's accounting value. *Reich v. Compton*, 57 F.3d 270 (3rd Cir. 1995).

The use of assets of an employee benefit plan to pay benefits to individuals who were not participants in that plan, or beneficiaries of such individuals, also contravened the exclusive purpose requirement. According to the Department of Labor, the payment of a gratuitous death benefit by plan trustees to the widow of a plan fiduciary would constitute a violation of the exclusive purpose standards of ERISA Sections 403(c)(1) and 404(a)(1)(A), since the payment could not be characterized as either compensation for services performed or as a reasonable expense of administration of the plan. Furthermore, the payment proposed to be made to the widow would not have been made to her as a participant or as a beneficiary of the plan; thus, such a payment would violate the requirements of ERISA Sections 403(c)(1) and 404(a)(1)(A) unless it constituted a reasonable expense of administering the plans. DOL Adv. Op. 81-52A. Likewise, trustees of collectively bargained pension and welfare benefit plans violated the exclusive purpose rule by improperly causing the plans to extend coverage and pay benefits to themselves and the plans' attorney as participants in the plans. *Donovan v. Daugherty*, 550 F. Supp. 390 (S.D. Ala. 1982).

The use of plan assets by corporate management either as an offensive or defensive tool in battles for corporate control also violates the exclusive purpose rule, and such attempts are particularly monitored by the Department of Labor. This was illustrated when plan fiduciaries invested a plan's assets in companies involved in corporate control contests. The fiduciaries themselves were actively engaged in the control contests, had substantial interests in them, and their investment decisions never deviated from their own best interests. In addition, where it might be possible to question the fiduciaries' loyalty, they are obliged at a minimum to engage in an intensive and scrupulous independent investigation of their options, in order to insure that they are acting in the best interests of the plan beneficiaries. *Leigh v. Engle*, 727 F.2d 113 (7th Cir. 1984); see also *Donovan v. Bierwirth*, above. Since ERISA requires plan fiduciaries to make investment decisions, including tender offer decisions, based on the facts and circumstances applicable to the investment and the plan, fiduciaries must take the course of action that is in the best economic interests of the pension plan, recognizing the pension trust as a separate legal entity designed to provide retirement income. DOL News Release No. 89-52 (1/31/89).

The exclusive purpose rule also was held to prohibit a fiduciary from granting preferences as between a plan's participants or its beneficiaries with respect to the administration of the plan. *Winpisinger v. Aurora Corp.*, 456 F. Supp. 559 (N.D. Ohio 1978). In carrying out this obligation, the trustees of a plan must exercise their discretion to serve the interests of all the participants of the plan. *Talarico v. United Furniture Workers Pension Fund A*, 479 F. Supp. 1072 (DC Neb. 1979). For example, the trustees of an employer sponsored pension plan failed to administer the plan for the exclusive purpose of providing retirement income benefits to all of the plan participants and beneficiaries when they extended credit to a limited number of plan participants at unreasonably low interest rates. The low rates of interest charged on the loans to the selected participants resulted in correspondingly low rates of return on the investment of the plan assets for all of the plan participants. By extending credit to a limited number of plan participants at unreasonably low rates, the plan trustees failed to administer the plan for the exclusive purpose of providing retirement income benefits to all plan participants and beneficiaries. *McLaughlin v. Rowley*, 698 F. Supp. 1333 (N.D. Texas 1988).

233. Is a fiduciary prohibited from holding positions of dual loyalty?

ERISA does not explicitly prohibit a fiduciary from holding positions of dual loyalty with conflicting interests; for example, an employer is permitted to act both as plan sponsor and plan administrator. See ERISA Sec. 408(c)(3). Employers who choose to administer their own plans assume responsibilities to both the company and the plan, and, accordingly, owe duties of loyalty and care to both entities. In permitting such arrangements, which ordinary trust law generally forbids due to the inherent potential for a conflict of interest, Congress understood that the interests of the plan might be sacrificed if an employer were forced to choose between the company and the plan. Hence, Congress imposed on plan administrators a duty of care that requires them to discharge their duties with respect to a plan solely in the interests of the participants and beneficiaries.

Congress never intended ERISA Section 404(a)(1) to establish a per se rule of fiduciary conduct. *Fentron Indus., Inc. v. National Shopmen Pension Fund*, 674 F.2d 1300 (9th Cir. 1982). Consequently, a court will not create a prohibited transaction and conflict of interest where Congress and precedent have not indicated one. *Ershick v. United Mo. Bank of Kansas City*, 948 F.2d 660 (10th Cir. 1991). See also *Brock v. Citizens Bank of Clovis*, 841 F.2d 344 (10th Cir. 1988), cert. denied, 488 U.S. 829 (1988), which pointed out that courts have been unwilling to create "a per se violation [of ERISA Section 406(b)] when Congress has not done so." Thus, for example, a bank does not commit a violation of ERISA Section 404(a)(1) by the mere act of becoming a trustee with conflicting interests, and a trustee does not necessarily violate ERISA Section 404(a)(1) by accepting a trusteeship with dual loyalties. *Friend v. Sanwa Bank Cal.*, 35 F.3d 466 (9th Cir. 1994).

234. Must a fiduciary with a conflict of interest resign?

Not necessarily. However, fiduciaries must be mindful that "outside pressure leading fiduciaries to consider anyone's interest other than that of the beneficiaries seriously undermines ERISA's core principles." *General American Life Ins. Co. v. Castonguay*, 984 F.2d 1518 (9th Cir. 1993). If a potential conflict of interest exists, a fiduciary must uphold its duty to act solely in the interests of the beneficiaries and for the exclusive purpose of providing them with benefits. Where the potential for conflicts is substantial, it may be difficult for a fiduciary to discharge his duties with an "eye single" to the interests of the beneficiaries, and the fiduciary may need to step aside, at least temporarily, from the management of assets where he faces potentially conflicting interests. *Leigh v. Engle*, 727 F.2d 113 (7th Cir. 1984).

Nevertheless, when a fiduciary has dual loyalties, the prudent person standard requires that he make a careful and impartial investigation of all investment decisions. *Schaefer v. Arkansas Medical Soc'y*, 853 F.2d 1487 (8th Cir. 1988), citing *Donovan v. Bierwirth*, 680 F.2d 263 (2nd Cir. 1982), cert. denied, 459 U.S. 1069 (1982). Where it might be possible to question the fiduciaries' loyalty, fiduciaries are obliged at a minimum to engage in an intensive and scrupulous independent investigation of their options to insure that they act in the best interests of the plan participants and beneficiaries. *Leigh v. Engle*, 727 F.2d 113 (7th Cir. 1984), citing *Donovan v. Bierwirth*, 680 F.2d 263 (2nd Cir. 1982), cert. denied, 459 U.S. 1069 (1982). In addition, courts may look closely at whether the fiduciaries investigated alternative actions and relied on outside advisors before implementing a challenged transaction. *Martin v. Feilen*, 965 F.2d 660 (8th Cir. 1992). See *Donovan v. Cunningham*, 716 F.2d 1467 (5th Cir. 1983); *Newton v. Van Otterloo*, 756 F. Supp. 1121 (N.D. Ind. 1991).

235. Is the payment of expenses by a plan subject to the exclusive purpose rule?

A payment that is not a distribution of benefits to participants or beneficiaries of a plan is not consistent with the requirements of ERISA unless it is used to defray a reasonable expense of administering the plan. ERISA Secs. 403(c)(1), 404(a)(1)(A). As a general rule, reasonable expenses of administering a plan include direct expenses properly and actually incurred in the performance of a fiduciary's duties to the plan. The determination of whether a particular expense is a reasonable administrative expense under ERISA Section 404(a)(1)(A) is the responsibility of the appropriate plan fiduciaries.

In making such a determination, a fiduciary must act prudently and solely in the interest of the plan participants and beneficiaries, and in accordance with the documents and instruments governing the plan insofar as they are consistent with the provisions of ERISA. In this regard, the fiduciary must assure that payment of the expenses by the plan is authorized by the plan and is in the interest of the plan participants and beneficiaries, as well as that the amount of the expense is reasonable. For example, the use of plan assets to pay fees and expenses incurred in connection with the provision of services would not be a reasonable expense of administering a plan if the payments are made for the employer's benefit or involve services for which an employer could reasonably be expected to bear the cost in the normal course of the employer's business or operations. DOL Opinion Letter to Kirk F. Maldonado (March 2, 1987).

236. Is the exclusive benefit rule violated if a plan pays expenses incurred in connection with business decisions, or "settlor" functions?

Yes. A plan may pay only those expenses incurred in connection with plan administration and fiduciary decision making, but may not pay expenses incurred in connection with business decisions, or "settlor" functions. These so-called "settlor" functions, which relate to the formation, rather than the management, of plans, include decisions relating to the establishment, design and termination of plans and generally are not fiduciary activities subject to Title I of ERISA. See Q 227; see also DOL Opinion Letter to John N. Erlenborn (March 13, 1986). Expenses incurred in connection with the performance of settlor functions are not reasonable plan expenses because they are incurred for the benefit of the employer and involve services for which an employer could reasonably be expected to bear the cost in the normal course of its business or operations. See DOL Opinion Letter to Kirk F. Maldonado (March 2, 1987).

237. Is the exclusive benefit rule violated if a plan pays expenses incurred in implementing the plan's termination?

Although the decision to terminate a plan is a settlor or business function, activities undertaken to implement the plan termination decision are generally fiduciary in nature. See DOL Adv. Op. 97-03A. Accordingly, reasonable expenses incurred in implementing a plan termination would generally be payable by the plan. These termination expenses include expenses incurred in auditing the plan, preparing and filing annual reports, preparing benefit statements and calculating accrued benefits, notifying participants and beneficiaries of their benefits under the plan, and, in certain circumstances, amending the plan to effectuate an orderly termination that benefits the participants and beneficiaries.

238. Is the exclusive benefit rule violated if an action intended to benefit the plan incidentally benefits the plan sponsor?

Not necessarily. Although a fiduciary has a duty under ERISA to act for the exclusive benefit of trust beneficiaries, "Congress did not intend ... [ERISA] to penalize employers for exercising their discretion to make rational economic decisions which are both in the best interests of the preservation of the fund and which are also not adverse to the employer's interests." *Holliday v. Xerox Corp.*, 732 F.2d 548 (6th Cir. 1984), cert. denied, 469 U.S. 917 (1984). Thus, the fact that a fiduciary's action incidentally benefits an employer does not necessarily mean that the fiduciary has breached his duty.

A transaction that incidentally benefits the plan sponsor or the fiduciaries does not violate the exclusive purpose requirements if: (a) after careful and impartial investigation, the fiduciaries reasonably conclude that the transaction is best to promote the interests of participants and beneficiaries, and (b) their decisions are made with an "eye single to the interests of the participants and beneficiaries." *Donovan v. Bierwirth*, 680 F.2d 263 (2nd Cir. 1982), cert. denied, 459 U.S. 1069 (1982).

For example, a plan sponsor did not violate the exclusive purpose requirement to participants in a merged pension plan by instituting a program designed to encourage early retirement through the payment of supplemental early retirement benefits from the plan, since any incidental economic benefit that the employer derived from the reductions in employees did not violate ERISA's exclusive benefit rule prohibiting plan assets from inuring to the employer's benefit. Thus, the exclusive benefit rule prohibits the use of plan assets for the primary benefit of an employer, but does not prohibit incidental benefits to an employer when the primary benefits go to participants. *In re Gulf Pension Litig.*, 764 F. Supp. 1149 (S.D. Tex. 1991). See also *United Steelworkers of America, Local 2116 v. Cyclops Corp.*, 860 F.2d 189 (6th Cir. 1988); *McDonald v. Pan Am. World Air., Inc.*, 859 F.2d 742 (9th Cir. 1988); *Morse v. Stanley*, 732 F.2d 1139 (2nd Cir. 1984).

239. What is the prudence requirement of ERISA Section 404?

ERISA requires that a fiduciary discharge his duties "with the care, skill, prudence, and diligence under the circumstances then prevailing that a prudent man acting in a like capacity and familiar with such matters would use in the conduct of an enterprise of like character and with like aims." ERISA Sec. 404(a)(1)(B). Known as the "prudent man" rule, this section defines the obligation of a trustee in investing the plan's assets. The prudent man standard, combined with the duty of loyalty imposes an unwavering duty on an ERISA trustee to make decisions with single-minded devotion to a plan's participants and beneficiaries and, in so doing, to act as a prudent person would act in a similar situation. These familiar principles evolved from the common law of trusts that Congress codified and made applicable to ERISA trustees. *Morse v. Stanley*, 732 F.2d 1139 (2nd Cir. 1984).

The case law gives meaning to the "prudence" standard and is replete with examples of imprudent behavior by plan fiduciaries. See, e.g., *Donovan v. Bierwirth*, 680 F.2d 263 (2nd Cir. 1982), cert. denied, 459 U.S. 1069 (1982); *Marshall v. Glass/Metal Ass'n*, 507 F. Supp. 378 (D. Haw. 1980); *Freund v. Marshall & Ilsley Bank*, 485 F. Supp. 629 (W.D. Wis. 1979). Courts have focused the inquiry under the "prudent man" rule on a review of the fiduciary's independent investigation of the merits of a particular investment.

For example, the Fifth Circuit Court of Appeals has ruled that the fiduciaries' decision to purchase stock for their plan in reliance upon a consultant's totally inaccurate appraisal of the stock's fair market value violated ERISA Section 404(a)(1)(B). The evidence showed that during the two years between the time of the appraisal and consummation of the transaction, the trustees failed to consider whether the facts and assumptions underlying the consultant's appraisal remained valid. See *Donovan v. Cunningham*, 716 F.2d 1455 (5th Cir. 1983).

Breaches of fiduciary duty constituting imprudent behavior are also recounted in *Katsaros v. Cody*, 744 F.2d 270 (2nd Cir. 1984). The trustees in *Katsaros* breached their fiduciary duty of prudence when they approved a $2 million loan to a bank which they knew was destined to fail based on its financial condition, performance and creditworthiness at the time of the transaction, as well as when they failed to collect the unreimbursed expenses incurred by the fund in connection with a second aborted loan. The trustees' handling of the $2 million loan was particularly imprudent, since they approved it without obtaining independent professional analysis of the bank's financial statements.

The records that should have been examined in *Katsaros* would have shown (1) that the bank had never earned enough money to service the debt and probably would not be able to do so in the future, (2) that the bank was undercapitalized, and (3) that the bank was deeply in debt. Moreover, several local banks, including the subject bank's principal creditor, had refused to extend credit to it, and some of the collateral that was to secure the loan had been seized for back taxes, while the remainder was worth one-third less than the stated value. The court found that the trustees who were involved in this transaction violated ERISA Section 404(a)(1)(B).

Patently imprudent behavior was also committed by plan trustees in *Donovan v. Mazzola*, 716 F.2d 1226 (9th Cir. 1983). The focus in *Mazzola*, as in *Katsaros*, was the prudence of a $1.5 million loan of pension fund assets to another fund secured by real estate. Of primary concern to the court was the trustees' retention and reliance upon the advice of a consultant whom they knew or should have known lacked the expertise to analyze the value of the collateral. The evidence showed that the consultant had never made a feasibility study of, or advised others about, property of the sort in question. He also failed to discuss the significance of his report with the trustees and did not submit an update when one was appropriate. An expert called by the DOL testified that the trustees' conduct prior to making the loan fell far short of industry standards because: (1) they failed to ascertain the value of the property deeded by the debtor as security for the loan; (2) they did not determine the extent to which the pension fund's interest in the collateral would be subordinate to other security interests; (3) they neglected to discover that the debtor had previously been unable to make regular payments on previous loans from the fund; and (4) they granted the loan at a rate below the prevailing interest rates for comparable mortgages at the time. See also, *Katsaros v. Cody*, 568 F. Supp. 360 (E.D. NY 1983).

In contrast, there was no imprudent behavior present where plan trustees charged participants who obtained mortgages from the plan more than two percentage points below the prevailing market rate. See *Brock v. Walton*, 609 F. Supp. 1221 (S.D. Fla. 1985), aff'd 794 F.2d 586 (11th Cir. 1986). In developing the loan program, the trustees consulted with lawyers, accountants, actuaries, and mortgage bankers over a 6-month period in 1979. The trustees examined loan rates charged by major commercial financial institutions in the area and determined that if they applied those rates they would have virtually no loan activity. The trustees also considered the rates of nontraditional mortgage loans in the area, such as owner financed loans. Each borrower's employment background was examined, and in addition to pledging their accrued pension benefits, borrowers whose equity was less than 20% were required to obtain mortgage insurance. The interest rates established were at a higher rate of return than any of the other assets in the fund's portfolio and were in excess of the fund's actuarial and funding requirements.

The loans accounted for about 10% of the portfolio. The court held that the term "reasonable rate of interest" is not synonymous with the term "prevailing or market rate of interest" and that a reasonable rate of interest may be below the prevailing market rate. See *Brock v. Walton*, above.

240. What is the standard for evaluating the prudence of a fiduciary's act?

Prudence is measured according to the objective "prudent person" standard developed in the common law of trusts. See *Donovan v. Mazzola*, 716 F.2d 1226 (9th Cir. 1983), cert. denied, 464 U.S. 1040 (1984); S. Rep. No. 93-127, 93rd Cong., 2nd Sess. The fiduciary responsibility section of ERISA, in essence, codifies and makes applicable to fiduciaries certain principles developed in the evolution of the law of trusts. "Consistent with these common law principles, the courts measure 'prudence' according to an objective standard, focusing on a fiduciary's conduct in arriving at an investment decision, not on its results, and asking whether a fiduciary employed the appropriate methods to investigate and determine the merits of a particular investment at the time they engaged in the challenged transactions." *Donovan v. Mazzola*, above. In addition, the prudence requirement is flexible, such that the adequacy of a fiduciary's independent investigation and ultimate investment selection is evaluated in light of the "character and aims" of the particular type of plan he serves. *Donovan v. Cunningham*, 716 F.2d 1455 (5th Cir. 1983), cert. denied, 467 U.S. 1251 (1984). Moreover, the fiduciary's subjective, good faith belief in an investment does not insulate him from the charges that he acted imprudently. *Donovan v. Bierwirth*, 538 F. Supp. 463 (E.D. NY 1981), aff'd, 680 F.2d 263 (2nd Cir. 1982), cert. denied sub nom., *Bierwirth v. Donovan*, 459 U.S. 1069 (1982).

Similarly, the Department of Labor regulations concerning the investment duties of ERISA fiduciaries provide that the requirements of ERISA Section 404(a)(1)(B) are satisfied if fiduciaries give "appropriate consideration to those facts and circumstances that, given the scope of such fiduciary's investment duties, the fiduciary knows or should know are relevant to the particular investment or investment course of action involved, including the role the investment plays in that portion of the plan's investment portfolio with respect to which the fiduciary has investment duties; and has acted accordingly." Labor Reg. §2550.404a-1(b)(1).

In reviewing a challenged transaction, the courts consider the prudence of a fiduciary's conduct at the time he engaged in the challenged transaction, rather than from the vantage point of hindsight. *American Comm. Ass'n, Local 10 v. Retirement Plan for Employees of RCA Corp.*, 488 F. Supp. 479 (S.D. NY 1980), aff'd, 646 F.2d 559 (2nd Cir. 1980).

241. What level of standard applies to ERISA fiduciaries under the prudent man rule?

The standard of prudence that applies to plan fiduciaries "is not that of a prudent lay person but rather that of a prudent fiduciary with experience dealing with a similar enterprise." *Marshall v. Snyder*, 430 F. Supp. 1224 (E.D. NY 1977); *Donovan v. Mazzola*, 716 F.2d 1226 (9th Cir. 1983), cert. denied, 464 U.S. 1040 (1984). Under the objective standard of the prudent person rule, fiduciaries are judged "according to the standards of others 'acting in a like capacity and familiar with such matters.'" *Marshall v. Glass/Metal Ass'n*, 507 F. Supp. 378 (DC Haw. 1980). These principles hold fiduciaries to a more exacting standard than the common law of trusts standards. *Donovan v. Mazzola*, 716 F.2d 1226 (9th Cir. 1983). The duties of an ERISA trustee are "the highest known to the law." *Donovan v. Bierwirth*, 680 F.2d 263 (2nd Cir. 1982), cert. denied, 459 U.S. 1069 (1982).

In the context of investing plan assets, the prudent person standard "requires that the fiduciary's behavior be measured as against the standards in the investment industry." *Lanka v. O'Higgins*, 810 F. Supp. 379 (N.D. NY 1992) citing

Jones v. O'Higgins, 736 F. Supp. 1243 (N.D. NY 1989). In contrast, the Fifth Circuit took exception to the premise that the reference in ERISA Section 404 to a prudent man "familiar with such matters" creates a "prudent expert" standard under ERISA. *Donovan v. Cunningham*, 716 F.2d 1455 (5th Cir. 1983). It was that court's view that the emphasis of ERISA Section 404 is on flexibility and that the level of knowledge required of a fiduciary will vary with the nature of the plan. The court agreed that the prudence requirement is flexible, such that the adequacy of a fiduciary's independent investigation and ultimate investment selection is evaluated in light of the "character and aims" of the particular type of plan he serves. See *Donovan v. Cunningham*, above; *In re Unisys Sav. Plan Litig.*, 74 F.3d 420 (3rd Cir. 1996), reh. denied 173 F.3d 145 (3rd Cir. 1999).

242. What is procedural prudence?

Procedural prudence, as distinguished from substantive prudence (see Q 243), is the conduct or process by which a fiduciary makes his decision. The focus of the inquiry is how the fiduciary acted in his selection of the investment; it considers the trustee's conduct and not the success or failure of the investment. *Donovan v. Cunningham*, 716 F.2d 1455 (5th Cir. 1983). In the context of investing the assets of a plan, procedural prudence requires that a fiduciary: (1) employ proper methods to investigate, evaluate, and structure the investment, (2) act in a manner as would others who have a capacity and familiarity with such matters, and (3) exercise independent judgment when making investment decisions. *Katsaros v. Cody*, 744 F.2d 270 (2nd Cir. 1984), cert. denied, 469 U.S. 1072 (1984).

243. What is substantive prudence?

In contrast to procedural prudence, which focuses on a fiduciary's conduct in arriving at an investment decision (see Q 242), substantive prudence concerns whether a fiduciary properly evaluated the merits of a particular investment. *Donovan v. Cunningham*, 716 F.2d 1455 (5th Cir. 1983); *Katsaros v. Cody*, 744 F.2d 270 (2nd Cir. 1984), cert. denied, 469 U.S. 1072 (1984).

244. What substantive factors must be considered by a fiduciary with respect to plan investments?

According to the Department of Labor, the prudence requirement is satisfied with respect to the investment duties of an fiduciary provided that the fiduciary "has given appropriate consideration to those facts and circumstances that, given the scope of such fiduciary's investment duties, the fiduciary knows or should know are relevant to the particular investment or investment course of action involved" and has acted accordingly. The substantive factors to which such consideration must be given include (but are not necessarily limited to):

1. A determination by the fiduciary that the particular investment or investment course of action is reasonably designed, as part of the portfolio, to further the purposes of the plan, taking into consid-

eration the risk of loss and the opportunity for gain associated with the investment or investment course of action; and

2. Consideration of the composition of the portfolio with regard to (a) diversification, (b) the liquidity and current return of the portfolio relative to the anticipated cash flow requirements of the plan; and (c) the projected return of the portfolio relative to the funding objectives of the plan (see Q 245 for further discussion). Labor Reg. §2550.404a-1(b).

In addition, the Department of Labor has advised that a prudent plan fiduciary "must consider, among other factors, the availability, riskiness, and potential return of alternative investments for his or her plan." Furthermore, it has indicated that investments will not be considered prudent if they provide a plan with less return, in comparison to risk, than comparable investments available to the plan, or if they involve a greater risk to the security of plan assets than other investments offering a similar return. DOL Adv. Op. 88-16A.

245. What are the general guidelines with respect to a fiduciary's investment duties?

Regulations under ERISA prescribe general guidelines with respect to an investment or investment course of action (i.e., any series or program of investments or actions related to a fiduciary's performance of his investment duties) taken by a fiduciary pursuant to his investment duties to a plan. In accordance with these regulations, the prudence requirements are satisfied if the fiduciary:

1. Has given appropriate consideration to those facts and circumstances that, given the scope of the fiduciary's investment duties, the fiduciary knows or should know are relevant to the particular investment or investment course of action involved, including the role the investment or investment course of action plays in that portion of the plan's investment portfolio with respect to which the fiduciary has investment duties; and

2. Has acted accordingly. Labor Reg. §2550.404a-1.

The regulation incorporates the views of the Department of Labor that generally, the relative riskiness of a specific investment or investment course of action does not render an investment or investment course of action either prudent or imprudent per se, and that the prudence of an investment decision should not be judged without regard to the role that the proposed investment or investment course of action plays within the overall plan portfolio. In addition, a fiduciary should not have to expend unreasonable efforts in discharging his duties, or to consider matters outside the scope of those duties. Thus, in accordance with the regulation, the scope of the fiduciary's inquiry is limited to those facts and circumstances that a prudent person having similar duties and familiar with such matters would consider relevant. See Labor Reg. §2550.404a-1.

246. What is "appropriate consideration"?

For purposes of the regulations under ERISA Section 404(a), "appropriate consideration" includes, but is not necessarily limited to, a determination by the fiduciary that the particular investment or investment course of action is reasonably designed, as part of the portfolio (or, where applicable, that portion of the plan portfolio with respect to which the fiduciary has investment duties), to further the purposes of the plan, taking into consideration the risk of loss and the opportunity for gain (or other return) associated with the investment or investment course of action, and consideration of the following factors as they relate to such portion of the portfolio:

1. The composition of the portfolio with regard to diversification ("diversification" is given its customary meaning as a mechanism for reducing the risk of large losses);

2. The liquidity and current return of the portfolio relative to the anticipated cash flow requirements of the plan (its principal subject matter is all anticipated cash requirements of the plan, and not solely those arising by reason of payment of benefits); and

3. The projected return of the portfolio relative to the funding objectives of the plan. Labor Reg. §2550.404a-1.

This includes giving appropriate consideration to the role that the investment or investment course of action plays (in terms of such factors as diversification, liquidity and risk/return characteristics) with respect to that portion of the plan's investment portfolio within the scope of the fiduciary's responsibility. Labor Reg. §2550.404a-1.

247. What is the meaning of the term "investment duties"?

The term "investment duties" refers to any duties imposed upon, or assumed or undertaken by, a person in connection with the investment of plan assets which make or will make the person a fiduciary, or which are performed by a fiduciary (as defined in ERISA Section 3(21)(A)(i) or ERISA Section 3(21)(A)(ii)).

248. Is there a "safe harbor" method of satisfying the prudence requirement?

Yes. In the view of the Department of Labor, the regulations at Section 2550.404a-1 act as a "safe harbor" provision, and fiduciaries who comply with its provisions (see Q 245) satisfy the requirements of the prudence rule. Although the "safe harbor" is a manner of satisfying the requirements of the prudence rule, it does not necessarily constitute the exclusive method for satisfying the requirements of the prudence rule, and does not impose any additional requirements or constraints upon plan fiduciaries. Labor Reg. §2550.404a-1.

249. What factors are included in an evaluation of an investment or investment course of action under the "safe harbor" provisions?

If a fiduciary desires to rely on the provisions of the "safe harbor," the fiduciary must consider the following factors, to the extent applicable, in its evaluation of an investment or investment course of action:

1. The composition of the portfolio with regard to diversification (as a mechanism for reducing the risk of large losses);

2. The liquidity and current return of the portfolio relative to the anticipated cash flow requirements of the plan (i.e., all anticipated cash requirements of the plan, and not solely those required for payment of benefits); and

3. The projected return of the portfolio relative to the funding objectives of the plan. Labor Reg. §2550.404a-1.

250. What investments are approved by the Department of Labor?

None. The Department of Labor does not consider it appropriate to develop any list of investments, classes of investment, or investment techniques that might be permissible under the "prudence" rule. In the Department's view, no such list could be complete; moreover, the Department does not intend to create or suggest a "legal list" of investments for plan fiduciaries.

251. Are high risk investments inherently imprudent?

Not necessarily. The risk level of an investment does not alone make the investment prudent or imprudent per se. Thus, an investment is not deemed imprudent merely because the investment, in isolation, is characterized by a relatively high degree of risk. However, a fiduciary must consider the risk characteristics of an investment in determining its suitability for the plan. Labor Reg. §2550.404a-1.

252. Are fiduciaries required to invest in expensive systems or analysis to make investment decisions?

Not necessarily. The prudence standard establishes a standard of conduct measured by how a prudent fiduciary with experience dealing in a similar capacity and familiar with administration of employee benefit plans would act. Under the "prudence" rule, the standard to which a fiduciary is held is defined, in part, by what a prudent person acting in a like capacity and familiar with such matters would do. Thus, for example, it would not seem necessary for a fiduciary of a plan with assets of $50,000 to employ, in all respects, the same investment management techniques as would a fiduciary of a plan with assets of $50,000,000. Labor Reg. §2550.404a-1.

253. Is a fiduciary "immunized" from liability once it has considered relevant facts and circumstances in the selection of an investment?

No. According to the Department of Labor, a trustee's ERISA responsibilities do not terminate solely because the fiduciary has given consideration to relevant facts and circumstances with regard to the initial decision to invest plan assets. Labor Reg. §2550.404a-1. Likewise, courts have agreed that upon the conclusion of a preliminary investigation and purchase of an investment, a fiduciary has a duty to monitor the performance of an investment with reasonable diligence and to withdraw an investment if it becomes clear that the investment is unsuitable for the plan. See *Whitfield v. Cohen*, 682 F. Supp. 188 (S.D. NY 1988), citing *Public Service Co. of Colo. v. Chase Manhattan Bank*, 577 F. Supp. 92 (S.D. NY 1983). "ERISA fiduciaries must monitor investments with reasonable diligence and dispose of investments which are improper to keep." *Hunt v. Magnell*, 758 F. Supp. 1292 (DC Minn. 1991). Thus, in accordance with the "prudent man" rule, a fiduciary has a duty to continually monitor the performance of an investment and dispose of any investment in the event it becomes undesirable for the plan.

254. Is a fiduciary liable for losses to a plan for failing to investigate and evaluate a proposed investment?

Not necessarily. A fiduciary's failure to investigate and evaluate an investment decision alone is not sufficient to make him liable for losses to a plan. Instead, efforts to hold the fiduciary liable for a loss attributable to inadequate investment decision must demonstrate a causal link between the failure to investigate and evaluate and the harm suffered by the plan. *Kuper v. Iovenko*, 66 F.3d 1447 (6th Cir. 1995).

The cases that hold a trustee liable for losses for failing to investigate and evaluate the merits of an investment have based the trustee's liability on findings of fact that clearly established the unsoundness of the investment decision at the time it was made. If a court determines that a trustee failed to investigate a particular investment adequately, it will examine whether, considering the facts that an adequate and thorough investigation would have revealed, the investment was objectively imprudent. *Fink v. National Sav. & Tr. Co.*, 772 F.2d 951 (DC D.C. 1985) (Scalia, J., concurring in part and dissenting in part).

"[T]he determination of an objectively prudent investment is made on the basis of what the trustee knew or should have known; and the latter necessarily involves consideration of what facts would have come to his attention if he had fully complied with his duty to investigate and evaluate." It is the imprudent investment rather than the failure to investigate and evaluate that is the basis of liability. A failure to investigate and evaluate the potential investment is merely evidence demonstrating that the trustee should have known more than he knew in selecting the imprudent investment. *Fink v. National Sav. & Tr. Co.*, above. Thus, a fiduciary may be held liable for losses to the plan for failure to perform his fiduciary obligations to investigate and evaluate a proposed investment of plan assets if the investment decision was objectively imprudent.

255. Is the prudent person rule subject to the business judgment rules?

No. It is not a business judgment rule that applies to the question of prudence in the management of an ERISA plan, but rather a prudent person standard. *Lanka v. O'Higgins*, 810 F. Supp. 379 (N.D. NY 1992), citing *Donovan v. Mazzola*, 716 F.2d 1226 (9th Cir. 1983) (which expressly rejected the business judgment rule).

256. Is a fiduciary an insurer of plan investments?

No. "[T]he prudence rule does not make the fiduciary an insurer of the plan's assets or of the success of its investments. ERISA does not require that a pension fund take no risk with its investments. Virtually every investment entails some degree of risk, and even the most carefully evaluated investments can fail while unpromising investments may succeed." *Donovan v. Mazzola*, 716 F.2d 1226 (9th Cir. 1983), cert. denied sub nom. *Mazzola v. Donovan*, 464 U.S. 1040 (1984). "The application of ERISA's prudence standard does not depend upon the ultimate outcome of an investment, but upon the prudence of the fiduciaries under the circumstances prevailing when they make their decision and in light of the alternatives available to them." *Marshall v. Glass/Metal Ass'n*, 507 F. Supp. 378 (DC Haw. 1980), aff'd, 895 F.2d 729 (11th Cir. 1990). The fiduciary duty of care requires prudence, not prescience. *Debruyne v. The Equitable Life Assurance Soc'y of the United States*, 720 F. Supp. 1342 (N.D. Ill. 1989).

In addition, the mere fact that a plan's investment portfolio declines in value or suffers a diminution of income does not by itself establish imprudence. Market values are untrustworthy indicia of value especially in times of economic decline. *American Comm. Ass'n, Local 10 v. Retirement Plan for Employees of RCA Corp.*, 488 F. Supp. 479 (S.D. NY 1980), aff'd, 646 F.2d 559 (2nd Cir. 1980). In that respect, whether a trustee is liable for losses to the plan depends upon the circumstances at the time when the investment is selected and not upon subsequent events. Thus, if at the time an investment is made, it is an investment a prudent person would make, there is no liability if the investment later depreciates in value absent a failure to monitor its performance.

257. Can a successor fiduciary be liable for the investment acts of its predecessor?

Yes. If the selection of plan investments by a predecessor fiduciary constitutes a breach of duty or a prohibited transaction, a successor fiduciary has a duty to dispose of these investments upon assuming his responsibilities as fiduciary. See *Morrissey v. Curran*, 567 F.2d 546 (2nd Cir. 1977). See also *McDougall v. Donovan*, 552 F. Supp. 1206 (N.D. Ill. 1983) (successor trustee has duty to dispose of prior improper investment upon becoming trustee); *Buccino v. Continental Assur. Co.*, 578 F. Supp.

1518 (S.D. NY 1983). A fiduciary has a continuing duty to advise the plan to divest of unlawful or imprudent investments and its failure to do so gives rise to a new cause of action each time the fund was injured. *PBGC v. Greene*, 570 F. Supp. 1483 (W.D. Pa. 1982), aff'd, 727 F.2d 1100 (3rd Cir. 1984).

258. Is a fiduciary's subjective good faith a defense to a breach of fiduciary duty?

No. The fact that a fiduciary may have acted in good faith is not a defense to a breach of fiduciary duties, because the sincerity of a fiduciary's belief that his actions are in the best interests of the plan are essentially irrelevant to a determination of the prudence of the fiduciary's conduct. *Donovan v. Daugherty*, 550 F. Supp. 390 (S.D. Ala. 1982); *Marshall v. Glass/Metal Ass'n*, 507 F. Supp. 378 (DC Haw. 1980). Thus, good faith alone is not recognized as a defense to a breach of fiduciary duties. *Reich v. King*, 867 F. Supp. 341 (DC Md. 1994) ("a fiduciary's subjective good faith belief of his prudence will not insulate him from liability"); see also *Lanka v. O'Higgins*, 810 F. Supp. 379 (N.D. NY 1992). See also *Donovan v. Bierwirth*, 538 F. Supp. 463 (E.D. NY 1981), aff'd as modified, 680 F.2d 263 (2nd Cir. 1982), cert. denied, 459 U.S. 1069 (1982).

259. Does the prudence requirement obligate a fiduciary to seek the assistance of an expert?

It depends. Although ERISA does not require a fiduciary to seek professional assistance in making plan investments, where a trustee does not possess the education, experience and skill required to make a decision concerning the investment of a plan's assets, he has an affirmative duty to seek independent counsel in making the decision. The failure to do so is imprudent and constitutes a violation of ERISA Section 404(a)(1)(B). *Donovan v. Bierwirth*, 538 F. Supp. 463 (E.D. NY 1981), aff'd as modified, 680 F.2d 263 (2nd Cir. 1982), cert. denied, 459 U.S. 1069 (1982).

The reasoning behind this requirement is that the investment selection process is an indication of the care and diligence of the trustee in arriving at an investment decision. Thus, while there is flexibility in the prudence standard, it is not a refuge for fiduciaries who are not equipped to evaluate a complex investment. If fiduciaries commit a pension plan's assets to investments which they do not fully understand, they will nonetheless be judged, as provided in the statute, according to the standards of others "acting in a like capacity and familiar with such matters." Consequently, a trustee's lack of familiarity with investments is no excuse to evaluating its prudence. *Marshall v. Glass/Metal Ass'n*, 507 F. Supp. 378 (DC Haw. 1980).

260. Can a fiduciary avoid liability by relying on the professional advice of others?

While a trustee has a duty to seek independent advice where he lacks the requisite education, experience and skill, the trustee, nevertheless, must make his own decision based on that advice. *Donovan v. Bierwirth*, 680 F.2d 263 (2nd Cir. 1982), cert. denied, 459 U.S. 1069 (1982); *Donovan v. Mazzola*, 716 F.2d 1226 (9th Cir. 1983). The conduct of a trustee in making an independent investigation is an indication of the care and diligence of the trustee in arriving at an investment decision. A trustee unfamiliar with an unusual or difficult investment decision is charged with making an "independent inquiry into the merits of particular investments rather than [relying] wholly upon the advice of others." *Withers v. Teachers' Retirement System*, 447 F. Supp. 1248 (S.D. NY 1978), aff'd mem., 595 F.2d 1210 (2nd Cir. 1979).

Although fiduciaries are not expected by the courts to duplicate their advisors' investigative efforts, fiduciaries are required to "review the data a consultant gathers, to assess its significance and to supplement it where necessary." *In re Unisys Sav. Plan Litig.*, 74 F.3d 420 (3rd Cir. 1996), *aff'd*, 173 F.3d 145 (3rd Cir. 1999). In addition, "[a]n independent appraisal is not a magic wand that fiduciaries may simply wave over a transaction to ensure that their responsibilities are fulfilled. It is a tool and like all tools, is useful only if used properly." However, as the source of the information upon which the experts' opinions are based, the fiduciaries are responsible for ensuring that the information is complete and up-to-date. *Donovan v. Cunningham*, 716 F.2d 1455 (5th Cir. 1983). Moreover, the thoroughness of a fiduciary's investigation is measured not only by the actions it took in performing it, but by the facts that an adequate evaluation would have uncovered. *In re Unisys Sav. Plan Litig.*, 74 F.3d 420 (3rd Cir. 1996), reh. denied, 173 F.3d 145 (3rd Cir. 1999), citing *Fink v. National Sav. & Tr. Co.*, 772 F.2d 951 (D.C. Cir. 1985) (Scalia, J., concurring in part and dissenting in part).

261. Do plan losses create a presumption of a breach of duty?

No. The test of prudence under the prudent man rule is one of conduct, and not a test of the result of performance of the investment. The focus of the inquiry is how the fiduciary acted in his selection of the investment, not whether his investments succeeded or failed. *Donovan v. Cunningham*, 716 F.2d 1455 (5th Cir. 1983).

262. What factors should be considered in the prudent selection of a person or entity to invest plan assets?

According to one court, there are "certain elements necessary to a prudent selection of a person or entity to invest ERISA plan assets." *Whitfield v. Cohen*, 682 F. Supp. 188 (S.D. NY 1988). Such considerations would require a prudent trustee to:

1. Evaluate the person's qualifications, including: (a) his experience in the particular area of investments under consideration and with other ERISA plans; (b) his educational credentials; (c) whether he is registered with the Securities and Exchange Commission under the Investment Advisors Act of 1940; (d) an independent assess-

ment of his qualifications by means of: (i) a widely enjoyed reputation in the business of investments; (ii) client references; and/or (iii) the advice of a professional third-party consultant; *and* (e) his record of past performance with investments of the type contemplated;

2. Ascertain the reasonableness of fees;

3. Review documents reflecting the relationship to be entered into; *and*

4. Ensure adequate, periodic accountings in the future. *Whitfield v. Cohen*, above.

263. May a fiduciary consider the collateral effects of an investment opportunity?

According to the Department of Labor, the requirements of ERISA Sections 403 and 404 do not exclude the consideration of collateral benefits in a fiduciary's evaluation of a particular investment opportunity. The DOL has stated that arrangements designed to bring areas of investment opportunity that provide collateral benefits to the attention of plan fiduciaries will not, in and of themselves, violate ERISA Section 403 or ERISA Section 404, provided that the arrangements do not restrict the exercise of the fiduciary's investment discretion. Labor Reg. §2509.94-1 (IB 94-1), 59 Fed. Reg. 32606 (June 23, 1994).

For example, in Advisory Opinion 88-16A, the DOL considered an arrangement whereby a company and union proposed to make recommendations, for up to 5% of the annual contributions, of investments with the potential for providing collateral benefits to union members. The DOL concluded that the arrangement would not be inconsistent with the requirements of ERISA Section 403(c) and ERISA section 404(a)(1), where the investment managers having responsibility with respect to these recommendations retained exclusive investment discretion and were required to secure, over the long term, the maximum attainable total return on investments in a manner consistent with the principles of sound pension fund management. Moreover, the DOL stated that in considering such investments, plan fiduciaries could be influenced by factors that were not related to the plan's expected investment return, only if such investments were equal or superior to alternative available investments. DOL Adv. Op. 88-16A.

Similarly, in a case involving construction project financing, the DOL also concluded that participation in an organization which presents investment opportunities but does not limit the investment alternatives available to the plans, and does not obligate the plans to invest in any project presented for consideration, did not, in itself, violate any of ERISA's fiduciary standards. Moreover, the DOL concluded that in enforcing the plan's rights after making an investment, the fiduciary could consider factors unrelated to the plan's investment return only if, in the fiduciary's judgment, the course of action taken would be at least as economically advantageous to the plan as any alternative course of action. DOL Opinion Letter to George Cox (January 16, 1981).

In other letters, the DOL has stated that the existence of such collateral benefits may be decisive in evaluating an investment only if the fiduciary determines that the investment containing the collateral benefits is expected to provide an investment return to the plan commensurate to alternative investments having similar risks. DOL Opinion Letters to Mr. Theodore Groom (January 16, 1981); Mr. Daniel O'Sullivan (August 2, 1982); Mr. James Ray (July 8, 1988), and Mr. Stuart Cohen (May 14, 1993).

Although the DOL has stated that a plan fiduciary may consider collateral benefits in choosing between investments that have comparable risks and rates of return, it has also consistently stated that fiduciaries who are willing to accept expected reduced returns or greater risks to secure collateral benefits are in violation of ERISA. Thus, while every investment may cause a plan to forgo other investment opportunities, an investment is not imprudent merely because it provides a plan with a lower expected rate of return than available alternative investments with commensurate degrees of risk, nor because it is riskier than alternative available investments with commensurate rates of return. See, DOL Opinion Letters to the Trustees of the Twin City Carpenters and Joiners Pension Plan (May 19, 1981); Mr. William Ecklund (December 18, 1985 and January 16, 1986); Mr. Reed Larson (July 14, 1986); and the Honorable Jack Kemp (November 23, 1990).

264. What are the fiduciary issues regarding economically targeted investments?

In the view of the Department of Labor, the fiduciary standards applicable to ETIs are no different than the standards applicable to plan investments generally. Therefore, the selection of an ETI, or the process of engaging in an investment course of action intended to result in the selection of ETIs for the collateral benefits derived from the investment, will not violate the loyalty and prudence standards or the exclusive purpose requirements of ERISA Section 404, provided the ETI has an expected rate of return that is commensurate with rates of return on alternative investments with similar risk characteristics that are available to the plan, and if the ETI is otherwise an appropriate investment for the plan in the context of such factors as diversification and the investment policy of the plan. However, an investment in ETIs is imprudent if it provides a plan with a lower expected rate of return than available alternative investments with commensurate degrees of risk or if it is riskier than alternative available investments with commensurate rates of return. Labor Reg. §2509.94-1 (IB 94-1), 59 Fed. Reg. 32606 (June 23, 1994). See Q 520 for an explanation of the asset management issues regarding economic targeted investments.

The DOL, in an Advisory Opinion letter states that the fiduciary investment standards of ERISA do not preclude the consideration of "collateral benefits," such as those offered under socially responsible investments, in a fiduciary's evaluation of a particular investment opportunity. However, such collateral benefits may be the deciding factor only if the fiduciary determines that the investment offering and collateral benefit is expected to provide an investment return commensurate with other investments having the same level of risk. DOL Advisory Opinion 98-04A.

265. May a fiduciary engage in shareholder activism with the intent to monitor or influence the management of corporations in which the plan owns stock?

Yes, in certain circumstances. In the view of the Department of Labor, it is consistent with a fiduciary's obligations in certain situations to engage in an investment policy that contemplates activities intended to monitor or influence the management of corporations (shareholder activism—see Q 266) in which the plan owns stock, provided that the fiduciary concludes that there is a reasonable expectation that such monitoring or communication with management, by the plan alone or together with other shareholders, is likely to enhance the value of a plan's investment in the corporation, after taking into account the costs involved. A reasonable expectation may be present in various circumstances, for example, where a plan invests in corporate stock as a long-term investment or where a plan investment is illiquid. Labor Reg. §2509.94-2(3) (IB 94-2), 59 Fed. Reg. 38860 (July 29, 1994).

266. What types of issues are involved in "shareholder activism"?

Shareholder activism can involve a variety of issues, including examining the independence and expertise of candidates for the corporation's board of directors and assuring that the board has sufficient information to carry out its responsibility to monitor management. Other issues may include such matters as consideration of the appropriateness of executive compensation, the corporation's policy regarding mergers and acquisitions, the extent of debt financing and capitalization, the nature of long-term business plans, the corporation's investment in training to develop its work force, other workplace practices and financial and non-financial measures of corporate performance. Active monitoring and communication may be carried out through a variety of methods including by means of correspondence and meetings with corporate management as well as by exercising the legal rights of a shareholder. Labor Reg. §2509.94-2(3) (IB 94-2), 59 Fed. Reg. 38860 (7-29-94).

267. May trustees be relieved from liability for the acts or omissions of an investment manager?

If an investment manager has been appointed, no trustee will be liable for the acts or omissions of such investment manager, nor will any trustee be under an obligation to invest or otherwise manage any asset of the plan that is subject to the management of the investment manager. ERISA Sec. 405(d).

However, this relief does not totally excuse from liability the named fiduciary who appointed the investment manager. If the named fiduciary violated Section 404(a)(1) (see Q 224) with respect to the allocation or designation, with respect to the establishment or implementation of procedures for allocating fiduciary duties, or in continuing the allocation or designation, then the named fiduciary will be liable for an act or omission of an appointed person. ERISA Sec. 405(c)(2)(A).

The limited relief from liability for the named fiduciary who has appointed the investment manager is also expressed in the legislative history of ERISA Section 405 as follows: "in choosing an investment manager, the named fiduciary must act prudently and in the interest of participants and beneficiaries, and also must act in this manner in continuing the use of the investment manager ... as long as the named fiduciary had chosen and retained the investment manager prudentially, the named fiduciary would not be liable for the acts or omissions of the investment manager." H.R. Conf. Rep. No. 93-1280, 93rd Cong., 2nd Sess., 301-302 (1974) (ERISA Conference Report).

Named fiduciaries and plan trustees may not avoid fiduciary liability by appointing an investment manager and delegating investment authority to him. Instead, plan fiduciaries and trustees retain oversight responsibility and have a duty to keep themselves apprised of plan investments to assure that they are prudent and legal. *Reich v. Hosking*, No. 94-CV-10363-BC, 20 EBC 1090 (E.D. Mich. 1996).

268. What are the duties and responsibilities of an investment manager?

The term "investment manager" means any fiduciary (other than a trustee or named fiduciary) who:

1. Has the power to manage, acquire, or dispose of any asset of a plan, and has acknowledged in writing that he is a fiduciary to the subject plan;

2. Is either (a) registered as an investment advisor under the Investment Advisors Act of 1940 (the 1940 Act), (b) a bank (as defined under the 1940 Act), or (c) an insurance company qualified to perform investment management services under the laws of more than one state; and

3. Has acknowledged in writing that he is a fiduciary with respect to the plan. ERISA Sec. 3(38).

The investment manager's duties and responsibilities, in addition to those discussed above (and in Q 504), are the same as those general provisions applicable to all fiduciaries under ERISA Sections 404 and 406. These obligations include the duty to diversify and follow the language of the plan.

The Court of Appeals for the Eleventh Circuit ruled that an investment manager had breached his fiduciary duties to a plan where he failed to investigate the cash flow needs of the plan and to adequately diversify the fund, which resulted in losses to the plan. See *GIW Indus., Inc. v. Trevor, Stewart, Burton & Jacobsen, Inc.*, 895 F.2d 729 (11th Cir. 1990). The Court of Appeals for the Second Circuit held that an investment firm was liable, and its owner was personally liable, for a breach of fiduciary duty due to the failure of the investment manager to follow the written agreement governing the investment management arrangement between the plan and the investment manager. See *Dardaganis v. Grace Capital, Inc.*, 889 F.2d 1237 (2nd Cir. 1989). The fact that the plan trustees in *Dardaganis* were aware of the investment manager's failure to follow the governing documents for more than 14 months, yet took no steps to correct the failure, did not relieve the investment manager from liability for the losses incurred as a result of his failure to follow the investment management agreement. In another case, the same court of appeals held that an investment manager was liable for losses incurred as a result of entering into a prohibited transaction with a plan, even though the plan trustees directed the investment manager to make the investments at issue. See *Lowen v. Tower Asset Mgmt., Inc.*, 829 F.2d 1209 (2nd Cir. 1987).

Investment managers, as fiduciaries, may receive reasonable compensation and reimbursement of expenses for services rendered to the plan. ERISA Sec. 408(c)(2).

PRACTITIONER'S POINTER

Most investment managers are compensated with a specified percentage of the assets they have under management, in accordance with an agreed-upon fee schedule. However, there has been a growing trend toward "performance based fees." Plan fiduciaries need to be cautious when entering into such performance based fee schedules because the Department of Labor has stated that where the fiduciary may use his authority, control or responsibility to cause the plan to pay additional fees, such a performance based fee agreement is a prohibited transaction. See DOL Adv. Op. 89-31A. Payment of performance based fees will not be a prohibited transaction where the fees depend solely upon the fluctuation of value of the plan's securities.

269. Are investment managers of pooled accounts required to comply with multiple investment policies?

Yes. It is the DOL's view that investment managers of pooled investment accounts holding the assets of more than one employee benefit plan under the direction of multiple investment policies, must to the extent possible, comply with each policy (assuming compliance with each policy would be consistent with ERISA Section 404(a)(1)(D)).

For example, an investment manager may be subject to a proxy voting policy from one plan that conflicts with the policy from another plan. If investment policies conflict, it may be necessary to vote proxies to reflect each policy in proportion to the respective plan's interest in the pooled account, unless in the particular situation voting in such a manner would be imprudent or otherwise inconsistent with applicable law. Nothing in ERISA, however, prevents such an investment manager from maintaining a single investment policy and requiring all participating investors to subject their assets to the policy as a condition of investing in the pooled account. As with policies originated by named fiduciaries, a statement of investment policy issued by an investment manager and adopted by the participating plans is regarded as an instrument governing the participating plans, and compliance with the policy is governed by Section 404(a)(1)(D). Labor Reg. §2509.94-2 (IB 94-2), 59 Fed. Reg. 38860 (7-29-94).

270. Does the prudence requirement extend to the resignation of a trustee?

Yes. The courts have held that a trustee's duty of prudence extends to his resignation, and that his resignation is valid only when he has made adequate provision for the continued prudent management of plan affairs. *Freund v. Marshall & Ilsley Bank*, 485 F. Supp. 629 (W.D. Wis. 1979). This resignation requirement is a component of the prudence standard imposed by ERISA Section 404(a)(1)(B). *PBGC v. Greene*, 570 F. Supp. 1483 (W.D. Pa. 1983) aff'd, 727 F.2d 1100 (3rd Cir. 1984), cert. denied, 469 U.S. 820 (1984); *Chambers v. Kaleidoscope, Inc., Profit Sharing Plan & Tr.*, 650 F. Supp. 359 (N.D. Ga. 1986); *Glaziers & Glassworkers Union Local 252 Annuity Fund v. Newbridge Sec., Inc.*, 93 F.3d 1171 (3rd Cir. 1996). See also *Ream v. Frey*, 107 F.3d 147 (3rd Cir. 1997) (bank that resigned as trustee of plan failed to provide a suitable and trustworthy successor, or advise the participants in advance of its termination and of the reasons for its termination).

271. May ERISA covered plans invest in derivatives?

Yes, but fiduciaries should exercise extreme caution and due diligence in considering derivatives as investment options for plan assets. A derivative investment is a security which that its value at any given time, in whole or in part, from the value of one or more underlying assets at the same point in time. Examples of derivatives include futures, options, collateralized mortgage obligations and forward contracts. See Q 528 for an explanation of asset management issues regarding derivative investments.

In a 1996 information letter, the Department of Labor advised fiduciaries of its concern with plan assets being invested in derivatives, due to the extreme price volatility, high degree of leverage and limited testing by markets associated with derivatives. In other words, the DOL expressed concern that the market value of derivatives is hard to establish due to the illiquid market conditions in which they exist. In considering the appropriateness of investments in derivatives, the DOL advised that fiduciaries must consider how they fit within a plan's investment policy, the plan's exposure to loss, and the role such derivatives would play in the plan's investment portfolio. DOL Information Letter to the Comptroller of the Currency (March 21, 1996).

Fiduciaries should carefully evaluate all information available on a potential derivative investment prior to making the investment. Review should be made of the credit risk and market risk, projected performance and the legal risk involved with the derivative being considered. Once an investment has been made in a derivative security, fiduciaries are required to exercise prudence in the monitoring of it to make certain that it is performing its expected function in regard to the plan's portfolio.

272. May fiduciaries purchase annuities for the purpose of distributing pension plan benefits?

Yes. It is appropriate for fiduciaries to purchase annuities for the purpose of transferring the plan's benefits liabilities to an annuity provider (i.e., the insurance company). These annuities are referred to as benefit distribution annuities. Benefit distribution annuity contracts are purchased for participants and beneficiaries under a variety of circumstances, such as in connection with the termination of a plan or, in the case of an ongoing plan, for participants who are retiring or separating from service with accrued vested benefits.

273. Is the purchase of distribution annuities subject to the fiduciary standards of ERISA?

Yes. The selection of an annuity provider for purposes of a pension benefit distribution, whether upon separation from service, retirement of a participant, or termination of a plan, is a fiduciary decision governed by ERISA. Thus, in choosing an annuity provider for the purpose of making a benefit distribution, fiduciaries must act solely in the interest of participants and beneficiaries and for the exclusive purpose of providing benefits to the participants and beneficiaries as well as defraying reasonable expenses of administering the plan. In addition, the fiduciary obligation of prudence requires that a fiduciary conduct an objective, thorough and analytical search in identifying and selecting the annuity providers, and must evaluate a potential annuity provider's claims paying ability and creditworthiness (see Q 274). Labor Reg. §2509.95-1(c).

274. What factors should be considered in the selection of an annuity provider?

The types of factors a fiduciary should consider include, among other things:

1. The quality and diversification of the annuity provider's investment portfolio;

2. The size of the insurer relative to the proposed contract;

3. The level of the insurer's capital and surplus;

4. The lines of business of the annuity provider and other indications of an insurer's exposure to liability;

5. The structure of the annuity contract and guarantees supporting the annuities, such as the use of separate accounts; and

6. The availability of additional protection through state guaranty associations and the extent of their guarantees.

Fiduciaries who do not possess the expertise necessary to evaluate the preceding factors should obtain the advice of a qualified, independent expert. In addition, a fiduciary must not rely solely on ratings provided by insurance rating services to identify the safest annuity. A fiduciary may conclude, after conducting an appropriate search, that more than one annuity provider is able to offer the safest annuity available. Labor Reg. §2509.95-1(c).

275. Must the safest annuity be purchased?

Yes, in the view of the DOL. The DOL believes that a fiduciary must obtain the safest annuity available, unless under the circumstances, it would be in the interests of participants and beneficiaries to do otherwise. Such a result may occur if the safest available annuity is only marginally safer, but disproportionately more expensive than competing annuities, and the participants and beneficiaries are likely to bear a significant portion of that increased cost. Other examples include:

1. It may be in the interest of the participants to choose a competing annuity where the participants in a terminating pension plan are likely to receive, in the form of increased benefits, a substantial share of the cost savings that would result from choosing the competing annuity; and

2. It may also be in the interest of the participants and beneficiaries to choose a competing annuity if the safest available annuity provider is unable to demonstrate the ability to administer the payment of benefits to the participants and beneficiaries.

However, the DOL believes that the increased cost or other considerations may not justify risking the benefits of annuitized participants and beneficiaries by purchasing an unsafe annuity. Labor Reg. §2509.95-1. In contrast, the Court of Appeals for the Fourth Circuit has rejected the proposition that fiduciaries must purchase the safest annuity available. *Riley v. Murdock*, 83 F.3d 415 (4th Cir. 1996). Similarly, the Fifth Circuit has stated that the DOL Interpretive Bulletin mandating purchase of "safest annuity available" exceeds the statutory mandate; however, it is a useful guide regarding the fiduciary process. *Bussian v. RJR Nabisco*, 25 EBC 1120 (5th Cir. 2000).

276. May a fiduciary consider the reversion of excess assets to the plan sponsor in selecting an annuity provider?

No. In the view of the DOL, a fiduciary may not purchase more risky, lower-priced annuities in order to ensure or maximize a reversion of excess assets that will be paid solely to the employer-sponsor in connection with the termination of an overfunded pension plan. Such a decision will violate the fiduciary's duties to act solely in the interest of the plan participants and beneficiaries, and will interfere with the fiduciary's ability to obtain the safest annuity available with no countervailing interests. Thus, a fiduciary in such circumstances must make diligent efforts to assure that the safest available annuity is purchased. Labor Reg. §2509.95-1.

277. May fiduciaries be relieved of liability by purchasing annuities for the distribution of plan assets to terminated participants or in connection with the termination of a plan?

In certain instances. The general rule is that liability for benefits promised under a plan is transferred from the plan where the provision of benefits has been arranged for through the purchase of an annuity contract. Once the contract is issued, the participants covered under it cease to be plan participants, and the liability for the provision of benefits is transferred to the insurance company issuing the annuity contracts if:

1. The contract has received transfer of the entire rights and benefits of the participant or beneficiary;

2. The benefits are guaranteed by the insurance company; and

3. The rights of the participants and beneficiaries are enforceable at law by the sole choice of the participant or beneficiary. Labor Reg. §2510.33(d)(2)(ii); PBGC Adv. Op. 91-1; PBGC Adv. Op. 85-9.

However, in the event that the purchase of an insurance contract or insurance annuity in connection with termination of an individual's status as a participant constitutes a violation of ERISA fiduciary obligations or the terms of the plan, the terminated participant or beneficiary has standing to seek relief. ERISA Sec. 502(a)(9). As such, these former participants and beneficiaries may sue the plan fiduciaries for any breaches that they may have committed in the termination of a pension plan, or in the purchase of annuity contracts.

278. Who is responsible for the voting of proxies?

The responsibility for voting proxies lies exclusively with the plan trustee except to the extent that either:

1. The trustee is subject to the directions of a named fiduciary, pursuant to ERISA Section 403(a)(1); or

2. The power to manage, acquire or dispose of the relevant assets has been delegated by a named fiduciary to one or more investment managers, pursuant to ERISA Section 403(a)(2).

If the authority to manage plan assets is delegated to an investment manager, only the investment manager has the authority to vote the proxies unless the named fiduciary has reserved to itself (or to another named fiduciary so authorized by the plan document) the right to direct a plan trustee regarding the voting of proxies. The investment manager also has the exclusive responsibility for voting proxies if the plan document or investment management agreement does not expressly preclude the investment manager from voting proxies. Labor Reg. §2509.94-2(1).

279. May a named fiduciary reserve the right to direct the voting of proxies?

Yes. A named fiduciary that delegates investment management authority to an investment manager may reserve to itself the right to direct a trustee with respect to the voting of all proxies or reserve to itself the right to direct a trustee as to the voting of only those proxies relating to specified assets or issues. In addition, a named fiduciary may also reserve to another named fiduciary the right to direct the trustee regarding proxy voting, provided that the plan document provides for procedures for allocating fiduciary responsibilities among named fiduciaries. Labor Reg. §2509.94-2(1).

280. Do the fiduciary standards apply to the voting of proxies?

Yes. The fiduciary duties of loyalty and prudence apply to the voting of proxies and require that the responsible fiduciary consider any factors that may affect the value of the plan's investment, and not subordinate the interests of the participants and beneficiaries in their retirement income to unrelated objectives. These duties also require the responsible fiduciary to vote proxies on issues that may affect the value of the plan's investment. In addition, a named fiduciary that appoints an investment manager must periodically monitor the activities of the investment manager with respect to the management of plan assets, including the investment manager's decisions and actions with respect to the voting of proxies. This responsibility must be carried out by the named fiduciary solely in the interest of the participants and beneficiaries and without regard to its relationship to the plan sponsor. Labor Reg. §2509.94-2(1).

281. How does a named fiduciary monitor an investment manager's proxy voting?

According to the Department of Labor, compliance with the duty to monitor an investment manager's proxy voting requires proper documentation. Thus, the investment manager or other responsible fiduciary is required to maintain accurate records as to proxy voting.

The proxy voting records must enable the named fiduciary to review not only the investment manager's voting procedure with respect to plan-owned stock, but also the actions taken in individual proxy voting situations. Labor Reg. §2509.94-2(1) (IB-94-2), 59 Fed. Reg. 38860 (7-29-94).

2002 ERISA Facts   200

282. What is the duty of diversification under ERISA?

A fiduciary has a duty to discharge his responsibilities with respect to an employee benefit plan by diversifying the investments of the plan, so as to minimize the risk of large losses, unless under the circumstances it is clearly prudent not to do so. ERISA Sec. 404(a)(1)(C). The diversification requirement imposes a duty on plan fiduciaries to spread the risk of loss to the plan. Just as ERISA Section 404(a)(1)(B) requires that a fiduciary be prudent in each investment decision, ERISA Section 404(a)(1)(C) requires that a fiduciary be prudent in deciding not to diversify a plan's investments. See *Reich v. King*, 867 F. Supp. 341 (DC Md. 1994). In general, a determination of whether the plan assets are sufficiently diversified is made by examining the ultimate investment of the plan assets. H.R. Conf. Rep. No. 93-1280, 93rd Cong., 2nd Sess., 304 (1974) (ERISA Conference Report).

Breaches of a fiduciary's duty to diversify plan assets have been found, for example, where the trustees invested 70% of the plan's assets in 30-year U.S. Treasury bonds without considering the plan's cash-flow requirements. See *GIW Indus., Inc. v. Trevor, Stewart, Burton & Jacobsen, Inc.*, 895 F.2d 729 (11th Cir. 1990). Similarly, the duty to diversify was breached where the plan had up to 85% of its assets invested in commercial real-estate first mortgages in a single geographic area. See *Brock v. Citizens Bank of Clovis*, 841 F.2d 344 (10th Cir. 1988), cert. denied, 488 U.S. 829 (1988).

A proposed loan constituting 23% of the plan's assets to finance a single, speculative, real estate venture amounted to a failure to diversify, considering the special risks of the venture (including the previous failure of the project, one participant being in bankruptcy, and the trustees' inexperience). *Marshall v. Glass/Metal Ass'n*, 507 F. Supp. 378 (DC Haw. 1980); see also *Donovan v. Guaranty Nat'l Bank of Huntington*, 4 EBC 1686 (S.D. W.Va. 1983). (In *Donovan*, a plan that invested entirely in residential real estate mortgages in one geographic area was not diversified because of risk associated with interest rates).

283. What is the purpose of diversifying the assets of a plan?

The purpose of diversifying the assets of a plan is to "distribute the risks of loss in order to maintain the trust principal, usually by limiting the proportion of total trust assets invested in any one stock or class of securities." G. Bogert, *The Law of Trusts & Trustees*, §612 at 18 (2nd Ed. 1980). See also *Marshall v. Glass/Metal Ass'n*, 507 F. Supp. 378 (DC Haw. 1980). By spreading asset purchases throughout a number of varying types of securities or investments, a fiduciary may protect the trust, to a certain extent, against adverse economic and market conditions or against the fortunes of a particular field of business or industry, and thereby minimize the risk of large losses. *GIW Indus., Inc. v. Trevor, Stewart, Burton & Jacobsen, Inc.*, 10 EBC 2290 (S.D. Ga. 1989).

By allocating funds to different types of investments, the potential losses that might occur in one area due to a particular economic event may be offset by gains in another area. Even if such a loss is not offset, its impact may be at least limited to a relatively small portion of the fund. In addition, by prudently diversifying investments and allowing for some degree of liquidity in a plan, trustees can prevent the risk of large losses and, at the same time, have funds available which can be shifted relatively quickly in order to profit from changes in economic conditions. *Donovan v. Guaranty Nat'l Bank of Huntington*, 4 EBC 1686 (S.D. W.Va. 1983).

Conversely, a plan fiduciary who pursues a strategy of non-diversification, runs a risk of incurring substantial losses if a particular investment vehicle, or one of a few large investments chosen, performs poorly. Under such circumstances, one particular negative economic event can devastate the entire plan, or a great portion of it. Thus, while diversification of plan assets is important as a prophylactic measure to guard against losses occasioned by unforeseeable events, it may also result in relatively stable earnings generated by those investments, as well as in the preservation of trust principal, by neutralizing the risk of a particular investment when that investment is combined with others. See *Investment Analysis & Portfolio Management*, Frank K. Reilly, The Dryden Press, p. 5. (1979).

When proper diversification is achieved, the risk inherent in the entire portfolio is less than that of any particular investment within that portfolio, with a result that the only risk remaining is primarily market risk. Moreover, "the return from a portfolio over time should be more stable than that of isolated investments within that portfolio." *Leigh v. Engle*, 858 F.2d 361 (7th Cir. 1988).

284. Who has the burden of proof in an action based on a breach of the duty of diversification?

The duty of diversification requires fiduciaries to diversify plan assets to minimize the risk of large losses, unless under the circumstances it is clearly prudent not to do so. However, Congress did not intend that a more stringent standard of prudence be established with the use of the term "clearly prudent." Instead, by using this term it intended that in an action for plan losses based on a breach of the diversification requirement, the plaintiff's initial burden will be to demonstrate that there has been a failure to diversify. H.R. Conf. Rep. No. 93-1280, 93rd Cong., 2nd Sess., 304 (1974) (ERISA Conference Report). To establish a violation, a plaintiff must demonstrate that the portfolio is not diversified "on its face." *Reich v. King*, 867 F. Supp. 341 (DC Md. 1994).

Once a plaintiff proves that non-diversification exists, the burden shifts to the fiduciary to demonstrate that the failure to diversify was prudent. *In re Unisys Sav. Plan Litig.*, 74 F.3d 420 (3rd Cir. 1996), reh. denied, 173 F.3d 145 (3rd Cir. 1999). The basic policy under ERISA Section 404(a)(1)(C) is to require diversification, and if diversification on its face does not exist, then the burden of justifying a failure to follow this general policy is on the fiduciary who engages in such conduct. The burden is not merely to prove that the investment was prudent, but that there was no risk of large loss resulting from the non-diversification. See ERISA Conference Report at p. 304; *Marshall v. Glass/Metal Ass'n*, 507 F. Supp.

378 (DC Haw. 1980). However, the "facts and circumstances" surrounding each plan and investment "ought to caution judicial review of investment decisions... and [i]t is clearly imprudent to evaluate diversification in hindsight." *Metzler v. Graham*, 112 F.3d 207 (5th Cir. 1997).

285. What is the proper degree of investment concentration necessary to satisfy the diversification requirement?

ERISA and the regulations thereunder do not specify what constitutes "diversification" of the investments of a plan. Congress, however, recognized that the diversification requirement of ERISA imposes a separate duty on plan fiduciaries to spread the risk of loss to the plan. In fashioning the diversification provisions of ERISA, Congress did not choose to establish a specific percentage requirement for investment concentration or a fixed percentage limit on any one investment. Instead, it imposed a requirement of diversification that requires a prudent fiduciary to consider the facts and circumstances surrounding each plan and investment, thereby providing plan fiduciaries discretion and latitude in selecting an investment portfolio for a plan. H.R. Conf. Rep. No. 93-1280, 93rd Cong., 2nd Sess., 304 (1974) (ERISA Conference Report).

286. What are the factors for diversification under the "facts and circumstances" test?

The extent to which a fiduciary has complied with the duty to diversify, as set forth in ERISA, is not measured by hard and fast rules or formulas. However, in prescribing that a prudent fiduciary consider the facts and circumstances surrounding each plan and investment, Congress established seven specific factors that should be considered by a plan fiduciary in determining the degree of concentration for prudent diversification. These factors are:

1. The purpose of the plan;

2. The amount of the plan assets;

3. Financial and industrial conditions;

4. The type of investment, whether mortgages, bonds or shares of stock or otherwise;

5. Distribution as to geographic location;

6. Distribution as to industries; and

7. The dates of maturity.

See H.R. Conf. Rep. No. 93-1280, 93rd Cong., 2nd Sess., 304 (1974) (ERISA Conference Report).

287. Is there a prohibition against a fiduciary investing a substantial portion of a plan's assets in a single security?

As a general proposition, ERISA's duty to diversify prohibits a fiduciary from investing disproportionately in a particular investment or enterprise. The key principle behind the requirements of ERISA Section 404(a)(1)(C) is to prevent plan assets from being exposed to certain shared risks through a concentration of plan assets in a single investment or a single class of investments. See, H.R. Conf. Rep. No. 93-1280, 93rd Cong., 2nd Sess., 304 (1974) (ERISA Conference Report); *Marshall v. Teamsters Local 282 Pension Tr. Fund*, 458 F. Supp. 986 (E.D. NY 1978).

Although a fiduciary may be authorized to invest in a particular type of investment, "[o]rdinarily the fiduciary should not invest the whole or an unduly large proportion of the trust property in one type of security or in various types of securities dependent upon the success of one enterprise or upon conditions in one locality since the effect is to increase the risk of large losses." ERISA Conference Report, above.

Disproportionate amounts of investment in a single security, industry, or class of property have been held to constitute a breach of the fiduciary's duty to diversify. For example, a fiduciary breached its duty to diversify where 23% of a pension plan's total assets were invested in a single loan. Committing a large percentage of plan assets to the loan violated the diversification requirement, since both on its face and according to standards of experienced lenders, it subjected a disproportionate amount of the plan's assets to the risk of a large loss. *Marshall v. Glass/Metal Ass'n*, 507 F. Supp. 378 (DC Haw. 1980). Similarly, the court in *Whitfield v. Tomasso* (682 F. Supp. 1287 (E.D. NY 1988)) held that the trustee's concentration of between 25% and 89% of the ERISA plan's assets to one type of investment also violated the diversification requirement. The trustees' investment of over 65% of the plan's assets in commercial real estate first mortgages was found to violate the diversification requirements in *Brock v. Citizens Bank of Clovis*, 841 F.2d 344 (10th Cir. 1988), cert. denied, 488 U.S. 829 (1988). In that case, the trustees were held liable since they failed to establish that such investments were prudent notwithstanding the lack of diversification. Conversely, a district court found that a fiduciary had *not* violated ERISA's diversification requirements where 18.5% of the trust's total market value had been invested in one corporation, approximately 11% in another, and nearly 14% in a third corporation. See *Sandoval v. Simmons*, 622 F. Supp. 1174 (C.D. Ill. 1985).

288. Is there a prohibition against a fiduciary investing a substantial portion of a plan's assets in a single geographic area?

Although concentrating a plan's investments in a particular geographic area is not prohibited by ERISA, such a strategy entails a great risk of loss to the plan by leaving the plan at the whimsy of the economic fate of the area. *Donovan v. Guaranty Nat'l Bank of Huntington*, 4 EBC 1686 (S.D. W.Va. 1983). Congress has stated that ordinarily the fiduciary should not invest the whole or an unduly large proportion of the trust property in one type of security, or in various types of securities that are dependent upon the success of one enterprise or conditions in one locality, since the effect is to increase the risk of large losses. See H.R. Conf. Rep. No. 93-1280, 93rd Cong., 2nd Sess., (1974) (ERISA Conference Report). If a fiduciary invests in mortgages on real estate, he should not invest a disproportionate amount of the trust fund in mortgages in a particular district or upon a particular class of property so that a decline in property values in that district or of that class might cause a large loss. See ERISA Conference Report, above.

For example, in *Donovan*, above, the plan trustees violated the diversification requirement by investing virtually all of the plan assets in real estate mortgage loans concentrated in a single geographic area of Huntington, West Virginia. By concentrating the plan assets in real estate mortgages in the single geographic area, the trustees were not able to take advantage of changing market conditions. Although the trustees attempted to spread the risk of large losses by making a large number of individual investments within a particular class (real estate mortgage loans), the degree of protection afforded the plan was not sufficient diversification under ERISA.

Similarly, in another case involving real estate mortgages, the trustees of a plan violated ERISA by investing over 65% of plan's assets in commercial real estate mortgages in the area of Clovis, New Mexico. See *Brock v. Citizens Bank of Clovis*, 841 F.2d 344 (10th Cir. 1988), cert. denied, 488 U.S. 829 (1988). The diversification requirement was not met because the trustees had chosen to invest in "one type of security" which did not protect against a multitude of risks, and the trustees failed to establish that the investments were prudent, notwithstanding the lack of diversification. In addition, the lack of diversification was not made moot by the trustees' reduction of the percentage of the plan's outstanding mortgages, because the trustees refused to assure the court that they would maintain a reduced level of real estate investments and insisted on maintaining independence in selecting plan investments.

289. Is non-diversification a per se violation of ERISA?

No. Non-diversification is not a per se violation of ERISA Section 404(a)(1)(C), and neither the case law nor the statutory language support the proposition that it is. "The degree of concentration in any asset or in any particular type of asset which would violate ERISA is determined on an ad hoc basis." *Brock v. Citizens Bank of Clovis*, 841 F.2d 344 (10th Cir. 1988), cert. denied, 488 U.S. 829 (1988). The language of ERISA Section 404(a)(1)(C), in effect, mandates a finding of fact that non-diversification is clearly imprudent before a finding of a fiduciary's liability. *Reich v. King*, 867 F. Supp. 341 (DC Md. 1994), citing *Lanka v. O'Higgins*, 810 F. Supp. 379 (N.D. NY 1992).

290. Is diversification required if it is clearly prudent not to diversify?

No. ERISA does not require the diversification of plan assets in circumstances when it is clearly prudent not to diversify. However, in charting a course of non-diversification, fiduciaries should be aware that the "heavy burden" on the plan fiduciary in a non-diversification challenge "is not merely to prove that [an] investment is prudent, but that there is no risk of large loss resulting from the non-diversification." *Marshall v. Glass/Metal Ass'n*, 507 F. Supp. 378 (DC Haw. 1980).

The diversification requirement and the clearly prudent exception are analyzed from the perspective of their purpose: to reduce the risk of large losses. Thus, if a course of non-diversification is clearly prudent, diversification is not required. For example, a pension plan administrator's purchase of a single tract of undeveloped land comprising 63% of the plan's assets was not in violation of his fiduciary duty to diversify, so as to minimize the risk of large losses. *Metzler v. Graham*, 112 F.3d 207 (5th Cir. 1997). The court held that the disproportionate amount of assets invested in undeveloped land was clearly prudent under all the circumstances. Even if the plan lacked diversification of its assets, the fiduciary did not imprudently introduce a risk of large loss to the plan by purchasing the property. The plan had adequate cash and short-term financial instruments to meet its projected long-term cash flows, the property was appropriate as a hedge against inflation, there was a significant cushion between the purchase price and the independent appraisal, and the fiduciary had expertise in the development of this type of property and the local real estate market. *Metzler v. Graham*, above; see also *Etter v. J. Pease Constr. Co.*, 963 F.2d 1005 (7th Cir. 1992).

Similarly, although the plan's trustee breached the diversification requirement by investing about 70% of a plan's assets in real estate mortgages located in single county in Maryland, the plan's trustee met the burden of showing that plan did not face risk of large losses due to the non-diversification. Thus, the plan's investments, though not diversified, were otherwise clearly prudent because expert testimony demonstrated that the mortgage loan investments had low loan to value ratios, mortgages were 5-year balloon mortgages (limiting the risk of inflation), and the trustee had knowledge of the local real estate market. In addition, the Department of Labor's expert had based his opinions on textbook-type theories that appeared far removed from actual realities of mortgages in the geographic area. *Reich v. King*, 867 F. Supp. 341 (DC Md. 1994).

Likewise, plan fiduciaries were clearly prudent in following a "contrarian" investment strategy even though the plan sustained heavy losses while 90% of the plan's assets were invested in stock of only three companies. Although the facts demonstrated a prima facie case of failure to diversify, the court held that the highly concentrated investments were prudent under the circumstances since the contrarian investment strategy was within industry standards. *Jones v. O'Higgins*, 736 F. Supp. 1243 (N.D. NY 1989).

291. Does the diversification requirement apply to the ultimate investment of plan assets?

Yes. Congress intended that, in general, whether the plan assets are sufficiently diversified is to be determined by examining the ultimate investment of the plan assets. For example, Congress understands that for efficiency and economy, plans may invest all their assets in a single bank or other pooled investment fund, but that the pooled fund itself could have diversified investments. Known as the "look-through" rule, it is the intent of Congress that the diversification rule is applied to the plan by examining the diversification of the investments in the pooled fund. The same is true with respect to investments in a mutual fund. Also, a plan may be invested wholly in insurance or annuity contracts without violating the diversification rules, since generally an insurance company's assets are invested in a diversified manner. H.R. Conf. Rep. No. 93-1280, 93rd Cong., 2nd Sess., 304-305 (1974) (ERISA Conference Report).

In addition, according to the Department of Labor, in the case of a plan which has invested in a single limited partnership, the underlying investments of the limited partnership are considered investments of the plan. DOL Adv. Op. 81-13A. Similarly, in the case of a plan which invests in a real estate investment trust (REIT), it is the Department of Labor's view that the investments of the REIT are considered investments of the plan to the extent of the plan's interest in the REIT. The DOL noted that the fiduciaries of a plan are also under a duty to consider and examine a REIT in the light of the facts and circumstances relevant to the plan and the particular investment or investment course of action involved, and the role the investment or investment course of action plays in the plan's investment portfolio. DOL Adv. Op. 78-30A.

This "look through" concept was not an adequate defense to a breach of a fiduciary duty by a trustee who failed to investigate the objectives and needs of the plan, and imprudently invested too large a portion of the plan's assets in a guaranteed investment contract ("GIC") issued by an insurer (Executive Life) that subsequently became insolvent. The court held that the investment in the Executive Life GIC did not meet the prudent person standard of diversification for the plan, considering the known risks of Executive life and the objectives and needs of the plan. *Bruner v. Boatmen's Tr. Co.*, 918 F. Supp. 1347 (E.D. Mo. 1996).

292. Is the requirement to diversify applicable to investment managers?

Yes. If the assets of a plan are managed by one or more investment managers, each investment manager must invest solely in accordance with the instructions of the named fiduciary and must diversify its portion of the plan investments in accordance with the diversification standard, the prudent man standard, and all other provisions applicable to the investment manager as a fiduciary.

For example, one investment manager, A, may be responsible for 10% of the assets of a plan and instructed by the named fiduciary or trustee to invest solely in bonds; another investment manager, B, may be responsible for a different 10% of the assets of the same plan and instructed to invest solely in equities. In these circumstances, A would invest solely in bonds in accordance with his instructions and would diversify the bond investments in accordance with the diversification standard, the prudent man standard, and all other provisions applicable to A as a fiduciary. Similarly, B would invest solely in equities in accordance with his instructions and these standards. Neither A nor B would incur any liability for diversifying assets subject to his management in accordance with his instructions. H.R. Conf. Rep. No. 93-1280, 93rd Cong., 2nd Sess., 304-305 (1974) (ERISA Conference Report).

293. How is the duty of diversification measured for an investment manager of a plan where the investments are distributed among several investment managers?

The Court of Appeals for the Eleventh Circuit, in keeping with the intent of Congress, and persuaded by the approach of the Third Circuit Court of Appeals, concluded that if a plan's investments are distributed among several investment managers, each responsible for the investment of a particular segment of the plan's investments, then the diversification requirements of an investment manager are properly assessed by examining the plan segment for which it is responsible rather than the plan's universe of investment funds. See *GIW Indus., Inc. v. Trevor, Stewart, Burton & Jacobsen, Inc.*, 895 F.2d 729 (11th Cir. 1990). Since the risk of loss managed by an individual investment manager is not distributed among the total investments of the plan, but only spread among the individual investments within that segment, the satisfaction of the duty to diversify is properly assessed by examining the particular segment managed by the investment manager. *In re Unisys Sav. Plan Litig.*, 74 F.3d 420 (3rd Cir. 1996), reh. denied, 173 F.3d 145 (3rd Cir. 1999).

294. How is the diversification requirement applied to eligible individual account plans?

The diversification requirement of ERISA Section 404(a)(1)(C) is eased somewhat in the case of an eligible individual account plan, which is defined under ERISA as an individual account plan that is a profit sharing, stock bonus, thrift or savings plan, an employee stock ownership plan (ESOP) or a pre-ERISA money purchase plan. ERISA Sec. 407(d)(3). ERISA provides that in the case of an eligible individual account plan, the diversification requirement is not violated by the acquisition or holding of qualifying employer real property or qualifying employer securities. See ERISA Sec. 404(a)(2).

295. How is the diversification requirement applied to segregated asset accounts underlying annuities?

Treasury regulations provide that investments of a segregated asset account which underlie a variable annuity, endowment, or life insurance contract are considered adequately diversified only if:

1.   No more than 55% of the value of the total assets of the account is represented by any one investment;

2.   No more than 70% of the value of the total assets of the account is represented by any two investments;

3. No more than 80% of the value of the total assets of the account is represented by any three investments; and

4. No more than 90% of the value of the total assets of the account is represented by any four investments. Treas. Reg. §1.817-5(b)(1)(i).

The regulation also provides for an alternative diversification requirement for variable life insurance contracts. Treas. Reg. §1.817-5(b)(3).

Segregated asset accounts are generally considered diversified during start-up and liquidation periods. For segregated accounts that are not invested in real property, the start up period is the 1-year period that begins on the date that any amount received under the life insurance or annuity contract is first allocated to the account. The liquidation period is the 1-year period that begins on the date the plan of liquidation is adopted. For segregated asset accounts which invest in real property, the start up period is the 5-year period beginning on the date that any amount received under the contract is first allocated. The liquidation period for real property accounts is two years. The start up period rules do not apply if more than 30% of the amount allocated to a segregated asset account as of the last day of a calendar quarter is attributable to contracts entered into more than one year before such date. Treas. Reg. §1.817-5(c).

296. What is the rule regarding diversification of 401(k) investments in employer securities or employer real property?

ERISA places certain restrictions on Section 401(k) plans that require 10% or more of employees' elective contributions to be invested in employer stock or employer real property. See ERISA Sec. 407(b)

Such plans must treat the portion of a 401(k) plan which consists of elective deferrals that are required to be invested in qualifying employer securities or qualifying employer real property as a separate plan.

In application, this rule restricts Section 401(k) plans from *mandating* that employees place more than 10% of their plan funds in company stock or real property; however, employees are free to *elect* to place more than 10% of their plan assets in employer stock or employer real property. See ERISA Sec. 407(a)(2)(A) through (C).

This restriction does not apply to ESOPs, nor to individual account plans where less than 1% of employee compensation is mandated to be invested in employer securities or employer real property.

ERISA Section 407(b) (as previously amended by the Tax Reform Act of 1997), was amended in 2001 to provide that it does not apply to any elective deferral that is invested in assets consisting of qualifying employer securities, qualifying employer real property, or both, if such assets were acquired before January 1, 1999. EGTRRA 2001, Sec. 665.

297. May an investment manager rely on information furnished by a fiduciary?

Yes. In the view of the DOL, an investment manager appointed to manage all or part of the assets of a plan, may, for purposes of compliance with his investment duties under ERISA Section 404(a)(1)(B), rely on and act upon the basis of information pertaining to the plan provided by or at the direction of the appointing fiduciary. However, the information must be provided for the stated purpose of assisting the manager in the performance of his investment duties, and the investment manager must not know or have reason to know that the information is incorrect. Labor Reg. §2550.404(a)-1(b)(3).

In addition, a prudent investment manager has a duty not to act in accordance with a delegation of plan investment duties to the extent that he either knows or should know that the delegation involves a breach of fiduciary responsibility. Once the investment manager has considered factors otherwise necessary to assure itself that the delegation of investment authority and related specific instructions are appropriate, he may, in exercising such authority and carrying out such instructions, rely upon information provided to him by or at the direction of the appointing fiduciary. See Preamble to Labor Reg. §2550.404(a)-1(b)(3).

298. What is a fiduciary's duty to act in accordance with the plan documents under ERISA?

ERISA requires that fiduciaries discharge their duties in accordance with the documents and instruments governing the plan insofar as such documents or instruments are consistent with the provisions of Titles I and IV of ERISA. ERISA Sec. 404(a)(1)(D). The duty to operate the plan "in accordance with the documents" is, however, *subject to* the prudent person standard of ERISA Section 404(a)(1)(B). See *Morgan v. Independent Drivers Ass'n Pension Plan*, 975 F.2d 1467 (10th Cir. 1992).

For example, a breach of the duty to operate the plan in accordance with the plan documents occurred in a case where the plan trustees allowed themselves and another defendant to participate in the plans and to cause the plans to make contributions on their behalf and on behalf of the defendant even though the plan documents made it clear that none of the trustees or the defendant was a proper participant. See *Donovan v. Daugherty*, 550 F. Supp. 390 (S.D. Ala. 1982). Similarly, a plan fiduciary acted contrary to the terms of a plan document where the evidence demonstrated that he participated in a decision on a transaction, and where the plan document provided that an administrative committee member having an interest in a transaction was not to vote or participate with respect to the transaction. *Donovan v. Cunningham*, 716 F.2d 1455 (5th Cir. 1983).

Likewise, an investment advisor violated ERISA Section 404(a)(1)(D) when he disregarded an agreement between himself and the plan's trustees to limit equity investments in the plan to 50% of the plan's investment portfolio. The agreement required the investment manager to sell the equity holdings if necessary to bring their proportion to within the prescribed portfolio limits. Regardless of whether the investment decisions seemed prudent when made, the investment advisor was required to act in accordance with plan documents. In addition, the plan's trustees could not waive the beneficiaries' right to have fiduciaries comply with the requirements of ERISA Section 404(a)(1)(D) by negligently enforcing the agreement. See *Dardaganis v. Grace Capital, Inc.*, 889 F.2d 1237 (2nd Cir. 1989).

299. Is a good faith but erroneous exercise of the trustees' powers under the plan agreement a breach of ERISA Section 404(a)(1)(D)?

Generally no. The fiduciary provisions of ERISA Section 404(a)(1)(D) are not violated simply because a fiduciary does not follow the terms of the plan, so long as the action is undertaken pursuant to a good faith (albeit erroneous) interpretation. Likewise, "trustees do not breach their fiduciary duties by interpreting the plan in good faith, even if their interpretation is later determined to be incorrect." *Challenger v. Local Union No. 1*, 619 F.2d 645 (7th Cir. 1980). To establish such a liability, willful or bad faith conduct must be proven. *Burke v. Latrobe Steel Co.*, 775 F.2d 88 (3rd Cir. 1985). In addition, "the mere fact that [a fiduciary] has made a mistake of fact or of law in the exercise of his powers or performance of his duties does not render him liable for breach of trust. In such a case [the fiduciary] is liable for breach of trust if he is negligent, but not if he acts with proper care and caution." However, a fiduciary could be liable under the law of trusts with respect to a mistake as to the extent of his duties and powers, even in good faith. *Morgan v. Independent Drivers Ass'n Pension Plan*, 975 F.2d 1467 (10th Cir. 1992). In support of the fiduciaries in the *Burke*, *Challenger* and *Morgan* cases, it should be noted that the plan provisions were somewhat ambiguous and subject to different reasonable interpretations.

300. Must a fiduciary follow the terms of a plan document if the terms are inconsistent with ERISA?

No. Fiduciaries are required to interpret their plans "in accordance with the documents governing the plan insofar as such documents and instructions are consistent with ERISA [Section 404(a)(1)]." *Pratt v. Petroleum Prod. Mgmt. Employee Sav. Plan*, 920 F.2d 651 (10th Cir. 1990). The duty to conform to the provisions of a plan is not intended to override the fiduciary's foremost duty to serve the interests of plan participants and beneficiaries. *Moench v. Robertson*, 62 F.3d 553 (3rd Cir. 1995), citing *Kuper v. Quantum Chemical Corp.*, 852 F. Supp. 1389 (S.D. Ohio 1994). Thus, ERISA Section 404(a)(1)(D) does not excuse fiduciaries who act in a manner inconsistent with ERISA merely because they act according to a provision of a plan document. *Central States, Southeast & Southwest Areas Pension Fund v. Central Transport, Inc.*, 472 U.S. 559 (1985).

For example, a provision for pass-through voting under the terms of a plan's trust agreement was held not in the best economic interest of the plan participants and their beneficiaries (and inconsistent with the requirements of ERISA). See *Central Tr. Co. v. American Avents Corp.*, 771 F. Supp. 871 (S.D. Ohio 1989).

Deviating from the terms of the trust provided the participants with the ability to sell the shares at $12.00 per share, in contrast to $5.00 per share, which they would have received if the pass-through voting provision had been followed. The court noted that in accordance with the *Restatement (Second) of Trusts* §167 (1959), a court may "direct or permit the trustee to deviate from a term of the trust if owing to circumstances not known to the settlor and not anticipated by him compliance would defeat or substantially impair the accomplishment of the purposes of the trust; and in such case, if necessary to carry out the purposes of the trust, the court may direct or permit the trustee to do acts which are not authorized or are forbidden by the terms of the trust." *Central Tr. Co. v. American Avents Corp.*, above.

301. Are statements of investment policy part of the documents governing a plan?

In the view of the Department of Labor, statements of investment policy issued by a named fiduciary are part of the "documents and instruments governing the plan" within the meaning of ERISA Section 404(a)(1)(D). In that respect, a fiduciary must discharge his duties with respect to the plan in accordance with the documents and instruments, including statements of investment policy governing the plan, insofar as such documents and instruments are consistent with the provisions of ERISA. Thus, an investment manager to whom an investment policy applies would be required to comply with such policy to the extent permitted by ERISA Section 404(a)(1)(D). See *Dardaganis v. Grace Capital, Inc.*, 664 F. Supp. 105 (S.D. NY 1987) (noncompliance with investment guidelines by an investment manager was held to violate ERISA Section 404(a)(1)(D)); *Marshall v. Teamsters Local 282 Pension Tr. Fund*, 458 F. Supp. 986 (E.D. NY 1978) (investment made in excess of trust percentage restrictions was held to violate ERISA Section 404(a)(1)(D)). See Labor Reg. §2509.94-2(2).

302. May a plan maintain the indicia of ownership of plan assets outside the jurisdiction of United States district courts?

No, with certain exceptions (see Q 303). In order to prevent "runaway assets," ERISA Section 404(b) prohibits an employee benefit plan from transferring or maintaining the indicia of ownership of plan assets outside the jurisdiction of United States district courts. The basic objective of this prohibition is to preclude frustration of adequate fiduciary supervision and remedies for breach of trust. H.R. Conf. Rep. No. 93-1280, 93rd Cong., 2nd Sess., 306 (1974) (ERISA Conference Report). This prohibition is limited to the "indicia of ownership" (i.e., evidence of ownership of plan assets such as bonds or stock certificates), which may not be maintained outside the United States. Thus, the investment of employee benefit plan assets outside the United States is not prohibited if the investments are in the best interests of plan participants and made under appropriate circumstances and with proper safeguards. DOL Adv. Op. 75-80.

303. What are the "indicia of ownership" rules regarding the maintenance of plan assets outside the jurisdiction of United States district courts?

Regulations under ERISA detail exceptions under which the indicia of ownership of plan assets may be held abroad, provided that the conditions described below are satisfied with respect to the nature of the assets *and* the maintenance of them. Labor Reg. §2550.404b-1(b).

Nature of Assets

The following assets may have indicia of ownership maintained outside of the United States:

1. Securities that are issued by a person, (other than an individual), which is not organized under the laws of the United States or a State and does not have its principal place of business within the United States;

2. Securities issued by a foreign government, State, or any political subdivision, agency or instrumentality of a foreign government;

3. Securities issued by a person (other than an individual) where the principal trading market for the securities is outside the jurisdiction of the district courts of the United States; *or*

4. Currency issued by a foreign government if the currency is maintained outside the jurisdiction of the district courts of the United States solely as an incident to the purchase, sale or maintenance of securities issued by a person which is organized under the laws of a foreign government and does not have its principal place of business within the United States. Labor Reg. §2550.404b-1(a)(1).

Maintenance of Assets

Furthermore, the requirements of either (1) or (2) as follow must be met with respect to the maintenance and the indicia of ownership of the assets:

1. The assets must be either under the management and control of a fiduciary which is a corporation or partnership organized under the laws of the United States or a State, and which has its principal place of business within the United States; however, the fiduciary must be either:

   a) a bank as defined in Section 202(a)(2) of the Investment Advisors Act of 1940 that has, as of the last day of its most recent fiscal year, equity capital in excess of $1,000,000,

   b) an insurance company which is qualified under the laws of more than one State to manage, acquire, or dispose of any asset of a plan, as of the last day of its most recent fiscal year, net worth in excess of $1,000,000 and which is subject to supervision and examination by the State authority having supervision over insurance companies, or

c) an investment advisor registered under the Investment Advisors Act of 1940 that has, as of the last day of its most recent fiscal year, total client assets under its management and control in excess of $50,000,000 and either: (1) shareholders' or partners' equity in excess of $750,000; or (2) all of its obligations and liabilities assumed or guaranteed by a bank, insurance company, investment advisor, or broker-dealer described in this regulation; *or*

2.   The indicia of ownership must be either:

a) in the physical possession of, or, as a result of normal business operations, in transit to the physical possession of, a person which is organized under the laws of the United States or a State. In addition, the person must have its principal place of business in the United States and must be:

(i) a bank as defined in section 202(a)(2) of the Investment Advisors Act of 1940 that has, as of the last day of its most recent fiscal year, equity capital in excess of $1,000,000,

(ii) a broker or dealer registered under the Securities Exchange Act of 1934 that has, as of the last day of its most recent fiscal year, net worth in excess of $750,000, or

(iii) a broker or dealer registered under the Securities Exchange Act of 1934 that has all of its obligations and liabilities assumed or guaranteed by a bank, insurance company, investment advisor, or broker-dealer described in the regulation, *or*

b) maintained by a broker or dealer in the custody of an entity designated by the Securities and Exchange Commission as a "satisfactory control location" with respect to such broker or dealer pursuant to Rule 15c3-3 under the Securities Exchange Act of 1934, provided that:

(i) such entity holds the indicia of ownership as agent for the broker or dealer, and

(ii) such broker or dealer is liable to the plan to the same extent it would be if it retained the physical possession of the indicia of ownership pursuant to paragraph (2)(a), above, *or*

c) maintained by a bank described in (2)(a)(i), above, in the custody of an entity that is a foreign securities depository, foreign clearing agency which acts as a securities depository, or foreign bank, which entity is supervised or regulated by a government agency or regulatory authority in the foreign jurisdiction having authority over such depositories, clearing agencies or banks, provided that:

(i) the foreign entity holds the indicia of ownership as agent for the bank,

(ii) the bank is liable to the plan to the same extent it would be if it retained the physical possession of the indicia of ownership within the United States,

(iii) the indicia of ownership are not subject to any right, charge, security interest, lien or claim of any kind in favor of the foreign entity except for their safe custody or administration,

(iv) beneficial ownership of the assets represented by the indicia of ownership is freely transferable without the payment of money or value other than for safe custody or administration, *and*

(v) upon request by the plan fiduciary who is responsible for the selection and retention of the bank, the bank identifies to the fiduciary the name, address and principal place of business of the foreign entity which acts as custodian for the plan, and the name and address of the governmental agency or other regulatory authority that supervises or regulates that foreign entity. Labor Reg. §2550.404b-1(a)(2).

The regulation also permits the maintenance in Canada of the indicia of ownership of certain plan assets; see Q 304.

304. What is the alternate "indicia of ownership" rule for Canadian based assets?

A fiduciary may maintain in Canada the indicia of ownership of plan assets that are attributable to a contribution made on behalf of a plan participant who is a citizen or resident of Canada, if such indicia of ownership must remain in Canada in order for the plan to qualify for and to maintain tax exempt status under the laws of Canada or to comply with other applicable laws of Canada or any Province of Canada. Labor Reg. §2550.404b-1(b).

305. May fiduciary responsibility be allocated among fiduciaries?

Yes, ERISA expressly permits certain fiduciary responsibilities not involving the management and control of plan assets to be allocated among named fiduciaries. Named fiduciaries may also designate persons other than named fiduciaries to carry out the fiduciary responsibilities, provided that the plan instrument expressly provides procedures for the allocation or designation of the fiduciary responsibilities. ERISA Sec. 405(c)(1); DOL Labor Reg. §2509.75-8, FR-12.

306. Is a named fiduciary relieved of liability for acts and omissions allocated to other named fiduciaries?

Yes, under certain conditions and to a limited extent. Named fiduciaries are not liable for the acts and omissions of other named fiduciaries in carrying out the fiduciary responsibilities which have been allocated to other named fiduciaries, provided that the allocation is made prudently and in accordance with procedures contained in the plan document. However, named fiduciaries are still liable for the acts and omissions of other named fiduciaries under ERISA Section 405(a) (relating to the general rules of co-fiduciary responsibility). In addition, if the plan document does not provide for a procedure for allocating fiduciary responsibilities among named fiduciaries, any allocation that the named fiduciaries made among themselves is ineffective to relieve an allocating named fiduciary from responsibility or liability for the acts and omissions of the other named fiduciaries. ERISA Sec. 405(c)(1); Labor Reg. §2509.75-8, FR-13.

307. May fiduciary responsibility be allocated to a person who is not a named fiduciary?

Yes, provided that the plan document provides for a procedure for designating the responsibilities of named fiduciaries to persons who are not named fiduciaries. In addition, the named fiduciaries of the plan will not be liable for the acts and omissions of the designated person except as provided in ERISA Section 405(a) (general rules of co-fiduciary liability), and Section 405(c)(2)(A) (designation of persons to carry out fiduciary responsibilities). However, the *selection* of a service provider to a qualified plan has been deemed by the DOL to be a fiduciary act for which named fiduciaries may be held liable. PWBA Information Letter to Theodore Konshak (12/1/97). However, if the plan document does not provide for a procedure for designating persons who are not named fiduciaries to carry out fiduciary responsibilities, then the designation will not relieve the named fiduciaries from responsibility or liability for the acts and omissions of the designated persons. Labor Reg. §2509.75-8, FR-14.

308. May a named fiduciary delegate the control and management of the plan assets?

Yes, subject to restrictions. A named fiduciary has the exclusive authority to control and manage the operation and administration of the plan. In accordance with that responsibility, the named fiduciary must appoint the trustees of a plan to manage and control the assets of the plan unless the plan document or trust agreement provides for that designation. In addition, only a named fiduciary may delegate the authority and discretion to manage and control the assets of a plan to others, provided that the plan document allows for the delegation. However, the authority and discretion to manage and control the assets of a plan may be delegated only to other named fiduciaries, trustees, investment managers, and plan participants under limited circumstances. See ERISA Secs. 402(a)(1), 402(c)(3), 403(a).

309. May a named fiduciary delegate responsibility for management and control of plan assets to anyone other than a person who is an investment manager?

No. ERISA does not allow named fiduciaries to delegate to others authority or discretion to manage or control plan assets. ERISA Sec. 405(c)(1). However, under the terms of ERISA Section 403(a)(2) and ERISA Section 402(c)(3), the authority and discretion may be delegated to persons who are investment managers as defined in ERISA Section 3(38). Further, under ERISA Section 402(c)(2), if the plan so provides, a named fiduciary may employ other persons to render advice to the named fiduciary to assist it in carrying out the named fiduciary's investment responsibilities under the plan. Labor Reg. §2509.75-8, FR-15.

310. Can a fiduciary who is not a named fiduciary with respect to an employee benefit plan be personally liable for all phases of the management and administration of the plan?

A fiduciary with respect to the plan who is not a *named* fiduciary is a fiduciary only to the extent that he performs one or more of the fiduciary functions described in ERISA Section 3(21)(A). In addition, any fiduciary may become liable for breaches of fiduciary responsibility committed by another fiduciary of the same plan under circumstances giving rise to co-fiduciary liability, as provided in ERISA Section 405(a). Labor Reg. §2509.75-8, FR-16.

311. What are the ongoing responsibilities of a fiduciary who has appointed trustees or other fiduciaries with respect to these appointments?

At reasonable intervals the performance of trustees and other fiduciaries must be reviewed by the appointing fiduciary in a manner that is reasonably expected to ensure that their performance has been in compliance with the terms of the plan, has met the statutory standards, and satisfies the needs of the plan. No single procedure will be appropriate in all cases; the procedure adopted may vary in accordance with the nature of the plan and other facts and circumstances relevant to the choice of the procedure. Labor Reg. §2509.75-8, FR-17.

312. Must a plan administrator solicit fee quotations in selecting a service provider to provide services to a plan?

Maybe. The selection of an actuary to provide the required services under Section 103(a)(4)(A) of ERISA is an exercise of discretionary authority or control with respect to the management and administration of the plan, within the meaning of Section 3(21) of ERISA, and therefore constitutes a fiduciary act subject to the general fiduciary responsibility standards and prohibited transaction provisions of Sections 404(a)(1) and 406(a)(1)(C) and (D) of ERISA, respectively. Information Letter to Theodore Konshak from Bette J. Briggs, December 1, 1997. Although this guidance addresses the issue within the context of selecting the services of an actuary, the information letter's rationale generally would seem to warrant its extension to the selection of any provider of services to a plan.

According to the DOL, in selecting a service provider such as an enrolled actuary, the responsible plan fiduciary must engage in an objective process designed to elicit information necessary to assess the qualifications of the service provider, the quality of the work product, and the reasonableness of the fees charged in light of the services provided. In addition, such a process should be designed to avoid self-dealing, conflicts of interest or other improper influence. What constitutes an appropriate method of selecting a service provider, however, will depend upon the particular facts and circumstances. In the view of the DOL, soliciting bids among service providers at the outset is a means by which the fiduciary can obtain the necessary information relevant to the decision-making process. Whether such a process is appropriate in subsequent years may depend, among other things, upon the fiduciary's knowledge of a service provider's work product, the cost and quality of services previously provided by the service provider, the fiduciary's knowledge of prevailing rates for the services, as well as the cost to the plan of conducting a particular selection process. Regardless of the method used, however, the DOL cautions that the fiduciary must be able to demonstrate compliance with ERISA's fiduciary standards. Information Letter to Theodore Konshak from Bette J. Briggs, December 1, 1997.

313. Must a plan administrator select the lowest quoted fee in selecting a service provider to provide services to a plan?

Not necessarily. Because a number of factors will necessarily be considered by a fiduciary when selecting a service provider, the DOL maintains that a fiduciary need not necessarily select the lowest bidder when soliciting bids, although the compensation paid to the service provider by the plan must be reasonable in light of the services provided. However, the fiduciary should not consider one factor, such as the lowest fee bid for services, to the exclusion of any other factor, such as the quality of the work product. Rather, the decision regarding which service provider to select should be based on an assessment of all the relevant factors, including both the quality and cost of the services. Information Letter to Theodore Konshak from Bette J. Briggs, December 1, 1997.

314. Is it appropriate for a trustee of an ERISA-covered health and welfare fund to consider quality in the selection of health care services?

Maybe. When the selection of a health care provider involves the disposition of employee benefit plan assets, such selection is an exercise of authority or control with respect to the management and disposition of the plan's assets within the meaning of Section 3(21)(A) of ERISA, and thus constitutes a fiduciary act subject to the general fiduciary responsibility standards and prohibited transaction provisions of Sections 404(a)(1) and 406(a)(1)(C) and (D) of ERISA, respectively. Information Letter to Diana Orantes Ceresi from Bette J. Briggs, February 19, 1998. Although this guidance addresses the issue within the context of selecting health care services, the same rationale would appear to apply to the selection of any provider of services to a plan.

According to the DOL, in selecting a health care provider in this context, as with the selection of any service provider under ERISA, the responsible plan fiduciary must engage in an objective process designed to elicit information necessary to assess the qualifications of the provider, the quality of services offered, and the reasonableness of the fees charged in light of the services provided. In addition, such a process should be designed to avoid self-dealing, conflicts of interest or other improper influence. What constitutes an appropriate method of selecting a health care provider, however, will depend upon the particular facts and circumstances. Soliciting bids among service providers at the outset is a means by which the fiduciary can obtain the necessary information relevant to the decision-making process. Whether such a process is appropriate in subsequent years may depend, among other things, upon the fiduciary's knowledge of the service provider's work, the cost and quality of the services previously provided by the service provider, the fiduciary's knowledge of prevailing rates for similar services, as well as the cost to the plan of conducting a particular selection process. Regardless of the method used, however, the DOL advises that the fiduciary must be able to demonstrate compliance with ERISA's fiduciary standards.

Because numerous factors necessarily will be considered by a fiduciary when selecting health care service providers, the DOL also notes that a fiduciary need not select the lowest bidder when soliciting bids, although the fiduciary must ensure that the compensation paid to a service provider is reasonable in light of the services provided to the plan. In addition, because "quality of services" is a factor relevant to selection of a service provider, it is the view of the DOL that a plan fiduciary's failure to take quality of services into account in the selection process would constitute a breach of the fiduciary's duty under ERISA when, in the case of a plan, the selection involves the disposition of plan assets.

In assessing "quality of services," the DOL believes that a plan fiduciary may, among other things, consider the scope of choices and qualifications of medical providers and specialists available to participants, ease of access to medical providers, ease of access to information concerning the operations of the health care provider, the extent to which internal procedures provide for timely consideration and resolution of patient questions and complaints, the extent to which internal procedures provide for the confidentiality of patient records, enrollee satisfaction statistics, and rating or accreditation of health care service providers by independent services or state agencies. Information Letter to Diana Orantes Ceresi from Bette J. Briggs, February 19, 1998.

2002 ERISA Facts

315. May a fiduciary be relieved of liability for investment losses resulting from participant-directed investments?

Yes, to a limited degree. Generally, ERISA provides that if a plan that provides for individual accounts permits a participant or beneficiary to exercise control over assets in his account, and that participant or beneficiary in fact exercises control over assets in his account, then the participant or beneficiary is not deemed to be a fiduciary by reason of his exercise of control, and no person who is otherwise a fiduciary will be liable for any loss, or by reason of any breach, which results from such exercise of control. ERISA Sec. 404(c); Labor Reg. §2550.404c. Details as to safe harbor means by which a fiduciary may avail itself of Section 404(c) relief are explained in Q 317.

316. Who enforces the fiduciary standards?

The Department of Labor has the sole authority for interpreting and enforcing the fiduciary provisions of ERISA, and it conducts investigations of violations thereof under its fiduciary investigations program. ERISA Secs. 502, 504, 505, 506; Reorganization Plan No. 4 of 1978, Sec. 102, 1979-1 CB 480; PWBA Enforcement Manual. A plan fiduciary who breaches any of the fiduciary obligations under ERISA Section 404 may be sued by the Secretary of Labor or other persons, and may be subjected to personal liability for losses to the plan and to all other appropriate equitable relief, including injunctive relief. See ERISA Secs. 409, 502(a)(2), 502(a)(5).

317. What is an ERISA Section 404(c) participant directed plan?

A participant directed plan is one under which individual plan participants or beneficiaries may exercise control over assets in individual accounts maintained for them under the plan. Under ERISA, a person who exercises authority or control over the assets of a plan is a fiduciary and, therefore, has specific duties and responsibilities with respect to the plan and its participants and beneficiaries.

Regulations under ERISA Section 404(c) state that where a participant or beneficiary exercises control over the assets in his individual account in an individual account plan (e.g., a 401(k), money purchase, profit sharing or 403(b) plan), then (1) the participant or beneficiary will not be deemed to be a fiduciary by reason of his exercise of control; and (2) no person who is otherwise a fiduciary will be liable under the fiduciary responsibility provisions of ERISA for any loss, or by reason of any breach, which results from such participant's or beneficiary's exercise of control, if certain requirements are met. Labor Reg. §2550.404c-1 (see Q 315).

The 404(c) regulations set forth specific rules that must be followed in order for plan fiduciaries to afford themselves the relief from liability allowed by ERISA Section 404(c).

In general, relief from liability is allowed under a 404(c) plan only if a participant or beneficiary actually exercises control over the assets in his account. A plan allows exercise of control if it provides the participant or beneficiary the opportunity under the plan to: (1) choose from a broad range of investment alternatives, which consist of at least three diversified investment alternatives, each of which has materially different risk and return characteristics; (2) give investment instructions with a frequency which is appropriate in light of the market volatility of the investment alternatives, but not less frequently than once within any three month period; (3) diversify investments within and among investment alternatives; and (4) obtain sufficient information to make informed investment decisions with respect to investment alternatives available under the plan. See Labor Reg. §2550.404c-1.

318. May defined benefit plan fiduciaries seek protection under the provisions of ERISA Section 404(c)?

No; the relief from fiduciary liability where participant direction of investments is allowed under ERISA Section 404(c) applies only to individual account plans. Individual account plans include: (1) profit sharing plans; (2) Section 401(k) plans; (3) money purchase pension plans; and (4) Section 403(b) retirement savings plans.

Defined benefit plans provide for the payment of actuarially determined benefits to participants and beneficiaries. As such, benefits under defined benefit plans are paid from a single trust which is managed by plan fiduciaries under the general fiduciary provisions of ERISA.

319. Is compliance with ERISA Section 404(c) mandatory?

Compliance with the provisions of ERISA Section 404(c) and its attendant regulations is optional. The preamble to Regulation §2550.404c-1 states that the transactional relief afforded under ERISA Section 404(c) is optional, and therefore, the regulations were not intended to establish standards for all ERISA covered plans concerning the types of investments a fiduciary must make.

The provisions of ERISA Section 404(c) do, however, present an opportunity for plan fiduciaries to limit their exposure to liability under certain fiduciary responsibility provisions of ERISA regarding participant direction of investments in an individual account plan. It is the Department of Labor's view that the protection allowed under ERISA Section 404(c) is "similar to a statutory exception to the general fiduciary provisions of ERISA and, accordingly, the person asserting applicability of the exception will have the burden of proving that the conditions of ERISA Section 404(c) and any regulation thereunder have been met." See Preamble (Part I) to Labor Reg. §2550.404c-1.

320. What are the "core investment alternatives"?

Regulations state that a participant in an ERISA Section 404(c) plan must be able to select among at least three investment alternatives:

1.   Each of which is diversified;

2.   Each of which has materially different risk and return characteristics;

3.   Which in the aggregate enable the participant or beneficiary, by choosing among them, to achieve a portfolio with risk and return characteristics at any point within the range normally appropriate for the participant or beneficiary; and

4.   Each of which, when combined with investment in the other alternatives, tends to minimize through diversification the overall risk of a participant's or beneficiary's portfolio. Labor Reg. §2550.404(c)-1(b)(3)(i)(B).

321. What is a "broad range of investment alternatives"?

An ERISA Section 404(c) plan satisfies the requisite provision of a broad range of investment alternatives if it provides the participant or beneficiary with a reasonable opportunity to:

1.   Materially affect the potential degree of risk and the potential return on amounts held in his account;

2.   Choose from at least three diversified investment alternatives, each of which has materially different risk and return characteristics (core investment alternatives — see Q 320); and

3.   Diversify the investment of the portion of his individual account with respect to which he is permitted to exercise control, so as to minimize the risk of large losses, taking into account the nature of the plan and the size of participants' or beneficiaries' accounts. Labor Reg. §2550.404c-1(b)(3)(i).

It is important to note that categories of investments must be diversified both between categories and within each category. See Labor Regs. §§2550.404c-1(b)(3)(i)(B)(1); 2550.404c-1(b)(3)(i)(C).

For plans that have small participant account balances, the broad range of investment alternatives requirement can be met by offering "look through" investment vehicles. See Labor Reg. §2550.404c-1(b)(3)(ii). The regulations define "look through" vehicles to include mutual funds, bank-maintained common or collective investment trust funds, bank deposits, guaranteed investment contracts, fixed rate investment contracts, and pooled separate accounts. Labor Reg. §2550.404c-(e)(1).

Only those alternatives for which sufficient information is available to participants can be taken into account in determining whether a plan provides a broad range of investment alternatives (for details as to the disclosure requirements, see Q 328).

The requirement of prudence will be applied to fiduciaries in the selection of "look through" investment vehicles and managers of "look through" vehicles.

322. What constitutes a "reasonable opportunity" to give investment instructions under an ERISA Section 404(c) plan?

With regard to the three core investments that create the broad range of investment alternatives (as mandated by Labor Reg. §2550.404c-1(b)(3)(i)(B); see Q 320), a 404(c) plan must give participants and beneficiaries a reasonable opportunity to give investment instructions no less frequently than once within any three month period. See Labor Reg. §2550.404c-1(b)(2)(ii)(C)(1).

The plan may impose reasonable restrictions on participants and beneficiaries as to the number of times they may give investment instructions. Such restrictions are reasonable only if they permit participants and beneficiaries to issue investment instructions with a frequency which is appropriate in light of the market volatility to which the investment alternative may reasonably be expected to be subject. See Labor Reg. §2550.404c-1(b)(2)(ii)(C).

In investment alternatives that are subject to a volatile market, the plan must permit the transfer of assets into one of the core investment alternatives with the same reasonable frequency as that which applies to the more volatile alternative (even if it is more frequent than once every three months). The preamble to the 404(c) regulations clearly states that the volatility rule allows more frequent transfers into the core alternatives and not in and out of the core alternatives. See Labor Reg. §2550.404(c)-1(b)(2)(ii)(C)(2)(i).

ERISA Section 404(c) plans may satisfy the volatility rule by permitting participants and beneficiaries to transfer their investments from volatile alternatives into "income producing, low risk, liquid funds" at least as often as they permit participants and beneficiaries to give investment instructions in the particular investment alternative. This allows for a safe place for participants and beneficiaries to place their assets (i.e., a "cash equivalency" vehicle), from which they may then direct assets into another investment vehicle when the next scheduled opportunity presents itself. See Labor Reg. §2550.404(c)-1(b)(2)(ii)(C)(2)(ii).

323. What is "opportunity to exercise control" in an ERISA Section 404(c) plan?

In an ERISA Section 404(c) plan, fiduciaries must provide specific instructions to participants and beneficiaries on how they may exercise control over the assets in their participant accounts. These instructions must be presented in writing.

Under the regulations, a participant or beneficiary is deemed to have exercised control over the assets in his account if the participant or beneficiary has:

1. A reasonable opportunity to give to an identified plan fiduciary investment instructions in writing (or by other means such as over the telephone) with an opportunity to receive a written confirmation that the instructions have been received and acted upon; and

2. The opportunity to obtain sufficient information to make an informed investment decision. Labor Reg. §2550.404c-1(b)(2)(A) and (B).

Instructions must be affirmatively given by participants and beneficiaries in order for the protections of ERISA Section 404(c) to cover plan fiduciaries. If a participant or beneficiary refuses to give investment instructions regarding his account under the plan, fiduciaries have an obligation to prudently invest those assets on behalf of the individual participant or beneficiary who refuses to exercise control. Preamble to Labor Reg. §2550.404c-1.

Plan fiduciaries may offer participants and beneficiaries an opportunity to exercise control over certain portions of their plan account assets and still maintain the protection available under ERISA Section 404(c). If fiduciaries limit such control for participants and beneficiaries, they will be afforded the protections of ERISA Section 404(c) only with regard to transactions over which they have provided participants and beneficiaries an opportunity to exercise control in conformity with the requirements of the regulations identified above.

Under the first prominent ERISA Section 404(c) case, the Third Circuit Court of Appeals ruled that any fiduciary who seeks protection under the ERISA provisions excusing a fiduciary from liability for any loss which results from a participant's exercise of control over an investment bears the burden of showing its application. Further, the court held that fiduciaries seeking protection must establish a causal nexus between the participant's exercise of control and the claimed loss. See *In re Unisys Sav. Plan Litig. v. Unisys Corp.*, 74 F.3d 420 (3rd Cir. 1996), reh. denied, 173 F.3d 145 (3rd Cir. 1999).

PRACTITIONER'S POINTER

It is recommended, when setting up an ERISA Section 404(c) program for a plan, that "identified fiduciaries" to whom investment instructions are to be delivered be identified by their position title. This saves the time and effort necessary to amend the documents if the fiduciaries are identified by name and they subsequently vacate their positions as fiduciaries.

324. To what extent may a fiduciary offer investment education and still maintain the protection from liability provided under ERISA Section 404(c)?

Fiduciaries are not required to offer investment advice under an ERISA Section 404(c) plan. Labor Reg. §2550.404c-1(c)(4). However, many plan sponsors recognize that some participants may not be able to make sound decisions regarding their plan accounts because they simply do not possess the investment expertise to do so. The DOL has provided guidance for plan sponsors who would like to provide some assistance for these participants and beneficiaries, while still maintaining their protection from liability (see Labor Reg. §2509.96-1 (IB-96-1), 61 Fed. Reg. 29586 (6-11-96)). For details of this guidance, see Q 214.

Regulations under ERISA Section 3(21)(A)(ii) provide in pertinent part that a fiduciary "renders investment advice" if:

1.   He renders advice as to the value of securities or other property, or makes recommendations as to the advisability of investing in, purchasing, or selling securities or other property; and

2.   He either directly or indirectly has discretionary authority or control with respect to purchasing or selling securities or other property for the participant or beneficiary, or renders any advice described in (1), above, on a regular basis to the participant or beneficiary pursuant to an agreement, arrangement, or understanding, written or unwritten, between the person and the participant or beneficiary that such services will serve as the primary basis for the participant's or beneficiary's investment decisions with respect to plan assets, and that the person will render individualized investment advice to the participant or beneficiary based on the particular needs of the participant or beneficiary.

The decision of whether the provision of investment education is the rendering of investment advice is made on a case by case basis, by considering the relevant facts and circumstances of the particular case. See Q 214 for a description of four "safe harbor" categories of information that may be provided which, in the opinion of the Department of Labor, will not constitute the rendering of investment advice under ERISA Section 3(21)(A)(ii) and Labor Regulation Section 2510.3-21(c).

The Securities and Exchange Commission has noted that plan sponsors (not third parties hired by the plan sponsor) who offer investment education under an ERISA Section 404(c) plan will not be considered investment advisors for purposes of the Investment Advisors Act of 1940. See IB 96-1, above.

325. Are fiduciaries of ERISA Section 404(c) plans required to exercise prudence in the selection and monitoring of educators and advisors?

Yes. In the context of an ERISA Section 404(c) plan, neither the designation of a person to provide education nor the designation of a beneficiary to provide investment advice to participants and beneficiaries will, in itself, give rise to fiduciary liability for loss with respect to any breach of the fiduciary responsibility provisions of ERISA (i.e., Part 4 of Title I) that is the direct and necessary result of a participant's or beneficiary's exercise of independent control over his account. Labor Reg. §2509.96-1 (IB 96-1), 61 Fed. Reg. 29586 (6-11-96).

Otherwise, the fiduciaries of an ERISA Section 404(c) plan are required to exercise the same prudence in the selection and monitoring of educators and advisors as is required with any designation of a service provider to a plan. Such a selection is an exercise of discretionary authority or control with respect to the management of the plan; consequently, persons making the selection must act solely in the interests of plan participants and beneficiaries (as required under ERISA Section 404(a)) in making the decisions regarding the appointment of persons to provide investment educational services or investment advice to participants and beneficiaries, as well as in continuing any such designations. Labor Reg. §2509.96-1(e) (IB 96-1(e)), above.

The DOL also notes in Interpretive Bulletin 96-1, that a plan sponsor or fiduciary will have no fiduciary responsibility or liability with respect to the actions of a third party selected by a participant or beneficiary to provide education or investment advice where the plan sponsor or fiduciary neither selects nor endorses the educator or advisor, nor otherwise makes arrangements with the educator or advisor to provide such services.

326. Which fiduciary responsibilities may not be relieved under ERISA Section 404(c)?

Fiduciaries of ERISA Section 404(c) plans retain responsibility under ERISA for the general fiduciary provisions regarding the selection and monitoring of investment alternatives and investment managers (unless the plan participants have been granted authority to select investment managers under the plan and have exercised that authority). Fiduciaries are also obligated to observe the ERISA Section 406 restrictions on prohibited transactions. Furthermore, plan fiduciaries are responsible for the provision of notice requirements under Labor Regulation Section 2550.404c-1, and the obligation to timely implement the written investment instructions of ERISA Section 404(c) plan participants.

Fiduciaries of an ERISA Section 404(c) plan are also responsible for any situations of co-fiduciary liability which may arise under ERISA Section 405, with the exception of breaches that are the direct result of a participant exercising direct control over the assets in his account. The regulations provide an example of this exception, where a participant independently exercises control over assets in his account by directing a fiduciary to invest 100% of his account balance in a single stock. In this situation, the participant will not be considered a fiduciary to the plan and the fiduciary will not be held liable for any losses that necessarily result from the participant's exercise of control. See Labor Reg. §2550.404c-1(f)(5).

327. Does ERISA Section 404(c) apply to SIMPLE plans?

The provisions governing SIMPLE (Savings Incentive Match Plans for Employees) plans were added to the Internal Revenue Code by the Small Business Job Protection Act of 1996. There are two different types of SIMPLE plans: SIMPLE IRA plans and SIMPLE 401(k) plans. Both are generally for employers who have 100 or fewer employees, and who do not sponsor any other qualified retirement plan (employers sponsoring a SIMPLE 401(k) plan may have another qualified plan provided it does not cover any of the same employees as the SIMPLE 401(k) plan).

Under both types of SIMPLE plans, eligible employees may defer up to $7,000 (in 2002) of earned income into their plan account on an annual basis. Generally, the employer must either provide a dollar-for-dollar matching contribution of up to 3% of compensation (a 1% match is available under limited circumstances in a SIMPLE IRA) or, alternately, a 2% of compensation nonelective contribution to all eligible participants, regardless of whether or not they are actively deferring earned income into the plan account. All contributions are immediately 100% vested in the plan participants. See IRC Secs. 408(p), 401(k)(11), both as amended by EGTRRA 2001. Furthermore, certain catch-up contributions by participants age 50 or over may be permitted. See IRC Sec. 414(v), as added by EGTRRA 2001.

SIMPLE plan fiduciaries are subject to the various fiduciary requirements of ERISA regarding the selection and monitoring of any financial institutions designated to receive plan contributions. A participant or beneficiary will be treated as exercising control over the assets in his account (and the protections of ERISA Section 404(c) will thus be extended to the SIMPLE plan fiduciaries) on the earliest of the following:

1. An affirmative election among investment options with respect to the initial investment of any contribution;

2. A rollover to any SIMPLE IRA or individual retirement plan; or

3. One year after the SIMPLE retirement account is established.

SIMPLE plans subject to ERISA Section 404(c) must also comply with all of the other requirements non-SIMPLE plans must satisfy in order to afford fiduciaries protection from liability.

328. What are the disclosure requirements for plan sponsors attempting to comply with ERISA Section 404(c) regulations?

If a participant, in fact, exercises control over the assets in his account, the regulations under ERISA Section 404(c) state that he is not treated as a fiduciary and fiduciaries of the plan will not be liable for any loss or for any breach of fiduciary duty which is the result of the participant's exercise of control over assets in his own account. Labor Reg. §2550.404(c)-1.

In order to be afforded the protection of this limited liability, fiduciaries must comply with the requirement that they provide a broad range of investment alternatives (see Q 321), the requirement that they provide sufficient opportunities to give investment instructions regarding a participant's individual account (see Q 322), and the mandatory disclosure requirement of the items described below.

An identified plan fiduciary, or duly appointed representative, must provide each plan participant or beneficiary the following information:

1. A written explanation that the plan is intended to be an ERISA Section 404(c) plan and that plan fiduciaries may be relieved of liability for losses that are a result of participant investment instructions;

2. A description of the investment alternatives under the plan and a general description of the investment objectives and risk/return characteristics of each alternative, including information relating to the type and diversification of assets comprising that portfolio;

3. Identification of any designated investment managers the plan might provide for the participants;

4. An explanation of how to give investment instructions, any limits/restrictions on giving instructions (including information of withdrawal penalties and valuation adjustments) as well as any restrictions on the exercise of voting, tender or similar rights;

5. A description of transaction fees or expenses that are charged to the participant's account (e.g., commissions);

6. If the plan provides for investment in employer securities, a description of those procedures established to provide for confidentiality to participants regarding their transactions in those securities. This requirement includes the name, address and telephone number of any fiduciary in charge of maintaining such confidentiality and information on independent fiduciaries that are required in transactions that involve employer securities where there is a high potential for a conflict of interest;

7. Shareholder information, subsequent to a specific investment, including any material the plan receives regarding the exercise of voting and ownership rights to the extent such rights are passed through to the participant, along with references to any plan provisions regarding the exercise of these rights;

8. A copy of the most recent prospectus must be provided participants immediately after they have made an initial purchase of an investment which is subject to the Securities Act of 1933 (this may also be satisfied by providing the prospectus prior to the initial purchase); and

9. A description of those materials available only upon request (see below) and the identification of the person responsible for providing that information. See Labor Reg. §2550.404c-1(b)(2)(i)(B)(1).

ERISA Section 404(c) plans must also provide the following information to participants and beneficiaries, but only if specifically requested:

1. A description of the annual operating expenses borne by plan investment alternatives, such as investment management fees. Also included would be any expense charges or record keeping fees, expressed as a percentage of the net assets of the investment, which may reduce the participant's return in the underlying investment;

2. Copies of financial statements, annual reports or other information relating to an investment alternative, to the extent it has been provided to the plan;

3. A list of assets in each designated investment alternative and the value of each asset, as well as the name of the contract issuer and the rate of return on fixed rate investment contracts (such as GICs and BICs);

4. Information concerning the share value or unit value of investment alternatives available to participants as well as information concerning the past and current investment performance of the investment option; and

5. The value of shares or units in investment alternatives held in the account of a participant. See Labor Reg. §2550.404c-1(b)(2)(i)(B)(2).

The Securities and Exchange Commission has issued a final rule which permits mutual funds to offer investors an easier to read and less technical summary disclosure document referred to as a "profile" which is intended to make it easier for investors to understand a fund's risks, strategies and performance. Mutual fund companies are permitted to tailor these profiles for 404(c) participants and to include enrollment forms for participating in the fund. The SEC appears to have considered the DOL's publicly stated concerns regarding the level of disclosure and understanding of information regarding risks and fees plan participants receive. SEC Final Rule, 63 Fed. Reg. 13968, (3-23-98).

329. May an ERISA Section 404(c) plan fiduciary refuse to follow affirmative investment instructions from a participant or beneficiary?

Identified ERISA Section 404(c) plan fiduciaries are generally required to follow any affirmative investment instructions they receive from participants or beneficiaries. However, identified plan fiduciaries are not required to follow affirmative investment instructions which, if carried out would:

1. Result in the occurrence of a prohibited transaction (see Chapter IV);

2. Result in the receipt of taxable income to the plan;

3. Place the plan in jeopardy of losing its tax-qualified status under IRC Section 401;

4. Violate the plan documents and the plan's governing instruments (insofar as they are consistent with the provisions of ERISA);

5. Result in the maintenance of any indicia of ownership outside of the United States or outside of the jurisdiction of the United States district courts;

6. Subject the participant's or beneficiary's account to a loss in excess of the actual account balance; or

7. Result in the occurrence of prohibited self-dealing under ERISA (see Chapter IV) such as a sale, exchange or leasing of property between a plan sponsor and the plan (except for ERISA Section 408 specified exemptions), a loan to a plan sponsor or affiliate, acquisition or sale of any employer real property, or the acquisition or sale of any employer securities (except for those specifically permitted under the regulations, see Q 330). Labor Regs. §§2550.404c-1(b)(2)(ii)(B), 2550.404c-1(d)(2)(ii).

330. When may a participant or beneficiary invest in employer securities under an ERISA Section 404(c) plan?

An ERISA Section 404(c) plan may permit the investment of participant or beneficiary assets in employer securities if the following requirements have been satisfied:

1. The securities are "qualifying employer securities" (see Chapter VIII);

2. The securities are (a) stock, or (b) an equity interest in certain publicly traded partnerships (as defined in IRC Section 7704(b) and Labor Reg. §2550.404c-1(d)(2)(ii)(E)(4)(ii));

3. The securities are publicly traded on a national exchange or other generally recognized market;

4. The securities are traded with sufficient frequency and in sufficient volume to assure that participant or beneficiary directions to buy and sell the security may be acted upon promptly and efficiently;

5. Information provided to shareholders of such securities is provided to participants and beneficiaries with accounts holding such securities;

6. Voting, tender and similar rights are passed through to participants and beneficiaries with accounts holding such securities;

7. Information is maintained regarding the confidentiality procedures that relate to the purchase, holding and sale of securities, and the exercise of voting, tender and similar rights with respect to such securities by participants and beneficiaries, except to the extent necessary to comply with Federal laws or state laws not preempted by ERISA;

8. The plan designates a fiduciary who is responsible for ensuring that the confidentiality procedures designed to satisfy the safeguards mandated under the preceding paragraph (7) are being followed; *and*

9. An independent fiduciary is appointed to carry out activities where there is the potential for undue influence on participants and beneficiaries with regard to the direct or indirect exercise of shareholder rights. Labor Reg. §2550.404c-1(d)(2)(ii)(E)(4).

Where an ERISA Section 404(c) plan does permit employer securities as an investment alternative, participants or beneficiaries must be allowed to transfer the assets invested in the employer securities alternative into any of the three mandated core investments as frequently as the participant or beneficiary is allowed to give investment instructions to the employer securities alternative. Participants and beneficiaries must also be permitted to transfer their assets out of the employer securities alternative into the low income producing cash equivalency alternative as often as the participant or beneficiary is permitted to give investment instructions to the employer securities alternative. Labor Reg. §2550.404c-1(b)(2)(ii)(C)(3)(ii).

2002 ERISA Facts

331. How are ERISA Section 404(c) plans affected by the use of investment managers?

Investment managers' decisions regarding the management of 404(c) plan participant assets "are not direct and necessary results" of their designation. In other words, the investment managers charged with the management and investment of ERISA Section 404(c) plan assets may not claim relief from their fiduciary obligations, and will retain responsibility for them, in spite of the fact that they have been appointed in accordance with the applicable regulations under ERISA Section 404(c). See Labor Reg. §2550.404c-1(d)(2)(iii).

ERISA Section 404(c) plans may permit the selection of investment managers by individual participants, or the plan may provide for the designation of investment managers from whom the participants may make a selection. If this is the case, the employer will retain its fiduciary obligations to prudently select and monitor the investment managers.

332. May ERISA Section 404(c) plan trustees override the investment directions of missing participants?

Yes. The Department of Labor has stated that an individual account plan will maintain ERISA Section 404(c) status where the plan's trustees prudently invest the funds of missing participants who could not be found after a diligent search. See DOL Adv. Op. 96-02A.

The employer seeking the opinion of the DOL in Opinion Letter 96-02A presented a history of hiring documented immigrants who were active participants in their 401(k) plan. Certain participants had unlawfully assumed the identities of properly documented workers. As a result of enforcement action by the Immigration and Naturalization Service, these employees were terminated and subsequently deported. The trustees made diligent efforts to locate the deported participants, but were unsuccessful.

The trustees were concerned that following the last investment instructions of missing participants would be imprudent due to a change in circumstances. The trustees proposed moving the missing participant account balances into a balanced mutual fund. The DOL advised that the plan would not lose its ERISA Section 404(c) status if the trustees prudently invested the assets of missing participants in a manner which contravened the last written investment instructions of missing participants.

The DOL cautioned, however, that ERISA Section 404(c) relief is provided only with respect to a transaction where a participant or beneficiary has exercised independent control "in fact" with respect to the investment of assets. Consequently, the DOL noted that any exercise of control by fiduciaries to override the last written investment instructions of a missing participant would not be afforded the transactional relief of ERISA Section 404(c). See DOL Adv. Op. 96-02A.

333. May ERISA Section 404(c) plan participants direct investments into collectibles?

No. The acquisition of any collectible by an individually directed account under a qualified plan (or by an IRA qualified under IRC Section 408) will be treated as a taxable distribution. IRC Sec. 408(m).

The term "collectible" generally means any work of art, rug or antique, metal or gem, stamp or coin, alcoholic beverage or any other tangible property specified by the Secretary of the Treasury as a collectible for purposes of IRC Section 408(m). However, certain bullion and certain gold, silver or platinum coins are not considered collectibles for this purpose. See IRC Secs. 401(m)(2), 401(m)(3).

334. What is the treatment of proceeds received by an employee welfare benefit plan in connection with a demutualization of an insurance company?

Generally, a mutual insurance company has no authorized, issued, or outstanding stock. Instead, the insurance and annuity policies issued by the mutual insurance company combine both insurance coverage and proprietary ownership rights in the company. The process of demutualization generally involves a reorganization that converts the company from a mutual insurance company to a stock insurance company. In such a case, the equity value of the company is distributed to eligible policyholders in the form of stock, cash, or policy credits in consideration of extinguishing the policyholders' membership interests in the company. Policyholder obligations generally remain unchanged and fully in force after the conversion. The amount of consideration each policyholder receives is generally dependent on various actuarial assumptions.

The U.S. Department of Labor ("DOL") issued guidance on the treatment of demutualization proceeds received by an employee benefit plan in the form of an Information Letter dated February 15, 2002, concurrently with two advisory opinion letters dealing with other issues involved in a demutualization. See DOL Opinion Letters 2001-02A, 2001-03A. The Information Letter addressed, in part, the applicability of ERISA's trust requirements to the treatment of proceeds received by an employee welfare benefit plan in connection with a demutualization of an insurance company and the alternatives available to a plan in such a case.

The DOL noted in the Information Letter that the application of the trust requirements of ERISA section 403 depends on whether the demutualization proceeds received by a plan constitute plan assets. In the view of the DOL, generally, some or all of the proceeds paid to an ERISA-covered employee welfare benefit plan in consideration of a demutualization may constitute plan assets if the proceeds would be deemed to be owned by the plan under ordinary notions of property rights. See Advisory Opinion 92-02A, Jan. 17, 1992 (assets of a plan generally are to be identified on the basis of ordinary notions of property rights under non-ERISA law). Additionally, if the plan participants pay a portion of the premiums to the plan, the portion of the demutualization proceeds attributable to participant contributions must be treated as plan assets. In determining what portion of the demutualization proceeds are attributable to participant contributions, the DOL noted that appropriate consideration should be made by the plan fiduciary to the facts and circumstances that the fiduciary knows or should know are relevant to the determination. Such a determination includes the documents and instruments governing the plan and the proportion of total participant contributions to the total premiums paid over an appropriate time period. Moreover, if the plan or trust is the policyholder, or where the policy is paid for out of trust assets, the DOL believes that all of the proceeds received by the policyholder in connection with a demutualization would constitute plan assets. DOL Information Letter, Groom Law Group, (2/18/2001).

The Information Letter also provides DOL guidance on how to apply demutualization proceeds received by a plan. The DOL notes that, consistent with ERISA section 403, the proceeds could be placed in trust until appropriately expended in accordance with the terms of the plan. Alternatively, prior to or simultaneous with the distribution of demutualization proceeds constituting plan assets, the DOL suggests that such assets could be applied to enhancing plan benefits under existing, supplemental or new insurance policies or contracts; applied toward future participant premium payments; or otherwise held by the insurance company on behalf of the plan without violating the requirements of section 403. DOL Information Letter, Groom Law Group, (2/18/2001).

Another issue involved in the treatment of proceeds received by an employee welfare benefit plan in connection with a demutualization of an insurance company is determining how to allocate the proceeds among the plan's participants. The DOL briefly addressed this issue in DOL Opinion Letter 2001-02A and noted that the general standards of fiduciary conduct under ERISA section 404 apply. In particular, a fiduciary of a plan making such a determination must act with impartiality to the plan's participants, and not select an allocation method that benefits the fiduciary (as a plan participant) at the expense of other participants in the plan. Furthermore, if a single policy covers multiple plans, the use of proceeds generated by one plan to benefit the participants of another plan may constitute a breach of the duty of loyalty to the plan's participants.

Finally, although the application of the trust requirement of ERISA section 403 may require that the proceeds of a demutualization be placed in trust for the benefit of plan participants and beneficiaries, the DOL addressed the issue of whether an employee welfare benefit plan funded solely by insurance contracts must establish a formal trust merely to receive and hold such proceeds for a limited period of time. In response to this issue, the DOL acknowledged that the costs and burdens involved in complying with ERISA's trust and reporting requirements for the one-time, receipt of demutualization proceeds could be burdensome in some cases. In consideration of the nature of the affected plans and expected short-term exhaustion of demutualization proceeds, the DOL found it appropriate to provide relief, pending the release of further guidance on the matter, in the form of not asserting a violation in any enforcement proceeding solely because of a failure to hold demutualization proceeds in trust if the following conditions are satisfied:

1. The plan is not otherwise required to maintain a trust under ERISA section 403.

2. The assets consist solely of proceeds received by the plan in connection with a demutualization.

3. The proceeds, and any earnings thereon, are placed in the name of the plan in an interest-bearing account, in the case of cash, or custodial account, in the case of stock, as soon as reasonably possible following receipt.

4. The assets are subject to the control of a designated plan fiduciary.

5. As soon as reasonably possible but no later than twelve (12) months following receipt, the proceeds are applied for:

    a) the payment of participant premiums; or

    b) applied to plan benefit enhancements; or

    c) distributed to plan participants.

6. The designated fiduciary maintains such documents and records as are necessary under ERISA with respect to the foregoing.

For those plans satisfying the above conditions, the DOL also will not assert a violation in any enforcement proceeding or assess a civil penalty with respect to such plans because of a failure to meet the reporting requirements by reason of not coming within the limited exemptions set forth in Labor Regulation sections 2520.104-20 and 2520.104-44 solely as a result of receiving demutualization proceeds constituting, in whole or in part, plan assets. DOL Information Letter, Groom Law Group, (2/18/2001).

The Information Letter and advisory opinion letters can be found at http://www.dol.gov/dol/pwba/public/programs/ori/advisory2001/opinion01.htm.

CHAPTER V

PROHIBITED TRANSACTIONS

335. In general, what are the fiduciary and prohibited transaction provisions of ERISA?

ERISA Section 406 supplements the general duties imposed on fiduciaries (discussed in detail in Chapter IV), by providing a list of specifically prohibited transactions between a plan and a "party in interest" (see Q 338). The questions in this chapter discuss the various types of prohibited transactions, who is subject to the prohibited transaction rules, the penalties for engaging in prohibited transactions, and how to correct prohibited transactions.

Both ERISA and the Internal Revenue Code statutorily exempt certain transactions from the prohibited transaction rules. In addition, the Department of Labor, and sometimes the Internal Revenue Service, may grant conditional and unconditional individual or class exemptions from all or part of the restrictions imposed by the prohibited transaction rules. Individual exemptions offer relief only to the person requesting the exemption, while class exemptions provide relief to parties who engage in transactions of the type specified by the class exemption. The exemptions and procedures to obtain exemptions are discussed in Chapter VI.

Rather than leaving all fiduciary transactions to be judged by the general standard of care found in ERISA Section 404, ERISA Section 406 was adopted by Congress to prevent plans from engaging in certain types of transactions that had been used previously to benefit other parties at the expense of the plans' participants and beneficiaries. *Reich v. Compton*, 57 F.3d 270 (3rd Cir. 1995). The prohibited transaction rules indicate a desire by Congress to prevent those transactions that offer a high potential for the loss of plan assets or for insider abuse, by prohibiting such transactions. *Cutaiar v. Marshall*, 590 F.2d 523 (3rd Cir. 1979); *Marshall v. Kelly*, 465 F. Supp. 341 (W.D. Okla. 1978).

The Internal Revenue Code maintains a nearly identical version of the prohibited transaction rules, which prohibit certain transactions between a plan and a "disqualified person." See IRC Sec. 4975. Although the terms party in interest and disqualified person are similar, a party in interest under ERISA encompasses a broader range of persons.

In order for a transaction to be considered a prohibited transaction under ERISA, a "fiduciary" must cause the plan to engage in the transaction, and must (or should) know that such a transaction constitutes a prohibited transaction. ERISA Sec. 406(a)(1). A fiduciary who violates the prohibitions set forth in ERISA is personally liable for any losses incurred by the plan and for any ill-gotten profits, and may be subject to other equitable and remedial relief that may be deemed appropriate by a court. ERISA Sec. 409. The Eleventh Circuit Court of Appeals has ruled that non-fiduciary parties in interest may be sued by the DOL for prohibited transaction violations due to ERISA Section 502(a)(5), which permits the DOL to seek equitable relief to redress such violations without restricting the types of parties who may be sued. *Herman v. South Carolina National Bank*, 140 F.3d 1413, (11th Cir. 1998), *cert. denied*, 119 S.Ct. 1030 (1999). In addition, a person who participates in a prohibited transaction may be subject to penalties and excise taxes under the IRC. These excise taxes are imposed automatically and significantly increase if the prohibited transaction is not timely corrected. IRC Sec. 4975. See Q 357.

336. What plans are subject to the prohibited transaction restrictions?

The prohibited transaction restrictions apply to all tax-qualified retirement plans, individual retirement accounts, individual retirement annuities, and medical savings accounts.

The prohibited transaction provisions do *not* apply to the following: (1) governmental plans; (2) church plans that have not elected to be subject to the participation, vesting, and funding standards under IRC Section 410; (3) plans maintained solely for the purpose of complying with applicable workmen's compensation, unemployment compensation, or disability insurance laws; (4) plans maintained outside of the United States primarily for the benefit of persons substantially all of whom are nonresident aliens; (5) unfunded excess benefit plans; (6) plans that are unfunded and maintained by an employer primarily for the purpose of providing deferred compensation for a select group of management or highly compensated employees; and (7) any agreement described in IRC Section 736, which provides payments to a retired partner or deceased partner or a deceased partner's successor in interest. In addition, under the Internal Revenue Code, the prohibited transaction restrictions do not apply to plans that are issued a guaranteed benefit policy, or to any assets of the insurance company, insurance service, or insurance organization merely because of its issuance of such policy. ERISA Secs. 4(b), 401(a); IRC Secs. 736, 4975.

337. What is a prohibited transaction?

Under ERISA, "prohibited transaction" means a transaction in which a plan fiduciary causes the plan to engage, if he knows (or should know) that such transaction constitutes a direct or indirect: (1) sale or exchange, or leasing, of any property between the plan and a party in interest; (2) lending of money or other extension of credit between the plan and a party in interest; (3) furnishing of goods, services, or facilities between the plan and a party in interest; (4) transfer to, or use by or for the benefit of, a party in interest, of any plan assets; or (5) acquisition, on behalf of the plan, of any employer security or employer real property in violation of ERISA Section 407. ERISA Sec. 406(a)(1).

Under the Internal Revenue Code, the term "prohibited transaction" means any direct or indirect: (1) sale or exchange, or leasing, of any property between a plan and a disqualified person; (2) lending of money or other extension of credit between a plan and a disqualified person; (3) furnishing of goods, services, or facilities between a plan and a disqualified person; (4) transfer to, or use by or for the benefit of, a disqualified person of plan income or assets; (5) act by a disqualified person who is a fiduciary whereby he deals with the income or assets of a plan in his own interest or for his own account; or (6) receipt of any consideration for a personal account by any disqualified person who is a fiduciary from any party dealing with the plan in connection with a transaction involving the income or assets of the plan. IRC Sec. 4975(c)(1). In contrast to ERISA, the IRC does not contain restrictions relating to employer securities.

These transactions described in ERISA are per se prohibited transactions, designed to prevent a trustee "from being put into a position where he has dual loyalties and therefore he cannot act exclusively for the benefit of a plan's participants and beneficiaries." *NLRB v. Amax Coal Co.*, 453 U.S. 950 (1981). The per se nature of the prohibitions is emphasized by the fact that the existence of a violation does not depend on whether any harm results from the transaction. *Marshall v. Kelly*, 465 F. Supp. 341 (W.D. Okla. 1978). Lack of harm to the plan or the good faith or lack of the same on the part of the borrower is not relevant, or controlling, under ERISA Section 406. *M & R Inv. Co., Inc. v. Fitzsimmons*, 484 F. Supp. 1041 (DC Nev. 1980). The transactions enumerated in ERISA Section 406(a)(1) are per se violations of ERISA regardless of the motivation that initiated the transaction, the prudence of the transaction, or the absence of any harm arising from the transaction. *Beck v. Levering*, 947 F.2d 639 (2nd Cir. 1991); *Donovan v. Cunningham*, 716 F.2d 1455 (5th Cir. 1983). However, acts that do not fall within the specific list of prohibitions proscribed by ERISA Section 406(a)(1) do not constitute per se violations of ERISA. *Brock v. Citizens Bank of Clovis*, 841 F.2d 344 (10th Cir. 1988).

338. Who is a party in interest or a disqualified person?

Party in Interest

The prohibited transaction rules under ERISA affect a party in interest. Under ERISA, a party in interest is defined as:

1. Any fiduciary (including, but not limited to, any administrator, officer, trustee, or custodian), counsel, or employee of such employee benefit plan;

2. A person providing services to such plan;

3. An employer any of whose employees are covered by such plan;

4. An employee organization any of whose members are covered by such plan;

5.   A direct or indirect owner of 50% or more of:

      a) the combined voting power of all classes of stock entitled to vote or the total value of shares of all classes of stock of a corporation,

      b) the capital interest or the profits interest of a partnership, or

      c) the beneficial interest of a trust or unincorporated enterprise,

which is an employer or an employee organization described in (3) or (4) above (the Secretary of Labor, after consultation and coordination with the Secretary of the Treasury, may, by regulation, prescribe a percentage lower than 50%);

6.   A relative of any individual described in (1), (2), (3), or (5) above (ERISA Section 3(15) defines "relative" to mean a spouse, ancestor, lineal descendant, or spouse of a lineal descendant);

7.   A corporation, partnership, or trust or estate of which (or in which) 50% or more of:

      a) the combined voting power of all classes of stock entitled to vote, or the total value of shares of all classes of stock of such corporation,

      b) the capital interest or profits interest of such partnership, or

      c) the beneficial interest of such trust or estate,

is owned directly or indirectly, or held by persons described in (1), (2), (3), (4), or (5) above (the Secretary of Labor, after consultation and coordination with the Secretary of the Treasury, may, by regulation, prescribe a percentage lower than 50%);

8.   An employee, officer, director (or an individual having powers or responsibilities similar to those of officers or directors), or a 10% or more shareholder (directly or indirectly), of a person described in (2), (3), (4), (5), or (7) above, or of the employee benefit plan (the Secretary of Labor, after consultation and coordination with the Secretary of the Treasury, may, by regulation, prescribe a percentage lower than 10%); or

9.   A 10% or more (directly or indirectly in capital or profits) partner or joint venturer of a person described in (2), (3), (4), (5), or (7) above (the Secretary of Labor, after consultation and coordination with the Secretary of the Treasury, may, by regulation, prescribe a percentage lower than 10%). ERISA Sec. 3(14).

Disqualified Person

Under the Internal Revenue Code, the prohibited transaction rules apply to a "disqualified person" rather than a party in interest. The term "disqualified person" covers a range of people, including employers, unions, and their officials, fiduciaries, persons providing services to a plan, and persons whose relationship to the plan is not immediately apparent. More specifically, a disqualified person is defined as a person who is:

1.   A fiduciary;

2.   A person providing services to the plan;

3.   An employer any of whose employees are covered by the plan;

4.   An employee organization any of whose members are covered by the plan;

5.   A direct or indirect owner of 50% or more of:

   a) the combined voting power of all classes of stock entitled to vote or the total value of shares of all classes of stock of a corporation,

   b) the capital interest or the profits interest of a partnership, or

   c) the beneficial interest of a trust or unincorporated enterprise,

   which is an employer or an employee organization described in (3) or (4) above (the Secretary of the Treasury, after consultation and coordination with the Secretary of Labor or his delegate, may, by regulation, prescribe a percentage lower than 50%);

6.   A member of the family of any individual described in (1), (2), (3), or (5) above (the family of an individual includes a spouse, ancestor, lineal descendant, and spouse of a lineal descendant);

2002 ERISA Facts

7. A corporation, partnership, or trust or estate of which (or in which) 50% or more of:

    a) the combined voting power of all classes of stock entitled to vote or the total value of shares of all classes of stock of such corporation,

    b) the capital interest or profits interest of such partnership, or

    c) the beneficial interest of such trust or estate,

    is owned directly or indirectly, or held by persons described in (1), (2), (3), (4), or (5) above (the Secretary of the Treasury, after consultation and coordination with the Secretary of Labor or his delegate, may, by regulation, prescribe a percentage lower than 50%);

8. An officer, director (or an individual having powers or responsibilities similar to those of officers or directors), a 10% or more shareholder, or a highly compensated employee (earning 10% or more of the yearly wages of an employer) of a person described in (3), (4), (5), or (7) above (the Secretary of the Treasury, after consultation and coordination with the Secretary of Labor or his delegate, may, by regulation, prescribe a percentage lower than 10%); or

9. A 10% or more (in capital or profits) partner or joint venturer of a person described in (3), (4), (5), or (7) above (the Secretary of the Treasury, after consultation and coordination with the Secretary of Labor or his delegate, may, by regulation, prescribe a percentage lower than 10%). IRC 4975(e)(2).

A party in interest under ERISA and a "disqualified person" under the Internal Revenue Code include generally the same group of individuals and entities, however, only employees who are highly compensated (earning 10% or more of the yearly wages of an employer) are disqualified persons under the Internal Revenue Code.

A recent Tax Court case held that while an individual may not be a fiduciary as defined under ERISA, he may still be liable for excise taxes as a disqualified person under the Internal Revenue Code for participating in a prohibited transaction. The court stated that although ERISA provides an exception for transactions conducted through individual account plans (ERISA Sec. 404(c)(1)), the Internal Revenue Code has no similar provisions preventing the attachment of liability. In so ruling, the court noted that under ERISA liability runs directly to the fiduciary for breaches of fiduciary duty. Under the Internal Revenue Code, however, liability runs to disqualified persons and applies whether or not a fiduciary has breached his duties under ERISA. *Flahertys Arden Bowl, Inc. v. Comm.*, 115 TC 269 (2000), *aff'd*, 88 AFTR 2d 2001-5547 (8th Cir. 2001).

Transaction Between a Plan and a Party in Interest

339. What are the rules regarding the sale, exchange, or leasing of property between a plan and a party in interest?

A plan fiduciary is prohibited from causing the plan to engage in a transaction if he knows (or should know) that the transaction constitutes a direct or indirect sale or exchange, or leasing, of any property between the plan and a party in interest. ERISA Sec. 406(a)(1)(A). ERISA protects a plan against influences exerted by a party in interest, as that term is defined in ERISA Section 3(14). *McDougall v. Donovan*, 552 F. Supp. 1206 (N.D. Ill. 1982). This prohibition is violated when, for example, one corporation's plan leases a building to a second corporation where both companies are 95% owned by the same individual. DOL Adv. Op. 76-14.

The acquisition of a jet by a plan from an aircraft firm, acting as a third party dealer, where the aircraft company acquired the jet from the same union that represented the participants of the plan was held to be an indirect sale prohibited by ERISA Section 406(a)(1)(A). Knowing that the union was trading in the airplane, the plan trustees prepared a bid equivalent to the trade-in value of the airplane, and purchased the airplane on the same day that the union traded it in. The presence of the aircraft company as an intermediary did not add an "arm's length" element to remove the transaction from the prohibitions of ERISA. This case illustrates that the prohibitions of ERISA Section 406 cannot be easily circumvented or legitimized by the insertion of a third party; a party who, incidentally, could profit from its role. *McDougall v. Donovan*, 552 F. Supp. 1206 (N.D. Ill. 1982).

According to a Department of Labor Opinion Letter, a transaction will not be prohibited if the transaction is an ordinary "blind" transaction purchase or sale of securities through an exchange where neither buyer or seller (nor the agent of either) knows the identity of the other party involved. DOL Adv. Op. 92-23A. That Opinion Letter addressed whether a bank would engage in a prohibited transaction if, in its capacity as directed trustee of an employee benefit plan, it purchased securities issued by its parent company on behalf of any such plan, at the proper direction of a named fiduciary having the authority to direct investments by the bank, or of an investment manager appointed by a named fiduciary.

According to the Opinion Letter, purchases and sales of a bank's stock in blind transactions executed by unaffiliated brokers at the proper direction of named fiduciaries of plans of its customers will not constitute transactions described in ERISA Section 406(a)(1)(A). The Opinion Letter reasoned that there is no reason to impose a sanction on a fiduciary (or party in interest) merely because, by chance, the other party turns out to be a party in interest (or plan). DOL Adv. Op. 92-23A.

In-kind contributions to a plan, which reduce the obligation of a plan sponsor or employer to make a contribution measured in terms of cash amounts, also constitute a prohibited transaction, unless a statutory or administrative exemption applies (see Chapter VI). For example, if a profit sharing plan required the employer to make annual contributions "in cash or in kind" equal to a given percentage of the employer's net profits for the year, an in-kind contribution used to reduce this obligation would constitute a prohibited transaction in the absence of an exemption, because the amount of the contribution obligation is measured in terms of cash amounts (a percentage of profits), even though the terms of the plan purport to permit in-kind contributions. Labor Reg. §2509.94-3.

An employer, as plan fiduciary, did not engage in a prohibited transaction with a party in interest, when, in the course of a corporate spinoff, it caused its plan to sell or transfer assets to the other company's plan. The successor company was not a party in interest, and the court said that to hold that the transfer was a prohibited transaction would be to construe the prohibited transaction rules to conflict with the permissive attitude of ERISA Section 208 towards plan mergers and transfers. *United Steelworkers of America, Local 2116 v. Cyclops Corp.*, 860 F.2d 189 (6th Cir. 1988).

340. What are the rules regarding the lending of money or other extension of credit between the plan and a party in interest?

A plan fiduciary is prohibited from causing a plan to engage in a transaction, if he knows (or should know) that such transaction constitutes a direct or indirect lending of money (or other extension of credit) between the plan and a party in interest. ERISA Sec. 406(a)(1)(B). This prohibition often extends to a loan made by a plan to a plan sponsor, to a union that is a party in interest, and to a business owned by a party in interest. In addition, a prohibited transaction occurs when a plan loan is made to a third party, where the fiduciaries know and intend that the proceeds of the loan are to be transferred to a party in interest. *Dole v. Lundberg*, 733 F. Supp. 895 (N.D. Texas 1989); *Donovan v. Bryans*, 566 F. Supp. 1258 (E.D. Pa. 1983).

For example, if a sole shareholder of the plan sponsor, acting as trustee of a plan, arranges loans from an employee benefit plan to a party in interest (in addition to making a loan to himself and causing the plan to renew outstanding loans to the plan sponsor), that transaction will violate the prohibition against lending of money or other extension of credit between a plan and a party in interest. *Marshall v. Kelly*, 465 F. Supp. 341 (W.D. Okla. 1978).

The statute prohibits lending between the plan and a party in interest, and although the intention behind the statute is to keep parties in interest from borrowing from the plan, its plain reading prohibits loans in both directions. *Brock v. Citizens Bank of Clovis*, 841 F.2d 344 (10th Cir. 1988), *cert. denied*, 488 U.S. 829 (1988); *Rutland v. Comm.*, 89 TC 1137 (1987). This was illustrated in a case where the owners of the plan sponsor, acting as trustees of the plan, loaned money to the plan and executed guarantees on behalf of the plan. The court held that loans made by disqualified persons (the equivalent of parties in interest under the Internal Revenue Code) to plans are absolutely prohibited. *Janpol v. Comm.*, 101 TC 518 (1993).

There is, however, no per se prohibition against a fiduciary lending money to an unrelated person who thereafter uses the loan proceeds to pay obligations to a party in interest. If a violation exists, it must arise by implication. This is the case if loans are made to third parties in order to avoid application of ERISA Section 406(a). *Brock v. Citizens Bank of Clovis*, 841 F.2d 344 (10th Cir. 1988).

A prohibited transaction under ERISA does not necessarily require that the assets of the plan be actually disbursed to a party in interest. In the case of a loan to a party in interest, even if the proceeds of the loan are never disbursed, there still may exist a lending of money where a contractually created right to the loan proceeds is not severable from the contract that created it.

In some cases, the culpability arises with the contract's creation, and not with the basically ministerial act of disbursing the funds. *M & R Inv. Co., Inc. v. Fitzsimmons*, 685 F.2d 283 (9th Cir. 1982).

Lack of knowledge on the part of a fiduciary (the fact that he does not know or should not have known that a borrower is a party in interest) is not a defense under ERISA Section 406(a)(1)(B). Knowledge is imputed to a fiduciary by the requirement that a "'thorough investigation' is mandated in any `significant transaction' to determine if the borrower is a party in interest," and knowledge, actual or constructive, on the part of fiduciary has no bearing on whether the transaction is prohibited. *M & R Inv. Co., Inc. v. Fitzsimmons*, 484 F. Supp. 1041 (DC Nev. 1980); see *Marshall v. Kelly*, 465 F. Supp. 341 (W.D. Okla. 1978).

341. What are the rules regarding furnishing goods, services, and facilities between the plan and a party in interest?

A plan fiduciary is prohibited from engaging in a transaction, if he knows (or should know) that such transaction constitutes a direct or indirect furnishing of goods, services, or facilities between the plan and a party in interest. ERISA Sec. 406(a)(1)(C). This prohibition is comprehensive and applies to the furnishing of living quarters, office space, equipment, and supplies, as well as accounting, legal, investment advisory, and computer services. This prohibition was illustrated where a corporation wholly owned by a union plan made excessive payments to the plan trustees for doing work for the local union as well as work for the corporation. *Marshall v. Snyder*, 572 F.2d 894 (2nd Cir. 1978).

On the other hand, a multiemployer plan was not seen as providing services to a participating employer merely because it undertook the task of directly reporting the third-party sick payments to recipient employees and to the IRS rather than providing the employers with the statements of those payments and obliging them to forward the information to the employees and to the IRS. DOL Adv. Op. 82-32A.

In addition, the furnishing of goods and services by the subsidiary of the sponsoring employer (and, thus, a party in interest) to an unrelated tenant of real property owned by the plan, for the repair and maintenance of the property was not a prohibited transaction. As the tenant was responsible for the maintenance of the property and only the tenant had enforceable rights under any service contracts it executed, the transaction was not between the plan and a party in interest, but was between a tenant and a provider of goods and services. DOL Adv. Op. 83-45A.

Under certain circumstances, a party in interest may be exempted from the prohibition of furnishing goods and services to a plan. ERISA exempts from the prohibition transaction rules a plan's payment to a party in interest, including a fiduciary, for office space or any service (or a combination of services) if (1) the office space or service is necessary for the establishment or operation of the plan; (2) the office space or service is furnished under a contract or arrangement which is reasonable; and (3) no more than reasonable compensation is paid for such office space or service. ERISA Sec. 408(b)(2); see Chapter VI.

342. What are the rules regarding transfers of assets of the plan?

The direct or indirect transfer to, or use by or for the benefit of, a party in interest of any plan assets is prohibited. ERISA Sec. 406(a)(1)(D). For example, the trustees of a union-sponsored pension plan engaged in prohibited transactions by loaning money to an association that was "closely-related" to the union. A prohibited transaction occurs when a fiduciary has subjective intent to benefit a party in interest, and the fiduciary knows (or reasonably should know) that the transaction represents a use of plan assets for the benefit of a party in interest. Where the trustees of a plan subjectively intended to benefit the union through the lending of plan assets to the association, and the union did, in fact, benefit from the loans, the transaction violated ERISA Section 406(a)(1)(D). *Reich v. Compton*, 57 F.3d 270 (3rd Cir. 1995).

A fiduciary does not necessarily need to have a culpable motive in order to have engaged in a prohibited transaction under ERISA Section 406(a)(1)(D). For example, a plan trustee transferred assets from the plan trust to his own bank account allegedly to protect the plan from a fraudulent scheme by plan participants. Because ERISA Section 406 on its face does not require culpable motive, the trustee's motive for the transfer of assets was not a defense to the prohibited transaction. *PBGC v. Fletcher*, 750 F. Supp. 233 (W.D. Texas 1990).

A prohibited transaction also occurs if there is an arrangement under which a plan invests in, or retains its investment in, an investment company, and, as part of the arrangement, it is expected that the investment company will purchase securities from a party in interest. Similarly, the plan's purchase of an insurance policy, pursuant to an arrangement under which it is expected that the insurance company will make a loan to a party in interest, is a prohibited transaction. Labor Reg. §2509.75-2.

A prohibited transaction also occurs if a fiduciary, acting as plan trustee: (1) renews outstanding loans with the sponsor of the plan (thus allowing continued use of plan assets by the plan sponsor); (2) causes the plan to make a loan to himself (thus transferring plan assets to himself for his own use and benefit); and (3) causes the plan to transfer its assets to the plan sponsor. *Marshall v. Kelly*, 465 F. Supp. 341 (W.D. Okla. 1978).

The trustees of collectively bargained pension and welfare plans violated ERISA, by authorizing monthly payments for each other from the plans' assets as compensation for their services as trustees and by authorizing the plans to make contributions on their behalf, so as to make each other eligible for the receipt of benefits from the plans. The trustees' receipt of the monthly payments from the plans, the contributions made on their behalf, and the receipt of benefits from the plans each constituted a separate prohibited transaction in violation of ERISA Section 406(a)(1)(D). *Donovan v. Daugherty*, 550 F. Supp. 390 (S.D. Ala. 1982).

In another case, plan trustees released parties in interest from guarantees of a plan loan. The court held that this constituted "a direct or indirect transfer" of "assets of the plan" to parties in interest, or the use of "assets of the plan" for the benefit of parties in interest, in violation of ERISA Section 406(a)(1)(D), because prior to their release, the guarantees were assets of the plan. In addition, the release benefited the guarantors at the expense of the plan, because the plan no longer had the same security to enable it to collect on the outstanding amount of its loan. Thus, assets of the plan were transferred for the benefit of parties in interest and the release of defendants' guarantees constituted a prohibited transaction under ERISA Section 406(a)(1)(D). *Reich v. Polera Bldg. Corp.*, 20 EBC 1100 (S.D. NY 1996).

In contrast, unless a transaction falls within the specific list of dealings proscribed by ERISA, it does not constitute a per se violation of the prohibited transaction rules. For example, a violation did not exist where a plan loaned money to unrelated persons, who then used all or a portion of the funds received to pay off loans to the employer of the plan's participants. Although the plan trustees were also employees of the plan sponsor, there was no evidence to support the hypothesis that they acted for their own benefit by approving the third party loans to protect their employment with the plan sponsor. *Brock v. Citizens Bank of Clovis*, 841 F.2d 344 (10th Cir.), *cert. denied*, 488 U.S. 829 (1988).

Likewise, a party in interest does not violate ERISA Section 406(a)(1)(D) merely because the party derives some incidental benefit from the investment of plan assets in shared investments that are made simultaneously with investments by a fiduciary for its own account on identical terms and in the same relative proportions. Any benefit that the fiduciary might derive from these circumstances is incidental and would not violate ERISA Section 406(a)(1)(D). PTE 88-93.

The United States Supreme Court held that the payment of benefits by an employer pursuant to an early retirement program conditioned on the participants' release of employment related claims did not constitute a prohibited transaction under ERISA Section 406(a)(1)(D). Although the amendments to the plan offered increased benefits in exchange for a release of employment claims, and the employer received an incidental benefit from the releases, the amendments did not constitute the use of plan assets to "purchase" a significant benefit for the employer. The Court held that the payment of benefits pursuant to an amended plan, regardless of what the plan requires of the employee in return for those benefits, does not constitute a prohibited transaction, because ERISA Section 406(a)(1)(D) does not, in direct terms, include the payment of benefits by a plan administrator. In addition, the surrounding provisions suggest that the payment of benefits is in fact not a "transaction" in the sense that Congress used that term in ERISA Section 406(a). The Court reasoned that the prohibited "transactions" identified in ERISA Section 406(a) have in common the use of plan assets in a manner that is potentially harmful to the plan. However, the "payment of benefits conditioned on performance by plan participants cannot reasonably be said to share that characteristic." *Lockheed Corp. v. Spink*, 517 U.S. 882 (1996).

343. What are the rules regarding the acquisition, on behalf of a plan, of employer securities or employer real property?

A fiduciary is prohibited from causing a plan to engage in a transaction, if he knows (or should know) that such transaction constitutes a direct or indirect acquisition, on behalf of the plan, of any employer security or employer real property in violation of ERISA Section 407. ERISA Sec. 406(a)(1)(E).

This prohibition seeks to protect the judgment of fiduciaries against influences exerted by employers in the context of security and real property purchases. The United States Supreme Court emphasized that the purpose of ERISA Section 406(a)(1)(E) and related provisions is to insulate the trust from the employer's interest, and to ensure that the exclusive authority and discretion to arrange and control the assets of the plan rest in the fiduciaries alone, and not in the employer or union who might be responsible for the fiduciaries' appointments. *N.L.R.B. v. Amax Coal Co.*, 453 U.S. 950 (1981). The purchase or sale of securities by a plan in an effort to manipulate the price of such securities to the advantage of a party in interest is an example of what would violate ERISA Section 406(a)(1)(E). H.R. Conf. Rep. No. 93-1280, 93rd Cong., 2nd Sess., 310 (1974).

TRANSACTIONS BETWEEN A PLAN AND A FIDUCIARY

344. What are the rules regarding self-dealing and conflicts of interest?

In addition to the five specific prohibited transactions involving parties in interest under ERISA Section 406(a), ERISA Section 406(b) prohibits fiduciaries from engaging in various acts of self-dealing or conflicts of interest, and transactions involving the plan in which the fiduciary personally profits. These transactions compromise the fiduciary's duties of loyalty to the plan and acting exclusively for the benefit of the plan or participants and beneficiaries. The purpose of ERISA Section 406(b) is to prevent a fiduciary from being put in a position where he has dual loyalties, and, therefore, cannot act exclusively for the benefit of a plan's participants and beneficiaries.

Under these prohibitions, a plan fiduciary may not: (1) deal with the assets of the plan in his own interest or for his own account; (2) in his individual or in any other capacity, act in any transaction involving the plan on behalf of a party (or represent a party) whose interests are adverse to the interests of the plan or the interests of its participants or beneficiaries; or (3) receive any consideration for his own personal account from any party dealing with such plan in connection with a transaction involving the assets of the plan. ERISA Sec. 406(b).

Similar to ERISA, under the Internal Revenue Code, a disqualified person who is a fiduciary may not: (1) deal with the income or assets of a plan in his own interests or for his own account; or (2) receive any consideration for his own personal account from any party dealing with the plan in connection with a transaction involving the income or assets of the plan. IRC Secs. 4975(c)(1)(E), 4975(c)(1)(F).

The prohibitions of ERISA Section 406(b) supplement the other prohibitions of ERISA Section 406(a), by imposing on parties in interest who are fiduciaries a duty of undivided loyalty to the plans for which they act. These prohibitions are imposed upon fiduciaries to deter them from exercising the authority, control, or responsibility that makes them fiduciaries when they have interests that may conflict with the interests of the plans. In such cases, the fiduciaries have interests in the transactions that may affect the exercise of their best judgment as fiduciaries. Labor Reg. §2550.408b-2(e)(1); *Gilliam v. Edwards*, 492 F. Supp. 1255 (DC N.J. 1980).

Thus, a fiduciary may not use the authority, control, or responsibility that makes such person a fiduciary to cause a plan to pay an additional fee to such fiduciary (or to a person in which such fiduciary has an interest that may affect the exercise of such fiduciary's best judgment as a fiduciary) to provide a service. Nor may a fiduciary use such authority, control, or responsibility to cause a plan to enter into a transaction involving plan assets whereby such fiduciary (or a person in which such fiduciary has an interest that may affect the exercise of such fiduciary's best judgment as a fiduciary) will receive consideration from a third party in connection with such transaction. A person in which a fiduciary has an interest that may affect the exercise of such fiduciary's best judgment as a fiduciary includes a person who is a party in interest. Labor Reg. §2550.408b-2(e)(1).

Thus, ERISA Section 406(b) is specifically directed at the problem of fiduciary self-dealing, and absolutely prohibits a fiduciary from acting in a conflict of interest situation where his loyalties to the plan may be compromised or divided. *Donovan v. Daugherty*, 550 F. Supp. 390 (S.D. Ala. 1982). The legislative history of ERISA Section 406(b) and relevant case law indicate that Congress sought to prevent "kickbacks," making "illegal per se the types of transactions that experience had shown to entail a high potential for abuse."

Donovan v. Cunningham, 716 F.2d 1455 (5th Cir. 1983), *cert. denied,* 467 U.S. 1251 (1984).

Additionally, even in the absence of bad faith, or in the presence of a fair and reasonable transaction, ERISA Section 406(b) creates a per se violation and establishes a blanket prohibition of certain acts, easily applied, in order to facilitate Congress' remedial interest in protecting employee benefit plans. *Gilliam v. Edwards,* 492 F. Supp. 1255 (DC N.J. 1980); see also *Brink v. DaLesio,* 496 F. Supp. 1350 (DC Md. 1980), *aff'd in part and rev'd in part,* 667 F.2d 420 (4th Cir. 1981).

345. What are the rules regarding dealing with the assets of the plan in one's own interest or for one's own account?

A fiduciary is prohibited from dealing with the assets of the plan in his own interest or for his own account. ERISA Sec. 406(b)(1). This prohibition is aimed at a fiduciary's use of a plan's assets as a vehicle for advancing his own interests. Fiduciaries that cause pension plans to invest in companies in which they have financial interests, and that accept consulting and other fees from such companies are examples of violations of this provision. *Lowen v. Tower Asset Mgmt., Inc.,* 653 F. Supp 1542 (S.D. NY 1987).

A fiduciary, acting as plan trustee, dealt with the plan assets in his own interest by actively negotiating and designing an employment contract under which a pension fund was to pay him for his services as its administrator. The prohibited transaction was supported when the trustee made no attempt to disqualify himself or extract himself from the plan trustees' considerations. He also actively participated in or initiated the discussions leading to his employment as administrator, and was a guiding force at the trustees' meetings, encouraging them to award him the contract. The final contract was decidedly one-sided in his favor, and he reserved the sole ability to terminate it. Because the trustee had actively pursued and discussed the design of his own employment contract without proper regard for the interests of the fund, he had abandoned his fiduciary obligation to the pension plan in order to secure the best contract, in violation of ERISA Section 406(b)(1). *Gilliam v. Edwards,* 492 F. Supp 1255 (DC N.J. 1980).

A plan fiduciary also cannot use any of his fiduciary authority to cause the plan to make a loan to an entity in which he has an interest. This occured where a plan fiduciary caused a plan to renew the loans to a company which he owned, caused the plan to make a loan to himself, and caused the plan to make a payment of plan assets to the same company that he owned. *Marshall v. Kelly,* 465 F. Supp 341 (W.D. Okla. 1978).

A violation also occured when plan trustees authorized monthly payments for themselves from a plan as compensation for services rendered to the plan (they received full-time pay from contributing employers and unions), and they authorized the plan to make contributions on their behalf, so as to make themselves eligible to receive benefits from the plan. *Donovan v. Daugherty*, 550 F. Supp 390 (S.D. Ala. 1982).

Although a fiduciary is prohibited from dealing with the assets of the plan in his own interests of a financial nature, the term "interests" is not limited to financial interests. The term "interest" is read broadly to prevent the use of plan assets for any interest, financial or nonfinancial, other than the interests of the plan and its beneficiaries. For example, in a contest for corporate control, actions of the plan trustees (who were also officers of either the "target" or the "raider") who bought shares in a target corporation, in order to assist either the target's management or the raider in the quest for either corporate control or a control premium, could be seen as having a significant "interest" of their own in the outcome of the contest. The officers of the "target" might well be immediately concerned about holding onto their jobs, and the officers of the "raider" might find it in their interest, in terms of maintaining good relations with their superiors, to assist their corporation in its acquisition efforts. *Leigh v. Engle*, 727 F.2d 113 (7th Cir. 1984).

Similarly, a fiduciary of a plan engages in a violation if he retains his child to provide, for a fee, various kinds of administrative services necessary for the operation of the plan. The fiduciary has engaged in an act described in ERISA Section 406(b)(1) because the fiduciary's child is a person in whom the fiduciary has an "interest" that may affect the exercise of the fiduciary's best judgment as a fiduciary. Labor Reg. §2550.408b-2(f), Ex. 6.

In contrast, a fiduciary does not engage in a violation of ERISA Section 406(b)(1), if the fiduciary does not use any of the authority, control, or responsibility (which makes such person a fiduciary) to cause a plan to pay additional fees for a service furnished by such fiduciary or to pay a fee for a service furnished by a person in which such fiduciary has an interest that may affect the exercise of such fiduciary's best judgment as a fiduciary. This may occur, for example, when one fiduciary is retained by a second fiduciary on behalf of a plan to provide a service for an additional fee. Labor Reg. §2550.408b-2(e)(2).

For example, a plan's investment advisor, who is a plan fiduciary, may also perform, for additional fees, services that are in addition to the services currently provided, if the provision of the services is arranged and approved by an independent plan fiduciary. The investment advisor has not engaged in a prohibited transaction described in ERISA Section 406(b)(1), because it does not use any of the authority, control, or responsibility that makes it a fiduciary (the provision of investment advisory services) to cause the plan to pay it additional fees for the provision of the additional services. Labor Reg. §2550.408b-2(f), Ex. 1.

Additionally, a plan may retain a bank, whose president is a trustee of the plan, to provide administrative services to it, if the bank president physically absents himself from all consideration of the bank's proposal to provide the services to the plan and does not otherwise exercise any of the authority, control, or responsibility that makes him a fiduciary to cause the plan to retain the bank.

Under these circumstances, the bank president has not engaged in an act described in ERISA Section 406(b)(1). Further, the other trustees have not engaged in an act described in ERISA Section 406(b)(1) merely because the bank president is on the board of trustees of the plan. This fact alone would not make them have an interest in the transaction that might affect the exercise of their best judgment as fiduciaries. Labor Reg. §2550.408b-2(f), Ex. 7.

However, because the authority, control, or responsibility that makes a person a fiduciary may be exercised "in effect" as well as in form, mere approval of the transaction by a second fiduciary does not mean that the first fiduciary has not used any of the authority, control, or responsibility that makes such person a fiduciary to cause the plan to pay the first fiduciary an additional fee for a service. For example, when plan fiduciary A retains fiduciary B to provide administrative services to the plan, and thereafter, fiduciary B retains fiduciary A to provide services to the plan for a fee in addition to the services currently provided to the plan by A, both A and B have engaged in a prohibited transaction. Regardless of any intent that he may have had at the time he retained B, A has engaged in a violation because A has, in effect, exercised the authority, control, or responsibility that makes A a fiduciary to cause the plan to pay A additional fees for the services. B, whose continued employment by the plan depends on A, has also engaged in a violation, because B has an interest in the transaction that might affect the exercise of B's best judgment as a fiduciary. As a result, B has dealt with plan assets in his own interest under ERISA Section 406(b)(1). Labor Reg. §2550.408b-2(f), Ex. 5.

346. What are the rules regarding transactions involving the plan on behalf of a party whose interests are adverse to the interests of the plan or the interests of its participants or beneficiaries?

Although not a prohibited transaction under the Internal Revenue Code, ERISA prohibits a plan fiduciary from acting in his individual or in any other capacity in any transaction involving the plan on behalf of a party (or representing a party) whose interests are adverse to the interests of the plan or its participants or beneficiaries. ERISA Sec. 406(b)(2).

This provision is a blanket prohibition against a fiduciary engaging in potential conflicts of interest. Like the prohibited transaction provisions of ERISA Section 406(a)(1), ERISA Section 406(b)(2) applies regardless of whether the transaction is "fair" to the plan.

An insurance company, as named fiduciary of a plan, violated ERISA Section 406(b)(2) when it engaged in a transaction involving a plan in which its interests were adverse to the plan's interests. The prohibited transaction occurred when the insurance company invested all of the plan's assets in annuity contracts issued by the insurance company. The insurance company's interest in the transaction involved the plan's purchase of its own group annuity contracts as investment vehicles to the insurance company's master pension plan. The insurance company maximized its profits by paying the lowest permissible return on the plan's investment and by charging the maximum permissible surrender charge. The plan's interest in the transaction was to maximize the sum of their investment by receiving the highest permissible rate of return and by minimizing or eliminating any surrender charges. *Arakelian v. National Western Life Ins. Co.*, 680 F. Supp. 400 (DC D.C. 1987).

The scope of the prohibition also encompasses the lending of money between a plan and another party. A fiduciary cannot act in a loan transaction on behalf of a party borrowing from the plan without violating ERISA Section 406(b)(2), because the interests of a lender and a borrower are, by definition, adverse. This was illustrated in a case where an identical group of trustees managed a union pension fund and a union welfare fund. Because of decreased employer contributions, the welfare fund began to run short of cash, and the trustees agreed to loan money from the pension fund to the welfare fund. Despite the fact that the transaction involved no allegations of misconduct or unfair terms, the court held that ERISA Section 406(b)(2) had been violated because when identical trustees of two employee benefit plans whose participants and beneficiaries are not identical effect a loan between the plans, a per se violation of ERISA exists. The violation existed because the borrower and lender in the same transaction had adverse interests and the fiduciaries acting on both sides of the loan transaction could not negotiate the best terms for either plan. *Cutaiar v. Marshall*, 590 F.2d 523 (3rd Cir. 1979); see also *Donovan v. Mazzola*, 606 F. Supp. 119 (N.D. Cal. 1981), aff'd, 716 F.2d 1226 (9th Cir. 1983).

A bank, in its capacity as plan fiduciary, violated ERISA Section 406(b)(2) when it arranged construction loans simultaneously with permanent loans using common trust funds that included employee plan assets. The bank received origination fees from the borrowers in exchange for the bank's assistance in obtaining the permanent loans funded by the employee benefit plan assets. In addition to having a conflict of interest in representing both parties to the permanent loan transactions, by arranging the permanent financing to retire the construction loans it had made, the bank assured itself that the construction loans would be virtually without risk, and was thus acting in its own economic interest. *Martin v. National Bank of Alaska*, 828 F. Supp. 1427 (DC Alaska 1992).

Just as a plan fiduciary cannot act in a loan transaction on behalf of the borrower who is obtaining a loan from the plan without violating ERISA Section 406(b)(2), likewise, a plan fiduciary cannot, without violating ERISA Section 406(b)(1), use any of his fiduciary authority to cause the plan to make a loan to an entity in which he has an interest. Such was the case when pension plan trustees approved the investment of virtually all of a pension plan's assets in loans to sponsoring companies of which they were officers. All of the plan trustees held an ownership or management interest in each of the borrowing companies, and the companies were so related and interdependent that each fiduciary had an interest in each borrower, and, in effect, represented both the borrowers and the lender in the transaction. Accordingly, the court concluded that in making and approving such loans, the trustees violated ERISA Section 406(b)(2). *Freund v. Marshall & Ilsley Bank*, 485 F. Supp. 629 (W.D. Wis. 1979).

347. What are the rules regarding receiving any consideration from any party dealing with a plan in connection with a transaction involving plan assets?

Commonly referred to as the "anti-kickback" provision, a plan fiduciary is prohibited from receiving any payments or other forms of consideration for his own personal account from any party dealing with such plan in connection with a transaction involving the assets of the plan. ERISA Sec. 406(b)(3).

This prohibition is illustrated in the case of a union official, acting as a trustee of union benefit funds, who accepted free tax preparation services from an accounting firm that served both the union and the benefit funds. Although the accounting services in controversy were valued at only $500, the court held that receipt of gratuities violated ERISA Section 406(b)(3), without regard to whether the costs attributable to those services were passed on to the union or the benefit funds, and without regard to whether there was any demonstrable effect on the trustee's discretion concerning the selection and retention of accountants to perform services for those entities. Even though it had not been proven that the transaction was a quid pro quo for the gratuities or that harm had resulted, the court also held that a fiduciary charged with violating ERISA Section 406(b)(3) must prove by clear or convincing evidence that the compensation he received was for services other than a transaction involving the assets of the plan. *Brink v. DaLesio*, 496 F. Supp. 1350 (DC Md. 1980), *aff'd in part and rev'd in part*, 667 F.2d 420 (4th Cir. 1981).

In another kickback case, health and welfare fund trustees violated ERISA's conflict of interest provisions when they received kickbacks, in the form of monthly payments and the free use of a boat, from an individual who provided the plans' insurance policies. *Donovan v. Tricario*, 5 EBC 2057 (S.D. Fla. 1984). Similarly, pension fund trustees violated ERISA Section 403(b)(3) when they received gratuities from the plan administrator that were used to give the trustees free trips and hotel rooms. Although no evidence was presented showing that the gratuity was made in connection with a transaction involving plan assets, the court held that logic dictates that the burden of proof should be placed on the trustees to prove the gratuity was not in connection with a transaction involving plan assets. *Secretary of Labor v. Carell*, 17 EBC 1159 (M.D. Tenn. 1993).

Receipt of 12b-1 Fees

12b-1 fees are those fees paid by mutual funds for administrative and other fees to service providers such as banks, consultants, record keepers, and directed plan trustees in connection with plan investments in mutual funds. Mutual funds are willing to pay these fees because such bundled service arrangements (the combination of trust, custodial, and administrative services along with mutual fund investment options) common within the industry reduce the mutual fund's own administrative costs of providing shareholder services.

Previously, the DOL had held that the receipt of 12b-1 fees by plan trustees as a result of plan investments made in the underlying mutual funds violated the anti-kickback provisions of ERISA. With the release of Advisory Opinions 97-16A (the "Aetna Letter") and 97-15A (the "Frost Letter"), the DOL has ruled that the receipt of 12b-1 fees by a directed trustee from mutual funds involved in such bundled service arrangements will not violate the anti-kickback provisions, so long as they do not exercise any fiduciary authority or control to cause the plans to invest in the mutual funds. The Aetna Letter applies this relief to recordkeepers from unrelated mutual funds which participate in the bundled service arrangement. The Frost Letter apples to bundled service products offered by a bank serving as trustee to customer plans as long as the bank acts according to investment directions from plan fiduciaries and participants, and does not otherwise exercise any authority or control to cause the plan to invest in the mutual funds. Further, the DOL ruled that where the bank exercises control over plan investments, there would be no violation of the anti-kickback provisions for the receipt of 12b-1 fees where the bank passes through to the plans a corresponding reduction in administrative fees in the amount of 12b-1 fees received by the bank from mutual funds to which it has directed plan investments.

348. Who enforces the prohibited transaction rules?

The Department of Labor (DOL) and the Internal Revenue Service (IRS) coordinate the administration of the prohibited transaction rules. In order to avoid unnecessary expense and duplication of these functions, the IRS transferred to the DOL general authority to issue regulations, rulings, opinions and exceptions with respect to the prohibited transaction rules while retaining the authority to enforce the excise tax provisions of IRC Section 4975(a) and IRC Section 4975(b). ERISA Reorganization Plan No. 4 of 1978, 1979-1 CB 480. The IRS and the DOL consult with each other with respect to the excise tax provisions of IRC Section 4975 and with respect to the provisions relating to prohibited transactions and exemptions therefrom. ERISA Sec. 3003(b). If the DOL obtains information indicating that a party in interest or disqualified person is violating the prohibited transaction rules, that information is transmitted to the IRS. ERISA Sec. 3003(c).

349. What is the DOL's Voluntary Fiduciary Correction Program?

On March 15, 2000, the Department of Labor (DOL) announced the implementation of the Interim Voluntary Fiduciary Correction Program (VFC). 65 Fed. Reg. 14164 (3-15-2000). On March 28, 2002, the Interim VFC Program was made permanent. 67 Fed. Reg. 15062 (3-28-2002). The VFC is designed to allow certain persons to avoid potential ERISA civil actions and the assessment of civil penalties under ERISA Section 502(l) in connection with investigations or civil actions by the DOL. The adoption of the VFC is the culmination of ongoing efforts between the DOL and the Department of Labor Enforcement Committee (on which the authors of this text serve) of the American Society of Pension Actuaries (ASPA), which had originally proposed this program to the DOL in 1997.

The VFC will be administered by each of the DOL's 10 regional offices.

The VFC is designed to benefit workers by encouraging the voluntary and timely correction of possible fiduciary violations of ERISA. Under the VFC, persons who are potentially liable for a breach of fiduciary duty will be relieved of the possibility of a civil investigation of that breach, or civil action by the DOL with respect to that breach, or both. If the conditions of the VFC are satisfied in the correction of a breach, there will be no imposition of civil penalties under ERISA Section 502(l). (ERISA Section 502(l) requires the assessment of a civil penalty in an amount equal to 20% of the amount recovered under any settlement agreement with the DOL or ordered by a court in an enforcement action under ERISA initiated by the DOL—see Q 430.)

Corrections under the program may be made without the determination that there is an actual breach; there need only be a possible breach. Each prohibited transaction eligible for remediation under the VFC has one established correction method (detailed in following questions). Applications concerning correction of breaches not described in the program will not be accepted. Also, the DOL reserves the right to reject an application when warranted by the facts and circumstances of a particular case.

350. What are the VFC eligibility and application procedures?

Plan officials and fiduciaries involved in a covered transaction may use the VFC program if neither the plan nor the applicant is currently under investigation by the DOL. "Currently under investigation," for this purpose, means being investigated pursuant to ERISA Section 504(a) or a criminal statute affecting an employee benefit plan. A plan under investigation includes any plan, plan official, or plan representative that has received oral or written notification from the DOL of a pending audit. A plan is not considered under investigation if it has been contacted regarding a complaint received, unless the complaint concerns the transaction described in the VFC application.

The DOL will reject any VFC application that it determines to contain any evidence of potential criminal violations. The proposed procedure elaborates that any material misrepresentation or omission will also be cause for rejection of an application or subsequent revocation of any "no-action" letter issued under the application.

According to the DOL, the application process consists of "five easy steps":

1.   Identify any violations and determine whether they fall within the transactions listed (detailed in Q 351):

2.   Follow the process for correcting the specific violations (also detailed in Q 351);

3. Calculate and restore any losses and profits with interest and distribute any supplemental benefits;

4. Notify participants and beneficiaries; and

5. File an application with the appropriate DOL regional office, including documentation of the corrected financial transactions.

The application must be prepared by a plan official or an authorized representative. If prepared by the latter, the application must include a signed statement authorizing the representative to act on behalf of the plan.

There must be a detailed narrative within the application that describes the violation and the corrective action taken. Details of the narrative must include pertinent identification numbers of the plan or plan sponsor and all persons materially involved in the violation, an explanation of the violation (including pertinent dates), an explanation of how the violation was corrected, and specific calculations demonstrating restoration of principal and lost earnings.

The supporting documentation that must accompany every application includes:

1. A current fidelity bond;

2. The plan document and all pertinent governing documents with relevant sections identified;

3. All documents supporting the narrative;

4. Documentation of lost earnings and calculations;

5. Documentation of restoration of profits;

6. Documentation required for the stated violation (as detailed in Q 351); and

7. Copy of the sample notice required to be provided to all participants.

The application must also include a "penalty of perjury" statement, which must be signed by a fiduciary with knowledge of the transaction addressed in the application and by the authorized representative, if any.

The detailed checklist of the proposed procedure provided in Appendix B must be completed and filed with the application. The checklist is designed to ensure that the above requirements have been satisfied prior to submission of the application package to the appropriate DOL regional office.

A complete copy of the application procedure is in the Federal Register at 65 FR 14164 (3-15-2000).

351. What are the covered transactions under the VFC Program?

In setting forth the five areas of violations covering the 13 specific prohibited transactions, the DOL advises that the correction methods are "strictly construed and are the only acceptable correction methods under the VFC program." The DOL will not accept applications concerning transactions not enumerated.

When filed with the DOL, each of the following correction methods must be accompanied by specific supporting documentation as required under the program.

Delinquent Participant Contributions

Where the employer has failed to remit participant salary deferral contributions to the plan trust within the permitted time period as provided under the plan's governing documents and under Labor Reg. §2510.3-102 (a reasonable period of time, but no later than the 15th day of the month following the month in which the contributions were made), the following correction is provided for under the procedure:

1. *Unpaid contributions.* Remit to the plan the outstanding principal amount along with the greater of (a) lost earnings, or (b) restoration of profits stemming from the employer's use of the principal amount. The loss date is the earliest date on which such contribution could have reasonably been segregated from the plan sponsor's general assets.

2. *Late contributions.* Pay the plan the greater of (a) lost earnings, or (b) restoration of profits resulting from the employer's use of the principal amount.

Plan Loans

There are four types of loans covered under the procedure: nonexempt loans at fair market rates made to a party in interest; nonexempt loans at below market rates made to a party in interest; below market interest rate loans made to a person who is not a party in interest; and loans made at below market interest rates due to a delay in perfecting the plan"s security interest.

Nonexempt loan at fair market interest rate made to a party in interest

Correction of these loans requires loan repayment in full, including any applicable prepayment penalties. An independent commercial lender is required to confirm, in writing, that the loan was made at a fair market interest rate for loans under similar terms to borrowers of similar creditworthiness.

A narrative describing the process used to determine the fair market interest rate at the time of the loan, validated in writing by an independent commercial lender, must be filed with the application.

Nonexempt loan at below market interest rates made to a party in interest

Correction of these loans requires the repayment in full of the amount of the loan to the plan plus the "principal amount" of the loan, and the greater of (1) lost earnings; or (2) the restoration of profits on the principal amount, if any. For below market rate loans, the principal amount is equal to the excess of the interest payments that would have been received had the loan been made at market rate, over interest payments actually received. The fair market interest rate must be determined by an independent financial institution. Finally, any supplemental distribution required as a result of the below market loan must be made.

Below market interest loan made to a non-party in interest

Correction of these loans involves payment to the plan of the "principal amount" plus lost earnings through the recovery date on the principal amount. Each loan payment will have a principal amount equal to the excess of interest on the principal amount payments that would have been received had the loan been executed at a fair market interest rate, over the interest actually received. An independent commercial lender must determine the fair market rate.

Loan at below market rate solely due to delay in perfecting plan's security interest (requiring higher market rate until unsecured loan security interest is perfected)

The acceptable correction method for this loan violation is the payment of the "principal amount" plus lost earnings on the principal amount through the date on which the loan is fully secured. The principal amount is the difference between the interest payments actually received and the interest payments that would have been received if the loan had been issued at a fair market rate for an unsecured loan. The fair market rate must be determined by an independent lender. If the delay in perfecting the security caused a permanent change in the risk characteristics of the loan, an independent commercial lender must establish the fair market rate for the remaining term of the loan.

Purchase, Sales and Exchanges

Purchase of an asset (including real property) by a plan from a party in interest

The acceptable correction is disposal of the asset through a sale back to the party in interest or to a disinterested third party. Either way, the plan must receive the higher of (1) fair market value at the time of resale, without a reduction for the costs of the sale; or (2) the principal amount (original purchase price) plus the greater of lost earnings on the principal amount or the restoration of profits on the principal amount, if any, as described in the program.

Sale of an asset (including real property) by a plan to a party in interest

Correction of the transaction requires the plan to receive the "principal amount" plus the greater of (1) lost earnings; or (2) the restoration of profits, if any. The principal amount is the amount by which the fair market value of the asset at the time of the original sale exceeds the sale price. As an alternative, the plan may repurchase the asset from the party in interest at the lower of the price for which it sold the property or the fair market value as of the recovery date, plus restoration of the party in interest's net profits from owning the property, to the extent that they exceed the plan's investment return from the proceeds of the sale. The determination as to which correction method is best for the plan must be made by an independent fiduciary.

Sale and leaseback of real property to the employer

The transaction is corrected by the sale of the property back to the plan sponsor or a non-party in interest. The plan must receive the higher of (1) fair market value at the time of the resale; or (2) the principal amount (original sale price), plus the greater of (a) lost earnings, or (b) the restoration of profits on the principal amount, if any.

If the plan has not been receiving rent at fair market value (as determined by a qualified independent appraisal), the sale price should not be based on the below market rent that was paid to the plan. If this is the case, the recovery amount must include the difference between the rent actually paid and the fair market rent that should have been paid. The additional rent payments, if any, must also include the greater of lost earnings or the restoration of profits.

Purchase of an asset by a plan from a person who is not a party in interest at a price other than fair market value

Correction of this transaction requires the plan to receive the principal amount (difference between the price paid and the fair market value at the time of the purchase), plus lost earnings.

Sale of an asset by a plan to a non-party in interest at a price less than fair market value

Correction of the transaction requires the plan to receive the principal amount (the amount by which the fair market value, as of the recovery date, exceeds the price at which the plan sold the property), plus lost earnings.

Payment of Benefits Without Properly Valuing Plan Assets

Correction of this transaction requires a corrected valuation of the plan assets for each plan year, starting with the first plan year for which the assets were improperly valued. The next step is to restore, directly to the plan for distribution to the affected plan participants, or directly to those participants, the amount by which all participants were underpaid distributions to which they were entitled, plus the higher of lost earnings or the underpayment rate (defined under IRC Section 6621(a)(2)). The plan must also file an amended Form 5500 for each of the last three plan years, or for all plan years in which the assets were improperly valued (whichever period is less).

According to the DOL, a plan official, rather than an independent fiduciary or independent expert, must determine the fair market value of the improperly valued asset for each year in which the asset was valued improperly. Once the assets are properly valued, participant accounts must be adjusted accordingly.

Plan Expenses

Duplicative, excessive, or unnecessary compensation paid by a plan

Correction of this transaction requires the restoration to the plan of the principal amount of the incorrect payment, plus the greater of (1) lost earnings; or (2) restoration of profits resulting from the use of the incorrect payments. The procedure defines "principal amount" as the difference between the amount actually paid during the six years prior to the discontinuation of the unnecessary payments and the reasonable market value of the services actually rendered.

Payment of dual compensation to a plan fiduciary

Correction requires payment to the plan of the principal amount of the dual payment, plus the greater of (1) lost earnings; or (2) restoration of profits resulting from the fiduciary's use of the principal amount. The principal amount is defined as the difference between the amount incorrectly paid during the six-year period prior to discontinuation of the payments and the amount that represents proper reimbursements of expenses actually incurred by the fiduciary.

EXCISE TAXES UNDER THE INTERNAL REVENUE CODE

352. What is the excise tax on prohibited transactions?

To induce the correction of a prohibited transaction, the Internal Revenue Code generally imposes a two-tier nondeductible excise tax on each prohibited transaction entered into by a disqualified person. IRC Sec. 4975. The DOL has proposed a Prohibited Transaction Class Exemption, which would relieve certain eligible transactions from these excise taxes under certain conditions. These eligible transactions are: (1) failure to timely remit participant contributions to the trust; (2) loans to a party in interest at fair market rates; (3) purchase or sale of an asset (including real property) between a plan and a party in interest; and (4) sale and leaseback of real property (at fair market value and fair rental value, respectively). Proposed Class Exemption, 67 Fed. Reg. 15083 (3-28-2002); see Q 351).

First Tier Tax

An initial tax is automatically imposed on a disqualified person (other than a fiduciary acting only as such) for each prohibited transaction. The tax imposed on the disqualified person is 15% of the "amount involved" in the transaction for each year or partial year (of the disqualified person) in the taxable period. Where a fiduciary participates in a prohibited transaction in a capacity other than as a fiduciary, he is treated as a disqualified person subject to the tax. IRC Sec. 4975(a). The initial excise tax was increased from 5% to 10% of the amount involved for prohibited transactions occurring after August 20, 1996, and increased from 10% to 15% of the amount involved for prohibited transactions occurring after August 5, 1997. TRA '97, Sec. 1074(a); SBJPA '96, Sec. 1453(a).

Second Tier Tax

If the prohibited transaction is not corrected within the taxable period, a tax of 100% of the "amount involved" is imposed on the disqualified person. IRC Sec. 4975(b). If the prohibited transaction is corrected during the correction period, the second tier tax imposed with respect to the prohibited transaction will not be assessed. If the tax has been assessed, it will be abated. If the tax has been collected, it will be credited or refunded as an overpayment. The tax imposed includes interest, additions to the tax, and additional amounts. IRC Sec. 4961(a). The correction period ends 90 days after a notice of deficiency is mailed under IRC Section 6212 with respect to the second tier tax and is extended by any periods during which the tax cannot be assessed due to a tax court proceeding and any period approved by the Secretary of the Treasury. IRC Sec. 4963(e).

Amount and Collection

The excise taxes under IRC Section 4975 are assessed annually and accumulate until the prohibited transaction is corrected. Pending the issuance of final regulations under IRC Section 4975, the excise tax is calculated in a similar manner as excise tax calculations with respect to private foundations under IRC Section 4941. In particular, the definitions of "amount involved" and "correction" are the same. Treas. Reg. §141.4975-13.

The excise taxes imposed under IRC Section 4975 are collected by the Internal Revenue Service (IRS). Unless the IRS finds that the collection of a tax is in jeopardy, it will notify the Department of Labor (DOL) before sending a notice of deficiency with respect to the excise tax. This is intended to provide the DOL with a reasonable opportunity to comment on the imposition or waiver of the excise tax or to obtain a correction of the prohibited transaction. In the event that the imposition of the excise tax imposed under IRC Section 4975 is based on a recommendation by the DOL, the IRS will not conduct a separate examination regarding the prohibited transaction. Upon receiving a written request to impose an excise tax from the DOL or from the Pension Benefit Guaranty Corporation (PBGC), the IRS will investigate whether the tax imposed by IRC Section 4975 should be applied to any person referred to in the request. ERISA Sec. 3003(a); IRC Sec. 4975(h).

Taxable Period

Generally, the term "taxable period" means the period beginning with the date on which the prohibited transaction occurs and ending on the earliest of: (1) the date of mailing of a notice of deficiency with respect to the tax imposed under IRC Section 4975(a); (2) the date on which correction of the prohibited transaction is completed; or (3) the date on which the tax imposed under IRC Section 4975(a) is assessed. IRC Sec. 4975(f)(2).

A prohibited transaction occurs on the date when the terms and conditions of the transaction and the liabilities of the parties have been fixed. When a notice of deficiency is not mailed because there is a waiver of the restriction on assessment and collection of a deficiency, or because the deficiency is paid, the date of filing of the waiver or the date of payment of the deficiency is treated as the end of the taxable period. Treas. Reg. §53.4941(e)-1(a).

Amount Involved—First Tier Tax

The "amount involved" in a prohibited transaction is the greater of (1) the amount of money and the fair market value of other property given; or (2) the amount of money and the fair market value of other property received in the transaction. The fair market value for first tier tax purposes is measured as of the date of the prohibited transaction. IRC Sec. 4975(f)(4).

Example. A corporation that maintains a plan purchases equipment from the plan for $12,000. The fair market value of the equipment is $15,000. The amount involved on first tier tax is $15,000. If the corporation pays $20,000 for the equipment, the amount involved is $20,000.

Exception—Excess Compensation

Services that are exempt from prohibited transaction treatment because they fall within the purview of the statutory exemptions relating to (1) arrangements for office space or certain other services necessary for the establishment or operation of the plan; or (2) reasonable compensation paid to a disqualified person for services rendered, are not subject to the excise tax penalty unless the compensation is deemed to be excessive. In such a case, the excessive compensation is the "amount involved" that is subject to the first tier tax. IRC Sec. 4975(f)(4).

Example. An investment advisor to a plan is paid $100 per day for each day worked. It is determined that $60 per day is a reasonable amount for the services rendered. The "amount involved" is $40 per day.

Exception—Use of Money or Property

Where the use of money or other property is involved, the "amount involved" is the greater of the amount paid for such use or the fair market value of such use for the period during which the money or other property is used. IRC Sec. 4975(f)(4).

Example 1. If a plan borrows $100,000 from an employer at 8% interest and the prevailing rate in the financial community for loans of a similar nature at the time of the loan is 15%, the "amount involved" is $15,000 ($100,000 loan x 15% interest rate). The amount of first tier excise tax is $2,250 (15% x $15,000).

Example 2. If the plan leases its building to a disqualified person for $10,000 a year and the fair rental value is $11,000, the "amount involved" is $11,000. However, if the fair rental value is $9,000, then the "amount involved" is $10,000.

Exception—Less than Fair Market Value Received

In the case of a prohibited transaction that would otherwise be protected from the imposition of the excise tax by virtue of a statutory or administrative exemption or a transitional rule, but fails to meet the conditions of such exemption or transitional rule solely because the plan paid more, or received less, than fair market value for the property transferred or a reasonable interest rate in the case of loans, the "amount involved" is the difference between the fair market value over the amount that the plan paid or received, provided that the parties made a good faith effort to determine fair market value. A good faith effort is ordinarily made when: (1) the person making the valuation is (a) not a disqualified person, (b) competent to make such valuations, and (c) not in a position to derive an economic benefit from the value used; and (2) the valuation method is a generally accepted one for valuing comparable property for purposes of arm's length business transactions. Treas. Reg. §53.4941(e)-1(b)(2)(iii).

Example. Assume that a good faith effort is made to determine the fair market value of property involved in a transaction, and it is valued at $5,000. The amount paid in the transaction is $5,000, but later the true fair market value is determined to be $5,500. The "amount involved" is $500. If a good faith effort had not been made, the amount involved would have been $5,500.

Amount Involved—Second Tier Tax

For determining the "amount involved" for second tier tax purposes, the first tier tax guidelines are applied except that the "amount involved" is the highest fair market value during the taxable period. IRC Sec. 4975(f)(4)(B). This provision is to ensure that the person subject to the tax will not postpone correction of the prohibited transaction in order to earn income on such amounts.

Correction Period

The correction period begins with the date on which the prohibited transaction occurs and ends 90 days after the date of mailing of a notice of deficiency with respect to the tax imposed by IRC Section 4975(b). The correction period is extended by any period in which a deficiency cannot be assessed under IRC Section 6213(a) (relating to notices of deficiency and tax court petitions) and may be extended by the Secretary of Treasury for any other period that is reasonable and necessary to bring about correction of the prohibited transaction (including, for taxes imposed under IRC Section 4975 and equitable relief sought by the Secretary of Labor). The correction period ordinarily will not be extended unless (1) the involved parties are actively seeking, in good faith, to correct the prohibited transaction; (2) adequate corrective action cannot reasonably be expected to result during the unextended correction period; and (3) the Secretary of Labor requests an extension because adequate corrective action cannot reasonably be expected to result during the unextended correction period. IRC Sec. 4963(e); Treas. Reg. §53.4963-1(e)(3).

If the first tier tax is paid within the unextended or normal correction period, the normal correction period is automatically extended to end on the later of: (1) 90 days after payment of the tax; or (2) the last day of the correction period, determined without regard to this extension. Treas. Reg. §53.4963-1(e)(4).

If a claim for refund is filed with respect to a tax imposed under IRC Section 4975(a) within the correction period, including extensions, the correction period is extended while the claim is pending, plus an additional 90 days. If a suit or proceeding referred to in IRC Section 7422(g) (regarding suits for the refund of certain excise taxes) is filed, the correction period will be extended while the suit or proceeding is pending. Treas. Reg. §53.4963-1(e)(5).

Settlement Agreement with DOL may not Preclude Excise Tax

The Ninth Circuit held that where a fiduciary enters into a consent agreement with the DOL after undertaking a transaction to reverse an existing prohibited transaction, the IRS may impose excise taxes under IRC Section 4975. *Baizer v. Comm.*, 204 F.3d 1231 (9th Cir. 2000). In that case, the court held that although the settlement agreement stated that it was the "final adjudication of all claims" made by the DOL, the IRS was free to impose the excise tax under its enforcement authority. Ironically, PTE 94-71 exempts a disqualified person/party in interest from excise taxes on a transaction authorized by the DOL which occurs *after* the agreement is reached with the DOL. If Baizer had undertaken the corrective transaction after reaching a settlement agreement with the DOL, he would have been relieved of the excise taxes imposed by the IRS.

353. How is a prohibited transaction corrected?

In order to avoid the imposition of the second level 100% excise tax, a prohibited transaction must be corrected within the taxable period. Correcting a prohibited transaction means undoing the transaction to the extent possible. In any case, the resulting financial position of the plan may be no worse than that in which it would have been had the disqualified person acted under the highest fiduciary standards. IRC Sec. 4975(f)(5).

The main significance of correcting a prohibited transaction is to avoid the second level 100% tax set forth by IRC Section 4975(b). Correcting the prohibited transaction does not constitute another prohibited transaction, and in correcting the prohibited transaction, the higher of the fair market value of the property given or received, either at the occurrence of each prohibited transaction or at the time of correction, must be utilized. Treas. Reg. §53.4941(e)-1(c).

Correction Involving Use of Money or Property by a Disqualified Person

If a disqualified person uses the property or money of a plan, correction includes, but is not limited to, the termination of such use. In addition, the disqualified person must pay to the plan the excess, if any, of the fair market value (the greater of the value at the time of the prohibited transaction or at the time of correction) for the use of the money or property over the amount paid for the use until termination, plus the excess, if any, of the amount that would have been paid by the disqualified person for the period such disqualified person would have used the property if such termination had not occurred, over the fair market value (at the time of correction) for the use for such period. Treas. Reg. §53.4941-1(c)(4).

Correction Involving Use of Property by a Plan

If a plan uses the property of a disqualified person, correction includes, but is not limited to, termination of such use. In addition, the disqualified person must pay to the plan the excess, if any, of the amount received from the plan over the fair market value (the lesser of the value at the time of the prohibited transaction or at the time of correction) for the use of the money or property until the time of termination, plus the excess, if any, of the fair market value at the time of correction for the use of the money or property (for the period that the plan would have used the money or property if termination had not occurred), over the amount that would have been paid by the plan after termination for use in such period. Treas. Reg. §53.4941(e)-1(c)(5).

Correction of Sales of Property by a Plan to a Disqualified Person

In the case of a sale of property by a plan to a disqualified person for cash, correcting the transaction includes, but is not limited to, rescinding the sale, if possible. The amount returned to the disqualified person must not exceed the lesser of the cash received by the plan or the fair market value of the property received by the disqualified person. The fair market value to be returned is the lesser of the fair market value on the date that the prohibited transaction occurred or at the time of the rescission of the sale. The disqualified person must also return to the plan any net income derived from the use of the property, to the extent that it exceeds any income derived by the plan during the correction period from its use of the cash received from the original sale, exchange, or transfer. Treas. Reg. §53.4941(e)-1(c)(2)(i).

Resale by a Disqualified Person Prior to the End of the Correction Period

If, prior to the end of the correction period, the disqualified person resells the property discussed immediately above in an arm's length transaction to a bona fide purchaser other than the plan or another disqualified person, rescission of the original sale is not required. The disqualified person must pay over to the plan the excess, if any, of the greater of the fair market value of the property on the date of correction (the date on which the money is paid over to the plan), or the amount realized by the disqualified person from the arm's length sale, over the amount that would have been returned to the disqualified person if rescission had been required. In addition, the disqualified person must pay over to the plan any net profits realized through the use of the property during the correction period. Treas. Reg. §53.4941(e)-1(c)(2)(ii).

Correction of Sales of Property by a Disqualified Person to a Plan

In the case of a sale of property to a plan by a disqualified person for cash, correcting the transaction includes, but is not limited to, rescission of the sale where possible. In order to avoid placing the plan in a position worse than if such rescission were not required, the amount received from the disqualified person pursuant to the rescission must be the greatest of: (1) the cash paid to the disqualified person; (2) the fair market value of the property at the time of the original sale; or (3) the fair market value of the property at the time of rescission. In addition to rescission, the disqualified person is required to pay over to the plan any net profits realized after the original sale with respect to the consideration received from the sale, to the extent that such income during the correction period exceeds the income derived by the plan during the correction period from the property that the disqualified person originally transferred to the plan. Treas. Reg. §53.4941(e)-1(c)(3)(i).

Resale by the Plan Prior to the End of the Correction Period

If the plan resells the property before the end of the correction period in an arm's length transaction to a bona fide purchaser, other than a disqualified person, no rescission is necessary. The disqualified person must pay over to the plan the excess, if any, of the amount that would have been paid to the plan in the case of a rescission over the amount that the plan realized on the resale of the property.

Also, the disqualified person is required to pay to the plan any net profits realized after the original sale with respect to the consideration received from the sale, to the extent that such income during the correction period exceeds the income derived by the plan during the correction period from the property that the disqualified person originally transferred to the plan. Treas. Reg. §53.4941(e)-1(c)(3)(ii).

Payment of Compensation to a Disqualified Person

If a plan pays compensation to a disqualified person for the performance of personal services that are reasonable and necessary to carry out the provisions of the plan, correction requires repaying any amount considered excessive to the plan. Termination of employment is not required. Treas. Reg. §53.4941(e)-1(c)(6).

Less than Fair Market Value Received

In the case of a transaction with respect to the exception for less than fair market value received (described in Q 352), correction will occur if the plan is paid an amount equal to the "amount involved," plus any additional amounts necessary to compensate it for the loss of the use of the money or other property during the period from the date of the prohibited transaction to the date of correction. Treas. Reg. §53.4941(e)-1(c)(7).

354. Who is liable for the excise tax?

Any disqualified person who participates in a prohibited transaction is liable for the excise taxes imposed under IRC Section 4975. However, a person who participates in a prohibited transaction only as a fiduciary is not liable for the excise tax. IRC Secs. 4975(a), 4975(b). If more than one disqualified person is liable for the prohibited transaction excise taxes, all such persons are jointly and severally liable with respect to the transaction. IRC Sec. 4975(f)(1).

355. What is the statute of limitations for assessing the excise tax under IRC Section 4975?

With respect to the excise taxes imposed under IRC Section 4975, the filing of Form 5500 starts the running of the statute of limitations for a prohibited transaction if the prohibited transaction is reported on the form. Form 5500 is the return for the plan only. Schedule P to Form 5500 is considered the annual return of the plan's trust. Filing Schedule P starts the running of the statute of limitations under IRC Section 6501(a) for any trust described in IRC Section 401(a).

The statute of limitations is three years if the prohibited transaction is disclosed on Form 5500; thus, the amount of any excise tax imposed by IRC Section 4975 must be assessed within three years after Form 5500 is filed. IRC Sec. 6501(a). If the Form 5500 fails to disclose the prohibited transaction, a 6-year statute of limitations applies. IRC Sec. 6501(e)(3).

The determination of the statute of limitations is different for a "continuing" transaction (e.g., a loan or lease) versus a "discrete" transaction (e.g., a sale). In the case of a continuing transaction, the prohibited transaction is deemed to recur on the first day of each subsequent taxable year. The filing of Form 5500 starts the statute of limitations running for transactions occurring in that year only; a separate determination as to the expiration of the statute of limitations must be made for each taxable year thereafter if the prohibited transaction has not been corrected. In the case of a discrete transaction, a determination need only be made for the taxable year in which the transaction occurred. See GCM 38846 (2-26-82), as modified by GCM 39475 (2-10-86).

The period of limitations on collection may be suspended, and assessment or collection of the first or second tier tax may be prohibited, during the pendency of administrative and judicial proceedings conducted to determine a taxpayer's liability for the second tier tax under IRC Section 4975(b). IRC Secs. 4961(b), 4961(c); Treas. Reg. §53.4961-2(a). Treasury Regulation §53.4961-2 provides rules relating to the suspension of the limitations period and the prohibitions on assessment and collection. It also describes the administrative and judicial proceedings to which these rules apply.

356. How are prohibited transactions and the excise taxes reported?

Any disqualified person who is liable for the excise tax under IRC Section 4975 due to participating in a prohibited transaction (other than a fiduciary acting only as such) for which there is no exception must file Form 5330 (Return of Excise Taxes Related to Employee Benefit Plans) by the last day of the seventh month after the end of his tax year. Form 5330 and tax payments are required for the year in which a disqualified person participates in a prohibited transaction and for each year (or part of a year) in the taxable period applicable to the prohibited transaction. A separate Form 5330 must be filed to report taxes with different filing due dates. In addition, failure to file or to pay the excise tax by the due dates (including extensions) subjects the individual to additional penalties on the unpaid tax unless the failure to file or pay on time was due to reasonable cause. Treas. Reg. §54.6011-1(b); Instructions to Form 5330.

EXCISE TAXES UNDER ERISA

357. What are the prohibited transaction excise taxes under ERISA?

In addition to the excise taxes imposed under IRC Section 4975, ERISA authorizes the Secretary of Labor to assess a civil penalty against a party in interest who engages in a transaction prohibited under ERISA Section 406 with regard to either an employee welfare benefit plan or a non-qualified plan. The initial penalty is 5% of the total "amount involved" in the prohibited transaction (unless a lesser amount is otherwise agreed to by the parties). However, if the prohibited transaction is not corrected during the "correction period," the civil penalty is

100% of the "amount involved" (unless a lesser amount is otherwise agreed to by the parties). ERISA Sec. 502(i); Labor Reg. §2560.502i-1(a).

The civil penalty under ERISA Section 502(i) complements the excise tax imposed on tax-qualified pension plans by IRC Section 4975 and is designed to achieve correction of the prohibited transaction. In contrast to the excise tax of the Internal Revenue Code, the assessment of the civil penalty under ERISA is not automatic, but is at the discretion of the Department of Labor (DOL).

The Pension and Welfare Benefits Administration (PWBA) of the DOL must notify a party in interest of its intention to assess the ERISA Section 502(i) penalty. The ability to assess an ERISA Section 502(i) penalty may be preserved by the DOL by the issuance of a voluntary compliance notice letter to a party in interest. See PTE 94-71.

First Tier Penalty

The first tier penalty under ERISA Section 502(i) is 5% of the amount involved. The ERISA regulations refer to the Treasury regulations to define "amount involved." In general, the amount involved means the greater of (1) the amount of money and the fair market value of the property given; or (2) the amount of money and the fair market value of the property received as of the date of the occurrence of the prohibited transaction. Labor Reg. §2560.502i-1(b); Treas. Reg. §53.4941(e)-1(b).

Amount Involved

When determining the amount involved, the DOL may distinguish between situations that involve the prohibited transfer of ownership (a sale or transfer of property) and the prohibited use of property (a lease or loan of property). Where the prohibited transaction involves the transfer of ownership, the penalty is based on the greater of the fair market value of the property or the actual amount of money that changed hands. In the situation where the prohibited transaction involves the use of money or property, the amount involved is the greater of the amount paid for the use or the fair market value of the use of the money or property. For example, in the event of a prohibited transaction that involves a prohibited loan, the amount involved is the greater of the interest actually paid or the fair market rate of interest for the loan. In the situation of a prohibited transaction involving a lease, the amount involved is the greater of the rent actually paid or the fair market rental value.

If a prohibited transaction involves the payment of compensation to a party in interest for services provided to the plan, the amount involved is limited to any excess compensation paid for those services. Treas. Reg. §53.4941(e)-1(b).

Discrete Transaction

The Department of Labor also may make a distinction between a discrete and continuing prohibited transaction in calculating the ERISA Section 502(i) civil penalty. In the case of discrete prohibited transactions (such as a sale of property), the first tier of the civil penalty is assessed simply as 5% of the amount involved for each taxable year (of the party in interest) or portion thereof until the prohibited transaction is corrected or the penalty is assessed. The penalty on discrete prohibited transactions is calculated on an annual basis and is not prorated for a portion of the year. Therefore, the amount of the penalty is not proportionately reduced for transactions that occur in the middle of a year.

Continuing Transaction

Where the prohibited transaction is continuing (such as a lease or loan), a new prohibited transaction is deemed to occur on the first day of each year or portion thereof during which the transaction remains uncorrected. This results in an assessment of an additional ERISA Section 502(i) penalty for each year during which the prohibited transaction remains outstanding. In contrast to discrete transactions, the penalty on a continuing transaction is calculated on an annual basis, but is prorated for a portion of any year involved. Labor Reg. §2560.502i-1(e); *PWBA Enforcement Manual*, Ch. 35.

Second Tier Penalty

The second tier of the ERISA Section 502(i) civil penalty (100% of the amount involved) may be assessed in addition to the first tier penalty if the prohibited transaction is not corrected within 90 days after a final agency order is issued with respect to such transaction. Labor Reg. §2560.502i-1(d). "Final order" means the final decision or action of the DOL concerning the assessment of a civil sanction against a particular party under ERISA Section 502(i). Such final order may result from a decision of an administrative law judge or the Secretary of Labor, or from the failure of a party to invoke the procedures for hearings or appeals. Labor Reg. §2570.2(g).

The "amount involved" in the transaction, for purposes of the second tier of the ERISA Section 502(i) penalty, is the highest fair market value during the correction period. Treas. Reg. §53.4941(e)-1(b)(3). In general, the correction period begins on the date when the prohibited transaction occurs and ends 90 days after a final agency order. Labor Reg. §2560.502i-1(d).

ERISA Section 502(i) Appeals

Upon receipt of a notice of assessment, a party in interest who elects to contest the PWBA's findings and assessment may request a hearing before an administrative law judge (ALJ). In general, the party in interest may file an answer and request for a hearing with the ALJ within 30 days of service of process. The failure to file a timely answer will be deemed to be a waiver of the right to appear as well as an admission of the facts alleged. Labor Reg. §2570.5.

Unless otherwise waived, the party in interest may file an appeal to the Secretary of Labor within 20 days of the issuance of the ALJ's final decision. Upon such appeal, the Secretary of Labor may affirm, modify, or set aside, in whole or in part, the decision on appeal. The Secretary of Labor's review is not a *de novo* proceeding, but rather a review of the record established before the ALJ. Labor Regs. §§2570.10, 2570.11, 2570.12.

358. What is the amount involved?

The term "amount involved" is defined as that term is defined under IRC Section 4975(f)(4). ERISA Sec. 502(i). Temporary excise tax regulations state that Treasury Regulation §53.4941(e)-1(b) is controlling with respect to the interpretation of the term "amount involved" under IRC Section 4975. Treas. Reg. §141.4975-13. Accordingly, the Department of Labor applies the principles set out in the Treasury Regulations to determine the "amount involved" in a transaction subject to the civil penalty provided under ERISA Section 502(i). Labor Reg. §2560.502i-1(b). See Q 352.

359. What is the correction period?

In general, the "correction period" begins on the date when the prohibited transaction occurs and ends 90 days after a final agency order with respect to the transaction. When a party in interest seeks judicial review within 90 days of a final agency order in an ERISA Section 502(i) proceeding, the correction period will end 90 days after the entry of a final order in the judicial action. Labor Reg. §2560.502i-1(d). The regulation provides the following examples to illustrate the operation of these rules:

A party in interest receives notice of the DOL's intent to impose the ERISA Section 502(i) penalty and does not invoke the ERISA Section 502(i) prohibited transaction penalty proceedings described in Labor Regulation §2570.1 within 30 days of such notice. As provided in Labor Regulation §2570.5, the notice of the intent to impose a penalty becomes a final order after 30 days. Thus, the "correction period" ends 90 days after the expiration of the 30-day period. Labor Reg. §2560.502i-1(d)(3)(i).

A party in interest contests a proposed ERISA Section 502(i) penalty, but does not appeal an adverse decision of the administrative law judge in the proceeding. As provided in Labor Regulation §2570.10(a), the decision of the administrative law judge becomes a final order of the DOL unless the decision is appealed within 20 days after the date of such order. Thus, the correction period ends 90 days after the expiration of such 20-day period. Labor Reg. §2560.502i-1(d)(3)(ii).

The Secretary of Labor issues a decision to a party in interest upholding an administrative law judge's adverse decision. As provided in Labor Regulation §2570.12(b), the decision of the Secretary of Labor becomes a final order of the DOL immediately. Thus, the correction period will end 90 days after the issuance of the Secretary's order, unless the party in interest judicially contests the order within that 90-day period. If the party in interest so contests the order, the correction period will end 90 days after the entry of a final order in the judicial action. Labor Reg. §2560.502i-1(d)(3)(iii).

360. How is the ERISA Section 502(i) penalty computed?

In general, the civil penalty under ERISA Section 502(i) is determined by applying the applicable percentage (5% or 100%) to the aggregate amount involved in the transaction. However, a continuing prohibited transaction, such as a lease or a loan, is treated as giving rise to a separate event subject to the sanction for each year (as measured from the anniversary date of the transaction) in which the transaction occurs. Labor Reg. §2560.502i-1(e)(1).

Labor regulations provide the following examples to illustrate the computation of the ERISA Section 502(i) penalty:

An employee benefit plan purchases property from a party in interest at a price of $10,000. The fair market value of the property is $5,000. The "amount involved" in that transaction, as determined under Treasury Regulation Section 53.4941(e)-1(b), is $10,000 (the greater of the amount paid by the plan or the fair market value of the property). The initial 5% penalty under ERISA Section 502(i) is $500 (5% of $10,000). Labor Reg. §2560.502i-1(e)(2)(i).

An employee benefit plan executes a 4-year lease with a party in interest at an annual rental of $10,000 (which is the fair rental value of the property). The amount involved in each year of that transaction, as determined under Treasury Regulation §53.4941(e)-1(b), is $10,000. The amount of the initial sanction under ERISA Section 502(i) would be a total of $5,000: $2,000 ($10,000 x 5% x 4 with respect to the rentals paid in the first year of the lease); $1,500 ($10,000 x 5% x 3 with respect to the second year); $1,000 ($10,000 x 5% x 2 with respect to the third year); $500 ($10,000 x 5% x 1 with respect to the fourth year). Labor Reg. §2560.502i-1(e)(2)(ii).

361. Can a prohibited transaction be authorized by the Department of Labor (DOL)?

Yes. In accordance with Prohibited Transaction Exemption 94-71 (PTE 94-71), a transaction will not be treated as a prohibited transaction under ERISA Section 406 and subject to the taxes imposed under IRC Section 4975 if the transaction is authorized by a settlement agreement with the DOL that results from an investigation of a plan by the DOL under ERISA Section 504, provided that: (1) the transaction is described in the settlement agreement; (2) the DOL is a party to the settlement agreement; (3) written notice is provided to the affected participants at least 30 days before the settlement agreement; (4) the notice and method of distribution is approved in advance by the DOL office that negotiated the settlement; and (5) the notice includes (a) a description of the corrective action, (b) the date when the action will occur, (c) the address of the DOL office that negotiated the settlement, and (d) a statement informing the participants of their right to forward comments to the DOL office. The relief offered under PTE 94-71 does not cover transactions prohibited under ERISA Section 406(b)(3) and IRC Section 4975(c)(1)(F) (i.e., receipt of kickbacks). However, action taken before an agreement is reached with the DOL may result in excise tax liability under IRC section 4975 (see Q 352).

CHAPTER VI

STATUTORY, CLASS, AND INDIVIDUAL EXEMPTIONS

362. What exemptions from prohibited transactions are provided under ERISA and its regulations?

The exemption provisions from the classes of prohibited transactions between ERISA-covered employee benefit plans and certain parties, identified as "parties in interest," are detailed in ERISA Section 408 and its attendant regulations. There are three different types of exemptions provided for under ERISA:

1. Statutory exemptions under ERISA Section 408;

2. Class exemptions, which are blanket exemptions issued by the Department of Labor (DOL) to grant relief to parties for common transactions, provided that they meet stated terms and conditions; and

3. Individual exemptions, which must be applied for on a case-by-case basis, in which the applicant seeks an exemption from the prohibited transaction provisions for a particular transaction he is contemplating.

The majority of transactions that are prohibited under ERISA are also prohibited under the Internal Revenue Code, although the latter refers to parties in interest as "disqualified persons." IRC Sec. 4975(e)(2). In 1978, the responsibility for granting exemptions to employee benefit plans was largely transferred to the DOL. Reorganization Plan No. 4 of 1978, 1979-1 CB 480. Therefore, the overwhelming majority of exemptions reviewed and granted in the past 20 years have come from the DOL.

In general, exemptions will be granted only if they are: (1) administratively feasible; (2) in the interest of the plan, its participants, and beneficiaries; and (3) protective of the rights of the participants and beneficiaries of the plan. ERISA Sec. 408(a).

This chapter explains in detail all three types of prohibited transaction exemptions (PTEs), as well as how to seek an exemption and what rights are available when the DOL denies an application for a PTE.

CLASS EXEMPTIONS

363. What are the class exemptions recognized by the Department of Labor and the Internal Revenue Service?

Class exemptions provide relief from the prohibited transaction provisions of ERISA for common transactions between parties in interest (as defined under ERISA Section 3(14)—see Q 338) and ERISA-covered employee benefit plans. In order for a class exemption to apply to a particular transaction, all of the requisite elements of the class exemption must be satisfied.

The DOL and IRS have recognized the following class exemptions:

- broker-dealers and banks (PTE 75-1, see Q 364);

- foreign exchange transactions (PTE 94-20, see Q 365);

- securities transactions by plan fiduciaries (PTE 86-128, replacing PTE 79-1 and PTE 84-46, see Q 366);

- purchase and sale of life insurance between a plan and its participants (PTE 92-5, PTE 92-6, and PTE 77-7, see Q 367);

- insurance agents and brokers as parties in interest (PTE 77-9, PTE 79-41, PTE 79-60, and PTE 90-1, see Q 368, Q 369, Q 371);

- insurance company pooled separate accounts (PTE 90-1, see Q 371).

- mutual fund "in-house" plans (PTE 77-3, see Q 372);

- closed-end investment companies (PTE 79-13, see Q 372);

- investment advisory firms (PTE 77-4, see Q 373);

- multiemployer plans (PTE 77-10, see Q 374);

- multiemployer apprenticeship plans (PTE 78-6, see Q 375);

- customer note sales (PTE 85-68, see Q 376);

- court ordered transactions (PTE 79-15, see Q 377);

- transactions authorized under DOL settlement agreements (PTE 94-71, see Q 378);

- interest free loans between plans and parties in interest (PTE 80-26, see Q 379);

- plan purchase of securities to retire debt owed to a party in interest (PTE 80-83, See Q 380);

- short-term plan investments (PTE 81-8, see Q 381);

- bank collective investment funds (PTE 91-38 and PTE 96-15A, see Q 382);

- transactions with mortgage pool investment trusts (PTE 81-7 and PTE 88-59, see Q 384);

- residential mortgage financing arrangements (PTE 88-59, see Q 385);

- qualified professional asset managers (PTE 84-14, see Q 386);

- in-house asset managers (PTE 96-23, see Q 387); and

- individual retirement accounts (PTE 97-11, see Q 391);

- accelerated exemption procedures (PTE 96-62, see Q 392);

- insurance company general accounts (PTE 95-60, see Q 393);

- compensation of fiduciaries for securities lending services (PTE 82-63);

This list, of course, is not intended to be an exhaustive review of all of the class exemptions granted by the DOL. It is merely a detailed overview of the more common situations among ERISA-covered employee benefit plans that have been granted a class exemption from the prohibited transaction provisions of ERISA.

364. What is the broker-dealer exemption?

Prohibited Transaction Exemption 75-1 provides a class exemption for transactions between plans and broker-dealers, reporting dealers, and banks that involve: (1) the extension of credit; (2) principal transactions; (3) agency transactions and services; (4) underwriting; and (5) market making, if certain specified conditions are met.

Much of the relief granted under PTE 75-1 was subsequently incorporated in regulations detailing the rules under which parties in interest may provide services to a plan. Labor Reg. §2550.408b-2. See Q 396.

Relief may also be available to a party in interest furnishing a plan with "any advice, either directly or through publications or writings, as to the value of

275 **2002 ERISA Facts**

securities or other property, the advisability of investing in, purchasing or selling securities or other property, or the availability of securities or other property or of purchasers or sellers of securities or other property, or of any analysis or reports concerning issuers, industries, securities or other property, economic factors or trends, or portfolio strategy, or the performance of accounts, under circumstances which do not make the party in interest a fiduciary with respect to the plan." PTE 75-1.

An advisor will become a fiduciary only if he renders the advice detailed above to the plan on a regular basis "pursuant to a mutual agreement...written or otherwise...that such service will serve as a primary basis for investment decisions with respect to plan assets." Labor Reg. §2510.3-21(c).

In order for the exemption to apply, such advice, analysis, and reports must be "furnished to the plan, on terms at least as favorable to the plan as an arm's length transaction with an unrelated party." PTE 75-1.

365. What is the foreign exchange class exemption?

If certain conditions are met, class exemption relief may be available to banks, broker-dealers, and their affiliates who purchase and sell foreign currencies on behalf of the plans to which they serve as parties in interest. Specifically, relief is provided if the transaction is directed for the benefit of a plan by a fiduciary that is independent of the bank, the broker-dealer, or any affiliate of the bank or broker-dealer. PTE 94-20.

At the time when the parties enter into the transaction, the general conditions of the exemption require that the terms of the transaction be "not less favorable to the plan than the terms generally available in comparable arm's length foreign exchange transactions between unrelated parties." The exemption also requires that "neither the bank, the broker-dealer, nor any affiliate thereof has any discretionary authority or control with respect to the investment of the plan assets involved in the transaction or renders investment advice with respect to the investment of those assets." PTE 94-20.

In addition to satisfying the general conditions detailed above, the following specific conditions must be satisfied in order for the exemption to apply:

1. At the time of the transaction, the terms must not be less favorable to the plan than the terms afforded by the bank, broker-dealer, or any of their affiliates in a comparable arm's length transaction involving unrelated parties;

2. The bank or broker-dealer must maintain, at all times, written policies and procedures detailing their handling of foreign exchange transactions with plans with respect to which the bank or broker-dealer is a trustee, custodian, fiduciary, or other party in

interest "which assure that the person acting for the bank or broker-dealer knows that he or she is dealing with a plan";

3.   Within five business days, the independent fiduciary who directs the covered foreign exchange transaction must be issued a written confirmation statement for the covered transaction that contains the account name, transaction date, exchange rates, settlement date, amount of currency sold, and the amount of currency purchased; and

4.   The bank or broker-dealer must maintain, within the United States or its territories, specific records of the transaction that would enable the DOL, the IRS, fiduciaries, plan sponsors, or contributing employers to "determine whether the applicable conditions of this exemption have been met." These records must be maintained for a period of six years from the date of the transaction. PTE 94-20.

The DOL has expanded PTE 94-20 to permit the foreign exchange transactions, discussed above, between plans and certain banks and broker-dealers that are parties in interest, provided that such transactions are executed under standing instructions. If specific conditions are satisfied, this rule may be applied retroactively to June 18, 1991. PTE 98-5.

366. What is the class exemption for securities transactions by plan fiduciaries?

Exemptive relief may be available to persons who serve as non-discretionary fiduciaries and trustees of plans executing securities transactions. Such relief is provided by PTE 86-128, which replaces PTE 79-1 and PTE 84-46.

Note that this exemption does not apply to plan trustees or to plan sponsors, unless they are executing covered transactions in which the plan is permitted to recapture (either through a direct return, or a credit to the plan) all profits earned in connection with the transaction.

Only agency transactions (e.g., a fiduciary selling on behalf of a third party) and cross transactions (e.g., both the buyer and seller utilizing the same broker) are authorized under PTE 86-128. In order for exemptive relief to apply to any cross transactions, the following conditions must be met: (1) the cross transaction must be for the purchase or sale for no consideration other than cash payment made against the prompt delivery of a security for which there is a readily available market quotation; (2) the cross transaction must be executed at a price between the current bid and current sale quotations; (3) the broker-dealer must not have any discretionary authority on either side of the transaction; (4) the fiduciary agent must disclose potentially conflicting loyalties regarding all parties involved in the transaction; and (5) the agent fiduciary must provide a summary of all cross transactions, commissions, and remuneration paid during the period being summarized. PTE 86-128, Section III(g).

There are, however, no special requirements under the exemption for cross transactions in which the agent fiduciary conducting the transaction: (1) does not render any investment advice to the subject plan for a fee; (2) has no investment discretion with respect to any of the plan's assets involved in the transaction; and (3) has no authority to engage, retain, or discharge any fiduciary regarding any plan assets. PTE 86-128, Section IV.

The exemption does not apply to principal transactions in which the fiduciary markets securities on his own; thus, this is still a prohibited transaction. See Q 364. The authorization requirement provides that the executing fiduciary must receive advance written authorization to complete the transaction on behalf of the plan.

For single customer accounts, the authorization must come from each plan that has assets involved in the transaction. The advance written authorization must be provided by a fiduciary that is independent of the fiduciary executing the trade. Further, at any time within a 3-month period prior to the granting of initial authorization, the independent fiduciary must have been furnished with reasonably available information that the agent believes to be necessary in order for the independent fiduciary to decide whether such authorization should be granted. Such information must include: (1) a copy of PTE 86-128; (2) a form for Termination of Authorization (which must be provided annually); (3) a description of the agent fiduciary's brokerage placement practices; and (4) any additional information that the agent fiduciary believes to be relevant to the decision to be made by the independent fiduciary. PTE 86-128, Sec. III(d).

The independent fiduciary must be able to terminate the authorization at will in writing and without penalty to the plan in order for it to be effective.

In addition, the exemption permits sponsors of pooled separate accounts and other pooled investment funds of more than one ERISA plan to execute transactions on behalf of a plan only if an independent fiduciary has provided advance authorization under the following circumstances:

1. At least 30 days prior to a grant of authorization, the independent fiduciary has been provided any information (including a description of any proposed material change to the arrangement) reasonably necessary to make a determination as to whether such authorization should be granted or continued;

2. The information provided contains a description of the fiduciary agent's brokerage placement practices; and

3. The independent fiduciary is able to terminate the investment in the agent fiduciary's collective fund, without penalty to the plan, by

the submission of a written notice to the fiduciary agent that there is an objection to the implementation of a material change in or a continuation of the arrangement. PTE 86-128, Section IV(d).

Where an independent fiduciary has terminated a plan's investment in the fiduciary agent's fund, it must be carried out within a time frame that allows for the withdrawal from the fund in such an orderly manner as to be equitable to all withdrawing and non-withdrawing plans. Such a withdrawal must be completed prior to the implementation of any material change in the brokerage arrangement.

The fiduciary agent must provide one of the following to each independent fiduciary:

1. A confirmation slip for each transaction covered under the broker-age arrangement (within 10 business days) that complies with Rule 10b-10(a) of the Securities Exchange Act of 1934; or

2. A quarterly report, furnished within 45 days of the end of the reporting period, which provides:

    a) a compilation of the information contained in the broker-age slips,

    b) a total of all transaction-related charges incurred within the reporting period,

    c) the amount of transaction-related charges retained by the agent, and

    d) the amount of such charges paid to third parties for appropriate services provided (such as executions).

PTE 86-128.

The agent fiduciary must also provide an annual report to each independent fiduciary with a summary of the information contained in the confirmation slips. This annual report must be provided within 45 days of the close of the reporting year and must contain the portfolio turnover ratio and the annual totals of the information required under the optional quarterly report.

The exemption permits the payment of additional fees to fiduciary agents, so long as the amount of transactions are not excessive as to size or frequency. The limits on the size and frequency of such transactions have been designed to prevent agent fiduciaries from generating excessive compensation through the churning of plan portfolios. PTE 86-128.

367. What are the class exemptions for the purchase and sale of life insurance?

There are two class exemptions that permit the purchase and sale of life insurance policies between a plan and its participants.

A plan may acquire an individual life insurance contract or annuity contract from (1) a participant for whom the contract was issued; or (2) an employer, any of whose employees are covered by the plan, if certain requirements are met. The exemptive relief will apply if:

1. The plan pays, transfers, or otherwise exchanges no more than the lesser of:

    a) the cash surrender value of the contract,

    b) the value of the participant's accrued benefit at the time of the transaction (if the plan is a defined benefit plan), or

    c) the value of the participant's account balance (if the plan is a defined contribution plan);

2. The sale, transfer, or exchange does not involve a contract that is subject to a lien or mortgage that the plan would assume;

3. The sale, transfer, or exchange does not violate any provision of the plan or trust documents; and

4. If the plan is a welfare benefit plan, the plan does not discriminate, in form or in operation, in favor of participants who are officers, shareholders, or highly compensated employees with respect to the sale, transfer, or exchange. PTE 92-5.

If certain conditions are met, a plan may sell an individual life insurance or annuity contract for its cash surrender value to any of the following:

1. A participant covered by the policy;

2. A relative of the participant who is the beneficiary under the contract;

3. The plan sponsor; or

4. Another plan.

In order for the exemption described above to apply to the sale of a contract, the following conditions must be met:

1.   The participant is insured under the contract;

2.   The "relative" is a spouse, ancestor, lineal descendant, or spouse of a lineal descendant (as defined under ERISA Sec. 3(15)), or is a brother or sister of the insured (or spouse of such brother or sister), *and is the beneficiary under the contract*;

3.   The insurance contract would be surrendered by the plan if it is not sold;

4.   The participant is first informed of the proposed sale and is given the first opportunity to purchase the contract from the plan, or he delivers to the plan a written statement that he elects not to purchase the contract and consents to the plan's sale of the contract to the plan sponsor, relative, or another plan;

5.   The amount received by the plan from the sale of the contract is at least equal to the amount necessary to put the plan in the same cash position as it would have been in had it kept the contract, surrendered it, and made any distribution owing to the participant of his vested interest under the plan; and

6.   If the selling plan is a welfare benefit plan, it must not discriminate, in form or operation, in favor of participants who are officers, shareholders, or highly compensated employees with respect to the sale of the contract. PTE 92-6.

The DOL has clarified PTE 92-6, so that, if all of its other conditions are met, then:

1.   Two or more relatives who are the sole beneficiaries under the contract may be considered a single "relative";

2.   The term "individual life insurance contract" may be read to include a contract covering the life of the participant and his spouse, to the extent that:

    a) applicable state insurance law permits an individual life insurance policy to cover the lives of an individual and his spouse, and

    b) "applicable law and pertinent plan provisions" permit the plan to acquire and hold such a policy; and

3.   The sale of a partial interest in a life insurance contract will constitute the sale of an "individual life insurance contract,"

provided that the portion of the interest in the contract sold and the portion of the interest in the contract retained would each:

a) have all of the characteristics of life insurance contracts,

b) be independently viable as life insurance contracts,

c) be available for purchase in the marketplace as life insurance contracts, and

d) qualify as life insurance contracts under applicable state law. DOL Adv. Op. 98-07A.

368. What is the class exemption regarding the sale of annuities, insurance, and annuity contracts by captive insurance companies?

Insurance companies that are related to a plan sponsor through substantial stock or partnership interests may be permitted to sell life insurance, health insurance, or annuity contracts designed to fund employee benefit plans sponsored by such related employer.

The exemptive relief will apply if:

1.   The insurance company making the sale:

      a) is a party in interest with respect to the plan by reason of a stock or partnership affiliation with the employer sponsoring the plan (including a joint venture),

      b) is licensed to sell insurance products in at least one of the United States or the District of Columbia, and

      c) has obtained a certificate of compliance from the insurance commissioner of its home state within 18 months of the sale (or, in the alternative, when the home state last issued such certificates);

2.   An independent certified public accountant has conducted a financial examination of the insurance company for its last completed taxable year, or its home state insurance commissioner has done so within the five years preceding the sale;

3.   The plan pays no more than "adequate consideration" for the insurance contracts or annuities;

4.   No commissions are paid with respect to the sale of such insurance contracts; *and*

5.   The total of all premiums and annuity considerations received by the insurance company for the sale of life and health insurance and annuity contracts to all employee benefit plans in which the insurance company is a party in interest does not exceed 50% of the premiums and annuity considerations it has received from all lines of insurance in that taxable year. PTE 79-41.

Note that this exemption does not provide relief from ERISA Section 406(b)(3), which prohibits a plan fiduciary from receiving "any consideration for his own personal account from any party dealing with a transaction involving the assets of the plan."

369. What is the class exemption regarding the sale of insurance or annuity contracts by agents or brokers that sponsor the plan making the purchase?

Exemptive relief is provided with respect to the sale of insurance or annuity contracts to employee benefit plans, and the receipt of commissions with respect to the sales by agents or brokers who are (or are related to) the employer sponsoring and maintaining the plan. In order for the exemptive relief to be granted, the following requirements must be met:

1.   The insurance agent or broker conducting the sale and receiving the commissions must be:

a) an employer whose employees are covered by the plan,

b) a 10% or more partner in the capital or profits of an employer whose employees are covered by the plan,

c) an employee, officer, director, or a 10% or more shareholder of an employer whose employees are covered by the plan, or

d) a party in interest with respect to the plan by reason of an affiliation with the employer who is the plan sponsor (including sole proprietor plan sponsors);

2.   The plan must pay no more than adequate consideration for the insurance contracts or annuities; and

3.   The total commissions received by the agent or broker for the taxable year in which the sales to the plan took place must not exceed 5% of the total insurance premiums he has earned in that year. PTE 79-60.

370. What is the class exemption relating to insurance company pooled separate accounts?

Exemptive relief allowing an insurance company pooled separate account to engage in transactions with persons who are parties in interest with respect to an employee benefit plan investing in the pooled separate account may be available. This includes pooled separate accounts that acquire or hold employer securities or employer real property.

The exemptive relief will apply only if, at the time of such transaction:

1. The assets of the plan in the pooled separate account do not exceed 10% of the total of all assets in the pooled separate account (if the transaction has occurred on or after July 1, 1988; different limitations apply in earlier years); *or*

2. The pooled separate account is a specialized account that has a policy of investing, and invests substantially all of its assets in short-term obligations, including, but not limited to: (a) corporate or governmental obligations or related repurchase agreements, (b) certificates of deposit, (c) bankers acceptances, or (d) variable amount notes of borrowers of prime credit; and

3. The party in interest is not (a) the insurance company that holds the plan assets in its pooled separate account, (b) any other account of the insurance company, or (c) any affiliate of the insurance company.

The exemption does not prohibit insurance company pooled separate accounts from engaging in transactions that exceed the previously described limits, if such transactions are with parties in interest with respect to an employee benefit plan that invests in the pooled separate account for the lease of real property and/or the incidental furnishing of goods. PTE 90-1.

371. Does the class exemption relating to insurance company pooled separate accounts apply to multiemployer plans?

In general, parties in interest may engage in transactions with the same insurance company pooled separate accounts in which a plan has invested. PTE 90-1; see Q 370.

This exemption also applies to any transaction between an employer (or its affiliates) of employees covered by a multiemployer plan and an insurance company pooled separate account in which the plan has an interest, or any acquisition or holding by the pooled separate account of employer securities or employer real property. In order for the exemption to apply, the following requirements must be satisfied at the time of the transaction:

1. The multiemployer plan assets invested in the pooled separate account do not exceed 10% of the pooled separate account's total assets; *and*

2.   The employer is not a "substantial employer," with respect to the plan, as defined under ERISA Section 4001(a)(2); *or*

3.   The multiemployer plan assets invested in the pooled separate account exceed 10% of the pooled separate account's total assets, *and* the employer is not a "substantial employer," with respect to the plan, and would not be a substantial employer if its contributions to the plan for each year constituting either

a) the two immediately preceding plan years, or

b) the first two of the three immediately preceding plan years,

totaled an amount greater than or equal to 5% of contributions required to be paid to the plan for that year.

This exemption does not prohibit insurance company pooled separate accounts from engaging in transactions that exceed the previously described limits with parties in interest that invest in pooled separate accounts for the lease of real property and/or the incidental furnishing of goods. PTE 90-1.

372. What are the class exemptions regarding mutual fund "in-house" plans?

Exemptive relief is provided for certain situations in which an "in-house" employee benefit plan (i.e., a plan covering only employees of the mutual fund, its investment advisor or principal underwriters, or any affiliate of the investment advisor or principal underwriter) invests the assets of the plan into its own open-end mutual funds.

In order for the exemptive relief to apply, such plans are prohibited from paying:

1.   Any investment management or investment advisory fees to the investment advisor, principal underwriter, or their affiliates;

2.   A sales commission for the acquisition or sale of shares; or

3.   A redemption fee for the sale of shares by the plan to the mutual fund, unless the fee is paid only to the investment company and the fee is disclosed in the mutual fund's prospectus, both at the time of the acquisition of the shares and at the time of the sale. PTE 77-3.

The DOL has extended relief under PTE 77-3 to include investment by a bank's in-house plan, through an in-kind exchange of assets for mutual fund shares, in a mutual fund advised by the bank. DOL Adv. Op. 98-06A.

Another exemption permits the acquisition and sale of shares of a closed-end mutual fund by employee benefit plans covering the employees of such closed-end mutual fund, its investment advisor, or an affiliate (as defined by Section 2(a)(3) of the Investment Company Act of 1940) of either. In order for this exemptive relief to apply, the plan *must not pay*:

1. Any investment management or investment advisory fee to the investment advisor or an affiliate; or

2. A sales commission in regard to the purchase or sale of shares to the closed-end fund, investment advisor, or affiliated person.

All other dealings between the plan and (1) the open-end and/or closed-end mutual fund; (2) its investment advisor or principal underwriter; or (3) any affiliated person of the mutual fund or underwriter, must be on a basis no less favorable to the plan than that found in such dealings with the mutual fund's other shareholders. PTE 79-13.

Section 15 of the Investment Advisors Act of 1940 permits both open-end and closed-end mutual funds to pay the investment advisory fees under the terms of the investment advisory agreement themselves (in place of the plan).

373. What is the class exemption regarding investment advisors who serve in a dual capacity to a plan?

Exemptive relief is provided for a plan's purchase and sale of shares of a registered open-end mutual fund when a plan fiduciary (e.g., the investment manager) is also the investment advisor for the mutual fund. In order for the exemptive relief to be applicable, the investment advisor must not be "an employer of employees covered by the plan."

In addition, the exemption will apply only if:

1. The plan does not pay any sales commissions regarding the purchase or sale of shares of the mutual fund;

2. The plan does not pay a redemption fee for the sale of shares from the plan to the mutual fund, unless: (a) the redemption fee is paid only to the mutual fund, and (b) the redemption fee is disclosed in the mutual fund prospectus at the time of the purchase and at the time of the plan's sale of those shares back to the mutual fund; and

3. The plan does not pay any investment management, investment advisory, or similar fees regarding the plan assets invested in the mutual fund "for the entire period of the investment"; however, the mutual fund may pay investment advisory fees, including fees for the entire portfolio of plan assets "from which a credit has been

subtracted representing the plan's pro rata share of investment advisory fees paid by" the mutual fund.

Further, a second plan fiduciary, "who is independent of and unrelated to the fiduciary/investment advisor" must receive a current plan prospectus for the mutual fund, along with a full and detailed written disclosure of all applicable fees, for the purpose of reviewing the investment advisor's decision to invest plan assets in the mutual fund and for the approval of the fee structure to which the plan will be subject.

The second independent fiduciary must also be notified of any change in any of the fees to which the plan is subject from the mutual fund. The second independent fiduciary must approve, in writing, any continued holding, purchase, or sale of shares of the mutual fund. PTE 77-4.

The DOL has expressed the opinion that PTE 77-4 does not provide exemptive relief for the purchase of shares in mutual funds that have not been paid for in cash. DOL Adv. Op. 94-35A. This would exclude asset exchanges between mutual funds from the exemption.

However, the DOL does extend the exemptive relief of PTE 77-4 to employee benefit plan investments in a master-feeder arrangement, even if the master fund has no prospectus available. Because a master fund is exempt from the prospectus requirements, the DOL has stated that Form N-1A must be provided to an independent plan fiduciary along with a detailed description of all relevant information necessary to determine the approval or disapproval of the plan's investment in the master-feeder arrangement. DOL Adv. Op. 94-35A. A master fund is one in which only other mutual funds (feeder funds) may invest. The master fund must be a registered investment company under the Investment Company Act of 1940 (the '40 Act), but not the Securities Act of 1933 (the '33 Act). The feeder funds must be registered under both the '40 Act and the '33 Act, and must be offered to the general public. DOL Adv. Op. 94-35A.

374. What are the class exemptions that specifically apply to transactions with multiemployer plans?

If certain conditions are met, PTE 76-1 exempts multiemployer plans from the prohibited transaction rules with respect to the following:

1. The extension of the period of time for submitting delinquent contributions;

2. The acceptance of less than the full amount that the employer is obligated to contribute; and

3. The termination of efforts to collect contributions deemed uncollectible, whether in whole or in part.

The exemption includes construction loans and the provision of office space, administrative services, and goods.

In order to qualify for this exemption, the decision to issue a construction loan from a multiemployer plan to a participating employer must be made by a bank, insurance company, or a savings and loan association. In addition, immediately after a construction loan is made: (1) the aggregate amount of plan assets invested in the loan to the participating employer must not exceed 10% of the fair market value of the plan's assets; and (2) the aggregate amount of plan assets invested in all loans to all participating employers of the multiemployer plan must not exceed 35% of the fair market value of the plan's assets. PTE 76-1.

Certain provisions of PTE 76-1 were extended, in PTE 77-10, to include circumstances in which a multiemployer plan shares office space and/or receives administrative services and goods. In order for the exemptive relief to apply, the following conditions must be satisfied:

1. The costs of sharing office space, services, and/or goods must be assessed and paid on a pro rata basis with respect to each party's use of the space, services, and goods;

2. The plan must receive "reasonable compensation" for the leasing of office space, or for the provision of administrative services or for the sale or lease of any goods (but the plan need not earn the profit that might otherwise have been realized in an arm's length transaction);

3. Any plan participating in such an arrangement must be able to terminate the transaction on reasonably short notice; and

4. Any plan involved in such an arrangement must maintain records, for a period of six years from the date of the termination of the arrangement, which would enable the DOL, plan participants and beneficiaries, participating employers, and employee organizations, or any duly authorized representative, to determine whether the conditions of the exemption have been met. PTE 77-10.

375. What is the class exemption regarding multiemployer apprenticeship plans?

The DOL has determined that multiemployer apprenticeship plans would not be able to operate in the manner for which they were designed without relief from the prohibited transaction rules. Thus, certain transactions between multiemployer apprenticeship plans and employers or employee organizations (unions) contributing to such plans are granted exemptive relief, provided that certain requirements are met.

The following classes of transactions between apprenticeship and training plans and employers and unions may be entitled to exemptive relief:

1.   The plan's purchase of personal property from a contributing employer or union;

2.   The plan's lease of personal property from a contributing employer or union;

3.   The plan's lease of real property from a contributing employer or union; and

4.   The plan's lease of personal property (incidental to the leasing of real property) from a contributing employer or union.

The classes of transactions described above are exempt only if:

1.   The terms of the transaction are at least as favorable to the plan as those found in an arm's length transaction;

2.   The transaction is appropriate and helpful to the plan in carrying out its purposes; and

3.   The plan maintains the appropriate records, for a period of six years from the termination of any exempted transaction, which would enable the DOL, any contributing employer (and its employees), any sponsoring union, or any person receiving benefits under the plan to determine if the requirements of the exemption have been satisfied. PTE 78-6.

376. What is the class exemption regarding the plan's purchase of customer notes?

A plan may acquire, hold, sell, and accept in-kind contributions of the plan sponsor's customer notes without violating the prohibited transaction provisions of ERISA, provided that the following conditions are satisfied:

1.   The terms of the transaction must be at least as favorable to the plan as those found under an arm's length transaction with an unrelated third party;

2.   Immediately following the acquisition, no more than 50% of the current value of the plan's assets may be invested in customer notes, nor may more than 10% of the current value of the plan's assets be invested in the notes of any one customer;

3.   An independent fiduciary must give written approval of the acquisition of the notes in advance of the purchase; and

4.   An independent fiduciary must monitor the investments in the notes to ensure that:

    a) payments are timely received,

    b) delinquencies are pursued, and

    c) the employer's guarantee to repurchase delinquent notes (with accrued interest) is enforced.

The employer must offer a written guarantee to repurchase delinquent notes from the plan in the event that the note is more than 60 days delinquent, or if the independent fiduciary has determined that other events have impaired the safety of the note as a plan investment. Upon a written request by the plan sponsor, the independent fiduciary may, in its discretion, extend the 60-day period by an additional 30 days.

"Other events" that may impair the safety of the note include: (1) faulty language in the note; (2) the obligor's insolvency; (3) the obligor's bankruptcy filing and/or its actions to reorganize; (4) appointment of a receiver of any property belonging to the obligor; and (5) the obligor's failure to maintain the property financed by the note.

A customer note is defined as "a two-party instrument, executed along with a security agreement for tangible personal property, which is accepted in connection with, and in the normal course of, an employer's primary business activity as a seller of such property." A two-party instrument is defined as "a promissory instrument used in connection with the extension of credit in which one party (the maker) promises to pay a second party (the payee) a sum of money."

The notes must be (1) secured by the property being financed; and (2) limited to a maximum term of five years. PTE 85-68.

377. What is the class exemption regarding court ordered transactions?

An exemption may be available for a transaction or activity ordered by a United States District Court.

The exemption provides that ERISA Section 406, ERISA Section 407(a), and IRC Section 4975(a) "shall not apply with respect to any transaction or activity which is authorized or required, prior to the occurrence of such transaction or activity, by an order of a United Stated District Court or by a settlement of litigation approved by such a court, provided that the nature of such transaction or activity is specifically described in such order or settlement, and provided further that the Secretary of Labor or the Internal Revenue Service is a party to the litigation at the time of such order or settlement." PTE 79-15.

378. What is the class exemption regarding Department of Labor settlement agreements?

The DOL determined that a class exemption was needed in order to eliminate the necessity of providing individual exemptions each time a transaction ordered under a settlement agreement would have otherwise violated the fiduciary or prohibited transaction provisions of ERISA. Accordingly, a class exemption is available to certain parties in interest whom the DOL has authorized to make transactions with a plan as part of a DOL settlement agreement.

The exemption requires that the activity required under the DOL settlement agreement be authorized in advance. Further, in order for the exemptive relief to apply, the following conditions must be satisfied:

1.   The nature of such transaction or activity is specifically described, in writing, by the terms of such settlement agreement;

2.   The DOL is a party to the settlement agreement;

3.   The party engaging in the transaction provides written notice to affected participants and beneficiaries at least 30 days prior to entering into the settlement agreement;

4.   The DOL field office that negotiated the settlement approves the notice and the method of its distribution in advance; and

5.   The notice contains:

       a) the date of the transaction,

       b) a description of the transaction,

       c) the address of the DOL field office that negotiated the settlement agreement, and

       d) a statement advising participants and beneficiaries that they have a right to provide their comments on the settlement agreement to the DOL field office.

Relief is not provided under this exemption for any transactions or activities in violation of fiduciary duties that gave rise to the DOL investigation, and which were cited as such in a Voluntary Compliance Letter (see Chapter XII for a discussion of DOL enforcement activities and Voluntary Compliance Letters). PTE 94-71.

379. What is the class exemption regarding interest free loans between a plan and parties in interest?

A party in interest may make an interest free loan or extension of credit to a plan if:

1. "No interest or other fee is charged to the plan, and no discount for payment in cash is relinquished by the plan" in connection with the loan;

2. The proceeds of the loan are restricted, to be used only: (a) for the payment of ordinary operating expenses of the plan, including benefits that are paid in accordance with the terms of the plan and insurance premiums under an insurance or annuity contract, or (b) for a period of no more than three days, for a purpose incidental to the ordinary operation of the plan;

3. The loan is unsecured; and

4. The loan is not directly or indirectly made by an employee benefit plan. PTE 80-26.

All of the remaining rules continue to apply to such a loan or extension of credit made to a party in interest. ERISA Secs. 404, 406.

The DOL issued a proposed amendment to PTE 80-26 regarding certain no interest loans and extensions of credit to plans affected by terrorists attacks from related parties.

In announcing the proposed exemption, the DOL stated their reasoning: "As a result of terrorist attacks on the World Trade Center and the Pentagon, all major stock markets in the United States were closed from Sept. 11 to Sept. 14, 2001. Among other things, the shutdown prevented buying, selling and/or trading of securities on these markets. In addition, temporary impairments to communication systems, pricing and valuation operations, and marketplace liquidity, may have interfered with the operations of employee benefit plans." PWBA Press Release 01-37, September 26, 2001.

The September 11, 2001 incidents may have caused temporary cash flow problems that affect essential plan operations. Interest free loans or extensions of credit could be used to facilitate (1) transfers of all or part of participants' accounts from one investment option to another; (2) participant loans; (3) temporary overdraft protection; or (4) participant withdrawal requests.

The proposed exemption would allow plans to receive temporary loans and extensions of credit from related parties (e.g., employers), if certain conditions are met. The conditions of the exemption allow loans and extensions of credit for no more than 120 days, beginning on September 11, 2001. All loans must be repaid by January 9, 2002. Among the conditions of the temporary exemption are requirements that:

- no interest or other fee is charged to the plan and no discount for payment in cash is relinquished by the plan;

- the loans and extensions of credit are unsecured;

- roceeds of the loans and extensions of credit are used only for purposes incidental to ordinary plan operations that are affected by the September 11 terrorist attacks and

- the loans or extension of credits are not directly or indirectly made by a plan.

66 Fed. Reg. 49703 (9-28-2001).

An interest free loan to a plan from a plan trustee was permitted in order for the plan to satisfy a payment obligation under a qualified domestic relations order (QDRO), which was issued pursuant to the trustee's divorce. The DOL stated that an alternate payee under a QDRO is a plan beneficiary and the plan must provide for the payment of benefits to participants and beneficiaries in accordance with the provisions of the plan document (requiring the plan to pay under the provisions of a QDRO). As such, the loan could be issued for the payment of benefits under a QDRO. DOL Adv. Op. 94-28A.

380. What is the class exemption regarding the purchase of securities by a plan in order to retire indebtedness to a party in interest?

An exemption may be available for a plan's purchase of securities, the proceeds of which may be used by the issuer to repay or reduce indebtedness to a party in interest.

In order for the exemption to apply, the following general conditions must be met:

1. The securities must be sold as part of a public offering and the price paid for the securities must not exceed the original offering price;

2. The fiduciary must maintain records relating to such transaction, sufficiently detailed to enable any authorized person reviewing them to determine whether the requisite elements of the exemption have been satisfied, for a period of six years from the date of the transaction;

3.   The records referenced above must be "unconditionally available at their customary location" for examination by:

    a) employees of the DOL or the IRS,

    b) any fiduciary who has authority to manage or control plan assets,

    c) any contributing employer,

    d) any participant or beneficiary to the plan, and

    e) the duly authorized representative of the persons listed in (a) through (d) above.

This exemption is only available to a party in interest who is a *fiduciary* if that fiduciary is a bank or bank affiliate. If such fiduciary has "knowledge" that the proceeds of the purchase will be used to reduce or retire a debt owed to the fiduciary, the exemption will apply to all otherwise prohibited transactions, with the exception of the restriction on the plan holding employer securities and the restriction on the receipt of kickbacks, provided the following requirements are met:

1.   The securities must generally be purchased prior to the end of the first full business day after the public offering, except that:

    a) if the securities are offered for subscription upon exercise of rights, then they may be purchased on or before the fourth day preceding the day on which the rights offering terminates, or

    b) if the securities are debt securities, they may be purchased on a day subsequent to the end of such first full business day after the public offering, if the effective interest rates on comparable debt securities offered to the public subsequent to such first full business day and prior to the purchase are less than the effective interest rate of the debt securities being purchased;

2.   The securities must be offered by the issuer pursuant to an underwriting agreement under which all of the members of the underwriting syndicate have committed to purchase all of the securities being offered, except where securities are purchased by others pursuant to a rights offering, or are offered pursuant to an over-allotment plan;

3.   The issuer must be in continuous operation for at least three years (including the operations of any predecessors), unless such securi-

ties are nonconvertible debt securities rated in one of the four highest rating categories by at least one nationally recognized statistical rating organization;

4.   The amount of securities acquired by the plan must not exceed 3% of the total amount of securities being offered;

5.   The consideration for the securities must not exceed 3% of the fair market value (as of the most recent valuation date prior to the purchase) of the plan assets that are subject to the control of the fiduciary; and

6.   The total amount of securities purchased in a single offering by the fiduciary on behalf of the plan (and on behalf of any other plan for which it serves as a fiduciary) may not exceed 10% of the total value of the offering.

A fiduciary will be deemed to have knowledge that the proceeds will be used to reduce or retire indebtedness to the fiduciary, if:

1.   Such knowledge is actually communicated to the fiduciary; or

2.   The officers or employees of the fiduciary, who are both authorized with respect to and actually involved in carrying out the fiduciary's investment responsibilities, obligations and duties regarding such purchase, possess information sufficient to cause them to believe that the proceeds will be so used.

This exemption does *not* provide relief for the following prohibited transactions in which the fiduciary does not know the proceeds will be used to reduce or retire indebtedness to the fiduciary, or in which such fiduciary is not involved in the decision to purchase the securities:

1.   The acquisition on behalf of the plan of any employer security in violation of ERISA Section 407(a) (ERISA Sec. 406(a)(1)(E));

2.   Fiduciaries with authority to control plan assets permitting the plan to hold any employer security if he knows, or should know, that such holding violates ERISA Section 407(a) (ERISA Sec. 406(a)(2));

3.   Dealing with plan assets in the fiduciary's own interest (ERISA Sec. 406(b)(1));

4.   Acting on behalf of any party whose interests are adverse to the interests of the plan, its participants, or its beneficiaries (ERISA Sec. 406(b)(2)); and

5.   Receiving any consideration for his own personal account (i.e., kickbacks) from any party dealing with the plan in connection with a transaction involving plan assets (ERISA Sec. 406(b)(3)). PTE 80-83.

381. What is the class exemption relating to short-term investments?

Employee benefit plans may engage in transactions involving certain short-term investments, notwithstanding the prohibited transaction provisions of ERISA. Specifically, plans may invest in banker's acceptances, commercial paper, repurchase agreements, certificates of deposit, and securities of banks that are parties in interest with respect to the plan, if the following requirements are satisfied:

1.   Banker's Acceptances: a plan may invest in these if:

  a) they are issued by a federal or state supervised bank,

  b) they have a stated maturity rate of one year or less, and

  c) neither the issuing bank, nor any of its affiliates, have any discretionary authority regarding the plan's assets;

2.   Commercial Paper: a plan may invest in commercial paper if:

  a) it is not issued by the plan sponsor or any of its affiliates,

  b) it has a stated maturity date of nine months or less,

  c) it has a rating that is one of the three highest rating categories by a nationally recognized statistical rating organization, and

  d) neither the issuer nor any guarantor has any discretionary authority over the plan's assets;

3.   Repurchase Agreements: a plan may invest in repurchase agreements if:

  a) they have a duration of one year or less,

  b) the plan receives written terms and an interest rate at least as favorable as in an arm's length transaction with an unrelated third party,

    c) the seller furnishes the plan with detailed financial statements, and

    d) neither the seller nor any of its affiliates has any discretionary authority over the plan's assets;

4.   Certificates of Deposit: a plan may invest in certificates of deposit if neither the issuing bank nor any of its affiliates have any discretion over the plan's assets; and

5.   Bank Securities: a plan may invest in a bank's securities, if the bank is considered a party in interest to the plan because it furnishes the plan with a checking account or related services (clearing, record keeping, etc.), provided that:

    a) the transaction is at least as favorable to the plan as an arm's length transaction with an unrelated third party would be, and

    b) the investment is not involved in an arrangement wherein the bank would cause a transaction to be made by the plan for the benefit of a party in interest. PTE 81-8.

This exemption does not extend relief with respect to prohibited transactions that result in the furnishing of goods, services, or facilities between the plan and a party in interest (ERISA Section 406(a)(1)(C)), an acquisition on behalf of the plan of any employer security or real property which violates ERISA Section 407 (ERISA Section 406(a)(1)(E)), or the prohibitions against fiduciaries dealing with the plan assets in their own interest, the interest of any individual whose interests are adverse to the plan, or the receipt of any kickbacks (ERISA Section 406(B)(1), ERISA Section 406(B)(2), and ERISA Section 406(B)(3)).

382. What is the class exemption for transactions between bank collective investment funds and parties in interest?

A bank collective investment fund in which plan assets are held may be permitted to engage in certain transactions with parties in interest, so long as the plan's assets in the collective investment fund do not exceed a specified percentage of the fund's total assets.

General Transaction Requirements

The exemption contains four sections, which detail general and specific rules. All transactions for which exemptive relief is sought must satisfy the following requirements:

1.   The terms of the transaction must not be less favorable to the collective investment fund than the terms of an arm's length transaction between unrelated parties; and

2.   For a period of six years from the date of the transaction, the bank must maintain the records necessary to enable the DOL, the IRS, plan fiduciaries, contributing employers, participants, and beneficiaries to ascertain whether the conditions of the exemption have been satisfied. PTE 91-38, Sec. III.

In general, exemptive relief is provided with respect to any transaction between a party in interest and a collective investment fund in which the plan has an interest, provided that:

1.   The party in interest is not the bank maintaining the collective investment fund, or an affiliate of such bank; and

2.   The plan's interest in the collective investment fund, when combined with the interests of any other employee benefit plans maintained by the same employer or employee organization, does not exceed 10% of all interests held in the collective investment fund (5% if the transaction occurs between September 23, 1980 and June 30, 1990); or

3.   The collective investment fund is a specialized fund investing in short term obligations, including, but not limited to: (a) corporate or governmental obligations, or related repurchase agreements, (b) certificates of deposit, (c) bankers' acceptances, or (d) variable amounts notes of borrowers of prime credit. PTE 91-38, Sec. I(a)(1)(A).

Specific Transaction Requirements

Transactions between (1) an employer of employees covered under a multiple employer plan; and (2) a collective investment fund holding plan assets may receive exemptive relief provided that:

1.   The combined assets in the collective investment fund *do not* exceed the 10% investment limitation, *and* the employer is not a "substantial employer" with respect to the plan (within the definition of ERISA Section 4001(a)(2)); or

2.   The combined assets in the collective investment fund *do* exceed the 10% investment limitation, *and* the employer is not a "substantial employer" and would not be a "substantial employer" if 10% were substituted for 5% in that definition. PTE 91-38, Sec. I(a)(2).

Exemptive relief is provided for the purchase, sale, or holding of employer securities and employer real property, which exceeds the investment limitations, by a collective investment fund in which the plan has an interest, provided that no commission is paid to the bank, the employer, or any affiliates of either with regard to the transaction. PTE 91-38, Sec. I(a)(3)(A).

Employer real property transactions must be for parcels of employer real property "and the improvements thereon" that are suitable for use by different tenants. If leased or held for lease to third parties, the property must be geographically dispersed. PTE 91-38, Sec. I(a)(3)(A)(i).

In the case of employer securities, the bank in whose collective investment fund the security is held cannot be an affiliate of the issuer. Further, if the security is an obligation of the issuer and the collective investment fund owns the obligation when the plan acquires an interest in the fund, the interests in the fund must be offered and redeemed in accordance with appropriate valuation procedures of the fund, which are applied on a reasonable and consistent basis. Alternatively, the exemption requirement is satisfied if, immediately after the acquisition of the obligation, the plan holds not more than 15% of the aggregate amount of the obligations issued and outstanding at the time of the acquisition. If the obligation is one that is a restricted security under Rule 144 of the Securities Act of 1933, at least 50% of the aggregate amount of obligations issued and outstanding at the time of the acquisition must be held by persons independent of the issuer. "The bank, its affiliates and any collective investment fund maintained by the bank shall be considered to be persons independent of the issuer if the bank is not an affiliate of the issuer." PTE 91-38, Sec. I(a)(3)(A)(ii).

For plans that are not eligible individual account plans (i.e., defined benefit plans), exemptive relief will be provided only if, immediately after the acquisition of securities or employer real property, the aggregate fair market value of the securities or employer real property over which the bank exercises investment discretion does not exceed 10% of the fair market value of all of the assets of the plan over which the bank has investment discretion. PTE 91-38, Sec. I(a)(3)(B).

Any transaction between a collective investment fund and parties in interest will be exempt if the service provider is not an affiliate of the bank maintaining the collective investment fund. For this purpose, "parties in interest" refers to those considered to be parties in interest simply because they provide services to the plan that has an interest in the collective investment fund or because they are related to a service provider to the plan and they do not have or exercise discretionary authority or control over the investment of plan assets in the collective investment fund. Such parties in interest will be provided exemptive relief if the service provider is not an affiliate of the bank maintaining the collective investment fund. PTE 91-38, Sec. I(b)(1)(A).

Exemptive relief will also be provided for the furnishing of goods or the leasing of employer real property if:

1.   The goods to be furnished are owned by the collective investment fund;

2. The party in interest is not the bank that maintains the collective investment fund, any of its affiliates, or any other collective investment fund maintained by the same bank; and

3. Any amount involved in the furnishing of goods or the leasing of real property does not exceed, in any calendar year, the greater of $25,000 or 0.5% of the fair market value of the assets of the collective investment fund. PTE 91-38, Sec. I(b)(1)(B).

Qualifying employer securities and qualifying employer real property held by a collective investment fund holding plan assets will not be taken into consideration when applying the prohibitions and restrictions on the holding of any employer real property or employer securities. ERISA Secs. 406(a)(1)(E), 406(a)(2), 407(a). This exemptive relief will only apply where the general 10% investment limitation has been satisfied (excepting the short-term securities collective investment fund that has no 10% limit). PTE 91-38, Sec. II.

The exemptive relief will not apply to prohibited transactions involving fiduciaries who deal with the plan assets in their interest or account, and the receipt of a kickback from any party dealing with the plan in connection with any transaction. ERISA Secs. 406(b)(1), 406(b)(3).

383. What is the class exemption that permits the conversion of collective investment funds transferred in-kind for shares of a registered investment company?

Plans may be permitted to purchase shares of a registered investment company (mutual funds), the investment advisor for which is a bank or plan advisor that also serves as a fiduciary of the plan, in exchange for plan assets transferred in-kind from a collective investment fund maintained by the bank or plan advisor. PTE 97-41. This exemption applies both retroactively and prospectively, if certain conditions are satisfied.

The exemption allows a bank or plan advisor that serves as a fiduciary to a plan, in addition to serving as an advisor to a mutual fund, to convert the plan's assets that are currently managed through a collective investment fund (CIF) into a mutual fund by the transfer of assets out of the CIF and into the mutual fund. The investment advisor must be registered under the Investment Advisors Act of 1940 in order for exemptive relief to be granted.

The exemption consists of four sections. Section I provides retroactive relief for transactions occurring from October 1, 1988 until August 8, 1997. Section II provides prospective relief for transactions that must meet certain additional conditions. Section III provides that a transaction meeting the applicable conditions of the exemption will be deemed a purchase by the plan of shares of an open-end investment company (mutual fund) registered under the Investment Advisors Act of 1940 for purposes of PTE 77-4 (see Q 373). Thus, a bank or advisor that complies with the terms of PTE 97-41 and PTE 77-4 is able to receive investment management and investment advisory fees from the mutual fund and the plan with respect to the plan's assets invested in shares of the mutual fund, to the extent permitted under PTE 77-4. Section III also provides that compliance with PTE 97-41 will constitute compliance with certain requirements of PTE 77-4. Section IV contains definitions for certain terms used in the exemption.

The operative language of the exemption emphasizes that it does not provide relief for any prohibited transactions that may arise in connection with terminating a CIF, permitting certain plans to withdraw from a CIF that is not terminating, liquidating, or transferring any plan assets held by the CIF. Therefore, the exemption only provides relief from ERISA Section 406(a), ERISA Section 406(b)(1), and ERISA Section 406(b)(2) for the purchase of mutual fund shares by a plan in exchange for assets that are transferred in-kind from a CIF.

Retroactive Exemptive Relief

Retroactive relief will be provided under Section I of the exemption if:

1.   No sales commissions or other fees have been paid by the plan in connection with the purchase of mutual fund shares;

2.   All transferred assets were cash or securities for which market quotations are readily available;

3.   The transferred assets constituted the plan's pro rata portion of all assets that were held by the CIF immediately prior to the transfer;

4.   The plan received mutual fund shares that had a total net asset value equal to the value of the plan's transferred assets on the date of the transfer (valued in accordance with SEC Rule 17a-7);

5.   An independent fiduciary of the plan received advance written notice of an in-kind transfer and purchase of assets and full written disclosure of information concerning the mutual fund, which included the following:

    a) a current prospectus for each mutual fund to which the CIF assets may be transferred,

    b) a statement describing the fees charged to, or paid by, the plan and the mutual funds to the bank or plan advisor, including the nature and extent of any differential between the rates of fees,

    c) a statement of the reasons why the bank or plan advisor considered the transfer and purchase to be appropriate for the plan, and

d) a statement of whether there were any limitations on the bank or plan advisor with respect to which plan assets may be invested in shares of the mutual funds, and, if so, the nature of such limitations;

6. On the basis of the foregoing information, the independent fiduciary gave prior approval, in writing, for each purchase of mutual fund shares in exchange for the plan's assets transferred from the CIF, consistent with the responsibilities, obligations, and duties imposed on fiduciaries under Part 4 of Title I of ERISA;

7. The bank or plan advisor sent a written confirmation of the transaction to the independent fiduciary by regular mail or personal delivery, no later than 105 days after the purchase, containing:

   a) the number of CIF units held by the client plan immediately before the in-kind transfer, the related per unit value, and the total dollar amount of such CIF units, and

   b) the number of shares in the mutual funds that were held by the plan immediately following the purchase, the related per share net asset value, and the total dollar amount of such shares;

8. As to each plan, the combined total of all fees received by the bank or plan advisor for the provision of services to the plan, and in connection with the provision of services to the mutual fund in which a plan holds shares purchased in connection with the in-kind transfer, was not in excess of "reasonable compensation," within the meaning of ERISA Section 408(b)(2); and

9. All dealings in connection with the in-kind transfer and purchase between the plan and a mutual fund were on a basis no less favorable to the plan than dealings between the mutual fund and other shareholders. PTE 97-41, Sec. I.

Prospective Exemptive Relief

All of the above conditions also apply to prospective relief, under Section II of the exemption. In addition, *prospective* relief will be granted only if:

1. The plan's independent fiduciary is provided with the following information in writing, in advance:

   a) the identity of all securities that will be valued in accordance with Rule 17a-7(b)(4) and allocated on the basis of the plan's pro rata portion of all assets that were held in the CIF immediately prior to the transfer, and

   b) the identity of any fixed-income securities that will be allocated on the basis of each plan's pro rata share of the aggregate value of such securities that were held in the CIF immediately prior to transfer;

2.   The bank or plan advisor sends a written confirmation (by regular mail or personal delivery or, if prior approval has been granted by the independent fiduciary, by facsimile or electronic mail) to the independent fiduciary of each plan that purchases mutual fund shares in connection with the in-kind transfer, no later than 30 days after completion of the purchase, which contains:

   a) the identity of each transferred security that was valued for purposes of the purchase of mutual fund shares in accordance with SEC Rule 17a-7(b)(4),

   b) the current market price, as of the date of the in-kind transfer, of each such security involved in the purchase of mutual fund shares, and

   c) the identity of each pricing service or market-maker consulted in determining the current market price of such securities;

3.   The bank or plan advisor provides the independent fiduciary of the plan with a current prospectus of each mutual fund in which the plan continues to hold shares acquired through the in-kind transfer, at least annually; and

4.   Upon request, the independent fiduciary is provided with a report or statement (which may take the form of the most recent financial report, the current Statement of Additional Information, or some other written statement) containing a description of all fees paid by the mutual fund to the bank or plan advisor. PTE 97-41, Sec. II.

384. What are the class exemptions regarding mortgage pool investment trusts?

Exemptive relief may be provided, under certain conditions, for transactions involving the origination, maintenance, and termination of mortgage pool investment trusts and the acquisition and holding of certain mortgage backed pass-through certificates of mortgage pools by plans. PTE 81-7. This exemption was updated and extended to transactions between plans and pools containing loans secured by mortgages or deeds of trust other than first lien loans, and contracts for the purchase or sale of one or more certificates that are to be determined at an agreed future settlement date (i.e., forward delivery commitments). PTE 83-1.

In these arrangements, sponsors establish investment pools, which invest in first and second mortgage notes originated by the sponsor of the pool or purchased from the mortgage loan originator. These loans are transferred to a trustee, who issues certificates of beneficial interest in the mortgages back to the investment pool. These certificates are issued to investors in the mortgage pool, including plans that invest their assets in the mortgage pool. In exchange for their investment, investors receive fixed monthly payments, which are funded (passed through) by the principal and interest payments of the mortgagors.

In order for this exemption to apply, these general conditions must be met:

1.   The sponsor and trustees of each mortgage pool must maintain a system for insuring and protecting the pooled mortgage loans and the underlying real property securing the loans, and for indemnifying certificate holders against reductions in pass-through payments due to defaults in loan payments or property damage;

2.   Except in the case of a governmental or quasi-governmental entity, such as the Federal National Mortgage Association, the trustee for each pool must not be an affiliate of the pool sponsor; and

3.   The sum of all payments made to and retained by the mortgage pool sponsor, as well as all funds inuring to the benefit of the pool sponsor as a result of their administration of the mortgage pool, must not represent more than adequate consideration for selling the mortgage loans, plus reasonable compensation for services provided by the pool sponsor to the pool. PTE 81-7.

The exemptions permit the sale, exchange, or transfer of the certificates of beneficial ownership between the plan and plan fiduciaries who are also either the pool sponsor, a plan trustee, or an insurer, provided that:

1.   The transaction is expressly approved by an independent fiduciary who has authority to manage and control those plan assets being invested in the certificates of the trust;

2.   The plan receives a price for the certificates that is at least as favorable to the plan as an arm's length transaction with an unrelated third party;

3.   There are no investment management, advisory, or underwriting fees or sales commissions paid to the pool sponsor;

4.   The plan has not purchased certificates with an aggregate value in excess of 25% of the total amount of the certificates issued; and

5.   At least 50% of the total value of the issue of certificates is purchased by persons independent of the pool sponsor, trustee, or insurer. PTE 81-7, PTE 83-1.

Any transaction of mortgage pool certificates between the plan and a sponsor of a mortgage pool, a trustee, or an insurer (where the pool sponsor, trustee, or insurer are parties in interest with respect to the plan, but are not fiduciaries) is permitted under PTE 81-7 and PTE 83-1 if the plan pays no more than fair market value for the pass-through certificates and the interests represented by the certificates purchased by the plan are not subordinated to the rights and interests of other certificates issued by the same pool.

The exemptive relief provided to fiduciaries under these exemptions does not extend to the prohibition on the receipt of kickbacks from any party dealing with the plan in connection with any transaction. ERISA Sec. 406(b)(3).

385. What is the class exemption regarding residential mortgage financing arrangements?

In 1982, the DOL issued PTE 82-87, which provided exemptive relief for the investment of qualified plan assets in certain residential mortgage financing arrangements. In 1988, the DOL amended PTE 82-87 and re-issued it as PTE 88-59. The amended class exemption expanded the types of mortgage transactions exempted from the prohibited transaction rules.

In order for the class exemption to apply, the following general conditions must be satisfied:

1.   Any mortgage purchased by the plan must qualify as a "recognized mortgage loan": a loan with respect to a residential unit which, at origination, was eligible for purchase by FNMA, GNMA, the FHLMC, or any FHA-insured GNMA project mortgage loan, or a participation interest in such a loan;

2.   All mortgages must be originated by an "established mortgage lender," with respect to which neither the plan nor the plan sponsor has controlling power over management or policies;

3.   The price paid for the mortgage by the plan must be at least as favorable as a similar transaction involving unrelated parties; and

4.   No developer, builder, or lender involved in the construction of the subject dwelling units has exercised any discretionary authority or control, or has rendered any investment advice, that would cause such person to be considered to be a fiduciary with respect to the plan's decision to purchase a mortgage loan or a participation interest therein or with respect to setting the terms of the loan.

The exemption defines "established mortgage lender" as an organized business enterprise, which has as one of its principal purposes, in the normal course of its business, the origination of loans secured by real estate mortgages or deeds of trust. In addition, to qualify as an established mortgage lender, a lender must have satisfied one of the following qualification requirement categories:

1.   Approval by the Secretary of the Department of Housing and Urban Development (HUD) for participation in any mortgage insurance program under the National Housing Act;

2.   Approval by the Federal National Mortgage Association of the Federal Home Loan Mortgage Corporation as a qualified Seller/ Servicer; or

3.   Approval by a state agency or independent state authority empowered by state law to raise capital to provide financing for residential dwelling units.

If the general conditions referenced above are satisfied, PTE 88-59 exempts the following transactions:

1.   Issuance of a commitment by one or more plans to provide mortgage financing to buyers of residential units, either by making or participating in loans directly to the buyers or by buying mortgages or participation interests in mortgages that have been originated by a third party;

2.   The plan's receipt of a fee in exchange for the issuance of a commitment;

3.   The making or purchase of a mortgage loan or participation interest pursuant to such commitment;

4.   The direct making or purchase by a plan of a mortgage loan or a participation interest other than where a commitment has been issued; and

5.   The sale, exchange, or transfer of a mortgage loan or participation interest by a plan prior to the maturity date of the instrument,

whether or not it was acquired pursuant to PTE 88-59, provided that the ownership interest sold, exchanged, or transferred represents the plan's entire interest in such investment.

When a plan enters into a commitment to purchase either a mortgage loan or a participation interest, the following specific conditions must be satisfied in order for exemptive relief to apply:

1.   The commitment must be (a) in writing, and (b) consistent with the customary practices in the residential finance industry;

2.   The commitment must be at least as favorable to the plan as an arm's length transaction between unrelated parties; and

3.   The commitment must provide for the use of underwriting guidelines and mortgage instruments, which will ensure that any mortgage loan originated under the commitment will be considered a "recognized mortgage loan."

When a plan commits to enter into a participation interest in mortgage loans, the following specific conditions must be satisfied in order for exemptive relief to apply:

1.   The participation agreement must provide that the rights and interests of the plan are not subordinated to the rights and interests of other holders in the participation agreement;

2.   The majority interest in the participation agreement must be owned by a person or entity independent of the person or entity selling the participation interest and/or servicing the underlying mortgages;

3.   In the event of an inability to collect on the payments on the underlying mortgages, the decision to foreclose must be directed by persons other than the seller/servicer; and

4.   The participation agreement must be:

       a) in writing,

       b) at least as favorable to the plan as a participation agreement involving unrelated parties, and

       c) consistent with the customary practices and procedures in the residential financing industry.

2002 ERISA Facts

Any retirement plan entering into a mortgage loan or a participation interest transaction must maintain records, for the duration of the obligation, that would enable any trustee, investment manager, participant, beneficiary, or any representative of the DOL or the IRS to determine whether the requirements of the exemption have been satisfied. No violation will be cited if the records were lost or destroyed due to circumstances beyond the control of the fiduciaries to the plan.

No exemptive relief will be provided, either retroactively or prospectively, if the transaction violates the self-dealing and anti-kickback provisions of ERISA Section 406(b). PTE 82-87; PTE 88-59.

386. What is the class exemption regarding qualified professional asset managers?

Relief may be provided to parties in interest, permitting them to engage in transactions involving plan assets, provided that those assets are managed by qualified professional asset managers (QPAMs) who meet specified financial standards and are independent of the parties in interest. PTE 84-14.

The exemption extends relief to employers for the furnishing of a limited amount of goods and services in the ordinary course of business to an investment fund in which the employer's plan has an interest, and which is managed by a QPAM.

Further, the exemption provides additional relief for the lease of office or commercial space between managed investment funds, QPAMs, and contributing employers.

QPAMs may be insurance companies, banks, or savings and loan associations. Additionally, a QPAM may be an insurance advisor that (1) is registered under the Investment Advisors Act of 1940; (2) has under his management, as of the last day of his most recent fiscal year, investor assets in excess of $50 million; and (3) could demonstrate either $750,000 in shareholder or partner equity, or a guarantee of payment of all liabilities by an affiliate that would satisfy the $750,000 equity requirement, including any liability for a breach of ERISA fiduciary duties. The QPAM must also acknowledge, in a written agreement, that he is a fiduciary with respect to each plan that has retained him.

It is the intent of the exemption to broadly expand the investment alternatives available to plans, while maintaining the protection of participants and beneficiaries.

Under the general provisions of the exemption, a party in interest and an investment fund in which the plan has an interest and which is managed by a QPAM may engage in transactions involving plan assets held in the investment fund, provided that:

1. At the time of the transaction, the party in interest, or its affiliate, does not have, and has not had, for the 1-year period immediately preceding the transaction, the authority to:

   a) appoint or terminate the QPAM as a manager of any plan assets, or

   b) negotiate, on behalf of the plan, the terms of the management agreement with the QPAM;

2. The terms of the transaction are negotiated on behalf of the investment fund by the QPAM, and either the QPAM or a property manager acting under written guidelines of the QPAM, makes the decision on behalf of the fund to enter into the transaction (so long as the transaction is not designed to benefit a party in interest);

3. The party in interest is neither the QPAM, nor a "related person" (a person who owns a 5% or more interest in the QPAM or in whom the QPAM owns a 5% or more interest);

4. The assets utilized in the transaction, when combined with all employer-established plan assets managed by the QPAM, do not exceed 20% of the assets managed by the QPAM at the time of the transaction;

5. The terms of the transaction are at least as favorable to the plan as an arm's length transaction between unrelated parties; and

6. Neither the QPAM, nor any of its affiliates, nor any person who owns 5% or more of the QPAM, has, within the 10-year period preceding the transaction, been convicted or released from prison as a result of any felony involving abuse of a position with a plan, labor organization, bank, broker-dealer, insurance company, or fiduciary (including tax evasion, larceny, theft, embezzlement, fraudulent conversion, misappropriation of funds, or conspiracy relating to any of the above). PTE 84-14.

Further, the exemption does not apply to transactions that have already received their own class exemptions, such as: (1) securities lending arrangements (PTE 81-6, see Q 388); (2) acquisitions by plans of interests in mortgage pools (PTE 83-1, see Q 384); and (3) mortgage financing arrangements (PTE 82-87).

Exemptive relief is available for the sale, leasing, or servicing of goods and the furnishing of services to an QPAM-managed investment fund by a party in interest if:

2002 ERISA Facts

1.   The party in interest is the plan sponsor, or its affiliate;

2.   The transaction is necessary for the administration or management of the fund;

3.   The transaction takes place in the ordinary course of a business engaged in by the parties in interest with the general public; and

4.   In the taxable year of the transaction, the amount earned through party in interest transactions engaged in with the investment fund does not exceed 1% of the gross receipts from all sources for the party in interest's prior taxable year. PTE 84-14.

Exemptive relief for the leasing of office space or commercial space by a QPAM-managed fund to a party in interest will be granted if:

1.   The party in interest is the plan sponsor, or its affiliate;

2.   No commission or other fee is paid by the fund to the QPAM, plan sponsor, or any affiliate;

3.   The space leased to the party in interest by the fund is suitable for use by different tenants;

4.   The space covered by the lease does not exceed 15% of the rentable space in the subject building, office park, or commercial center; and

5.   In the case of defined benefit plans, immediately after the transaction is entered into, the fair market value of employer real property and employer securities held by funds of the QPAM in which the plan has an interest does not exceed 10% of the fair market value of the plan assets held in those funds. PTE 84-14.

The specific exemptions for both the provision of goods and services and the leasing of office space must also comply with the general exemption requirements detailed above.

QPAMs will receive specific exemptive relief for the leasing of office or commercial space by a QPAM-managed fund to the QPAM or its affiliates, if:

1.   The amount of space covered by the lease does not exceed the greater of 7,500 square feet or 1% of the rentable space of the office building, office park, or commercial center in which the investment fund has an investment;

2.   The space leased is suitable for use by different tenants;

3.   The terms of the lease are not more favorable to the lessee than an arm's length transaction between unrelated parties; and

4.   No commission or other fee is paid to the QPAM by the investment fund. PTE 84-14.

Exemptive relief is extended for the transactions involving places of public accommodation (e.g., hotels) that are owned by a QPAM-managed fund for the furnishing of services and facilities to parties related to plans that participate in a QPAM-managed fund, if the services and facilities are made available to the general public on a comparable basis. PTE 84-14.

387. What is the class exemption relating to in-house asset managers?

The prohibited transaction class exemption relating to qualified professional asset managers (QPAMs—see Q 386) does not extend exemptive relief to transactions involving the assets of plans managed by in-house asset managers (INHAMs). PTE 84-18.

Previously, when an INHAM wished to conduct a transaction similar to that authorized for QPAMs, he was required to seek an individual exemption from the DOL, or hire a QPAM to execute the transaction.

The DOL recognized the need for a class exemption to provide relief to INHAMs in a manner similar to the relief afforded QPAMs, and issued Prohibited Transaction Exemption 96-23. This exemption provides relief with respect to otherwise prohibited transactions with party in interest service providers (except the INHAM, or parties related to the INHAM) regarding the portion of plan assets managed by the INHAM, as follows:

- the sale, exchange, or leasing of property between a plan and a party in interest (ERISA Sec. 406(a)(1)(A));

- the lending of money or the extension of credit to a party in interest (ERISA Sec. 406(a)(1)(B));

- the furnishing of goods, services, or facilities between a plan and a party in interest (ERISA Sec. 406(a)(1)(C)); and

- the transfer to, or use by, a party in interest, of any assets of a plan (ERISA Sec. 406(a)(1)(D)).

The exemption also permits a plan to lease office and commercial space to the plan sponsor. It extends exemptive relief to the furnishing of goods and services to a party in interest by places of public accommodation (e.g., hotels, motels) that are owned by the plan and managed by the INHAM.

The exemption defines an INHAM as an organization that is:

1. Either a direct or indirect wholly owned subsidiary of (a) an employer, or (b) a parent corporation of such employer; *or*

2. A member of a non-profit corporation, a majority of whose members are officers or directors of the parent corporation or employer; *and*

3. A registered investment advisor that, as of the last day of its most recent fiscal year, had INHAM affiliate plan assets of at least $50 million under its management.

In addition, the aggregate amount of all employee benefit plan assets under management by the INHAM or its affiliates must be at least $250 million as of the last day of the INHAM's most recent fiscal year. PTE 96-23.

The exemption requires that the INHAM have discretionary authority or control with respect to the plan assets involved in the transaction. If this is the case, exemptive relief will be extended to transactions between a party in interest, if:

1. The terms of the transaction are negotiated on behalf of the plan by the INHAM, and either the INHAM or a property manager acting under written guidelines established by the INHAM, makes the determination to enter into the transaction (provided the INHAM retains fiduciary responsibility where the property manager makes the decision). But if the transaction involves plan assets of $5,000,000 or more, the plan sponsor must retain veto rights over the INHAM's approval of the transaction;

2. The transaction is not part of an agreement that has been established to benefit a party in interest;

3. The terms of the transaction are at least as favorable to the plan as an arm's length transaction between unrelated parties;

4. The party in interest: (a) is a party in interest solely by reason of being a plan service provider, or an affiliate of such service provider, and (b) does not have discretionary authority or control over the plan assets and does not render investment advice regarding plan assets involved in the transaction;

5. The party in interest is neither the INHAM nor a person related to the INHAM;

6.   The INHAM has implemented written policies and procedures that govern the compliance with the conditions of the exemption; and

7.   An exemption audit is conducted, on an annual basis, by an independent auditor who (a) documents sufficient technical training and experience with the fiduciary responsibility provisions of ERISA, and (b) issues a written report to the plan detailing its findings regarding compliance with the written policies and procedures. PTE 96-23.

Note that, if the independent audit referenced in item 7, above, reveals a failure to satisfy the conditions of the exemption on a specific transaction, exemptive relief will not be extended to that transaction. Further, the INHAM's failure to comply with the general exemption requirements (detailed above) will result in no exemptive relief for such any transaction.

Further, the exemptive relief will not be extended to the following transactions, because they have already been granted specific class exemptions: (1) securities lending arrangements (PTE 81-6, see Q 388); (2) acquisitions by plans of interests in mortgage pools (PTE 83-1, see Q 384); and (3) mortgage financing arrangements (PTE 88-59; see Q 385).

The exemption also specifically applies to the leasing of office or commercial space, owned by a plan managed by an INHAM, to a plan sponsor or sponsor affiliate, if:

1.   The plan acquires the office or commercial space as a result of foreclosure on a mortgage or deed of trust;

2.   The INHAM makes the decision, on behalf of the plan, to foreclose on the mortgage or deed of trust in the exercise of its discretionary authority; and

3.   The amount of space covered by the lease does not exceed 15% of the rentable space of the office building or commercial center.

Exemptive relief is also extended for the leasing of residential space by a INHAM-managed plan to a party in interest, if:

1.   The party in interest is an employee of the plan sponsor or its affiliate;

2.   The leasing employee has no discretionary authority or control with respect to the investment of the assets involved in the lease transaction and does not render investment advice with respect to those assets;

3. The leasing employee is not an officer, director, or a 10% or more shareholder of the plan sponsor or its affiliate;

4. The terms of the transaction are not less favorable to the plan than an arm's length transaction between unrelated parties; and

5. The amount of space covered by the lease does not exceed 5% of the rentable space in the apartment building or multi-unit residential subdivision, and the aggregate amount of space leased to all employees of the plan sponsor, or sponsor affiliate, does not exceed 10% of the rentable space. PTE 96-23.

Both the lease of office/commercial space and the lease of residential space must also comply with the general exemptive provisions detailed above.

Finally, a place of public accommodation (e.g., hotel, motel) that is owned by a plan and managed by an INHAM may furnish services and facilities to parties in interest, if the services and facilities are furnished on a comparable basis to the general public. PTE 96-23.

388. What is the class exemption regarding the lending of securities by employee benefit plans?

In the financial services industry, the lending of securities to broker-dealers and banks is commonplace. Absent an exemption, such practices, when entered into by plans and parties in interest, would violate the prohibited transaction provisions of ERISA. For this reason, requests for individual and class exemptions permitting plans to lend securities to broker-dealers and banks who were parties in interest had been filed by such prominent organizations as Morgan Guaranty and Trust, Salomon Brothers, The American Bankers Association, and the Grumman Corporation.

In response to these requests, the DOL issued Prohibited Transaction Exemption 81-6, which was subsequently amended into its current form on May 19, 1987.

The exemption, as amended, provides relief with regard to the lending of securities that are plan assets to a broker-dealer registered under the Securities Exchange Act of 1934 (the '34 Act) or a broker-dealer exempted from registration under Section 15(a) of the '34 Act as a dealer in exempted government securities, or to a bank, if the following conditions are satisfied:

1. The entity borrowing the securities, or any of its affiliates, has no discretionary authority or control over the investment of plan assets involved in the transaction, and does not render investment advice regarding those assets;

2.   Either by physical delivery or by book entry in an appropriate securities depository, the subject plan receives collateral from the borrower consisting of: (a) cash, (b) securities issued or guaranteed by the U.S. Government, or (c) irrevocable bank letters of credit issued by an entity other than the borrower or its affiliates, and having a market value equal to not less than 100% of the market value of the securities being loaned (The collateral must be delivered by the close of the lending fiduciary's business on the day when the securities are borrowed. The market value of the collateral must be determined as of the close of the business day preceding the business day on which the securities are borrowed.);

3.   Prior to the borrowing of any securities, the borrower has provided to the lending fiduciary:

   a) the most recent available audited statement of the borrower's financial condition,

   b) the most recent available unaudited statement of the borrower's financial condition (if more recent than the audited statement), and

   c) a statement that there has been no material adverse change in its financial condition since the date of the most recent financial statement furnished to the plan that has not already been disclosed to the lending fiduciary;

4.   The loan is made in accordance with a written loan agreement (which may be a master agreement covering a series of securities lending transactions), the terms of which are as favorable to the plan as a comparable arm's length transaction with an unrelated third party;

5.   The plan providing the securities to be borrowed receives:

   a) an opportunity to earn compensation through the investment of any cash collateral, or

   b) a reasonable fee that is earmarked to the value of the securities borrowed and the duration of the loan, and

   c) an amount equal to all distributions made to the holders of the borrowed securities during the term of the loan (such distributions include cash dividends, interest payments, shares of stock from stock splits, and any rights to purchase additional securities);

6. If, as of the close of any business day within the term of the loan, the value of the collateral should ever fall below 100% of the market value of the borrowed securities, the borrower must deliver, by the close of the following business day, an additional amount of collateral, which, when combined with the fair market value of the existing collateral, equals at least 100% of the market value of the borrowed securities;

7. The loan must be terminable at any time by the plan, and the borrower must deliver certificates for securities, identical to the borrowed securities, to the plan within the customary delivery period for such securities, five business days, or within the time negotiated for delivery by the plan and the borrower; and

8. In the event of a failure to return the borrowed securities, if the loan is terminated within the time frames described in (7) above, the plan may use the collateral provided by the borrower to purchase securities identical to the borrowed securities, and may also use the collateral to pay any other obligations of the borrower and any expenses related to the purchase of replacement securities. The borrower is obligated to pay to the plan any remaining obligations and expenses not covered by the collateral, plus a reasonable rate of interest. PTE 81-6.

In reviewing the terms of any potential letters of credit under the terms of a securities lending arrangement, plan fiduciaries are not relieved of their duties under ERISA Section 404(a) (see Q 224), which require them to assure, among other things, that they have made prudent decisions. Also, fiduciaries retain their general responsibility to continually monitor the market value of the securities and the collateral to ensure that the plan is adequately protected during the entire term of the loan.

The exemption does not provide exemptive relief from the self-dealing and kickback prohibitions of ERISA Section 406(b).

389. What is the class exemption that permits banks to offer IRA, SEP, and Keogh plans services at reduced fees or no cost?

If certain conditions are met, a self-employed individual for whose benefit a Keogh plan (see Q 21) is established or maintained (or members of his family) may receive services at reduced or no cost from a bank that bases the eligibility to receive such services upon the account balance of the plan. This exemption may also apply to services received by an individual for whose benefit an individual retirement account (IRA) is established or maintained (or members of his family). In addition, this exemption applies to Simplified Employee Pension plans (SEPs), including those SEPs that provide participants with an unrestricted authority to transfer the assets in their accounts to IRAs sponsored by different financial institutions. The DOL has amended PTE 93-33 to expand coverage of the exemption to SIMPLE retirement accounts and education IRAs. 64 Fed. Reg. 11044 (3-8-1999). In the preamble to the proposal of this amendment to PTE 93-33, the DOL indicated that Advisory Opinion 98-03A (see Q 391) should be read to extend the coverage of PTE 93-33 to include Roth IRAs. 63 Fed. Reg. 56233 (10-21-1998).

These conditions must be met for the exemption to apply:

1.   The Keogh plan, SEP, or IRA is established and maintained for the exclusive benefit of the participant or IRA owner, his spouse, or beneficiaries;

2.   The service is of the type that the bank itself could offer consistent with applicable federal and state banking law;

3.   The services are provided by the bank (or an affiliate) in the ordinary course of business to customers who qualify for reduced or no cost services but do not maintain IRAs, SEPs, or Keogh plans with the bank;

4.   In the determination of eligibility, the Keogh plan, SEP, or IRA account balance required is equal to the lowest balance required by the bank for any other type of account that the bank includes to determine eligibility to receive reduced or no cost services; and

5.   The rate of return on the Keogh plan, SEP, or IRA investment is no less favorable than the rate of return on an identical investment that could have been made at the same time at the same branch of the bank by a customer who is not eligible for (or who does not receive) reduced or no cost services.

The term "service" includes incidental products of a *de minimis* value provided by third persons pursuant to an arrangement with the bank, which are directly related to the provision of banking services covered by the exemption.

The exemption specifically excludes relief from the prohibited transaction provisions of ERISA to investments in securities offered by the bank exclusively to Keogh plans and IRAs. PTE 93-33.

390. What is the class exemption regarding the payment of consideration to IRA and Keogh account holders?

Banks and financial institutions traditionally offer incentives to new customers, in order to encourage them to open new accounts. Incentives have included products (such as radios and toasters), services (such as free checking accounts and free check cashing privileges), and cash incentives (such as the payment of a set fee for the deposit of certain dollar amounts). In addition, credit unions traditionally provide group life insurance policies for their members, free of charge, in an amount equal to the value of the assets that the member has on deposit, up to a predetermined amount (usually $5,000).

Exemptive relief is granted for the provision of these goods and services to IRA account holders and Keogh plan sponsors by banks and financial institutions, which would otherwise be prohibited transactions. In order for exemptive relief to apply, the following conditions must be satisfied:

1.   The IRA or Keogh plan must be established solely for the purpose of providing benefits to the participant, his spouse, or beneficiaries;

2.   The cash, property, or other consideration must be offered only in regard to the establishment of the IRA or Keogh plan, or additional contributions made to, or the transfer of assets from another plan to the IRA or Keogh plan;

3.   The total of the fair market value of the property or other consideration provided to the sponsor of the Keogh plan or to the IRA owner must not be more than $10 in any taxable year for deposits of less than $5,000, and not more than $20 in any taxable year for deposits of more than $5,000; and

4.   In the case where the consideration provided is group term life insurance, the limitations set forth in (2) and (3) will not apply, if, during any taxable year, no more than $5,000 of the face value of the insurance is attributable, on a dollar for dollar basis, to the assets of the IRA or Keogh plan. PTE 93-1.

391. What is the class exemption permitting broker-dealers to offer IRA, Roth IRA, Education IRA, SEP, SIMPLE, and Keogh plans' services to clients at reduced fees or no cost?

Broker-dealers registered under the Securities Exchange Act of 1934 are permitted to offer reduced or no-cost services to their IRA, Simplified Employee Pension (SEP) plan, and Keogh plan clients. PTE 97-11. Subsequently, the DOL amended PTE 97-11 to expand its relief to education IRAs and SIMPLE retirement accounts. 64 Fed. Reg. 11042 (3-8-1999). In the preamble to the proposal of this amendment to PTE 97-11, the DOL indicated that Advisory Opinion 98-03A should be read as extending the coverage of PTE 97-11 to include Roth IRAs. 63 Fed. Reg. 56231 (10-21-1998).

The exemption was issued in order to place broker-dealers on a level playing field with banks, which have been permitted to offer these services to their clients under PTE 93-33. See Q 389. The conditions established under PTE 97-11 are essentially the same as those required under PTE 93-33, except for the necessary changes to reflect the terminology and operations of broker-dealers.

Brokers may now take into consideration retirement plan assets when determining whether an individual is eligible for free or low cost brokerage services, without running afoul of the prohibited transaction rules. The services permitted under the exemption include financial planning, direct deposit/debit and automatic fund privileges, enhanced account statements, toll-free access to client service centers, check-writing privileges, debit/credit cards, special news-letters, and reduced brokerage and asset management fees.

Under the exemption, the following conditions apply with respect to the balances under IRAs (including education IRAs, SIMPLE IRAs, and Roth IRAs), SEPs, and Keogh plans:

1. The balance taken into account for purposes of determining eligibility to receive relationship brokerage arrangement services must be established and maintained for the exclusive benefit of the clients, their spouses, and beneficiaries;

2. The relationship brokerage services must be of the type that the broker-dealer could offer, consistent with all applicable federal and state laws regulating broker dealers;

3. The relationship brokerage services must be provided by the broker-dealer (or an affiliate) in the ordinary course of business, to clients who otherwise qualify for reduced or no cost services, but do not maintain these types of plans with the broker-dealer;

4. For purposes of determining eligibility to receive services, the relationship brokerage arrangement must have eligibility require-ments that:

    a) if based on the balance, must be as favorable as any such requirements based on the value of any other type of account that the broker-dealer includes to determine eligibility,

    b) if based on fees, must be as favorable as any requirements based on the amount of fees incurred by any other type of account that the broker-dealer includes to determine eligibility;

5. The combined total of all fees for the provision of services must not exceed "reasonable compensation," as defined under IRC Section 4975(d)(2);

2002 ERISA Facts

6.   The investment performance must be no less favorable than the investment performance on an identical investment that could have been made at the same time by a client of the broker-dealer who is not eligible for (or does not receive) reduced or no-cost services; and

7.   The services offered under the arrangement to a participant must be the same as are offered to non-plan clients with account values of the same amount or the same amount of fees generated. PTE 97-11.

392. What is the class exemption relating to accelerated exemption procedures?

The DOL has issued an exemption that permits ERISA plans to seek approval, on an accelerated basis, of certain transactions that would otherwise be prohibited transactions under ERISA. PTE 96-62.

The exemption also provides a general exemption for the accelerated approval of transactions prohibited under ERISA Section 406(a) and a specific exemption for the accelerated approval of transactions involving a fiduciary's self-dealing and the representation of a party whose interests are adverse to a plan, which would otherwise be prohibited under ERISA Sections 406(b)(1) and 406(b)(2).

Under these general and specific exemption provisions, relief will be extended to cover transactions between a plan and a party in interest, which would otherwise violate the general exemption provision and the self-dealing or adverse interest restrictions of ERISA, if:

1.   The proposed transaction is substantially similar to transactions described in at least two individual exemptions that were granted by the DOL, and which provided relief from the same restriction, within the 5-year period ending on the date on which the written submission for an accelerated approval is filed;

2.   There is little risk of abuse or loss to the participants and beneficiaries as a result of the transaction; and

3.   Prior to executing the transactions, a written submission has been filed with the DOL regarding the proposed transactions, which contains the following information:

a) a separate written declaration, from the party who wishes to engage in the transaction, that the submission has been made in order to demonstrate compliance with the conditions of the exemption,

b) all required information for an individual exemption (see Q 782, Q 783),

c) a specific statement demonstrating that the proposed transaction poses little, if any, risk of loss or abuse to plan participants or beneficiaries,

d) a comparison of the proposed transaction(s) to at least two other substantially similar transactions that have been granted individual exemptions by the DOL within the 5-year period ending on the date of the submission, as well as an explanation that any differences should not be considered material for the purpose of granting the exemption, and

e) a complete draft of the required notice to be issued to interested persons (discussed below), and a description of the method to be used in distributing the notice.

For the specific transactions involving self-dealing or adverse interests, the written submission must contain the following information:

1.   Identification of the independent fiduciary;

2.   A description of that fiduciary's independence from the parties in interest involved in the transaction;

3.   A written statement by the independent fiduciary, which details why the independent fiduciary believes the transaction is in the interest of and protective of the participants and beneficiaries;

4.   An agreement by the independent fiduciary to represent the interests of the plan in the transaction; and

5.   A description of how the independent fiduciary will be replaced, if necessary, during the term of the transaction. PTE 96-62.

Following a tentative authorization of the transaction by the DOL, the party requesting an accelerated approval of a requested exemption must provide written notice of the proposed transaction in such a manner that it is likely that (1) interested persons will (a) receive the notice, and (b) be informed of the date of expiration for the comment period; and (2) all substantial adverse comments that interested persons have submitted within the comment period will be resolved to the satisfaction of the DOL. PTE 96-62.

The notice to interested persons must include a description of the proposed transaction, including all material terms and conditions, the approximate date on which the transaction will occur and a statement that the proposed transaction has satisfied the requirements for a tentative authorization by the DOL.

393. What is the class exemption regarding life insurance company general accounts?

In 1993, the U.S. Supreme Court ruled that assets of a plan allocated to the general accounts of an insurance company are plan assets for purposes of ERISA, and thus are subject to the ERISA's fiduciary provisions, including the prohibition of certain transactions involving plan assets. As such, insurance companies holding plan assets in their general accounts are considered fiduciaries under ERISA if they exercise discretionary authority or control over such plan assets. *John Hancock Mut. Life Ins. Co. v. Harris Tr. & Sav. Bank*, 510 U.S. 86 (1993). This holding exposed life insurance companies to heretofore unheard of levels of liability regarding their dealings with their qualified retirement plan clients.

In response, the American Council of Life Insurance requested that the DOL issue a prohibited transaction exemption to counteract the effects of the *Hancock* ruling. The DOL complied with this request and issued Prohibited Transaction Exemption 95-60, which permits (prospectively and retroactively to January 1, 1975) certain transactions engaged in by insurance company general accounts in which plan assets are invested. The exemption also extends relief to plans that engage in transactions with people who provide services to insurance company general accounts. The exemption also provides relief for transactions relating to the origination and operation of certain asset pool investment trusts in which an insurance company general account has an interest as a result of the acquisition of certificates issued by the trust.

The basic exemption provides relief from the restrictions of ERISA which prohibit the sale, exchange, or leasing of plan property, the extension of credit between the plan and a party in interest, the furnishing of goods and services or transfer to or use by a party in interest of plan assets, and which prohibit the plan from holding employer real property or employer securities. ERISA Secs. 406(a), 407(a). The exemption applies to the following:

1.   Any transaction between an insurance company general account (in which a plan has an interest) and a party in interest, or any acquisition or holding by the general account of employer securities or employer real property, if, at the time of the transaction, the amount of reserves and liabilities for the general account contracts held on behalf of the plan, together with the amount of reserves and liabilities for the general account contracts held on behalf of any other plans maintained by the same employer (or the same employee organization) in the general account do not exceed 10% of the total reserves and liabilities of the general account, plus surplus; and

2.   Any acquisition or holding of qualifying employer real property or qualifying employer securities by a plan (other than through an insurance company general account) if: (a) the acquisition or holding violates the restrictions of ERISA Sections 406(a)(1)(E), 406(a)(2), and 407(a), solely because they are aggregated with employer real property or employer securities held by an insurance company general account in which the plan has an interest, and (b) the percentage limitation of section (1) (above) is satisfied.

The exemption provides relief from ERISA Sections 406(a)(1)(A) through 406(a)(1)(D) for transactions with parties in interest if they are parties in interest solely because they provide certain services to an insurance company general account in which the plan has an interest, or are affiliates of such service providers.

The exemption also provides relief from ERISA restrictions upon the furnishing of services, facilities, and any goods incidental to services and facilities to a party in interest by a place of public accommodation owned by an insurance company general account. ERISA Secs. 406(a), 406(b), 407(a). Such services and facilities must be available to the general public on a comparable basis in order for the exemptive relief to apply.

For the above transactions to receive exemptive relief, the following conditions must be satisfied at the time when the parties entered into the transaction:

1.   The terms of the transaction must be at least as favorable to the plan as an arm's length transaction between unrelated parties;

2.   The transaction must not be designed, as part of an agreement or arrangement, to benefit a party in interest; and

3.   The party in interest must not be the insurance company, a pooled separate account of the insurance company, or an affiliate of the insurance company.

The specific exemption for the operation of asset pool investment trusts provides relief from ERISA Sections 406(a), 406(b), and 407(a) for transactions in connection with the servicing, management, and operation of a trust in which an insurance company general account has an interest, if:

1.   The trust is described in PTE 83-1 or in one of the "Underwriter Exemptions" (referring to specific exemptions identified in PTE 95-60);

2.   The conditions of PTE 83-1 or the applicable underwriter exemption are met, except that:

a) the rights and interests evidenced by the trust certificates that were acquired by the general account are not subordinated to the rights and interests of the other certificates of the same trust, and

b) the certificates of the trust acquired by the general account, at the time of the acquisition, have earned a rating that is one of the three highest generic rating categories from Standard & Poors, Moody's, Duff & Phelps, or Fitch Investors Service.

Exemptive relief will be extended to those who are parties in interest as a result of being a service provider to the plan solely because of the plan's ownership of certificates issued by a trust.

This exemption does not relieve a fiduciary or party in interest from the other provisions of ERISA, including any prohibited transaction provisions to which the exemption does not apply, and the general fiduciary provisions of ERISA Section 404. PTE 95-60.

STATUTORY EXEMPTIONS

394. What are the statutory exemptions to the prohibited transaction provisions of ERISA?

ERISA Section 408 details several specific exemptions, which permit employee benefit plans to engage in transactions that would otherwise be prohibited under various provisions of ERISA, the Internal Revenue Code, and other sources of governing authority. ERISA Section 408 generally provides statutory exemptions for:

1. Loans to participants (ERISA Sec. 408(b)(1), see Q 395);

2. Provision of office space or services reasonably necessary for the operation of the plan (ERISA Sec. 408(b)(2), see Q 396);

3. Loans to employee stock ownership plans (ERISA Sec. 408(b)(3), see Q 397);

4. Deposits in bank investments where the bank is a plan fiduciary (ERISA Sec. 408(b)(4), see Q 398);

5. Purchase of insurance and annuity products from an insurance company that is the sponsor of the plan (ERISA Sec. 408(b)(5), see Q 399);

6. The provision of ancillary bank services to a plan by a bank that is a party in interest (ERISA Sec. 408(b)(6), see Q 400);

7.   Certain transactions between the plan and owner-employees (ERISA Sec. 408(d), see Q 401);

8.   The conversion of securities (ERISA Sec. 3(18), ERISA Sec. 408(b)(7), see Q 402);

9.   Transactions between a plan and a pooled investment fund maintained by a bank that is a party in interest (ERISA Sec. 408(b)(8), see Q 403);

10.   The receipt of benefits by a disqualified person (IRC Sec. 4975(d)(9), IRC Sec. 4975(d)(10), see Q 404);

11.   Distribution of plan assets in accordance with the plan documents upon plan termination (ERISA Sec. 408(b)(10), see Q 405); and

12.   The merger and transfer of assets and liabilities between multiemployer plans (ERISA Sec. 408(b)(11), see Q 406).

395. What is the statutory exemption regarding plan loans to parties in interest?

The lending of money or other extension of credit between a plan and a party in interest is prohibited under ERISA Section 406(a)(1)(B). However, a statutory exemption permits loans from plans to parties in interest who are participants or beneficiaries if:

1.   The loans are made available to all participants and beneficiaries on a reasonably equivalent basis;

2.   The loans are not made available to highly compensated employees (as defined under IRC Section 414(g)) in an amount greater than the amount made available to other employees;

3.   The loans are made in accordance with specific provisions regarding participant loans, which are set forth in the plan;

4.   The loans bear a reasonable rate of interest; and

5.   The loans are adequately secured. ERISA Sec. 408(b)(1).

A "participant loan" is defined as a loan arranged and approved by the fiduciary administering the loan program, which has been prudently established and administered primarily in the interest of the participants and beneficiaries. Labor Reg. §2550.408b-1(a)(3). The existence of a written loan program and supporting loan documents will not qualify as a participant loan for which exemptive relief is available under ERISA Section 408(b)(1), if, upon consideration of all relevant facts and circumstances, the DOL determines that the parties to the loan agreement did not intend for the loan to be repaid.

Section 408(d)(2) of ERISA has been amended to provide for the provision of loans from qualified plans to certain S corporation shareholders, partners and sole-proprietors. This expanded availability of participant loans is effective for plan years beginning after December 31, 2001. Title VI, Subtitle E, Section 612(b) and (c) of EGTRRA.

In order for loans to be made available on a reasonably equivalent basis, they must be available to all participants and beneficiaries without regard to race, color, religion, sex, age, or national origin. Labor Reg. §2550.408b-1(a)(3). That same regulation also requires that consideration be given only to those factors that would be considered in a normal setting by an entity in the business of making similar types of loans. Such factors may include a review of the applicant's credit worthiness and financial need.

A participant loan program will not fail to qualify for exemptive relief under ERISA Section 408(b)(1) merely because it has established a minimum loan amount. Plans may not establish minimum loan amounts in excess of $1,000. Labor Reg. §2550.408b-1(b)(2).

Participant loan programs contained within the plan's governing documents must include (but need not be limited to) the following provisions: (1) The identification of the person or positions authorized to administer the loan program; (2) The procedure for applying for loans; (3) The basis on which loans will be approved or denied; (4) Limitations on the types and amount of loans offered; (5) The procedure under the program for determining a reasonable rate of interest; (6) The types of collateral that may be used to secure a participant loan; and (7) The events that would constitute default and the steps that will be taken to preserve plan assets in the event of such default. Labor Reg. §2550.408b-1(d)(2).

A reasonable rate of interest is one that provides the plan with a return that is commensurate with the interest rates charged by persons in the business of lending money under similar circumstances. Labor Reg. §2550.408b-1(e).

Adequate security is defined under the regulations as "something in addition to and supporting a promise to pay, which is so pledged to the plan that it may be sold, foreclosed upon, or otherwise disposed of upon default of repayment of the loan, the value and liquidity of which security is such that it may reasonably be anticipated that the loss of principal or interest will not result from the loan." Labor Reg. §2550.408b-1(f).

See IRC Section 72(p) and its attendant regulations for further details regarding the official restrictions on the number and amount of loans that can be made available under a participant loan program.

396. What is the statutory exemption for the provision of services or office space?

ERISA Section 408(b)(2) permits a plan to contract for or make reasonable arrangements with a party in interest for the provision of office space, or legal, accounting, or other services necessary for the establishment or operation of the plan, if no more than reasonable compensation is paid for such services or office space.

A necessary service is a service that is appropriate and helpful to the plan in carrying out the purposes for which the plan is established or maintained. A person providing such services may furnish goods that are necessary for the establishment or operation of the plan in the course of, and incidental to, the furnishing of such services to the plan. Labor Reg. §2550.408b-2(b).

A reasonable contract or arrangement is one that permits the termination of services by the plan, without penalty, on reasonably short notice under the circumstances, in order to prevent the plan from becoming locked into an arrangement that has become disadvantageous. However, a contract provision that reasonably compensates the service provider or lessor for loss upon early termination of a contract, arrangement, or lease is not a penalty. A lease provision for termination fees covering reasonably foreseeable expenses related to the vacancy and re-letting of the office space upon early termination of the lease (not to exceed the actual loss) is also not a penalty; however, provisions for lease termination fees must also provide for mitigation of damages in order to avoid a DOL ruling that it is a penalty. Labor Reg. §2550.408b-2(c).

Reasonable compensation may be paid to a party in interest or a fiduciary for services rendered to the plan or for the provision of office space if the services or office space are reasonable and necessary for the establishment and ongoing operation of the plan. Labor Reg. §2550.408c-2. Under the regulations, the DOL will determine the reasonableness of compensation under a review of the particular facts and circumstances of each case. The payment of fees to a fiduciary who is already a paid full-time employee of the plan sponsor is not considered reasonable unless it is paid as reimbursement of direct expenses properly and actually incurred. Labor Reg. §2550.408b-2(d); DOL Adv. Op. 83-07A. A fiduciary may also be granted an advance to cover direct expenses that it reasonably expects to incur in the immediate future. The fiduciary must provide an accounting of such expenses at the end of the period covered by the advance. DOL Adv. Op. 89-28A.

The statutory exemption does not permit fiduciaries to use their authority, control, or responsibility to cause the plan to pay additional fees to the fiduciary for the provision of services. Labor Reg. §2550.408b-2(e)(1). Such an act would be considered a prohibited transaction in violation of the self-dealing prohibitions of ERISA Section 406(b). However, the regulations provide that it is not, in and of itself, a violation of the self-dealing prohibitions for a fiduciary to provide services to the plan without receiving compensation. Labor Reg. §2550.408b-2(e)(3).

A fiduciary is forbidden from using his authority, control, or responsibility to cause a plan to pay additional fees for a service provided by an entity in which the fiduciary has an interest. Labor Reg. §2550.408b-2(e)(2).

The statutory exemption found under ERISA Section 408(b)(2) for the payment in settlement of a claim arising from a service arrangement has been extended. This exemption applies if:

1. The service arrangement initially qualified for, and continues to qualify for the exemption found under ERISA Section 408(b)(2), after considering: (a) the settlement agreement, (b) the alleged conduct of the service provider giving rise to the claims, and (c) where appropriate, the ability of the plan to obtain a guarantee from the service provider that the conduct resulting in the claim will not be repeated, and the fiduciaries' ability to protect the plan from abuse that may be inherent in the relationship between the parties to the settlement claim and the plan;

2. The party in interest relationship arises only from the provision of services under the exemption; and

3. The fiduciaries have prudently determined that settlement would be reasonable because the plan will receive payment at least equal to the amount of the plan's claims, taking into account the risks of litigation and credit worthiness of any party who has received an extension of credit. DOL Adv. Op. 95-26.

397. What is the statutory exemption regarding ESOP loans?

Plan fiduciaries are prohibited from receiving any consideration for their own account from any party dealing with the plan in connection with a transaction involving the income or assets of the plan. ERISA Sec. 406(b). However, exemptive relief is provided for a loan from a fiduciary or other party in interest to an employee stock ownership plan (ESOP) (as defined in ERISA Section 407(d)(6)) where: (1) the loan is primarily for the benefit of participants and beneficiaries of the plan; and (2) the loan's interest rate is not in excess of a reasonable rate of interest. ERISA Sec. 408(b)(3).

If the plan provides collateral for a loan, such collateral may only consist of qualifying employer securities, as defined under ERISA Section 407(d)(5).

The terms of the loan must be at least as favorable to the plan as the terms of a comparable loan resulting from an arm's length transaction between unrelated third parties. Labor Reg. §2550.408b-3(c)(3).

The proceeds of an exempt loan may only be issued by the plan in order to: (1) acquire qualifying employer securities; (2) repay the loan; or (3) repay a prior exempt loan. Labor Reg. §2550.408b-3(d). No securities purchased with such loan may be subject to a put, call, or other option, or a buy-sell or similar arrangement while held by, or when distributed from, the plan.

An ESOP loan must be made without recourse against the plan. No one who is entitled to payment under the loan should have any right to assets of the plan other than: (1) collateral given for the loan; (2) contributions made to satisfy the ESOP's loan obligation; and (3) earnings attributable to the collateral and the investment of such contributions. Labor Reg. §2550.408b-3(e).

Where there has been a default upon an exempt loan, the value of plan assets transferred in satisfaction of the loan must not exceed the value of the default amount. Labor Reg. §2550.408b-3(f).

In considering what constitutes a reasonable rate of interest on an ESOP loan, all relevant factors will be considered, including the amount and duration of the loan, the security and guarantee involved, the credit worthiness of the plan and the guarantor, and the interest rate available on comparable loans. Labor Reg. §2550.408b-3(g).

The regulations provide a complicated formula to calculate the number of securities released from encumbrance as collateral for the loan. Basically, for each plan year during the life of the loan, the number of securities released from encumbrance must equal the number of encumbered securities held immediately before release for the current plan year, when multiplied by a fraction. The numerator of that fraction is the amount of principal and interest paid for the year. The denominator is the sum of the numerator plus the principal and interest to be paid in all future years. Labor Reg. §2550.408b-3(h).

Securities acquired with the proceeds of an ESOP loan may be subject to a right of first refusal. Securities subject to such a right of first refusal must be stock or an equity security, or a debt security convertible into stock or an equity security. In addition, securities subject to a right of first refusal must not be publicly traded at the time when the right may be exercised. The right of first refusal must be in favor of the plan sponsor, the plan, or both. Labor Reg. §2550.408b-3(i).

398. What is the statutory exemption regarding investments in deposits of banks?

The investment of all or part of a plan's assets in deposits that bear a reasonable interest rate in a bank or similar financial institution supervised by the United States or a State is exempted from the prohibited transaction restrictions of ERISA Sections 406(a), 406(b)(1), and 406(b)(2), if that bank or institution is a plan fiduciary, and:

1. The plan covers only employees of the bank or institution; *or*

2. The investment is expressly authorized by a provision of the plan or by a fiduciary (other than the bank, institution, or an affiliate

thereof) who is expressly empowered by the plan to instruct the plan trustee regarding the investment. ERISA Sec. 408(b)(4).

However, ERISA Section 408(b)(4) does not provide an exemption from the prohibited transaction provision of ERISA Section 406(b)(3), which prohibits a fiduciary from receiving consideration for his own account from any party dealing with a plan in connection with a transaction involving plan assets. Further, the regulations provide that the fiduciary provisions of ERISA Section 404 continue to apply to the exempt transaction. In other words, the transaction must comply with the prudence and diversification requirements of ERISA. Labor Reg. §2550.408b-4(a).

399. What is the statutory exemption regarding the purchase of insurance from an employer?

A plan is permitted to purchase any contract for life insurance, health insurance, or annuities with one or more insurers qualified to conduct business in a state, provided that:

1.   The plan pays no more than adequate consideration; and

2.   Each insurer is:

         a) the plan sponsor, *or*

         b) a party in interest wholly owned (either indirectly or directly) by the plan sponsor, or by any person who is a party in interest to the plan, but only if the total premiums and annuity considerations written by such insurer for all plans (and their employers) with respect to which the insurer is a party in interest do not exceed 5% of the total premiums and annuity considerations written for all lines of insurance in that year by the insurer.

The 5% limitation excludes all premiums and annuity considerations paid for a plan that the insurer maintains. ERISA Sec. 408(b)(5).

400. What is the statutory exemption regarding the provision of ancillary bank services?

Exemptive relief is provided for any ancillary service provided to a qualified plan by a bank or similar financial institution that is supervised by the United States or a state, if the bank or institution is a plan fiduciary, and:

1.   The bank or financial institution has adequate internal safeguards that assure that the ancillary service is consistent with sound

banking and financial practice (as determined by a federal or state supervisory authority); and

2. Stated guidelines provided by the bank or financial institution hold that ancillary services may not be provided in an excessive or unreasonable manner, or in a fashion that is inconsistent with the best interests of participants and beneficiaries of the plans.

Under this statutory exemption, ancillary services may not be provided at more than reasonable compensation. ERISA Sec. 408(b)(6).

This exemptive relief extends to services provided by the bank or financial institution which would not meet the requirements of the statutory exemption of ERISA Section 408(b)(2) (regarding the contracting by a plan for necessary services) because the provision of these ancillary services involves an act otherwise prohibited under either ERISA Section 406(b)(1) (the prohibition against fiduciaries dealing with plan assets in their own interest), or ERISA Section 406(b)(2) (the prohibition against fiduciaries acting in any transaction involving the plan on behalf of a party whose interests are adverse to the interests of the plan). ERISA Section 408(b)(6) provides exemptive relief from ERISA Sections 406(b)(1) and 406(b)(2) because it contemplates the provision of such ancillary services without the approval of a second fiduciary. Labor Reg. §2550.408b-6(a).

However, ERISA Section 408(b)(6) does not provide exemptive relief from ERISA Section 406(b)(3), the prohibition for fiduciaries receiving consideration for their own personal account from any party dealing with a plan in connection with a transaction involving assets of a qualified plan.

PRACTITIONER'S POINTER

The transfer of idle cash balances in plan accounts to short-term investment vehicles (commonly referred to as "sweep services" or "overnight sweeps") by the party in interest bank or financial institution will not be a prohibited transaction in violation of the self-dealing rules if the plan is not required to pay an additional fee for the service. If the plan is required to pay a fee for any sweep services, the DOL is likely to consider the payment of fees to be a prohibited transaction. DOL Adv. Op. 88-2A.

401. What is the statutory exemption regarding owner-employee transactions?

ERISA Section 408(d) provides that certain provisions of ERISA (enumerated below) do not apply to transactions in which a plan (either directly or indirectly): (1) lends any part of the corpus or income of the plan; (2) pays any compensation for personal services rendered to the plan; or (3) acquires for the plan any property from, or sells any property to, any person who is an owner-employee of the plan sponsor, a member of the family of any such owner-employee (defined under ERISA Section 267(c)(4) as brothers, sisters, spouse, ancestors, and lineal descendants), or a corporation controlled by an owner-employee through the direct or indirect ownership of 50% or more of the total combined voting power of all classes of stock entitled to vote, or 50% or more of the total value of shares of all classes of stock of the corporation.

The ERISA provisions that will not apply to the transactions described above are:

1.   The 10% limit on the acquisition of employer securities and employer real property (ERISA Sec. 407(d));

2.   The statutory exemptions (ERISA Sec. 408(b));

3.   The provision permitting parties in interest to receive benefits earned under a plan (ERISA Sec. 408(c)); and

4.   The statutory exemption for the purchase, sale or lease of qualifying employee securities or real property (ERISA Sec. 408(e)).

These rules also apply to shareholder-employees of a Subchapter S corporation, an owner of an IRA, individual retirement annuity, or bond (or his beneficiary), and an employer or association of employers that establishes such an account or annuity under IRC Section 408(c).

ERISA Section 408(d), however, does not prohibit an owner-employee from receiving benefits under the plan as a participant or beneficiary. The premature distribution of assets to an owner-employee was permitted when the amount distributed was calculated according to the plan document, the same calculation method was applied to all of the other participants and beneficiaries and the method used to calculate the benefit did not provide a greater benefit to the owner-employee than other methods of payment. Let. Rul. 7933029.

The owner-employees and 50% shareholders who are restricted from receiving plan loans are permitted to qualify for the exemption regarding plan loans if a special exemption is approved by the DOL. Labor Reg. §2550.408b-1(a)(2). The DOL will consider individual exemption applications for such loans on a case-by-case basis.

402. What is the statutory exemption for the conversion of securities?

The exercise of a privilege to convert securities is permitted, but only if the plan receives no more than adequate consideration pursuant to such conversion. ERISA Sec. 408(b)(7).

"Adequate consideration," for securities in which there is a generally recognized market, means "the price of the security prevailing on a national securities exchange." In the case of securities for which there is no recognized market, "adequate consideration" means "a price not less favorable to the plan than the offering price for the security as established by the current bid and asked prices" quoted by persons independent of the issuer and parties in interest. ERISA Sec. 3(18).

A plan may hold or acquire certain employer securities. Some of these securities may be convertible (for example, from bonds to stock). The statutory exemption permits these conversions if the plan receives at least fair market value under the conversion. The ERISA Conference Report provides that "it is expected that a conversion will be permitted if all the securities of the class held by the plan are subject to the same terms." These terms must be as favorable to the plan as an arm's length transaction, so that conversions cannot be tailored to apply only to a particular plan. H.R. Conf. Rep. No. 93-1280, 93rd Cong., 2nd Sess., 323 (1974) (ERISA Conference Report).

403. What is the statutory exemption regarding pooled investment funds?

Any transaction between a plan and either: (1) a common or collective trust fund or pooled investment fund maintained by a party in interest that is a bank or trust company supervised by a state or federal agency; or (2) the pooled investment fund of an insurance company qualified to do business in a state is exempt from the prohibited transaction provisions of ERISA if:

1. The transaction is a sale or purchase of an interest in the fund;

2. The bank, trust company, or insurance company does not receive more than reasonable compensation; and

3. Such transaction is expressly permitted by the instrument under which the plan is maintained, or by a fiduciary (other than the bank, trust company, or insurance company, or any of their affiliates) who has authority to manage and control assets of the plan. ERISA Sec. 408(b)(8).

The DOL has ruled that the investment of plan assets by a trustee bank in common trust funds maintained by the bank would not violate the prohibited transaction provisions of ERISA, since the bank trustee would not be exercising any of the authority, control, or responsibility that makes it a fiduciary to cause a plan to pay an additional fee. DOL Adv. Op. 88-11A.

Further, fiduciaries may not use any of the authority, control, or responsibility that makes such a person a fiduciary to cause a plan to pay additional fees to the fiduciary (or to an entity in which such fiduciary has an interest that may affect the exercise of his best judgment as a fiduciary) for the provision of a service. Labor Reg. §2550.408b-2(e)(2).

404. What is the statutory exemption for the receipt of benefits?

Parties in interest may receive any benefit to which they may be entitled as a participant or beneficiary of the plan. IRC Secs. 4975(d)(9), 4975(d)(10). Further, parties in interest may receive compensation for services rendered to the plan and for the reimbursement of reasonable expenses incurred in providing services to the plan. DOL Adv. Op. 89-9A.

The payment of benefits must be computed and paid on the same basis that benefits are computed and paid to the other participants and beneficiaries.

405. What is the statutory exemption regarding termination distributions?

The decision to terminate a qualified retirement plan is exempt from ERISA's fiduciary provisions. ERISA Sec. 408(b)(10). As such, the prohibited transaction provisions do not apply to a fiduciary's distribution of assets during the termination of the plan, if they are distributed in accordance with the written provisions of the plan's governing documents. *District 65, UAW v. Harper & Row, Inc.*, 576 F. Supp. 1468 (S.D. NY 1983).

406. What is the statutory exemption for the merger of multiemployer plans?

A merger of multiemployer plans, or the transfer of assets or liabilities between multiemployer plans, will be exempt from the prohibited transaction provisions of ERISA if the same requirements that must be satisfied in order for the Pension Benefits Guaranty Corporation (PBGC) to approve a merger of multiemployer plans (see ERISA Section 4231) are satisfied. ERISA Sec. 408(b)(11).

This statutory exemption does not provide relief from ERISA Section 406(b)(1), which prohibits a fiduciary from dealing with the plan assets in his own interest, or from ERISA Section 406(b)(3), which prohibits a fiduciary from receiving any consideration for his own account from any party dealing with such plan in connection with a transaction involving plan assets.

INDIVIDUAL EXEMPTIONS

407. What is an "individual prohibited transaction exemption," and how is such an exemption granted?

An individual prohibited transaction exemption is an administrative exemption, granted under ERISA Section 408(a) and IRC Section 4975(c)(2). An individual prohibited transaction exemption applies only to specific parties in interest, named or otherwise defined in the exemption. Labor Reg. §2570.31(e).

Under ERISA Section 408, the Department of Labor (DOL) is authorized to issue exemptions to the prohibited transaction rules under both ERISA and the Internal Revenue Code. Since 1978, the DOL has been the sole entity granting exemptions. Reorganization Plan No. 4 of 1978, 1979-1 CB 480. Prior to 1978, the IRS would issue exemptions from the prohibited transaction provisions of the Internal Revenue Code and the DOL would issue exemptions from the prohibited transaction provisions of ERISA. As it stands today, any exemption application received by the DOL expressly seeking an exemption under the Internal Revenue Code or ERISA will be treated as an application filed under both law sections, if it relates to any transaction prohibited under both the Internal Revenue Code and ERISA. Labor Reg. §2570.30(b).

The DOL will review each application on its own merits. Even if an application satisfies all of the requirements as to content (which are detailed under the applicable regulation), there is no guarantee that the DOL will grant the relief requested. All exemptions granted by the DOL must be: (1) administratively feasible; (2) in the best interests of the plan and its participants and beneficiaries; and (3) protective of the rights of participants and beneficiaries of the plan. ERISA Sec. 408(a).

Some examples of individual prohibited transaction exemptions that the DOL has granted include:

- the extension of credit between the plan and parties in interest;

- the sale, transfer, and use of plan assets by parties in interest;

- the payment of commissions to parties in interest;

- leases between a plan and parties in interest;

- loans between a plan and parties in interest;

- the provision of services between a plan and parties in interest;

- transactions involving collective investment funds;

- transactions between investment managers and parties in interest;

- the sale of leases, letters of credit, loans, and memberships in clubs; and

- transactions between Keogh plans and IRAs.

408. How does one apply for an individual prohibited transaction exemption?

The DOL has issued final regulations, which describe the procedures for the filing and processing of applications for individual prohibited transaction exemptions under ERISA and the Internal Revenue Code. These regulations detail the procedural and content requirements for filing an application for an individual prohibited transaction exemption. See Labor Reg. §2570.1, et seq.

The DOL may initiate exemption proceedings on its own, usually where there is a need for a class exemption that has been recognized by the DOL as applicable on an industry-wide basis. Labor Reg. §2570.32(a).

The DOL will not issue exemptions that have been requested orally. Although an applicant for an individual exemption may request and receive oral advice from DOL representatives in preparing an exemption application, the DOL has indicated that such advice does not constitute a part of the administrative record of the application and is not binding upon the DOL in processing an individual exemption application procedure.

The following questions explain the procedures for seeking an individual exemption application, including:

- where to file an individual exemption application (see Q 414);

- who may apply for an individual exemption (see Q 409);

- what information an exemption application must contain (see Q 411, Q 412);

- which individual exemption applications the DOL will not consider (see Q 410);

- what to do if you wish to withdraw an individual exemption application (see Q 422);

- what your rights are should the DOL notify you that they intend to reject your individual exemption application (see Q 416, Q 417);

- what are the limits and effect of an individual exemption once it has been granted (see Q 426); and

- whether the DOL may revoke or modify an individual exemption once it has been granted (see Q 427).

409. Who may apply for an individual exemption?

Regulations detail persons who may apply for individual exemptions. Labor Reg. §2570.32. In addition to the DOL initiating exemption procedures on their own, the DOL will initiate exemption proceedings upon the receipt of an application from the following entities:

1.   Any party in interest who is or may be a party to the transaction upon which the individual exemption is sought;

2.   Any plan that is a party to the transaction for which the individual exemption is being sought; and

3.   Regarding an application for an exemption that will affect a class of parties in interest or a class of transactions, (in addition to those persons described in (1) and (2), above), an association or organization representing parties in interest who may be parties to the transaction for which the individual exemption is being sought. Labor Reg. §2570.32(a).

If an application is being submitted on behalf of any of the above parties by an authorized representative of the applicant, the representative must submit proof of his authority in an executed Power of Attorney or a written certification from the applicant. Labor Reg. §2570.32(b).

If the authorized representative submits the individual exemption application with proof of his authority to represent the applicant to the DOL, the DOL will direct all correspondence and inquiries regarding the application to the authorized representative, unless requested to do otherwise by the applicant. Labor Reg. §2570.32(c).

410. What type of individual exemption applications will the Department of Labor ordinarily not consider?

The DOL will ordinarily not consider any individual prohibited transaction application that does not include all of the required information contained under the application procedures (see Q 411, Q 412). Labor Reg. §2570.33. The DOL will also not consider any application that does not conform to the requirements of the individual exemption application procedures.

The DOL will not consider for approval any application for an individual exemption that involves transactions that the DOL is currently investigating for possible violations of ERISA. The DOL will also not consider any application that involves any party in interest who is the subject of a DOL investigation, or is a defendant in any court action, whether brought by the DOL or the IRS, to enforce Parts 1 or 4 of Subtitle B of ERISA, Sections 8477 and 8478 of the Federal Employees' Retirement System Act of 1986, or the Internal Revenue Code. Labor Reg. §2570.33(a).

If the DOL is considering a class exemption relating to the type of transaction in which they have received an individual exemption application, they will ordinarily not consider the individual application on a separate basis. Labor Reg. §2570.33(c).

If the DOL determines that they will not consider an individual exemption application, they will inform the applicant of that decision in writing, including the reasons for which they have declined to consider the application. Labor Reg. §2570.33(b).

APPLICATIONS FOR EXEMPTIONS

411. What information must be contained in every exemption application?

In the summary of the final regulations for prohibited transaction exemption procedures, the DOL notes that the efficiency of the exemption application program could be greatly improved "if the quality of exemption applications filed were improved." The DOL further states that, "In the past, applications have been incomplete, have omitted or misstated facts or legal analysis needed to justify requests for exemptive relief, and, in some cases, have been so poorly drafted that the details of the transactions for which exemptive relief is sought are unclear." Prohibited Transaction Exemption Procedures; Employee Benefit Plans, 55 Fed. Reg. 32836. In an effort to improve the quality of the applications received, the regulations require that an application for exemption contain more detailed information, and that certain documents be included when such application is filed with the DOL.

Regulations detail the information that must be included in every exemption (class and individual) application submitted to the DOL. Labor Reg. §2570.34. For a detailed review of the additional information that must accompany individual exemption applications, see Q 412. *Every* exemption application must contain the following information:

1.   The names of all applicants;

2.   A detailed description of the proposed transaction for which exemptive relief is sought and the parties in interest for whom the exemption is being requested, including a description of any larger integrated transactions, of which the transaction at issue may be a part;

3.   Whether there will be a dual representation of the plan and any of the parties in interest by the same person in regard to the exemption application;

4.   The plan's reasons for entering into the proposed exempted transaction;

5.   The provisions of ERISA that would otherwise prohibit the proposed transaction and the reason why the proposed transaction would violate each such provision;

6.   Whether the proposed transaction is a type that is customary for the industry or class involved;

7.   A statement detailing whether the proposed transaction is or has been the subject of an investigation or enforcement action by the DOL or the IRS; and

8.   The hardship or economic loss that a denial of the application would cause to (a) the person(s) filing the exemption application, (b) the plan(s), and (c) participants and beneficiaries. Labor Reg. §2570.34(a).

In addition, all exemption applications must contain:

1.   A statement explaining that the requested exemption would be: (a) administratively feasible, (b) in the interests of the plan(s), participants, and beneficiaries, and (c) protective of the rights of plan participants and beneficiaries; and

2.   A required notification (see Q 420), which must contain: (a) a detailed description of those interested individuals to whom the applicant will provide notice of the application, (b) the manner in which the notice will be provided, and (c) an estimate of the length of time that the applicant must provide the notice to all interested parties following publication of a notice of the proposed exemption in the Federal Register. Labor Reg. 2570.34(b).

If an advisory opinion has been requested regarding any issue related to the exemption application, the application must contain: (1) a copy of the response from the DOL, which states its action on the advisory opinion request; or (2) if the DOL has not concluded its action on the request, both (a) a copy of the request (or the date on which it was submitted, along with the DOL's correspondence control number assigned in its acknowledgment letter), and (b) an explanation of what effect the granting of a favorable advisory opinion would have upon the proposed exemption transaction. Labor Reg. §2570.34(b).

If the application is to be signed by anyone other than those parties in interest for whom the exemption is sought, a statement must be provided, which identifies the individual who will be signing the application and that individual's relationship to the applicant(s). The statement will also need to contain a brief explanation of the signing party's familiarity with the matters discussed in the application. Labor Reg. §2570.34(b)(4).

An exemption application may, but is not required to, include a draft of the requested exemption defining the proposed transaction for which relief is sought and the parties in interest to the proposed transaction along with an explanation of those specific conditions under which the exemption would apply. Labor Reg. §2570.34(c).

Finally, all exemption applications must contain the following declaration, which must be made under penalty of perjury:

"I declare that I am familiar with the matters discussed in this application, and, to the best of my knowledge and belief, the representations made in this application are true and correct."

This declaration must be signed and dated by:

1.   The individual party in interest seeking the exemption;

2.   A corporate officer (if the applicant is a corporation);

3.   A partner (if the applicant is a partnership); or

4.   A plan fiduciary who will have authority and control regarding the exempted transaction (if the applicant seeking exemptive relief is a plan). Labor Reg. §2570.34(b)(5).

Specialized statements from third party experts submitted in support of an exemption application must also contain a statement of consent from the expert, acknowledging that the statement is being submitted to the DOL as part of an exemption application. The specialized statements may include, but are not limited to, appraisals or analyses of market conditions that support the proposed transaction. Labor Reg. §2570.34(b)(5)(iii).

Where an exemption application requires an independent fiduciary to represent the plan with respect to the proposed transaction, that independent fiduciary must file a declaration, made under penalty of perjury, that to the best of his knowledge and belief, the representations made in the statement are true and correct. Labor Reg. §2570.34(b)(5)(iv).

412. What information is required to be included in an individual exemption application?

In addition to the material required for *all* exemption applications (see Q 411), individual exemption applications are required to include the following information:

1.   The name, address, telephone number, and type(s) of plan to which the requested exemption will apply;

2. The Plan Number and the Employer Identification Number (EIN) used by the plan(s) on all reporting and disclosure requirements filed with the DOL;

3. Whether any plan or trust involved in the requested exemption has ever been found by the DOL, the IRS, or a court to have violated the exclusive benefit rule (of IRC Section 401(a)), or to have engaged in a prohibited transaction (under ERISA Sections 406, 407(a), or IRC Section 503(b));

4. Whether any statutory relief under ERISA Section 408 or IRC Section 4975(c)(2) has been provided to, or requested by, the applicant or any of the parties for whom the exemption is being sought, and, if so, the exemption application number or the prohibited transaction exemption number;

5. Whether the applicant or any party in interest involved in the proposed transaction has been (or is currently) a defendant in any lawsuit or criminal action regarding his conduct as a fiduciary or party in interest with respect to any plan within the last five years;

6. Whether the applicant or any party in interest with respect to the proposed transaction has been convicted of any crime prohibited under ERISA Section 411 (prohibition against certain persons holding fiduciary positions) within the last 13 years;

7. Whether, within the last five years, any of the affected plans or any party in interest has been under investigation or examination by, or has been involved in litigation or a continuing controversy with the DOL, the IRS, the PBGC, or the Federal Retirement Thrift Investments Board involving compliance with any of the provisions of ERISA, the employee benefit provisions of the Internal Revenue Code, or the provisions of the Federal Employees Retirement System Act of 1986 (FERSA) relating to the Federal Thrift Savings Fund (if so, the affected parties must submit copies of all correspondence with the DOL, the IRS, the PBGC, the Justice Department or the Federal Retirement Thrift Investment Board relating to the substantive issues involved in the investigation, examination, litigation, or controversy);

8. Whether any of the plans affected by the exemption application have experienced a reportable event under ERISA Section 4043 (plan mergers, consolidation, partial termination, termination, failure to meet minimum funding standards, etc.);

9. Whether a Notice of Intent to Terminate has been filed under ERISA Section 4041 relating to any of the plans affected by the proposed exemption;

10. The name, address, and taxpayer identification number of each party in interest with respect to the proposed transaction;

11. An estimate of the number of participants and beneficiaries in each plan affected by the proposed transaction (as of the date of the application);

12. What percentage of the assets of each affected plan, by fair market value, will be involved in the proposed transaction;

13. Whether the proposed transaction has been consummated or will be consummated only if the exemption is granted;

14. If the transaction has already been consummated, the circumstances under which fiduciaries caused the transaction to be consummated prior to seeking an exemption from the DOL, whether the transaction has been terminated, whether the transaction has been corrected (IRC Sec. 4975(f)(5)), whether Form 5330, *Return of Excise Taxes Related to Employee Benefit Plans* has been filed with the IRS, in relation to the transaction and whether all excise taxes due with respect to the transaction have been paid to the IRS (IRC Secs. 4975(a), 4975(b));

15. The identity of every person with investment discretion over any of the assets involved in the proposed transaction and their relationship to the parties in interest and their affiliates with respect to the proposed transaction;

16. If the assets of the plan are invested in (i) loans to any party in interest with respect to the transaction, (ii) property that is leased to a party in interest, or (iii) in any securities issued by a party in interest, a statement with respect to each of these three types of investments, which details: (a) to which of the three investment types the investment pertains, (b) the fair market value of all of the plan investments of this type (as of the most recent plan valuation), (c) the overall percentage of plan assets represented by this type of investment (as of the most recent plan valuation), and (d) any applicable statutory or administrative exemption which covers the investments;

17.   The aggregate fair market value of the assets of all of the plans involved in the proposed transaction;

18.   The individuals responsible for the costs of the exemption application and the notification of interested persons; and

19.   The identity of the independent fiduciaries involved in the transaction, if any, and the identity of those individuals bearing the responsibility for any fee payable to the independent fiduciary. Labor Reg. §2570.35(a).

All applications for individual exemptions must also include true copies of all contracts, deeds, agreements, and instruments, as well as relevant portions of each plan's governing documents, trust agreements, and any other documents that relate to the proposed transaction. Along with the relevant documents, there must also be an explanation of the relevant facts in these documents that have a bearing on the transaction, as well as an analysis of their relevance to the transaction. Labor Reg. §2570.35(b).

All applications must also be accompanied by a copy of the most recent financial statements of all plans affected by the requested exemption. Labor Reg. §2570.35(b)(3).

413. What are the special rules for applications for individual exemptions involving pooled funds?

Individual prohibited transaction exemption applications involving pooled funds have specific requirements as to the information that they must contain. Labor Reg. §2570.35(c). Much of the information required for other individual exemption applications must also be provided in applications submitted by pooled funds. In addition, individual exemption applications submitted by pooled funds must contain an estimate of the number of plans that are participating (or will participate) in the pooled fund and the minimum and maximum limits imposed on participating plans regarding the total assets of each plan that may be invested in the pooled fund.

As noted above, the following information must be furnished with reference to the pooled funds seeking the individual exemption:

1.   The name, address, and telephone number of the pooled fund(s) to which the requested exemption applies;

2.   The Employer Identification Number (EIN) used by such pooled fund(s);

3.   Whether the DOL, the IRS, or a court has ever found any pooled fund affected by the requested exemption to have violated the

exclusive benefit rule of IRC Section 401, or to have engaged in a prohibited transaction in violation of ERISA Sections 406, 407(a), or IRC Section 503(b);

4. Whether relief under ERISA Section 408(a) or IRC Section 4975(c)(2) has been requested by, or provided to, the applicant of any of the parties on behalf of whom the application is sought, and, if so, the prohibited transaction exemption number or the exemption application number;

5. Whether presently, or in the past five years from the date of the application, the applicant or a party in interest with respect to the proposed exemption has been a defendant in any lawsuit or criminal action concerning his conduct as a fiduciary or party in interest with respect to plan assets invested in the pooled fund;

6. Whether the applicant or a party in interest with respect to the transaction has been convicted, within the last 13 years from the date of the application, of any crime described in ERISA Section 441 (prohibition against certain persons holding fiduciary positions);

7. Whether, in the last five years from the date of the application, any plan affected by the transaction or any party in interest involved in the transaction has been under investigation or engaged in litigation or a continuing controversy with the DOL, the IRS, the PBGC, the Department of Justice, or the Federal Retirement Thrift Investment Board involving issues that relate to compliance with the provisions of Part 1 or 4 of Subtitle B of Title I of ERISA, IRC Section 4975, or Federal Employees Retirement System Act (FERSA) Sections 8477 or 8478 (excluding routine audits under FERSA Section 8477(g));

8. Whether the transaction has been consummated or will be consummated only if the exemption is granted;

9. If the transaction has been consummated: (a) the circumstances that resulted in the pooled fund engaging in the transaction before an exemption has been granted, (b) whether the transaction has been terminated, (c) whether the transaction has been corrected in accordance with IRC Section 4975(f)(5), (d) whether Form 5330, *Return of Excise Taxes Related to Employee Benefit Plans*, has been filed with the IRS with respect to plans involved in the transaction, and (e) whether any excise taxes, due by reason of the transaction under IRC Sections 4975(a) and 4975(b), have been paid;

10.   The name of every person who has investment discretion over any assets involved in the transaction and the relationship of each of these people to the parties in interest involved in the transaction and their affiliates;

11.   Whether assets of the affected plan are invested in loans to any party in interest, in property leased to any such party in interest, or in securities issued by any such party in interest involved in the transaction, and, if such investments exist, a statement with respect to each of these three types of investments, which details: (a) the type of investment to which the statement pertains, (b) the aggregate fair market value of all investments of this type, (c) the approximate percentage of the fair market value of the funds' total assets represented by all investments of this type, and (d) the statutory or administrative exemption covering plan assets involved in these investments, if any;

12.   The approximate fair market value of the total assets of each of the pooled funds affected by the transaction;

13.   The person(s) responsible for the costs of the exemption application and for notifying interested persons; and

14.   Whether an independent fiduciary is, or will be, involved in the exemption transaction and, if so, the names of the persons who will bear the cost of the fee payable to such fiduciary. Labor Reg. §2570.35(a).

Each applicant for an individual exemption involving a pooled asset fund must also include copies of all contracts, deeds, agreements, and instruments, as well as all relevant portions of qualified retirement plan-related documents, trust agreements, and other documents with respect to the transaction. Labor Reg. §2570.35(b)(1).

Applicants must also provide a discussion of the relevant facts to the transaction that are reflected in these documents, an analysis of their bearing on the requested exemption, and a copy of the most recent financial statement of each plan affected by the requested exemption. Labor Regs. §§2570.35(b)(2), 2570.35(b)(3).

More detailed informational requirements apply to exemption applications that involve one or more pooled asset funds in which the investment of any participating plan is more than 20% of the total assets of the pooled fund or which covers employees of the party, or its affiliates, sponsoring the pooled fund or any fiduciary with investment discretion over the pooled fund's assets. Under these circumstances, the exemption application must include, with respect to each plan involved in the transaction: (1) the names, addresses, and taxpayer identification numbers of all parties in interest with respect to the plan involved in the transaction; (2) the percentage of the fair market value of the total assets of each affected plan that is involved in the transaction; and (3) the information required to be disclosed by pooled asset funds detailed above in paragraphs (1), (2), (3), (5), (6), (7), (8), (9), (10), (11), (13), and (14), but only to the extent that the requested information applies to the plans involved in the transaction. Labor Reg. §2570.35(c).

414. Where are individual exemption applications filed?

The Department of Labor's prohibited transaction exemption program is administered by the Pension and Welfare Benefits Administration (PWBA). Labor Reg. §2570.36. As such, all individual exemption applications, filed in accordance with the application procedures detailed under Labor Regulations §§ 2570.32 through 2570.47, should be delivered to:

> Exemption Application
> PWBA, Office of Exemption Determinations
> Division Of Exemptions
> U.S. Department of Labor
> 200 Constitution Avenue, N.W.
> Washington, DC 20210

415. When do applicants have a duty to amend and supplement an individual exemption application?

After the initial filing of an individual exemption application, the applicant must notify the DOL Division of Exemptions, in writing, if it discovers that any material fact or representation contained in the original application is inaccurate. The applicant must also promptly notify the Division of Exemptions if any of the facts or representations in the application have changed, or if anything has occurred, while the application is pending, which may have an effect on the accuracy of the facts or representations contained in the application. Labor Reg. §2570.37(a).

The DOL Division of Exemptions must be promptly notified if any of the parties in interest with respect to the proposed transaction have become the subject of an investigation regarding issues of compliance with ERISA, the employee benefit provisions of the Internal Revenue Code, or the portions of the Federal Employees Retirement System Act (FERSA) relating to the Federal Thrift Savings Fund. The notification must be made when the investigation or enforcement action has been undertaken by the DOL, the IRS, the Department of Justice, the PBGC, or the Federal Retirement Thrift Savings Fund. Labor Reg. §2570.37(b).

The DOL may also require applicants to provide any additional documentation that it believes may be necessary in order to verify statements in the application or its supporting documents. Labor Reg. §2570.37(c).

416. What options are available to individual exemption applicants when they receive a tentative denial letter from the Department of Labor?

The DOL notifies individual exemption applicants in writing of a tentative denial of an exemption application. The DOL also provides a brief written statement, which lists its reasons for the tentative denial. Labor Reg. §2570.38(a).

Applicants who receive a tentative denial letter may, within 20 days from the date of the letter, request a conference or notify the DOL of their intent to submit, in writing, additional information to be considered under the exemption application. See Q 417, Q 418. If, within the 20-day period, the DOL has not received a written request for a conference or a written notice of the applicant's intention to submit additional written information, the DOL will issue a final denial letter. See Q 419. Labor Reg. §2570.38(b).

The DOL is under no obligation to issue a tentative denial letter where it has conducted a hearing on the exemption application pursuant to either a hearing held by interested persons in objection to the proposed exempted transaction (see Q 424), or where the DOL has scheduled and conducted a hearing on the application on its own volition due to its determination that issues within the application must be more fully explored (see Q 425). Labor Reg. §2570.38(c).

417. When may an applicant take the opportunity to submit additional information in support of an exemption application?

An applicant may submit additional information to the DOL regarding his exemption application according to the specific procedures outlined in the regulations. Labor Reg. §2570.39. If an applicant intends to submit additional information in support of his exemption application, he must notify the DOL of this intent. This notice may be made over the telephone, or in writing to the address provided within a tentative denial letter (see Q 416). The notice should detail the type of additional information being provided. Labor Reg. §2570.39(a).

After the applicant has provided notice to the DOL, he has 30 days from the date of that notice to submit in writing all of the additional material that he intends to provide to the DOL in support of his individual exemption application. The applicant must also submit a written declaration, made under penalty of perjury, which attests to the truth and correctness of the information provided, and which is signed and dated by either the applicant or a person qualified to sign such a declaration. Labor Regs. §§2570.39(b), 2570.34(b)(5).

The applicant may request an extension of the 30-day period if, for reasons beyond his control, he is unable to submit, in writing, all additional information he intends to provide in support of his application. Requests for extensions beyond the 30-day period must be made prior to the close of the 30-day period, and will be granted only in unusual circumstances. Labor Reg. §2570.39(c).

If the applicant is unable to submit the additional written information that he had previously notified the DOL he intended to submit, the applicant may withdraw his exemption application before the expiration of the 30-day period, plus any additional extension that may have been granted. By withdrawing the exemption application before the expiration of the applicable time period, he may later reinstate the application when he has prepared the additional information to be submitted in support of his application. Labor Reg. §2570.39(d).

The DOL will issue a final denial letter of an exemption application where the DOL has not received the additional information that the applicant intended to submit within the 30-day period (plus any additional extension that has been granted). The DOL will also issue a final denial letter if the applicant did not file a request for a conference after the receipt of a tentative denial letter (see Q 416), or where the applicant has not withdrawn his exemption application. Labor Reg. §2570.39(e).

418. What are the procedures for an exemption application conference with the Department of Labor?

All conferences between the applicant(s) and the DOL regarding a pending individual exemption application will be held at the Washington, D.C. offices of the DOL. The DOL will, however, conduct a conference over the telephone at the applicant's request. Labor Reg. §2570.40(a).

The DOL will schedule conferences, at a mutually convenient time, within 45 days following the later of:

1.   The date when the DOL receives the applicant's request for a conference; or

2.   The date when the DOL notifies the applicant that it is still not prepared to propose the requested exemption, after the review of additional material presented by the applicant, in accordance with the provisions of Labor Regulation §2570.39 (see Q 417).

If an applicant fails to appear at a scheduled conference, or if he fails to attend a conference at any time within the 45-day period, the DOL will deem the applicant to have waived his right to a conference, unless the applicant is unable to appear due to circumstances beyond his control. Labor Reg. §2570.40(d).

If the DOL has held a hearing on an individual exemption application pursuant to a request filed in opposition to the exemption application from an interested person, or a hearing scheduled by the DOL, on its own initiative, in an effort to develop further information regarding a pending exemption application (see Q 424), an applicant will not be entitled to an exemption application conference with the DOL. Otherwise, an applicant is entitled to one conference with respect to any exemption application. Labor Reg. §2570.40(b).

The DOL will consolidate conferences, with all applicants being present, where there is more than one applicant under an individual exemption application or where more than one applicant has filed an application with respect to similar types of transactions, which the DOL is considering together as a request for a class transaction. The DOL will also hold joint conferences where more than one applicant has requested a conference and where the DOL is contemplating the rejection of an application. Labor Reg. §2570.40(c).

Within 20 days after the date of a conference, an applicant may submit a written record to the DOL, containing any additional information, arguments, or precedents discussed during the conference, but which were not previously or adequately presented in writing. Labor Reg. §2570.40(e).

419. When will the Department of Labor issue a final denial letter?

The DOL will issue a final denial letter regarding an individual exemption application, in situations where:

1. The applicant has either failed to request a conference with the DOL, or failed to notify the DOL of his intent to submit additional information within the 20-day period following the date of a tentative denial letter;

2. The applicant has failed to appear at a requested conference or to submit additional information;

3. The applicant has not withdrawn his application as permitted by Labor Regulation §2570.39(d);

4. After issuing a tentative denial letter and receiving additional information, and after considering the entire record of the application, the DOL decides not to propose an exemption or to withdraw an exemption already proposed; or

5. After proposing and conducting a hearing on the exemption, and after considering the entire record of the application, the DOL decides to withdraw the proposed exemption. Labor Reg. §2570.41.

420. How will the Department of Labor publicize its intention to tentatively grant an individual exemption application?

If, after consideration of all information submitted by an applicant, the DOL has made a tentative decision to grant an individual exemption application, it will publish a notice of proposed exemption in the Federal Register. Labor Reg. §2570.42. This notice will explain the exemption transaction along with a summary of the information submitted to the DOL in support of the exemption application. Labor Reg. §2570.42(a).

The notice published in the Federal Register will also specify all conditions under which the exemption is proposed, and serves to inform interested persons of their rights to submit written comments to the DOL regarding the proposed exempt transaction, as well as to establish a deadline for the receipt of such comments. Labor Regs. §§2570.42(b), 2570.42(c).

If the proposed exemption provides relief from the prohibited transaction provisions of ERISA Section 406(b), or the prohibitions found under IRC Sections 4975(c)(1)(E) or 4975(c)(1)(F), the notice published in the Federal Register will serve to inform interested persons of their rights to request a hearing in opposition to the exemption and to establish a deadline for the receipt of such opposition hearing requests. Labor Reg. §2570.42(d).

421. When will an applicant be required to provide notice to interested persons of a proposed prohibited transaction exemption?

If the DOL determines that the publication of a proposed prohibited transaction exemption in the Federal Register will not provide sufficient notice to interested persons, the DOL is required to notify the applicant and to secure the applicant's written agreement to provide adequate notice to interested persons under the circumstances. Labor Reg. §2570.43(a).

If a notice of the proposed exemption is published in the Federal Register as a result of the DOL's tentative decision to grant the exemption, the applicant must notify interested persons of the pending exemption in the manner and time specified in the exemption application, or in any superseding agreement with the DOL. The notification must include a copy of the Notice of Proposed Exemption and a supplemental statement that provides the following statement:

> "You are hereby notified that the United States Department of Labor is considering granting an exemption from the prohibited transaction provisions of the Employee Retirement Income Security Act of 1974, the Internal Revenue Code of 1986, or the Federal Employees' Retirement System Act of 1986. The exemption under consideration is explained in the enclosed Notice of Proposed Exemption. As a person who may be affected by the exemption, you have the right to comment on the proposed exemption by [date]. [If you may be adversely affected by the grant of the exemption, you also have the right to request a hearing on the exemption by [date]].

> "Comments or requests for a hearing should be addressed to: Office of Exemption Determinations, Pension and Welfare Benefits Administration, Room N-5671, U.S. Department of Labor, 200 Constitution Avenue, N.W., Washington, D.C. 20210, ATTENTION: Application No. _____.

> "The Department will make no final decision on the proposed exemption until it reviews all comments received in response to the enclosed notice. If the Department decides to hold a hearing on the exemption before making its final decision, you will be notified of the time and place of the hearing." Labor Reg. §2570.43(b).

The method elected for the notice to interested persons must be "reasonably calculated" to ensure that all interested persons will actually receive the notice. In all cases, personal delivery and delivery by first-class mail will be considered reasonable methods of furnishing the required notice. Labor Reg. §2570.43(c).

After furnishing the required notice, an applicant must provide a statement to the DOL confirming that the required notice was furnished to the persons in the manner and time designated in its exemption application, or in any superseding agreement with the DOL.

The statement must also contain a declaration stating that, under penalty of perjury, the applicant attests to the truth of the information provided in the statement. This declaration must be signed by the applicant or a person qualified to sign such a declaration. Labor Reg. §2570.34(b)(5).

The DOL will not grant an exemption until such statement and accompanying declaration have been furnished to the DOL. Labor Reg. 2570.43(d).

422. What is involved in the withdrawal of an exemption application?

Applicants may wish to withdraw an exemption application where they have been notified of a tentative denial of the application by the DOL, or where the applicant will require additional time beyond the 30-day period to compile and submit additional information in support of his application to the DOL (see Q 417). Withdrawing an application prior to an official denial from the DOL will permit the applicant to re-submit the application at a later time for reconsideration. An official denial will preclude the applicant from seeking an exemption from the DOL at any time thereafter. An applicant may withdraw his individual exemption application at any time by informing the DOL, either orally or in writing, of his intent to withdraw the application. Labor Reg. §2570.44(a).

The DOL will confirm the applicant's request for withdrawal of the application for an exemption by letter and will terminate all proceedings regarding the withdrawn application. The DOL will also publish a notice of the withdrawn application in the Federal Register if a notice of the proposed exemption had been published therein. Labor Reg. §2570.44(b).

Where the applicant proposes to withdraw an application that has been considered with other applications under a request for a class exemption, or where the application itself is for a class exemption, the DOL will inform all other applicants with respect to the exemption of the individual withdrawal. The DOL will continue to process remaining applications seeking the same exemption. Where all applicants provide notice of an intent to withdraw an application, the DOL will either terminate all proceedings related to the exemption, or it will propose the exemption upon its own motion. Labor Reg. §2570.44(c).

At any time after the timely withdrawal of an application, the applicant may seek to reinstate the application by submitting a letter to the DOL requesting that the application be reinstated and by referring to the application number assigned to the original application. If there was any additional information outstanding at the time of the withdrawal of the application (see Q 417), that information must accompany the letter that requests reinstatement of the original application. The information submitted to the DOL at the time of the original application does not need to be re-submitted with the request for reinstatement unless the application had been withdrawn more than two years prior to the request for reinstatement. Labor Reg. §2570.44(d).

The DOL will reinstate any application upon a request made in accordance with these procedures, and the DOL will take whatever steps remained at the time the application was withdrawn to process the application. Labor Reg. §2570.44(e).

423. What is involved in a request for the reconsideration of an exemption application?

Once a final denial has been issued, the DOL will grant one request for reconsideration of the denied exemption application if the applicant presents significant new information or arguments in support of the application which could not have been submitted for consideration during the DOL's initial review of the application. Labor Reg. §2570.45(a).

Such a request for reconsideration must be filed with the DOL within 180 days of the issuance of the final denial letter and must be accompanied by a copy of the final denial letter, along with a statement setting forth the new facts and arguments that provide the basis for the request for reconsideration. Labor Reg. §2570.44(b). The request for reconsideration must also contain a statement declaring that, under the penalty of perjury, the new information provided is true. This statement must be signed by either the applicant or a person qualified to sign such a declaration. Labor Regs. §§2570.45(c), 2570.34(b)(5).

If, after reviewing the additional facts and arguments, the DOL decides that the facts do not warrant reversal of the original denial, it will submit a letter to the applicant reaffirming the original denial. Labor Reg. §2570.45(d).

If, after reviewing the additional facts and arguments, the DOL decides that the facts *do* warrant reconsideration, the DOL will notify the applicant of this decision in writing. The DOL will then initiate whatever steps remained in order to process the original exemption application at the time it issued its original denial letter. Labor Reg. §2570.45(e). If, at any time during the reconsideration of an exemption application, the DOL again determines that the facts and arguments do not warrant the granting of the exemption, the DOL will issue a letter to the applicant reaffirming the original decision to deny the application. Labor Reg. §2570.45(f).

424. May either interested persons who oppose an exemption application, or the Department of Labor seek a hearing regarding an exemption application on its own initiative?

Any interested person that may be adversely affected by an exemption that the DOL proposes to grant from the prohibited transaction provisions of ERISA Section 406(b) (prohibitions against self-dealing), Internal Revenue Code Sections 4975(c)(1)(E) and 4975(c)(1)(F), or Federal Employees Retirement System Act (FERSA) Section 8477(c)(2) may request a hearing before the DOL within the deadline specified in the notice of the proposed transaction published in the Federal Register. Labor Reg. §2570.46.

All requests for hearings in opposition to exemptions must provide: (1) the name, address, and telephone number of the person making the request; (2) the person's interest in the exemption and how they would be adversely affected by the exemption; and (3) a written presentation of the issues to be addressed and a description of the evidence to be presented at the hearing. Labor Reg. §2570.46(a).

The DOL may grant a request for a hearing where it determines it is necessary to fully explore material and factual issues raised by the person requesting the hearing. However, the DOL may decline a request for an opposition hearing where: (1) the request fails to satisfy the above requirements; (2) the only issues raised by the party seeking the opposition hearing are matters of law; or (3) the factual issues raised can be adequately explored through the submission of written evidence. Labor Reg. §2570.46(b).

The DOL, in its discretion, may schedule a hearing on its own where it believes that issues relevant to the proposed exemption would be most fully or expeditiously explored in such a hearing. Labor Reg. §2570.47.

If the DOL grants a hearing in opposition to an exemption application, or of its own volition, the applicant seeking the exemption must notify interested persons in the form, time, and manner prescribed by the DOL. Ordinarily, adequate notification can be provided by giving interested persons a copy of the notice of hearing published by the DOL in the Federal Register within 10 days of its publication, or using any method reasonably calculated to ensure that interested persons actually receive the notice. In all cases, the DOL considers personal delivery and delivery by first class mail to be reasonable methods of furnishing notice. Labor Reg. §2570.46(c).

After providing the required notice, the applicant must provide the DOL with a written statement confirming that the notice was issued in the form, manner, and time prescribed. The statement must be accompanied by a declaration stating that, under penalty of perjury, the information provided in the written statement is true. This declaration must be signed by either the applicant or a person qualified to sign such a declaration. Labor Regs. §§2570.46(d), 2570.34(b)(5).

425. What steps will the Department of Labor take if it decides to grant an exemption?

If the DOL decides to grant an exemption, after taking into consideration all of the facts and representations presented by the applicant(s) in support of an exemption application and all comments received in response to the notice of proposed exemption, it will publish a notice in the Federal Register granting an exemption. Labor Reg. §2570.48(a).

The Federal Register notice of the grant of the exemption will provide a summary of the transaction or transactions for which the exemptive relief has been granted. The notice will also specify the conditions under which the exemptive relief is available. Labor Reg. §2570.48(b).

426. What are the limits on the effect of exemptions once they have been granted?

Once an exemption has been granted, it is effective only for the period of time specified in the exemption, and remains in effect only if the specific conditions contained within the exemption are satisfied. Generally, the exemption will only provide exemptive relief for those parties specifically identified within the exemption. If the notice of the granted exemption does not limit the exemptive relief to specific identified parties, all parties to the exemption transaction may rely on the exemption. Labor Reg. §2570.49.

Such an exemption will not take effect or provide exemptive relief to parties involved in the transaction(s) unless the material facts and representations contained in the original application and all subsequent materials and documents submitted in support of the application are true and complete.

427. What will cause the revocation or modification of an exemption?

After the DOL has granted an exemption, it may take steps to revoke or modify the exemption if certain changes in the law or official DOL policy occur after an exemption has taken effect, and such changes have a potential bearing upon the continuing validity of the DOL's original decisions regarding the granting of the exemption. Labor Reg. §2570.50(a).

When the DOL has decided to revoke or modify an exemption, it will give written notice to the original applicant at least 30 days in advance of the revocation or modification. This notice will detail the DOL's reasons for taking the proposed action and will provide the applicant with an opportunity to comment on such revocation or modification. The DOL will also publish a notice of its intended actions in the Federal Register. This notice will provide interested persons with an opportunity to comment on the proposed revocation or modification. Labor Reg. §2570.50(b).

When the DOL goes forward with an exemption modification or revocation, it will have only prospective effect. Labor Reg. §2570.50(c).

CHAPTER VII

FIDUCIARY LIABILITY ISSUES

428. When, for what, and to whom may a fiduciary be held personally liable for a fiduciary breach?

Fiduciaries may be held personally liable only for breaches that occurred during their tenure as a fiduciary. ERISA states that "[n]o fiduciary shall be liable with respect to a breach of fiduciary duty under this title if such breach was committed *before he became a fiduciary or after he ceased to be a fiduciary*." ERISA Sec. 409(b) (Emphasis added).

Anytime a plan fiduciary is found to have violated his fiduciary duties to a plan under the provisions of ERISA (see Chapter IV for a discussion of fiduciary duties), the Department of Labor, participants, beneficiaries, and certain former participants (see discussion of The Pension Annuitants Protection Act of 1994, below) may seek to enforce personal liability against the offending fiduciary for damages caused as a result of the breach.

A person who is a fiduciary with respect to a plan who breaches any of the responsibilities, obligations, or duties imposed upon fiduciaries will be personally liable to make good to such plan any losses resulting from each breach. A breaching fiduciary also must "restore to such plan any profits" that have been earned through the use of plan assets. ERISA Sec. 409(a).

In addition, a fiduciary who breaches a fiduciary duty "shall be subject to such other equitable or remedial relief as the court may deem appropriate, including removal of such fiduciary." ERISA Sec. 409(a). The Secretary of Labor, participants, or beneficiaries may bring a civil action under ERISA Section 502(a)(2) "for appropriate relief" under ERISA Section 409.

Further, civil penalties may be imposed against a fiduciary who has breached his fiduciary duty whenever the plan he holds fiduciary status with recovers an amount through a settlement agreement or judicial proceeding as a result of the breach. (See Q 430 for more detail on the application of civil penalties.) ERISA Sec. 502(l). However, the Ninth Circuit has ruled that a liability for breach of fiduciary duty under ERISA is dischargeable in bankruptcy if it does not involve the misappropriation of funds or failure to provide a proper accounting of funds. *Blyler v. Hemmeter*, 2001 U.S. App. LEXIS 4559 (9th Cir. 2001).

The Pension Annuitants Protection Act of 1994 (P.L. 103-401) allows former participants and beneficiaries to seek "appropriate relief" from the fiduciaries of their former plan who violated their fiduciary duty in regard to the purchase of annuities that terminated the participants' and beneficiaries' active status under the plan (i.e., the termination removed them from the protections afforded active participants and beneficiaries under ERISA). Although the term "appropriate relief" is not defined, the statute does state that appropriate relief includes "the posting of security if necessary, to assure receipt by the participant or beneficiary of the amounts provided by such . . . annuity, plus reasonable prejudgment interest on such amounts." ERISA Sec. 502(a)(9). This statute was a direct response to the failures of life insurance companies that sold lesser rated annuities to large pension plans for the benefit of terminated and retired participants (thereby removing them from active status under their plan), and then went bankrupt, leaving the annuities worthless and the annuitants without recourse to plan fiduciaries under ERISA. See *Kayes v. Pacific Lumber Co.*, 51 F.3d 1449 (9th Cir. 1995).

The Supreme Court has held that ERISA Section 409(a) was designed to protect the entire plan. Consequently, ERISA's authorization of other appropriate relief (equitable or remedial) does not provide relief other than for the plan itself. In other words, disgorgement of profits and recoveries are not forms of relief available to individual participants or beneficiaries. *Massachusetts Mut. Life Ins. Co. v. Russell*, 473 U.S. 134 (1985).

In a different case, the Court held that participants and beneficiaries may seek individual equitable relief for a breach of fiduciary duty under ERISA Section 502(a)(3), which authorizes appropriate equitable relief to "redress such violations or . . . to enforce any provisions of this title or the terms of the plan." In its ruling, the Court rejected the claim that ERISA Section 409 provides the exclusive remedy for a breach of fiduciary duty. The Court determined ERISA Section 502(a)(3) to be a "catch all" provision that was consistent with ERISA's purpose of protecting the best interests of participants and beneficiaries. The holding authorized relief under ERISA Section 502(a)(3) only where appropriate equitable relief was not otherwise available. *Varity Corp. v. Howe*, 514 U.S. 1082 (1996).

429. What are successor fiduciary responsibilities in regard to an actual or potential breach of fiduciary duty committed by a former fiduciary?

A successor fiduciary is obligated to take "reasonable steps" to remedy an outstanding breach committed by a predecessor fiduciary if he discovers sufficient information to determine that the actions of the prior fiduciary resulted in the outstanding breach. A failure to take remedial action constitutes a separate, current breach of fiduciary duty by the successor fiduciary. DOL Adv. Op. 76-95.

A successor fiduciary also has a duty to notify plan trustees or the Department of Labor if he has developed enough information to believe that a breach of fiduciary duty by a former fiduciary may have taken place. DOL Adv. Op. 77-79.

430. What are ERISA Section 502(l) penalties and how are they applied?

In 1989 ERISA was amended to provide for a mandatory civil penalty against a fiduciary who breaches a fiduciary responsibility, or commits a violation of ERISA. Civil penalties are also imposed upon other persons who knowingly participate in such a breach or violation. The civil penalty is equal to 20% of the "applicable recovery amount" paid pursuant to a settlement agreement with the Department of Labor (DOL) or a court ordered payment to a plan, participant, or beneficiary in a judicial proceeding instituted by the DOL. ERISA Sec. 502(l).

The DOL Regional Directors have been delegated authority in their respective geographic jurisdictions for assessing these civil penalties. This includes the authority to waive or reduce the penalty based upon a determination that the subject would be unable to restore all losses to the plan, or participant or beneficiary of the plan, without incurring "severe financial hardship." The DOL Director of the Office of Exemption Determinations is delegated the authority to waive or reduce the civil penalties based upon a determination that an individual acted reasonably and in good faith in engaging in the fiduciary breach. *PWBA Enforcement Manual*, Ch. 35.

The amount of the civil penalty is reduced by the amount of any penalty or tax imposed on the fiduciary or other person with respect to the transaction under ERISA Section 406 and ERISA Section 502(i) (5% of any amount involved in an ERISA Section 406 prohibited transaction, see Q 357), or IRC Section 4975. ERISA Sec. 502(l)(4).

PRACTITIONER'S POINTER

In order for the DOL to impose civil penalties, the penalties must be applied against any recovery amount paid pursuant to a settlement agreement or court order. In other words, the plan fiduciaries must be placed on "official notice" that a prohibited transaction is outstanding and the DOL or court is ordering the reversal of the violation. If an outstanding violation is discovered prior to the plan being placed on official notice of its existence, it is important that the prohibited transaction be reversed prior to the issuance of an official notice (usually in the form of a "Notice Letter" from the Regional Office of the DOL). In reversing the violation prior to official notice, the 20% penalty may not be imposed by the DOL or a court.

431. What is the applicable recovery amount under ERISA Section 502(l)?

The term "applicable recovery amount" is defined as any amount that is recovered by an employee benefit plan, a participant or beneficiary of a plan, or a legal representative of a plan, from a fiduciary or other person who knowingly participated in a breach of fiduciary duty or violation of the rules regarding fiduciary responsibility. The amount may be recovered pursuant to a settlement agreement with the Department of Labor (DOL) or a court order resulting from a judicial proceeding instituted by the DOL. ERISA Sec. 502(l)(2). The applicable recovery amount with regard to a continuing violation is the total amount recovered pursuant to a settlement agreement or court order, reduced by the amount attributable to any element of the violation that occurred prior to December 19, 1989. Prop. Labor Reg. §2560.502l-1(c).

432. What is a settlement agreement and court order?

A "settlement agreement" is an agreement between the Department of Labor (DOL) and a person whom the DOL alleges has committed a breach of fiduciary duty or violation of the rules regarding fiduciary responsibility. The agreement is pursuant to a claim for the breach or violation that is released in return for cash or other property being tendered to a plan, a participant or beneficiary of a plan, or the legal representative of a plan or participants and beneficiaries. Prop. Labor Reg. §2560.502l-1(e).

A "court order" is a judicial decree that either awards monetary damages or provides equitable relief. Prop. Labor Reg. §2560.502l-1(e).

According to the Pension and Welfare Benefits Administration (PWBA), in the absence of a signed agreement, but where corrective actions are taken by the recipient of a Voluntary Correction (VC) notice letter, the circumstances dictate whether a settlement agreement has been effected. A settlement agreement is deemed to occur in situations where the recipient of a VC notice letter, in response to that letter, corrects the described violations. *PWBA Enforcement Manual*, Ch. 34, p. 5.

433. How is the ERISA Section 502(l) penalty assessed?

The ERISA Section 502(l) penalty is assessed subsequent to the payment of the applicable recovery amount in accordance with a settlement agreement or court order. The civil penalty may be assessed against only the person who is required by the terms of the judgment or the settlement agreement to pay the applicable recovery amount, and can be assessed only for breaches or violations of ERISA that occurred on or after December 19, 1989. ERISA Sec. 502(l)(2); Labor Reg. §2570.83. With regard to a continuing violation, the 20% penalty may be assessed upon only that portion of the recovery that is attributable to violations occurring on or after December 19, 1989. The Pension and Welfare Benefits Administration (PWBA) offers this example: if only one of a group of fiduciaries agrees to restore losses to a plan pursuant to a settlement agreement, the civil penalty may be assessed against only that fiduciary. In certain circumstances, the penalty may be assessed against fiduciaries or knowing participants where the restitution to the plan is made on their behalf by a third party. Specifically, the penalty may be assessed when the third party has no independent obligation under ERISA to correct the violations. *PWBA Enforcement Manual*, Ch. 35, p. 5.

The regional office of the PWBA serves on the person liable for making the payment a notice of assessment (Notice) of a civil penalty equal to 20% of the applicable recovery amount. Labor Reg. §2570.83(a). The Notice sent by the regional office is a document that contains a specified assessment, in monetary terms, of the civil penalty. The Notice contains a brief factual description of the violation for which the assessment is being made, the identity of the person being assessed, the amount of the assessment, and the basis for assessing that particular person that particular penalty amount. *PWBA Enforcement Manual*, Ch. 35, p. 4.

The service of the Notice is made by delivering a copy to the person being assessed, by leaving a copy at the principal office, place of business, or residence of such person, or by mailing a copy to the last known address of the person. Service by certified mail is completed upon mailing the notice; service by regular mail is completed upon receipt by the addressee. Labor Reg. §2570.83(b); *PWBA Enforcement Manual*, Ch. 35, pp. 4-5.

434. How is the ERISA Section 502(l) penalty calculated?

The penalty under ERISA Section 502(l) is equal to 20% of the "applicable recovery amount" paid pursuant to a settlement agreement with the Department of Labor (DOL) or a court order in a judicial proceeding instituted by the DOL under ERISA Section 502(a)(2) or ERISA Section 502(a)(5). The penalty is calculated as a percentage of the amount paid to a plan, participant, or beneficiary that represents losses incurred by the plan, disgorged profits, and amounts necessary to achieve correction of the ERISA violation. If correction is achieved without actual payment to a plan, participant, or beneficiary, no penalty may be assessed. An example of such an action is a fiduciary taking administrative action to prevent future violations. *PWBA Enforcement Manual*, Ch. 35, p. 5.

435. What is the time period to pay the ERISA Section 502(l) penalty?

A person liable for the ERISA Section 502(l) penalty has 60 days from the service of the notice of assessment to pay the assessed amount. Subject to any tolling of the 60-day payment period during the consideration of a waiver or reduction petition (see Q 436), the notice of assessment becomes a final agency action (meaning it is reviewable by a court (see 5 U.S.C. 704)) on the first day following the 60-day period. At any time prior to the expiration of that 60-day period, a person may request one conference, per assessment, with the Department of Labor (DOL) to discuss the calculation of the assessment. If a conference is requested, the DOL will schedule one as soon as administratively feasible. The 60-day payment period will not, however, be tolled upon such request. Labor Reg. §2570.84; *PWBA Enforcement Manual*, Ch. 35, pp. 5-6.

436. May the ERISA Section 502(l) penalty be reduced or waived?

At any time prior to the expiration of the 60-day payment period, a person may petition the Department of Labor (DOL) to waive or reduce the assessed penalty on one of two grounds: (1) that the person acted reasonably and in good faith in engaging in the breach or violation; or (2) the person will not be able to restore all losses to the plan, participants, or beneficiaries of the plan without severe financial hardship unless the waiver or reduction is granted. Labor Reg. §2570.85(a). The petition for waiver or reduction of the penalty is submitted to the Regional Director who issued the notice of assessment of the penalty. *PWBA Enforcement Manual*, Ch. 35, p. 6.

As to whether a person acted reasonably and in good faith, the DOL examines the decision-making process with respect to the transaction in question to determine whether it was designed to adequately safeguard the interests of the participants and beneficiaries of the plan.

A person may request a financial hardship waiver not only with regard to actual losses to the plan, but also with regard to any disgorgement of profits gained through the relevant breach or violation, or amounts necessary for transfer to the plan in order to correct the relevant breach or violation. Preamble to Labor Reg. §2570.80, nn. 4 & 5, 55 Fed. Reg. 25284.

If the petition is based wholly on financial hardship, a written determination of whether to reduce or waive the penalty is made by the regional director within 60 days of receipt of the petition. If the petition is based in part on financial hardship and in part on good faith, the regional director makes a written determination of whether to reduce or waive the penalty only on the basis of financial hardship within 60 days of receipt. If the petitioner remains liable for any portion of the penalty after the regional director's written determination, the regional director forwards the petition to the Pension and Welfare Benefits Administration's (PWBA) Office of Exemption Determinations for a determination of whether to reduce or waive the remaining portion of the penalty based on good faith. If the petition is based in whole on good faith, the regional director forwards the petition to the PWBA's Office of Exemption Determinations for a determination of whether to reduce or waive the penalty. *PWBA Enforcement Manual*, Ch. 35, p. 6.

If the petition for waiver or reduction of penalty is submitted during the 60-day payment period, the payment period for the penalty in question will be tolled pending the DOL's consideration of the petition. During the consideration, the petitioner is also entitled to one conference with the DOL. The DOL may, however, in its sole discretion, schedule or hold additional conferences with the petitioner concerning the actual allegations contained in the petition. Labor Reg. §2570.85(c).

Once the DOL has made a decision with regard to the petition, the petitioner will be served a written determination briefly informing him of the DOL's decision and the grounds for that decision. The determination is solely within the DOL's discretion and is a final, non-reviewable order. In the event that the DOL concludes that no waiver or reduction is granted, the payment period for the penalty in question, if previously tolled, will resume as of the date of service of the written determination on the petitioner. Labor Reg. §2570.85(d).

437. What are the required contents of a petition for a waiver of the ERISA Section 502(l) penalty?

A petition to waive or reduce the ERISA Section 502(l) civil penalty must be in writing and contain the following information: (1) the name of the petitioner; (2) a detailed description of the fiduciary duty, breach, or violation that is the subject of the penalty; (3) a detailed recitation of the facts that support the bases for waiver or reduction (see Q 436), accompanied by underlying documentation supporting such factual allegations; and (4) a declaration, signed and dated by the petitioner, which states, under penalty of perjury, that the petitioner is making true and correct representations to the best of his knowledge and belief. Labor Reg. §2570.85(b).

438. May the ERISA Section 502(l) penalty be offset by other penalties?

Yes. The ERISA Section 502(l) civil penalty assessed on a fiduciary or other person with respect to a transaction is reduced by the amount of a penalty or tax imposed on the fiduciary or other person with respect to ERISA Section 502(i) or Internal Revenue Code Section 4975. Labor Reg. §2570.86. ERISA Section 502(i) provides for a civil penalty against a party in interest who engages in a prohibited transaction with respect to an employee benefit plan. See Q 357. IRC Section 4975 provides for an excise tax against a disqualified person who engages in a prohibited transaction with a plan. See Q 352.

In order to reduce the ERISA Section 502(l) penalty, a person must provide proof to the Department of Labor that an offsetting penalty was paid. The entire IRC Section 4975 excise tax or ERISA Section 502(i) penalty may offset an ERISA Section 502(l) civil penalty imposed due to the same transaction. The offset is limited to the identical parties on whom the excise tax or penalty is imposed. Any interest accrued on an ERISA Section 502(i) penalty or IRC Section 4975 excise tax assessment is not allowed as an offset to the ERISA Section 502(l) penalty. ERISA Sec. 502(l); Labor Reg. §2570.86; *PWBA Enforcement Manual*, Ch. 35, pp. 6-7.

439. Must the Department of Labor prove a breach of fiduciary duty to assess the ERISA Section 502(l) penalty?

Yes. Absent a court order, in order to assess the penalty, the Department of Labor (DOL) must prove a breach of fiduciary duty rather than unilaterally determine that a breach occurred because the statute does not contemplate punishment where no violation has occurred. ERISA Section 502(l) provides, in pertinent part, that in the case of any breach of fiduciary responsibility by a fiduciary, the DOL must assess a civil penalty against the fiduciary in an amount equal to 20% of the "applicable recovery amount" (any amount recovered from a fiduciary in accordance with a settlement agreement or court order). *Rodrigues v. Herman*, 121 F.3d 1352 (9th Cir. 1997).

The DOL has contended that it is not required to prove a breach to assess the penalty when it has secured a settlement agreement, even if, in that settlement agreement, the party does not admit it breached a fiduciary duty. The DOL has argued that the words "in the case of any breach" are merely an instruction as to when to assess the penalty, and not an element of the penalty itself. The courts have rejected this argument because it would provide the DOL the unilateral determination of when a fiduciary breach has occurred and the "unchecked authority to impose a penalty," so long as there was a recovery through a settlement agreement. One court noted that a fiduciary may agree to a settlement to avoid an expensive legal battle even in the absence of a fiduciary breach. In such a case, under the DOL's proposed reading of the statute, a fiduciary would subject itself to the 20% penalty because of the enforceable settlement agreement. In rejecting the DOL's contention, the court noted that in seeking the imposition of the ERISA Section 502(l) penalty, a trial may not be necessary to prove a breach of fiduciary duty if the facts (already developed in the course of the settlement negotiations) could establish a breach of fiduciary duty as a matter of law, or alternatively, if the DOL settled the case and required a sentence in the consent decree admitting that a violation occurred. *Rodrigues v. Herman*, 121 F.3d 1352, 1355 (9th Cir. 1997); *Citywide Bank of Denver v. Herman*, 978 F. Supp. 966 (DC Colo. 1997).

440. Is a settlement agreement required for the assessment of an ERISA Section 502(l) penalty?

Yes. According to one court, absent a court order, the Department of Labor (DOL) may not impose an ERISA Section 502(l) penalty on fiduciaries who voluntarily correct a breach without entering into a settlement agreement. The DOL must assess a civil penalty against the fiduciary in an amount equal to 20% of the "applicable recovery amount" (any amount that is recovered from a fiduciary in accordance with a settlement agreement or court order). ERISA Sec. 502(l). According to the court, the applicable recovery amount does not include amounts that are recovered by a voluntary correction that are not recovered pursuant to a settlement agreement.

The essential elements of a settlement agreement are "a definitive offer and acceptance, consideration, and parties who have the capacity and authority to agree." As a contract, a settlement agreement is construed using ordinary principles of contract interpretation. In one case, a contract was not formed simply by an exchange of letters between the fiduciary and the DOL, including a voluntary correction letter issued by the DOL. Also, the fiduciary repeatedly used precatory language in the letters, demonstrating that there was no definite offer upon which the parties could have a meeting of the minds, nor was there the presence of the essential elements of a contract. As no contract or settlement agreement had been formed between the fiduciary and DOL, the district court held that there was no statutory basis on which to impose the ERISA Section 502(l) penalty. *Citywide Bank of Denver v. Herman*, 978 F. Supp. 966 (DC Colo. 1997).

441. What is the scope of protection offered under the ERISA prohibition against interference with participant rights?

ERISA Section 510 provides that "[i]t shall be unlawful for any person to discharge, fine, suspend, expel, discipline, or discriminate against a participant or beneficiary for exercising any right to which he is entitled" under the provisions of an employee benefit plan or ERISA.

The Supreme Court has held that ERISA Section 510 does not distinguish between rights that vest under ERISA and those that do not. Therefore, ERISA Section 510 prohibits the interference with the attainment of any right to which a participant may become entitled. Further, the Court held that a plan sponsor's power to amend or eliminate a welfare benefit plan does not include the power to discharge, fine, suspend, expel, discipline, or discriminate against the plan's participants and beneficiaries for the purpose of interfering with the attainment of rights under the plan. *Inter-Modal Rail Employees Ass'n v. Atchison, Topeka & Santa Fe Railway*, 520 U.S. 510 (1997).

This would appear to be an extension of an earlier Supreme Court ruling that a plan sponsor's right to amend its plans exists in balance with participant rights under ERISA Section 510 and may only be exercised in accordance with the plan's formal amendment procedures. See *Ingersoll-Rand Co. v. McClendon*, 498 U.S. 133 (1990).

ERISA Section 510 protects existing employees and does not extend to any issues involving a claim of a discriminatory refusal to hire an individual. Further, ERISA provides plan sponsors considerable discretion in the design and administration of qualified plans that they sponsor. Part of this discretion is a right to offer varying degrees of benefits to participants under the plans they sponsor. Previously laid-off employees, who were not re-hired in spite of an upsurge in business because of the negative financial impact they would have on their former employer's retirement plans, were held to have no standing under ERISA section 510 as it does not apply to former employees. *Williams v. Mack Trucks*, 2000 U.S. Dist. LEXIS 18758 (E.D. PA 2000).

The Sixth Circuit expanded the coverage of ERISA Section 510 beyond the traditional plan sponsor or employer-employee relationship. The court held that ERISA Section 510 was primarily, but not exclusively, aimed at employment situations. The holding by the court is that a Section 510 claim may be brought against any person who discharges, fines, expels, disciplines, or discriminates against a participant or beneficiary for exercising any right to which they are entitled under an employee benefit plan or ERISA. The case involved the widow of a participant who had signed a prenuptial agreement that provided that if she survived her husband she would be entitled to remain in the marital residence and receive a weekly allowance of $300 from the decedent's estate. In return, she surrendered all other claims against his estate. The widow learned of the decedent's benefits under a plan to which she, as the surviving spouse, was entitled. The plan administrator paid the widow those benefits in a lump-sum.

The decedent's estate determined that the widow's receipt of the lump-sum benefit from the plan was in violation of the prenuptial agreement and ceased the $300 weekly living stipend. The court held that, under ERISA Section 510, where a case does not involve an employment relationship, the list of proscribed actions should be read to mean adverse actions that affect the claimant's rights under the plan. The court held that the widow had met this threshold in that the estate had the power to interfere with her enjoyment of the survivor benefits under the plan by offsetting them against the weekly payments made available under the prenuptial agreement. Such alleged retaliation has a logical linkage to the widow's status as an ERISA beneficiary. *Mattei v. Mattei*, 126 F.3d 794 (6th Cir. 1997).

The Ninth Circuit has expanded the coverage of ERISA Section 510 to include a whistleblower claim brought by a former participant because the claimant was an active participant at the time of the alleged violation of ERISA Section 510. The claimant was terminated from his employment with the plan sponsor three weeks after he, as a member of the ESOP committee, strongly urged that the DOL investigate the plan sponsor's proposed termination of the ESOP. The opinion of the Court states that "[t]o hold otherwise would allow an employer simply by wrongfully firing a whistleblowing employee and then terminating the Plan, wrongfully or otherwise, to deprive that employee of the right to sue the employer for retaliation prohibited by ERISA." *McBride v. PLM International Inc.*, 179 F.3d 737 (9th Cir. 1999).

Any attempt to interfere with, or prevent the exercise of, participant rights under an employee benefit plan that involves "the use of fraud, force, violence, or threat of the use of force or violence" is a criminal act to which the perpetrator may be fined up to $10,000, imprisoned for up to one year, or both. ERISA Sec. 511.

442. Does ERISA restrict an employer's right to discharge an employee for cause?

No. Courts have held that an employee's discharge for cause is not interference with participant rights under ERISA Section 510. This includes discharge for breach of company policy, misconduct, and criminal activities. See *Furcini v. Equibank NA*, 660 F. Supp. 1436 (W.D. Pa. 1987).

443. Who has the burden of proof with respect to establishing intentional interference with participant rights?

In order for a participant to establish a prima facie case of a violation of ERISA Section 510, the participant must show that the plan sponsor: (1) undertook prohibited action; (2) which was undertaken in an effort to interfere; (3) with the attainment of any right to which the participant may become entitled. *Rush v. United Technologies Otis Elevator Div.*, 930 F.2d 453 (6th Cir. 1991); *Hendricks v. Edgewater Steel Co.*, 898 F.2d 385 (3rd Cir. 1990); *Baker v O'Reilly Automotive, Inc.* 2001 U.S. Dist. LEXIS 15085 (N.D. Tex. 2001).

The burden of proof requires the complainant to demonstrate specific intent on the part of the plan sponsor to interfere with the attainment of rights under the plan. If this is established, the plan sponsor must establish a nondiscriminatory purpose for the actions it undertook. If the plan sponsor can do this, the participant must be able to demonstrate that the stated reasons of the plan sponsor are pretextual.

444. Are an employer's efforts to reduce costs by capping lifetime health benefits a violation of ERISA Section 510?

The Fifth Circuit has held that retroactive modifications to the lifetime benefits available under an employer's health plan do not violate the anti-discrimination provisions of ERISA Section 510. The plan sponsor placed a cap on the lifetime benefits under its health plan in an effort to reduce health care costs associated with AIDS treatment. The court decided that the plan sponsor's action in capping benefits was not discriminatory in that it affected all participants in the plan and not just those participants who were under treatment for AIDS. *McGann v. H & H Music Co.*, 946 F.2d 401 (5th Cir. 1991).

445. Do participants and beneficiaries have a right to seek civil enforcement of ERISA Section 510?

Yes. A participant, beneficiary or fiduciary may bring a civil action to enjoin any act or practice that violates any provision of ERISA or the terms of the plan's governing documents, or to obtain other equitable relief to redress such violations and enforce any provision of ERISA (including ERISA Section 510). ERISA Sec. 502(a)(3). Actions that may be brought by participants and beneficiaries include efforts to recover benefits due under the plan, enforce rights under the plan, or clarify rights to future benefits under the plan. Participants and beneficiaries may also bring suit against plan administrators for failure to comply with the notice requirements of ERISA.

Alleged violations of the fiduciary provisions of ERISA may be the subject of civil actions to enforce those provisions. Civil actions under these circumstances may be brought by the Department of Labor, participants, beneficiaries and other plan fiduciaries.

In any civil action regarding causes of action under ERISA: (1) the party filing the action must have standing to sue; (2) the court to which the suit has been filed must have jurisdiction over the claim; and (3) the action must be brought in the proper venue.

446. Do participants and beneficiaries have a right to seek criminal enforcement of ERISA?

No. The criminal provisions of ERISA Section 511 (prohibiting the interference with participant rights through the use or threat of force or intimidation) may be brought before the courts only by the Department of Justice. *West v. Butler*, 621 F.2d 240 (6th Cir. 1980).

This does not mean, however, that participants and beneficiaries who reasonably believe they have experienced an intentional interference with their rights under ERISA as a result of the use or threat of force or intimidation are without recourse. The aggrieved participants or beneficiaries have the right to present the evidence they have gathered, which led them to believe that a criminal violation of ERISA Section 511 occurred, to the Pension and Welfare Benefits Administration (PWBA) field office that has jurisdiction for review and investigation. If the PWBA field office investigates the claims of criminal interference and establishes probable cause to believe that a participant or beneficiary has been the victim of criminal intimidation, the PWBA field office will present its findings to the appropriate U.S. Attorney's Office for consideration of prosecution. The U.S. Attorney's Office will review the results of the investigation, and if it agrees with the PWBA's findings, present the case to a grand jury to seek an indictment of the alleged perpetrators.

REMEDIES

447. What remedies are available to participants, beneficiaries, and plans when a fiduciary duty is breached?

Federal courts have broad discretion to fashion appropriate relief on behalf of plans, participants, beneficiaries, other fiduciaries, and the Department of Labor to remedy a breach of fiduciary duty, including the return of any profits earned through the use of plan assets. ERISA also provides for the legal remedy of monetary damages for the restoration of plan losses. Courts may fashion whatever equitable or remedial relief they deem appropriate, including the removal of an individual from his position of fiduciary. ERISA Sec. 409(a).

ERISA Section 206(d)(4) permits the offset and alienation of benefits of fiduciaries who have been convicted or held liable for a criminal or civil judgment against the plan to which they serve as fiduciaries if the requirement to pay arises from:

1.   A judgment of conviction for a crime involving the plan;

2.   A civil judgment (or consent order or decree) that is entered by a court in an action brought in connection with a breach (or alleged breach) of fiduciary duty under ERISA; or

3.   A settlement agreement entered into by the participant and either the Secretary of Labor or the PBGC in connection with a breach of fiduciary duty.

The court order, judgment, decree or settlement agreement must specifically require that all or a part of the amount to be paid to the plan be offset against the participant's plan benefits. According to the Conference Committee Report, such an offset is includable in the breaching fiduciary's income as of the date of the offset. H.R. Conf. Rep. No. 220, 105th Cong., 1st Sess., at 756-57 (1997).

The Eighth Circuit Court of Appeals has ruled that a 401(k) plan participant is not entitled to monetary damages from the plan sponsor for a three and one-half year delay he incurred in obtaining his 401(k) distribution. *Kerr v. Charles F. Vatterott & Co.*, 184 F.3d 938 (8th Cir. 1999).

The Tenth Circuit Court of Appeals has ruled that a plaintiff's failure to exhaust remedies regarding a claim for disability benefits results in judgment in favor of the defendant plan. *Getting v. Fortis Benefits*, 2001 U.S. App. LEXIS 3070 (10th Cir. 2001).

448. Can the DOL sue a fiduciary for money damages even though an identical claim brought by a class of participants against the same fiduciary has been the subject of a court-approved settlement?

Yes. Under the 1998 Eleventh Circuit holding in *Herman v. South Carolina Nat'l Bank*, 140 F.3d 1413 (11th Cir. 1998), *cert. denied*, 119 S. Ct. 1030 (1999), the Department of Labor (DOL) may sue a plan fiduciary for monetary damages even though an identical claim brought by a class of participants against the same fiduciary has been the subject of a court-approved settlement. The court ruled that the DOL may bring their identical suit even though they had prior notice of the participant's suit and the pending settlement.

In considering the fiduciary's argument that the DOL's actions were barred under the doctrine of res judicata, the court stated that it did not apply because the Secretary of Labor was not a party to the settlement and has "national public interests" that are "wholly distinct and separate from those of private litigants."

PRACTITIONER'S POINTER

When negotiating any settlement with a class of participants who have brought suit against a plan, the attorneys are strongly urged to have the DOL join the action through ERISA Section 502(h). Unless and until ERISA is amended to eliminate this "double jeopardy," fiduciaries will be discouraged from settling participant suits, or will settle them for less (in anticipation of the later action by the DOL on the same issue).

449. Does a fiduciary breach that causes no damages mandate a remedy?

No, in limited circumstances. The Seventh Circuit issued a very narrow ruling that held that the fact that a transaction is prohibited by ERISA, or violates some other provision of the Act, does not necessarily mandate a remedy. *Etter v. J. Pease Constr. Co.*, 963 F.2d 1005 (7th Cir. 1992).

In that case, a participant sued the plan and the trustees alleging that the trustees violated ERISA by engaging in two prohibited transactions and by failing to diversify plan investments. The alleged prohibited transactions included a loan from the plan to a party in interest (see Q 338), and a large investment in a real estate venture in which the plan trustees had a 63% financial stake.

The district court denied relief as to the prohibited loan because it was well secured, carried an above market rate of interest, and was timely repaid. The district court further found that the real estate venture, which represented 88% of the plan's assets, did not constitute a prohibited transaction, and that there was no duty to diversify because, under the circumstances, it was prudent not to do so. The court based this decision on the experience and attention of the trustees and the significant profit of a 97% return the plan earned on its investment.

The Seventh Circuit affirmed the district court's decision, stating, "the fact that a transaction is prohibited under ERISA does not necessarily mandate a remedy." Citing its decision in *Leigh v. Engle*, 727 F.2d 113 (7th Cir. 1984), the court further stated that the remedy of damages is not appropriate where there is no injury to the plan. In addition, the remedy of divestment is not possible where the plan cashed out of an investment, nor is the remedy of disgorgement of profits appropriate in the absence of evidence that the trustees engaged in self-dealing or transferred assets for their own personal interest.

PRACTITIONER'S POINTER

This holding should be strictly construed and narrowly applied. The Department of Labor (DOL) will aggressively enforce the prohibited transaction provisions (ERISA Section 406) and the diversification provisions (ERISA Section 404(a)(1)(C)) of the Act. In the *Etter* case, the DOL was not involved in the detection of the investments in question, nor in the enforcement efforts under ERISA to correct them. Had the DOL discovered such violations in the course of a routine investigation of the subject plan, the trustees probably would have been subject to an official enforcement order to correct the outstanding violations, and they would have been subject to the possibility of ERISA Section 502(l) penalties (see Q 430) once they were placed on notice to reverse the prohibited transaction. The Seventh Circuit issued a caution in the *Etter* case that lends support to the DOL's enforcement position by saying that while prohibited transactions that do not result in losses may not be appropriate for a remedy, "it is a very dangerous area for trustees to explore, let alone attempt to exploit."

In addition, the Fifth Circuit has held that although a fiduciary breach that did not result in a loss to a plan is not subject to monetary damages, there is available equitable relief such as the suspension or removal of a violating fiduciary. *Donovan v. Cunningham*, 716 F.2d 1455 (5th Cir. 1983), *cert. denied*, 467 U.S. 1257 (1984).

450. How are the losses determined if a breaching fiduciary is held personally liable?

The measure of damages to be applied to a breaching fiduciary is determined by establishing what the plan would have earned in an investment in the absence of the fiduciary's breach. This concept is referred to as "making the plan whole." Where there are several alternative returns that could have been earned in the absence of the fiduciary breach, the court applies the one that is most favorable to the plan and its participants and beneficiaries. This has been established and upheld repeatedly by the courts. See *Leigh v. Engle*, 858 F.2d 361 (7th Cir. 1988); *Donovan v. Bierworth*, 754 F.2d 1049 (2nd Cir. 1985); *Dardaganis v. Grace Capital, Inc.*, 755 F. Supp. 85 (S.D. NY 1985).

A breaching fiduciary is not held liable for all profits earned while acting in the capacity of a fiduciary. *American Fed'n of Unions, Local 102 v. Equitable Life Assurance Soc'y*, 841 F.2d 658 (5th Cir. 1988). A breaching fiduciary is liable for only those profits earned through the use of plan assets in a breach of fiduciary duty, regardless of whether or not the plan suffered a loss as a result of the breach. ERISA Sec. 409(a); *Donovan v. Mazzola*, 716 F.2d 1226 (9th Cir. 1983), *cert. denied*, 464 U.S. 1040 (1984).

Further, plan losses incurred through a fiduciary breach may not be offset by gains earned by the fiduciary in a separate and distinct transaction. *Leigh v. Engle*, 858 F.2d 361 (7th Cir. 1988).

451. Can a fiduciary be subject to punitive damages for a breach of fiduciary duty?

ERISA does not expressly permit the imposition of punitive damages. However, some courts had held that the imposition of punitive damages to be paid to a plan is within a court's discretion. See *Monson v. Century Mfg. Co.*, 739 F.2d 1293 (8th Cir. 1984). The United States Supreme Court had left this question open. See *Massachusetts Mut. Life Ins. Co. v. Russell*, 473 U.S. 134 (1985).

The Supreme Court later held that participants and beneficiaries may not recover punitive damages from a fiduciary for a breach of fiduciary duty. The only available remedies are the restoration of losses and disgorgement of profits, both of which must be paid to the plan. *Mertens v. Hewitt Assocs.*, 508 U.S. 248 (1993).

452. Are fiduciaries subject to civil liability for the interference with ERISA protected rights?

ERISA Section 510 states that "[i]t shall be unlawful for any person to discharge, fine, suspend, expel, discipline, or discriminate against a participant or beneficiary for exercising any right to which he is entitled under the provisions of an employee benefit plan" or ERISA or to interfere with the attainment of such rights. The provisions of ERISA Section 502 (Civil Enforcement) govern the enforcement of ERISA Section 510.

Courts have held that where such interference with ERISA protected rights has been committed by a fiduciary that is also the employer, participants and beneficiaries may recover damages. See *Ingersoll-Rand Co. v. McClendon*, 498 U.S. 133 (1990); *Byrd v. MacPapers, Inc.*, 961 F.2d 157 (11th Cir. 1992).

453. What are the rules regarding co-fiduciary liability?

In addition to liability for their own conduct, plan fiduciaries may also be liable for a breach of fiduciary duty committed by co-fiduciaries. A fiduciary with respect to a plan may be liable for a breach of a fiduciary duty by another fiduciary with respect to the same plan in the following circumstances: (1) if he participates knowingly in, or knowingly undertakes to conceal, an act or omission of another fiduciary, knowing that the act or omission is a breach; (2) if, by a failure to comply with ERISA Section 404(a)(1) (requiring fiduciaries to discharge their duties solely in the interest of participants and their beneficiaries) in the administration of his responsibilities that give rise to his status as a fiduciary, *he enables another fiduciary to commit a breach*; or (3) if he has knowledge of a breach by another fiduciary, unless he makes reasonable efforts under the circumstances to remedy the breach. ERISA Sec. 405(a).

The ERISA Conference Report, as well as the Seventh Circuit, established the "knowing participation" rule that holds that in order for a co-fiduciary to be held liable, he must know that: (1) the other person is a fiduciary with respect to the plan; (2) the other person participated in the act that constituted the breach; and (3) the act itself constituted a breach. H.R. Conf. Rep. No. 93-1280, 93rd Cong., 2nd Sess., 323 (1974) (ERISA Conference Report); *Thornton v. Evans*, 692 F.2d 1064 (7th Cir. 1982).

The ERISA Conference Report also states that a co-fiduciary is liable "if he knowingly undertakes to conceal a breach committed by the other [fiduciary]." In order for liability to be imposed for the concealment of a breach the "knowing participation" rule is applied, as the Conference Report provides: "[f]or the first fiduciary to be liable, he must know that the other is a fiduciary with regard to the plan, must know of the act, and must know it is a breach."

The First Circuit has held that, where an investment manager is involved, ERISA Section 405(d) specifically limits co-fiduciary liability to actions that involve a "knowing participation or concealment of" an act or omission of another fiduciary. Thus, where a nondiscretionary trustee bank expressed concern over the real estate valuations of plan assets by the investment manager (which later proved to be inappropriately inflated), the bank did not assume the liability to assure that the assets were properly valued. The court held that ERISA does not impose a Good Samaritan liability that would cause an institution to volunteer itself as a fiduciary regarding matters to which it would otherwise have no fiduciary liability simply because it undertakes reporting responsibilities that exceed its official mandate. *Beddall v. State St. Bank & Trust Co.*, 137 F.3d 12 (1st Cir. 1998).

A bank acting as a co-fiduciary was held liable under ERISA Section 405(a)(2) when it resigned as plan fiduciary and assigned the plan's assets to the administrator without taking the necessary steps to protect the assets of participants and beneficiaries, enabling the administrator to embezzle the plan's assets. The resigning fiduciary had reason to be concerned about the administrator (the plan sponsor's president) in that the administrator was repeatedly late in making remittances of the participant's 401(k) salary deferrals to the plan trust. *Ream v. Frey*, 107 F.3d 147 (3rd Cir. 1997).

In applying the "reasonable efforts" to remedy the breach requirement of ERISA Section 405(a)(3), regulations state that where a majority of plan fiduciaries plan on taking action that would clearly violate the prudence requirement of ERISA Section 404(a)(1)(B), the minority fiduciaries must take "all reasonable and legal steps" to prevent the majority fiduciaries from taking the planned action. If the minority fiduciaries can demonstrate that they unsuccessfully took all reasonable and legal steps to prevent the imprudent actions of the majority fiduciaries, they will not be held liable for the breach committed by the majority fiduciaries. Labor Reg. §2509.75-5, FR-10.

A successor fiduciary is required to take whatever action is "reasonable" under the circumstances to remedy a breach by a former fiduciary if he knows of the existence of a breach by the prior fiduciary. The failure to take whatever steps are reasonable to remedy the breach will result in the successor fiduciary being held liable for a separate breach of fiduciary responsibility. DOL Adv. Op. 76-95.

454. Is there a right of co-fiduciary contribution?

A civil action may be brought by a plan fiduciary, on behalf of the plan, against another plan fiduciary in an effort to "enjoin any act or practice which violates" ERISA or the terms of the plan to which they serve as fiduciaries. He may also bring a civil action on behalf of the plan to seek appropriate equitable relief and to enforce any provisions of ERISA that a co-fiduciary may be violating. ERISA Sec. 502(a)(3).

ERISA, however, does not provide for, or preclude a right of contribution between co-fiduciaries. Consequently, the issue has been settled on both sides by different courts and is, for all intents and purposes, unresolved.

One court held that a federal right of contribution may only arise where Congress has expressly provided for it, has clearly implied a right of contribution, or has granted the courts power to fashion a right of contribution under federal common law. Since, under ERISA, there has been no such right of contribution expressed, there can be no right of contribution by a co-fiduciary. *Mutual Life Ins. Co. v. Yampol*, 706 F. Supp. 596 (N.D. Ill. 1988). In a similar holding, another court held that a plan administrator who has been found liable for a breach of fiduciary duty by engaging in prohibited transactions does not have a right of contribution against the plan's trustees. *Daniels v. National Employee Benefit Services, Inc.*, 877 F. Supp. 1067 (N.D. Ohio 1995). The Supreme Court has held that ERISA Section 409 only establishes a right of remedy on behalf of the plan. *Massachusetts Mut. Life Ins. Co. v. Russell*, 473 U.S. 134 (1985). The Ninth Circuit applied this holding when it held that a plan fiduciary is liable to the plan for any losses the plan suffers as a result of a breach, and because ERISA Section 409 only provides a remedy for the benefit of the plan, the breaching fiduciary has no right to the equitable remedy of contribution from co-fiduciaries. *Kim v. Fujikawa*, 871 F.2d 1427 (9th Cir. 1989).

In holding that ERISA does not preclude a right of contribution from co-fiduciaries, a court held that traditional trust law does provide for contribution under ERISA's federal common law. *Cohen v. Baker*, 845 F. Supp. 289 (E.D. Pa. 1994). The Seventh Circuit has held in two separate cases that there is a right of contribution against more culpable trustees and that a district court has equitable power to require a more culpable fiduciary to indemnify passive co-fiduciaries for losses incurred by the plan. Also, a federal court may not refuse to approve a settlement agreement between the Department of Labor and certain fiduciaries where certain third party defendants who file an objection to the settlement agreement are not adversely affected by it. *Donovan v. Robbins*, 752 F.2d 1170 (7th Cir. 1985); *Free v. Briody*, 732 F.2d 1331 (7th Cir. 1984).

455. May nonfiduciaries who participate in a breach of fiduciary duty be held liable for monetary damages?

No. The Supreme Court has held that participants are not permitted to recover monetary damages from nonfiduciaries who knowingly participate in a fiduciary's breach of duty. The available relief to be applied against nonfiduciaries who knowingly participate in a fiduciary breach is found in equity. *Mertens v. Hewitt Assocs.*, 508 U.S. 248 (1993). Restitution has been deemed to be an appropriate equitable remedy that will require nonfiduciaries who are found liable for their active participation in a fiduciary breach to return to the plan all money earned through their active participation in the breach. ERISA Sec. 502(a)(3); *Landwehr v. DuPree*, 72 F.3d 726 (9th Cir. 1995)).

Likewise, nonfiduciaries are not subject to right of contribution for their active participation in a breach. *Glaziers & Glassblowers Union Local 252 Annuity Fund v. Newbridge Sec., Inc.*, 823 F. Supp. 1191 (E.D. Pa. 1993).

The First Circuit has held that nonfiduciaries who do not benefit from their actions may not be subject to non-monetary equitable remedies for their active participation in a fiduciary breach. Under this holding the Department of Labor could not seek an injunction to bar a nonfiduciary consultant from providing his services to plans even though the consultant had previously advised plan fiducia-ries to violate ERISA. *Reich v. Rowe*, 20 F.3d 25 (1st Cir. 1994).

The Supreme Court has reconciled contradicting Circuit Court opinions on this issue in a recent ruling. In that case, the Supreme Court ruled unanimously that a fiduciary (even those culpable in the prohibited transaction at issue), participant or beneficiary can sue a nonfiduciary party in interest for equitable relief for engaging in a prohibited transaction. Where the nonfiduciary party in interest engages in an ERISA Section 406 violation with a fiduciary, both may be held liable under ERISA Section 502(a)(3). The Supreme Court took a plan-based approach to this issue when reviewing ERISA Section 502(a)(3) by holding that it imposes a duty on nonfiduciary parties in interest that is separate and distinct from individual duties specifically imposed on fiduciaries under ERISA Sections 404 and 406. *Harris Trust and Savings Bank, etc., et al. v. Salomon Smith Barney Inc., et al.,* 530 U.S. 238 (2000). This ruling may have a dramatic impact on future litigation stemming from prohibited transactions because it creates a potential second class of defendants in service providers (many of whom have much deeper pockets than individual fiduciaries) who knowingly participate in a fiduciary breach. The Supreme Court indicated in the *Harris Trust* ruling that an action for restitution under ERISA Section 502(a)(3) could be considered one for "equitable relief" as required in the *Mertens* case discussed above.

456. May a fiduciary enter into an agreement that relieves him from liability?

Generally speaking, no. Except as allowed by ERISA Section 405(b)(1) (a trust agreement that allocates specific duties) and ERISA Section 405(d) (delegation of authority to an investment manager), any provision in an agreement or instrument that purports to relieve a fiduciary from responsibility or liability for any responsibility, obligation or duty under ERISA is void as against public policy. ERISA Sec. 410(a). However, plans and fiduciaries are allowed to purchase fiduciary insurance that provides coverage for potential liability for a fiduciary breach occurring in regard to an employee benefit plan. ERISA Sec. 410(b).

Plan fiduciaries are permitted to indemnify their employees who actually perform fiduciary services for the plan because this does not relieve the fiduciaries of their responsibilities under ERISA. An indemnification agreement that maintains a fiduciary's liability, but permits another party to satisfy any liability incurred by the fiduciary in a manner such as insurance coverage would provide, is permissible. Labor Reg. §2509.75-4.

Further, the Seventh Circuit has held that ERISA permits a plan trustee to be indemnified by a more culpable trustee for plan losses incurred due to a breach of fiduciary duty. *Free v. Briody,* 732 F.2d 1331 (7th Cir. 1984).

Releases have been allowed from participants that relieve a fiduciary from past liability for a fiduciary breach where the releases were used to settle a bona fide dispute and had been given in exchange for consideration. *Blessing & Grossman v. Struthers-Dunn, Inc.,* 1985 U.S. Dist. LEXIS 14159 (E.D. Pa. Nov. 5, 1985). A release that conditions the distribution of a vested interest from a plan in exchange for the execution of the release must be provided for in the plan document in order for it to be valid under ERISA. *Haberern v. Kaupp Vascular Surgeons Ltd. Defined Benefit Plan & Tr. Agreement,* 24 F.3d 1491 (3rd Cir. 1994), *cert. denied,* 513 U.S. 1149 (1995).

457. May liquidated damages be awarded in a civil action for a breach of fiduciary duty?

There is case precedent that in civil actions under ERISA's civil enforcement provisions, reasonable liquidated damages may be awarded at the discretion of the court. See *Doolan v. Doolan Steel Corp.*, 591 F. Supp. 1506 (E.D. Pa. 1984).

Federal common law principles require the satisfaction of two conditions in order to award liquidated damages: (1) the damages caused by the breach must be difficult or impossible to estimate; and (2) the amount of the award must be a reasonable forecast of just compensation for the harm caused. *Idaho Plumbers Funds v. United Mechanical Contractors, Inc.*, 875 F.2d 212 (9th Cir. 1989).

STATUTE OF LIMITATIONS

458. What is the statute of limitations for bringing a civil action for a fiduciary breach?

ERISA Section 413 provides that "[n]o action may be commenced under this title with respect to a fiduciary's breach of any responsibility, duty, or obligation under this part, after the earlier of—

(1) six years after (A) the date of the last action which constituted a part of the breach or violation, or (B) in the case of an omission, the latest date on which the fiduciary could have cured the breach or violation, or

(2) three years after the earliest date on which the plaintiff had actual knowledge of the breach or violation; except that in the case of fraud or concealment, such action may be commenced not later than six years after the date of discovery of such breach or violation."

The Department of Labor (DOL) distinguishes fiduciary violations as either discrete or continuing violations. A discrete violation is one that occurs at a single moment in time. An example of a discrete violation would be the purchase of real property for more than fair market value. For a single discrete violation, the period for the statute of limitations is computed in a straightforward manner.

A continuing violation is one that continues past the initial moment when it occurs. An example of a continuing violation is an outstanding loan to a party in interest (which continues to be an ongoing violation so long as the loan is outstanding). With continuing violations, the DOL has argued the theory that the statute of limitations should have no direct effect other than making monetary relief unavailable with respect to pre-limitation portions of a violation.

In response to this argument, the Ninth Circuit has stated, "[t]he application of the continuing violation theory founders on the plain language of [ERISA Section 413(a)(2)]. This section requires the plaintiff's knowledge to be measured from the 'earliest date' on which he or she knew of the breach. . . . Once a plaintiff knew of one breach, an awareness of later breaches would impart nothing materially new. . . . The earliest date on which a plaintiff became aware of any breach would thus start the limitation period of [ERISA Section 413(a)(2)] running." *Phillips v. Alaska Hotel & Restaurant Employees Pension Fund*, 944 F.2d 509 (9th Cir. 1991).

In an earlier similar ruling, the Ninth Circuit held that a continuous series of breaches may allow a plaintiff to argue for a new cause of action with each new breach. However, if the breaches are of the same nature and the plaintiff had actual knowledge of one of the breaches more than three years before bringing the civil action, ERISA Section 413(a)(2) bars the action. *Ziegler v. Connecticut Gen. Life Ins. Co.*, 916 F.2d 548 (9th Cir. 1990).

The Second Circuit has accepted the "continuing violation" theory allowing for a claim beyond the original 3- and 6-year statute of limitations under a specific application of the "prudent investor rule" (ERISA Section 404(a)(1)(B), see Q 239). Under the prudent investor rule, fiduciaries have a continuing obligation to monitor plan investments and to review and advise the subject plan to divest itself of unlawful or imprudent investments. The court held that a fiduciary obligation to continually monitor plan investments effectively permits actions under ERISA Section 404(a)(1)(B) to be brought after the initial 3- or 6-year statute of limitations. *Morrissey v. Curran*, 567 F.2d 546 (2nd Cir. 1977).

PRACTITIONER'S POINTER

The DOL is likely to continue in its efforts to establish cases that accept the "continuing violation" theory to extend the statute of limitations when there is a failure to correct outstanding breaches that are of the same kind and nature as those that have been outstanding beyond the ERISA Section 413(a)(2) limits. Because of this, should plan representatives become aware of any outstanding violations, or of a series of actions by plan fiduciaries that may be violations of the same kind and nature, they should take remedial action to reverse or correct the violations that would create isolated violations and clearly establish the time frame under which the statute of limitations would run.

459. How is the statute of limitations affected by an act of fraud or concealment by a fiduciary?

If a breaching fiduciary has taken affirmative steps to hide his breach of fiduciary duty, the statute of limitations for bringing a civil action against him is six years from the discovery of the breach or violation. In determining if the 6-year statute of limitations applies, the issue is whether or not the fiduciary took affirmative steps to conceal his breach, not whether or not the civil complaint actually alleges fraud. ERISA Sec. 413; *Kurz v. Philadelphia Elec. Co.*, 96 F.3d 1544 (3rd Cir. 1996).

The plan or participant bringing a civil action must prove that the fiduciary undertook a course of conduct designed to conceal evidence of the wrongdoing, and that the plan and the participants did not have actual or constructive knowledge of evidence of the violation, despite the exercise of reasonable diligence. *J. Geils Band Employee Benefit Plan v. Smith Barney Shearson, Inc.*, 76 F.3d 1245 (1st Cir. 1996).

460. When does an ERISA cause of action accrue for purposes of the statute of limitations?

ERISA is silent as to what event constitutes the fiduciary breach at issue or the knowledge of that breach. There are, however, two different theories that have developed. The "discovery rule" holds that the statute of limitations begins to run when the violation is discovered. *Connors v. Hallmark & Sons Coal Co.*, 935 F.2d 336 (D.C. Cir. 1991). The "actual knowledge of breach or violation" rule states that the participant plaintiff must have knowledge of all of the relevant facts that are sufficient to provide the participant knowledge that a fiduciary duty has been breached or that a provision of ERISA has been violated. *Gluck v. Unisys Corp.*, 960 F.2d 1168 (3rd Cir. 1992).

461. When does the statute of limitations begin to run for a denial of benefits claim?

The statute of limitations for a denial of benefits claim begins to run when the participant receives notice of the denial. *Price v. Provident Life & Accident Ins. Co.*, 2 F.3d 986 (9th Cir. 1993). Where a participant has made no formal request for benefits, the statute of limitations begins to run at the time that the participant "should have known" they were entitled to benefits. *Brown v. Cuttermill Bus Service*, 1991 U.S. Dist. LEXIS 9487 (E.D. NY June 20, 1991).

A claim for denial of benefits is time barred where the plaintiff could have obtained knowledge, through due diligence, that the denial of benefits was a fiduciary violation. *Vernau v. Vic's Market*, 896 F.2d 43 (3rd Cir. 1990).

462. Is knowledge of a breach by a former fiduciary imputed to a successor fiduciary for purposes of the statute of limitations?

The statute of limitations for a fiduciary breach begins to run when the plaintiff has actual knowledge of the breach. As such, knowledge of a fiduciary breach by a former fiduciary cannot be imputed to a successor fiduciary. A claim for a fiduciary breach by a successor trustee more than three years after the prior trustees had knowledge of the violation is not time barred. *District 65 Retirement Tr. v. Prudential Sec.*, 925 F. Supp. 1551 (N.D. Ga. 1996).

463. What is the statute of limitations in fiduciary cases where ERISA does not provide one?

ERISA specifically provides for a specific time limit under which suits to enforce certain fiduciary standards may be brought. Where ERISA does not expressly provide a statute of limitations for bringing a civil action relating to a plan, courts have applied state statutes of limitation that are most analogous to the claim. *Kennedy v. Electricians Pension Plan IBEW #995*, 954 F.2d 1116 (5th Cir. 1992); *Meade v. Pension Appeals & Review Comm.*, 966 F.2d 190 (6th Cir. 1992); *Tolle v. Touche, Inc.*, 977 F.2d 1129 (7th Cir. 1992); *Lumpkin v. Envirodyne Indus., Inc.*, 933 F.2d 449 (7th Cir.), *cert. denied*, 502 U.S. 939 (1991); *Held v. Manufacturers Hanover Leasing Corp.*, 912 F.2d 1197 (10th Cir. 1990); *Giuffre v. Delta Airlines*, 746 F. Supp. 238 (D.C. Mass. 1990); *Bologna v. NMU Pension Tr.*, 654 F. Supp. 637 (S.D. NY 1987); *Nolan v. Aetna Life Ins. Co.*, 588 F. Supp. 1375 (E.D. Mich. 1984).

In a civil action under ERISA Section 510 that alleges discrimination or interference with a protected right, the analogous state statute of limitations is that governing employment discrimination, wrongful termination or wrongful discharge. *Sandberg v. KPMG Peat Marwick, LLP*, 111 F.3d 331 (2nd Cir. 1997); *Rich v. Zeneca, Inc.*, 845 F. Supp. 162 (DC Del. 1994).

When a state statute of limitations expresses a hostile stance towards federal causes of action, it will not be applied to an action brought under ERISA. The Tenth Circuit has held that a very brief state statute of limitations that governed civil actions "seeking to impose liability based on a federal statute" would not be applied. *Trustees of the Wyo. Laborers Health & Welfare Plan v. Morgan & Oswood Constr. Co.*, 850 F.2d 613 (10th Cir. 1988).

464. How can the statute of limitations be tolled?

Tolling the statute of limitations (delaying it from running) can be accomplished by filing a civil action relating to the fiduciary issue in a state court. However, if the issue is one that should be filed in a federal court, the statute of limitations will not be tolled by the state action for purposes of filing a subsequent ERISA claim in federal court. *Shofer v. The Stuart Hack Co.*, 970 F.2d 1316 (4th Cir. 1992).

ATTORNEY'S FEES

465. When does a court have discretion to award attorney's fees?

A court has discretion to award reasonable attorney's fees to participants, beneficiaries or fiduciaries. ERISA Sec. 502(g)(1). This has been interpreted to include the costs of a civil action through appeal, paralegal fees, and the costs of collecting a post-judgment ERISA award. *Free v. Briody*, 793 F.2d 807 (7th Cir. 1986); *Mendez v. Teachers Ins. & Annuity Ass'n & College Retirement Equities Fund*, 789 F.Supp 139 (S.D. NY 1993); *Parise v. Ricelli Haulers, Inc.*, 672 F. Supp. 72 (N.D. NY 1987).

Courts have the discretion to deny attorney's fees in cases that are not timely filed. *Schake v. Colt Indus. Operating Corp. Severance Plan*, 960 F.2d 1188 (3rd Cir. 1992).

In determining what are "reasonable" attorney's fees under ERISA Section 502(g)(1), courts will utilize what is commonly referred to as the "lodestar method." Using the lodestar method, the court determines a reasonable number of hours spent on the case and then multiplies the hours by a reasonable hourly rate. The court may take into consideration such factors as the complexity of the case and the prevailing hourly rates of local attorneys. *D'Emanuaelle v. Montgomery Ward & Co.*, 904 F.2d 1379 (9th Cir. 1990); *Bowen v. Southtrust Bank of Ala.*, 760 F. Supp. 889 (M.D. Ala. 1991); *Motion Picture Indus. Pension Plan v. The Klages Group*, 757 F. Supp. 1082 (C.D. Cal. 1991).

The Eleventh Circuit has held that a district court abuses its discretion regarding the decision whether or not to award attorney's fees when it denies a motion for fees without stating the reasons for doing so. *Evans v. Bexley*, 750 F.2d 1498 (11th Cir. 1985).

The Fifth Circuit has ruled that a dismissal of an action under ERISA for lack of subject matter jurisdiction precludes an award of attorney fees under ERISA Section 502(g)(1). *Cliburn v. Police Jury Assoc. of Louisiana*, 165 F.3d 315 (5th Cir. 1999).

466. Who may be awarded attorney's fees in an ERISA civil action?

ERISA Section 502(g)(1) provides that "[i]n any action under [ERISA] by a participant, beneficiary, or fiduciary, the court in its discretion may allow a reasonable attorney's fee and costs of action *to either party*" (emphasis added). Some courts have strictly interpreted this and have limited the recovery of attorney's fees to only a participant, beneficiary or fiduciary. See *Self Ins. Inst. of America, Inc. v. Korioth*, 53 F.3d 694 (5th Cir. 1995); *Saladino v. I.L.G.W.U. Nat'l Retirement Fund*, 754 F.2d 473 (2nd Cir. 1985); *M & R Inv. Co., Inc. v. Fitzsimmons*, 685 F.2d 283 (9th Cir. 1982).

However, there have been cases where attorney's fees were awarded to employers, pension plans and insurance companies as prevailing parties. See *Credit Managers Ass'n v. Kennesaw Life & Accident Ins. Co.*, 25 F.3d 743 (9th Cir. 1994); *Continental Can Co. v. Chicago Truck Drivers & Warehouse Workers Union Pension Fund*, 921 F.2d 126 (7th Cir. 1990).

Further, out of court settlements of ERISA actions are not a bar to the awarding of attorney's fees. *Cefali v. Buffalo Brass Co.*, 748 F. Supp. 1011 (W.D. NY 1990).

The Eighth Circuit awarded attorney fees to an employee benefit plan administrator (under the Equal Access to Justice Act) because the administrator was the victim of a "baseless claim" filed by the Department of Labor (DOL). The DOL filed suit claiming that the administrator should have done more to ensure medical claim payments from the bankrupt plan sponsor of an ERISA covered health plan. The Court stated that the DOL failed to show that it was "justified in substance or in the main" in filing suit against the administrator because it knew that the administrator had made "reasonable, prudent, and largely successful efforts to obtain as much funding as possible" for the health plan. *Herman v. Schwent*, 177 F.3d 1063 (8th Cir. 1999).

467. What factors will a court consider in awarding attorney's fees?

The majority of courts have applied a 5-factor test for determining whether or not to award attorney's fees in an ERISA civil action. The five factors are: (1) the degree of the offending party's culpability (bad faith); (2) the ability of the offending party to pay an award of attorney's fees; (3) the deterrent factor of such an award; (4) whether or not the motion for an award of attorney's fees is to benefit all participants and beneficiaries, or if the action was brought forth to resolve a significant legal question regarding ERISA; and (5) the relative merits of the parties' positions. *Kimbro v. Atlantic Richfield Co.*, 889 F.2d 869 (9th Cir. 1989); *Gray v. New England Tel. & Tel. Co.*, 792 F.2d 251 (1st Cir. 1986); *Ironworkers Local No. 272 v. Bowen*, 695 F.2d 531 (11th Cir. 1983); *Eaves v. Penn*, 587 F.2d 453 (10th Cir. 1978).

All five factors need not be present in order for a court to award attorney's fees. However, one court held that the element of bad faith did not need to be established in all instances in order for the court to exercise its discretion in awarding attorney's fees. *Gennamore v. Buffalo Sheet Metals, Inc. Pension Plan & Tr.*, 568 F. Supp. 931 (W.D. NY 1983).

Another court held that attorney's fees could be awarded on behalf of a plaintiff seeking payment of his vested interest in the plan after his termination where the plaintiff had limited financial resources and a favorable judgment would otherwise leave the plaintiff with an empty victory. *Morales v. Plaxall, Inc.*, 541 F. Supp. 1387 (E.D. NY 1982).

The Supreme Court held that an award of attorney's fees should not be reduced if a party has garnered substantial relief on the majority of the claims where the lawsuit consists of a number of related claims. *Hensley v. Eckerhart*, 461 U.S. 424 (1983).

Attorney's fees may be awarded if the plaintiff succeeds on any significant issue that achieves part of the benefits sought in filing the initial action. *Int'l Bhd. of Teamsters Local No. 710 Pension Fund v. Janowski*, 812 F.2d 295 (7th Cir. 1987).

An ERISA Section 502(g) award of attorney fees is inappropriate when such fees are specified as being contingent based. *Martin v. Arkansas Blue Cross/Blue Shield*, 2001 U.S. App. LEXIS 22940 (8th Cir. 2001).

In applying the 5-factor test, the Ninth Circuit ruled that a plan participant who filed suit seeking correction of a miscalculation of her benefits was entitled to a recovery of attorney fees in spite of the fact that her employer had filed for IRS approval of a correction of the miscalculation at issue under what was then called the IRS' Voluntary Compliance Resolution (VCR) program. The Court awarded attorney fees because it deemed the employer to have "relative culpability and bad faith" by refusing to advise the participant of the VCR submission, thereby making it necessary for her to file her civil action under an expiring statute of limitations in order to guarantee that her claim was protected. *McElwaine v. U.S. West, Inc.*, 176 F.3d 1167 (9th Cir. 1999).

468. Does ERISA provide for the recovery of reasonable costs in addition to attorney's fees?

ERISA provides for the recovery of "reasonable attorney's fees and costs of action." ERISA Sec. 502(g)(1). The Ninth Circuit held that the term "reasonable" applies as a modifier to the term "legal fees" and not to the term "costs." As such, the plaintiff was not permitted to recover "reasonable costs" for the full amount of fees charged by an expert witness. The court stated that the awarding of expert witness fees is governed by the Federal Rules of Civil Procedure (FRCP). *Agredano v. Mutual of Omaha Cos.*, 75 F.3d 541 (9th Cir. 1996).

Under the FRCP, an award of attorney's fees may only be for the actual fees and costs that were incurred as a result of the conduct at issue. *Browning v. Kramer*, 931 F.2d 340 (5th Cir. 1991).

469. Can an award of attorney's fees be discharged in bankruptcy?

If a fiduciary has been held accountable for an award of attorney's fees for conduct that goes beyond mere negligence, the attorney's fees may not be discharged in a bankruptcy proceeding. Further, there must be a fiduciary relationship between the parties to the suit, and the offending action must have occurred as a result of a breach of, or a failure to satisfy, a fiduciary obligation. *In re Eisenberg*, 189 BR 725 (1995).

When plan sponsors of defined benefit plans file for bankruptcy protection, the Pension Benefits Guaranty Corporation (PBGC) becomes a creditor. In 1992 the PBGC established its Bankruptcy Fee Monitoring Section to monitor attorney's fees that are charged in large bankruptcy proceedings in which the PBGC is a major creditor (obligated to pay any unfunded liability to the bankrupt corporation's defined benefit plan). Established within the PBGC's General Counsel office, the program is designed to prevent excessive attorney and other professional fees from being charged in large bankruptcy cases. *Dep't of Labor News Release*, USDL 92-343, (June 5, 1992).

MULTIEMPLOYER PLANS

470. What special remedies exist for multiemployer plans?

Fiduciaries, participants, beneficiaries, employer organizations, and plan sponsors may bring civil actions to seek legal or equitable relief for damages caused by an act or omission of a party in relation to an ERISA covered multiemployer plan. Such actions may not be brought against the Department of Labor or the Pension Benefits Guaranty Corporation. ERISA Sec. 4301(a).

The majority of cases against multiemployer plans involve actions seeking the payment of unpaid or delinquent plan contributions into the plan trust. Participating employers are required to make contributions to a multiemployer plan trust in accordance with "the terms of the plan or under the terms of a collectively bargained agreement." ERISA Sec. 515. Such actions may only be brought by fiduciaries to the multiemployer plan, not participants or beneficiaries. ERISA Sec. 502(g). Multiemployer plans are permitted to utilize the defense that they have relied on the terms of the collective bargaining agreement as it has been written. Therefore, any provision within the collective bargaining agreement that may have been incorrectly written may, nonetheless, be relied upon by the parties to the action. *Central Pa. Teamsters Pension Fund v. McCormack Dray Line, Inc.*, 85 F.3d 1098 (3rd Cir. 1996).

The National Labor Relations Board (NLRB) has exclusive jurisdiction in determining liability for delinquent multiemployer plan contributions under an expired collective bargaining agreement. This is based on the theory of unfair labor practices. Unless, and until, the collective bargaining agreement has expired, federal district courts retain jurisdiction to hear cases against multiemployer plans for delinquent contributions. *Smith v. Candler Coffee Shop*, 1996 U.S. Dist. LEXIS 10935 (S.D. NY 1996). If the NLRB determines that a collective bargaining agreement is invalid, the participating employers are not obligated to continue making contributions to the plan under the agreement. If the collective bargaining agreement has not been invalid from inception, participating employers must continue to make contributions to the plan unless, and until, the NLRB has ruled on the validity of it. Participating employers may not unilaterally cease making contributions to a multiemployer plan on the basis of a complaint filed with the NLRB regarding the validity of the collective bargaining agreement. *MacKillop v. Lowe's Market, Inc.*, 58 F.3d 1441 (9th Cir. 1995).

In cases seeking the payment of delinquent contributions to a multiemployer plan brought by a fiduciary against a participating employer, the court *must* award attorney's fees and costs of the action where a judgment was awarded in favor of the plan. ERISA Sec. 502(g)(2); *O'Hare v. General Marine Transp. Corp.*, 740 F.2d 160 (2nd Cir. 1984); *Greater Kansas City Laborers Pension Fund v. Thummel*, 738 F.2d 926 (8th Cir. 1984); *Operating Eng'rs Pension Tr. v. Reed*, 726 F.2d 513 (9th Cir. 1984).

Actions to enforce ERISA's multiemployer plan provisions must be brought (1) within six years after the date on which the cause of action arises, or (2) three years after the earliest date on which the plaintiff acquires actual knowledge of the existence of the cause of action, whichever is later. As in any ERISA case where there has been an act of fraud or concealment regarding the fiduciary violation, the 3-year limit is extended to six years after the date of discovery of the act of fraud or concealment. ERISA Sec. 4301(f).

Member employers in a multiemployer plan are required to make contributions to the plan under the terms of the collective bargaining agreement. ERISA Sec. 515. In a civil action to recover delinquent employer contributions wherein the plan emerges victorious on its claim, the court must award prejudgment interest on the delinquent contributions. ERISA Sec. 502(g)(2)(B); *Bricklayers Pension Tr. Fund v. Taiariol*, 671 F.2d 988 (6th Cir. 1982). Further, the court must award the plan under such a judgment the greater of interest on the unpaid contributions or liquidated damages that have been provided for under the terms of the plan, plus reasonable attorney's fees and costs of the action to enforce the contribution obligation. Liquidated damages are limited to 20% of the total amount of the outstanding delinquency. ERISA Secs. 502(g)(2)(C), 502(g)(2)(D); *Teamsters Pension Tr. Fund v. John Tinney Delivery Serv., Inc.*, 732 F.2d 319 (3rd Cir. 1984).

In a civil action to force a participating employer to make payments to a multiemployer plan under the terms of a collective bargaining agreement, a court must award, if it rules in favor of the plan, an amount equal to the greater of interest on the unpaid liability or liquidated damages (paid to the plan), reasonable attorney's fees, and the costs of bringing the civil action. ERISA Sec. 502(g).

CHAPTER VIII

FIDELITY BONDING, FIDUCIARY LIABILITY INSURANCE, AND EXCULPATORY PROVISIONS

471. Does ERISA require bonding or insurance for plans or plan fiduciaries, administrators, officers, or employees?

ERISA requires that every administrator, officer, and employee of any employee welfare benefit plan or employee pension benefit plan who handles funds or other property of the plan be bonded, in order to protect benefit funds against loss by acts of fraud or dishonesty. ERISA Sec. 412. A bond that covers against loss resulting from dishonest or fraudulent acts of bonded employees is generally known as a fidelity bond.

ERISA permits a plan to purchase fiduciary insurance for its fiduciaries or for itself to cover liability or losses resulting from acts or omissions of the fiduciary. However, ERISA prohibits any agreement or instrument that purports to relieve a fiduciary from responsibility or liability for any obligation or duty under ERISA.

472. What are the bonding requirements of ERISA?

With exceptions, ERISA mandates that every fiduciary of an employee benefit plan and every person who "handles" (see Q 478) funds or other property of such a plan (a "plan official") be bonded, in order to protect the plan against loss by reason of acts of fraud or dishonesty on the part of the plan official, directly or through connivance with others. ERISA Sec. 412(a).

ERISA also provides that it is unlawful for any plan official to receive, handle, disburse, or otherwise exercise custody or control of any of the funds or other property of any employee benefit plan without being properly bonded. Additionally, it is unlawful under ERISA for any plan official, or any other person with authority, to permit a plan official who is not bonded to receive, handle, disburse, or otherwise exercise custody or control of any of the funds or other property of any employee benefit plan. ERISA Sec. 412(b); *Brock v. Ardito*, 8 EBC 2303 (E.D. NY 1987). The required bond must be in an approved form or type, and is required to have as surety an acceptable corporate surety company. ERISA Sec. 412(a).

Pending the issuance of permanent regulations with respect to the bonding provisions of ERISA Section 412, the DOL has concluded that plan officials will be in compliance with ERISA's bonding requirements if they are in compliance with Section 13 of the Welfare and Pension Plans Disclosure Act (WPPDA), as amended, and its regulations, as well as the temporary bonding rules of ERISA.

These temporary bonding rules apply to all employee benefit plans covered by ERISA. Any bond (or rider thereto) that contains a reference to the WPPDA is construed as referring to ERISA, provided that the surety company agrees. References to the WPPDA in the temporary bonding regulations are intended to refer to ERISA Section 412, and the language in ERISA supersedes similar language with a different meaning in the WPPDA and its regulations. Labor Reg. §2550.412-1.

473. What plans are exempt from the bonding requirements?

The bonding requirements of ERISA Section 412 do not apply to an administrator, officer, or employee of a plan if the benefits of the plan are paid from the general assets of an employer or a union. This exception from the bonding provisions applies only to completely unfunded plans in which the plan benefits derive solely from the general assets of a union or employer, and in which the plan assets are not segregated from the general assets of a employer or union, and remain solely within the general assets until the time of distribution of benefits. ERISA Sec. 412(a)(1); Labor Reg. §2580.412-2.

The plan itself is not exempt from the bonding requirements if the plan is one in which: (1) any benefits are provided or underwritten by an insurance carrier or service or other organization; (2) there is a trust or other separate entity to which contributions are made or out of which benefits are paid; (3) employees make contributions to the plan, either through withholding or otherwise, or from any source other than the employer or union involved; or (4) there are separately maintained bank accounts or separately maintained books and records for the plan, or other evidence of the existence of a segregated or separately maintained or administered fund out of which plan benefits are to be provided. Labor Reg. §2580.412-2.

As a general rule, the presence of special ledger accounts or accounting entries for plan funds as an integral part of the general books and records of an employer or union will not, in and of itself, be deemed sufficient evidence of segregation of plan funds to take a plan out of the exempt category, but will be considered along with the other factors and criteria discussed above in determining whether the exemption applies. The fact that a plan is not exempt from the bonding requirements does not necessarily mean that its administrators, officers, or employees are required to be bonded. This will depend in each case on whether or not they "handle" funds or other property of the plan within the meaning of ERISA Section 412, and under the standards set forth in the regulations (see Q 478). Labor Regs. §§2580.412-2, 2580.412-6.

474. What are the exceptions to the bonding requirements for fiduciaries?

The bonding requirements do not apply to a fiduciary (or any director, officer, or employee of such fiduciary) if the fiduciary: (1) is a corporation organized and doing business under federal or state law; (2) is legally authorized to exercise trust powers or to conduct an insurance business; (3) is subject to supervision or examination by federal or state authorities; and (4) at all times has a combined capital and surplus of at least $1,000,000. ERISA Sec. 412(a)(2).

A bank or other financial institution that is authorized to exercise trust powers and the deposits of which are not insured by the Federal Deposit Insurance Corporation (FDIC) may satisfy this exception if it meets bonding or similar requirements under state law that are at least equivalent to those imposed on banks by federal law. ERISA Sec. 412(a)(2).

475. Who must be bonded?

Every administrator, officer, and employee of any benefit plan subject to ERISA who "handles" (see Q 478) funds or other property of such plan must be bonded. ERISA Sec. 412(a).

A plan "administrator" is either: (1) the person or persons designated under the terms of the plan or the collective bargaining agreement with responsibility for the ultimate control, disposition, or management of the money received or contributed; or (2) in the absence of such designation, the person or persons actually responsible for the control, disposition, or management of the money received or contributed, irrespective of whether such control, disposition, or management is exercised directly or through an agent or trustee designated by such person or persons. Labor Reg. §2580.412-3(a)(1).

If the term *administrator* (as defined above, or in regulations, interpretations, or opinions in regard to this definition) embodies natural persons such as members of the board of trustees of a trust, the bonding requirements will apply to such persons. However, if the term (as defined above, or in regulations, interpretations, or opinions in regard to this definition) is deemed to apply to an entity such as a partnership, corporation, mutual company, joint stock company, trust, unincorporated organization, union, or employees' beneficiary association, the term will apply, in meeting the bonding requirements, only to those natural persons: (1) who are vested under the authority of the entity-administrator with the responsibility for carrying out functions constituting control, disposition, or management of the money received or contributed within the definition of administrator, or who, acting on behalf of or under the actual or apparent authority of the entity-administrator, actually perform such functions; and (2) who *handle* (see Q 478 for the definition of "handle") funds or other property of the plan within the meaning of the regulations to ERISA Section 412. Labor Regs. §§2580.412-3(a)(2), 2580.412-3(a)(3).

The term "officer," for purposes of the bonding provisions, includes any person designated under the terms of a plan or collective bargaining agreement as an officer, any person performing or authorized to perform executive functions of the plan, or any member of a board of trustees or similar governing body of a plan. The term includes such persons, regardless of whether they are representatives of or selected by an employer, employees, or an employee organization. In its most frequent application, the term *officer* encompasses those natural persons appointed or elected as officers of the plan or as members of boards or committees performing executive or supervisory functions for the plan, but who do not fall within the definition of *administrator*. Labor Reg. §2580.412-3(b).

For purposes of the bonding provisions, the term "employee," to the extent a person performs functions not falling within the definition of *officer* or *administrator*, includes any employee who performs work for or directly related to a covered plan, regardless of whether, technically, he is employed, directly or indirectly, by or for a plan, a plan administrator, a trust, or by an employee organization or employer. Labor Reg. §2580.412-3(c).

For purposes of the bonding requirements, the terms "administrator, officer, or employee" also include any persons performing functions for the plan normally performed by administrators, officers, or employees of a plan. As such, the terms include persons indirectly employed, or otherwise delegated, to perform this type of work for the plan, such as pension consultants and planners, and attorneys who perform handling functions, within the meaning of the regulations. In contrast, the terms do not include those brokers or independent contractors who have contracted for the performance of functions that are not ordinarily carried out by the administrators, officers, or employees of a plan, such as securities brokers who purchase and sell securities, or armored motor vehicle companies. Labor Reg. §2580.412-3(d).

In November, 2000, the PWBA announced that it is undertaking a review of the temporary bonding regulations under ERISA Section 412 for the purpose of developing a regulation which would exempt certain investment advisors and broker-dealers from the definition of "plan officials" required to be bonded under ERISA Section 412(a). 65 Fed. Reg. 74071 (11-30-00).

476. What are "funds or other property" of a plan?

The term "funds or other property" is intended to include all property that is used or may be used as a source for the payment of benefits to plan participants. It does not include permanent assets used in the operation of the plan (e.g., land and buildings, furniture and fixtures, or office and delivery equipment). It does include all items in the nature of quick (i.e., liquid) assets (e.g., cash, checks, and other negotiable instruments, government obligations, and marketable securities).

Funds or other property also includes all other property or items convertible into cash or having a cash value and held or acquired for the ultimate purpose of distribution to plan participants or beneficiaries. In the case of a plan that has investments, this would include all the investments of the plan, even though such investments are not in the nature of quick assets (e.g., land and buildings, mortgages, and securities in closely held corporations). However, in a given case, the question of whether a person was *handling* (see Q 478 for the definition of "handling") such *funds or other property* so as to require bonding depends upon whether his relationship to this property is such that there is a risk that he, alone or in connivance with others, could cause a loss of such *funds or other property* through fraud or dishonesty. Labor Reg. §2580.412-4.

477. When do items contributed to a plan become the "funds or other property" of the plan?

The point at which any item or amount contributed to a plan from any source (including employers, employees, or employee organizations) becomes *funds or other property* (see Q 476) of a plan for purposes of the bonding provisions is determined according to whether the plan administrator is the employer or employee organization that established the plan.

If the plan administrator is a board of trustees, person, or body *other than* the employer or employee organization establishing the plan, a contribution to the plan from any source becomes *funds or other property* of the plan at the time it is received by the plan administrator. Employee contributions collected by an employer and later turned over to the plan administrator would not become *funds or other property* of the plan until the funds are received by the plan administrator.

If the employer or employee organization establishing the plan is itself the plan administrator, the following rules apply:

1. Contributions from employees or other persons who are plan participants would normally become *funds or other property* of the plan when the contributions are received by the employer or employee organization; however, contributions made by withholding from employees' salaries are not considered *funds or other property* of the plan for purposes of the bonding provisions, so long as they are retained in and not segregated in any way from the general assets of the withholding employer or employee organization; and

2. Contributions made to a plan by an employer or employee organization and contributions made by withholding from employees' salaries would normally become *funds or other property* of the plan if and when they are: (a) taken out of the general assets of the employer or employee organization and placed in a special bank account or investment account, (b) identified on a separate set of books and records, (c) paid over to a corporate trustee or used to purchase benefits from an insurance carrier or service or other organization, or (d) otherwise segregated, paid out or used for plan purposes, whichever occurs first. Thus, if a plan is operated by a corporate trustee and no segregation from general assets is made of monies to be turned over to the corporate trustee prior to the actual transmittal of such monies, the transmitted contribution becomes *funds or other property* of the plan at the time when the corporate trustee receives it. On the other hand, if a special fund is first established, from which monies are paid

over to the corporate trustee, a contribution would become *funds or other property* of the plan when it is placed in the special fund. Similarly, if plan benefits are provided through an insurance carrier or service or other organization and no segregation from general assets of monies used to purchase such benefits is made prior to turning such monies over to the organization contracting to provide benefits, status as *funds or other property* comes into being when the insurance carrier or service or other organization receives payment for such benefits. In these circumstances, the *funds or other property* of the plan would be represented by the insurance contract or other obligations to pay benefits, and would not be normally subject to *handling* (see Q 478). Bonding would not be required for any person with respect to the purchase of such benefits directly from general assets nor with respect to the bare existence of the contract obligation to pay benefits. However, if the particular arrangement were such that monies derived from, or by virtue of, the contract subsequently flowed back to the plan, bonding may be required if such monies returning to the plan are *handled* by plan *administrators, officers, or employees.* Labor Reg. §2580.412-5.

478. When are funds or other property "handled" so as to require bonding?

A plan administrator, officer, or employee will be considered to be "handling" funds or other property of a plan, and, thus, required to be bonded under ERISA, whenever the person's duties or activities with respect to the plan's *funds or other property* present a risk that the plan's funds or other property could be lost in the event of fraud or dishonesty on the part of the person, whether acting alone or in collusion with others. Generally, plan administrators, officers, and employees who *handle* funds within the meaning of ERISA will be persons with duties related to the receipt, safekeeping, and disbursement of funds; however, the scope of the term *handles* and the prohibitions of ERISA are deemed to include any relationship of an administrator, officer, or employee with respect to funds or other property, which can give rise to a risk of loss through fraud or dishonesty. This includes relationships such as those that involve access to funds or other property or decision making powers with respect to funds or property that can give rise to such risk of loss. Labor Reg. §2580.412-6(a)(1).

The determination of the existence of risk of loss is not based on the amount involved or the amount or value of funds or other property *handled.* A given duty or relationship to funds or other property is not considered *handling*, and bonding is not required, where it occurs under conditions and circumstances in which the risk of loss through fraud or dishonesty is negligible, regardless of the amount involved. For example, where the risk of mishandling is precluded by the nature of the funds or other property (e.g., checks, securities, or title papers, which cannot be negotiated by the persons performing duties with respect to them), and where significant risk of mishandling in the performance of duties of an essentially clerical character is precluded by fiscal controls. Labor Reg. §2580.412-6(a)(2).

General Criteria

The regulations detail the general criteria (see below) for determining whether there is *handling* so as to require bonding, subject to the application of the basic standard of risk of loss to each situation.

Physical contact with cash, checks, or similar property generally constitutes handling. However, persons who, from time to time, perform counting, packaging, tabulating, messenger, or similar duties of an essentially clerical character involving physical contact with funds or other property would not be *handling* when they perform these duties under conditions and circumstances where risk of loss is negligible because of factors such as close supervision and control, or the nature of the property. Labor Reg. §2580.412-6(b)(1).

The power to exercise physical contact or control is also determinative of *handling.* Whether or not physical contact actually takes place, the power to secure physical possession of cash, checks, or similar property through factors such as access to a safe deposit box or similar depository, access to cash or negotiable assets, powers of custody or safekeeping, power to withdraw funds from a bank or other account generally constitutes *handling*, regardless of whether the person in question has specific duties in these matters and regardless of whether the power or access is authorized. Labor Reg. §2580.412-6(b)(2).

The power to transfer to oneself or a third party or to negotiate for value is also an example of *handling*. With respect to property such as mortgages, title to land and buildings, or securities, while physical contact or the possibility of physical contact may not, of itself, give rise to risk of loss so as to constitute handling, a person shall be regarded as handling such items where he, through actual or apparent authority, could cause those items to be transferred to himself or to a third party or to be negotiated for value. Labor Reg. §2580.412-6(b)(3).

The disbursement of funds or other property by persons such as officers or trustees who are authorized to sign checks or other negotiable instruments, or persons authorized to make cash disbursements, will be considered *handling*. Whether other persons who may influence, authorize, or direct disbursements or the signing or endorsing of checks or similar instruments will be considered to be *handling* funds or other property will be determined by reference to the particular duties or responsibilities of such persons as applied to the basic criteria of risk of loss. Labor Reg. §2580.412-6(b)(4).

The signing or endorsing of checks or other negotiable instruments by persons with the power to do so, or to otherwise render them transferable, in connection with disbursements or otherwise, whether individually or as co-signers with one or more persons, are each considered to be *handling* of such funds or other property. Labor Reg. §2580.412-6(b)(5).

To the extent that the *supervisory or decision making responsibility* of a person factors in relationship to funds discussed above, such persons will be considered to be *handling* in the same manner as any person to whom the criteria of those paragraphs apply. These persons are considered to be *handling* whenever the facts of the particular case raise the possibility that funds or other property of the plan are likely to be lost in the event of their fraud or dishonesty, to the extent that only general responsibility for the conduct of the business affairs of the plan is involved, including such functions as approval of contracts, authorization of disbursements, auditing of accounts, investment decisions, determination of benefit claims, and similar responsibilities. The existence of general supervision would not necessarily, in and of itself, mean that such persons are *handling*. Factors to be considered are the system of fiscal controls, the closeness and continuity of supervision, who is in fact charged with, or actually exercising final responsibility for determining whether specific disbursements, investments, contracts, or benefit claims are bona fide, regular, and made in accordance with the applicable trust instrument or other plan documents.

For example, certain persons with supervisory or decision making responsibility would be considered to be *handling* to the extent they: (1) act in the capacity of plan *administrator* and have ultimate responsibility for the plan (within the meaning of "administrator" (see Q 475)), except to the extent that it can be shown that such persons could not, in fact, cause a loss to the plan through fraud or dishonesty; (2) exercise close supervision over corporate trustees or other parties charged with dealing with plan funds or other property, or exercise such close control over investment policy that they, in effect, determine all specific investments; (3) conduct, in effect, a continuing daily audit of the persons who *handle* funds; or (4) regularly review and have veto power over the actions of a disbursing officer, whose duties are essentially ministerial.

However, persons having supervisory or decision making responsibility would not be *handling* to the extent that: (1) they merely conduct a periodic or sporadic audit of the persons who *handle* funds; (2) their duties with respect to investment policy are essentially advisory; (3) they make a broad general allocation of funds or general authorization of disbursements intended to permit expenditures by a disbursing officer who has final responsibility for determining the propriety of any specific expenditure and making the actual disbursement; (4) a bank or corporate trustee has all the day-to-day functions of administering the plan; or (5) they are in the nature of a board of directors of a corporation or similar authority acting for the corporation, rather than for the plan, and do not perform specific functions with respect to the operations of the plan. Labor Reg. §2580.412-6(b)(6).

Finally, *insured plan arrangements* that would not normally be subject to bonding except to the extent that monies returned by way of benefit payments, cash surrender, dividends, credits, or otherwise, and which by the terms of the plan belonged to the plan (rather than to the employer, employee organization, insurance carrier, or service or other organization) were subject to *handling* by plan administrators, officers, or employees. In many cases, plan contributions made by employers or employee organizations or by withholding from employees' salaries are not segregated from the general assets of the employer or employee organization until payment for purchase of benefits from an insurance carrier or service or other organization. No bonding is required with respect to the payment of premiums or other payments made to purchase such benefits directly from general assets, nor with respect to the bare existence of the contract obligation to pay benefits. Labor Reg. §2580.412-6(b)(7).

SCOPE AND FORM OF THE BOND

479. What is the meaning of "fraud or dishonesty" in terms of the scope of the protection provided by the bond?

The scope of coverage under ERISA Section 412 requires that the bond protect the plan against loss by reason of acts of fraud or dishonesty on the part of a plan administrator, officer, or employee, directly or through connivance with others. This coverage is limited to protection for those duties and activities from which loss can arise through *fraud or dishonesty*.

The term "fraud or dishonesty" encompasses all those risks of loss that might arise through dishonest or fraudulent acts in *handling* plan funds (see Q 478 for the definition of "handling"). "As such, the bond must provide recovery for loss occasioned by such acts even though no personal gain accrues to the person committing the act and the act is not subject to punishment as a crime or misdemeanor, provided that within the law of the state in which the act is committed, a court would afford recovery under a bond providing protection against fraud or dishonesty." Labor Reg. §2580.412-9. The term *fraud or dishonesty*, as usually applied under state laws, encompasses such matters as larceny, theft, embezzlement, forgery, misappropriation, wrongful abstraction, wrongful conversion, willful misapplication, or any other fraudulent or dishonest acts. Other fraudulent or dishonest acts also include acts where losses result through any act or arrangement that violates the federal law prohibiting offers, acceptances, or solicitations to influence the operations of an employee benefit plan. Labor Reg. §2580.412-9.

480. What is an individual or schedule or blanket form of bonds?

ERISA provides that bonds are to be "in a form or of a type approved by the Secretary of Labor, including individual bonds or schedule or blanket forms of bonds which cover a group or class." ERISA Sec. 412(a). An individual, schedule, or blanket bond, or combination thereof, is acceptable under ERISA Section 412, provided that the form of the bond, in its particular clauses and application, is not inconsistent with meeting (1) the substantive requirements of ERISA for the persons and plan involved; and (2) the specific requirements of the regulations.

Basic types of bonds in general usage are: (1) individual bonds, covering a named individual in a stated penalty; (2) name schedule bonds, covering a number of named individuals in the respective amounts set opposite their names; (3) position schedule bonds, covering each of the occupants of positions listed in the schedule in the respective amounts set opposite such positions; and (4) blanket bonds, covering all of the insured's officers and employees with no schedule or list of those covered being necessary and with all new officers and employees becoming bonded automatically, in a blanket penalty that takes two forms, an aggregate penalty bond and a multiple penalty bond.

The aggregate penalty blanket bond, such as the commercial blanket bond, is a bond in which the amount of the bond is available for dishonesty losses caused by persons covered by the bond, or losses in which such person is concerned or implicated. Payment of loss on account of any such person does not reduce the amount of coverage available for losses other than those caused by such person or in which he was concerned or implicated.

The multiple penalty bond, such as the blanket position bond, gives separate coverage on each person for a uniform amount, the net effect being the same as though a separate bond were issued on each person covered by the bond and all of such bonds being for a uniform amount.

For the purpose of ERISA Section 412, blanket bonds (which are either aggregate penalty or multiple penalty in form) are permissible only if they otherwise meet the requirements of ERISA and the regulations.

"Bonding, to the extent required, of persons indirectly employed, or otherwise delegated, to perform functions for the plan which are normally performed by `administrators, officers, or employees'... may be accomplished either by including them under individual or schedule bonds or other forms of bonds meeting the requirements of [ERISA], or naming them in what is known under general trade usage as an `Agents Rider' attached to a Blanket Bond." Labor Reg. §2580.412-10.

AMOUNT OF THE BOND

481. What is the amount of the bond?

Each individual must be bonded for at least 10% of the amount of funds he *handles* (see Q 478 for a definition of "handles"). The amount of the bond is fixed at the beginning of each calendar, policy, or other fiscal year that constitutes the plan year. The amount of the bond is subject to a minimum of $1,000 and a maximum of $500,000. The Secretary of Labor may prescribe that a person be bonded for an amount in excess of $500,000, subject to the 10% limitation of the funds handled, upon due notice, opportunity for hearing to all interested parties, and after consideration of the record. ERISA Sec. 412(a)(2)(D); Labor Reg. §2580.412-11.

482. How is the amount of the bond determined?

For purposes of fixing the amount of the bond, the amount of funds handled must be determined by the funds handled by the person, group, or class covered by the bond, and by their predecessor or predecessors, if any, during the preceding plan year; however, if the plan has no preceding plan year, the amount of the bond is determined by estimating the amount of funds to be handled during the current plan year by such person, group, or class. ERISA Sec. 412(a); Labor Reg. §2580.412-11.

483. What are the required recovery provisions of a bond?

The bond must meet certain requirements relating to reimbursement for loss. Reimbursement to a plan suffering a loss must be from the first dollar of loss up to the full amount for which the person causing the loss is bonded. The regulations do not permit the use of a deductible or any feature by which a portion of the risk with the amount of the bond is assumed by the insured. If a plan is already insured under a blanket bond covering all employees of the employer, but the bond has a deductible provision, the deductible provision must be either eliminated or modified so as not to apply to loss of plan funds caused by an administrator, officer, or employee of the plan; otherwise, a new bond must be secured covering the plan. Labor Reg. §2580.412-11.

484. What is the relationship between determining the amount of the bond and the "handling" of funds or other property?

The determination of whether an administrator, officer, or employee is required to be bonded depends on whether they *handle* funds or other property. (See Q 478 for a definition of "handle.") Determining the amount of the bond requires a determination of which funds or other property are being *handled* or which amounts of funds or other property are subject to risk of loss with respect to the duties or powers of an administrator, officer, or employee of a covered plan. Once this calculation is made, the required amount for which that person must be covered by a bond, either by himself or as a part of a group or class being bonded under a blanket or schedule bond, is not less than 10% of the amount *handled* or $1,000, whichever is the greater amount, except that a bond is not required in an amount greater than $500,000. Labor Reg. §2580.412-12.

485. What is the meaning of "funds" in determining the amount of the bond?

The amount of the bond depends on the amount of *funds handled* (see Q 478 for a definition of "handle"), and must be sufficient to provide bonding protection against risk of loss through fraud or dishonesty for all plan funds, including other property similar to funds or in the nature of funds. As such, the term "funds" is deemed to include and be equivalent to *funds and other property* of the plan. (See Q 476 for a definition of "funds or other property.") With respect to any item of *funds or other property* that does not have a cash or readily ascertainable market value, the value of such property may be estimated on such basis as will reasonably reflect the potential loss to the plan if it were mishandled. Labor Reg. §2580.412-13.

486. How is the amount of funds "handled" during the preceding reporting year determined?

The amount of funds *handled* by an administrator, officer, or employee (or his predecessors) during the preceding reporting year is the total of funds subject to risk of loss, within the meaning of the definition of handling (see Q 478), through acts of fraud or dishonesty, directly or in connivance with others, by such person or his predecessors during the preceding reporting year.

The relationship of the determination of the amount of funds *handled* to the determination of who is *handling* them can best be illustrated by a situation that commonly arises with respect to executive personnel of a plan, where a bank or corporate trustee has the responsibility for the receipt, safekeeping, physical handling, and investment of a plan's assets and the basic function of the executive personnel is to authorize payments to beneficiaries and payments for services to the corporate trustee, the actuary, and the employees of the plan itself. Normally, in any given year, only a small portion of the plan's total assets is disbursed, and the question arises as to whether an administrator or executive personnel are *handling* only the amounts actually disbursed each year or whether they are *handling* the total amounts of the assets. The answer to this question depends on the same basic criterion that governs all questions of *handling*, namely, the possibility of loss. If the authorized duties of the persons in question are strictly limited to disbursements of benefits and payments for services, and the fiscal controls and practical realities of the situation are such that these persons cannot gain access to funds that they are not legitimately allowed to disburse, the amount on which the bond is based may be limited to the amount actually disbursed in the reporting year. This would depend, in part, on the extent to which the bank or corporate trustee that has physical possession of the funds also has final responsibility for questioning and limiting disbursements from the plan, and on whether this responsibility is embodied in the original plan instruments.

On the other hand, where insufficient fiscal controls exist, so that the persons involved have free access to, or can obtain control of, the total amount of the fund, the bond must reflect this fact and the amount *handled* must be based on the total amount of the fund. This would generally occur with respect to persons such as the *administrator* (see Q 475 for a definition of "administrator"), regardless of which functions are performed by a bank or corporate trustee, since the *administrator*, by definition, retains ultimate power to revoke any arrangement with a bank or corporate trustee. In such a case, the *administrator* would have the power to commit the total amount of funds involved to his control, unless the plan itself or other specific agreement: (1) prevents the *administrator* from so doing; or (2) requires that revocation cannot be had unless a new agreement providing for similar controls and limitations on the *handling* of funds is entered into simultaneously.

Where the circumstances of *handling* are such that the total amount of a given account or fund is subject to *handling*, the amount *handled* must include the total of all the funds on hand at the beginning of the reporting year, plus any items received during the year for any reason, such as contributions or income, or items received as a result of sales, investments, reinvestment, interest, or otherwise. It would not, however, be necessary to count the same item twice in arriving at the total funds *handled* by a given person during a reporting year.

For example, a given person may have various duties or powers involving receipt, safekeeping, or disbursement of funds, which would place him in contact with the same funds at several times during the same year. Different duties, however, would not make it necessary to count the same item twice in arriving at the total *handled* by such person. Similarly, where a person has several different positions with respect to a plan, it would not be necessary to count the same funds each time that they are *handled* by him in these different positions, so long as the amount of the bond is sufficient to meet the 10% requirement with respect to the total funds *handled* by him subject to risk or loss through his fraud or dishonesty, whether acting alone or in collusion with others. In general, once an item that is properly within the category of *funds* has been counted as *handled* by a given person, it need not be counted again even though it is subsequently *handled* by the same person acting in another capacity during the same year. Labor Reg. §2580.412-14.

487. What are the procedures to be used for estimating the amount of funds to be "handled" during the current reporting year in those cases where there is no preceding reporting year?

If, for any reason, a plan does not have a complete preceding reporting year, the amount *handled* (see Q 478 for a definition of "handle") by persons required to be covered by a bond is estimated at the beginning of the calendar, policy, or other fiscal year that would constitute either the operating year or the reporting year of the plan, whichever occurs first, according to the rules below.

In the case of a plan having a previous experience year, even though it has no preceding reporting year, the estimate of the amount to be handled for any person who must be covered is based on the experience in the previous year, by applying the same standards and criteria as in a plan that has a preceding reporting year. Similarly, where a plan is recently established, but has had, at the time when a bond is obtained, sufficient experience to reasonably estimate a complete year's experience for persons who must be bonded, the amount of funds to be handled is projected for the complete year on the basis of the period in which the plan has had experience, unless, to the knowledge of the plan administrator, the given period of experience is so seasonal or unrepresentative of a complete year's experience as not to provide a reasonable basis for projecting the estimate for the complete year.

Where a plan does not have any prior experience sufficient to allow it to estimate the amount handled in the manner outlined above, the amount to be handled by the administrators, officers, and employees of the plan during the current reporting year is that amount initially required to fund or set up the plan, plus the amount of contributions required under the plan formula from any source during the current reporting year. In most cases, the amount of contributions will be calculated by multiplying the total yearly contribution per participant (required by the plan formula from either employers, employees, employer organizations, or any other source) by the number of participants in the plan at the beginning of such reporting year. In cases where the per capita contribution cannot readily be determined, such as in the case of certain insured plans covered by ERISA, the amount of contributions are estimated based on the amount of insurance premiums that are actuarially estimated as necessary to support the plan, or on such other actuarially estimated basis as may be applicable. In the case of a newly formed profit sharing plan covered by ERISA, if the employer establishing the plan has a previous year of experience, the amount of contributions required by the plan formula are estimated on the basis of the profits of the previous year. The amount of the bond is then fixed at 10% of this calculation, but not more than $500,000. A bond for this amount is obtained in any form the plan desires on all of the persons who are administrators, officers, or employees of the plan and who handle funds or other property of the plan. Labor Reg. §2580.412-15.

488. What is the amount of bond required in certain types of bonds or where more than one plan is insured in the same bond?

ERISA permits the use of blanket, schedule, and individual bonds, so long as the amount of the bond is sufficient to meet the requirements of ERISA for any person who is an administrator, officer, or employee of a plan handling funds or other property of the plan (see Q 480). Each person must be bonded for 10% of the amount he handles, and the amount of the bond must be sufficient to indemnify the plan for any losses in which the person is involved up to that amount.

When individual or schedule bonds are written, the amount of the bond for each person must represent not less than 10% of the funds *handled* (see Q 478 for a definition of "handle") by the named individual or by the person in the named position. When a blanket bond is written, the amount of the bond must be at least 10% of the highest amount handled by any administrator, officer, or employee to be covered under the bond. If an individual (or group or class) covered under a blanket bond "handles" a large amount of funds or other property, while the remaining bondable persons "handle" only a smaller amount, it is permissible to obtain a blanket bond in an amount sufficient to meet the 10% requirements for all except the individual, group, or class handling the larger amounts. For those individuals handling larger amounts, an excess indemnity must be secured in an amount sufficient to meet the 10% requirement.

ERISA does not prohibit more than one plan from being named as insured under the same bond. However, the bond must allow for recovery by each plan in an amount at least equal to that which would be required if bonded separately. This requirement is applicable where a person (or persons) to be bonded has handling functions in more than one plan covered under the bond. In such a case, the amount of the bond must be sufficient to cover the persons having functions in more than one plan for at least 10% of the total amount handled by them in all of the plans covered under the bond.

For example, X is the administrator of two welfare plans sponsored by the same employer, and he handled $100,000 in the preceding reporting year for Plan A and $500,000 in the preceding reporting year for Plan B. If both plans are covered under the same bond, the amount of the bond with respect to X must be at least $60,000, or 10% of the total handled by X for both plans covered under the bond in which X has powers and duties of handling, since Plan B is required to carry a bond of at least $50,000 and Plan A is required to carry a bond of at least $10,000.

Additionally, in order to meet the requirement that each plan be protected, it is necessary that an arrangement be made either by the terms of the bond or rider to the bond or by separate agreement among the parties concerned that payment of a loss sustained by one of the insureds must not work to the detriment of any other plan covered under the bond with respect to the amount for which that plan is required to be covered.

For example, if Plan A (as described above) suffered a loss of $30,000, and such loss was recompensed in its entirety by the surety company, it would receive $20,000 more than the $10,000 protection required under ERISA, and only $30,000 would be available for recovery with respect to further losses caused by X. In a subsequently discovered defalcation of $40,000 by X from Plan B, it would be necessary that the bond, rider, or separate agreement provide that such amount of recovery paid to Plan A in excess of the $10,000 for which it is required to be covered be made available by such insured to, or held for the use of, Plan B in such amount as Plan B would receive if bonded separately. Thus, in this example, Plan B would be able to recover the full $40,000 of its loss. Where the funds or other property of several plans are commingled (if permitted by law) with each other or with other funds, such an arrangement must allow recovery to be attributed proportionately to the amount for which each plan is required to be protected. Thus, in this example, if funds or other property were commingled, and X caused a loss of these funds through fraud or dishonesty, one-sixth of the loss would be attributable to Plan A and five-sixths of the loss attributable to Plan B.

The maximum amount of any bond with respect to any person in any one plan is $500,000, but bonds covering more than one plan may be in excess of $500,000 in order to meet the requirements of ERISA Section 412, since persons covered by such a bond may have handling functions in more than one plan. The $500,000 limitation for such persons applies only with respect to each separate plan in which they have such functions. The minimum bond coverage for any administrator, officer, or employee handling funds or other property of a plan is $1,000 with respect to each plan in which he has handling functions. Labor Reg. §2580.412-16.

General Bonding Rules

489. What are the general bonding rules?

Naming of Insureds

Where a single plan is the only insured under a bond, that plan is entitled to receive reimbursement for loss as the named insured. However, where a plan is insured jointly with other plans, or with an employer or an employee organization, the plan must be afforded the same protection that it would have under its own separate bond. A plan must receive preference (up to 10% of funds handled) when a loss is common to the plan and to the employer or employee organization. It is possible to achieve this result through a pay-over rider, an agreement among the parties that any reimbursement collected on a bond will be for the benefit and use of the plan suffering the loss (at least up to the statutory bonding minimum), or a combination of the two. Such rider or agreement must clearly be enforceable by all plans that do not have other direct recourse on the bond. Such a rider or agreement is always required: (1) where the employer or employee organization is first named joint insured with one or more plans; or (2) two or more plans are named joint insureds under a single bond with the first named acting for all insureds for the purpose of orderly servicing of the bond. Payment to one plan must not reduce the amount another plan is entitled to up to the bond amount required by ERISA for the other plan. Labor Reg. §2580.412-18.

Term of the Bond

The amount of any required bond must be based on the amount of funds "handled," and must be fixed or estimated at the beginning of the plan's reporting year; that is, as soon after the date when this year begins as the necessary information from the preceding reporting year can practicably be ascertained. This does not mean, however, that a new bond must be obtained each year. ERISA does not prohibit a bond for a term longer than one year, with whatever advantages such a bond might offer by way of a lower premium. However, at the beginning of each reporting year, the bond must be in at least the requisite amount. If, for any reason, the bond is below the required level at that time, the existing bond must either be increased to the proper amount, or a supplemental bond must be obtained. Labor Reg. §2580.412-19.

Discovery Period

The bond must provide a discovery period of no less than one year after the termination or cancellation of the bond in which to discover the loss. A discovery period is the period after termination of the bond during which the insured is allowed to uncover a loss that occurred while the bond was in force. Any standard form written on a "discovery" basis (i.e., providing that a loss must be discovered within the bond period as a prerequisite to recovery of such loss) will not be required to have a discovery period if it contains a provision giving the insured the right to purchase a discovery period of one year in the event of termination or cancellation and the insured has already given the surety notice that it desires such a discovery period. Labor Reg. §2580.412-19.

Additional Rules

A bond does not adequately meet the requirements of ERISA Section 412 if it contains a clause in contravention of the law of the state in which it is executed, or is otherwise in contravention of the law of such state. Labor Reg. §2580.412-19(c).

As long as a particular bond meets the requirements of ERISA Section 412 as to the persons who must be bonded, and provides coverage for these persons in at least the minimum required amount, additional coverage as to persons or amount may be taken in any form, either on the same or separate bond.

If an existing bond is adequate to meet the bonding requirements or if it is modified to meet these requirements through a rider, modification, or separate agreement between the parties, no further bonding is required.

The choice of whether persons required to be bonded are bonded separately or under the same bond, whether given plans are bonded separately or under the same bond, whether existing bonds are used or separate bonds are obtained, or whether the bond is underwritten by a single surety company or more than one surety company, either separately or on a co-surety basis, is left to the judgment of the parties concerned, so long as the bonding program adopted meets the requirements of ERISA and the regulations thereunder.

More than one plan may be insured under the same bond, but the bond providing the coverage must allow for recovery by each plan in an amount at least equal to that which would be required if the plans were bonded separately. If a person handles the funds of more than one plan, he should be bonded in a manner that provides protection in the total of the amounts required by ERISA for each plan. Labor Reg. §2580.412-20.

490. What is an approved surety company?

ERISA Section 412(a) requires that bonds be written only by a corporate surety approved by the Treasury Department as an acceptable surety of federal bonds. In order for a surety company to be eligible for a grant of authority, it must be incorporated under the laws of the United States or of any state, and the Secretary of the Treasury must be satisfied of certain facts relating to its authority and capitalization. Approved surety companies are evidenced by certificates of authority issued by the Secretary of the Treasury, and which expire and are renewable annually. Companies holding certificates of authority as acceptable sureties on federal bonds are also acceptable as reinsuring companies.

A list of the companies holding such certificates of authority is published annually in the Federal Register, usually in May or June. This list is also published annually in the Department of the Treasury's Listing of Approved Sureties (Department Circular 570). Changes in the list, occurring between May 1 and April 30, either by addition to or removal from the list of companies, are also published in the Federal Register following each such change. Labor Reg. §2580.412-21.

If the bond is for a term of more than one year, the plan administrator must confirm that the surety is on the approved list at the beginning of each year. When a company is removed from the approved list, the plan administrator must secure a new bond from an approved company as soon as he learns of such removal.

491. What are the party in interest restrictions with respect to procuring the bond?

A bond for a plan may not be placed with any surety or other company or through any agent or broker in whose business operations such plan or any party in interest in the plan has any significant control or financial interest, direct or indirect. ERISA Sec. 412(c). The application of this prohibition requires a determination of whether the financial interest or control held is sufficiently significant to disqualify the agent, broker, or surety. Although no rule of guidance is established to govern each and every case in which this question arises, in general, the essential test is whether the existing financial interest or control held is incompatible with an unbiased exercise of judgment in regard to procuring the bond or bonding the plan's personnel. Lack of knowledge or consent on the part of persons responsible for procuring bonds with respect to the existence of a significant financial interest or control rendering the bonding arrangement unlawful is not deemed a mitigating factor where the persons have failed to make a reasonable examination into the pertinent circumstances affecting the procuring of the bond. Labor Reg. §2580.412-35.

The party in interest prohibition appears to indicate that the intent of Congress was to eliminate those instances where the existing financial interest or control held by the party in interest in the agent, broker, surety, or other company is incompatible with an unbiased exercise of judgment in regard to procuring the bond or bonding the plan's personnel. Accordingly, not all parties in interest are disqualified from procuring or providing bonds for the plan. Thus, where a party in interest or its affiliate provides multiple benefit plan services to plans, persons are not prohibited from availing themselves of the bonding services provided by the party in interest or its affiliate merely because the plan has already availed itself, or will avail itself, of other services provided by the party in interest. In this case, it is inherent in the nature of the party in interest or its affiliate as an individual or organization providing multiple benefit plan services, one of which is a bonding service, that the existing financial interest or control held is not, in and of itself, incompatible with an unbiased exercise of judgment in regard to procuring the bond or bonding the plan's personnel. In short, there is no distinction between this type of relationship and the ordinary arm's length business relationship that may be established between a plan customer and an agent, broker, or surety company, a relationship that Congress could not have intended to disturb.

However, where a party in interest in the plan or an affiliate does not provide a bonding service as part of its general business operations, ERISA Section 412 would prohibit any person from procuring the bond through or with any agent, broker, surety, or other company, with respect to which the party in interest has any significant control or financial interest, direct or indirect. In this case, the failure of the party in interest or its affiliate to provide a bonding service as part of its general business operations raises the possibility of less than an arm's length business relationship between the plan and the agent, broker, surety, or other company, since the objectivity of either the plan or the agent, broker, or surety may be influenced by the party in interest. Labor Reg. §2580.412-36.

The application of the principles discussed above is illustrated by the following examples:

> *Example 1*: B, a broker, renders actuarial and consultant service to plan P. B has also procured a group life insurance policy for plan P. B may also place a bond for P with surety company S, provided that neither B nor P has any significant control or financial interest, direct or indirect, in S, and provided that neither P nor any other party in interest in P (e.g., an officer of the plan) has any significant control or financial interest, direct or indirect, in B or S.

Example 2: I, a life insurance company, has provided a group life insurance policy for plan P. I is affiliated with S, a surety company, and has a significant financial interest or control in S. P is not prohibited from obtaining a bond from S, since I's affiliation with S does not ordinarily, in and of itself, affect the objectivity of P in procuring the bond or the objectivity of S in bonding P's personnel. However, if any other party in interest (as defined in ERISA Section 3(14)), such as the employer whose employees are covered by P, should have a significant financial interest or control in S, S could not write the bond for P, since the employer's interest affects the objectivity of P and S. Labor Reg. §2580.412-36.

EXEMPTIONS

492. What is the exemption to the bonding requirements for bonds placed with certain reinsuring companies?

Although all bonds required under ERISA must be issued by a corporate surety company that is an acceptable surety on federal bonds, an exemption exists for companies authorized by the Secretary of the Treasury as acceptable reinsurers on federal bonds. The exemption is conditioned on the fact that if, for any reason, the authority of any such company to act as an acceptable reinsuring company is terminated, the administrator of an insured plan will, upon knowledge of the fact, be responsible for securing a new bond with a company acceptable under ERISA. In obtaining or renewing a bond, or if the bond is for a term of more than one year, the plan administrator, at the beginning of each reporting year, must ascertain that the surety satisfies the requirements of ERISA. Labor Regs. §§2580.412-23, 2580.412-24.

493. What is the exemption to the bonding requirements for bonds placed with underwriters at Lloyds, London?

Bonding arrangements (which otherwise comply with the requirements of ERISA Section 412 and its attendant regulations) placed with the underwriters at Lloyds, London will be deemed to satisfy the bonding requirements of ERISA if certain requirements are met. This exemption applies only to the requirements of ERISA Section 412(a), which requires that all bonds required thereunder have as surety thereon a corporate surety company that is an acceptable surety on federal bonds under authority granted to the Secretary of the Treasury. ERISA Sec. 412(a)(2)(D).

The exemption will be granted if the following conditions are met:

1. Underwriters at Lloyds, London must continue to be licensed in a state of the United States to enter into bonding arrangements of the type required by ERISA.

2. Underwriters at Lloyds, London must file two copies of each annual statement, required to be made to the Commissioner of Insurance of those states in which underwriters at Lloyds, London are licensed, with the Office of Pension and Welfare Benefit Programs. Copies of annual statements must be filed with the Office of Pension and Welfare Benefit Programs within the same period required by the respective states.

3.   All bonding arrangements entered into by underwriters at Lloyds, London under ERISA Section 412 must contain a "Service of Suit Clause" in substantial conformity with that set forth in the petition for exemption. Labor Regs. §§2580.412-25, 2580.412-26.

494. What are the exemptions to the bonding requirements for banking institutions and trust companies?

Banking institutions and trust companies subject to regulation and examination by (1) the Comptroller of the Currency; (2) the Board of Governors of the Federal Reserve System; or (3) the Federal Deposit Insurance Corporation (FDIC) are exempt from the bonding requirements with respect to welfare and pension benefit plans. Labor Regs. §§2580.412-27, 2580.412-28.

495. What are the exemptions to the bonding requirements for savings and loan associations subject to federal regulation?

Savings and loan associations (including building and loan associations, cooperative banks, and homestead associations) that are subject to regulation and examination by the Federal Home Loan Bank Board are exempt from the bonding requirements, if such associations are the administrators of welfare and pension benefit plans benefiting their own employees. Labor Regs. §§2580.412-29, 2580.412-30.

496. What are the exemptions to the bonding requirements for insurance carriers, service, and other similar organizations?

Insurance carriers or service or other similar organizations that provide or underwrite welfare or pension plan benefits in accordance with state law are exempt from the bonding requirements with respect to welfare or pension plans established or maintained for the benefit of persons other than the employees of the insurance carrier or service or other similar organization. Labor Regs. §§2580.412-31, 2580.412-32.

497. What are the exemptions to the bonding requirements for broker-dealers?

The DOL proposes to amend the temporary bonding regulations for broker-dealers and investment advisors subject to federal regulation. Under the proposed regulation, if a broker-dealer maintains a fidelity bond covering the broker-dealer and/or an affiliated investment advisor that complies with the bonding requirements of its governing self-regulatory organization, and the bond meets minimum limits of coverage, the following persons will be considered bonded under ERISA Section 412: (1) any broker-dealer registered under the Securities Exchange Act of 1934 (Exchange Act); and (2) any investment advisor registered under the Investment Advisors Act of 1940 who controls, is controlled by, or is under common control with a broker-dealer registered under the Exchange Act (investment advisor affiliate), and does not maintain actual custody or possession of assets of employee benefit plans, and is named as an additional insured on the registered broker-dealer's bond.

As indicated above, the bond must meet minimum limits of coverage, irrespective of the limits prescribed by the governing self-regulatory organization. These limits are:

Securities and money values in possession and control	Basic minimum coverage
$0 - 50 million	$1 million
$50 - 100 million	$3 million
$100 - 500 million	$5 million
$500 million - 1 billion	$10 million
$1 - 2 billion	$25 million
Above $2 billion	$50 million

For purposes of this proposed exception, a "broker-dealer" and "investment advisor" include any partner, director, officer, or employee of such broker-dealer or investment advisor. The term "control" means the power to exercise a controlling influence over the management or policies of a person other than an individual. The bond must have a corporate surety company that is an acceptable surety on federal bonds under authority granted by the Secretary of the Treasury. Prop. Labor Reg. §2580.412-33.

498. What are the exemptions to the bonding requirements for other bonding arrangements or adequate financial conditions of the plan?

The Secretary of Labor may exempt a plan from the bonding requirements in circumstances where other bonding arrangements or the overall financial condition of the plan is adequate to protect the interests of the beneficiaries and participants. For example, if the Secretary of Labor determines that the plan administrator presents adequate evidence of the financial responsibility of the plan, or that other bonding arrangements would provide adequate protection of the beneficiaries and participants, the plan may be exempted from the bonding requirements. ERISA Sec. 412(e).

Although the Secretary of Labor is authorized to exempt plans from the bonding requirement in specified situations, depositing plan-owned assets with the Secretary of Labor in lieu of obtaining a fiduciary bond from a corporate surety company does not satisfy the bonding requirement of ERISA. This was illustrated in a case where the plan trustees proposed that a plan set aside certain amounts of its own assets to provide a source from which "reimbursements" could be made to the fund in the event that one of the fund fiduciaries breached a duty to the plan. The court held that such a scheme did not protect the assets of the fund in the event of a breach of fiduciary duty by one of the fund's trustees, because the plan's assets would be diminished by the amount of the damage caused by the breach. *Musso v. Baker*, 834 F.2d 78 (3rd Cir. 1987), *cert. denied*, 487 U.S. 1205 (1988).

Fiduciary Liability Insurance

499. May a plan purchase insurance to cover liability or losses due to the acts or omissions of a fiduciary?

Yes. ERISA allows, but does not require, a plan to purchase fiduciary insurance for its fiduciaries (or for itself) to cover liability or losses resulting from acts or omissions of the fiduciary. However, the insurance policy must permit recourse by the insurer against the fiduciary for a breach of its fiduciary obligation. ERISA Sec. 410(b). Therefore, if, under an insurance agreement, a fiduciary remains liable to the extent that there is a breach of fiduciary responsibility, such agreement would not be exculpatory and would be permissible under ERISA Section 410(a). The decision to purchase fiduciary insurance, as well as the particular arrangement entered into, can be made only by the appropriate plan fiduciaries, consistent with their fiduciary responsibilities in accordance with ERISA Section 404(a)(1). DOL Adv. Op. 76-3.

500. May a fiduciary purchase insurance to cover his own liability or to cover liability or losses resulting from his own acts or omissions?

Yes. ERISA Section 410(b) also permits plan fiduciaries to purchase insurance to protect themselves from any liability or losses resulting from their own acts or omissions. However, it is not necessary for the insurance policy to provide the insurer with recourse against the fiduciaries. ERISA Sec. 410(b)(2); Labor Reg. §2509.75-4.

501. May an employer or an employee organization purchase insurance to cover potential liability of persons who serve in a fiduciary capacity?

Yes. An employer or an employee organization may purchase insurance to cover potential liability of persons serving in a fiduciary capacity with respect to an employee benefit plan. It is not necessary for the insurance policy to provide the insurer with recourse against the fiduciaries. ERISA Sec. 410(b)(3); Labor Reg. §2509.75-4.

The liability of an employer for its decision to terminate a welfare plan was not recoverable under the employer's fiduciary liability insurance policy, because the policy covered the corporate employers' fiduciary violations in the administration and management of the plan, and did not cover the everyday business decisions of the employer. The decision of the employer to terminate the welfare plan was considered a "business decision," rather than a fiduciary decision, and, thus, was not covered as a breach of fiduciary duty under the policy. *Gulf Resources & Chem. Corp. v. Gavine*, 763 F. Supp. 1073 (DC Idaho 1991).

CHAPTER IX

INVESTMENT ISSUES

502. Must fiduciaries adhere to the plan's governing documents in managing and investing plan assets?

Yes, fiduciaries must discharge their duties with respect to a plan in accordance with the documents and instruments governing the plan (insofar as they are consistent with the provisions of ERISA). ERISA Sec. 404(a)(1)(D). This duty is reviewed in the overall context of the "prudent man" standard of care established under ERISA Section 404(a)(1)(B).

503. What are the general guidelines for a prudent investment program?

The requirements of ERISA Section 404(a)(1)(B) (the prudent man standard) are satisfied with regard to an investment course of action taken by a fiduciary if the fiduciary has given appropriate consideration to those facts and circumstances that the fiduciary knows or should know are relevant to the particular investment, or to the role the investment course of action plays in that portion of the plan's investment portfolio with respect to which the fiduciary has investment duties, and he has acted accordingly. Labor Reg. §2550.404a-1.

"Appropriate consideration" includes (but is not limited to) a determination by the fiduciary that the particular investment course of action is reasonably designed, as part of the portfolio, to further the purposes of the plan, taking into consideration the risk of loss and the opportunity for gain associated with the investment or investment course of action. "Adequate consideration" also means consideration of the following factors as they relate to such portion of the plan's investment portfolio:

1. The composition of the portfolio with regard to diversification;

2. The liquidity and current return of the portfolio relative to the anticipated cash flow requirements of the plan; and

3. The projected return of the portfolio relative to the funding objectives of the plan. Labor Reg. §2550.404a-1(b)(2).

In carrying out a plan's investment program, a fiduciary's failure to investigate the investments it administers violates the prudent man standard of care *only* if adequate investigation would have revealed to a prudent fiduciary that the investment at issue was inappropriate, or somehow not in the best interests of the participants and beneficiaries of the plan. See *Katsaros v. Cody*, 744 F.2d 270 (2nd Cir. 1984); *Roth v. Sawyer-Cleator Lumber Co.*, 16 F.3d 915 (8th Cir. 1994). In other words, ERISA does not state that a fiduciary is prohibited from making a bad investment; rather, it states that a fiduciary may not make an imprudent investment.

504. May plan fiduciaries delegate investment management responsibilities to others?

The plan documents may provide that the named fiduciaries (see below) have the authority to delegate the management and investment of plan assets (including the power to acquire and dispose of plan assets) to an investment manager. ERISA Sec. 402(c)(3). These individuals need not be specifically identified within the plan documents.

A *named fiduciary* is a fiduciary who is identified in the plan's governing documents, or who, pursuant to a procedure specified in the plan, is identified as a fiduciary by: (1) a person who is an employer or employee organization with respect to the plan, or (2) the employer and employee organization acting jointly. ERISA Sec. 402(a)(2).

The ongoing responsibilities of named fiduciaries who have appointed trustees or other fiduciaries, such as investment managers, include a continuing obligation to monitor the performance of the appointed individuals at reasonable intervals. Their performance should be reviewed in such a manner as may be reasonably expected to ensure that it has been in compliance with the terms of the plan and statutory standards, and that it satisfies the needs of the plan. No single procedure will be appropriate in all cases. The procedures adopted for the monitoring of investment managers may vary in accordance with the nature of the plan and other facts and circumstances. relevant to the choice of procedure. See Labor Reg. §2509.75-8, Q&A FR-17.

505. What is a "statement of investment policy"?

A "statement of investment policy" is defined as a written statement that provides the fiduciaries who are responsible for plan investments with guidelines or general instructions concerning various types or categories of investment management decisions, which may include proxy voting decisions. A statement of investment policy provides general instructions or guidelines to be applied in all applicable situations, such as identification of acceptable classes or types of investments, limitations on investment categories as a percentage of the plan's portfolio, or generally applicable guidelines regarding voting positions in proxy contests (e.g., criteria regarding the support of or opposition to recurring issues, such as proposals to create classified boards of directors or to provide for cumulative voting for board members). A statement of investment policy does not provide specific instructions as to the purchase or sale of a specific investment at a specific time or specific instructions to vote specific plan proxies a certain way. In addition, since the fiduciary act of managing plan assets that are shares of corporate stock includes the voting of proxies appurtenant to those shares of stock, a statement of proxy voting policy is an important part of any comprehensive statement of investment policy. Labor Reg. §2509.94-2(2) (IB 94-2), 59 Fed. Reg. 38860 (7-29-94).

506. Are statements of investment policy required by ERISA?

No. The maintenance of a statement of investment policy is not specifically required under ERISA. However, the Department of Labor believes that statements of investment policy serve a legitimate purpose in many plans by helping to assure that investments are made in a rational manner and are designed to further the purposes of the plan and its funding policy. For example, a statement of investment policy that includes a statement of proxy voting may increase the likelihood that proxy voting decisions are consistent with other aspects of the investment policy. Additionally, in plans with multiple investment managers, a written proxy voting policy may also prevent (where such prevention is desirable) the managers from taking conflicting positions on a given voting decision. Labor Reg. §2509.94-2(2) (IB 94-2), 59 Fed. Reg. 38860 (7-29-94).

507. Is a statement of investment policy consistent with the duty of loyalty and prudence?

Yes. The Department of Labor issued Interpretive Bulletin 94-2, in part, to clarify that the maintenance by an employee benefit plan of a statement of investment policy designed to further the purposes of the plan and its funding policy is consistent with the fiduciary obligations of loyalty and prudence. In the view of the DOL, a named fiduciary's determination of the terms of a statement of investment policy is an exercise of fiduciary responsibility and, as such, statements may need to take into account factors such as the plan's funding policy and its liquidity needs as well as issues of prudence, diversification and any other fiduciary requirements of ERISA. Labor Reg. §2509.94-2(2) (IB 94-2), 59 Fed. Reg. 38860 (7-29-94).

508. Does the maintenance of a statement of investment policy by a named fiduciary relieve the named fiduciary of its fiduciary duties with respect to the appointment and monitoring of an investment manager or trustee?

No. In the view of the DOL, maintenance of a statement of investment policy by a named fiduciary does not relieve the named fiduciary of its obligations under ERISA Section 404(a) with respect to the appointment and monitoring of an investment manager or trustee. In this respect, the named fiduciary appointing an investment manager must periodically monitor the investment manager's activities with respect to management of the plan assets. Moreover, complying with the duty of prudence requires maintenance of proper documentation of the activities of the investment manager and of the named fiduciary in monitoring the activities of the investment manager. In addition, as it exercises its fiduciary responsibility in determining the terms of a statement of investment policy, a named fiduciary may need to consider factors such as the plan's funding policy, liquidity needs, prudence, diversification and the other fiduciary requirements of ERISA. Labor Reg. §2509.94-2(2) (IB 94-2), 59 Fed. Reg. 38860 (7-29-94).

509. May a fiduciary expressly require, as a condition of an investment management agreement, that an investment manager comply with the terms of a statement of investment policy?

Yes. According to the DOL, the named fiduciary responsible for the appointment of investment managers in plans that delegate investment management responsibility to one or more investment managers has the authority to condition the appointment on acceptance of a statement of investment policy. Thus, the named fiduciary may expressly require, as a condition of the investment management agreement, that an investment manager comply with the terms of a statement of investment policy that sets forth guidelines concerning investments and investment courses of action that the investment manager is authorized to make or is precluded from making. However, in the absence of an express requirement of compliance with an investment policy, the authority to manage the plan assets placed under the control of an investment manager would lie exclusively with the investment manager. Labor Reg. §2509.94-2(2) (IB 94-2), 59 Fed. Reg. 38860 (7-29-94).

510. Does ERISA Section 404(a)(1)(d) shield an investment manager from liability for imprudent actions taken in compliance with a statement of investment policy?

No. According to the DOL, acting in accordance with the plan documents does not shield an investment manager from liability for imprudent actions taken in compliance with a statement of investment policy. Even though a trustee may be subject to the directions of a named fiduciary pursuant to ERISA Section 403(a)(1), an investment manager who has authority to make investment decisions is not relieved of its fiduciary responsibility if it followed directions as to specific investment decisions from the named fiduciary or any other person. However, an investment manager who operates under an investment policy is required to comply with the policy, pursuant to ERISA Section 404(a)(1)(D), insofar as the policy's directives or guidelines are consistent with ERISA. If compliance with the guidelines is imprudent, then the investment manager's refusal to follow the guidelines is not a violation of ERISA Section 404(a)(1)(D). Labor Reg. §2509.94-2(2) (IB 94-2), 59 Fed. Reg. 38860 (7-29-94).

511. When will an employer be regulated as an investment advisor?

If an employer is "in the business of providing investment advice," it is subject to the registration requirements and regulation under the Investment Advisors Act of 1940 if it:

1.   Holds itself out to the public as providing investment advice; or

2.   Receives separate or additional compensation from employees or third parties that represents a clearly definable charge for providing investment advice. Letter from Jack W. Murphy, Associate Director of the SEC, to Olena Berg, Assistant Secretary of the Pension and Welfare Benefits Administration, dated December 5, 1995.

If an employer is merely offering various investment options under a defined contribution plan, it will not be considered an investment advisor, unless it is otherwise in the business of providing investment advice.

If any money or other property of an employee benefit plan is invested in securities issued by an investment company registered under the Investment Company Act of 1940, the investment will not by itself cause the investment company or its investment advisor or principal underwriter to be deemed to be a fiduciary or party in interest, except to the extent that the advisor or underwriter acts in connection with an employee benefit plan covering employees of the investment company, of the investment advisor or of the principal underwriter. ERISA Sec. 3(21)(B).

512. May a financial institution include the business of investment management of ERISA covered plan assets under its control in the sales price of a fiduciary?

The Department of Labor (DOL) has strongly cautioned financial firms not to use employee benefit plan assets in negotiating corporate sales. In PWBA News Release 97-82, the DOL stated that it is an abuse of fiduciary duty for a financial institution to hire investment managers and service providers for plans by including the business of managing plans under their control in the sales price of a subsidiary or division.

The news release quotes Assistant Secretary Alan D. Lebowitz as saying, "The department is concerned that other financial institutions may be using their plans to barter for higher purchase prices. There is no gray area under the law. Employers cannot promise prospective buyers that they will get plan business, especially if they stand to profit by reaping a higher price on the sale of an affiliate."

The DOL cautions that financial institutions that include in the sale price of a related subsidiary the business of managing plans under their control could be placing their interest ahead of plans and participants in violation of ERISA Section 404(a)(1) and ERISA Section 406(b)(1).

513. What are "plan assets"?

ERISA defines plan assets in two contexts: plan investments and employee contributions.

Plan Investments

When a plan invests in another entity, the *plan assets* generally include its own investments but do not, solely by reason of such investment, include any of the underlying assets of the entity. However, there is a "look through" rule, that provides that in the case of a plan's investment in an equity interest of an entity that is neither a publicly offered security nor a security issued by an investment company registered under the Investment Company Act of 1940 (i.e., generally mutual funds), that plan's assets will include both the equity interest and an undivided interest in each of the underlying assets of the entity, unless it is established that:

1.   The entity is an operating company; or

2.   Equity participation in the entity by benefit plan investors is not significant. See Labor Reg. §2510.3-101(a).

If the look through rule does apply, any person who exercises authority or control over the management and disposition of the underlying assets, or who provides investment advice with respect to such assets is a fiduciary of the investing plan.

Generally, an investment by a plan in securities of a corporation or partnership will not, solely by reason of such investment, be considered an investment in the underlying assets of the corporation or partnership so as to make the assets of the entity "plan assets." Consequently, a subsequent transaction between the party in interest and the corporation or partnership generally would not constitute a prohibited transaction merely on account of such an investment. See Labor Reg. §2509.75-2(a).

Employee Contributions

Under applicable regulations, plan assets include amounts (other than union dues) that a participant or beneficiary pays to an employer, or amounts that a participant has withheld from his wages by an employer, for contribution to the plan as of the earliest date on which such contributions can reasonably be segregated from the employer's general assets. Labor Reg. §2510.3-102(a). However, in no case may such employee contributions be paid to the plan later than the 15th business day of the month following the month in which the contributions were withheld or received by the employer. Labor Reg. §2510.3-102(b).

NOTE: The 15-day business rule for participant contributions does not apply to welfare benefit plans. Therefore, participant contributions to a welfare benefit plan become plan assets as of the earliest date on which they can reasonably be segregated from the employer's general assets, but in no event later than 90 days from the date on which contributions are received or withheld by the employer. Labor Reg. §2510.3-102(c).

The regulations do not provide any further guidance regarding plan assets. The Department of Labor has stated that in all other issues regarding plan assets, it will apply the rules of property rights for the determination of what constitutes plan assets. Plan assets will generally include any property, tangible or intangible, in which the plan holds a beneficial ownership interest. Beneficial ownership exists where:

1. An employer has established a trust on behalf of the plan;

2. The employer has set up a separate account with a bank or third party in the name of the plan; *and*

3. The plan documents state that separately maintained funds belong to the plan. DOL Adv. Op. 92-24A.

514. When do contributions to SIMPLE plans become plan assets?

The answer depends on whether the plan is a SIMPLE IRA or a SIMPLE 401(k) plan. In the case of SIMPLE IRAs, the Internal Revenue Code states that an employer must make salary reduction contributions to the financial institution maintaining the SIMPLE IRA plan no later than the close of the 30-day period following the last day of the month with respect to which the contributions are to be made. IRC Sec. 408(p)(5)(A)(i). Regulations under ERISA mirror this provision. See Labor Reg. §2510.3-102(b)(2).

The maximum period for holding SIMPLE 401(k) plan salary deferral contributions prior to their becoming plan assets is the same as under traditional 401(k) plans (see Q 513); thus, such amounts become plan assets no later than the 15th business day of the month following the month in which the contributions are received by the employer or would have otherwise been payable to the employee. See Labor Reg. §2510.3-102(b)(1).

515. What are the plan asset rules with respect to insurance company general accounts?

The U.S. Supreme Court has ruled that certain retirement plan assets held in the general accounts of insurance companies are plan assets under the rules of ERISA. See *John Hancock Mut. Life Ins. Co. v. Harris Tr. & Sav. Bank*, 510 U.S. 86 (1993). As such, these assets are subject to the fiduciary and prohibited transaction provisions of ERISA. This ruling contradicted two decades of insurance company practices that had been supported through DOL guidance indicating that the consideration paid by an employee benefit plan for a contract or policy of insurance that is placed into the insurance company's general account was not to be considered plan assets. See IB 75-2; Labor Reg. §2509.75-2.

Insurance company general accounts are assets held by, and commingled with the assets of, an insurance company that are not legally segregated and allocated to separate accounts.

Final regulations issued in January, 2000, clarify the application of the provisions of ERISA to insurance company general accounts. These regulations offer guidelines for determining what percentage of insurance company general account assets may be considered ERISA "plan assets" where the insurer has provided a policy for the benefit of an ERISA covered employee benefit plan that is supported by the insurer's underlying general account. Labor Reg. §2550.401c-1.

The general rule is that when a plan acquires a policy issued by an insurer on or before December 31, 1998 (i.e., a "transition policy"), that is supported by assets of the insurer's general account, the plan's assets include the policy, but do not include any of the underlying assets of the insurer's general account if the insurer satisfies the following general requirements (see Labor Regs. §§2550.401c-1(a)(2), 2550.401c-1(h)(6)(i)):

1.   An independent plan fiduciary with appropriate authority expressly authorizes the purchase of the transition policy;

2.   Certain disclosure requirements detailed under the regulations are satisfied both prior to the issuance of the transition policy and on an annual basis thereafter, including:

     a) a description of the method by which any income, ongoing fees, and expenses of the insurer's general account are allocated to the policy during the term of the policy and upon policy termination,

     b) a report of the actual return to the plan under the policy,

     c) a description of the policyholder's rights to transfer or withdraw amounts credited to any "accumulation fund" established under the policy,

     d) a statement of the method used to calculate any charges, fees credits or market value adjustments that may be imposed with connection to the transfer or withdrawal, and

3.   Mandatory statement language provided for under the regulations is provided for with the disclosure material. Such statements must provide information regarding the difference in risks and legal rights between insurance company general accounts and insurance company separate accounts (which are segregated funds not commingled with the general account).

In general, the provisions of the final regulations were applicable on July 5, 2001; however, the initial annual disclosure requirements (from the insurance company to the independent fiduciary) became effective on January 5, 2000.

516. Must plan documents provide for a written funding policy?

Yes. Every employee benefit plan must provide a procedure for establishing and carrying out a funding policy and a method consistent with the objectives of the plan and the requirements of ERISA. ERISA Sec. 402(b)(1). There has been a great deal of debate as to whether this policy must be in writing, but due to the emphasis the Department of Labor places on plan funding and investment issues, it is strongly recommended that the funding policy be formalized in a written document.

The Conference Committee Report to ERISA states that the procedures relating to funding are to enable plan fiduciaries to determine the plan's long-term and short-term financial needs (growth vs. liquidity) and to use this information in establishing the funding and investment policy for the plan. See H.R. Conf. Rep. No. 93-1280, 93rd Cong., 2nd Sess. (1974) (ERISA Conference Report). As noted in Q 503, the funding and investment policy should take into consideration the composition of the portfolio with regard to diversification and the projected return of the portfolio relative to the funding objectives of the plan (in addition to the liquidity and return characteristics).

The funding policy should also take into consideration:

1. The general investment philosophy and objectives of the plan;

2. Standards for the identification and selection of appropriate investments;

3. Acceptable risk/return ratios;

4. Benchmarks for the measurement of investment performance;

5. The size of the plan; and

6. Appropriate procedures for the monitoring and evaluation of investments.

PRACTITIONER'S POINTER

Plan fiduciaries should periodically review the plan's funding and investment policies to evaluate the necessity of any changes that may be required due to the changing circumstances of the plan as it grows. It is recommended that fiduciaries review the funding and investment policies at least once a year.

517. Are there any restrictions on the types of investments that are permissible for a plan?

ERISA does not mandate any specific investments or investment portfolio for employee benefit plans. The only restrictions on plan investments are the requirements that the investments be prudent, for the exclusive benefit of participants and beneficiaries, and that they not violate the prohibited transaction provisions of ERISA (see Chapters IV and V for details on fiduciary issues and prohibited transactions, respectively). Otherwise, fiduciaries are free to select any investment they deem to be within the funding and investment policies of the plan.

518. Are plan assets required to be held in a trust?

Yes, except as explained in Q 519. ERISA states that all assets of an employee benefit plan shall be held in a trust by one or more trustees. ERISA Sec. 403(a). Such trustees must either be named in the trust instrument or plan document, or appointed by a person who is a named fiduciary. The trustee has the exclusive authority and discretion to manage and control the assets of the plan, except where:

1. The plan expressly provides that the trustee is subject to the direction of a named fiduciary who is not a trustee (in which case the trustee will be subject to the proper directions of the named fiduciary); and

2. Authority to manage, acquire, or dispose of assets has been delegated to one or more investment managers pursuant to ERISA Section 402(c)(3).

The Conference Committee Report to ERISA provides that a plan may allow for an investment committee to manage plan investments. Because investment decisions are basic to plan operations, the members of the investment committee must be named fiduciaries (see Q 504). They may be named by title (President, Vice-President, etc.), which would result in any person holding that position becoming a named fiduciary to the plan. Trustees are obligated to follow the investment committee's recommendations (if the plan permits the appointment of such committee), unless the recommendations are contrary to the terms of the plan document or the provisions of ERISA. See H.R. Conf. Rep. No. 93-1280, 93rd Cong., 2nd Sess. (1974) (ERISA Conference Report).

519. What are the exceptions to the requirement that plan assets be held in a trust?

The requirement that plan assets be held in a trust does not apply to:

1. Any assets that consist of insurance contracts or policies issued by an insurance company qualified to do business in a state;

2. Any assets of such an insurance company or any assets of a plan that are held by the insurer;

3.   A plan in which some or all of the participants are self-employed or that consists of IRAs, to the extent that such plan's assets are held in one or more custodial accounts;

4.   A plan that the Secretary of Labor exempts from the requirement that plan assets be held in a trust, and that is not subject to the participation, vesting, funding and plan termination insurance provisions of ERISA; and

5.   A tax sheltered annuity contract established and maintained under Internal Revenue Code Section 403(b) to the extent that such assets are held in one or more custodial accounts pursuant to Internal Revenue Code Section 403(b)(7). ERISA Sec. 403(b).

The ERISA Conference Committee Report states that although assets consisting of insurance contracts and policies are not required to be held in a trust, any individual who holds these contracts is a fiduciary and must act in accordance with the fiduciary provisions of ERISA. H.R. Conf. Rep. No. 93-1280, 93rd Cong., 2nd Sess. (1974) (ERISA Conference Report). As such, plan assets held by an insurance company are "plan assets" and the insurance company is to be treated as a fiduciary with respect to the plan whose assets it is holding.

The trust requirement will not be violated merely because securities of a plan are held in the name of a nominee or in a street name, provided such securities are held on behalf of the plan by a bank or trust company, a broker-dealer registered under the Securities Exchange Act of 1934, or a clearing agency (as defined in Section 3(a)(23) of the Securities Exchange Act of 1934). Labor Reg. §2550.403a-1(b)(1).

The trust requirement will also be satisfied for any real property held in an IRC Section 501(c)(2) tax exempt corporation on behalf of a plan if the stock of the corporation is held in trust on behalf of the plan. Labor Reg. §2550.403a-1(b)(2).

Finally, if the assets of an entity in which a plan invests (e.g., a partnership) include plan assets by reason of the plan's investment in the entity, the trust requirement will be satisfied with respect to that entity if the indicia of ownership of the plan's interest in the entity are held in trust on behalf of the plan by one or more trustees. Labor Reg. §2550.403a-1(b)(3).

520. May a plan participate in economically targeted investments? What are the asset management issues involved in economically targeted investments?

Yes, under limited circumstances. An economically targeted investment (ETI) is an investment that is selected for the economic benefit it creates, in addition to the investment return to the employee benefit plan investor.

Interpretive Bulletin 94-1 (Labor Regulation §2509.94-1) provides that "ETIs fall within a wide variety of asset categories, including real estate, venture capital and small business investments. Although some of these asset categories may require a longer time to generate significant investment returns, may be less liquid, and may not have as much readily available information on their risk and returns as other asset categories, nothing in ERISA precludes trustees and investment managers from considering ETIs in constructing plan portfolios." The Department of Labor (DOL) believes that while some of these asset categories may require special expertise to evaluate, they may be attractive to sophisticated, long-term investors "including many pension plans." For an explanation of the *fiduciary* issues involved in economically targeted investments, see Q 264.

521. May an employer offer investment advice without incurring fiduciary liability?

Yes, within certain limitations. The Department of Labor has noted that with the growth of participant-directed individual account plans, more employees are directing the investment of their retirement plan assets and thereby assuming more responsibility for ensuring the adequacy of their retirement income. Simultaneously, the DOL has expressed increasing concern that many participants may not have sufficient understanding of investment principles and strategies to make their own informed investment decisions.

An Interpretive Bulletin (IB 96-1, see Q 214) provides final guidance on the provision of investment education for participants who are entitled to direct their own investments in an individual account plan. This guidance sets forth the views of the DOL regarding the circumstances under which the provision of investment related information to participants will not constitute the "rendering of investment advice" under ERISA Section 3(21)(A)(ii). See Labor Reg. §2509.96-1 (IB 96-1).

The regulation establishes a series of graduated safe harbors for plan sponsors and service providers who provide participants and beneficiaries with the following specific categories of investment information and materials:

1.   Investment education (see Q 522);

2.   General financial and investment education (see Q 523);

3.   Asset allocation models (see Q 524); and

4.   Interactive investment materials (see Q 525).

For details as to what constitutes the "rendering of investment advice" see Q 324. See Q 526 regarding other types of information that may be covered under Interpretive Bulletin 96-1.

522. What is the "plan information" safe harbor under Interpretive Bulletin 96-1?

Interpretive Bulletin 96-1 provides a safe harbor for the provision of investment education to participants in an individual account plan by an employer or service provider without such information constituting the "rendering of investment advice" (which results in certain persons, under ERISA Section 3(21)(A)(ii) and Labor Regulation Section 2510.3-21(c), becoming a fiduciary with respect to the plan).

This first of the four safe harbors under Interpretive Bulletin 96-1 states that providing information and materials that inform a participant or beneficiary about the benefits of plan participation, the benefits of increasing plan contributions, the impact of preretirement withdrawals on retirement income, the terms of the plan, or the operation of the plan, that are made without reference to the appropriateness of any individual investment option for a participant or beneficiary will not be considered the rendering of investment advice. Furthermore, the regulation allows for the provision of information regarding investment alternatives, including descriptions of investment objectives, risk and return characteristics, historical performance information, prospectuses and basic asset classes (such as bonds, equities and cash equivalents) of such alternatives. See Labor Reg. §2509.96-1(d)(1).

523. What is the "general financial and investment information" safe harbor under Interpretive Bulletin 96-1?

Interpretive Bulletin 96-1 states that the provision of general financial and investment information by a plan sponsor or service provider will not constitute the rendering of investment advice if the materials inform participants and beneficiaries concerning:

1. General financial and investment concepts, such as risk and return, diversification, dollar cost averaging, compounded return, and tax deferred investments;

2. Historic differences in rates of return between different asset classes (e.g., equities, bonds and cash) based on standard market indices;

3. The effects of inflation;

4. Estimating future retirement income needs;

5. Determining investment time horizons; and

6. Assessing risk tolerance.

This information is considered, under the regulation, to be general financial and investment information that has no direct relationship to investment alternatives available to participants and beneficiaries under a plan. As such, the provision of it is not considered the rendering of investment advice or the making of recommendations to a participant or beneficiary. Labor Reg. §2509.96-1(d)(2).

524. What is the "asset allocation model" safe harbor under Interpretive Bulletin 96-1?

Interpretive Bulletin 96-1 establishes a safe harbor under which the provision of asset allocation models will not be considered the rendering of investment advice or the making of recommendations for purposes of conferring fiduciary status upon the plan sponsor or service provider offering such information. See Labor Reg. §2509.96-1(d)(3).

Under the safe harbor, this applies to information and materials (e.g., pie charts, graphs, or case studies) that provide participants and beneficiaries with models of asset allocation portfolios of hypothetical individuals with different time horizons and risk profiles where:

1. Such models are based on generally accepted investment theories that take into account the historic returns of different asset classes (e.g., equities, bonds, or cash) over defined periods of time;

2. All material facts and assumptions on which such models are based (e.g., retirement ages, life expectancies, income levels, financial resources, replacement income ratios, inflation rates, and rates of return) accompany the models;

3. To the extent that an asset allocation model identifies any specific investment alternative available under the plan, the model is accompanied by a statement that indicates that other investment alternatives with similar risk and return characteristics may be available under the plan, and that identifies where information on those investment alternatives may be obtained; and

4. Such asset allocation models are accompanied by a statement that indicates that, in applying particular asset allocation models to their individual situations, participants or beneficiaries should consider their other assets, income, and investments (e.g., home equity, IRAs, savings accounts and other qualified plan account balances) in addition to their interests in the plan.

The DOL advises, under the regulation, that because the information and materials described above would enable a participant or beneficiary to assess the relevance of an asset allocation model to his individual situation, the furnishing of such information would not be considered the rendering of investment advice or the making of recommendations for the purposes of ERISA Section 3(21)(A)(ii).

525. What is the "interactive investment materials" safe harbor under Interpretive Bulletin 96-1?

Interpretive Bulletin 96-1 establishes an "interactive investment materials" safe harbor under which the provision of questionnaires, worksheets, software and similar materials, which provide a participant or beneficiary the means to estimate future retirement income needs and assess the impact of different asset allocations on retirement income, will not be considered the rendering of investment advice or the making of recommendations, where:

1. Such materials are based on generally accepted investment theories that take into account the historic returns of different asset classes (e.g., equities, bonds, or cash) over defined periods of time;

2. There is an objective correlation between the asset allocations generated by the materials and the information and data supplied by the participant or beneficiary;

3. All material facts and assumptions (e.g., retirement ages, life expectancies, income levels, financial resources, replacement income ratios, inflation rates, and rates of return) that may affect a participant's or beneficiary's assessment of the different asset allocations accompany the materials, or are specified by the participant or beneficiary;

4. To the extent that an asset allocation generated by the material identifies any specific investment alternative available under the plan, the asset allocation is accompanied by a statement indicating that other investment alternatives having similar risk and return characteristics may be available under the plan, and identifying where information on those investment alternatives may be obtained; and

5. The materials either take into account or are accompanied by a statement indicating that, in applying particular asset allocations to their individual situations, participants or beneficiaries should consider their other assets, income, and investments (e.g., home equity, IRAs, savings, and interests in other qualified plans) in addition to their assets under the plan. Labor Reg. §2509.96-1(d)(4).

The information provided through the use of interactive investment materials enables participants and beneficiaries to independently design and assess multiple asset allocation models, but otherwise these materials do not differ from asset allocation models based on hypothetical assumptions. Accordingly, such information does not constitute the rendering of investment advice or the making of recommendations for purposes of ERISA Section 3(21)(A)(ii).

526. Are there any other types of information covered by Interpretive Bulletin 96-1?

In Interpretive Bulletin 96-1, the Department of Labor points out that the information and materials described in the four graduated safe harbors detailed within the bulletin (see Q 522 to Q 525) merely represent examples of the type of information and materials that may be furnished to participants and beneficiaries without such information and materials constituting "investment advice" for purposes of ERISA Section 3(21)(A)(ii).

Further, in IB 96-1, the DOL states that there may be many other examples of information, materials and educational services which, if furnished to participants and beneficiaries, would not constitute the provision of investment advice. Accordingly, the DOL advises, no inferences should be drawn from the four graduated safe harbors with respect to whether the furnishing of any information, materials or educational services not described therein may constitute the provision of investment advice. The DOL cautions that the determination as to whether the provision of any information, materials or educational services not described within IB 96-1 constitutes the rendering of investment advice must be made by reference to the criteria set forth in Labor Regulation 2510.3-21(c)(1). That regulation establishes that a person will be deemed to be rendering "investment advice" to an employee benefit plan, within the meaning of ERISA Section 3(21)(A)(ii), only if:

1. Such person renders advice to the plan as to the value of securities or other property, or makes recommendations as to the advisability of investing in, purchasing, or selling securities or other property; and

2. Such person either directly or indirectly has discretionary authority or control, whether or not pursuant to agreement, arrangement or understanding, with respect to purchasing or selling securities or other property for the plan; or renders any advice described in (1), above, on a regular basis to the plan pursuant to a mutual agreement, arrangement or understanding, written or otherwise, between such person and the plan or a fiduciary with respect to the plan, that such services will serve as a primary basis for investment decisions with respect to plan assets, and that such person will render individualized investment advice to the plan based on the particular needs of the plan regarding such matters as, among other things, investment policies or strategy, overall portfolio composition, or diversification of plan investments.

527. When will the underlying assets of an insurance company issuing group annuity contracts be considered, or not considered, to be plan assets?

The assets of a plan to which a guaranteed benefit policy is issued by an insurer will be deemed to include that policy, but will not, solely by reason of the issuance of the policy, be deemed to include any assets of the insurer. ERISA Sec. 401(b)(2)(B). The term "guaranteed benefit policy" means an insurance company or contract to the extent that such policy or contract provides for benefits the amount of which is guaranteed by the insurer. The Court of Appeals for the Second Circuit has ruled that the insurer is a fiduciary with respect to plan assets invested in a policy that are not guaranteed benefits. See *Harris Tr. & Sav. Bank v. John Hancock Mut. Life Ins. Co.*, 970 F.2d 1138 (2nd Cir. 1992). The court held that the insurer was a plan fiduciary with respect to nonguaranteed benefits even though they are not considered plan assets for purposes of the prohibited transaction provisions of ERISA.

The Department of Labor has stated that if the assets that back a group annuity contract issued to a plan are placed in a separate account that provides for the crediting of income on the group annuity contract based upon the investment performance of the separate account, then the assets of the separate account will be deemed to be plan assets. DOL Adv. Op. 83-51A.

In general, under the *Harris Trust* decision, any group annuity contract that provides for the provision of variable payments will be deemed "not guaranteed," and that variable portion will be considered plan assets that are subject to ERISA's fiduciary provisions.

The American Council on Life Insurance applied to the DOL for a prohibited transaction class exemption retroactively effective to January 1, 1975 that would provide for exemptive relief from the holdings of the *Harris Trust* case. In response to the application, the DOL issued Prohibited Transaction Class Exemption 95-60, which provides relief, prospectively and retroactively, for certain transactions engaged in by insurance company general accounts containing qualified plan asset investments. The exemption also extends relief to transactions relating to the origination and operation of certain asset pool investment trusts in which insurance company general accounts have an interest as a result of the acquisition of certificates issued by the trust. Further, the exemption extends relief to people who provide services to insurance company general accounts. For a detailed review of the retroactive and prospective relief from the holdings of the *Harris Trust* case provided for under PTE 95-60, see Q 393.

The DOL has issued regulations to clarify the application of ERISA to insurance company general accounts. See Q 515.

528. What are the asset management issues regarding investments in derivatives?

The DOL defines "derivatives" as financial instruments whose performance is derived in whole or in part from the performance of an underlying asset (such as a security or index of securities). Examples of these financial instruments include, but are not limited to, futures, options, options on futures, forward contracts, swaps, structured notes and collateralized mortgage obligations. DOL Information Letter to Comptroller of the Currency (March 21, 1996). (See Q 271 for details regarding fiduciary obligations when investing plan assets into derivatives.)

According to the DOL, investments in derivatives are subject to the fiduciary responsibility rules in the same manner as are any other plan investments. In determining whether to invest in a particular derivative, plan fiduciaries must engage in the same general procedures and undertake the same type of analysis that is made in any other investment decision. This includes, but is not limited to, considering how the derivative fits within the plan's investment policy, the role the particular derivative plays in the plan's portfolio, and the plan's potential exposure to losses. See DOL Information Letter, above; see also Q 271.

In the view of the DOL, derivatives may be a useful tool for managing a variety of risks and for broadening investment alternatives in a plan's portfolio. However, investments in certain derivatives, such as structured notes and collateralized mortgage obligations, may require a higher degree of sophistication and understanding on the part of plan fiduciaries than other investments. Characteristics of such derivatives may include extreme price volatility, a high degree of leverage, limited testing by markets, and difficulty in determining the market value of the derivative due to illiquid market conditions. Thus, it is possible the DOL may hold fiduciaries who invest in high risk derivatives to a higher standard of fiduciary responsibility than that established under the "prudent person" rule.

The DOL also explained that plan fiduciaries who invest in derivatives must secure sufficient information to understand the investment prior to making the investment. For example, plan fiduciaries must secure sufficient information to allow an independent analysis of the credit risk and market risk being undertaken by the plan in making the investment in the particular derivative. The market risks presented by the purchased derivatives must be understood and evaluated in terms of the effects that they will have on the relevant segments of the plan's portfolio as well as the portfolio's overall risk. See DOL Information Letter, above.

Likewise, plan fiduciaries have a duty to determine the appropriate methodology used to evaluate market risk and the information needed to do so. Among other things, this includes stress simulation models showing the projected performance of the derivatives in the plan's portfolio under various market conditions. The DOL believes that stress simulations are particularly important because assumptions that may be valid for normal markets may not be valid in abnormal markets, resulting in significant losses. To the extent that there may be little pricing information available with respect to some derivatives, reliable price comparisons may be necessary. In addition, after purchasing a derivative, a plan fiduciary must obtain timely information from the derivatives dealer regarding the plan's credit exposure and the current market value of its derivatives positions, and, where appropriate, obtain this information from third parties to determine the current market value of the plan's derivatives positions with a frequency that is appropriate to the nature and extent of these positions. If the plan invests in a pooled fund that is managed by a party other than the plan fiduciary, then that plan fiduciary must obtain, among other things, sufficient information to determine the pooled fund's strategy with respect to use of derivatives in its portfolio, the extent of investment by the fund in derivatives, and any other information that is appropriate under the circumstances. See DOL Information Letter, above.

In addition, the DOL believes that a fiduciary must analyze the operational risks being undertaken in selecting a derivative as part of its evaluation of the investment. Among other things, the DOL believes that the fiduciary must determine whether it possesses the necessary expertise, knowledge, and information to understand and analyze the nature of the risks and potential returns involved in a particular derivative investment. In particular, the fiduciary must determine whether the plan has adequate information and risk management systems in place given the nature, size and complexity of the plan's derivatives activity, and whether the plan fiduciary has personnel who are competent to manage these systems. If the investments are made by outside investment managers hired by the plan fiduciary, that fiduciary must consider whether the investment managers have sufficient personnel and controls and whether the plan fiduciary has personnel who are competent to monitor the derivatives activities of the investment managers. See DOL Information Letter, above.

Plan fiduciaries also have a duty to evaluate the legal risk related to the investment. In the DOL's view, this includes assuring proper documentation of the derivative transaction and, where the transaction is pursuant to a contract, assuring written documentation of the contract before entering into the contract. Also, as with any other investment, plan fiduciaries must properly monitor their investments in derivatives to determine whether they are still appropriately fulfilling their role in the portfolio. The frequency and degree of the monitoring depends on the nature of the derivatives and their role in the plan's portfolio. See DOL Information Letter, above.

529. Is the cash asset value of a split dollar life insurance policy considered a plan asset?

Split dollar life insurance generally refers to a variety of arrangements between an employer and employees where interests in, and proceeds payable under, a whole life insurance policy are split, and the obligation to pay premiums may be split.

The Department of Labor has advised that the cash value portion of a welfare plan's split dollar life insurance policy that provides life insurance coverage for employees (with premiums paid for by the employees on a voluntary basis through payroll deduction while actively employed, and through direct payment to the carrier after separation from service) and a separate cash value portion providing benefits to the employer and paid for on a discretionary basis by the employer, would not be a plan asset for purposes of Title I of ERISA. DOL Adv. Op. 92-22A.

The DOL stated that, the use of a split dollar policy as described above does not, in itself, appear to violate ERISA Section 406(a)(1)(D) (the prohibition against the use of plan assets for the benefit of a party in interest) because the use of the insurance policy to fund the cash value death benefit does not provide any direct or indirect benefit to the employer.

In closing, the DOL stated that a plan fiduciary may, under appropriate facts and circumstances, provide benefits under a death benefit plan through a life insurance policy whose cash value element belongs exclusively to the sponsoring employer, without violating requirements that the selection and retention of the policy be prudent and made solely in the interests of participants and beneficiaries. However, the DOL continued, if a split dollar life insurance policy were selected to fund a death benefit without due regard to both the cost to the plan of the pure insurance and the financial soundness and claims-paying ability of the insurer, or if such a policy were acquired for the benefit of the employer, this would not meet the fiduciary standards of ERISA Section 404.

530. May plans engage in securities lending arrangements utilizing plan assets?

Yes, but fiduciaries must be cautious that such ventures do not violate the prohibited transaction provisions regarding parties in interest. Securities lending involves the lending of securities to broker-dealers, investment managers, banks, or financial institutions for the purpose of assisting the borrower in covering "short" positions. A "short sale" is an investment practice where the borrower believes the market for a particular stock will go down in the near future. Thus, the borrower sells stock that has been borrowed and holds the proceeds of the sale to purchase an equivalent number of the same shares at the future, lower price. The borrower gets to retain the difference in the sale and purchase price that has been realized due to a drop in the market price of the stock, less any interest on the that is repaid along with delivery of the borrowed stock.

Securities lending is also a common practice for assistance in covering positions where delivery of promised stock has been delayed, as well as to assist in limited arbitrage situations.

In the absence of an exemption, it would be a prohibited transaction for an ERISA covered plan to engage in the lending of securities to a financial institution, investment manager, bank or broker-dealer that is a party in interest to the plan. Fortunately, the Department of Labor has issued Prohibited Transaction Exemption (PTE) 81-6, which permits the lending of securities by a plan to domestic parties in interest that are:

1. Broker-dealers registered under the Securities Exchange Act of 1934;

2. A dealer in government securities who is exempt from the Securities Exchange Act of 1934; or

3. A bank.

This exemptive relief applies only if all of the requirements detailed in the exemption are satisfied. For a detailed review of the lending and collateral requirements of PTE 81-6, see Q 388.

531. May plans engage in repurchase agreements utilizing plan assets?

A repurchase agreement involving a retirement plan is a method utilized by securities dealers to raise cash. These arrangements involve finding a plan to act as a temporary buyer for securities and simultaneously executing a contract with the securities dealer to sell back the securities at a later date at a predetermined price, plus interest (in effect, these are fully collateralized loans). As with securities lending arrangements, plan fiduciaries must exercise caution when entering into repurchase agreements with parties in interest, as they may be prohibited transactions.

The Department of Labor has issued Prohibited Transaction Exemption (PTE) 81-8, which provides exemptive relief for repurchase agreements where the securities are sold to the plan by a party in interest under a written agreement to sell them back to the party in interest at a later date for a predetermined price, provided that the requirements spelled out under the exemption are satisfied. Parties in interest who may enter into such repurchase agreements with a plan are:

1. Broker-dealers registered under the Securities Exchange Act of 1934;

2. A bank supervised by the United States or a State thereof; or

3. A government securities dealer who has complied with specific requirements detailed under the exemption.

For a detailed review of the permissible parties, permissible securities, collateral and other required elements to be satisfied for such exemptive relief, see PTE 81-8.

Other types of repurchase agreements may be structured as securities lending arrangements (see Q 530 and Q 388), transactions involving bank collective trust funds (see the explanation of PTE 91-38 in Q 382), and those involving insurance company pooled separate accounts (see the explanation of PTE 90-1 in Q 370).

A reverse repurchase agreement involves a dealer agreeing to buy securities from a plan and then selling them back to the plan later at a higher price. Although there is exemptive relief for plans entering into repurchase agreements, there is no class exemption available for plans that enter into reverse repurchase agreements with parties in interest.

532. May plans enter into "soft dollar" and directed commission arrangements?

"Soft dollar" and directed commission arrangements typically involve situations in which an investment manager purchases goods or services with a portion of the brokerage commissions paid by the investor to a broker for executing a securities transaction. Soft dollar and directed commission arrangements with ERISA covered plans involve the payment of a portion of brokerage fees involved in transactions with plan assets to a broker for the provision of goods or services, in addition to the basic execution of the underlying transaction. Soft dollar arrangements benefit retirement plans by allowing them access to investment research that they may not otherwise be able to afford if they were required to pay for them with "hard" dollars.

In ERISA Technical Release 86-1, the Department of Labor set forth its policies regarding soft dollar and directed commission arrangements under the limited safe harbor of Section 28(e) of the Securities Exchange Act of 1934 (i.e., "the 1934 Act"). In 1975 Congress added Section 28(e) to the 1934 Act, eliminating the fixed commission rates on stock exchange transactions. Prior to the elimination of fixed commission rates, investment managers often purchased additional services with commission dollars beyond simple execution, clearance and settlement of securities transactions. Section 28(e) of the 1934 Act provides a limited safe harbor from ERISA's fiduciary responsibility rules. It provides that no person who exercises investment discretion with respect to securities transactions will be deemed to have acted unlawfully or to have breached a fiduciary duty solely by reason of paying brokerage commissions for effecting a securities transaction in excess of the amount of the commission another broker-dealer would have charged, if such person determined in good faith that the commission was reasonable in relation to the value of brokerage and research services provided by the broker-dealer. In addition to these requirements, the DOL permits plans to enter into soft dollar arrangements where the plan has received "best execution" of the transactions.

"Best execution" is defined as a money manager executing transactions in such a manner that the investor's total cost or proceeds in each transaction is the most favorable under the circumstances. Securities and Exchange Act Release No. 34-23170 (April 23, 1986). This Release further advises that the investment manager should take into consideration the full range and quality of the broker's services in placing brokerage transactions including, among other things, the value of the research provided as well as execution capability, commission rate, financial responsibility, and responsiveness to the investment manager. Obviously, "best execution" does not always mean the lowest commission fees; the investment manager must make an evaluation of the relevant facts of each transaction to determine what constitutes "best execution."

In addition to the relief from the general fiduciary provisions, the safe harbor provides relief from the prohibited transaction provisions of: ERISA Section 406(a)(1)(D) (restricting the transfer to, or use by or for the benefit of, a party in interest of any of the assets of the plan); ERISA Section 406(b)(1) (restricting the use of plan assets by a fiduciary in his own interest or for his own account); and ERISA Section 406(b)(3) (prohibiting the receipt by a fiduciary of any consideration for his own account from any party involved in a transaction involving plan assets).

The DOL points out that the Securities and Exchange Commission has ruled that the limited safe harbor provided by Section 28(e) is available only for the provision of brokerage and research services to persons who exercise investment discretion with respect to an account. The investment manager with discretion is still required to act prudently both with respect to a decision to buy or sell securities as well as with respect to the decision as to who will execute the transaction. The named fiduciary to the plan retains the fiduciary obligation for the oversight responsibility of periodically reviewing the investment manager's performance.

533. May plans enter into "soft dollar" and directed commission arrangements where the plan sponsor has directed brokerage transactions?

Yes, the Department of Labor has established in Technical Release 86-1, that plan sponsors may direct brokerage transactions or direct them to specific broker-dealers where the plan trustees have determined that the broker-dealer is able to provide the plan "best execution" (see Q 532) for the brokerage transactions. Trustees are also responsible for the monitoring of services provided by the broker-dealer so as to assure that the best execution has occurred and that the commissions paid are reasonable in relation to the value of the brokerage and other services received by the plan.

The DOL has stated that where a plan sponsor or other plan fiduciary directs the investment manager to execute securities trades for the plan through one or more specified broker-dealers, the direction generally requires the investment manager to execute a specified percentage of the plan's trades or a specified amount of the plan's commission business through the particular broker-dealers, consistent with the investment manager's duty to secure best execution for the transactions. The DOL also advises that the plan sponsor's decision to direct brokerage transactions must be made prudently and solely in the interest of the participants and beneficiaries.

However, the DOL advises that the Securities and Exchange Commission has indicated that the limited safe harbor of Section 28(e) is not available for directed brokerage transactions (as defined under Section VI of Securities

Exchange Act Release No. 34-23170, April 23, 1986) where plan sponsors who do not have investment discretion with respect to a plan direct the plan's securities trades to one or more broker-dealers in return for research, performance evaluation, other administrative services or discounted commissions.

534. What types of "soft dollar" and directed commission arrangements fall outside of Technical Release 86-1 and the limited safe harbor?

In ERISA Technical Release 86-1, the Department of Labor states that there are several types of "soft dollar" and directed commission arrangements that do not qualify for the limited safe harbor established under Section 28(e) of the Securities Exchange Act of 1934. The Securities and Exchange Commission has indicated that if a plan fiduciary does not exercise investment discretion with respect to a securities transaction, or uses "soft dollars" to pay for non-research related services, the transaction falls outside of the protection afforded by the limited safe harbor and may be in violation of the securities laws and the fiduciary responsibility provisions of ERISA.

Some examples of improper transactions cited by the DOL include the use of a percentage of brokerage commissions by investment managers or plan sponsors to pay for travel, hotel rooms and other goods and services that do not qualify as research within the meaning of the limited safe harbor. Such prohibited services would include the provision of bookkeeping services for the benefit of an investment manager from a broker-dealer who has directed plan brokerage transactions through the broker-dealer. Another example would be the provision of tax-exempt securities research services to an investment manager from a broker-dealer in exchange for the execution of plan related brokerage transactions.

In consideration of such transactions, Technical Release 86-1 states that "soft dollar" and directed commission arrangements must take the prohibited transaction provisions of ERISA into account. A fiduciary is generally prohibited from causing the plan to engage in a transaction in which he has an interest that may affect his best judgment as a fiduciary. See ERISA Sec. 406(b)(1). The Release cites as an example that an employer who is the named fiduciary and who does not exercise investment discretion would normally be prohibited from directing the plan's brokerage transactions through a designated broker-dealer who agrees to utilize a portion of the brokerage commissions received from the plan to procure goods or services for the benefit of the plan sponsor.

535. Does the limited safe harbor for "soft dollar" arrangements apply to recapture provisions?

A recapture arrangement involves the rebating of commissions from a broker-dealer to one of the parties involved in the brokerage transaction. These arrangements may be permissible under Technical Release 86-1 if the plan is the party receiving the recaptured commissions, and all other fiduciary and prohibited transaction provisions have been satisfied (see Q 532 to Q 534 for details). An improper fiduciary interest in a recapture arrangement that will result in a prohibited transaction is the direction of brokerage transactions through a broker-dealer who, in turn, rebates a portion of the commissions to the employer or trustee to reduce his fees.

536. Are there any proposed changes regarding the rules on "soft dollar" and commission recapture arrangements?

In December, 1997, the Department of Labor's ERISA Advisory Council Working Group on Soft Dollars and Commission Recapture (i.e., "the Advisory Council") issued its final report. The Advisory Council is a statutorily mandated aggregation of employee benefit plan professionals, including representatives from private sponsors, governmental plan sponsors and the financial services industry, who issue reports and recommendations to the Department of Labor.

The Advisory Council reviewed current industry practices on soft dollar arrangements and applicable ERISA regulations in an effort to determine whether employee benefit plan sponsors and other plan fiduciaries are being provided sufficient disclosure to allow them to adequately protect plan assets. In its report, the Advisory Council reviewed all of the written and oral testimony it had received throughout 1997. That report contains the following recommendations to the Department of Labor, the Securities and Exchange Commission (SEC) and the employee benefits plan industry as a whole:

1.   To the Department of Labor the following recommendations were made:

    a) modify Annual Report Form 5500 so that it requires all plan sponsors to detail all fees greater than $5,000 paid under directed brokerage arrangements, and

    b) list an additional question to the Annual Report Form 5500 that requires plan sponsors to certify compliance with the requirements of ERISA Technical Release 86-1 regarding directed brokerage programs.

2.   To the Securities and Exchange Commission the following recommendations were made:

    a) apply a more stringent definition of the term "research" to Section 28(e) of the Securities Exchange Act of 1934,

    b) establish a detailed list that specifies those brokerage and research services that may be purchased under a soft dollar or directed commission arrangement,

c) require investment managers to disclose to each client the investment manager's soft dollar policies, all transactions executed for the client in which soft dollars were involved, and details of the benefits received by the investment manager from the soft dollar arrangement, and

d) establish a requirement that investment managers disclose, on their Form ADV, any external research received.

To the employee benefits plan industry the Advisory Council recommended further efforts to educate plan sponsors on the legal requirements and industry practices of soft dollar and directed brokerage arrangements. Further recommendations include 10 guidelines for education efforts on industry practices and appropriate conduct regarding soft dollar and directed brokerage arrangements.

The report issued to the Department of Labor by the Advisory Council also included minority positions, which recommended the repeal of Section 28(e) of the Securities Exchange Act of 1934 as it applies to employee benefit plans (which would eliminate the research safe harbor; see Q 532), and the "unbundling" of services by brokerage firms, which would eliminate the use of soft dollars for employee benefit plans. This final minority recommendation would also require investment managers to pay separately for execution and investment research with "hard dollars."

In October 1998, the SEC released the results of its examination of soft dollar commission practices of the investment advisory and broker-dealer industries. The SEC advised that inadequate disclosure of soft dollar practices is prevalent. This inadequacy was cited in that the general level of disclosure fails to provide adequate information to enable clients to understand the advisors' soft dollar practices and policies. The SEC states that advisors and plan sponsors may violate the exclusive purpose provisions of ERISA Sections 403(c)(1) and 404(a)(1) where soft dollar or directed brokerage benefits are not received by the benefit plan account whose transactions generated the benefits. The full text of the SEC's report is available on the internet at: www.sec.gov/news/studies/softdolr.htm.

537. What are "qualifying employer securities"?

A "qualifying employer security" is defined as an employer security that is (a) stock, (b) a marketable obligation or (c) an interest in a publicly traded partnership (as described under Internal Revenue Code Section 7704(b)) that is issued by an employer of employees covered by a plan or an affiliate of such employer. ERISA Secs. 407(d)(1), 407(d)(5). After December 17, 1987, a stock or an interest in a publicly traded partnership is a "qualifying employer security" only if, immediately following the acquisition of such stock:

1. No more than 25% of the aggregate amount of stock of the same class issued and outstanding at the time of the acquisition is held by the plan; and

2. At least 50% of the aggregate amount referred to in (a) is held by persons independent of the issuer. ERISA Secs. 407(d)(5), 407(f)(1).

Qualifying employer securities may also include "marketable obligations" that are bonds, debentures, notes or certificates, or other evidence of indebtedness if:

1. The obligation is acquired:

   a) on the market, either (i) at the price of the obligation prevailing on a national securities exchange that is registered with the SEC, or (ii) if the obligation is not traded on a national securities exchange, at a price not less favorable to the plan than the offering price for the obligation as established by current bid and asked prices quoted by persons independent of the issuer,

   b) from an underwriter, at a price (a) not in excess of the public offering price for the obligation as set forth in a prospectus or offering circular filed with the SEC, and (b) at which a substantial portion of the same issue is acquired by persons independent of the issuer, or

   c) directly from the issuer, at a price not less favorable to the plan than the price paid currently for a substantial portion of the same issue by persons independent of the issuer; and

2. Immediately following the acquisition:

   a) not more than 25% of the aggregate amount of obligations issued in such issue and outstanding at the time of acquisition is held by the plan, and

   b) at least 50% of the aggregate amount outstanding is held by persons independent of the issuer; and

3. Immediately following acquisition of the obligation, not more than 25% of the assets of the plan are invested in obligations of the employer or an affiliate of the employer. ERISA Sec. 407(e).

538. What is "qualifying employer real property"?

"Employer real property" is real property (and related personal property) that is leased to an employer of employees covered by a plan, or to an affiliate of such employer. ERISA Sec. 407(d)(2) "Qualifying employer real property" is defined as parcels of employer real property:

1. Where a substantial number of the parcels are dispersed geographically;

2. Where each parcel of real property and the improvements thereon are suitable (or adaptable without excessive cost) for more than one use;

3. Even if all such real property is leased to one lessee (which may be an employer, or an affiliate of an employer); and

4. Where the acquisition and retention of such property comply with the fiduciary provisions of ERISA (except for the diversification and prohibited transaction provisions of ERISA Section 404(a)(1)(C) and ERISA Section 406). ERISA Sec. 407(d)(4).

539. What rules apply to the acquisition and holding of employer securities and employer real property?

The general rule is that a plan may not acquire or hold any employer security that is not a qualifying employer security (see Q 537) or any employer real property that is not qualifying employer real property (see Q 538). ERISA Sec. 407(a). Furthermore, a plan may not hold or acquire qualifying employer securities or qualifying employer real property if immediately after such acquisition, the fair market value of employer securities and employer real property held by the plan exceeds 10% of the fair market value of the assets of the plan. ERISA Sec. 407(a)(2).

"Eligible individual account plans" may invest in qualifying employer securities and qualifying employer real property, provided that the plan explicitly provides for acquisition and holding of qualifying employer securities and qualifying employer real property. ERISA Sec. 407(d)(3)(B). Eligible individual account plans include profit sharing, stock bonus, thrift, and savings plans, as well as employee stock ownership plans (see Q 540 through Q 552 for a review of the special rules and restrictions that are applicable to ESOPs). Pre-ERISA money purchase plans, which invested primarily in employer securities prior to the enactment of ERISA, are also included in the definition of eligible individual account plans. ERISA Sec. 407(d)(3)(A). Eligible individual account plans are not subject to the 10% restriction on the holding of qualifying employer securities or qualifying employer real property. ERISA Sec. 407(b)(1). Finally, the 25%/50% restriction of ERISA Section 407(f)(1)(A) and ERISA Section 407(f)(1)(B) (see Q 537 for details) does not apply to eligible individual account plans with respect to their investments in qualifying employer securities.

Section 401(k) plans are restricted from mandating that employees place more than 10% of their plan funds in company stock or employer real property. ERISA Sec. 407(b)(2)(A). (See Q 296 for details of this provision.) Participants in Section 401(k) plans that permit investments into qualifying employer securities or qualifying employer real property may elect, of their own volition, to place more than 10% of their plan assets in such qualifying employer investment vehicles.

540. What is an employee stock ownership plan (ESOP)?

An "employee stock ownership plan" is an individual account plan (Section 401(k), profit sharing or money purchase) that is a stock bonus plan or a stock bonus plan and money purchase plan, which is qualified under Internal Revenue Code Section 401(a), is designed to invest primarily in qualifying employer securities, and that satisfies the requirements regarding ESOPs provided for under the Internal Revenue Code and regulations thereunder. ERISA Sec. 407(d)(6). A provision requiring that more than 50% of plan assets be invested in employer stock satisfies the requirement that the plan "be designed to invest primarily in employer securities." ESOPs may require that 100% of the assets in the plan be invested in qualifying employer securities. DOL Adv. Op. 83-6A.

ESOPs are designed to invest primarily in employer stock, and may borrow the funds necessary to purchase such stock from a bank, the plan sponsor or its shareholders (creating a "leveraged ESOP"; see Q 541, Q 543 and Q 552 for details). Employer stock purchased by the ESOP is held in trust for the participants, and is distributed to them after their employment with the plan sponsor ends and they cease to be active participants in the plan. Employer stock acquired by an ESOP can never revert to the employer.

Because an ESOP is a qualified plan, annual contributions to it by the plan sponsor are generally tax deductible, subject to the 25% limitation under IRC Section 404(a)(3)(A), as amended by EGTRRA 2001. In the case of a leveraged C corporation ESOP, the deductible limit is also 25% to the extent of ESOP contributions used to repay principal of a loan incurred to acquire employer securities. Furthermore, contributions applied by the plan to the repayment of interest on a loan used to acquire employer securities may be deducted without limit. IRC Sec. 404(a)(9). The plan sponsor is also permitted to make additional annual contributions of cash or stock to the ESOP. These additional contributions are also tax deductible if they satisfy the limitation requirements imposed by IRC Section 404(a)(3)(A), as amended by EGTRRA 2001. Finally, limited carry-forward rules permit unused deductions for those years where the employer contributes less than the 25% limit to be carried forward into subsequent plan years.

All cash and employer stock contributed to or purchased by an ESOP is allocated on an annual basis to the individual accounts of the participants. Securities purchased by a leveraged ESOP are held in a suspense account and are allocated as the loan is paid off.

541. What is the difference between a stock bonus plan and a leveraged ESOP?

An employee stock ownership plan (ESOP) is a stock bonus plan or a combination of a stock bonus and a money purchase plan qualified under Internal Revenue Code Section 401(a) and designed to invest primarily in qualifying employer securities. ERISA Sec. 407(d)(6); IRC Sec. 4975(e)(7), as amended by EGTRRA 2001. A stock bonus plan is one that "is established and maintained by an employer to provide benefits similar to those of a profit sharing plan, except that the contributions by the employer are not necessarily dependent upon profits and the benefits are distributable in stock of the employer company." Treas. Reg. §1.401-1(b)(1)(iii).

A leveraged ESOP is used primarily as a financing vehicle for the plan sponsor. Generally, the plan sponsor will direct the ESOP to borrow money to purchase qualifying employer securities from the plan sponsor or outstanding shareholders. See IRC Secs. 4975(d)(3), 4975(e)(7), as amended by EGTRRA 2001. The ESOP then repays the loan using tax deductible cash contributions made by the plan sponsor. These contributions are traditionally mandated at a fixed rate (similar to the mandatory funding requirements of a money purchase plan). As the stock loan is paid off, the shares purchased with the proceeds from the loan are released from a suspense account and allocated to the individual participant accounts.

See Q 543 for details on the loan requirements for an ESOP, and Q 552 regarding the fiduciary issues involved in the management of a leveraged ESOP.

542. May an ESOP be maintained by an S corporation?

An ESOP (a qualified plan trust) may be a shareholder of an S corporation. IRC Sec. 1361(a). Furthermore, ESOPs that are established and maintained by S corporations do not need to provide participants the right to demand their distributions in the form of employer securities if the plan permits them the right to receive distributions in cash. IRC Sec. 409(h)(2)(B).

S corporation sponsored ESOPs are also exempt from the prohibited transaction restriction that forbids the sale of employer securities to an ESOP by certain parties (i.e., a shareholder employee, family member of a shareholder employee, or corporation in which the shareholder employee owns at least 50% of the stock). IRC Sec. 4975(f)(6)(B), as amended by EGTRRA 2001.

S Corporation sponsored ESOPs have a series of new restrictions designed to limit the application of them to S corporations that will offer them to rank and file employees in addition to the highly compensated employees. Where there is a non-allocation year in an S corporation ESOP (the plan holds employer securities of an S corporation, and disqualified persons hold at least 50% of the number of shares in the S corporation), three penalty provisions apply:

1. Any amount allocated to a disqualified person in a prohibited allocation (any allocation under the plan to a disqualified person in a non-allocation year), is treated as a distribution in that year to the disqualified person, so, the value of such allocation must be included in the disqualified person's income;

2. The S corporation involved in the prohibited allocation will be subject to a 50% excise tax on the amount of the prohibited allocation; and

3. The S corporation will also be subject to a 50% excise tax on the value of any "synthetic equity" owned by a disqualified person. IRC Section 409(p), as added by Title VI, Subtitle E, Section 656 of EGTRRA (H.R. 1836).

A "synthetic equity" means any stock option, warrant, restricted stock, deferred issuance stock right, or similar interest or right that gives the holder the right to acquire or receive stock of the S corporation in the future. Synthetic equity also includes a stock appreciation right, phantom stock unit, or similar right to a future cash payment based on the value of such stock or appreciation in such value. Title VI, Subtitle E, Section 656(a)(6)(C) of EGTRRA.

These new penalty provisions go into effect for plan years beginning after December 31, 2004. However, in the case of an S corporation ESOP established after March 14, 2001, or an ESOP established on, or before March 14, 2001 if employer securities held by the plan consist of stock in a corporation for which an "S" election was not in effect on that date, these rules apply to plan years ending after March 14, 2001. Title VI, Subtitle E, Section 656(d) of EGTRRA.

543. What are the requirements of an "exempt loan" used for the purchase of qualifying employer securities by an ESOP?

The prohibited transaction provisions of ERISA Section 406 and the restrictions on the holding of qualified employer securities found under ERISA Section 407 do not apply to the acquisition and sale by a plan of qualifying employer securities by an ESOP, if such acquisition is in exchange for adequate consideration (see below) and no commission is charged for the transaction. ERISA Sec. 408(e). An ESOP may use the proceeds of a loan from a party in interest for the acquisition of qualifying employer securities if certain regulatory provisions have been satisfied in the making of the loan. Labor Reg. §2550.408b-3.

Adequate Consideration: Adequate consideration is defined under ERISA Section 3(18). If there is a generally recognized market for employer stock, adequate consideration is the price prevailing on a national securities exchange that is registered under Section 6 of the Securities Exchange Act of 1934 (if applicable), or the offering price for the security as established by the current bid and ask prices quoted by persons independent of the issuer and party in interest. In the case of a security for which there is no generally recognized market (e.g., closely held stock), the fair market value of the asset is as determined in good faith by the trustee or named fiduciary pursuant to the terms of the plan, in accordance with generally accepted methods of valuing closely held stock, and in accordance with the regulations provided under ERISA. Where there is no generally recognized market for employer stock, it is very important that a valuation be conducted by an independent appraiser who will apply objective standards of conduct, and who is experienced in the valuation of closely held corporations, in order to establish the adequate consideration to be paid by the ESOP. Prop. Labor Reg. §2510.3-18.

Exclusive Benefit Requirement: Exempt loans for the purchase of qualifying employer securities by an ESOP must be for the primary benefit of ESOP participants and their beneficiaries. Labor Reg. §2550.408b-3; see also IRC Sec. 4975(d)(3); Treas. Reg. §54.4975-7(b)(3)(I). All surrounding facts and circumstances will be considered in determining whether such a loan satisfies this requirement. At the time the loan is made, the interest rate for the loan and the price of the securities to be acquired should not be such that the plan assets might be drained off. Treas. Reg. §54.4975-7(b)(3)(ii).

At the time the loan is made, the terms of an exempt loan to an ESOP must be at least as favorable to the ESOP as a comparable loan resulting from arm's-length negotiations between independent parties, whether or not the loan is between independent parties. IRC Sec. 4975(d)(3); Treas. Reg. §54.4975-7(b)(3)(iii); Labor Reg. §2550.408b-3(c)(3).

Use of Exempt Loan Proceeds: The proceeds of an exempt loan must be used, within a reasonable time after their receipt, only for any, or all, of the following purposes:

1.   To acquire qualifying employer securities;

2.   To repay such loan; and

3.   To repay a prior exempt loan (a new loan, the proceeds of which are so used, must satisfy these requirements). Labor Reg. §2550.408b-3(d).

Reasonable Rate of Interest: The interest rate of an exempt loan must not be in excess of a reasonable rate of interest. All relevant factors will be considered in determining a reasonable rate of interest, including the amount and duration of the loan, the security and guarantee involved (if any), the credit standing of the ESOP and the guarantor (if any), and the interest rate prevailing for comparable loans. When these factors are considered, a variable interest rate may be reasonable. IRC Sec. 4975(d)(3); Labor Reg. §2550.408b-3(g).

Collateral Restrictions: An exempt loan must be without recourse against the ESOP. The only assets of the ESOP that may be given as collateral on an exempt loan are qualifying employer securities of two classes:

1.   Those acquired with the proceeds of the exempt loan; and

2.   Those that were used as collateral on a prior exempt loan repaid with the proceeds of the current exempt loan. Labor Reg. §2550.408b-3(e).

No person entitled to payment under an exempt loan may have any right to assets of the ESOP other than collateral for the loan, contributions made under an ESOP to meet its obligations under the loan, and earnings attributable to such collateral and the investment of such contributions. Labor Regs. §§2550.408b-3(e)(1), 2550.408b-3(e)(2), 2550.408b-3(e)(3).

Suspense Account Requirement: Employer securities purchased with the proceeds of an exempt loan must be maintained in a suspense account. Treas. Reg. §54.4975-11(c). As the exempt loan is repaid, the shares held in the suspense account are released and allocated to participants in accordance with the Treasury regulations. Treas. Regs. §§54.4975-7(b)(8), 54.4975-7(b)(15).

The payments made on an exempt loan during a plan year must not exceed an amount equal to the sum of such contributions and earnings received during or prior to the year less such payments in prior years. These earnings and contributions must be accounted for separately in the books of account of the ESOP until the loan is repaid. An exempt loan must provide for the release from encumbrance of plan assets used as collateral. For each plan year during the duration of the loan, the number of securities released must equal the number of encumbered securities held immediately before release for the current plan year multiplied by a fraction. The numerator of the fraction is the amount of principal and interest paid for the year. The denominator of the fraction is the sum of the numerator plus the principal and interest to be paid for all future years (which must be definitely ascertainable without taking into account possible extension or renewal periods). Labor Reg. §2550.408b-3(h).

PRACTITIONER'S POINTER

Contributions used by an ESOP to pay the loan are treated as annual additions to participants' accounts and are subject to the Internal Revenue Code Section 415 limits on account contributions. Further, the release of shares from encumbrance in annually varying numbers may reflect a failure on the part of the employer to make substantial and recurring contributions to the ESOP, which may lead to the loss of plan qualification under IRC Section 401(a). The IRS will observe closely the operation of ESOPs that release encumbered securities in varying annual amounts, particularly those that provide for the deferral of loan payments or for balloon payments. Labor Reg. §2550.408b-3; Treas. Reg. §54.4975-7(b)(8)(iii).

Default: In the event of a default, the value of plan assets transferred in satisfaction of the loan must not exceed the amount of the default. Treas. Reg. §54.4975-7(b)(6). If the lender is a party in interest, a loan must provide for a transfer of plan assets upon default only upon and to the extent of the failure of the plan to meet the payment schedule of the loan. Treas. Reg. §54.4975-7(b)(6); Labor Reg. §2550.408b-3(f).

Scope of the exemption: The scope of the exemption includes the prohibited transaction provisions of ERISA Section 406(a) and ERISA Section 406(b)(1) (relating to fiduciaries dealing with assets in their own interest or for their own account) and ERISA Section 406(b)(2) (relating to fiduciaries in their individual or in any other capacity acting in any transaction involving the plan on behalf of a party whose interests are adverse to the interests of its participants or beneficiaries). ERISA Section 403(b)(3) does not provide an exemption from the prohibitions of ERISA Section 406(b)(3) (relating to fiduciaries receiving consideration for their own personal account from any party dealing with a plan in connection with a transaction involving the income or assets of the plan). Labor Reg. §2550.408b-3(b).

PRACTITIONER'S POINTER

The exemption under ERISA Section 408(b)(3) includes within its scope certain transactions in which the potential for self-dealing by fiduciaries exists and in which the interests of fiduciaries may conflict with the interests of participants. The Department of Labor advises that, to guard against these potential abuses, it will subject these transactions to special scrutiny to ensure that they are primarily for the benefit of participants and their beneficiaries. Although the transactions need not be approved by an independent fiduciary, fiduciaries are cautioned to scrupulously exercise their discretion in approving them. Labor Reg. §2550.408b-3(b)(2).

Also, the purchase of qualifying employer securities will always be subject to the general fiduciary provisions of ERISA Section 404.

544. Does the use of an independent appraiser by an ESOP fiduciary ensure compliance with ERISA?

Not necessarily. The prohibited transaction provisions of ERISA Section 406 and ERISA Section 407(a) do not apply to the acquisition or sale by a plan of qualifying employer securities, if, among other conditions, the acquisition or sale is for adequate consideration. ERISA Sec. 408(e). The definition of the term "adequate consideration" under ERISA is of particular importance to the establishment and maintenance of ESOPs because, under ERISA Section 408(e), an ESOP may acquire employer securities from a party in interest only under certain conditions, including that the plan pay no more than adequate consideration for the securities.

The term "adequate consideration" when used in the case of an ESOP holding securities without a recognized market, means that the fair market value of the securities must be determined in good faith by the trustee or named fiduciary pursuant to the terms of the plan. ERISA Sec. 3(18)(B). Regulations addressing the concept of fair market value, as it relates to a determination of "adequate consideration" under this section, state that the good faith requirement of adequate consideration may be determined by the use of an independent appraisal in connection with the determination of good faith. Prop. Labor Reg. §2510.3-18(b)(2). In addition, the Internal Revenue Code provides that all valuations of non-publicly traded employer securities with respect to activities carried on by the plan must be conducted by an independent appraiser. IRC Sec. 401(a)(28)(C).

ERISA's requirement that ESOP fiduciaries pay "adequate consideration" for employer stock is interpreted by the courts so as to give effect to the fiduciary requirements of ERISA Section 404, to which ESOP fiduciaries remain subject. In this regard, the adequate consideration test, like the prudent man rule of ERISA Section 404(a)(1)(B), focuses on the conduct of the fiduciaries. Thus, in determining the value of employer securities, an ESOP fiduciary is required to act with the care, skill, and diligence that a prudent person would undertake in acting on behalf of ESOP beneficiaries. In reviewing the acts of ESOP fiduciaries under the objective prudent person standard, courts examine both the process used by the fiduciaries to reach their decision as well as an evaluation of the merits. *Donovan v. Cunningham*, 716 F.2d 1455 (5th Cir. 1983). Thus, whether an ESOP received adequate consideration depends on the thoroughness of the ESOP fiduciaries' investigation.

However, the mere use of an independent appraiser by an ESOP fiduciary does not guarantee thoroughness or compliance with the fiduciary requirements of ERISA. According to the courts, retaining a financial advisor or legal consultant to secure an independent assessment of the value of the ESOP shares is mere evidence of a prudent investigation and not a complete defense to a charge of imprudence. *Howard v. Shay*, 100 F.3d 1484 (9th Cir. 1996); *Martin v. Feilen*, 965 F.2d 660 (8th Cir. 1992). Moreover, " [a]n independent appraisal is not a magic wand that fiduciaries may simply wave over a transaction to ensure that their responsibilities are fulfilled. It is a tool and, like all tools, is useful only if used properly." *Donovan v. Cunningham*, above. In addition, since securing the advice of an independent third party appraiser might not insulate a fiduciary from liability per se, a fiduciary also must (according to the court in *Howard v. Shay*): (1) investigate the expert's qualifications; (2) provide the expert with complete and accurate information; and, (3) make certain that reliance on the expert's advice is reasonably justified under the circumstances.

An ESOP fiduciary need not become an expert in the valuation of a closely held company; it is entitled to rely on the expertise of others. *Donovan v. Cunningham*, above. However, to justifiably rely on an independent appraiser, an ESOP fiduciary must make an honest, objective effort to read the valuation, carefully review and understand it, discuss it with the appraiser, inquire into questionable methods and assumptions and seek the review of a second firm if uncertainties remain. *Howard v. Shay*, above. "The degree to which an [ESOP] fiduciary makes an independent inquiry is crucial." *Eyler v. Commissioner*, 88 F.3d 445 (7th Cir. 1996). Thus, a fiduciary is responsible to ensure that the methodologies, projections, and assumptions are correct and the appraisal is based on information that is complete and up-to-date. *Donovan v. Cunningham*, above. Otherwise, in failing to do so, an ESOP fiduciary breaches its duty of prudence under ERISA Section 404 and likewise cannot establish that it paid adequate consideration. For liberal and conservative views, respectively, of fiduciary breaches involving ESOP security transactions, see *Ershick v. United Mo. Bank of Kansas City*, 705 F. Supp. 1482 (D.C. Kan. 1990) *aff'd*, 948 F.2d 660 (10th Cir. 1991) and *Reich v. Valley Nat'l Bank of Ariz.*, 837 F. Supp. 1259 (S.D. NY 1993).

545. What are the "pass through" voting rights applicable to ESOPs?

The Internal Revenue Code requires that shares of qualifying employer securities that are held in an ESOP and that are readily tradable on an established securities exchange "pass through" full voting rights on all shares allocated to participants so they may direct the voting of their shares on those issues presented to shareholders for consideration and vote. IRC Secs. 409(e)(2), 4975(e)(7), as amended by EGTRRA 2001. If the shares are not readily tradable on an established securities exchange, participants have the right to vote only on "significant transactions" (e.g., mergers, acquisitions, liquidations, reclassification, sale of substantially all assets, etc.) passed through to them. IRC Sec. 409(e)(3). Where shares are not readily tradable on an established securities exchange, an ESOP may satisfy the limited pass through voting requirement by allowing each participant in the ESOP one vote with respect to an issue presented to shareholders by the corporate board of directors regardless of the actual number of votes allocated to a participant's account. IRC Sec. 409(e)(5). The plan must provide for this "one vote" rule within the plan documents if the plan fiduciaries decide to allow for it. This "one vote per participant" rule is permitted only where the ESOP trustee votes unallocated shares of the ESOP stock in proportion to the allocated shares voted by the participants. See IRC Sec. 409(e)(5).

PRACTITIONER'S POINTER

The voting of shares held in an ESOP is subject to the general fiduciary rules of ERISA; thus, fiduciaries may not use pass through voting rights to relieve themselves of liability regarding the obligations to oversee the plan in a prudent manner and for the exclusive benefit of participants and beneficiaries. *O'Neill v. Davis*, 721 F. Supp. 1013 (N.D. Ill. 1989). Consequently, fiduciaries are cautioned to carefully review any pertinent issues passed through under the "one vote" rule. The Department of Labor states that the voting of allocated shares is considered a management and control issue over plan assets. If fiduciaries believe that the result of votes presented under the "one vote" rule is not in the best interest of the plan, its participants and beneficiaries, they should consult competent legal counsel in order to review the possibility of overriding these votes, even if such a move would violate the written provisions of the plan document. In the case of *Danaher Corp. v. Chicago Pneumatic Tool Co.*, 635 F. Supp. 246 (S.D. NY 1986), the court, in relying on Scott's *Law of Trusts*, stated that "it would be inappropriate (and perhaps a breach of fiduciary obligation) for a trustee to put aside his personal judgment in favor of carrying out the wishes of the [ESOP's] participants." The *Danaher* court instructed that a "neutral trustee" of the ESOP should be appointed, and that this trustee must make an independent evaluation of the tender offer for takeover of the plan sponsor before implementing the participant's instructions. On the other hand, in *Martin*

Marietta Corp. v. Bendix Corp., 697 F.2d 293 (2nd Cir. 1982), the court ordered the pass through of a tender offer to employees, despite the fact that the plan document did not call for it. A Sixth Circuit Court of Appeals decision held that ESOP fiduciaries who directed ESOP trustees to vote the ESOP stock for themselves in an election of corporate board members, without permitting pass through of the voting to ESOP participants, did not breach the fiduciary provisions of ERISA. The Court ruled that such refusal to pass through the voting on this issue was not a prohibited "self-dealing" issue because the right to vote ESOP stock is not a plan "asset" for prohibited transaction purposes. *Grindstaff v. Green*, 1998 U.S. App. LEXIS 203 (1998).

546. What special diversification rules apply to ESOPs?

ESOP participants must be provided an opportunity to diversify their individual accounts under the plan as they approach retirement age. For qualifying employer securities purchased by the ESOP after December 31, 1986, the plan must permit an employee who is at least 55 years of age and has completed at least 10 years of participation in the ESOP an option to diversify 25% of his ESOP stock. A participant who qualifies for this treatment must be provided the diversification option annually during a 90-day election period for six years after the employee attains age 55 and ending with the fifth succeeding plan year. At the sixth plan year, the participant must be provided with an option to make a one-time diversification of up to 50% of his account balance (less any prior diversified amount). IRC Sec. 401(a)(28)(B).

The ESOP must offer at least three investment options in addition to the employer stock, in order to satisfy the diversification requirement. IRC Sec. 401(a)(28)(B)(ii). Within 90 days after the diversification election by the eligible participant, the plan must invest that portion of the participant's account covered by the election in accordance with the eligible participant's expressed wishes. See Conference Committee Report, TRA '86, P.L. 99-514. As an alternate to providing the three investment options, the ESOP may satisfy the diversification obligation by making a distribution to the participant of an amount equal to the diversification request. Also, failure of an eligible participant to make an election to diversify is considered an election under the required diversification option.

For employer stock held in an ESOP that is not readily tradable on a recognized securities exchange, the plan must acquire a valuation of the stock from an independent appraiser, as defined under Internal Revenue Code Section 170(a)(1). IRC Sec. 401(a)(28)(C).

547. What rules apply to the distribution of ESOP benefits?

ESOPs generally must begin to distribute vested benefits to a participant not later than (a) one year after the close of the plan year in which the participant either retires, is disabled, or dies, or (b) the close of the sixth plan year following the participant's separation from service for other reasons. See IRC Sec. 409(o)(1)(A). The timing of these ESOP distributions must be specifically outlined in the plan's governing documents; thus, ERISA Section 404(a)(1)(D) (which requires fiduciaries to govern the plan in accordance with its governing documents) mandates that plan fiduciaries adhere to these requirements. Different rules apply in the case of a leveraged ESOP in which the loan used to purchase qualifying employer securities remains outstanding. See IRC Sec. 409(o)(1)(B).

The ESOP must also provide that the distribution of the participant's account balance will be in substantially equal periodic payments (not less frequently than annually) over a period of time not to exceed five years. IRC Sec. 409(o)(C). If the participant's account balance exceeds $500,000, there is an extension of the distribution period of one year for every $100,000 by which the participant's account balance exceeds $500,000. IRC Sec. 409(o)(1)(C). These limits are adjusted annually for inflation; for 2002 the indexed amounts are $160,000 and $800,000, respectively. Notice 2001-84, 2001-53 IRB 642; IRC Sec. 409(o)(2).

Participants may elect to receive their distribution in a different manner than the substantial equal periodic payment method (e.g., lump-sum). Where the employer stock allocated to the participant's account has been purchased in connection with a loan, the distribution of such stock may be restricted until after the loan has been fully repaid. Under this rule, the distribution is not required to be made available to the participant until the close of the plan year following the plan year in which the loan has been fully repaid. IRC Sec. 409(o)(1)(B).

Where the participant has not made an affirmative election regarding his distribution rights, the payment of benefits must begin no later than the sixtieth day after the latest of the close of the plan year in which:

1.   The participant attains the earlier of age 65 or the normal retirement age established under the plan documents;

2.   The tenth anniversary of the participant's participation in the plan occurs; or

3.   The participant terminates employment. IRC Sec. 401(a)(14).

Distributions from ESOPs are traditionally made in the form of employer securities, which the participant may sell on an open market at his discretion, or in cash if the participant does not exercise his option to receive stock. The participant in an ESOP may demand that his benefits be distributed in the form of employer securities. IRC Sec. 409(h)(1)(A).

Put Option: If the employer securities are not readily tradable on an established securities market, the participant has a right to require that the plan sponsor repurchase the employer securities under a fair valuation formula (this is commonly referred to as a "put option"). IRC Sec. 409(h)(1)(B). These put options must be exercisable only by a participant, the participant's donees, or by a person to whom the security passes by reason of the participant's death. Labor Reg. §2550.408b-3(j). The put option must permit a participant to "put" the security to the employer. Under no circumstances may the put option bind the ESOP; however, the put option may grant the ESOP an option to assume the rights and obligations of the employer at the time the put option is exercised. A put option must be exercisable for at least a 15-month period that begins on the date the security subject to the put option is distributed by the ESOP. Treas. Reg. §54.4975-7(b)(11).

Right of First Refusal: The stock may also be subject to a right of first refusal, which permits the plan sponsor or the ESOP to purchase the stock back from the participant before it may be sold to a third party. Treas. Reg. §54.4975-7(b)(9). The plan sponsor exercising a right of first refusal must pay the participant a price no less favorable to the participant than the greater of the value of the security (as determined in accordance with Treas. Reg. §54.4975-11(d)(5)) or the purchase price offered by a third party who has made a good faith offer to purchase the securities. The right of first refusal will lapse no later than 14 days after the participant provides written notice to the ESOP or the plan sponsor (whichever holds the right of first refusal) that an offer by a third party to purchase the securities has been received.

ESOPs may require the distribution of benefits in the form of cash where the plan sponsor's charter or by-laws mandate that only active employees may own corporate stock and the company is, in fact, "substantially owned" by employees. See IRC Sec. 409(h)(2)(B).

548. Does the "put option" apply to bank sponsored ESOPs?

The Internal Revenue Code provides a special rule for banks, which states that "In the case of a plan established and maintained by a bank (as defined in [IRC] Section 581) that is prohibited by law from redeeming or purchasing its own securities," the put option provision "shall not apply if the plan provides that participants entitled to a distribution from the plan shall have a right to receive a distribution in cash." IRC Sec. 409(h)(3).

549. What are the responsibilities of an ESOP fiduciary where there is a contest for corporate control?

Among the matters that have been addressed by the case law that follows, analyzing fiduciary conduct in the context of a takeover bid, are the effects of: the standard of prudence under ERISA, the exclusive benefit rule, the "business judgment rule" under the state corporate law, the effect of fiduciaries benefiting from incidental benefits that arise in the management of an ESOP, and the timing of the decision to adopt the ESOP.

The Tenth Circuit Court of Appeals held that an ESOP fiduciary must satisfy ERISA's standard of prudence and the exclusive benefit rule. See *Eaves v. Penn*, 587 F.2d 453 (10th Cir. 1978). In *Eaves v. Penn.*, the defendant wanted to take control of a corporation using assets of the corporation's profit sharing plan. He had the profit sharing plan converted into an ESOP and had himself appointed as trustee of that newly formed ESOP. Simultaneously, the defendant had himself appointed as treasurer of the corporation and, in that capacity, instructed the corporation to pay a $491,000 contribution to the ESOP. The defendant then used the proceeds of that contribution and the existing profit sharing plan assets to purchase control of 97% of the corporation's stock. He then purchased the remaining 3% of corporate stock with the proceeds of a $25,000 loan, which he ordered the corporation to extend to him as an individual, and with $5 of his own money. In other words, the defendant took control of the corporation for a total personal expenditure of $5, while the plan spent $1,013,000 for the 97% of stock placed into trust as ESOP assets, which had a book value of $76,000 at the time of purchase. The court concluded that the defendant had violated the exclusive benefit rule of ERISA and that he had not acted in a prudent manner in the best interests of the plan, its participants and beneficiaries.

The responsibilities imposed by ERISA do not preclude fiduciaries from benefiting from incidental benefits that arise in the management of an ESOP, provided that they acted "with an eye single to the interests of participants and beneficiaries" in considering a course of action regarding plan assets involved in a tender offer for control of a corporation. The Second Circuit Court of Appeals has ruled that officers of a corporation who were trustees of an employee benefit plan would not violate their duties as trustees by taking action which, after careful investigation, would best promote the interests of participants even though this action might incidentally benefit the corporation or themselves as corporate officers. See *Donovan v. Bierworth*, 680 F.2d 263 (2nd Cir. 1982). However, the court advised that fiduciaries have a duty to avoid placing themselves in a position where their acts as officers and directors would prevent their functioning with complete loyalty to the participants. Where there is such a conflict of interest, the court suggested that trustees either resign for the duration of the takeover attempt or employ independent legal and investment counsel for advice, and conduct an intensive and scrupulous investigation of the facts regarding the takeover attempt.

The adoption of an ESOP in response to a hostile takeover bid (as a defensive maneuver) is protected by the "business judgment rule" under the laws governing corporations (which, in general, protect corporate directors from liability for decisions they have made regarding corporate governance if they have acted on an informed basis, in good faith and in the honest belief that the action taken by the board was in the best interests of the company). *NCR Corp. v. American Telephone and Telegraph Co.*, 761 F. Supp. 475 (S.D. Ohio 1991). It is important to note, however, that the court in the *NCR* case invalidated the ESOP established by the NCR Board on the grounds that, although they were acting in good faith, they had not been properly informed about the substantive elements of the ESOP. These elements included potential adverse tax consequences involved in the ESOP, the NCR Human Resources Department's concern that there would be difficulty in getting the employees to enroll in the ESOP, and whether or not the terms of the ESOP were fair to common stockholders of the company. The court also pointed out that NCR always viewed the ESOP as a defensive response to a hostile takeover attempt and that it was used as a tool to entrench the current management.

The court in *NCR* advised that the business judgment rule will be evaluated on the basis of the following factors:

1.   The timing of the formation of the ESOP (e.g., whether it was in response to a hostile takeover attempt);

2.   Consideration of the ESOP's establishment by the Board (i.e., by reviewing committee minutes and applicable corporate resolutions);

3.   History of employee participation in the company;

4.   Shareholder neutrality of the ESOP; and

5.   Other legitimate business reasons that may exist for the establishment of an ESOP.

The Delaware Chancery Court upheld the establishment of an ESOP by a plan sponsor who was in the middle of a hostile takeover attempt in *Shamrock Holdings v. Polaroid Corp.*, 559 A.2d 278 (Del. 1989). The court in this case determined that the sale of plan sponsor shares to the ESOP was fundamentally fair to the Polaroid shareholders because it involved no increased cost to Polaroid (the ESOP was funded through pay cuts to employees and the elimination of other benefits). In contrast to the NCR rejection of the ESOP attempt, Polaroid Corporation had actually adopted a 5% ESOP before it was contacted by Shamrock Holdings regarding their intention to attempt a hostile takeover.

While it may be permissible to establish an ESOP in the midst of a takeover attempt, one federal district court determined that the factors relevant to an evaluation of whether or not the ESOP was created to benefit employees and simply not to entrench management include: the timing of the establishment, the identity of the trustees and voting control of the ESOP shares (in this case they were all insiders), and the financial impact upon the company. See *Buckhorn, Inc. v. Ropack Corp.*, 656 F. Supp. 209 (S.D. Ohio 1987).

As the foregoing rulings indicate, in the event there has been a takeover attempt, the *timing* of the decision to establish an ESOP is very important in the eyes of the courts in determining whether the establishment of the ESOP will be validated as an effort to act in a prudent manner for the exclusive benefit of plan participants and beneficiaries. Still, timing is not the only matter to be considered. There is no hard and fast rule regarding the establishment of an ESOP where there has been a tender offer for purposes of obtaining corporate control.

The DOL can bring legal action to enjoin any transaction that violates ERISA. Where there has been a filing of a proxy statement with the SEC regarding a buyout that involves an ESOP, the SEC will provide a copy of the filing to the DOL. The DOL will review the transaction to ensure that participants are treated as fairly as all other shareholders. If they are not, the DOL may intervene seeking different terms or negation of the deal.

550. What are the fiduciary issues regarding the voting of unallocated and non-voting allocated shares in an ESOP?

As noted earlier (see Q 545), the voting of shares held in an ESOP is always subject to the general fiduciary rules of ERISA, including the duty to oversee the plan in a prudent manner and for the exclusive benefit of participants and beneficiaries. *O'Neill v. Davis*, 721 F. Supp. 1013 (N.D. Ill. 1989). Regarding allocated shares, the plan fiduciaries must pass through certain voting rights to participants to whose accounts the shares have been allocated. The general rule regarding these shares requires plan trustees to follow participant instructions. (See Q 545 regarding the voting of allocated shares.)

Plan trustees must take careful consideration with respect to the voting of shares that are unallocated or of the shares that have been allocated, but with respect to which the participants to whom they have been allocated have refused, or failed, to vote. It is a common practice for ESOPs to provide in the governing documents for the "mirror voting" of unallocated and unvoted shares. "Mirror voting" means that the trustee is instructed to tender unallocated and unvoted shares held by the plan in the same proportion as it tenders allocated shares. However, mirror voting rules have not always protected trustees from liability for violations of their fiduciary obligations.

In a 1997 ruling, the Eleventh Circuit Court of Appeals provided some much-needed clarification to this issue. See *Herman v. NationsBank Tr. Co.*, 126 F.3d 1354 (11th Cir. 1997). There, the court reviewed the voting of unallocated and non-voting allocated shares in the takeover fight for Polaroid Corporation (this case resulted from the attempted takeover of Polaroid by Shamrock Holdings, Inc.). The Polaroid ESOP's trustee bank, NationsBank, had received a letter from the Secretary of Labor in the midst of the takeover attempt that outlined the DOL's view of NationsBank's fiduciary responsibilities in light of the competing tender offers (this letter is reprinted at 16 BNA 390 (1989)). The DOL insisted that an ESOP trustee bears the final responsibility for making tender offer decisions with regard to the plan's unallocated shares and its allocated non-voting shares.

In following the mirror voting provisions, the trustees tendered the majority of unallocated and non-voting shares to Polaroid Corporation, leaving the remaining shares to be tendered to Shamrock Holdings, or not tendered (in accordance with participant wishes, including a like percentage withheld under mirror voting rules). Polaroid paid to the ESOP $72,762,200 for the 482,073 shares it accepted that were tendered by NationsBank on behalf of the ESOP. If NationsBank had tendered all of the unallocated shares to Polaroid, the ESOP would have obtained an additional 332,917 shares at a price between $37.41 and $37.67 per share.

The DOL filed suit against NationsBank in 1992, complaining that NationsBank had violated ERISA Section 404(a)(1)(A) and ERISA Section 404(a)(1)(B) by failing to tender all of the unallocated shares and the allocated non-voted shares to Polaroid. In Count Two of the complaint, the DOL alleged that an indemnification provision in the ESOP created a disincentive for

NationsBank to exercise its independent judgment and, therefore, encouraged NationsBank to breach its fiduciary obligations under ERISA. The district court held that NationsBank could not rely on the mirror voting provisions under the ESOP in determining how it would vote unallocated shares.

The Eleventh Circuit was concerned with the issue of whether Polaroid ESOP participants, under the mirror voting provisions of the plan document, could become named fiduciaries who could direct NationsBank's asset management decisions with regard to unallocated and nonvoting shares.

The DOL took the position that ESOP participants may be named fiduciaries *only* with respect to allocated shares for which participants give explicit directions (Ian D. Lanoff Letter, 22 BNA 2249 (1995)). The DOL also took the position that participants may never be named fiduciaries with regard to unallocated and non-voted shares and cannot direct a trustee with regard to those shares. The DOL expressed the view that ERISA Section 404(a)(1) must govern the trustee decisions with respect to unallocated and non-voting shares. As such, the DOL argued that NationsBank's only prudent course of action would have been to tender all non-voted and unallocated shares to Polaroid.

NationsBank countered that it was acting prudently in following the plan's mirror voting rules and that, consequently, the ESOP participants had the discretion to vote the ESOP's unallocated and non-voting shares in accordance with their fiduciary obligations in voting the pass through rights. The DOL responded that Polaroid ESOP participants could not satisfy the definition of fiduciary because whatever control they had regarding the unallocated and nonvoting shares was unknown to them. This left the responsibility for the voting of those shares with NationsBank.

The Eleventh Circuit ruled that fiduciaries must know that they can decide an issue and be aware of the choices they have. "Based on the plain language of ERISA, ESOP participants are not fiduciaries when they do not knowingly decide how assets will be managed." Accordingly, (because Polaroid ESOP participants were not aware of their fiduciary responsibility regarding unallocated and non-voting shares) NationsBank retained exclusive fiduciary authority to manage those shares in accordance with the fiduciary standards of ERISA. The Eleventh Circuit further noted that mirror voting language in an ESOP plan document is not per se incorrect. However, blindly following mirror voting provisions that lead to an imprudent result is incorrect (citing the holding under *Ershick v. Greb X-Ray Co.*, 705 F. Supp. 1482 (D. Kan. 1989), that trust documents cannot excuse trustees from their duties under ERISA if following them results in an imprudent result). The Eleventh Circuit Court stated that where plan participants are not sufficiently informed to be named fiduciaries "ERISA dictates that a mirror voting provision that leads to an imprudent result is invalid as applied."

In remanding the case to the district court for final disposition, the Eleventh Circuit stated that NationsBank was required to act solely in the interest of participants in voting unallocated shares.

551. May pre-tax salary reduction contributions be used to repay an exempt loan to a leveraged employee stock ownership plan?

It depends. On October 13, 1994, the Internal Revenue Service issued a national office technical advice memorandum regarding the use of pre-tax salary reduction contributions (i.e., 401(k) elective deferrals) to repay an exempt loan to a leveraged ESOP under the exclusive benefit rule of Section 401(a)(2) of the Internal Revenue Code and the regulation that sets forth the permissible assets for repayment of an exempt loan. See Treas. Reg. §54.4975-7(b)(5). The IRS concluded that because the applicable regulations designate such contributions as employer contributions, they could be applied to payments under an exempt loan without violating the exclusive benefit rule under the Internal Revenue Code. See TAM 9503002; Treas. Reg. §1.401(k)-(a)(4)(ii).

In contrast to the IRS's view based on Internal Revenue Code provisions, the DOL takes the position that amounts that a participant pays to or has withheld by an employer, whether pursuant to a salary reduction agreement or otherwise, for contribution to an employee benefit plan constitute participant contributions subject to ERISA's general provisions governing the protection of employee benefit rights (Subtitle A of Title I) as well as ERISA's reporting and disclosure provisions (Part 1 of Subtitle B) and fiduciary responsibility provisions (Part 4 of Subtitle B), and for the purposes of the prohibited transaction provisions of IRC Section 4975. Consequently, the DOL believes that the use of pre-tax salary reduction contributions for payments under an exempt loan raises issues with respect to the primary benefit test under ERISA Section 408(b)(3) and the exclusive purpose requirements of Sections 403 and 404 of ERISA.

Since it is generally understood that an exempt loan to an ESOP is secured primarily by an employer's guarantee of the loan and its agreement to make annual contributions to the plan sufficient to meet the plan's obligation to repay the principal and interest due under the loan arrangement, the use of participant contributions to satisfy part of the loan obligation serves directly to relieve the employer of its obligation to contribute to the plan. For this reason, the DOL does not believe that a loan that is structured to be repaid with participant contributions will satisfy the general requirements under ERISA section 408(b)(3) that an exempt loan must be primarily for the benefit of the ESOP's participants and beneficiaries. In addition, when a primary benefit requirement is not met, the DOL takes the position that there is also a violation of the "exclusive purpose" and "solely in the interest" requirements of ERISA Sections 403 and 404. DOL Letter to Evelyn Petschek, Internal Revenue Service, January 16, 1996; see also TAM 9503002.

552. What are the fiduciary issues regarding ESOP leveraged buyouts?

The most common situation involving an ESOP in a leveraged buyout is the coordination of key management personnel in the existing corporation with outside investors in the formation of a new corporation to purchase the outstanding shares of the existing corporation. The investor group will typically furnish a minor initial investment of equity capital (approximately 10%) into the new corporation and raise the balance of the necessary funds in a loan from a financial institution or from the issuance of new stock. The new corporation then establishes a leveraged ESOP at the time it is establishing financial arrangements for the takeover of the existing corporation. The newly established ESOP will then borrow funds from a financial institution for the purchase of stock from the new corporation. The new corporation will use the funds received from the purchase of stock by the ESOP, in addition to the equity capital contributed by the investor group and the outside funds borrowed by the new corporation, to complete the purchase of the existing company. In establishing the ESOP, the fiduciaries need to be cognizant of the fact that they are bound by the general fiduciary duties under ERISA. *Danaher Corp. v. Chicago Pneumatic Tool Co.*, 635 F. Supp. 246 (S.D. NY 1986).

If the Department of Labor has objections (due to perceived violations of ERISA) in an ESOP leveraged buyout, it may intervene in an effort to secure better arrangements for the ESOP, or to stop the completion of the buyout where the terms of the transaction violate ERISA. DOL concerns tend to focus on the valuation of the stock purchased by the ESOP when compared to the price paid by other investors. The DOL also focuses on the adequacy of the consideration (see Q 543 regarding the definition of "adequate consideration") involved in the transaction. In reviewing these two issues, the DOL will ascertain whether the transactions also satisfy the fiduciary duties of general prudence, exclusive purpose, and the prohibited transaction provisions which are not extended the statutory exemptions for ESOPs (conflict of interest, self-dealing, etc.).

The acquisition of employer securities must be for adequate consideration. ERISA Sec. 408(e). Trustees and other fiduciaries have the obligation to investigate the reasonableness of the appraisal value of employer stock purchased by the ESOP. *Donovan v. Cunningham*, 716 F.2d 1455 (5th Cir. 1983). Furthermore, the DOL will view a valuation as reflecting fair market value where there has been an appropriate demonstration of the level of expertise demonstrated by the parties making the valuation.

Proposed regulations state that the adequacy of consideration paid by an ESOP for privately held employer securities must satisfy a 2-part test (Prop. Labor Reg. §2510.3-18(b)(1)(I)):

1.   The consideration must reflect fair market value; and

2.   The valuation must be made in "good faith" (as stated under ERISA Section 3(18)).

The determination of the fair market value of privately held securities must include an assessment of the following factors:

1.   The nature of the business and the history of the enterprise from its inception;

2. The economic outlook in general and the condition and the outlook of the specific industry in particular;

3. The book value of the stock and the financial condition of the business;

4. The earning capacity of the company;

5. The dividend paying capacity of the company;

6. Whether or not the enterprise has goodwill or other intangible value;

7. The market price of securities of corporations engaged in the same or a similar line of business, which are traded in a free and open market, either on an exchange or over the counter; and

8. Sales of the stock and the size of the block of stock to be valued. Prop. Labor Reg. §2510.3-18(b)(4)(ii)(H).

Examples of DOL intervention in leveraged buyouts include objections over ESOP trustees violating the exclusive benefit rule in paying an excessive consideration for ESOP shares after the exercise of options and warrants (DOL letter to Scott & Fetzer ESOP Trustees, July 30, 1985; 12 BNA Pens. Rep. 1182); the investment of ESOP sale proceeds to be used in a leveraged buyout and restructuring in a highly leveraged firm creating an unreasonable risk of loss (DOL Letter to C.R. Smith, Blue Bell, Inc., November 23, 1984; 12 BNA Pens. Rep. 52); and the payment of a per share price by the ESOP that was in excess of that paid by other leveraged buyout investors (*Reich v. Valley Nat'l Bank of Ariz.*, 837 F. Supp. 1259 (S.D. NY 1993)). In the *Valley Nat'l Bank* case, the DOL attempted to force recovery of all losses incurred by the ESOP. The DOL has also intervened in a leveraged ESOP situation in which there were conflicting interests by ESOP trustees because they also served as officers in a target or raider corporation. The court ruled that they had a significant personal interest in the outcome of the takeover involving the ESOP, which would have violated the provisions of ERISA Section 406(b)(1). The court ordered the trustees to resign their positions until the control issue was settled. See *Freund v. Marshall & Ilsley Bank*, 485 F. Supp. 629 (W.D. Wis. 1979).

The DOL is not always successful in its interventions. In a 1990 case, the DOL took the position that the value of the stock involved in an ESOP should be valued on a post-transaction basis in order to establish whether more than adequate consideration was paid by the ESOP. This position received an intense amount of widespread criticism because such hindsight analysis makes it too easy to determine that excessive consideration was paid. In response to this widespread disapproval, the DOL withdrew the complaint on October 4, 1990. See *Dole v. Farnum*, Civil No. 900371, (D.C. RI 1990).

Chapter X

TAFT-HARTLEY PLANS

(Multiemployer Plans)

553. What is a "Taft-Hartley" plan?

A "Taft-Hartley" plan, so called after the landmark 1947 collective bargaining legislation, is the same type of plan as a "multiemployer plan," discussed in more detail in Q 554.

554. What is a multiemployer plan?

A multiemployer plan is a plan (1) that is maintained pursuant to a collective bargaining agreement (between one or more employee organizations, see Q 555, and more than one employer); and (2) to which more than one employer is required to contribute. ERISA Secs. 3(37)(A)(i), 3(37)(A)(ii).

Note that both elements must be present in order for a plan to be a multiemployer plan. In contrast, for example, a plan subject to a collective bargaining agreement that benefits the employees of two or more members of a controlled group is simply a collectively bargained single-employer plan, while a plan that benefits the employees of two or more unrelated employers, but is not subject to a collective bargaining agreement, is a "multiple employer plan."

ERISA Section 3(37)(A) provides that a multiemployer plan must also satisfy "other requirements as the Secretary [of Labor] prescribes by regulation." See Labor Reg. §2510.3-37.

Substantially the same definition of multiemployer plan applies for purposes of the rules relating to the Pension Benefit Guaranty Corporation (PBGC). ERISA Sec. 4001(a)(3).

555. What is an employee organization?

"Employee organization" means (1) any labor union; (2) any organization of any kind; (3) any agency or employee representation committee, association, group, or plan in which employees participate and which exists for the purpose, in whole or in part, of dealing with employers concerning an employee benefit plan, or other matters incidental to employment relationships; or (4) any employees' beneficiary association organized, in whole or in part, for the purpose of establishing such a plan. ERISA Sec. 3(4).

556. Who are the fiduciaries in a multiemployer plan?

The general definition of a fiduciary is applicable to multiemployer plans. In general, in order to achieve fiduciary status, an individual or entity must either: (1) exercise discretionary authority or control regarding the management of the plan or its assets; or (2) exercise discretionary authority or responsibility in the administration of the plan. ERISA Sec. 3(21)(A). See Q 186. This would include the power to appoint a plan's trustees.

In order for a participating employer to be considered a fiduciary of a multiemployer plan, it would have to exercise the sort of discretion and authority provided under ERISA Section 3(21)(A). Note that a participating employer in a multiemployer plan would be included in the definition of a party in interest under ERISA Section 3(14)(C). See Q 338.

Because they traditionally have the power, under Labor Management Relations Act Section 302(c)(5), to appoint a portion of a multiemployer plan's trustees, employee organizations (i.e., unions) are considered to be fiduciaries. As is the case with participating employers, an employee organization would be included in the definition of a party in interest under ERISA Section 3(14)(C). See Q 338.

The trustees appointed to operate a multiemployer plan satisfy the statutory definition of fiduciary under ERISA Section 3(21)(A) because they are charged with the power to exercise discretionary authority regarding the control and administration of the plan and its assets. Investment committee members and union-employed plan administrators are usually fiduciaries of a multiemployer plan (unless their duties are limited to ministerial functions) by virtue of performing duties that involve the discretion and authority provided under ERISA Section 3(21)(A).

Other individuals or entities that may be considered to be fiduciaries of a multiemployer plan include service providers who have been granted limited authority regarding the control and administration of the plan or its assets. Such service providers include: third party administrators, investment managers, broker-dealers, and insurance companies.

Fiduciaries of a multiemployer plan are obligated to conduct themselves in accordance with the fiduciary standards of ERISA, which are delineated under ERISA Section 404 (see Chapter IV for details).

557. What is the funding structure of multiemployer plans?

The level of benefits to be funded through a multiemployer plan is traditionally determined by the formula contained within the collective bargaining agreement (CBA) established between the union and the participating employers. Contributions are submitted to plan fiduciaries who either:

1.   Administer the type and amount of benefits as they are defined in the CBA; or

2.   Establish the type and amount of benefits provided under the plan.

Multiemployer pension plans are funded through an IRC Section 501(a) tax-exempt trust. Multiemployer welfare plans are traditionally funded through an IRC Section 501(c)(9) tax-exempt trust. Fiduciaries of both types of trusts are charged with investing and managing trust assets in accordance with the general provisions of ERISA (Q 245). See PBGC Adv. Op. 94-39A.

Multiemployer pension plans must satisfy the minimum funding standard, which is satisfied if, as of the end of such plan year, the plan does not have a minimum funding deficiency. ERISA Sec. 302(a). Multiemployer welfare plans are not subject to funding limits. IRC Sec. 419A(f)(5).

Multiemployer pension plans must establish and maintain a funding standard account. Each year, such account is:

1.   Charged with the sum of the normal cost of the plan, the unfunded past service liabilities, net experience losses, net losses resulting from changes in the plan's actuarial assumptions, and the amount necessary to amortize each waived funding deficiency for each prior plan year; and

2.   Credited with the sum of employer contributions, the amount necessary to amortize, in equal annual installments, the net decrease of unfunded past service liabilities, the plan's net experience gains, gains due to changes in the plan's actuarial assumptions, and waived funding deficiencies. ERISA Sec. 302(b).

The provisions of ERISA Sections 302(a) and 412(b) are mirrored under IRC Sections 412(a) and 412(b).

IRC Section 413(c)(4) requires pension funding requirements to be applied to multiemployer plans as if all of the participants are employed by a single employer.

558. How can a multiemployer plan be terminated?

There are three ways in which a multiemployer plan can be terminated:

1.   By the adoption of one of two types of amendment:

a) an amendment that provides that participants will receive no credit under the plan for any period of service for an employer after the date specified by the amendment (ERISA Sec. 4041A(a)(1)), or

b) an amendment that results in the plan being converted to a defined contribution plan (ERISA Sec. 4041A(a)(3));

2. By the mass withdrawal of every employer participating in the plan (ERISA Sec. 4041A(a)(2)); and

3. Through proceedings instituted by the PBGC (ERISA Sec. 4042).

Where a multiemployer plan has been terminated through an amendment, the termination is effective on the date when the amendment is adopted or goes into effect, whichever is later. ERISA Sec. 4041A(b)(2). In the case of a termination by mass withdrawal, the termination is effective on the earlier of the date when the last employer has withdrawn from the plan or the first day of the first plan year for which no employer contributions are required under the plan. ERISA Sec. 4041A(b)(2).

In the case of termination by amendment, the plan must file a termination notice with the PBGC. See Q 580.

For details regarding the termination of a plan by the PBGC, see Chapter XII. Generally, involuntary terminations of single employer defined benefit plans and multiemployer plans are covered by the same rules as delineated under ERISA Section 4042 (applications specific to each type of plan are spelled out in those rules).

559. What is withdrawal liability? Who is responsible for withdrawal liability?

An employer that withdraws from a multiemployer pension plan is responsible for an allocable share of the multiemployer plan's unfunded vested benefits (sometimes referred to as "UVBs"). ERISA Sections 4201 through 4225 set forth a series of rules that require the withdrawing employer to fund a proportional share of unfunded vested benefits in the plan through a series of annual withdrawal payments to the plan.

For purposes of a multiemployer plan, "employer" means a participating employer, and includes "all trades or businesses (whether or not incorporated) which are under common control within the meaning of section 4001(b)(1)." ERISA Sec. 3(37)(B). An individual who owns the entire interest in an unincorporated trade or business is treated as his own employer, and a partnership is treated as the employer of each partner who is an employee within the meaning of IRC Section 401(c)(1). ERISA Sec. 4001(b)(1).

560. What constitutes a withdrawal for this purpose?

There are two types of withdrawals: a complete withdrawal and a partial withdrawal.

In general, a *complete withdrawal* occurs when an employer:

1. Permanently ceases to have an obligation to contribute under the multiemployer plan; or

2. Permanently ceases all covered operations under the plan. ERISA Sec. 4203(a).

The cessation of an obligation to contribute occurs when the employer is no longer required to make any contributions under the terms of the collective bargaining agreement. *Parmac, Inc. v. I.A.M. National Pension Fund Benefit Plan*, 872 F.2d 1069 (D.C. Cir. 1989).

In order for the employer to have permanently ceased all covered operations under the plan, the contributing employer must have completely ceased all operations that are covered by the collective bargaining agreement. *Trustees of the Iron Workers Local 473 v. Allied Products Corp.*, 872 F.2d 208 (7th Cir. 1989).

Special rules apply in making the determination of whether a complete withdrawal has occurred for multiemployer pension plans that cover employees in the building and construction industries (ERISA Section 4203(b)), the entertainment industry (ERISA Section 4203(c)), and the trucking, moving, and warehousing industries (ERISA Section 4203(d)).

A *partial withdrawal* occurs when, on the last day of the plan year, there is either (1) a 70% contribution decline; or (2) a partial cessation of the employer's contribution obligation. ERISA Sec. 4205(a).

A *70% contribution decline* occurs if the employer's contribution base units do not exceed 30% of the employer's contribution base units for the high base year during each plan year in the 3-year testing period. ERISA Sec. 4205(b)(1)(A).

The *3-year testing period* is the period consisting of the current plan year and the immediately preceding two plan years. The number of *contribution base units for the high base year* is the average number of units for the two plan years (within the five plan years immediately preceding the beginning of the 3-year testing period) for which the employer's contribution base units were the highest. ERISA Sec. 4205(b)(1)(B).

Partial cessation of the employer's contribution base units occurs if, during such plan year, the employer permanently ceases to have an obligation to contribute:

1. Under one or more (but fewer than all) collective bargaining agreements under which the employer has been obligated to contribute under the plan, but continues to perform work (of the type for which contributions were previously required) in the jurisdiction of the collective bargaining agreement, or transfers such work to another location; or

2.   With respect to work performed at one or more (but fewer than all) of its facilities, but continues to perform the type of work for which the obligation to contribute ceased at the facility. ERISA Sec. 4205(b)(2)(A).

However, an employer that has permanently ceased to perform covered work under one of its collective bargaining agreements but contracts to buy that same service or product from an independent third party has not transferred that work to another location for the purposes of this rule. PBGC Adv. Op. 86-17.

A cessation of obligations under a collective bargaining agreement shall not be considered to have occurred solely because, with respect to the same plan, one agreement that requires contributions to the plan has been substituted for another agreement. ERISA Sec. 4205(b)(2)(B).

According to Section 108(c)(2) of the Multiemployer Pension Plan Amendments Act of 1980 (Public Law 96-364), the liability incurred by an employer for a partial withdrawal is a pro rata portion of the liability that the employer would otherwise incur if there had been a complete withdrawal on the same date. See Q 567.

561. Is there withdrawal liability for withdrawal from a multiemployer welfare benefit plan?

ERISA is silent on the imposition of withdrawal liability against employers that have withdrawn from multiemployer welfare benefit plans, but the issue has been subject to litigation.

Courts have held that multiemployer welfare benefit plans have no authority, either under the law of trusts or under ERISA, to unilaterally impose withdrawal liability upon an employer. *Manchester Knitted Fashions, Inc. v. Amalgamated Cotton Garment and Allied Industries Fund*, 967 F.2d 688 (1st Cir. 1992). In that case, the First Circuit Court of Appeals indicated that participating employers in a multiemployer welfare benefit plan may contract for the imposition of withdrawal liability for the funding of post retirement welfare benefits. The court cautioned, however, that such a contractual arrangement must be reasonable under the general construction of contracts and must be interpreted in such a way as to "give effect to the expressed intentions of the parties," citing *Rothenberg v. Lincoln Farm Camp, Inc.*, 755 F.2d 1017 (2nd Cir. 1985).

562. How is withdrawal liability computed?

The basic method for computing withdrawal liability is the presumptive method. See Q 563. In addition, there are three alternative methods for computing withdrawal liability: the modified presumptive method (see Q 564), the rolling-5 method (see Q 565), and the direct attribution method (see Q 566). Note that, in order for any of the alternative methods to be used, the plan must be amended to permit the use of such alternative method. See PBGC Regs. §§4211.1 through 4211.13.

As a practical matter, the plan's actuary will calculate an employer's with-drawal liability. The withdrawing employer may also wish to engage its own actuary in order to dispute the withdrawal liability determination of the plan's actuary.

563. What is the presumptive method for calculating withdrawal liability?

Under the presumptive method, the amount of unfunded vested benefits (UVBs) allocable to a withdrawing employer (that is, the employer's withdrawal liability) is the sum of:

1.   The employer's proportional share of the unamortized amount of the change in the plan's UVBs for plan years ending after September 25, 1980;

2.   The employer's proportional share, if any, of the unamortized amount of the plan's UVBs at the end of the plan year ending before September 25, 1980; and

3.   The employer's proportional share of the unamortized amounts of the reallocated unfunded vested benefits. ERISA Sec. 4211.

Determining the employer's proportional share of the unamortized amount of the change in the plan's UVBs. This determination is a four-step process. First, the *change in the plan's UVBs* must be determined. For any plan year, this is the amount by which the UVBs at the end of the plan year exceeds the sum of:

1.   The unamortized amount of the UVBs for the last plan year ending before September 26, 1980; and

2.   The sum of:

      a) the unamortized amounts of the change in UVBs for each plan year ending after September 25, 1980, and

      b) the unamortized amounts of the change in UVBs for the year preceding the plan year for which the change is determined. ERISA Sec. 4211(b)(2)(B).

Second, the *unamortized amount of the change in the plan's UVBs,* with respect to a plan year, is determined by reducing the change in UVBs for the plan year, as determined in step one, by 5% for each succeeding plan year. ERISA Sec. 4211(b)(2)(C).

Third, the *employer's proportional share of the unamortized amount of the change in a plan's UVBs* is determined by multiplying the amount determined in step two, above, by this fraction:

> Numerator: the sum of the contributions that the employer must make to the plan for the year in which such change arose, and for the four preceding plan years.

> Denominator: the sum (for the plan year in which such change arose and the four preceding plan years) of all contributions made by all employers that had an obligation to contribute under the plan for the plan year in which such change arose, reduced by the contributions made in such years by employers that had withdrawn from the plan in the year in which the change arose.

Finally, to complete the calculation, add the employer's proportional share amount, determined above, for each plan year. The sum is the employer's proportional share of the unamortized amount of the change in the plan's unfunded benefit obligations for plan years beginning after September 25, 1980.

Determining the employer's proportional share of the unamortized amount of the UVBs for the last plan year ending before September 26, 1980. This is a three-step process. First, establish the *amount of the UVBs* as of the end of that plan year.

Second, determine the *unamortized amount of the UVBs* by reducing the amount of UVBs by 5% for each succeeding plan year. ERISA Sec. 4211(b)(2)(B).

Next, calculate the *employer's proportional share of the unamortized amount of the UVBs* by multiplying the unamortized amount, determined above, by this fraction:

> Numerator: the sum of all contributions required to be made by the employer under the plan for the most recent five plan years ending before September 26, 1980.

> Denominator: the sum of all contributions made for the most recent five plan years ending before September 26, 1980 by all employers that had an obligation to contribute under the plan for the first plan year ending on or after such date, and that had not withdrawn from the plan before such date. ERISA Sec. 4211(b)(3).

Determining the employer's proportional share of the unamortized amounts of the reallocated UVBs. This is a three-step process. First, determine the amount of the *reallocated UVBs*. In general, this is the sum of:

1.   Amounts that the plan sponsor determines are uncollectible for that year, due to bankruptcy or similar proceedings;

2.   Amounts that the plan sponsor determines will not be assessed for that year, due to the operation of the *de minimis* rule of ERISA Section 4209 (see Q 571), the 20-year limit of ERISA Section 4219(c)(1)(B) (see Q 575), or the limitation on withdrawal liability of ERISA Section 4225 (see Q 591 and Q 592), with respect to employers that have received a notice under ERISA Section 4219 (see Q 573); and

3.   Amounts that the plan sponsor determines are uncollectible or unassessable for that plan year, for other reasons that are consistent with applicable regulations. ERISA Sec. 4211(b)(4)(B).

Second, determine the *unamortized amount of the reallocated UVBs* by reducing the reallocated unfunded vested benefits, determined above, by 5% for each succeeding plan year. ERISA Sec. 4211(b)(4)(C).

Finally, determine the *employer's proportional share of the unamortized amount of the reallocated UVBs* by multiplying the unamortized amount of the reallocated UVBs by this fraction:

Numerator: the sum of the contributions that the employer must make to the plan for the year in which such change arose, and for the four preceding plan years.

Denominator: the sum (for the plan year in which such change arose and the four preceding plan years) of all contributions made by all employers that had an obligation to contribute under the plan for the plan year in which such change arose, reduced by the contributions made in such years by employers that had withdrawn from the plan in the year in which the change arose. ERISA Sec. 4211(b)(4)(D).

564. What is the modified presumptive method for calculating withdrawal liability?

ERISA Section 4211(c) provides for the modified presumptive method. This method, like the presumptive method discussed in Q 563, provides for different calculations for plan years ending before September 26, 1980, and plan years ending after September 25, 1980.

Under the modified presumptive method, the amount of the unfunded vested benefits (UVBs) allocable to an employer is the sum of (1) and (2), below:

1.   The plan's UVBs as of the end of the last plan year ending before September 26, 1980:

    a) reduced, as if those obligations were being fully amortized in level annual installments over 15 years, beginning with the first plan year ending on or after such date,

    b) multiplied by the following fraction:

Numerator: the sum of all contributions required to be made by the employer for the last five plan years ending before September 25, 1980.

Denominator: the sum of all contributions made for the last five plan years ending before September 26, 1980, by all employers that had an obligation to contribute under the plan for the first plan year ending after September 25, 1980 and had not withdrawn from the plan before such date; and

2.   The plan's UVBs as of the end of the plan year preceding the plan year in which the employer withdraws, minus the sum of:

    a) the value, as of such date, of all outstanding claims for withdrawal liability that can reasonably be expected to be collected, with respect to employers withdrawing before such plan year, and

    b) that portion of the amount to be determined under (1)(a), above, which is allocable to employers that have an obligation to contribute under the plan in the plan year preceding the plan year in which the employer withdraws, and also had an obligation to contribute under the plan for the first plan year ending after September 25, 1980,

    c) multiplied by the following fraction:

Numerator: the total amount required to be contributed under the plan by all employers for the last five plan years ending before the date on which the employer withdraws.

Denominator: the total amount contributed under the plan by all employers for the last five plan years ending before the date on which the employer withdraws, increased by the amount of any employer contributions owed with respect to earlier periods, which were collected in those plan years, and decreased by any amount contributed by an employer that withdrew from the plan during those plan years. ERISA Sec. 4211(c)(2).

In the case of an employer that did not contribute to the plan for plan years ending prior to September 26, 1980, the amount of the UVBs allocable to the employer is the amount established under item (2), above.

565. What is the rolling-5 method for calculating withdrawal liability?

The rolling-5 method for determining withdrawal liability is a statutory alternative to the presumptive method discussed in Q 563. The amount of the unfunded vested benefits (UVBs) allocable to an employer under the rolling-5 method is equal to the product of:

1. The UVBs as of the end of the plan year preceding the plan year in which the employer withdraws, less the value, as of the end of such year, of all outstanding claims for withdrawal liability that can reasonably be expected to be collected from employers withdrawing before such year;

2. Multiplied by this fraction:

    Numerator: the total amount required to be contributed by the employer under the plan for the last five plan years ending before withdrawal.

    Denominator: the total amount contributed under the plan by all employers for the last five years ending before the withdrawal, increased by any employer contributions owed with respect to earlier periods that were collected in those plan years, and decreased by any amount contributed to the plan during those plan years by employers that withdrew from the plan during those plan years. ERISA Sec. 4211(c)(3).

566. What is the direct attribution method for calculating withdrawal liability?

The direct attribution method for calculating withdrawal liability is a statutory alternative to the presumptive method, discussed in Q 563. The amount of the unfunded vested benefits (UVBs) allocable to an employer under the direct attribution method is equal to the sum of:

1. The plan's UVBs that are attributable to participants' service with the employer (determined as of the end of the plan year preceding the plan year in which the employer withdraws); and

2.   The employer's proportional share of any UVBs that are not attributable to service with the employer or other employers who are obligated to contribute to the plan in the plan year preceding the plan year in which the employer withdraws (determined as of the end of the plan year preceding the plan year in which the employer withdraws). ERISA Sec. 4211(c)(4).

567. How is the pro rata determination of partial withdrawal liability calculated?

When there has been a partial withdrawal, the amount of liability for the employer is calculated on a pro rata basis. This pro rata amount of withdrawal liability is determined by multiplying the amount of withdrawal liability that would have been applied in the case of a complete withdrawal by a stipulated fraction.

When there has been a *partial cessation of an employer's obligation* (see Q 559), the withdrawal liability is determined by multiplying the withdrawal liability that would have applied (in the case of a complete withdrawal on the date of the partial withdrawal) by a number, which is one minus this fraction:

Numerator: the employer's contribution base units for the plan year following the plan year of the partial withdrawal.

Denominator: the average of the employer's contribution base units for the five plan years preceding the plan year of partial withdrawal. ERISA Sec. 4206(a)(2).

When there has been a *70% decline in employer contributions*, withdrawal liability is determined as of the last day of the first plan year in the 3-year testing period. This amount is multiplied by a number, which is one minus this fraction:

Numerator: the employer's contribution base units for the plan year following the plan year of the partial withdrawal.

Denominator: the average of the employer's contribution base units for the five plan years immediately preceding the 3-year testing period. ERISA Sec. 4206(a)(2)(B).

PBGC Advisory Opinion 93-2 provides that the contribution base units for the plan year following the plan year in which the partial withdrawal occurs are the contribution base units for the plan year following the last plan year in the 3-year testing period, and not the plan year that follows the hypothetical withdrawal.

568. What are the plan sponsor's responsibilities when an employer withdraws from a multiemployer plan?

When an employer withdraws from a multiemployer plan, the plan sponsor must:

1.   Determine the amount of the employer's withdrawal liability (see Q 562);

2.   Notify the employer of the amount of the withdrawal liability; and

3.   Collect the amount of the withdrawal liability from the employer. ERISA Sec. 4202.

569. Does the sale of the assets or stock of a contributing employer, or a merger constitute a plan withdrawal?

Yes and no. In certain situations, a withdrawal has been deemed to have occurred as a result of the sale or merger of the contributing employer. Under other circumstances, no withdrawal has been found to have occurred.

An employer is not deemed to have withdrawn from a multiemployer plan because it ceases to exist by reason of a change in corporate structure through reorganization, liquidation into a parent corporation, merger, consolidation, division, or as a result of a change to an unincorporated form of business enterprise. ERISA Sec. 4218(1).

Normally, the sale of a contributing employer's assets *does* constitute a withdrawal from a multiemployer pension fund. See, for example, *I.A.M. National Pension Fund Benefit Plan A v. Cooper Industries, Inc.*, 635 F. Supp. 335 (DC D.C. 1986), rev'd 825 F.2d 415 (D.C. Cir. 1987). However, a withdrawal will not occur where a seller ceases covered operations or ceases to have an obligation to contribute for such operations as a result of a bona fide, arm's length sale of assets to an unrelated party, provided that:

1.   The purchaser has an obligation to contribute to the plan with respect to the operations for substantially the same number of contribution base units for which the seller had an obligation to contribute to the plan;

2.   For a period of five plan years (commencing with the first plan year beginning after the sale of assets), the purchaser provides the plan with:

a) a bond issued by a corporate surety company that is listed in IRS Circular 570 as an approved surety provider, or

b) an amount held in escrow by a bank or similar financial institution satisfactory to the plan, in an amount equal to the greater of (i) the average annual contributions that the seller must make with respect to operations under the plan for the three plan years preceding the plan year in which the sale of assets occurs, or (ii) the annual contribution that the seller must make with respect to the operations under the plan for the last plan year before the plan year in which the sale of employer assets occurs; and

3.   The contract for sale provides that, if the purchaser withdraws (in either a complete withdrawal, or a partial withdrawal with respect to operations) during the first five plan years following the sale, the seller is secondarily liable for any unpaid liability of the purchaser. ERISA Sec. 4204(a)(1).

If the purchaser withdraws before the last day of the fifth plan year beginning after the sale and fails to make any withdrawal liability payment when due, then the seller shall pay to the plan an amount equal to the payment that would have been due from the seller, but for the sale. ERISA Sec. 4204(a)(2).

If all, or substantially all, of the seller's assets are distributed, or if the seller is liquidated before the end of the five plan year period following the sale, then the seller must provide a bond or escrow an amount equal to the present value of the withdrawal liability that it would have had but for the sale of assets. ERISA Sec. 4204(a)(3).

Under certain circumstances, an employer may request a "variance" or waiver from the bond or escrow account requirement. See PBGC Regs. §§4204.11, 4204.12, and 4204.13. Note, however, that a failure to strictly adhere to the requirements of ERISA Section 4204 and the regulations thereunder will result in the asset sale being treated as a withdrawal from the multiemployer plan. See, for example, *Brentwood Fin. Corp. v. Western Conference of Teamsters Pension Trust Fund*, 902 F.2d 1456 (9th Cir. 1990).

A second sale of the same business within the 5-year period will not result in withdrawal liability, provided that the subsequent sale also meets the requirements of ERISA Section 4204. PBGC Adv. Op. 90-1.

570. Does the interruption of business as a result of a labor dispute constitute a withdrawal from a multiemployer pension plan?

No. An employer is not deemed to have withdrawn from a multiemployer pension plan solely because it suspends making contributions to the plan during a labor dispute involving its employees. ERISA Sec. 4218(2).

571. What are the de minimis and permissive reduction rules of ERISA Section 4209?

The *de minimis reduction rule* provides that the amount of the unfunded vested benefits (UVBs) allocated to an employer that withdraws from a multiemployer pension plan shall be reduced by the lesser of:

1. Three-fourths of 1% (.0075) of the plan's unfunded vested obligations (determined as of the end of the plan year preceding the date of withdrawal); or

2. $50,000,

reduced by the amount, if any, by which the employer's portion of UVBs exceeds $100,000. ERISA Sec. 4209(a).

The *permissive reduction rule* provides that a plan may be amended to provide for reduction of the UVBs allocated to a withdrawing employer by not more than the greater of:

1. The amount established under the *de minimis* rule, above; or

2. The lesser of:

    a) Three-fourths of 1% (.0075) of the plan's unfunded vested obligations (determined as of the end of the plan year preceding the date of withdrawal), or

    b) $100,000,

reduced by the amount, if any, by which the employer's withdrawal liability amount would otherwise exceed $150,000. ERISA Sec. 4209(b).

572. What is the "free look" rule of ERISA Section 4210?

Under certain circumstances, discussed below, withdrawal liability may be eliminated for:

1. Employers first obligated to contribute to the plan after September 26, 1980;

2. Employers obligated to contribute to the plan for no longer than the lesser of:

    a) six consecutive plan years preceding the date of the employer's withdrawal, or

    b) the number of years required for vesting under the plan;

3. Employers required to contribute (for each plan year) less than 2% of the sum of all employer contributions made to the plan for each year; and

4.   Employers that have never previously avoided withdrawal liability under these provisions. ERISA Sec. 4210(a).

This "free look" rule applies only to multiemployer plans that:

1.   Are amended to provide that the provisions of ERISA Section 4210(a), discussed above, apply;

2.   Provide (or are amended to provide) that the reduction under IRC Section 411(a)(3)(E) applies to the withdrawing employer's employees; and

3.   Have a ratio of plan assets to benefit payments made, during the plan year preceding the first plan year for which the employer was required to contribute to the plan, of at least eight to one. ERISA Sec. 4210(b).

Note also that the relief afforded under ERISA Section 4210(a) does not apply to multiemployer plans that primarily cover employees in the building and construction industry. ERISA Sec. 4210(b)(1).

573. What is the notice requirement of withdrawal liability?

As soon as practicable after an employer's complete or partial withdrawal, the plan sponsor must notify the employer of the amount of the withdrawal liability and the schedule for liability payments, and demand payment in accordance with the schedule for liability payments. ERISA Sec. 4219(b)(1).

After receiving the notice of withdrawal liability from the plan sponsor, the employer has 90 days in which to:

1.   Request that the plan sponsor review any specific matter relating to the determination of the employer's liability and the schedule of payments (see Q 574);

2.   Identify any inaccuracy in the plan sponsor's determination of the amount of the unfunded vested benefits allocable to the employer; and

3.   Furnish any additional relevant information to the plan sponsor. ERISA Sec. 4219(b)(2)(A).

574. What is the plan sponsor's responsibility after receipt of a request from a contributing employer for a review of the notice of withdrawal liability?

After the receipt of a request from an employer for a review of its withdrawal liability, and reasonable review of any matter raised, the plan sponsor (see Q 573) shall notify the employer of:

1. The plan sponsor's decision;

2. The basis for the decision; and

3. The reason for any change in the determination of the employer's liability or the schedule of liability payments. ERISA Sec. 4219(b)(2)(B).

575. When and how are withdrawal liability payments to be made?

Withdrawal liability payments must begin no later than 60 days after the date on which the plan sponsor demands payment. ERISA Sec. 4219(c)(2).

The withdrawing employer must pay the withdrawal liability over the period of years necessary to amortize the amount in annual level payments, calculated as if the first payment were made on the first day of the plan year following the plan year in which the withdrawal occurs, and as if each subsequent payment were made on the first day of each subsequent plan year. This amortization period may not exceed 20 years. ERISA Sec. 4219(c)(1).

The Supreme Court has ruled that interest begins to accrue on the amortization as of the first day of the plan year after withdrawal, holding that the withdrawing employer's obligation does not begin to accrue until the first day of the year after withdrawal. *Milwaukee Brewery Workers' Pension Plan v. Jos. Schlitz Brewing Co. and Stroh Brewing Co.*, 513 U.S. 414 (1995).

Annual withdrawal liability payments must be made in four equal payments, due quarterly, or at other intervals specified in the plan. Interest accrues on late payments from the due date until the date when actually paid. ERISA Sec. 4219(c)(3).

There is no prepayment liability if the employer prepays all or a part of the outstanding amount of the unpaid withdrawal liability obligation. If a prepayment has subsequently been determined to be a part of a mass withdrawal (see Q 579), the employer's liability will not be limited to the amount of the prepayment. ERISA Sec. 4219(c)(4).

The amount of the annual withdrawal liability payment equals:

1. The average number of contribution base units for the three consecutive plan years during the 10-year plan period ending before the plan year of withdrawal, in which the number of such units was the highest

multiplied by

2.   The highest contribution rate for required contributions of the employer during the 10-year period ending with plan year of withdrawal. ERISA Sec. 4219(c)(1)(C)(i).

576. What happens in the event of a default on withdrawal liability payments?

Default on withdrawal liability payments occurs when the withdrawing employer has failed to make a payment on its withdrawal liability when due, and then fails to make payment within 60 days after receiving written notice from the plan sponsor of such failure. ERISA Sec. 4219(c)(5)(A); PBGC Reg. §4219.31(b)(1)(i). The plan sponsor may also establish rules that include, within the definition of default, other events that indicate a substantial likelihood that an employer would be unlikely to pay its withdrawal liability. ERISA Sec. 4219(c)(5)(B); PBGC Reg. §4219.31(b)(1)(ii).

If an employer defaults on the payment of scheduled withdrawal liability, the plan sponsor may require the immediate payment of all or a portion of the outstanding balance of the employer's liability, plus accrued interest from the due date of the first payment in default. Should the plan sponsor accelerate only a portion of the outstanding balance owed, the plan sponsor must establish a new schedule of payments for the remaining amount owed. ERISA Sec. 4219(c)(5); PBGC Reg. §4219.31(b)(2).

577. Does interest accrue on delinquent withdrawal liability payments?

ERISA Section 4219(c)(3) requires that each annual payment that is in default shall accrue interest from the due date until the date on which the payment is made. Such interest rates shall be based on prevailing market rates for comparable obligations, in accordance with PBGC regulations. ERISA Sec. 4219(c)(6).

Interest on defaulted amounts is charged or credited for each calendar quarter at an annual rate, equal to the average quoted prime rate on short term commercial loans quoted by large banks (as published by the Federal Reserve Board) on the 15th day (or the following business day, if the 15th day is not a business day) of the month preceding the beginning of the calendar quarter. PBGC Reg. §4219.32(b).

Plans may adopt procedures for establishing interest rates that are different from those established under PBGC regulations. However, the alternative rates must be consistent with ERISA and reflect "prevailing market rates for comparable obligations." PBGC Reg. §4219.33.

Any overpayment of withdrawal liability must be refunded with interest at the same rate as that applied to overdue payments. Such overpayments must be refunded in a lump sum, with interest, and may not be applied to future payment obligations. PBGC Reg. §4219.31(d).

578. Are payments made by an employer for withdrawal liability deductible?

Yes. IRC Section 404(g)(1) provides that an employer's payments made under part 1 of subtitle E of Title VI of ERISA (that is, the withdrawal liability provisions) are treated as deductible employer contributions.

The deduction will be permitted when paid, without regard to the limitation on employer deductions for contributions to tax-qualified plans found elsewhere in IRC Section 404. Treas. Reg. §1.404(g)-1(a). Withdrawal liability payments will be included in the employer's total plan contributions for purposes of establishing the maximum allowable deduction under the full funding limitation (see Q 53). Treas. Reg. §1.404(g)-1(c)(3).

579. What happens when substantially all of the employers withdraw from a plan?

When every employer withdraws from a multiemployer plan, or when substantially all employers withdraw from a multiemployer plan pursuant to an agreement or arrangement, a "mass withdrawal" occurs and there is a plan termination. In the event of a plan termination triggered by such a mass withdrawal, the liability of each withdrawing employer is determined without regard to the 20-year cap on payments under ERISA Section 4219(c)(1)(B) and the total unfunded vested benefits of the plan will be fully allocated among all of the employers, in a manner "not inconsistent" with PBGC regulations. ERISA Sec. 4219(c)(1)(D).

Withdrawal from a plan by an employer during a period of three consecutive plan years within which substantially all of the employers withdraw from the plan is presumed to be a withdrawal pursuant to an agreement or arrangement, unless the employer proves otherwise by a preponderance of the evidence. ERISA Sec. 4219(c)(1)(D).

The termination date of a multiemployer plan subject to mass withdrawal is the earlier of (1) the date on which the last employer withdraws; or (2) the first day of the first plan year in which no employer contributions are required under the plan. ERISA Sec. 4041A(b)(2).

When there is a termination of a multiemployer plan as a result of a mass withdrawal of employers (or by a plan amendment, see ERISA Section 4041A(a)(2)), three notice requirements must be satisfied:

1.   The notice of termination (see Q 580);

2.   The notice of benefit reductions (see Q 581); and

3.   The notice of insolvency (see Q 582).

580. What is involved in filing the notice of termination for a multiemployer plan?

When a multiemployer plan has been terminated (whether by mass withdrawal or by a plan amendment), a notice of termination must be filed with the PBGC. In this notice, the plan sponsor is required to certify that all documents and information submitted are true and correct to the best of its knowledge and belief. PBGC Reg. §4041A.11(c).

If a multiemployer plan is terminated by a mass withdrawal (see Q 579), the notice of termination must contain the following information:

1. The name of the plan;

2. The name, address, and telephone number of the plan sponsor and its duly authorized representative;

3. The name, address, and telephone number of the person who will administer the plan after the date of termination (if other than the plan sponsor);

4. A copy of the plan's most recent annual report (Form 5500) and any schedules attached thereto;

5. The date of plan termination;

6. A copy of the plan document that was in effect five years prior to the termination date, and copies of any amendments adopted after that date;

7. A copy of the trust agreement authorizing the plan sponsor to control and manage the operation and administration of the plan;

8. A copy of the most recent actuarial statement and opinion (if any) relating to the plan;

9. A statement of any material change in plan assets or liabilities after the date of either:

    a) the most recent actuarial statement, or

    b) the annual report (Form 5500) submitted with the notice;

10. Copies of any IRS determination letters relating to establishment of the plan, disqualification of the plan and any subsequent requalification, and termination of the plan; and

11.   A statement indicating whether the plan assets will cover all benefits in pay status during the 12-month period following the termination date. PBGC Regs. §§4041A.11(a), 4041A.11(b).

If the plan assets are sufficient to pay all nonforfeitable benefits, the notice is required to contain a brief description of the proposed method of distributing them. Should the plan have insufficient assets to pay all nonforfeitable benefits, the notice must contain the name and address of all employers who have contributed to the plan within three plan years before the termination date. PBGC Regs. §§4041A.11(b)(7), 4041A.11(b)(8).

The notice is required to be filed with the PBGC by the plan sponsor or its duly authorized representative. PBGC Reg. §4041A.11. The notice of termination may be filed with the PBGC by mailing it to the following address:

> Reports Processing, Insurance Operations Department
> Pension Benefit Guaranty Corporation
> 1200 K Street, NW
> Washington, DC 20005-4026

In the case of the termination of a multiemployer plan by mass withdrawal, the notice of termination must be filed within 30 days after the earlier of: (1) the date on which the last employer withdrew from the plan; or (2) the first day of the first plan year for which no employer contributions were required under the plan. PBGC Reg. §4041A.11(c)(2).

For further details on PBGC participation in the termination of a multiemployer plan, including questions on guaranteed limits and benefit payment rules, see Chapter XII, CIVIL COMPLIANCE AND ENFORCEMENT ISSUES.

581. What is involved in filing the notice of benefit reductions?

When a multiemployer plan is terminated (whether through a mass withdrawal or by amendment), a notice of benefit reductions must be filed with the PBGC and provided to participants and beneficiaries whose benefits are reduced by the termination. PBGC Reg. §4281.32(a).

The notice of benefit reductions *to be filed with the PBGC* must contain:

1.   The name of the plan;

2.   The name, address, and telephone number of the plan sponsor;

3.   The Employer Identification Number (EIN) and the plan number (PN) assigned to the plan by the plan sponsor;

4.   The case number assigned by the PBGC when the plan's notice of termination was filed;

5. A statement that a plan amendment reducing benefits has been adopted, including the adoption and effective dates of the amendment; and

6. A certification, signed by the plan sponsor, that the notice of benefit reductions (containing all of the required information) has been provided to all participants and beneficiaries. PBGC Reg. §4281.32(d).

The notice of benefit reductions *to be provided to participants and beneficiaries* must contain:

1. The name of the plan;

2. A statement that a plan amendment reducing benefits has been adopted, including the adoption and effective dates of the amendment;

3. A summary of the amendment, including a description of the effect of the amendment on the benefits to which it applies; and

4. The name, address, and telephone number of the plan administrator or other person designated by the plan sponsor to answer inquiries regarding benefits. PBGC Reg. §4281.32(e).

The notice of benefit reductions must be filed with the PBGC, and provided to participants and beneficiaries, no later than the earlier of: (1) 45 days after the amendment is adopted; or (2) the date of the first reduced benefit payment. PBGC Reg. §4281.32(b). The notice of benefit reductions must be provided to the PBGC and to participants and beneficiaries who are in pay status (or who are reasonably expected to enter pay status in the plan year after the plan year in which the amendment is adopted) either through regular mail delivery or hand delivery. PBGC Reg. §4281.32(c). The plan sponsor may use any method of delivery reasonably calculated to reach participants and beneficiaries not in pay status.

The notice of benefit reductions provided to the PBGC must be mailed or hand delivered to:

Reports Processing, Insurance Operations Department
Pension Benefit Guaranty Corporation
1200 K Street, NW
Washington, DC 20005-4026

582. What is involved in filing the notice of insolvency?

When there has been a plan termination through mass withdrawal, the plan sponsor who has determined that the plan is, or will soon be, insolvent for a plan year must file a notice of insolvency with the PBGC. A notice of insolvency must also be sent to plan participants and beneficiaries. PBGC Reg. §4281.43(a).

Thereafter, the plan sponsor must provide annual updates to the PBGC and participants and beneficiaries for each plan year beginning after the plan year for which the notice of insolvency was issued. The plan sponsor need not issue revised annual updates to participants and beneficiaries who have received a notice of insolvency benefit level under PBGC Regulation §4281.45 for that plan year. PBGC Reg. §4281.43(b). After the plan sponsor has issued annual updates for the plan year, it need not provide revised annual updates if the plan sponsor determines, under PBGC Regulation §4041A.25(b), that the plan is, or will be, insolvent for that plan year. PBGC Reg. §4281.43(b).

The notice of insolvency *to be filed with the PBGC* must contain:

1. The plan sponsor's Employer Identification Number (EIN) and the plan number (PN) assigned to the plan;

2. The IRS Key District Office that has jurisdiction over determination letters for the plan;

3. The PBGC case number assigned to the filing of the plan's notice of termination;

4. The plan year for which the plan sponsor has determined that the plan is or may be insolvent;

5. A copy of the plan's most recent actuarial valuation;

6. A copy of the plan document currently in effect;

7. The estimated amount of annual benefit payments under the plan for the insolvency year;

8. The estimated amount of the plan's available resources for the insolvency year;

9. The estimated amount of benefits guaranteed by the PBGC for the insolvency year;

10. A statement indicating whether the notice of insolvency is the result of an insolvency determination under the insolvency determination requirements (see Q 591); and

11. A certification signed by the plan sponsor that notices of insolvency have been provided to all participants and beneficiaries containing all required information. PBGC Reg. §4281.44(a).

The notice of insolvency *to be provided to participants and beneficiaries* must contain the following:

1.   The name of the plan;

2.   A statement of the plan year for which the plan sponsor has determined that the plan is or may be insolvent;

3.   A statement that benefits above the amount that can be paid from available resources or the level guaranteed by the PBGC, whichever is greater, will be suspended during the insolvency year, with a brief explanation of which benefits are guaranteed by the PBGC; and

4.   The name, address, and telephone number of the plan administrator or other person designated by the plan sponsor to answer inquiries concerning benefits. PBGC Reg. §4281.44(b).

"Available resources" for a plan year are the plan's cash, marketable assets, contributions, and withdrawal liability payments and earnings, less reasonable administrative expenses owed to the PBGC for the plan year under provisions relating to financial assistance repayments. ERISA Secs. 4245(b)(3), 4261(b)(2); PBGC Reg. §4281.2.

The plan sponsor must deliver the notices of insolvency no later than 30 days after it determines that the plan is or may be insolvent. The notice to plan participants and beneficiaries in active pay status may be delivered along with the first benefit payment made after the determination of insolvency. PBGC Reg. §4281.43(c)

The notice of insolvency must be mailed or hand delivered to the PBGC and to plan participants and beneficiaries in pay status. Participants and beneficiaries who are not in pay status may be provided their notice of insolvency in any manner reasonably calculated to reach them (including the posting of notices at work sites, placing notice in union newsletters, or by placing a notice in a newspaper of general circulation). PBGC Reg. §§4281.43(e), 4281.43(f).

583. What is the penalty for failure to provide any of the required notices under the multiemployer plan provisions of ERISA?

Any person who fails, without reasonable cause, to provide a notice required under the multiemployer plan provisions of ERISA or applicable regulations, shall be liable to the PBGC in an amount up to $100 for each day during which such failure continues. The PBGC may bring a civil action against any person who fails to provide a required notice in the U.S. District Court for the District of Columbia, or in any district court of the U.S. within the jurisdiction in which (1) the plan assets are located; (2) the plan is administered; or (3) a defendant resides or does business. Process may be served in any district where a defendant resides, does business, or may be found. ERISA Sec. 4302.

584. Is the plan sponsor's determination of withdrawal liability presumed to be correct? How can a withdrawing employer challenge the plan sponsor's determination?

Yes. Any determination of withdrawal liability made by a plan sponsor is presumed correct, unless the party contesting the determination shows, by a preponderance of the evidence, that the determination was unreasonable or clearly erroneous. ERISA Sec. 4221(a)(3).

A dispute between an employer and the plan sponsor of a multiemployer plan regarding the calculation or imposition of withdrawal liability must be resolved through arbitration. See Q 585.

585. What are the rules regarding arbitration of multiemployer plan withdrawal liability disputes?

ERISA Section 4221 mandates that any dispute between an employer and a plan sponsor of a multiemployer plan regarding the calculation or imposition of withdrawal liability be resolved through arbitration. Either party may initiate arbitration within the 60-day period after the earlier of:

1. The date when the plan sponsor notifies the employer of its decision (see Q 574), following the employer's request for a review of the withdrawal liability determination (see Q 573); or

2. 120 days after the date of the employer's request for review of the withdrawal liability determination (see Q 573).

Both parties may jointly initiate arbitration within the 180-day period after the date of the plan sponsor's initial notice and demand of payment in accordance with the schedule for liability payments. ERISA Sec. 4221(a)(1). The parties may also waive or extend the statutory time limits at any time by mutual agreement. PBGC Reg. §4221.3(b).

Any failure to initiate arbitration within the 60-day period will result in the employer waiving the right to contest the assessment of the withdrawal liability (*Phila. Marine Trade Assoc.-Int'l. Longshoreman's Assoc. Pension Fund v. Rose*, 85 F.3d 612 (3rd Cir. 1996)) which, consequently, becomes immediately due and payable (*Robbins v. Admiral Merchants Motor Freight, Inc.*, 846 F.2d 1054 (7th Cir. 1988)).

In the absence of an equitable tolling of the deadlines, the employer will be deemed to have waived the right to contest the merits of an assessment if it fails to comply with the statutory time limits.

Where the employer requests arbitration, it must include in its notice of initiation of arbitration a statement that it disputes the plan sponsor's determination of its withdrawal liability, and that it is initiating arbitration. This notice must also contain a copy of the demand for payment of withdrawal liability, any request for reconsideration of the withdrawal liability determination, and any response to such request received from the plan sponsor. PBGC Reg. §4221.3(d).

Where any other party initiates arbitration, the notice of intent to arbitrate must include a statement that the party is initiating arbitration, along with a brief description of the questions that it seeks to resolve through arbitration. PBGC Reg. §4221.3(d).

Where both parties jointly initiate arbitration, the agreement to arbitrate must include a description of the questions that are being submitted to arbitration for resolution. PBGC Reg. §4221.3(d).

A party that fails to promptly object to an incomplete or faulty request for arbitration waives its right to object to any filing deficiencies later. PBGC Reg. §4221.3(e).

The parties must select an arbitrator within 45 days after the arbitration is initiated, unless the parties mutually agree upon a different time limit. The parties must provide a notice of appointment to the arbitrator they have selected, which includes (1) a copy of the notice of initiation of arbitration; (2) a statement that the arbitration is to be conducted in accordance with the arbitration rules in the PBGC regulations; and (3) a request for a written acceptance by the arbitrator. PBGC Reg. §4221.4(a).

If the arbitrator selected by the parties refuses or fails to accept an appointment within 15 days after the notice of appointment has been mailed or delivered, the arbitrator is considered to have declined to act. The parties must then select another arbitrator. If the parties fail to select an arbitrator within the statutory time limits, either party may request the appointment of an arbitrator in a United States district court. PBGC Reg. §4221.4(a).

An accepting arbitrator is required to disclose to the parties any facts or circumstances that are likely to have an affect upon his impartiality. PBGC Reg. §4221.4(b).

If any of the parties to the arbitration believe that the arbitrator should be disqualified because of the information disclosed, that party is required to notify all other parties, as well as the arbitrator, within 10 days after the arbitrator makes the disclosure. The arbitrator must withdraw and the parties must then select another arbitrator. PBGC Reg. §4221.4(b).

Any party may also request an arbitrator to withdraw from the proceedings at any time prior to the issuance of a final award on the grounds that the arbitrator is unable to render an impartial award. PBGC Reg. §4221.4(c). The request for withdrawal must be provided to all parties and to the arbitrator, either by hand delivery or by certified or registered mail, and must include a statement of the circumstances that have caused the requesting party to question the arbitrator's impartiality, as well as a statement that the requesting party has brought these circumstances to the attention of the arbitrator and the other parties at the earliest practicable point in the proceedings. If, after review, the arbitrator determines that the circumstances raised by the objecting party are likely to affect his impartiality, and that the request was timely presented, the arbitrator must withdraw from the proceedings and notify the parties of the reasons for the withdrawal. PBGC Reg. §4221.4(c).

In all cases of an arbitrator vacancy, the parties must select another arbitrator within 20 days after they receive notice of the vacancy. PBGC Reg. §4221.4(d).

586. What are an arbitrator's powers and duties?

An arbitrator must conduct an arbitration hearing on withdrawal liability in accordance with arbitration rules found in the PBGC regulations, which provide that an arbitrator has the following powers and duties:

1. An arbitrator must follow applicable law in reaching a decision, including, but not limited to: statutes, regulations, court decisions, and interpretations of those agencies charged with the enforcement of ERISA;

2. An arbitrator may allow any party to conduct pre-hearing discovery, through interrogatories, depositions, requests for documents, and other traditional means, but such attempts at discovery must be shown to be likely to lead to the production of relevant evidence and not to be disproportionately burdensome;

3. An arbitrator may impose sanctions if he determines that a party has failed to respond to good faith discovery requests or has proceeded with discovery in bad faith, or for the purpose of harassment;

4. An arbitrator may require all parties to provide advance notice of the use of expert witnesses or other witnesses upon which they intend to rely;

5. An arbitrator may determine the admissibility and relevance of evidence presented, but there is no mandate of conformity to the legal rules of evidence; and

6. An arbitrator may subpoena witnesses or documents on his own initiative, or upon request of any of the parties. PBGC Reg. §4221.5(a)

If an arbitrator should conclude that a pre-hearing conference would expedite the proceedings, he may direct the parties to appear at a pre-hearing conference at any time before the arbitration hearing commences, in order to consider any of the following items:

1.   Settlement of the case;

2.   Clarification of issues and stipulation of facts not in dispute;

3.   Admission of documents to avoid unnecessary proof;

4.   Limitations on the number of expert or other witnesses; and

5.   Any other matters that may hasten the disposition of the proceedings. PBGC Reg. §4221.5(b).

An arbitrator is permitted to render an award without conducting a hearing if all parties so agree, and file with the arbitrator all evidence necessary to enable the arbitrator to render an award. PBGC Reg. §4221.5(c).

In the absence of a pre-hearing settlement, the arbitrator and the parties must establish a date and a place for the hearing, no later than 15 days after the arbitrator's written acceptance (see Q 585). PBGC Reg. §4221.6(a). The hearing must be scheduled to take place within 50 days after the mailing date of the arbitrator's written acceptance. The arbitrator is then required to provide all parties with written notification of the time and place for the hearing, to be delivered by hand or by certified or registered mail. PBGC Reg. §4221.6(b).

At the request of either party, the arbitrator must provide a record of the arbitration hearing, prepared by either stenographic means or by tape recording. The cost of preparing the record, including transcription and copying, is considered part of the cost of arbitration. PBGC Reg. §4221.6(d).

No later than 30 days after the proceedings have closed, the arbitrator must render the award regarding the withdrawal liability dispute. The award must:

1.   State the basis for the award, including findings of fact and conclusions of law;

2.   Adjust the amount or schedule of withdrawal liability payments to reflect overpayments or underpayments made before the award was rendered, or require the plan sponsor to refund overpayments; and

3.   Provide for an allocation of costs. PBGC Regs. §§4221.8(a), 4221.8(b).

A party may seek a modification or reconsideration of the award by filing a written motion with the arbitrator and all opposing parties within 20 days after the award has been issued. PBGC Reg. §4221.9(a). Such motion will be granted only if:

1. There is a numerical error or mistake in the description of any person, thing, or property referred to in the award;

2. The arbitrator made the award based upon a matter not submitted to the arbitrator, and the matter affects the merit of the decision; or

3. The award is imperfect with respect to a matter of form not affecting the merits of the dispute. PBGC Reg. §4221.9(b).

The arbitrator must render an opinion or denial of the request for a rehearing within 20 days after the request has been filed with him. If an objection to the motion for a rehearing has been filed, the arbitrator must respond in writing within 30 days with a denial of the motion for a rehearing, or render a revised award. PBGC Reg. §4221.9(c).

587. How are the awards and costs of arbitration handled?

In general, all costs of the hearing are shared equally by the parties, but each party must bear the costs for their own witnesses, and the cost of tapes or transcripts of the proceedings (see Q 586) is borne by the party requesting them. The parties may agree to a different allocation of costs, provided that they enter into such agreement after the employer has been notified of its withdrawal liability. PBGC Reg. §4221.10.

The arbitrator may, however, allocate the costs in an unequal fashion if it deems such an award necessary. PBGC Reg. §4221.10(b). For example, the arbitrator may award reasonable attorneys fees where he has determined that one of the parties has acted in bad faith. PBGC Reg. §4221.10(c).

588. May a party to an arbitration bring a post-award court action seeking enforcement, modification, or vacation of the award?

Yes. "Upon completion of the arbitration proceedings in favor of one of the parties, any party thereto may bring an action, no later than 30 days after the issuance of an arbitrator's award, in an appropriate United States district court...to enforce, vacate, or modify the arbitrator's award." ERISA Sec. 4221(b)(2).

In any post-award court action, there is a rebuttable presumption that the findings of fact made by the arbitrator were correct. Such presumptions are rebuttable only by a preponderance of the evidence. ERISA Sec. 4221(c).

589. Is a withdrawing employer entitled to a refund for the overpayment of withdrawal liability payments?

Yes. If the plan sponsor or an arbitrator determines that an employer has made an overpayment of its withdrawal liability, the plan sponsor must refund the overpayment and pay the employer interest thereon. The rate of interest to be paid is "based on prevailing market rates for comparable obligations, in accordance with regulations," or the rate applied to overdue payments. ERISA Sec. 4219(c)(6); PBGC Reg. §4219.31(d).

If a withdrawal liability overpayment is refunded to the employer within six months, it will not be considered a prohibited transaction (see Q 342). ERISA Sec. 403(c)(3).

590. Must a plan sponsor seek PBGC approval of a plan amendment to utilize a nonstatutory, alternative method for computing withdrawal liability? What information must a request for approval of such an amendment contain?

Yes. An amendment to utilize a nonstatutory, alternative method for computing withdrawal liability under ERISA Section 4211(c)(5)(A) must be approved by the PBGC. ERISA Sec. 4220(b).

The PBGC will disapprove an amendment to a multiemployer plan "only if the...[PBGC] determines that the amendment creates an unreasonable risk of loss to plan participants and beneficiaries or to the...[PBGC]." ERISA Sec. 4220(c). Likewise, an amendment that provides for an alternative allocation method or modification of allocation will be approved if the PBGC finds that the change will not significantly increase the risk of loss to plan participants and beneficiaries or to the PBGC. PBGC Reg. §4211.23(a). Specifically, the amendment will be approved if it meets the following criteria:

1. The method allocates a plan's total unfunded vested benefits (UVBs), on both a current and prospective basis, to the same extent as any of the statutory allocations or permitted modifications;

2. The method calculates the amount allocated to an employer either on the basis of that employer's share of total contributions to the plan over a specified period, or on the basis of UVBs attributable to employers; and

3. The method provides a procedure for fully allocating: (a) amounts of uncollectible employer liability, and (b) amounts not assessed against withdrawn employers because of the *de minimis* rule, the 20-year cap, and the insolvent employer provision among employers that have not withdrawn from the plan. PBGC Reg. §4211.23(b).

A request for approval of an alternative allocation method, or a modification to an existing method, must contain the following information:

1. The name, address, and telephone number of the plan sponsor and the duly authorized representative of the plan sponsor;

2. The name of the multiemployer plan;

3. The plan sponsor's Employer Identification Number (EIN) and the plan number (PN);

4. The date when the amendment was adopted;

5. A copy of the amendment that sets forth the full text of the alternative allocation method (or modification);

6. The allocation method that the fund currently uses and a copy of the plan amendment that adopted the method; and

7. A certification that notice of the adoption of the amendment has been given to all employers that have an obligation to contribute under the plan and to all employee organizations that represent covered employees. PBGC Reg. §4211.22(d).

A request for approval of an alternative allocation method, or a modification to an existing method, should be sent by first class mail or courier to:

Reports Processing, Insurance Operations Department
Pension Benefit Guaranty Corporation
1200 K Street, NW
Washington, DC 20005-4026

PBGC Reg. §4211.22(c).

The PBGC may request additional information from the plan sponsor that it may need in order to conduct an adequate review of the request for approval of an alternative allocation method or modification of allocation method. PBGC Reg. §4211.22(e).

591. What is the 50% insolvency rule?

Special rules apply to a withdrawing employer that is insolvent and going through liquidation or dissolution. ERISA Sec. 4225(b). In such a case, the employer is minimally liable for the first 50% of the normal withdrawal liability, see Q 559 and Q 562. After paying 50% of this amount, the employer is liable for that portion of the remaining 50% of the allocable unfunded vested benefits not in excess of the liquidation or dissolution value of the employer, as determined at the beginning of the liquidation or dissolution.

An employer is "insolvent" for this purpose if its liabilities (including withdrawal liability) exceed its assets. ERISA Sec. 4225(d)(1). The liquidation or dissolution value of the employer shall be determined without regard to the withdrawal liability under the plan. ERISA Sec. 4225(d)(2).

In the case of one or more withdrawals of an employer attributable to the same sale, liquidation, or dissolution, all withdrawals shall be treated as a single withdrawal for the purpose of the 50% insolvency rule, and the rule will be applied proportionally to all plans from which the employer has withdrawn. ERISA Sec. 4225(e).

Reorganization (under Chapter 11 of the Bankruptcy Code) will not qualify a plan for the application of the 50% insolvency rule. The employer must be undergoing a process of *liquidation* (under Chapter 7 of the Bankruptcy Code) in order to avail itself of the rule. *Granada Wines, Inc. v. New England Teamsters and Trucking Industry Pension Fund*, 748 F.2d 42 (1st Cir. 1984); *Trustees of Amalgamated Cotton Garment and Allied Industries Fund v. Baltimore Sportswear, Inc.*, 632 F. Supp. 641 (S.D. NY 1986).

592. What rules apply to the sale of assets to an unrelated employer?

In the case of a bona fide sale of substantially all assets, in an arm's length transaction to an unrelated party, for an amount not in excess of $2 million, an employer's withdrawal liability will not be greater than:

1.   30% of the liquidation or dissolution value of the employer; or

2.   The unfunded vested benefits attributable to the employees of the employer. ERISA Sec. 4225(a).

Where the sale of assets exceeds $2 million, ERISA Section 4225(a)(2) provides the following sliding scale for determining the withdrawal liability of the employer:

If the liquidation/dissolution value after the sale/exchange is:	The portion is
$2 million to $4 million	$600,000 plus 35% of that amount in excess of $2 million
$4 million to $6 million	$1,3000,000 plus 40% of that amount in excess of $2 million
$6 million to $7 million	$2,100,000 plus 45% of that amount in excess of $2 million

$7 million to $8 million	$2,550,000 plus 50% of that amount in excess of $2 million
$8 million to $9 million	$3,050,000 plus 60% of that amount in excess of $2 million
$9 million to $10 million	$3,650,000 plus 70% of that amount in excess of $2 million
More than $10,000,000	$4,350,000 plus 80% of that amount in excess of $2 million

In cases where withdrawal from two or more plans has occurred, the withdrawal liability is apportioned among all of the plans involved. ERISA Sec. 4225(e).

593. What are the rules applicable to the merger of multiemployer plans?

A merger is defined as the combining of two or more multiemployer plans into a single multiemployer plan. PBGC Reg. §4231.2. A plan sponsor may not cause a multiemployer plan to merge with one or more multiemployer plans, or engage in a transfer of assets and liabilities to or from another multiemployer plan, unless the following requirements are satisfied:

1. One of the plan sponsors notifies the PBGC at least 120 days before the effective date of the merger or transfer;

2. The accrued benefits of participants and beneficiaries will not be decreased as a result of the merger;

3. The benefits of participants and beneficiaries are not reasonably expected to be suspended under insolvency provisions; and

4. An actuarial valuation of each of the affected plans has been performed during the plan year preceding the effective date of the merger or transfer. ERISA Sec. 4231.

The effective date of the merger or transfer is defined, for this purpose, as the earlier of:

1. The date on which one plan assumes liability for the benefits accrued under another plan involved in the transaction; or

2. The date on which one plan transfers assets to another plan involved in the transaction. PBGC Reg. §4231.8(a)

Where a plan assumes obligations for the payment of benefits to a group of participants as a result of a merger or transfer, that plan must preserve the accrued benefits as determined under the vesting requirements of ERISA Section 411. PBGC Reg. §4231.4.

594. What occurs if there is a withdrawal following a merger?

In the case of a withdrawal following a merger of multiemployer plans, the withdrawal liability rules of ERISA Section 4211 (see Q 560) will be applied in accordance with PBGC regulations, except that if a withdrawal occurs within the first plan year beginning after a merger of multiemployer plans, withdrawal liability is determined as if each of the multiemployer plans had remained separate. ERISA Sec. 4211(f).

Withdrawal liability is determined using one of the four methods provided in ERISA Section 4211 (see Q 560); a non-statutory allocation method that has been adopted by the plan and approved by the PBGC (see Q 590); or one of the allocation methods that have been prescribed by the PBGC specifically for use by merged multiemployer plans (see Q 593). PBGC Reg. §4211.31.

Merged plans may choose from among four allocation methods:

1.   The presumptive method (see Q 563);

2.   The modified presumptive method (see Q 564);

3.   The rolling-5 method (see Q 565); or

4.   The direct attribution method (see Q 566). PBGC Reg. §4211.31

Note that a plan must be amended in order to utilize one of these methods; however, PBGC approval of the amendment is not required. See Q 562.

595. How is "transfer of assets or liabilities" defined?

"Transfer of assets or liabilities" is defined, for this purpose, as a reduction of assets or liabilities for one plan and the acquisition of those assets or assumption of those liabilities by another plan or plans. The shifting of assets or liabilities under a written reciprocity agreement between two multiemployer plans, in which one plan assumes the liabilities of another plan, is not a transfer of assets or liabilities. Likewise, the transfer of assets among multiple funding media (for example, trusts) of a single plan does not constitute a transfer of assets or liabilities. PBGC Reg. §4231.2.

A "significantly affected plan" is defined as a plan that:

1.   Transfers assets that equal or exceed 15% of its assets before the transfer;

2. Receives a transfer of unfunded accrued benefits that equals or exceeds 15% of its assets before the transfer;

3. Is created by a spin-off of another plan; or

4. Engages in a merger or transfer (other than a *de minimis* merger or transfer, see Q 597) either:

> a) after such plan was terminated by mass withdrawal under ERISA Section 4041A(a)(2) (see Q 579), or

> b) with another plan that has so terminated. PBGC Reg. §4231.

596. Is the transfer of assets or liabilities between plans a prohibited transaction?

Generally speaking, no. The merger or transfer of assets or liabilities between multiemployer plans does not constitute a prohibited transaction under ERISA Section 406(a) or ERISA Section 406(b)(2) if the PBGC determines that the merger or transfer has otherwise satisfied the requirements of ERISA Section 4231 (see Q 593). ERISA Sec. 4231(c).

597. What are the asset transfer rules for multiemployer plans?

A multiemployer plan must adopt asset transfer rules. ERISA Sec. 4234(a). The rules adopted must not unreasonably restrict the transfer of plan assets in connection with the transfer of plan liabilities. Such rules are to operate and be uniformly applied with respect to each proposed transfer, except that the rules may provide for reasonable variation taking into account the potential financial impact of a proposed transfer on each affected multiemployer plan. Plan rules authorizing asset transfers under the "in and out" rule between multiemployer and single employer plans (see Q 598) are deemed to satisfy these requirements. ERISA Sec. 4234.

The transfer of assets provision will only apply where there has been a transfer of assets in connection with a voluntary transfer of liabilities. Under *Vornado, Inc., t/a Two Guys v. Trustees of the Retail Store Employees Union Local 1262*, 829 F.2d 416 (3rd Cir. 1987), a multiemployer association fund could not be compelled, under ERISA, to transfer a share of its assets into a new fund established by employers that had withdrawn from the old association fund. The court found that the transfer of assets provision was inapplicable, because there had been no such transfer of liabilities from the old fund to the new fund.

The PBGC has issued regulations providing that *de minimis* transfers of assets are exempt from the general asset transfer rules of ERISA Section 4234(a). A transfer of assets or liabilities is *de minimis* if:

1. The fair market value of the assets transferred is less than 3% of the fair market value of the transferor plan's total assets;

2. The present value of the accrued benefits transferred (whether or not vested) is less than 3% of the fair market value of the transferee plan's total assets; and

3. The transferee plan is not a plan that has been terminated pursuant to ERISA Section 4041A(a)(2). PBGC Reg. §4231.7(c).

In making the determination of whether a transfer is *de minimis*, assets and accrued benefits transferred in previous *de minimis* transfers within the same plan year must be aggregated. A transfer is not *de minimis*, if, when aggregated:

1. The value of the assets *transferred from a plan* equals or exceeds 3% of the value of the plan's assets; or

2. The present value of all accrued benefits *transferred to a plan* equals or exceeds 3% of the plan's assets. PBGC Reg. §4231.7(e)(2).

The asset transfer rules do not apply to a transfer of assets that has occurred in accordance with written reciprocity agreements, except to the extent provided in any regulations that may be prescribed by the PBGC. ERISA Sec. 4234(c).

598. What rules apply to the transfer of assets between multiemployer and single employer plans?

Where there is a transfer of assets or liabilities, or a merger, between a multiemployer plan and a single employer plan, the accrued benefit of any participant or beneficiary may not be less immediately after the transfer or merger than it was immediately before. ERISA Sec. 4232(b). A multiemployer plan that transfers liabilities to a single employer plan shall be liable to the PBGC if the single employer plan terminates within 60 months after the transfer. The amount of such liability is the lesser of:

1. The amount of the plan asset insufficiency of the terminated single employer plan, minus 30% of the net worth of the employer maintaining the single employer plan; or

2. The value of the unfunded benefits, as of the effective date of the transfer, which are transferred to the single employer plan and are guaranteed by the PBGC. ERISA Sec. 4232(c)(1).

The PBGC must make a determination as to the multiemployer plan's liability within 180 days after the PBGC has received an application from the multiemployer plan seeking such determination. There will be no liability where the PBGC determines that the interests of participants and beneficiaries are adequately protected, or if the PBGC fails to issue a determination within the 180 day time frame. ERISA Sec. 4232(c)(2).

Under the "in and out" rule, there is an exception to liability where a multiemployer plan merges with, and later "spins off," a single employer plan. The "in and out" rule eliminates liability to the multiemployer plan because of the transfer of liabilities to a single employer plan if:

1. The value of the liabilities transferred to the single employer plan does not exceed the value of the liabilities for benefits that accrued before the merger; and

2. The value of the assets transferred to the single employer plan is substantially equal to the value of the assets that would have been in the single employer plan if the employer had maintained and funded it as a separate plan under which no benefits accrued after the merger. ERISA Sec. 4232(c)(3).

The PBGC may make equitable arrangements with a multiemployer plan for the satisfaction of the plan's liability. ERISA Sec. 4232(c)(4).

599. What special asset transfer rules apply to multiemployer welfare benefit plans?

In distinguishing between cases involving welfare benefits and those involving retirement benefits, one court has ruled that a multiemployer welfare benefit fund must transfer assets to a successor fund if those assets were contributed pursuant to a collective bargaining agreement. The transfer must take place after the affected members are no longer covered by the transferring plan. *Trapani v. Con. Ed. Employees Mutual Aid Society*, 891 F.2d 48 (2nd Cir. 1989).

600. What rules apply to transfers where there has been a change in bargaining representatives?

Where an employer completely or partially withdraws from one multiemployer plan (the "old plan") as a result of a certified change of collective bargaining representatives, and the employer's employees who participated in the old plan will, as a result of that change, participate in another multiemployer plan (the "new plan"), the old plan shall transfer assets and liabilities to the new plan. ERISA Sec. 4235(a).

The following rules must be satisfied in order to execute an appropriate transfer of assets pursuant to a change in the certified bargaining representative:

1. The employer must notify the plan sponsor of the old plan of the change in multiemployer plan participation no later than 30 days after the employer determines that the change will occur;

2.   The plan sponsor of the old plan must notify the employer of the amount of its withdrawal liability, the old plan's intent to transfer the nonforfeitable benefits of employees (no longer in covered service under the old plan because of the change of bargaining representative) to the new plan, and the amount of assets and liabilities that are to be transferred to the new plan; and

3.   The plan sponsor of the old plan must notify the plan sponsor of the new plan of the benefits, assets, and liabilities that will be transferred to the new plan. ERISA Secs. 4235(b) and 4235(c).

Within 60 days of receiving the notice of the benefits, assets, and liabilities to be transferred, the new plan may file an appeal with the PBGC to prevent the transfer. The transfer will not be made if the PBGC determines that the new plan will suffer substantial financial harm as a result of the transfer. ERISA Sec. 4235(b)(3).

If (1) the employer fails to object to the transfer within 60 days after receiving notice; or (2) the new plan fails to file an appeal; or (3) the PBGC fails to find, within 180 days after the appeal is filed, that the new plan would suffer substantial financial harm as a result of the transfer, then the plan sponsor of the old plan must transfer the appropriate amount of assets and liabilities to the new plan. ERISA Secs. 4235(b)(3)(A) and 4235(b)(3)(B).

In a transfer of assets pursuant to a change in the certified bargaining representative, only those assets allocated to active participants shall be transferred. PBGC Adv. Op. 88-6.

The plan sponsor shall not transfer any assets to the new plan if the old plan is in reorganization, or if the transfer of assets would cause the old plan to go into reorganization. ERISA Sec. 4234(e)(1). Where a transfer is so prohibited, the old plan may make a limited transfer to the new plan. If the value of such benefits does not exceed the employer's withdrawal liability, the old plan shall transfer nonforfeitable benefits of all employees who have transferred to the new plan. If, on the other hand, the value of such benefits exceeds the withdrawal liability of the employer, only the portion of such nonforfeitable benefits that is equal to the employer's withdrawal liability is to be transferred. ERISA Sec. 4234(e)(2).

The plan sponsors of the old plan and the new plan may agree to a transfer of assets and liabilities, so long as their agreement complies with the rules for mergers and transfers between multiemployer plans under ERISA Section 4231 and the asset transfer rules of ERISA Section 4234, and provided that the employer's withdrawal liability under the old plan shall be reduced by the amount by which the value of the unfunded vested benefits allocable to the employer that were transferred to the new plan exceeds the value of the assets transferred. ERISA Sec. 4235(f).

601. What rules apply where an employer withdraws from a plan after a transfer due to a change in bargaining representatives?

If an employer withdraws from the new plan within 240 months after the effective date of a transfer of assets and liabilities due to a change in certified collective bargaining representatives (see Q 600), the amount of the employer's withdrawal liability to the new plan shall be the greater of:

1.   The employer's withdrawal liability, as determined under applicable withdrawal liability provisions; or

2.   The amount by which the employer's withdrawal liability to the old plan was reduced by the amount by which the value of the unfunded vested benefits allocable to the employer that were transferred from the old plan exceeds the value of the assets transferred, reduced by 5% for each 12-month period following the effective date of the transfer and ending before the date of the withdrawal from the new plan. ERISA Sec. 4235(f)(2).

602. Do the rules regarding the transfer of assets and liabilities as a result of a change in collective bargaining representatives apply to a transfer to a defined contribution plan?

No. Where there has been a merger between a defined benefit plan and a defined contribution plan, the rules that govern transfers relating to changes in collective bargaining representatives do not apply to the defined contribution plan, because such plans are not subject to Title IV of ERISA's plan termination rules. PBGC Adv. Op. 87-13.

603. When will the PBGC order the partitioning of a multiemployer plan?

A plan sponsor may request that the PBGC order the partition of a multiemployer plan. ERISA Secs. 4233(a) and 4233(b).

In the partitioning of a plan, a portion of the plan's assets and liabilities are segregated and held in a separate trust as the new partitioned plan. The plan created by the partition is the successor plan for the purpose of benefit guarantees under ERISA Section 4022A, and as a plan terminated by mass withdrawal under which only the employer involved in the bankruptcy has withdrawal liability. ERISA Sec. 4233(e).

Prior to ordering a partition of a plan, the PBGC must find that:

1.   A substantial reduction in the amount of aggregate contributions under the plan has resulted, or will result, from a bankruptcy proceeding filed by an employer;

2.   The plan is likely to become insolvent;

3.   Contributions will have to be increased significantly in reorganization to meet the minimum contribution requirement and prevent insolvency; and

4.   Partition would significantly reduce the likelihood that the plan will become insolvent. ERISA Secs. 4233(b)(1) through 4233(b)(4).

The PBGC must provide notice to the plan sponsor and the participants and beneficiaries whose vested benefits will be affected by the ordered partitioning of a plan. ERISA Sec. 4233(c).

The PBGC's partition order shall provide for a transfer of no more than the nonforfeitable benefits directly attributable to service with the employer that has undergone bankruptcy proceedings and an equitable share of the plan's assets. ERISA Sec. 4233(d).

The PBGC may seek a court decree partitioning the plan in lieu of ordering the partition. The court must make the findings detailed above in items (1) through (4) before it can order the partitioning of the plan. The court order will result in the appointment of a trustee for the terminated portion of the plan. ERISA Sec. 4233(f).

604. Does ERISA require contributions to a multiemployer plan?

Every employer that is obligated to make contributions to a multiemployer plan under the terms of (1) the plan; or (2) a collective bargaining agreement must make such contributions in accordance with the terms and conditions of the plan or agreement. ERISA Sec. 515.

A fiduciary (see Q 186 through Q 221) may bring suit to compel contributions under ERISA Section 502(g)(2). If the court awards judgment in favor of the plan in such a suit, the court must award the plan the following:

1.   The unpaid contributions;

2.   Interest on the unpaid contributions;

3.   The greater of the unpaid contributions or liquidated damages, as provided in the plan document (but not to exceed 20% of the unpaid contributions);

4.   Reasonable attorneys fees and court costs; and

5.   Such other legal or equitable relief as the court deems appropriate. ERISA Sec. 502(g)(2).

Interest on unpaid contributions is determined by using the rate set forth in the plan document, or, if no rate is specified therein, the rate under IRC Section 6621. ERISA Sec. 502(g)(2)(E).

Financial hardship is not a legal excuse for failure to make contributions; the employer will be excused from its obligation only if (1) the contributions are illegal; or (2) the collective bargaining agreement is void. *Onondaga County Laborers' Health, Welfare, Pension, Annuity, and Training Funds v. Sal Masonry Contractors, Inc.*, 1992 US Dist. LEXIS 4715 (N.D. NY 1992).

605. How are claims for contributions and withdrawal liability handled in bankruptcy?

The Bankruptcy Code gives priority to the expenses and claims for contributions to an employee benefit plan arising from services rendered within 180 days before (1) the date for the filing of the petition; or (2) the date of the cessation of the debtor's business, whichever occurs first. 11 USC 507(a)(4)(A). However, priority is given only to the extent of:

1. The number of employees covered by each plan, multiplied by $4,300

2. Minus:

   a) the aggregate amount paid to such employees as pre-petition wages (under U.S. Bankruptcy Code Section 507(a)(3)), and

   b) the aggregate amount paid by the bankruptcy estate on behalf of such employees to any other employee benefit plan. 11 USC 507(a)(4)(B).

In a case that extended the rules of 11 USC 507(a)(4) to non-collectively bargained plans, the court held that the insurer was entitled to receive directly the priority payment of employee group life, health, and disability insurance premiums as "unsecured claims for contributions to employee benefit plans." The court observed that it was simpler to grant the priority directly to the insurer, rather than to require employees to seek the premium amount and then pay it over to the insurer, and noted that the employees were protected because 11 USC 507(a)(4) expressly subordinates the plan contribution priority to the employees' wage priority. *In re Saco Local Development Corp.*, 711 F.2d 441 (1st Cir. 1983).

In the case of a reorganization (Chapter 11 bankruptcy), administrative expenses, including the cost of carrying on the debtor's business after the bankruptcy filing, are given the first priority. 11 USC 507(a)(1). A claim for withdrawal liability is not an administrative expense, because the debtor's withdrawal liability to a multiemployer plan is deemed to have accrued prior to the filing of the bankruptcy petition, even if the actual withdrawal occurs after the filing. Thus, withdrawal liability has the status of a general unsecured claim. *Amalgamated Insurance Fund v. William B. Kessler, Inc.*, 55 BR 735 (1985).

606. What happens if an employer that has previously withdrawn from a multiemployer plan re-enters the plan?

An employer that has completely withdrawn from a multiemployer plan, and subsequently re-enters the plan, may have its withdrawal liability "abated" if certain requirements are met. PBGC Reg. §4207.5(a).

A re-entering employer must formally apply for abatement by the due date of the first withdrawal liability payment following the date when the employer resumes covered operations, or, if later, the 15th day after the employer resumes covered operations. PBGC Reg. §4207.5(a). This application must contain the following information:

1.   The identity of the withdrawing employer;

2.   The date when the employer withdrew;

3.   The identity of the re-entering employer (if different from the withdrawing employer), and all entities under common control with the employer, as of both the date of the withdrawal and the date when covered operations resumed;

4.   A list of the operations for which the employer is obligated to make contributions to the plan; and

5.   The date when the employer resumed covered operations. ERISA Sec. 4207; PBGC Reg. §4207.3(a).

While the abatement determination is pending, an employer may be relieved from its obligation to make withdrawal liability payments if it (1) posts a bond; or (2) establishes an escrow account, in an amount equal to 70% of the withdrawal liability payment that the employer would have otherwise been required to make. PBGC Reg. §4207.4.

The plan sponsor determines whether a re-entering employer has met these requirements of abatement:

(1)   Resumption of covered operations under the plan; and

(2)   Assumption of a post-entry level of contribution base units (see Q 560) that exceeds 30% of the employer's pre-withdrawal amount. PBGC Reg. §4207.5(a).

If the plan sponsor determines that a re-entering employer is eligible for abatement, then the employer no longer has an obligation to make payments on its withdrawal liability, and the employer's liability for any subsequent withdrawal will be calculated under modified rules under Labor Regulations §§4207.7 or 4207.8, as applicable. PBGC Reg. §4207.3(c). Under these circumstances, the employer's bond will be canceled, or amounts held in escrow will be returned to the employer. PBGC Reg. §4207.3(c)(3). Finally, any withdrawal liability payments that the employer made after reentry will be refunded by the multiemployer plan. PBGC Reg. §4207.4(c)(4).

If the plan sponsor determines that a re-entering employer is not eligible for abatement, then the plan sponsor must so notify the employer. Within 30 days of the date of the plan sponsor's notice, the bond posted by the employer, or the escrow accounts established by the employer, must be paid over to the multiemployer plan, and the employer must also pay the balance of the withdrawal liability that was not satisfied by the bond or escrow account. PBGC Regs. §§4207.3(d)(1), 4207.3(d)(2). Thereafter, the employer must resume its schedule for making withdrawal liability payments. PBGC Reg. §4207.3(d)(3). The employer will be treated as a new employer for purposes of any future application rules. PBGC Reg. §4207.3(d)(4).

607. Who has standing to bring a civil action regarding a multiemployer plan?

A plan fiduciary, employer, plan participant, or beneficiary who is adversely affected by the act or omission of any party under the multiemployer plan provisions of ERISA with respect to a multiemployer plan, or an employee organization that represents such a plan participant or beneficiary for purposes of collective bargaining has standing to bring a civil action. Such a suit may seek appropriate legal or equitable relief, or both. ERISA Sec. 4301(a)(1).

ERISA does not authorize any civil actions against the PBGC, the Secretary of Labor, or the Secretary of the Treasury. ERISA Sec. 4031(a)(2).

608. What is the statute of limitations for civil actions regarding multiemployer plans?

A civil action may not be brought after the later of:

1.   Six years after the date on which the cause of action arose; or

2.   Three years after the earliest date on which the plaintiff acquired, or should have acquired, actual knowledge of the existence of such cause of action, except that, in the case of fraud or concealment, such action may be brought not later than six years after the date of discovery of the existence of such cause of action. ERISA Sec. 4301(f).

CHAPTER XI

MULTIPLE WELFARE BENEFIT ARRANGEMENTS

609. What are the issues regarding Multiple Welfare Benefit Arrangements?

Multiple Welfare Benefit Arrangements (MEWAs), also known as Multiple Employer Trusts, have been used for years to market health and welfare benefits to employers for their employees. MEWAs are established by two or more employers for the purpose of pooling resources in a cost-saving manner to provide benefits to their employees. Oftentimes, a MEWA is established by a third party, who will then market it to small employers as an attractive low-cost alternative source of health insurance. Typical clients of MEWAs are small employers, who would otherwise have difficulty in obtaining health and welfare benefits coverage for their employees from a traditional insurer. The economies of scale presented by a MEWA allow for the spreading of risk and the resulting decrease in the cost of coverage.

Because MEWAs specifically offer insurance coverage for participants, state insurance regulators have attempted to regulate them, in an effort to eliminate the potential for fraud and abuse that unscrupulous promoters of MEWAs could unleash upon unwitting employers. Many MEWA promoters have represented to employers that MEWAs are employee benefit arrangements subject to the jurisdiction of ERISA and are, therefore, exempt from state insurance regulations under ERISA's preemption provisions. In the past, a number of MEWAs have been unable to pay claims as a result of insufficient funding or inadequate reserves. A few of the more notorious situations of MEWA failures involved individuals who drained the assets out of the MEWA through excessive administration fees and embezzlement.

State regulators who attempted to prevent this type of abuse through administrative and judicial actions were often thwarted by claims that, because the MEWA at issue paid for the type of benefits traditionally covered by an ERISA plan out of a tax exempt trust (just like an ERISA plan), the MEWA was subject to ERISA preemption. Some plans even filed ERISA-required documents to enhance the appearance of being an ERISA-covered plan. In 1983, Congress amended ERISA, in order to provide relief from the preemption provisions often applied to the regulation of MEWAs for state insurance commissions seeking to establish, apply, and enforce state insurance laws.

On December 16, 1998, Sherwin Kaplan, Deputy Associate Solicitor for the DOL's Plan Benefits Security Division, stated that fraudulent MEWAs are one of the top enforcement issues for the field offices of the Pension and Welfare Benefits Administration. Kaplan spoke at a meeting of a proposed rulemaking committee developed by the DOL for the purpose of developing rules expected to provide guidance in determining when a MEWA has been developed under a collective bargaining agreement. Unscrupulous MEWA operators often attempt to evade state regulation by claiming to have been established under collective bargaining agreements, thereby making them subject to ERISA and exempt from state regulation. Kaplan said that the DOL was conducting 200 to 300 investigations of fraudulent MEWAs.

Unfortunately, there is still a great deal of confusion regarding the enforcement of state and federal laws against MEWAs. The following questions have been designed to help provide a better understanding of MEWAs, how they operate, and how they are subject to the coverage and enforcement provisions of ERISA.

610. What is a Multiple Employer Welfare Arrangement (MEWA)?

The term "multiple employer welfare arrangement" means an employee welfare benefit plan or other arrangement that is established or maintained for the purpose of offering or providing welfare benefit plans to the employees (or their beneficiaries) of two or more employers (including self- employed individuals), except that the term does not include any plan or arrangement that is established or maintained: (1) by one or more collective bargaining agreements; (2) by a rural electric cooperative; or (3) by a rural telephone cooperative association. ERISA Sec. 3(40).

The definition of a MEWA includes employee welfare benefit plans and other arrangements that provide coverage for medical, surgical, hospital care, or benefits in the event of sickness, accident, disability or any other benefit described in ERISA Section 3(1) (see Q 1).

611. Are welfare benefit plans maintained by one employer or a group of employers under common control considered to be provided by two or more employers?

In situations where a single employer with multiple locations provides a plan maintained to provide benefits to that employer's employees or retirees, or beneficiaries of those employees or retirees, the plan will be considered a single employer plan and not a MEWA.

Certain groups of employers that share a common ownership interest are treated as a single employer. Two or more trades or businesses, whether or not incorporated, are considered to be a single employer if those trades or businesses are within the same control group. ERISA Sec. 3(40)(B)(i).

The term "control group" means a group of trades or businesses under common control. ERISA Sec. 3(40)(B)(ii). In defining "common control," ERISA Section 3(40)(B)(iii) refers to the regulations defining common control under ERISA Section 4001(b), with a statutory exception that common control may not be based on an interest of less than 25%.

The regulations under ERISA Section 4001(b) incorporate the regulations under IRC Section 414(c). These regulations provide that "common control" generally means, in the case of a parent-subsidiary group of trades or businesses, an 80% ownership interest, or, in the case of organizations controlled by five or fewer persons who are the same persons with respect to each organization, more than 50% ownership interest by such persons in each organization. PBGC Reg. §4001.3; Treas. Reg. §1.414(c)-2.

612. Is a welfare benefit arrangement maintained by a group or association of unrelated employers considered to be provided by two or more employers?

Yes. The term "employer" is defined as "any person acting directly as an employer, or indirectly in the interest of an employer, in relation to an employee benefit plan; and includes a group or association of employers acting for an employer in such capacity." ERISA Sec. 3(5).

In order for a group or association to constitute an "employer" within the meaning of ERISA Section 3(5), there must be a bona fide group or association of employers acting in the interest of its employer members to provide benefits for their employees. However, unlike the specified treatment of a controlled group of employers as a single employer, there is no indication in ERISA Section 3(40), or the legislative history accompanying the MEWA provisions, that Congress intended that such groups or associations be treated as "single employers" for purposes of determining the status of arrangements such as MEWAs.

The Department of Labor has said that while a bona fide group or association of employers may constitute an "employer" within the meaning of ERISA Section 3(5), the individuals typically covered by the group- or association-sponsored plan are not employed by the group or association, and, therefore, are not employees of the group or association. The covered participants are actually employees of the employer members of the group or association. Accordingly, to the extent that a plan sponsored by a group or association of employers provides benefits to the employees of two or more employer members (which are not a part of a controlled group), the plan would constitute a MEWA within the meaning of ERISA Section 3(40). DOL Adv. Op. 92-05A.

613. Are welfare benefit plans established by employee leasing organizations considered to be provided by "two or more employers"?

Employee leasing organizations often must wrestle with the question of who is the employer of the employees involved in its leasing arrangements. Are they employees of the leasing organization, or of the client employer who is actually receiving the services of these employees? If all of the employees participating in the leasing organization's welfare benefit plan are determined to be employees of the leasing organization, the plan would constitute a "single employer" plan and would not be considered a MEWA. If the employees participating in the welfare benefit plan are considered employees of two or more recipient employers, or employees of the leasing organization and at least one recipient employer, the welfare benefit arrangement would be considered a MEWA, because it would provide benefits to the employees of two or more organizations. DOL Adv. Op. 92-05A.

The term "employee" is defined as "any individual employed by an employer." ERISA Sec. 3(6). The Department of Labor takes the position that an individual is employed by an employer when an employee-employer relationship exists. Like a bona fide group or association of employers, an employee leasing organization may be an employer to the extent it is acting directly or indirectly in the interests of an employer. See Q 612. Employer status does not by itself mean that the individuals covered by the leasing organization welfare benefit plan are "employees" of the leasing organization. There must be an employee-employer relationship. In determining the existence of an employee-employer relationship, the payment of wages, federal, state, and local employment taxes, and the provision of health or pension benefits are not solely determinative of an employee-employer relationship. Rather, the application of established common-law principles "taking into account the remedial purposes of ERISA" is used to determine the existence of an employee-employer relationship. A contract purporting to create an employee-employer relationship will not be determinative where the facts and circumstances establish that the relationship, in fact, does not exist. DOL Adv. Op. 92-05A. For more on the employee-employer relationship, see Q 614.

614. How is employee status determined when considering employers under a MEWA?

The term "employee" is defined to mean "any individual employed by an employer." ERISA Sec. 3(6). The Department of Labor takes the position that an individual is employed by an employer when an employee-employer relationship exists. In most instances, the existence of an employee-employer relationship is easy to determine. In general, the existence of an employee-employer relationship is determined on the basis of the facts and circumstances of the particular situation. Common law principles are applied in addition to facts and circumstances, such as the payment of wages, the payment of federal, state, and local employment taxes, and the provision of health or retirement benefits. The common law principles to be applied include, among other things, "whether the person for whom services are being performed has the right to control and direct the individual who performs the services, not only as to the result to be accomplished by the work, but also as to the details and means by which the result is to be accomplished; whether the person for whom services are being performed has the right to discharge the individual performing the services; and whether the individual performing the services is, as a matter of economic reality, dependent upon the business to which he or she renders services . . ." DOL Adv. Op. 92-05A.

In reviewing whether a welfare benefit plan is sponsored by a single employer or two or more employers, the above process for determining employee status must be applied in establishing whether or not the subject plan is sponsored by a person, group, or association that constitutes a single employer, or if the plan benefits the employees of two or more employers. If the plan benefits the employees of two or more employers, it is a MEWA.

Certain individuals are not considered "employees" for purposes of ERISA. An individual and his spouse are not "employees" with respect to a trade or business that is wholly owned by the individual or the individual and his spouse. Further, a partner in a partnership and his spouse are not "employees" with respect to the partnership. Labor Reg. §2510.3-3(c).

615. Is it mandatory that a plan be established by an employer in order for it to be considered a MEWA?

An advisory opinion held that a welfare benefit arrangement that was established by an association to provide health benefits to its members, who were full-time ministers, and other full-time employees of certain schools and churches, was a MEWA, even though there was no employer involvement in the development, adoption, and administration of the plan. The definition of a MEWA refers to an arrangement that offers to provide benefits to the employees of two or more employers; it is not limited to arrangements established or maintained by employers. MEWA status is not affected by the absence of a connection between the plan and the employers of the employees who are covered by the plan. DOL Adv. Op. 88-5A.

616. Which welfare benefit arrangements are excluded from the definition of a MEWA?

There are three types of welfare benefit arrangements that are specifically excluded from the definition of a "multiple employer welfare arrangement," even though such arrangements may provide benefits to the employees of two or more employers. The three types of arrangements are plans established and maintained: (1) pursuant to collective bargaining agreements; (2) by rural electric cooperatives; and (3) by rural telephone cooperative associations. ERISA Sec. 3(40)(A).

Plans Maintained Pursuant to Collective Bargaining Agreements

Any plan or arrangement that is established and maintained "pursuant to one or more agreements which the Secretary [of Labor] finds to be collective bargaining agreements" is excluded from the definition of a MEWA. ERISA Sec. 3(40)(A)(i). This includes those arrangements commonly referred to as "Multiemployer Plans" (not to be confused with the term "Multiple Employer Welfare Arrangement"). See Chapter X for a discussion of multiemployer plans.

Multiemployer plans are established pursuant to collective bargaining agreements that are negotiated by representatives of unions and employers or an association of employers. Collective bargaining agreements must be negotiated "in good faith" and in accordance with other provisions of the Labor Management Relations Act. 29 U.S.C. Sec. 151, et seq. Contributions to a plan established by a collective bargaining agreement are held in a trust that is administered jointly by trustees appointed from both the union (labor trustees) and the participating employers or association of employers (management trustees).

A collective bargaining agreement is a contract that, as mentioned above, is arrived at through the process of good faith bargaining between bona fide employee representatives (usually selected through a vote of rank and file union members) and one or more employers (where the union has been certified as the bona fide representative of the employees by the National Labor Relations Board, or has been elected by a majority of employees of the signatory employers as the exclusive bargaining representative of the employees). In deciding whether or not a collective bargaining agreement was reached through the process of good faith bargaining, the Department of Labor (DOL) will examine the relevant facts and circumstances (such as the provisions for wages, benefits, working conditions and grievance resolution), taking into consideration the pertinent provisions of the National Labor Relations Act.

In October 2000, the DOL issued two proposed rules to assist in the determination of collective bargaining status for welfare benefit plans. 65 Fed. Reg. 64481 and 64498 (10-27-2000). Under the first proposed rule, the following criteria must be satisfied in any applicable plan year in order for there to a collective bargaining agreement:

1. The plan satisfies the criteria of an employee welfare benefit plan as required under ERISA Section 3(1);

2. At least 80% of the participants in the plan include those who are (a) actively employed under the collective bargaining agreement (b) retirees who participated in the plan at least five of the 10 years preceding their retirement, or are receiving pension benefits under a plan maintained pursuant to the same bargaining agreement and have at least five years of service under the pension plan, or (c) receiving extended coverage under the plan through COBRA or another applicable statute, or court or administrative agency decision;

3. The plan is incorporated or referenced in a written agreement between two or more employers and one or more employee organizations, and the agreement: (a) is the product of a bona fide collective bargaining agreement, (b) identifies employers and employee organizations bound by the agreement, (c) identifies the personnel, job classifications and/or work jurisdiction covered by the agreement, (d) provides terms and conditions of employment in addition to coverage under the plan, and (e) is not unilaterally terminable or automatically terminated solely for non-payment of benefits or contributions. Prop. Labor Reg. §2510.3-40(b).

The second proposed rule establishes procedures for hearings for entities seeking individual determinations of collective bargaining status. Where the jurisdiction or law of a state has been asserted against a plan, the plan may petition the Secretary of Labor for a hearing, before an administrative law judge, to determine whether, under ERISA Section 3(40), it is established and/or maintained pursuant to a collective bargaining agreement and thereby exempt from the state law or jurisdiction being applied. Prop. Labor Reg. §2570.131.

For purposes of a final decision as to collective bargaining status, the plan has the burden of proof in establishing satisfaction of the requisite elements of a collectively bargained plan (see above). Prop. Labor Reg. §2570.137. However, in the discussion of the proposed rules, the DOL notes that the plan would meet its burden of proof going forward when it makes a prima facie showing that it satisfies the criteria spelled out above. 65 Fed. Reg. 64498, 64501 (10-27-2000).

Rural Electric Cooperatives

Any plan or arrangement established or maintained by a "rural electric cooperative" is excluded from the definition of a MEWA. ERISA Sec. 3(40)(A)(ii). A rural electric cooperative is (1) an organization exempt from tax under IRC Section 501(a) and engaged primarily in providing electric service on a mutual or cooperative basis; and (2) an organization described in IRC Section 501(c)(4) or IRC Section 501(c)(6), exempt from tax under IRC Section 501(a), and at least 80% of the members are organizations described in (1) above. ERISA Sec. 3(40)(B)(iv).

Rural Telephone Cooperative Associations

Any plan or other arrangement established or maintained by a "rural telephone cooperative association" is excluded from the definition of a MEWA. ERISA Sec. 3(40)(a)(iii). A rural telephone cooperative association is an organization, described in IRC Section 501(c)(4) or IRC Section 501(c)(6), that is exempt from tax under IRC Section 501(a) and at least 80% of the members of which are organizations engaged primarily in providing telephone service to rural areas of the United States on a mutual, cooperative, or other basis. ERISA Sec. 3(40)(B)(v).

617. To what extent may states regulate MEWAs covered by ERISA?

States are generally precluded from treating an ERISA-covered plan as an insurance company for purposes of state insurance laws. ERISA Sec. 514(b)(2)(B). However, there is an exception to the restriction on treating an ERISA-covered plan as an insurance company with respect to any employee welfare benefit plan that satisfies the statutory definition of a MEWA. ERISA Sec. 514(b)(6)(A).

The extent to which state insurance laws may be applied to a MEWA that is an ERISA-covered plan depends upon whether or not the plan is fully insured. An employee welfare benefit plan that is a multiple employer welfare arrangement and is fully insured (or is a multiple employer welfare arrangement subject to certain exemptions) may be subject to state laws regulating insurance to the extent that a state law provides (1) standards requiring the maintenance of specified levels of reserves and specified levels of contributions, which any plan, or any trust established under such a plan must meet in order to be considered, under the state law, able to pay benefits in full when due; and (2) provisions to enforce these standards. ERISA Sec. 514(b)(6)(A)(i).

The Department of Labor (DOL) has said that nothing in ERISA Section 514(b)(6)(A) limits the application of state insurance laws to only those laws that specifically reference the terms "MEWA" or "Multiple Employer Welfare Arrangement." DOL Adv. Op. 90-18A.

States may apply and enforce any state insurance law requiring the maintenance of specific reserves or contributions that have been established to ensure that a fully insured MEWA will be able to satisfy its benefit obligations in a timely manner. ERISA Section 514(b)(6)(A)(i) also permits states to subject MEWAs to licensing, registration, certification, financial reporting, examination, audit, and other requirements of state insurance law necessary to ensure compliance with insurance reserve, contribution, and funding requirements. The DOL has stated that "it would be contrary to Congressional intent to conclude that states, while having the authority to apply insurance laws to such plans, do not have the authority to require and enforce . . . requirements necessary to establish and monitor compliance with those laws." DOL Adv. Op. 90-18A.

State insurance laws may require ERISA-covered MEWAs to meet more stringent standards of conduct, or to provide more protections to plan participants and beneficiaries than required by ERISA. DOL Adv. Op. 90-18A.

Conversely, ERISA preempts any applicable state insurance law that would "adversely affect a participant's or beneficiary's rights under Title I of ERISA" to review or receive documents, receive continuation of health coverage, or to pursue claims procedures established under ERISA. Further, ERISA preempts any state insurance law that makes compliance a physical impossibility. DOL Adv. Op. 90-18A.

Welfare benefit plans that have been established pursuant to a collective bargaining agreement are also exempt from state laws governing MEWAs. In October 2000, the DOL published two proposed rules designed to assist the DOL and states in determining whether a welfare benefit arrangement is established or maintained pursuant to a collective bargaining agreement and, therefore, exempt from state regulation. See Q 616 for details on these proposed rules.

618. What is a fully insured MEWA?

A multiple employer welfare arrangement is considered fully insured only if the terms of the arrangement provide for benefits and the Department of Labor (DOL) determines that these benefits are guaranteed under a contract or policy of insurance, issued by an insurance company, insurance service, or insurance organization qualified to conduct business in a state. ERISA Sec. 514(b)(6)(D).

Under ERISA Section 514(b)(6), it is not mandatory for the DOL to make a determination as to whether a MEWA is fully insured in order for a particular state to treat a MEWA as fully insured and apply its state insurance laws.

619. Which state insurance laws may be enforced against a MEWA that is not fully insured?

If a MEWA is not fully insured, the only limitation on the applicability of state insurance laws to the MEWA is that the state law may not conflict with ERISA. ERISA Sec. 514(b)(6)(A).

The Department of Labor will consider a state insurance law to be in conflict with ERISA if: (1) compliance with the law would abolish or abridge an affirmative protection or safeguard available to participants and beneficiaries under ERISA (such as a state law that would impede a participant's or beneficiary's right to obtain required disclosure documents under the plan, limit a right to pursue claims procedures described in ERISA, or restrict the right to obtain continuation health coverage under COBRA); or (2) would conflict with any provision of ERISA making compliance with ERISA impossible (such as a state law requiring an ERISA-covered plan to make an imprudent investment). DOL Adv. Op. 90-18A.

A state insurance law generally will not be considered in conflict with ERISA if it requires ERISA-covered MEWA plans to meet more stringent standards of conduct or to provide greater protection to plan participants and beneficiaries than required by ERISA. State laws that require a license or certificate of authority to transact insurance business or that subject persons who fail to comply with these requirements to taxation, fines, and other civil penalties are not, when considered by themselves, in conflict with ERISA. DOL Adv. Op. 90-18A.

620. To what extent will the DOL enforce ERISA-governed activities of a MEWA that is not an employee welfare benefit plan?

Persons who exercise discretionary authority or control over the management of ERISA-covered plans or the assets of such plans are considered fiduciaries and are subject to ERISA's fiduciary responsibility provisions. ERISA Sec. 3(21)(A). When the sponsor of an ERISA-covered plan purchases health care coverage from a MEWA for its employees and its employee's dependents, the assets of the MEWA are considered to include "plan assets," unless the MEWA is a state licensed insurance company. Labor Regs. §§2510.3-101, 2510.3-102. In exercising discretionary authority or control over plan assets (e.g., the payment of administration fees or making benefit claim determinations), the individuals operating the MEWA are considered to be conducting fiduciary acts that are subject to ERISA's fiduciary provisions. When a fiduciary breaches a statutorily mandated duty under ERISA (see Q 239, Q 337), or when an individual knowingly participates in such breach, the Department of Labor (DOL) may investigate and, if such violation is proven, pursue civil sanctions.

The DOL does not have any direct regulatory authority over the insurance business and, as such, ERISA does not cover the typical MEWA as a welfare benefit plan. Because of this, the DOL, through its Pension and Welfare Benefits Administration, focuses its MEWA investigations solely on whether individuals operating MEWAs have breached their fiduciary duties to employee plans that purchase health coverage from a MEWA.

Because of the complex nature of MEWAs, investigations of alleged fiduciary breaches typically require a detailed review of financial records and transactions, as well as a detailed review of the documents relating to the establishment and operation of the MEWA and the contracts between the MEWA, service providers, and participating employers and associations. This is a time consuming and cumbersome process that can result in a determination that the questionable activities of the individuals operating the MEWA have not violated any provisions of ERISA. This is a result of the narrow scope of ERISA's authority over MEWAs. States are usually in a better position to take swift enforcement action against MEWAs, based upon failures to comply with specific statutory requirements such as licensing, reserve, and taxation requirements.

621. What is the scope of ERISA's preemption provisions in regard to MEWA regulation under state insurance laws?

ERISA generally preempts any and all state laws that "relate to any employee benefit plan" subject to ERISA. ERISA Sec. 514(a). There are a number of exceptions to the broad preemptive effect of ERISA. They are set forth in ERISA Section 514(b) and are commonly referred to as the "savings clause."

In reviewing the phrase "relate to any employee benefit plan," the Supreme Court held that the phrase should be construed broadly. In the ruling, the Court said that a "law 'relates to' an employee benefit plan, in the normal sense of the phrase, if it has a connection with or reference to such plan." *Shaw v. United Airlines, Inc.*, 463 U.S. 85 (1983).

While a state law may be found to "relate to" an employee benefit plan, that law may be saved from preemption to the extent that the exceptions contained in ERISA Section 514(b) are applicable. ERISA Section 514(b)(2) contains two relevant exceptions to the broad based preemption found in ERISA. They specifically apply to insurance, banking, and securities regulation at the state level. ERISA provides that nothing in ERISA should be construed to exempt or relieve a person from any law of a state that regulates insurance (the "savings clause"). However, neither an employee benefit plan, nor any trust established under such a plan, is considered an insurance company or other insurer for purposes of a law of a state purporting to regulate insurance companies, or insurance contracts (the "deemer clause"). ERISA Sec. 514(b)(2). See *Metropolitan Life Ins. Co. v. Massachusetts*, 471 U.S. 724 (1985) for a discussion of the criteria applied by the Supreme Court to determine if a state law regulates insurance.

The "savings clause" of ERISA Section 514(b)(2) reserves to the states the right to regulate the insurance business and persons engaged in that business. On the other hand, the "deemer clause" of ERISA Section 514(b)(2) makes it clear that a state law regulating insurance may not consider an employee benefit plan to be an insurance company in order to establish jurisdiction over such a plan.

Consequently, a state's ability to regulate MEWAs was dependent upon the determination as to whether or not the particular MEWA was an ERISA-covered plan. MEWAs often claimed to be ERISA-covered plans in order to evade state regulation and enforcement activities brought against them under state insurance laws. Congress then added ERISA Section 514(b)(6), which allows for a special exception to the broad preemption provisions of ERISA for the application of state insurance laws to ERISA-covered welfare benefit plans that are "multiple employer welfare arrangements." Specifically, ERISA Section 514(b)(6)(A) provides:

1) In the case of an employee welfare benefit plan that is a multiple employer welfare arrangement and is fully insured, any law of any state that regulates insurance may apply to such arrangement to the extent that such law provides— (a) standards requiring the maintenance of specified levels of reserves and specified levels of contributions, which any such plan, or any trust established under such a plan, must meet in order to be considered under such law able to pay benefits in full, when due, and)(b) provisions to enforce such standards; and

2. In the case of any other employee welfare benefit plan that is a multiple employer welfare arrangement, in addition to this title, any law of any state that regulates insurance may apply to the extent not inconsistent with the preceding sections of this title.

622. What is the Form M-1?

The Form M-1 is a reporting form issued by the Department of Labor (DOL). It is an annual reporting form for MEWAs and certain collectively bargained plans that provide health coverage to the employees of two or more employers. 65 Fed. Reg. 7152 (2-11-2000).

According to the DOL, Form M-1 is designed to assist MEWAs in complying with recent health care-related legislation such as the Women's Health and Cancer Rights Act, the Newborns' and Mothers' Health Protection Act and HIPAA (see Chapter II). In effect, the reporting required on Form M-1 will make it more difficult for MEWA operators to manage the plans in an unscrupulous manner by taking premium payments from participants and failing to provide the promised coverage. The information required to be reported on the form will assist the DOL in identifying plans that require closer scrutiny and will assist the DOL in coordinating compliance and enforcement efforts with respect to these plans with state insurance departments.

Under the final rules, administrators of the following plans must file Form M-1: (1)MEWAs that offer or provide benefits consisting of medical care, regardless of whether the entity is a group health plan; and (2) Multiemployer collectively bargained group health plans, or entities that claim they are not MEWAs due to collectively bargaining status as an "entity claiming exemption" (ECE). Labor Reg. §2520.101-2(c).

ECEs are generally not considered MEWAs under ERISA Section 3(40)(A)(i). However, the DOL is requiring ECEs that have been in existence for three or fewer years to file Form M-1. Labor Reg. §2520.101-2(c)(1)(ii). The DOL advises that this requirement is because of a recurring problem with administrators of ECEs attempting to avoid state insurance regulations by mischaracterizing their arrangements as established or maintained pursuant to collective bargaining agreements. Therefore, requiring them to file Form M-1 for the first three years assures a proper review and analysis of operations by the DOL. The MEWA administrator determination that a particular plan is an ECE does not affect the applicability of state law to the entity during, nor after, the initial 3-year reporting period.

The Form M-1 filing requirement does not apply to a MEWA or ECE if it is licensed or authorized to operate as a health insurance issuer in every state in which it offers or provides medical care to employees. Labor Reg. §2520.101-2(c)(2).

All newly formed MEWAs and ECEs are required to file Form M-1 within 90 days of origination. Labor Reg. §2520.101-2(e)(2)(iii)(A). However, this rule does not apply if the origination date occurs between October 1 and December 1 (Labor Reg. §2520.101-2(e)(2)(iii)(B)) due to the mandatory Form M-1 filing deadline of March 1 for all required Form M-1 filings. Labor Reg. §2520.101-2(e)(2)(i).

A copy of Form M-1 is available on the DOL website at: www.dol.gov/dol/pwba. Completed copies of Form M-1 are to be filed with the DOL at:

> Public Documents Room
> Pension and Welfare Benefits Administration, Room N-5638
> U.S. Department of Labor
> 200 Constitution Avenue, NW
> Washington, DC 20210

CHAPTER XII

CIVIL COMPLIANCE AND ENFORCEMENT ISSUES

623. What is involved in the civil compliance and enforcement process?

This chapter will review the administration and enforcement of the civil provisions of ERISA, from the individual participant benefits dispute through the investigation and enforcement procedures of the Pension and Welfare Benefits Administration ("PWBA") to the administration and enforcement of the plan termination insurance provisions of ERISA and the Pension Benefits Guaranty Corporation ("PBGC").

The Department of Labor ("DOL"), through the PWBA, is charged with the enforcement of the reporting, disclosure and fiduciary provisions of ERISA. The DOL undertakes the majority of its enforcement efforts through the investigative process. This usually results in an administrative settlement of any issues discovered through the course of an investigation. If administrative enforcement efforts fail, the DOL may bring civil actions to compel plan administrators to satisfy their reporting obligations to the DOL and the IRS, as well as their disclosure obligations (i.e., to provide participant statements, summary annual reports and summary plan descriptions). Likewise, the DOL may bring, or join, civil actions to enforce the fiduciary provisions of ERISA and to recover losses incurred by the plan as a result of fiduciary breaches.

The DOL conducts four major types of investigations: (1) targeting and limited reviews; (2) fiduciary investigations; (3) prohibited person investigations; and (4) criminal investigations. These various actions are reviewed in detail in this chapter, from the targeting and conduct of the investigations through the negotiation process used to settle any outstanding violations identified in the investigation.

Title IV of ERISA (Plan Termination Insurance) was established to provide for the timely and uninterrupted payment of pension benefits under defined benefit plans that are subject to the jurisdiction of Title IV. The PBGC maintains two pension protection programs that provide termination insurance protection to single employer defined benefit plans and multiemployer defined benefit plans. The PBGC collects premiums from participating plans that are placed into "revolving funds" that are managed by investment managers selected by the PBGC through a process of competitive bidding. The provisions of Title IV and the termination of defined benefit plans through the plan termination insurance program as well as the PBGC enforcement procedures are reviewed in this chapter.

This chapter closes with a brief review of how the DOL and other federal agencies (particularly the IRS) will refer issues identified through their various enforcement efforts to those federal agencies with appropriate jurisdiction. Finally, this chapter will review how and when ERISA will and will not preempt state laws.

PENSION AND WELFARE BENEFITS ADMINISTRATION

624. What is the Pension and Welfare Benefits Administration?

The Pension and Welfare Benefits Administration ("PWBA") is an agency within the DOL that administers and enforces the provisions of Title I of ERISA (Protection of Employee Benefit Rights). PWBA is directed by an Assistant Secretary, a Presidential appointee, who reports directly to the Secretary of Labor. Headquartered in Washington, D.C., PWBA's enforcement activities are conducted primarily in its field offices—10 regional offices and five district offices, located in 15 cities throughout the United States. There are over 300 investigators and auditors working out of these offices, many of whom are attorneys, certified public accountants, or individuals holding advanced degrees in business and finance. PWBA's Office of Enforcement, located in PWBA's national office, supports the activities of the regional and district offices. A list of field offices is located in Appendix C.

PWBA shares responsibility with the IRS and the Pension Benefit Guaranty Corporation ("PBGC") for the administration and enforcement of ERISA. Under ERISA, the Secretary of Labor is responsible for protecting the rights and financial security of employee benefit plan participants and beneficiaries and for assuring the integrity and effective management of the private pension and welfare benefit system. In carrying out its enforcement responsibilities, PWBA conducts a wide range of activities (including civil and criminal investigations) to determine whether the provisions of ERISA have been violated or whether any crimes have been committed with respect to employee benefit plans. PWBA also issues regulations and interpretations under Title I of ERISA (Protection of Employee Benefit Rights), grants class or individual exemptions regarding the prohibited transactions of ERISA, receives and discloses to the public required annual financial reports filed by employee benefit plans, provides educational, technical and compliance assistance to the public, and assists plan participants and beneficiaries regarding their plan benefits. *PWBA Enforcement Manual.*

625. What is the mission of the Pension and Welfare Benefits Administration?

The PWBA protects the integrity of pensions, health plans, and other employee benefits for more than 200 million people. According to PWBA, its mission is to:

1.   Assist workers in getting the information they need to protect their benefit rights;

2.   Assist plan officials in understanding the requirements of the relevant statutes in order to meet their legal responsibilities;

3.   Develop policies and laws that encourage the growth of employ-
        ment-based benefits; and

4.   Deter and correct violations of the relevant statutes.

See Appendix C for contact information and a list of PWBA Officers and
Directors.

626. What is PWBA's policy for recruiting and training investigators and auditors?

PWBA prefers to recruit individuals for investigator and auditor positions
whose educational and employment background indicates a familiarity with
ERISA-related fields of knowledge, such as law, accounting, and finance. The
agency's training objectives for newly hired as well as experienced investigators
and auditors lie in the areas of: (1) basic training; (2) specialized training and skills
development; and (3) ongoing continuing education.

Each new investigator or auditor attends a 3-week mandatory "Basic
Training Course." It consists of an intensive lecture and discussion period,
supplemented by practical exercises, to familiarize new employees with the
provisions of the federal law that PWBA enforces, as well as presentations and
practice sessions to acquaint the investigators and auditors with investigative
techniques. This "basic training" course is supplemented by a self-teaching course
in the provisions of ERISA, which is mandatory for all new enforcement
investigators and auditors.

After basic training, experienced investigators and auditors also attend a
seven day formal classroom presentation in "Financial Institutions." The course
provides an understanding of the structure and operation of institutional investment managers, such as banks, registered investment advisors and insurance
companies. Investigators who have no substantial training in accounting also
attend a 7½ day formal classroom course in "Employee Benefit Plan Accounting."
The course concentrates on accounting for employee benefit plans. A formal 1-
week course in criminal investigation also is presented. In this course, students
learn about the applicable criminal statutes and techniques of criminal investigations. These in-house classroom programs are supplemented by additional
training. Investigators and auditors may attend these additional training courses,
as required in the course of their assignments.

PWBA also provides on-the-job training that is intended primarily for new
employees and can range from the use of structured training material to ad hoc
discussions between employees and supervisors. It also includes actual case work
in the field under the supervision of a supervisor or senior investigator and is
primarily designed to address specific needs of individual investigators. PWBA
uses continuing education for the purpose of updating the technical knowledge
and skills of both new and experienced employees. Legislative changes, regulatory
developments, enforcement initiatives, and new investigative techniques are
examples of such training.

PWBA also offers investigators and auditors individual development courses that are typically presented at institutions of higher learning or similar establishments. Included are courses of study leading to professional certification, such as Certified Employee Benefit Specialist (CEBS). *ERISA Enforcement Strategy Implementation Plan,* Sept. 1990, pp. 25-26.

627. What is the Office of Enforcement of the Pension and Welfare Benefits Administration?

The PWBA Office of Enforcement is responsible for overseeing the planning and implementation of the investigative programs of the agency. The office is headquartered in Washington, D.C. Fifteen PWBA Regional and District Offices are responsible for conducting the actual investigations to detect civil and criminal violations of Title I of ERISA (Protection of Employee Benefit Rights), related DOL regulations, and other criminal laws that relate to employee benefit plans.

628. What is the Office of the Chief Accountant of the Pension and Welfare Benefits Administration?

The PWBA's Office of the Chief Accountant ("OCA") is responsible for enforcing the reporting and disclosure provisions of ERISA and administering a program to audit compliance with the fiduciary requirements of the Federal Employees' Retirement System Act of 1986 ("FERSA").

In order to leverage its limited resources, OCA implements a multifaceted program to improve compliance with ERISA's reporting and disclosure requirements. One component of this program is a set of traditional enforcement initiatives involving civil penalties imposed against plan administrators for their failure to submit complete and accurate Form 5500 Series Annual Reports with the Department. OCA reviews Form 5500 Annual Reports to ensure that the information contained therein is complete and accurate. The Non-Filer Enforcement Program is an effort to proactively target employee benefit plans that are required to file annual reports, but have not done so.

According to PWBA, non-filers are generally companies and corporations, large and small, that have illegally elected not to file annual reports for various reasons. In PWBA's view, the failure to file annual reports could be a signal that participants' benefits are in jeopardy. The program seeks both retroactive (back to 1988) and prospective compliance. Employee benefit plans targeted through the Non-Filer Enforcement Program, or that are referred to the program through a DOL investigation or IRS or Pension Benefit Guaranty Corporation ("PBGC") referral, are not eligible to participate in other DOL voluntary or reduced penalty programs.

OCA also has established an on-going quality review program for employee benefit plan audits to address the concern that independent qualified public accountant audits ("IQPA") do not consistently meet professional standards.

This program involves a random selection of plan audits for review to ensure that the level and quality of audit work performed supports the opinion rendered by the IQPA on the plan's financial statements, and that such work is adequately documented in the IQPA's work papers as required by established professional standards.

See Appendix C for contact information for the Office of the Chief Accountant.

629. What is the Office of Exemption Determinations of the Pension and Welfare Benefits Administration?

The Office of Exemption Determinations of the PWBA administers the program for the granting of administrative exemptions from the prohibited transaction provisions of ERISA. The office has two divisions, one of which is responsible for class exemptions, and the other of which administers the program for individual exemptions.

The office reviews applications for such exemptions and determines whether to grant relief. Individual exemptions relate to a particular plan or applicant; class exemptions are applicable to anyone engaging in the described transactions, provided the enumerated conditions are satisfied. (See Chapter V for information on prohibited transaction exemption requests.)

630. What is the Office of Regulations and Interpretations of the Pension and Welfare Benefits Administration?

The Office of Regulations and Interpretations of the PWBA plans, directs, and implements a program for the development and issuance of policies, regulations, opinions, and interpretive bulletins regarding the reporting and disclosure, fiduciary, and coverage provisions of ERISA. It also develops and implements a regulatory program to meet the requirements assigned to the DOL by the Federal Employees' Retirement Security Act.

OFFICE OF THE SOLICITOR

631. What is the United States Department of Labor's Office of the Solicitor?

The Solicitor of Labor, who is subject to presidential nomination and Senate confirmation, serves as the chief legal officer of the DOL. The Solicitor's responsibilities include enforcing the laws under the Department of Labor's jurisdiction through litigation and providing a full range of legal services to the Secretary of Labor and the numerous agencies and bureaus that comprise the DOL.

Within the immediate Office of the Solicitor, there are three Deputy Solicitors, with each one having his own responsibility. The different responsibilities are: (1) National Operations; (2) Regional Operations; and (3) Planning and Coordination.

The attorneys in the Washington, D.C. National Office are divided into 11 Divisions, nine of which are program specific. The program specific divisions are:

- The Division of Black Lung Benefits;

- The Division of Civil Rights;

- The Division of Employee Benefits;

- The Division of Employment and Training Legal Services;

- The Labor-Management Laws Division;

- The Fair Labor Standards Division;

- The Division of Mine Safety and Health;

- The Division of Occupational Safety and Health; and

- The Plan Benefits Security Division.

The two other function-related divisions are: (1) the Division of Special Appellate and Supreme Court Litigation; and (2) the Division of Legislation and Legal Counsel. There are also 15 Regional and Branch Offices throughout the United States.

632. What is the Plan Benefits Security Division of the Office of the Solicitor?

The Plan Benefits Security Division ("PBSD") of the Office of the Solicitor is responsible for the legal work arising out of the DOL's administration and enforcement of ERISA and the Federal Employees' Retirement Security Act ("FERSA"). The Division is headed by an Associate Solicitor and Deputy Associate Solicitor.

PBSD litigates matters that arise under ERISA in federal court. This litigation consists of: (1) District Court enforcement cases arising out of investigations conducted by the PWBA; and (2) an amicus curiae program. This program was designed to clarify and provide consistency to judicial interpretations of ERISA. In addition, the program: (1) expands participant access under ERISA to the federal courts; (2) assures that adequate remedies are available to them under ERISA once they secure standing; and (3) interprets the scope of federal preemption of state law in the way intended by the drafters of ERISA.

PBSD is also actively involved in all regulatory and legislative departmental activity involving ERISA and health care reform. PBSD provides technical assistance and support to congressional staffs, departmental and administration policy makers and to interested trade and professional groups. Additionally, PBSD is involved in drafting and reviewing legislative proposals, interpretive bulletins, advisory opinions, class exemptions and other policy initiatives involving ERISA.

ERISA ADVISORY COUNCIL

633. What is the ERISA Advisory Council?

The Advisory Council (Council) on Employee Welfare and Pension Benefit Plans is provided for under ERISA Section 512. The Council's members, appointed by the Secretary of Labor, include:

- three representatives of employee organizations (at least one of whom represents an organization whose members are participants in a multiemployer plan);

- three representatives of employers (at least one of whom represents employers maintaining or contributing to multiemployer plans);

- one representative from each of the following fields: (1) insurance; (2) corporate trust, (3) actuarial counseling; (4) investment counseling; (5) investment management; (6) accounting; and

- three representatives of the general public (one of whom represents those receiving benefits from a pension plan).

The 15 members of the Council are appointed for 3-year terms, with five terms expiring each year. Additionally, no more than eight members of the Council may be from the same political party.

Members of the Council must be qualified to appraise the programs instituted under ERISA. The duties of the Council are to advise the Secretary and submit recommendations regarding the Secretary's functions under ERISA. The Council customarily holds four meetings each year, which are open to the public. ERISA Secs. 512(a), 512(b). See Appendix C for a list of current ERISA Advisory Council members.

634. How are members of the ERISA Advisory Council appointed?

Each year, vacancies for the Council are announced in the Federal Register. Any person or organization who desires to recommend one or more individuals for appointment to the Council may submit recommendations on or before a specified time and date.

The recommendations may be in the form of letters, resolutions or petitions signed by the person making the recommendation, or by an authorized representative of the organization, if the recommendation is made by an organization. The recommendations should contain the candidate's name, occupation or position, telephone number and address, as well as a brief description of the candidate's qualifications and the group or field that he or she would represent. The candidate's political party affiliation must be noted because of the requirement that no more than eight Council members may be members of the same political party. Additionally, the recommendation must state whether the candidate is available and would accept appointment to the Council.

The nomination or recommendation letters are evaluated for completeness and qualifications of the candidate. The letters are acknowledged and the nominees are requested to declare their political affiliation. Letters supporting candidates are welcomed and acknowledged. This process continues until the close of business on the termination date previously announced in the Federal Register for receiving nominations.

Upon the completion of the nomination process, the Assistant Secretary of the PWBA reviews the nominations and submits his recommendations to the Secretary, who then appoints the five new members. In addition, the Secretary selects the chair and vice-chair of the full Council and working groups, based upon the advice and recommendation of the Assistant Secretary. ERISA Sec. 512(a).

635. Who is the Executive Secretary of the ERISA Advisory Council?

ERISA Section 512 establishes the position of the Executive Secretary for the ERISA Advisory Council. It is the responsibility of the Executive Secretary to: (1) provide staff support to the Office of the Assistant Secretary of Labor and the PWBA regarding Council activities; (2) schedule, coordinate and provide administrative support to all Council and Working Group meetings; (3) plan and coordinate the selection process for new members of the Council; (4) prepare reports regarding the Council's activities; and (5) establish and maintain the archives of the Council. ERISA Sec. 512(c).

636. How does the ERISA Advisory Council work?

After considering and debating various issues that are important to the administration of ERISA, the Council forms a number of working groups to focus on such issues. Additional issues for the Council to examine during the year may be suggested by the Office of the Assistant Secretary of PWBA. The Council usually forms three or four such working groups per year.

The Council receives the working groups' progress reports, discusses the findings, poses questions and makes recommendations to the working groups during the Council meetings. However, the Council retains the responsibility for all final decisions made in regard to working group reports, and makes its decisions at scheduled meetings open to the general public.

The working groups: (1) identify and define the various issues; (2) investigate and take testimony from witnesses; and (3) submit final or interim reports of their findings and recommendations to the Council.

The working group usually uses its first meeting to organize itself. Additionally, during this meeting, a wide variety of witnesses are identified with a view to inviting them to testify before the working group. The working group devises the approach and strategy it will use to study the relevant issue, and reports to the Council for advice and consent. The working groups continue to report their progress to the Council during the course of the Council term, and the Council may offer input and guidance. The Council encourages joint consultation among members of the working groups and their chairs.

A typical working group meeting follows the same general schedule. First, the chair or vice chair calls the meeting to order, welcomes the general public, introduces members of the working group, and states the purpose of the meeting. Next, the chair invites any members who have been given a work assignment to provide a report. Then, any witnesses who have been invited to testify are called forward and requested to speak for a maximum of 10 minutes. Also, some witnesses submit written testimony that is distributed to the working group and made part of the official record of the meeting. Members of the working group are invited to pose questions to each witness, and when the working group has no further questions, the chair thanks the witness and excuses him. The process continues with the next witness, until all witnesses scheduled for the meeting have been heard.

Members of the working group are encouraged to discuss the events of the meeting, and to express their views and concerns. After the discussion is completed, the chair invites statements from the general public. When the general public has completed its statements and any subsequent discussion has been completed, the chair asks for a motion to adjourn.

During the Council year, the working group studies testimony received and deliberations that took place on various issues. The working group continues to meet and to report to the Council until early November of each year. Near the end of the Council term, members of the working group may be requested to summarize witness testimonies and deliberations of the group in preparation of a final report of findings and recommendations to the Council.

Members of the working groups continue to consult informally with other members and chairs between formal meetings. During this time, members may be called upon to review materials submitted by witnesses, prepare summaries of witness testimonies, research and prepare documents for an upcoming meeting, or seek additional witnesses for appearance at working group meetings.

The Council term ends on November 14, at which time the working groups present their final or preliminary findings and recommendations to the full Council. The Council then discusses each working group's report, and either accepts or modifies the report. Finally, the Council Chair transmits the working groups' reports as accepted by the Council to the Secretary of Labor.

GENERAL INVESTIGATIVE AUTHORITY

637. What is the Department of Labor's general investigative authority?

ERISA Section 504(a) grants the Secretary of Labor broad discretion to investigate whether any person has violated or is about to violate any provision of Title I of ERISA (Protection of Employee Benefit Rights), or its attendant regulations. Such investigations may require the submission of reports, books and records, and the filing of data in support of any information required to be filed with the Department of Labor.

The DOL may also "enter such places, inspect such books and records and question such persons" as it deems necessary to determine the facts relative to the investigation. ERISA Secs. 504(a)(1), 504(a)(2). This authority extends beyond plans and plan sponsors — it also includes service providers to plans and financial institutions (e.g., banks, savings and loans, insurance companies and investment management companies) who conduct business with ERISA covered plans.

The DOL may not require any plan to submit to an investigation more than once in any 12-month period, unless the DOL has "reasonable cause" to believe that there may exist a violation of Title I of ERISA, or its attendant regulations. ERISA Sec. 504(b).

The enforcement of Title I of ERISA is handled by the PWBA. The PWBA has regional and district offices throughout the United States. Under the DOL's 1990 Enforcement Strategy Implementation Plan, the DOL, in an effort to allocate its limited resources in the most effective manner, so as to protect the largest number of plan participants and plan assets, has developed an enforcement strategy designed to:

1.   Identify and investigate those areas most prone to abuse;

2.   Detect and obtain correction of ERISA violations;

3.   Respond to participant complaints, public inquiries and referrals received from other governmental agencies;

4.   Disseminate information and promote voluntary compliance with Title I of ERISA; and

5.   Establish a presence in the regulated benefits community.

Under ERISA Section 504(c), the DOL has administrative subpoena authority regarding testimony and the production of books, records and documents; however, the DOL is required to seek a grant of authority from the Department of Justice to conduct criminal investigations (see Chapter XIII for details). In criminal investigations, the DOL has no subpoena authority. If the DOL requires a subpoena in the course of a criminal investigation, it must request it through the Department of Justice, specifically, a U.S. Attorney in the district in which the investigation is being conducted.

638. Does the Department of Labor possess the power to subpoena?

Yes. In accordance with its investigative authority pursuant to ERISA Section 504(c), the DOL has the power to subpoena when conducting investigations under Title I of ERISA (Protection of Employee Benefit Rights). This subpoena power is in accordance with the provisions of Sections 9 and 10 of the Federal Trade Commission Act, which relate to the attendance of witnesses and the production of books, records, and documents, and is applicable to the jurisdiction, powers, and duties of the DOL or its designees. Accordingly, these provisions provide the DOL with: (1) the authority to administer oaths; (2) the power to compel the attendance of witnesses; and (3) the access to and the right to copy documentary evidence. ERISA Sec. 504(c).

The authority of the DOL to execute and issue administrative subpoenas is delegated to the regional directors of PWBA under the guidance and direction of the Director of Enforcement. Through the use of their subpoena powers, the regional directors issue subpoenas as a method of requiring an individual or entity to produce certain documents and records and to appear for the purpose of providing sworn testimony in connection with an investigation. Prior to its issuance, a subpoena is reviewed by a regional solicitor of the DOL for its legal sufficiency. *PWBA Enforcement Manual*, Ch. 33, pp. 1-3.

639. What is a subpoena duces tecum?

A subpoena duces tecum is a command to a person or organization to appear at a specified time and place and: (1) to bring certain designated documents in his custody or control; (2) to produce the documents; and (3) to testify as to their authenticity, as well as any other matter concerning the documents to which proper inquiry is made. *PWBA Enforcement Manual*, Ch. 33, p. 1.

640. What is a subpoena ad testificandum?

A subpoena ad testificandum is a command to a named individual or corporation to appear at a specified time and place to give oral testimony under oath. A verbatim transcript is made of this testimony. *PWBA Enforcement Manual*, Ch. 33, p. 1.

641. What is an accommodation subpoena?

An accommodation subpoena is a subpoena issued by the PWBA to persons or entities who are willing to testify or to produce the documents requested but are concerned about protecting themselves from any potential adverse consequences of doing so without a legal requirement. These subpoenas are often issued by PWBA as an accommodation to service providers and financial institutions for the foregoing reasons. *PWBA Enforcement Manual,* Ch. 33, p. 1.

642. What methods are used to serve the subpoena?

Subpoenas are generally served by certified or registered mail, with return receipt requested. PWBA investigators or auditors often arrange service by prior telephone conversation or through the individual's or entity's legal counsel. In all cases, a letter, with references to any earlier telephone discussions, accompanies the subpoena. (See *PWBA Enforcement Manual,* Ch. 33, Figures 1, 2, 3, 4, and 5 for model letters.)

In instances where it proves impractical or impossible to serve the subpoena on an individual by mail, PWBA may arrange to have the subpoena served personally, and a copy also may be sent by mail. The DOL instructs its investigators or auditors that personal service is complete when the subpoena: (1) is delivered directly to the individual or entity; or (2) is delivered to the individual's residence with a person of suitable age and discretion residing there full-time, such as a spouse; or (3) is delivered to the person in charge at the office or place of business of the entity. *PWBA Enforcement Manual,* Ch. 33 pp. 3-4.

643. What types of investigations are conducted by the Department of Labor?

The DOL conducts investigations of plans, service providers, plan sponsors and multiemployer organizations. Investigations of these entities are classified by the DOL, depending upon the actual issues being investigated. The classifications are based upon the chapters within the *PWBA Enforcement Manual.* The DOL refers to these investigations as: Program 53, Program 48, Program 52 and Program 47.

Program 53 — Targeting and Limited Reviews

Most investigations are initially opened as Program 53 investigations. The initial on-site investigations for the majority of DOL field audits are conducted as Program 53 investigations (known internally as a "P-53"). (See Q 667 though Q 671 for the details of how the DOL conducts an initial on-site investigation.) The purpose of a P-53 is to investigate the issues upon which the case was targeted and opened (as identified on a Case Opening Form 205), as well as the bonding, reporting and disclosure obligations applicable to all plans. (See Q 667 for details on how the DOL targets investigations). If a P-53 reveals evidence that a fiduciary violation has occurred, the investigation is converted to a Program 48 ("P-48") investigation. P-53 investigations that fail to uncover any outstanding fiduciary or criminal investigations are quickly closed, and a brief case closing letter is issued. *PWBA Enforcement Manual,* Ch. 53.

Program 48 — Fiduciary Investigation

Chapter 48 of the *PWBA Enforcement Manual* details the procedures to be followed in conducting fiduciary investigations. If, in the course of targeting an investigation, the DOL has sufficient evidence to believe that a fiduciary violation has occurred, they will open the investigation as a P-48 and dispense with the formality (and paperwork) involved in a P-53 investigation. P-48 investigations are usually very detailed and involve an in-depth analysis of plan records as well as interviews of, and requests for records from, plan service providers. If the DOL uncovers alleged fiduciary violations of ERISA, the targets of the investigation will likely receive a Voluntary Compliance ("VC") letter from the DOL which details: (1) the facts of the alleged violations identified by the DOL; (2) the provisions of ERISA that are alleged to have been violated; and (3) a request that the target of the investigation provide to the DOL, within 10 days, a written explanation of the target's plan to reverse the outstanding alleged violations and restore to the plan any alleged losses and lost opportunity costs.

In cases of extreme or egregious violations of ERISA, the target of a P-48 investigation may receive from the Pension Benefits Security Division ("PBSD") of the DOL, or from the DOL's Regional Solicitor, a Notice of Intent to Litigate. At this point, the DOL is of the opinion that achieving voluntary compliance from the investigative target is highly unlikely, or that the outstanding violations are of a nature that warrant immediate judicial intervention in order to protect plan assets for the benefit of participants and beneficiaries. (See Q 694 regarding information on how investigation subjects should proceed in responding to the DOL voluntary compliance letter). *PWBA Enforcement Manual*, Ch. 48.

Program 52 — Criminal Investigation

If a P-53 discovers evidence of criminal activity regarding the subject plan, the evidence will be documented and presented to the United States Attorney's Office for the jurisdiction in which the plan is located. *PWBA Enforcement Manual*, Ch. 52. The DOL will present evidence of criminal activity regarding employee benefit plans to the U.S. Attorney along with a request for a Grant of Authority to conduct a criminal investigation. (This is necessary because the DOL does not, by itself, have the authority to issue subpoenas in criminal matters.) All subpoenas issued in the course of a P-52 are issued from the Department of Justice and are carried out by the DOL.

If a P-52 investigation establishes sufficient evidence that criminal activity has occurred in regard to the subject employee benefit plan, and that a certain subject or subjects have committed the violations, the Department of Justice will present the results of the investigation to a federal grand jury for the purpose of securing an indictment against the subject or subjects with respect to whom the investigation has established probable cause to believe that they have committed the crimes for which the indictments were sought.

The most common criminal acts for which indictments are sought under a P-52 investigation are:

1.   Theft or embezzlement from an employee benefit plan;

2.   Making of false statements and concealment of facts in relation to ERISA required documents;

3.   Acceptance or solicitation of funds to influence the operation of employee benefit plans; and

4.   Mail fraud.

Program 47 — Prohibited Person Investigation

The final type of investigation routinely conducted by the DOL is outlined in Chapter 47 of the *PWBA Enforcement Manual*. That chapter deals with the investigation of certain persons holding certain positions in relation to an employee benefit plan, although they are statutorily barred from serving in a such capacity. This prohibited person investigation is referred to within the DOL as a "P-47" investigation. This chapter is guided by the statutory provisions of ERISA Section 411, which states that "[n]o person who has been convicted of, or has been imprisoned as a result of his conviction for, robbery, bribery, extortion, embezzlement, fraud, grand larceny, burglary, arson, a felony violation of federal or State law" involving controlled substances, "murder, rape, kidnapping, perjury, assault with intent to kill" or any crime under the Investment Company Act of 1940, may serve or be permitted to serve:

1.   As an administrator, fiduciary, officer, trustee, custodian, counsel, agent, employee, or representative in any capacity of an employee benefit plan;

2.   As a consultant or advisor to an employee benefit plan, including, but not limited to, any entity whose activities are, in whole or substantial part, devoted to providing goods or services to any employee benefit plan; or

3.   In any capacity that involves decision making authority or custody or control of the monies, funds, assets or property of any employee benefit plan.

PRACTITIONER'S POINTER

This prohibition under ERISA Section 411 is not permanent. It is a restriction that is in place for 13 years after the conviction, or after the term of incarceration, whichever is later. The 13-year restriction can be circumvented if the sentencing judge (in federal court) or a U.S. District court judge (for a state level conviction) has determined that the subject serving in a restricted capacity would not be contrary to ERISA's provision regarding the protection of employee benefit rights. ERISA Sec. 411(a). The court reviewing the restoration request must hold a hearing and provide notice by certified mail to the state, county, and federal prosecuting officials in the jurisdiction(s) in which the conviction took place.

If the P-47 investigation establishes that such a prohibited person is serving an employee benefit plan in one of the statutorily defined positions, he may be fined (not more than $10,000) or imprisoned (for not more than five years) or both.

INVESTIGATIONS OF SERVICE PROVIDERS

644. Does the PWBA investigate service providers to employee benefit plans?

Yes. As a result, the DOL investigates service providers, as a national enforcement priority, under the Strategic Enforcement Plan ("StEP"). The focus on service providers as a national investigative priority under the StEP is not new, but a continuation of the DOL's long-standing practice under the ERISA Enforcement Strategy Implementation Plan of 1990 (ESIP). Under the ESIP, the PWBA devoted 50% of PWBA fiduciary investigative time to abusive practices in the areas of welfare plan service providers and financial institutions that provide services to employee benefit plans. By continuing its focus on service providers under the StEP, the PWBA is maintaining its position under the ESIP that service provider investigations generally result in larger recoveries for more plans and more participants, and provide a mechanism whereby the PWBA can leverage its resources and obtain the maximum impact for the benefit of plan participants and beneficiaries. As under the ESIP, the investigation of service providers generally focuses on the abusive practices committed by the specific service providers rather than on the plans. In contrast to the ESIP, the allocation of appropriate resources under the StEP, however, does not mandate that any specific percentage of fiduciary investigative time be devoted to the targeting and investigation of these issues or entities.

645. What types of issues and service providers are investigated by PWBA?

According to PWBA, a number of different types of abuses can be identified that involve service providers. These include, but are not limited to: (1) the payment by plans of large sums of money for the provision of benefits to very few participants; (2) the hiring of individuals as consultants who receive money for no services rendered through an arrangement with plan officials; (3) the purchase of inappropriate, unnecessary, or expensive insurance products for plan participants; (4) the payment of excessive or duplicative administrative fees; (5) the payment of kickbacks to plan fiduciaries by service providers; and (6) the retention of parties in interest to provide services not exempted by ERISA Section 408. The focus of PWBA service provider investigations is on abuses committed by the actual providers of specific services to welfare plans, rather than on the plans themselves.

According to the PWBA, a "service provider" is defined as any person or entity who provides a service, directly or indirectly, to an employee benefit plan for compensation. The following are service providers common to employee benefit pension and welfare plans and a brief description of the types of services that they offer to plans:

1. *Contract Professional Services.* This category includes those individuals, groups of individuals or firms who enter into a contract with a plan to provide a specific type of professional service (e.g., legal, dental or vision care) to participants.

2. *Third Party Administrators.* Most Taft-Hartley plans (see Chapter X) as well as other welfare and pension plans, employ third party administrators to provide a full line of administrative services. Such services include: (a) receiving and depositing contributions; (b) maintaining participant records; (c) processing participant claims; (d) preparing benefit statements; (e) attending trustee meetings; and (f) providing general advice on the day-to-day operation of the plan. Fees are computed in a number of different ways, depending upon the service being provided.

3. *Attorneys.* Employee benefit plans generally have one or more attorneys on retainer, to: (a) prepare plan documents; (b) attend board meetings; (c) review contracts; (d) collect delinquent contributions; (e) provide legal advice in disputes between the plan and its participants or other third parties; and (f) give legal advice in the day-to-day operation of the fund.

4. *Consultants.* Consultants serve a multitude of purposes in the employee benefit plan industry. A consultant might become involved in any of the following matters: (a) analyzing insurance contracts in an insured program; (b) preparing plan documents and benefit booklets; (c) monitoring adherence on the part of an insurance carrier to the contract terms; (d) interpreting the plan documents; and (e) reviewing experience reports in either insured or self-insured programs.

5. *Insurance Brokers and Agents.* Insurance brokers and agents are often involved in the packaging and selling of insurance coverage and benefits to a plan and may work through a consultant hired by the trustees or a plan administrator responsible for operating the fund.

6. *Computer Services.* More and more employee benefit plans are becoming involved with companies set up to provide computer

services to plans. Such services can vary significantly, ranging from tracking participant eligibility records and utilization data to monitoring investments.

7.   *Accountants.* Accountants, as service providers to plans, generally perform a full line of bookkeeping and accounting activities. They may prepare Form 5500 filings and plan financial statements.

Service provider investigations may have been targeted as a result of evidence discovered in the course of a routine investigation of one of the service providers of ERISA plan clients. Conversely, an investigation of an ERISA service provider that indicates evidence of violations committed by the service provider's client plans may result in the opening of investigations of those client plans by the DOL, or a referral of administrative violations to the IRS for investigation by their Employee Plans Division. ERISA Enforcement Strategy Implementation Plan, Sept. 1990; Strategic Enforcement Plan.

646. What are PWBA's goals and objectives in the investigation of service providers?

According to the ERISA Enforcement Strategy Implementation Plan of 1990, PWBA's objectives involving the investigation and audit of service providers are as follows:

- identifying and conducting investigations of service providers who have the most potential for abuse;

- establishing a presence in the service provider field nationwide by identifying and conducting investigations of at least one major service provider in each of the 50 states;

- establishing a presence in areas of high concentration of employee benefit plan service providers by identifying and conducting investigations of at least one major service provider in each of the 20 major population centers in the country;

- establishing a presence in the entire service provider community by identifying and conducting investigations of service providers based on size (small, medium and large) and type of service;

- identifying ERISA violations and obtaining corrections of those violations;

- developing data through investigations of service providers that form a basis for establishing targeting guidelines and for use in pursuing, when violations exist, the correction of those violations; and

- ensuring the most widespread possible dissemination of knowledge of PWBA's correction of employee abuses through publicity, speeches, etc.

647. What methods are used by PWBA in targeting service providers for investigation?

As a general rule, each regional office independently targets service providers for investigation. The service providers selected for audit usually represent a cross-section of the service providers within the jurisdiction, both geographically and by type of provider. The methods used by the regional offices in targeting service providers include the following:

- access to all Schedule C filings attached to Forms 5500 processed on the PWBA ERISA Access System (or equivalent);

- computer generated reports from Form 5500 filings of service providers servicing multiple plans;

- computer generated reports from Form 5500 filings analyzing plan administrative expenses;

- computer generated reports from Form 5500 filings for various specific health and welfare plans, including: (a) prepaid legal; (b) dental; and (c) vision;

- office intelligence files, including case filings for various identified potential problem areas with service providers;

- contacts with other state and federal government agencies to identify potential abusive service providers (e.g., the Federal Bureau of Investigation, Office of Inspector General, Department of Justice, and State Insurance Commissioners);

- any congressional subcommittee hearing transcripts that may identify potential abusive service providers; and

- interviews with individuals, companies, and others who might have knowledge of violations in the service provider field.

648. What is the focus of DOL service provider audits?

The Strategic Enforcement Plan and ERISA Enforcement Strategy Implementation Plan of 1990 provide that service provider investigations conducted by the DOL will focus on abusive practices committed by actual providers of specific services to employee benefit plans rather than on the plans themselves. According to the ESIP, each investigation is conducted to determine whether:

1. A legitimate service is being rendered to the plan or its participants;

2. The service is necessary to the administration of the plan or the payment of benefits;

3. The service is being duplicated by other service providers; and

4. The cost of providing the service is reasonable under the circumstances.

Any entity who provides a service, directly or indirectly, to an employee benefit plan for compensation may be subjected to an investigation by the DOL to determine if a violation of ERISA has been, or is about to be, committed. ERISA Sec. 504(a).

Such investigations may have been targeted as a result of evidence discovered in the course of a routine investigation of one of the service providers of ERISA plan clients. Conversely, an investigation of an ERISA service provider that indicates evidence of violations committed by the service provider's client plans may result in the opening of investigations of those client plans by the DOL, or a referral of administrative violations to the IRS for investigation by their Employee Plans Division. *ERISA Enforcement Strategy Implementation Plan*, Sept. 1990.

INVESTIGATIONS OF FINANCIAL INSTITUTIONS

649. Does the DOL investigate financial institutions that serve employee benefit plans?

Yes. Financial institutions provide services to employee benefit plans in many different capacities. Typically, they provide checking and savings accounts for plans, contribution collection services, and custodial services. With respect to the direct investment of plan assets, financial institutions serve as investment managers and advisors, directed trustees, and co-trustees to plans. In addition, they provide plans with investment vehicles, such as participation loans, pooled or collective investment funds and deposit administration contracts. Some financial institutions are involved in broker-dealer activities, particularly with discount broker operations.

In accordance with the ERISA Enforcement Strategy Implementation Plan of 1990, PWBA has previously selected abusive practices by financial institutions for investigation for a variety of reasons. First, ERISA is a very complex law and other regulatory agencies cannot be expected to fully understand the interrelationships among applicable law, ERISA, and the numerous ERISA exemptions and regulations. The absence of any federal regulations in the insurance industry and the unevenness of state regulation provide an additional reason for PWBA to protect the interests of employee benefit plans from abusive practices committed by a relatively small number of insurance companies. Finally, and presumably because of resource limitations, federal and state bank regulators have emphasized the commercial operations of banks in their examination activities, as opposed to bank trust department operations where most employee benefit plan assets are held and where most abusive practices relating to employee benefit plans occur. *ERISA Enforcement Strategy Implementation Plan*, Sept. 1990, pp. 12 - 13.

650. What are the types of issues involving violations of ERISA and financial institutions?

According to the DOL, generally, substantive issues involving violations of ERISA committed by financial institutions acting as fiduciaries to employee benefit plans fall into two categories. The first category involves the financial institution's management of plan assets. Despite the professionalism of many institutions, there exists the possibility of improper and imprudent management and investment of plan assets. The second, and more serious, category of violations concerns conflict of interest and self-dealing situations. Examples of these violations include: (1) transfers of bad loans from a bank's commercial department to its trust department; (2) the charging of excessive fees (either directly or through a related entity, such as a stock broker); and (3) the use of plan assets for permanent financing of risky construction projects for which the financial institution has provided interim financing. Also, financial institutions may extend certain "favors" to employee benefit plan fiduciaries in order to retain plan or plan sponsor business. Examples of these "favors" include the making of low interest or unsecured loans to plan fiduciaries, agreement to plan sponsors' directions of imprudent investments, and the promise of gifts or other gratuities to plan fiduciaries. *ERISA Enforcement Strategy Implementation Plan*, Sept. 1990, p. 13.

651. What types of financial institutions are investigated by PWBA?

PWBA has investigated the following financial institutions:

1. *Banks.* Many employee benefit plans receive services from state or nationally chartered banks. These services range from a bank providing a simple checking account to a bank serving as a plan's sole discretionary trustee. Banks are involved in both the short-term and long-term investment of plan assets. Banks provide pooled investments and other collective trusts for plans.

2. *Savings and Loan Associations.* Similar to banks, savings and loan associations provide a variety of services to employee benefit plans. They manage plan cash in the short-term and provide certificates of deposit for long-term investing. In addition, savings and loan

associations provide many investment vehicles for plans such as participation loan packages.

3. *Trust Companies.* Trust companies are primarily involved in managing trust assets and sometimes act as a conduit for plans investing in real estate, mortgages, and other types of investments. Trust companies frequently serve as fiduciaries to employee benefit plans.

4. *Investment Management Companies.* These entities, although not banks, savings and loan associations or trust companies, receive large sums of money from employee benefit plans and are responsible for the investment of that money. Often these companies also have money from non-ERISA accounts that they are also responsible for investing. Mutual funds and other investment vehicles are expressly excluded from this category as they do not involve the investment of plan assets.

5. *Insurance Companies.* In addition to the provision of insurance, insurance companies provide a large variety of services and investments to plans, sometimes in a fiduciary capacity, such as deposit administration contracts, annuities, and collective or pooled investment arrangements. *ERISA Enforcement Strategy Implementation Plan*, Sept. 1990, p. 14.

652. What are PWBA's goals and objectives in investigating financial institutions?

By investigating abuses committed by financial institutions, PWBA attempts to protect participants and beneficiaries of employee benefit plans by ensuring that these institutions are holding, managing and investing plan assets in accordance with ERISA. The objectives of PWBA in such investigations are as follows:

- targeting enforcement efforts on plan assets held by at least two financial institutions located in each state;

- concentrating PWBA investigative resources on individuals and entities believed to be involved in the most egregious conflicts of interest and self-dealing violations;

- where violations of ERISA are uncovered, seeking to promptly protect and preserve plan assets, recover plan losses and, if appropriate, remove violators from activities associated with employee benefit plans; and

- seeking the assistance and cooperation of federal agencies that regulate financial institutions. *ERISA Enforcement Strategy Implementation Plan*, Sept. 1990, pp. 14-15.

653. What is the focus of DOL financial institution audits?

The Enforcement Strategy Implementation Plan of 1990 required the DOL to allocate 50% of its investigative resources to investigations of significant issues. Consequently, in the years following the issuance of the ESIP, the DOL has focused a tremendous amount of time and resources on conducting investigations of financial institutions. Since the Strategic Enforcement Plan (StEP) does not mandate that any specific percentage of fiduciary investigative time be devoted to the targeting and investigation of these issues or entities, it is presumably at the discretion of the PWBA Regional Office to determine the amount and percentage of its investigative resources that will be allocated to investigations of financial institutions.

Financial institutions that are subject to the DOL's service provider investigations include banks, savings and loans, trust companies, investment management companies and insurance companies.

The issues and documents reviewed in a financial institution audit by the DOL include the following:

1. *The relationship between the commercial department and the trust department.* This issue involves the review of potentially improper arrangements or relationships between commercial and trust departments of banks or similar departments of other financial institutions.

2. *Prudence and exclusive purpose of the bank as trustee.* This issue involves the failure of financial institutions to act independently or in the sole interest of plans when acting in the capacity of a co-trustee, directed trustee, or fiduciary.

3. *Investment vehicles.* This issue involves the investment of client plan assets in collective investment funds with low earnings and a high concentration of plan asset investments in real estate or other similar investments in a specific geographic or economic area.

4. *Plan equity portfolio management and proxy voting.* This issue involves the failure of financial institutions to manage plan equity portfolios, or to vote plan stock in the sole interest of participants and beneficiaries.

5. *Fees charged by the bank.* This issue deals with the appropriateness and reasonableness of fees and other charges of financial institutions to employee benefit plans.

6.   *"Soft dollar arrangements."* This issue involves the propriety of "soft dollar" arrangements involving financial institutions that manage and invest plan assets.

In the conduct of a financial institution audit, the investigation will review a sample of the institution's ERISA plan client files. A rule of thumb for determining how many client files to review is the "25 plus 10" rule. The "25 plus 10" rule requires the investigator to randomly select, from the ERISA plan client list provided by the financial institution, 25 client plans plus 10% of the overall number of ERISA client plans serviced by the financial institution. For example, if a financial institution services 200 ERISA covered plans, the "25 plus 10" rule will result in the review of 45 ERISA plan client files. In the review of these files, the investigator will review: (1) the trust agreement and amendments; (2) the plan document and amendments; (3) the plan adoption agreement and amendments; (4) the applicable agency agreements; (5) the IRS determination letter; (6) the correspondence file; (7) the trust annual reports (for a minimum of three years); and (8) the Annual Report Forms 5500 (for a minimum of three years).

For a review of specific questions asked by the investigator in reviewing individual ERISA plan client files, see Q 656.

654. How does PWBA select financial institutions as targets of investigation?

PWBA has viewed the selection of financial institutions to be investigated for potential abuse as crucial to the protection of employee benefit plan assets, the efficient use of investigative resources, and the detection of ERISA violations. PWBA selects investigative targets through a detailed review of intelligence data available from a wide variety of sources. These sources include, but are not limited to, the following:

- PWBA case files, and other intelligence files that identify financial institutions providing services to employee benefit plans;

- data contained in Master Trust and Common Trust Annual Report filings;

- information contained in Form 5500 Annual Report filings;

- applications and comments submitted by financial institutions and other interested parties in connection with individual or class exemptions proposed or granted;

- information on problem institutions obtained from federal and state regulatory agencies, such as state insurance commissioners; and

- information identified in public sources, such as legislative committee hearings and trade publications. *ERISA Enforcement Strategy Implementation Plan*, Sept. 1990, p. 15.

655. What factors are considered by the PWBA in selecting financial institutions for investigation?

The selection of financial institutions for investigation takes into consideration the following: (1) the size of the financial institution in terms of plan assets held, managed or invested; (2) the number and size of employee benefit plan clients; (3) the geographic location of the financial institution; (4) the type and variety of financial services offered to plans; (5) the reputation and standing of the financial institution in the community, as determined by industry professionals and government regulators; and (6) the likelihood of finding ERISA violations involving selected areas of significant concern to PWBA. *ERISA Enforcement Strategy Implementation Plan*, Sept. 1990, pp. 15-16.

656. What are the issues covered in a review of individual ERISA plan client files in a financial institution investigation?

Financial institution investigations by the DOL require the investigator to carefully review a specific number of ERISA plan client files. In the review of those files, the investigator is guided by an account examination sheet that details the issues to be examined. The following is a review of the questions detailed in the financial institution account examination checklist:

1. Is the financial institution named as trustee?

2. Does the financial institution have investment responsibility? According to which trust agency/agreement section?

3. Does the plan sponsor direct the financial institution on investment of assets?

   • According to which trust agency/agreement section?

   • Are written investment instructions contained in the file?

4. Does the client plan have an outside investment manager? On all or a part of the assets?

5. What percentage of plan assets are invested in CTFs and/or government securities?

6. Is the trustee/custodian/agency fee paid by the plan?

   • Which section of the trust/agency agreement permits the plan to pay this fee?

• Does the fee appear to be reasonable for the services rendered?

7.   Is the plan charged sweep fees?

• What was the time period for which the fees were incurred?

• What were the total sweep fees for the last three years?

8.   Does the plan hold investments in Bank CTFs? Which trust agreement section permits this?

9.   Does the plan hold participant loans?

• Which section of the plan document permits this?

• Are all payments current?

• Are the loans adequately secured?

• Is the rate of interest reasonable?

• Is the loan within statutorily defined limits?

10.   Does the plan hold employer securities?

• Which section of the trust agreement permits this?

• Are the securities qualifying?

• Are the holdings within the ERISA Section 407 limits?

11.   Does the plan hold employer real property?

• Which section of the trust agreement permits this?

• Is the property geographically dispersed?

• Is the rent charged adequate and current?

• What are the dates of the latest appraisals?

• What are the terms of the leases?

• Are the lease(s) apparently from an arm's-length transaction?

12. Does the plan own any interests in limited partnerships?

  • Which section of the trust agreement permits this?

  • Is the prospectus in the file?

13. Does the plan own real estate?

  • Which section of the trust agreement permits this?

  • Is it carried on the books at market value?

  • What was the date of latest appraisal?

  • Was it appraised free of encumbrance?

  • Is the real property leased or occupied by a party in interest?

  • Does the lease appear to be at an arm's-length?

  • Is the rent adequate and current?

  • What are the terms of the lease?

14. Does the plan own mortgages?

  • Which section of the trust agreement permits this?

  • Is the mortgage adequately secured?

  • Is the property adequately insured?

  • Are mortgage payments current?

  • Are the interest rate and terms of the mortgage reasonable?

  • How was the mortgage obtained?

15. Does the plan hold promissory notes other than on participant loans?

  • Which section of the trust agreement permits this?

  • Does the note represent a loan to a party in interest?

  • Is the loan adequately secured?

- Are payments on the note current?

- Are the terms and interest rate on the note reasonable?

16.   Does the plan hold precious metals, art, or collectibles?

- Which section of the trust agreement permits this?

- What percentage of plan assets were represented by the purchase when made?

- What percentage of plan assets are currently represented by these holdings?

- Are current appraisals of these holdings in the plan file?

- What is the appraised value of these holdings?

- Where and when were these holdings obtained by the plan?

17.   Does the plan invest in commercial paper?

- Is the commercial paper issued by a party in interest?

- If so, does it satisfy the requirements of PTE 81-8?

18.   Does the plan invest in repurchase agreements?

- Are the repurchase agreements with a party in interest?

- If so, do they satisfy the requirements of PTE 81-8?

19.   Does the plan invest in certificates of deposit?

- Are they with a party in interest?

- If so, do they satisfy the requirements of PTE 81-8?

This checklist and the general financial institution investigative guidelines are designed to identify improper or imprudent instances of plan asset management, as well as violations involving conflicts of interest and self-dealing between the plan and the financial institution service provider. Such violations include:

1.   Transfers of bad loans from the financial institution's commercial loan department to the trust department;

2.   The charging of excessive fees; and

3.   The use of plan assets for the permanent financing of risky construction projects for which the financial institution has provided interim financing.

The ESIP also cautions that financial institution investigations have discovered situations wherein the financial institution has extended favors to clients who are ERISA plan fiduciaries, in order to retain the plan or the plan sponsor as a client. Such "sweetheart deals" include gifts, gratuities and unsecured or low interest loans. *ERISA Enforcement Strategy Implementation Plan*, Sept. 1990.

657. What are the issues covered under the DOL's HIPAA service provider enforcement/compliance review?

In mid-1999, the use of HIPAA enforcement/compliance questionnaires originated in one of the DOL's Regional Offices as an added aspect of their service provider investigations. On June 11, 1999, at the IRS Midwest Benefits Conference in Cincinnati, Ohio, the DOL announced that they would be launching a National Office directed HIPAA Compliance/Enforcement project in October, 1999. The DOL National Office Project is based upon the regional office efforts identified above, and the enforcement checklist will either be, or closely resemble, the checklist detailed below.

The questionnaire has been designed for use in a "desk audit" situation. That is, the target of the inquiry will receive the checklist in the mail or via facsimile, along with a request that a written response and supporting documentation be forwarded to the issuing office within 10 business days. The cover letter also advises that "submission of relevant documents to our office prior to the inception of on-site field investigation can lessen the time subsequently spent with, and the administrative burden placed upon (service provider target) personnel."

Compliance with the HIPAA Provisions in Part 7 of Subtitle B of Title I of ERISA

(Specific lines of inquiry presented by DOL Field Offices in conducting investigations)

If any of the below requested items are voluminous in nature, the DOL advises that the recipient may submit the relevant parts of the requested items that relate to the specific question or following questions.

1.   Provide a copy of the Plan's (a) Summary Plan Description, (b) Plan Document, and (c) Plan Group Policy.

2.   Does the group health plan automatically issue complete certificates of creditable coverage free of charge to individuals who lose coverage under the plan, and to individuals upon request? Labor Regs. §§2590.701-5(a)(2)(ii), 2590.701-5(a)(2)(iii).

3. Does the group health plan have a written procedure for individuals to request and receive certificates? Labor Reg. §2590.701-5(a)(4)(ii).

4. If the group health plan imposes a preexisting condition exclusion period, does the plan or issuer issue a notice informing individuals of such exclusion period, the terms of such exclusion period, and the right of individuals to demonstrate creditable coverage (and any applicable waiting or affiliation periods) to reduce the preexisting condition exclusion period? Labor Reg. §2590.701-3(c). [The plan sponsor may be asked to provide copies of the General Notice of Preexisting Condition Exclusions sent to two different plan participants.]

5. If the group health plan imposes a preexisting condition exclusion period, does it issue letters of determination and notification of creditable coverage within a reasonable time after the receipt of individuals' creditable coverage information? Labor Regs. §§2590.701-5(d)(1), 2590.701-5(d)(2). [The plan sponsor may be asked to provide a list or log of Individualized Determination of Preexisting Condition Exclusion letters sent out in the last 12 months.]

6. Were any of the above individuals *not* provided a certificate of creditable coverage from their prior plan? [If so, the plan sponsor must identify them and explain and provide supporting documentation as to how the matter was resolved. If there have been more than three individuals, the issuing DOL Investigator will select the individuals for which supporting documentation must be applied.]

7. If the group health plan imposes a preexisting condition exclusion period, does it comport with HIPAA's limitations on preexisting condition exclusion periods? Labor Regs. §§2590.701-2(a), 2590.701-2(b). [The plan sponsor may be asked to provide a list of all claims that were denied in the last 12 months due to the imposition of a preexisting condition exclusion period, as well as records showing the enrollment dates of the individuals involved.]

8. Does the group health plan have written provisions notifying individuals who are ineligible to enroll in the plan of coverage of special enrollment rights, and issue notices of special enrollment rights? Labor Reg. §2590.701-6(c).

9. Does the group health plan have written procedures that provide special enrollment rights to individuals who lose other coverage

and to individuals who acquire a new dependent, if they request enrollment within 30 days of the loss of coverage, marriage, birth, adoption, or placement for adoption? Labor Regs. §§2590.701-6(a), 2590.701-6(b).

10.   Do the group health plan's rules for eligibility to enroll under the terms of the plan or coverage (including continued eligibility) comply with the nondiscrimination requirements that prohibit discrimination against any individual or a dependent of an individual based on any health status-related factor? ERISA Sec. 702(a)(1); Labor Reg. §2590.702(a)(1). [The plan sponsor may be asked to provide a list of any applicants or participants denied eligibility to enroll during the last 12 months.]

11.   Does the group health plan comply with the nondiscrimination requirements that prohibit requiring any individual (as a condition of enrollment or continued enrollment) to pay a premium or contribution that is greater than the premium or contribution for a similarly situated individual enrolled in the plan on the basis of any health status-related factor? ERISA Sec. 702(b)(1); Labor Reg. §2590.702(b)(1).

12.   If the group health plan is a multiemployer plan or a multiple employer welfare arrangement (MEWA), does it comply with Part 7 (guaranteed renewability requirements), which generally prohibit it from denying an employer whose employees are covered under a group health plan continued access to the same or different coverage under the terms of the plan? ERISA Sec. 703 (accompanying regulation cite has been reserved). [The plan sponsor may be asked to provide a list of any employers who have not renewed coverage during the last 12 months.]

General PWBA Investigations

658. What is the general framework that governs PWBA's enforcement resources?

The general framework through which PWBA enforcement resources are efficiently and effectively focused to achieve its policy and operational objectives is the Strategic Enforcement Plan (StEP), released on April 6, 2000. The StEP identifies and describes the PWBA's enforcement priorities and informs the public of the PWBA's current goals, priorities, and methods. The StEP promotes compliance with Title I of ERISA. The PWBA's enforcement strategy is designed to support the Department of Labor's goal of a secure workforce by deterring and correcting violations of ERISA and related statutes.

The PWBA's enforcement programs are primarily carried out through civil investigations. The civil investigative program is organized by the PWBA using two main approaches: (I) national projects, which are investigative projects that further more broadly established long-range national investigative priorities; and (ii) regional projects, which are localized investigative projects undertaken by individual PWBA regional offices. A critical part of PWBA's enforcement program under the Strategic Enforcement Program also includes the prosecution of criminal acts relating to employee benefit plans. Criminal investigations are discussed in detail in Chapter XIII.

659. What are PWBA's National Investigative Priorities?

The PWBA establishes priorities in order to ensure that its enforcement program focuses on the areas that are critical to the well-being of employee benefit plans. Generally, the PWBA designates and identifies over several years the various types of plans, benefits, or other broad segments of the regulated employee benefit plan universe that will be emphasized under the enforcement program. Within these national investigative priorities, the PWBA annually identifies national investigative projects, to which it dedicates enforcement resources. These national investigative projects are designed to identify and correct the ERISA violations that the PWBA believes may be widespread or to focus upon abusive practices that affect many plans. The StEP identifies the following three current national investigative priorities: plan service providers; health care plans; and defined contribution pension plans.

Plan Service Providers

As discussed in the preceding questions, the DOL defines a "plan service provider" as any person or entity that provides a direct or indirect service to an employee benefit plan for compensation. The DOL considers third party administrators, accountants, attorneys, and actuaries to be plan service providers. The definition also includes financial institutions such as banks, trust companies, investment management companies, and insurance companies, as well as others that manage or administer (directly or indirectly) funds or property owned by employee benefit plans. The DOL believes that the investigation of plan service providers offers the opportunity to address abusive practices that may affect more than one plan. Thus, by focusing investigative resources on plan service providers, the PWBA can address violations involving many plans.

The focus on service providers as a national investigative priority under the StEP is not new, but a continuation of the DOL's long-standing practice under the ERISA Enforcement Strategy Implementation Plan of 1990 (ESIP). Under the ESIP, the PWBA devoted 50% of PWBA fiduciary investigative time to abusive practices in the areas of welfare plan service providers and financial institutions that provide services to employee benefit plans. By continuing its focus on service providers under the StEP, the PWBA is maintaining its position under the ESIP that service provider investigations generally result in larger recoveries for more plans and more participants, and provide a mechanism whereby the PWBA can leverage its resources and obtain the maximum impact for the benefit of plan participants and beneficiaries.

As under the ESIP, the investigation of service providers generally focuses on the abusive practices committed by the specific service providers rather than on the plans. For example, where a third party administrator has systematically retained an undisclosed fee, the focus of the investigation will be on the third party administrator rather than the plan that contracted for the services. Although the StEP does not mandate that any specific amount of investigative time be devoted to the investigation of service providers, the PWBA is encouraging the field offices to allocate appropriate resources to the targeting and investigation of these issues as a method to leverage its available staffing.

Health Benefit Issues

The DOL estimates that there are a total of 2.6 million ERISA-covered health plans that cover approximately 122 million participants and beneficiaries. In the view of the DOL, several factors have combined in recent years to make the management and administration of ERISA-covered health plans a matter of vital national importance, including: increased health care costs (due in part to improved technology and accessibility); changes in the health care delivery and funding systems; and the evolution of the legal standard under which health plans and their service providers must operate. Additionally, as the cost of health care has increased, the methods for delivering that care have changed. Further, the DOL generally regards the increase in health care costs to be a key factor in the move toward managed care, the stated purpose of which is to control access to health care and its related costs.

Under the StEP, the PWBA seeks to ensure that the benefits of participants and beneficiaries under welfare plans are protected. The application of available remedies under ERISA is critical in those cases where federal preemption leaves participants with no other effective statutory or common law cause of action. The PWBA seeks to apply the full extent of ERISA's remedies and to promote a legal standard that will increase the availability of appropriate remedies to protect welfare plan participants and beneficiaries.

Because the PWBA views health benefits as critically important, in recent years it has applied substantial resources to addressing abusive practices that violate ERISA. For example, the PWBA has pursued enforcement actions involving multiple employer welfare arrangements (MEWAs), and insurers and service providers that receive hidden discounts. Moreover, the PWBA's role in health care has also expanded as a result of the enactment of new legislation, such as the Health Insurance Portability and Accountability Act of 1996 (HIPAA); the Newborns' and Mothers' Health Protection Act of 1996 (NMHPA); the Mental Health Parity Act of 1996 (MHPA); and the Women's Health and Cancer Rights Act (WHCRA). The PWBA is charged with implementing new regulatory and enforcement requirements that are found in these laws. In response to its expanding role in the health care area, the StEP provides that the

PWBA will continue to devote substantial enforcement resources to the targeting and investigation of fiduciary issues relating to health benefit plans. The PWBA has also established the Office of Health Plan Standards and Compliance Assistance to develop regulations, interpretive bulletins, opinions, forms, and rulings relating to health care portability, nondiscrimination requirements, and other related health provisions in furtherance of this role.

Defined Contribution Plans

In the StEP, the PWBA has identified defined contribution plans as a national investigative project. In recent years there has been a tremendous growth in 401(k) defined contribution plans in terms of the number of plans, number of participants, and amount of assets in these plans. The PWBA has decided that this growth and the related administrative and investment practices that have developed to accommodate these plans warrant scrutiny, in order to ensure the safety of this large volume of assets. Moreover, because defined contribution plans are not covered by PBGC insurance, plan losses due to a fiduciary breach directly affect plan participants and such losses are irrevocable unless the funds can be recovered through enforcement or other legal actions. Accordingly, the PWBA has identified defined contribution plans as a national enforcement priority because the risk of loss in such plans rests entirely on the plan participants.

660. What are PWBA's National Projects?

According to the StEP, national projects are investigative projects that focus on a selected issue or group of related issues of national scope and significance that fall within the established national enforcement priorities. Generally, a PWBA field office must give priority to conducting investigations and dedicating appropriate resources to the project during the fiscal year. On occasion, however, national projects may address issues that are not necessarily prevalent in all areas of the country, and then only a selected group of PWBA field offices are required to participate in the project. According to the PWBA, the issues selected for implementation as national projects are determined in annual planning sessions (or reviewed, since an individual national project may extend over more than one fiscal year), including commentary from the PWBA's field offices. National projects may be an expansion of a successful regional project or may arise in connection with field office investigations. Coordination and enforcement policy determinations for national projects are generally directed through the Office of Enforcement (OE), although the field office managers have substantial opportunities to participate and comment. The OE's involvement in national projects includes monitoring and evaluating the project's progression, and, where appropriate, issuing procedural directives and technical guidance.

661. What are some of the national enforcement projects identified by the PWBA?

The field offices have been ordered to place particular investigative emphasis upon the following national enforcement projects identified by the PWBA.

Multiple Employer Welfare Arrangements (MEWAs)

A Multiple Employer Welfare Arrangement (MEWA) is a welfare benefit plan or other arrangement established to benefit the employees of two or more employers. The PWBA has found that small employers may use MEWAs when they are either unable to obtain health care coverage for their employees or cannot afford the cost of such coverage. PWBA investigations continue to reveal instances where MEWAs have failed to pay claims as a result of insufficient funding and inadequate reserves. In the worst situations, MEWAs have been operated by individuals who drained the MEWA's assets through excessive administrative fees or by outright theft. According to the StEP, the PWBA's emphasis is on abusive and fraudulent MEWAs created by unscrupulous promoters, who default on their obligations after promising inexpensive health benefit insurance.

The DOL believes that MEWAs may also be involved in criminal violations.

Administrative Services Only (ASO) Project

This national project involves investigations of insurance companies that provide administrative services only to self-funded welfare plans. These investigations focus on whether fee reductions or discounts obtained from medical service providers have been passed on to the plans or their participants.

401(k) Fees

Although it does not presently appear to be an investigative-type project, the PWBA intends the 401(k) Fees Project to educate both plan participants and plan sponsors about the impact of fees on participants' return on investments. An in-depth discussion of this subject appears in Chapter IV. The PWBA developed a consumer information brochure on plan investment fees in support of this project, which is designed to educate participants on important ways to monitor investment fees and to remind plan sponsors of their fiduciary obligations to monitor these fees. The PWBA reports that this investigative project has increased its knowledge of how 401(k) plans monitor and analyze their investment fees (particularly where the fees are paid from plan assets rather than by the plan sponsor), and how fiduciaries oversee the administration of these types of plans.

Orphan Plans

In response to situations where plans have been abandoned by plan sponsors and fiduciaries, or fiduciaries have completely abdicated their responsibilities to administer plans prudently and in the sole interest of the participants, the PWBA began the Orphan Plans project in October 1999. According to the PWBA, the objectives of this project are to: (1) locate orphan plans that have been abandoned by fiduciaries as a result of death, neglect, bankruptcy, or incarceration; (2) determine if the fiduciary is available to make fiduciary decisions, such as the termination of the plan and the distribution of plan assets; (3) require fiduciaries to fulfill their duties, file appropriate compliance forms, and ensure that proper actions are undertaken to protect promised benefits; and, where possible, (4) to identify and penalize plan officials that have not fulfilled their responsibilities to plan participants.

662. What is the Employee Contributions Project?

Since 1995, the PWBA has used the Employee Contributions Project to pursue an aggressive enforcement program that is intended to safeguard employee contributions made to 401(k) plans and health care plans. The PWBA investigates situations in which employers delay depositing employee contributions made to these plans. Pursuant to the revised participant contribution regulations, effective February 3, 1997, employee pension benefit plan contributions become plan assets as soon as they can reasonably be segregated from the employer's general assets, but in no event later than 15 business days after the end of the month in which the contributions are withheld from employees' pay. Employee welfare benefit plan contributions become plan assets as soon as they can reasonably be segregated from the employer's general assets, but in no event later than 90 days after the date when the employer receives them (in the case of amounts that a participant or beneficiary pays to the employer), or the date on which such contributions would otherwise be payable in cash (in the case of amounts withheld by an employer from a participant's wages). The PWBA has determined that in some cases, employers do not promptly deposit the contributions in the appropriate funding vehicle, as required by the regulations. In other cases, the PWBA has found that the employer simply converts the contributions to other uses, such as business expenses. In the PWBA's view, both scenarios may occur when the employer is having fiscal problems and turns to the plan for unlawful financing.

663. Are any other enforcement projects aimed at health benefit plans?

In recent years, the PWBA has applied substantial enforcement resources to the targeting and investigation of fiduciary violations, as well as criminal violations relating to health benefit plans. The PWBA's role with respect to health plans has also expanded as a result of legislation that increased the regulatory and enforcement requirements to be implemented by the PWBA. These statutes include the Health Insurance Portability and Accountability Act of 1996 (HIPAA), the Mental Health Parity Act of 1996 (MHPA), the Newborns' and Mothers' Health Protection Act of 1996 (Newborns' Act), and the Women's Health and Cancer Rights Act of 1998 (WHCRA). The PWBA's focus with regard to health plans is primarily to ensure that funded plans are financially sound and that plans are administered prudently and in the participants' sole interest.

664. What are Regional Projects?

Enforcement initiatives are also conducted as projects by individual regional field offices. Each year, the regional field office managers submit their project proposals to the Office of Enforcement (OE) for review and approval. The subjects selected for regional projects are generally topics that have been identified by a particular region as an enforcement issue that may be unique or particularly problematic within its geographic jurisdiction. Because regional field office staff may be able to identify potential issues through their investigative activities, they have the unique opportunity to observe industry practices firsthand and select issues for development as regional projects that may ultimately be appropriate for adoption as national projects. According to the PWBA, an issue selected as a regional project will normally be:

- well-defined both in terms of scope and focus (rather than couched in terms of broad categories, such as "small plan issues");

- identified in the context of a type of transaction or industry practice; or

- an emerging concern or involving a legal position that is precedential in nature.

In addition, a regional project should have the potential to develop an effective targeting method so that an appropriate number of subjects can be identified for investigation. As noted previously, any number of targeting methods may be used. The PWBA considers regional projects that satisfy the criteria listed above to provide a foundation for identifying cutting-edge issues that may ultimately involve matters of national scope and importance. If an issue is subsequently selected as a national project, the PWBA believes that the experience and insight gained at the field office level will provide a substantive basis for guiding other field offices in conducting similar investigations. Some regional projects address practices that are more localized in their scope and impact. Because the demographics of each region differ with respect to the concentrations of various types of plans and service providers, the same strategy may not be effective for all regional field offices.

665. What factors are considered by PWBA in targeting cases?

In developing priorities for meeting the objectives for targeting cases, the PWBA considers the following factors:

- preventing dissipation of plan assets;

- obtaining restitution on behalf of employee benefit plans;

- removing harmful individuals from contact with plans, through both civil measures and criminal sanctions;

- establishing legal precedent for the guidance of the public;

- enlisting the assistance of others, such as plan accountants, in PWBA enforcement efforts;

- encouraging private initiatives (as contemplated by ERISA Section 502) by fostering greater awareness by plan participants of their rights and increasing their ability to obtain meaningful information about their plans;

- assisting the public;

- promoting legislative and public awareness of PWBA enforcement efforts and seeking legislative and regulatory solutions to enforcement problems; and

- encouraging inter-agency cooperation. *ERISA Enforcement Strategy Implementation Plan*, Sept. 1990, pp. 19-20.

666. What targeting methods are used in selecting plans for investigations?

PWBA uses the following targeting methods in selecting cases for investigation:

- plan directories for each area office's jurisdiction, based upon its designated geographical territories, participant size, and asset dollar size;

- specifically designed Form 5500 computer based targeting reports;

- comparison of data from the ERISA database to data merged or generated from other databases befitting the criteria under review or investigation (i.e., (1) the Federal Deposit Insurance Corporation (FDIC) database reporting statistical information on financial institutions holding employee benefit trust assets; (2) the Master Trust database maintained by PWBA; (3) the common and collective trusts database; (4) the Office of Labor Management Standards database; and (5) other databases deemed appropriate by PWBA);

- continued review of significant answers to Form 5500 narrative questions that warrant further inquiry by the appropriate regional office for investigation;

- targeting techniques to measure whether plan assets are adequately diversified as to decrease the risk of losses to plans using investment strategies;

- specific "on-line" targeting for special plan characteristics;

- information from PWBA's Office of Exemption Determinations and Office of Regulations and Interpretations, such as exemption applications and related comments;

- complaints of abuse in employee benefit plans received from participants, trustees, and interested third parties;

- information obtained from other federal and state agencies, including the Office of Inspector General, Federal Bureau of Investigation, and state insurance commissioners; and

- referrals from the Pension Benefit Guaranty Corporation (PBGC) for consideration for investigation by PWBA of those cases relating to areas of potential exposure for PBGC, such as severely underfunded plans, abandoned plans, and special classes of preferred stock by employers to their plans. *ERISA Enforcement Strategy Implementation Plan*, Sept. 1990, pp. 20-21.

667. How does the PWBA target a plan for investigation?

The DOL's Pension and Welfare Benefits Administration ("PWBA") has approximately 300 auditors and investigators located within its 10 regional and five district offices. With the amount of private sector benefit plans in the United States numbering in the hundreds of thousands, the DOL, with such a relatively small investigative staff, does not randomly target plans for investigation. Consequently, any plan, sponsor, or service provider identified as a target for investigation has been determined to have a high probability of violating ERISA.

There is one exception to this general rule. Plans may be selected for a limited review under the DOL's national computer targeting program, which targets plans based on the information reported on the Annual Report Form 5500. The DOL's national office periodically sends its regional field offices a list of plans within their respective geographic jurisdictions that meet the current targeting criteria for a limited review. At its discretion, the regional office may send an inquiry letter requesting certain information to the plans listed on the targeting report in order to determine whether any violations exist with respect to the issues targeted. A timely response to the regional office, indicating that no violation exists, is likely to result in a closed case.

DOL field offices primarily use the following sources of information to select a plan, sponsor or service provider for an investigation:

1. *Complaints.* The DOL may receive information that indicates or alleges that a violation of ERISA has occurred or is about to occur. Complaints may be written or oral and they may be received from individuals, news media, or other governmental agencies. If infor-

mation in the complaint is indefinite, general, or grounded in rumor or conjecture, an investigation likely will not be conducted. Nevertheless, if a participant complaint indicates and documents ERISA violations that affect a class of participants, the DOL will be interested in investigating. Many of the more egregious civil and criminal violations are brought to the attention of the DOL through participant complaints to the DOL field offices.

2. *Issues Identified Through Other Investigations.* DOL auditors and investigators are trained to identify and investigate evidence of ERISA violations discovered in investigations of plan service providers. If a service provider is being investigated and the provider's actions have left client plans in violation of ERISA, or if violations exist in the plans regardless of the service provider's actions, the DOL may open investigations of the individual plans. Similarly, if a single plan investigation details an ERISA violation that may involve other plans or service providers, further investigations may result.

PRACTITIONER'S POINTER

This is why service providers are strongly encouraged to request an accommodation subpoena from the DOL when notified that they are the target of a DOL investigation. An accommodation subpoena is a subpoena issued to persons or entities who are willing to testify or to produce the documents requested, but are concerned about the potential adverse consequences of doing so without a legal requirement. It is not good business to volunteer potentially damaging information to the DOL about one's clients.

Additionally, the attorney-client privilege may protect plan records that have been subpoenaed from plan legal counsel. However, under *Dole v. Milonas*, 889 F.2d 885 (9th Cir. 1989), it has been held that the attorney-client privilege does not permit an attorney to refuse to identify plan participants to the DOL absent a showing that the release of such names would be tantamount to the provision of protected communications protected by the attorney-client privilege. The *Milonas* case also established that the plan (or its service providers) may petition the court to issue a protective order that restricts the use of the subpoenaed information to the agency conducting the investigation and the use of the information solely for the purpose of conducting the ERISA investigation.

3. *Other Government Agency Referrals.* The DOL shares information with the IRS, Office of Inspector General, and other federal agencies about evidence of violations under their respective jurisdictions discovered in the course of investigations.

4. *Field Office Computer Targeting.* The DOL field offices currently receive digitally scanned images of Annual Report Forms 5500,

attached accountants' opinions, and audited financial statements filed with the IRS. The information reported on the Annual Report Form 5500 is entered into a computer database known as "FEDS," and is distributed to the DOL field offices on electronic media, accessible through their computer network. The system does not have the capability to conduct searches or inquiries using targeted criteria. It can only generate a reproduction of the actual Annual Report Forms 5500, attached accountants' opinions, or audited financial statements. Using FEDS, the DOL targets plans for investigation, based upon Annual Report Forms 5500 contained in its database. The targeting criteria are usually determined by the investigators who conduct searches.

5.   *Annual Report Form 5500 Review.* Some of the DOL regional offices may periodically send a team of investigators and auditors to an IRS regional storage facility to manually select and review the hard copy filings of Annual Report Forms 5500, accountants' opinions, and audited financial statements filed by employee benefit plans within their regional jurisdiction. The DOL team then screens, selects, and copies the documents that indicate potential violations of ERISA, according to their experience and judgment. The copied documents are returned to the regional office and used as targeting sources for potential future investigations.

6.   *ESIP Targeting Programs.* An enforcement strategy implementation plan ("ESIP") is periodically undertaken by the DOL, in an effort to allocate limited resources in the most effective manner to achieve and maintain compliance with ERISA. The 1990 ESIP directs the DOL to allocate 50% of its investigative resources to investigations of "significant issues": specific areas that have the highest potential for abuse. The objectives of the ESIP are to:

a) provide protection for the largest number of plan participants and amount of plan assets, given the available resources,

b) identify and investigate areas with the most potential for abuse,

c) detect and obtain corrections of ERISA violations,

d) establish a presence in the regulated community,

e) disseminate information and promote voluntary compliance, and

f) respond to participant complaints, public inquiries, and referrals from other government agencies.

In the years immediately following the announcement of the 1990 ESIP, the DOL focused its investigations on financial institutions. Since many of the larger financial institutions across the country have been investigated, the DOL is now focusing its ESIP resources on service providers, such as insurance companies, brokerage houses, third-party administrators, and, most recently, home health care agencies. *ERISA Enforcement Strategy Implementation Plan*, Sept. 1990.

PREPARING FOR THE INVESTIGATION

668. How can an employee benefit plan prepare for a pending Department of Labor investigation?

The target of a pending DOL investigation will be contacted, generally one to three weeks in advance, in order to schedule a convenient date and time for the initial on-site investigation. Unless the situation is urgent, the DOL is usually flexible regarding the scheduling. After the date has been established, the DOL will confirm the appointment with a follow-up letter that includes a list of documents the auditor/investigator will want to review. The auditor/investigator uses this list to prepare for the investigation by identifying the information requested, conducting a pre-investigation analysis of the plan or its operations, and preparing any other necessary documentation and support.

All service providers to the plan should be notified as soon as possible. This allows them time to review their records pertaining to the plan and prepare for any potential inquiries they may receive from the DOL. It also allows the entity and its service providers to obtain a uniform understanding of all of the facts regarding the operation of the plan. It is not uncommon for a DOL investigator/auditor to make unannounced visits to a service provider to follow up on a line of inquiry initiated with the plan sponsor. Preparation may allow these unscheduled visits to confirm, rather than contradict, the information presented by the plan sponsor.

All relevant materials and documents should be organized. Having well-organized documents may result in shorter investigations and minimize follow-up questions that could lead to problems. It may also give the DOL investigator/auditor the impression that the plan is well run and operated in compliance with ERISA. All requested documents may be placed into binders with a labeled dividing tab indicating each document, or if the records are voluminous, using separate, labeled file folders. A copy of the investigator's list of requested records should be placed on the front of the binder or folder with the records it contains highlighted on the list.

The plan sponsor should conduct a thorough pre-investigation internal audit. Depending upon the level of sophistication required to review complex documents, obtaining professional assistance to conduct such an internal audit should be considered. Regardless of who conducts the audit, questionable entries, vague or confusing information, or unanswered questions about plan records should be identified and answers prepared. Many DOL investigations are targeted through an analysis of the information reported on the Annual Report Forms 5500, attached schedules, accountants' opinions and audited financial statements.

Explanations should be prepared for any unanswered questions or vague or confusing information. DOL investigations are usually based on specific issues that indicate possible ERISA violations. Investigators or auditors must document these possible violations in order to open up an investigation. In that respect, a thorough pre-investigation audit may disclose any possible violations that may be present. If any issues that may support possible violations are identified, responses should be formulated and supporting documentation amassed to deflect or quell the DOL inquiry. Rapid, steadfast, and defensible responses may convince the investigator to disregard the issue. Conversely, hesitant or vacillating responses may indicate that the issue is worth pursuing. See Q 671 through Q 681 for detailed guidance on where to begin a pre-investigation audit.

Any defects identified in the internal audit should be corrected prior to the initial on-site investigation. A targeted entity may minimize its exposure to DOL sanctions and penalties if ERISA violations and defects are corrected before being discovered (or confirmed) during an investigation. In correcting violations, corrections should not be backdated, and documents should never be falsified. This may not only compound civil penalties, it may also be considered a criminal act. If there is a time-related issue, it should be corrected with the current date. Nevertheless, if the violation was also a violation of the Internal Revenue Code, the DOL may notify the IRS under its examination referral program.

PRACTITIONER'S POINTER

Although a violation may have existed, penalties may be reduced or eliminated if the underlying violation is corrected. If a breach of a fiduciary responsibility under ERISA is corrected prior to the receipt of a voluntary compliance ("VC") letter advising of a violation by the DOL, the 20% penalty of ERISA Section 502(l) may be inapplicable. That is because, in order for the the 20% penalty to apply, the applicable recovery amount must be paid pursuant to a settlement agreement with the Secretary of Labor or pursuant to court order in a judicial proceeding instituted by the Secretary of Labor. Note, however, that if a recipient of a VC letter performs the requested action in order to obtain the benefit of the DOL's promise to take no further action, a settlement agreement may be deemed to have occurred, thereby subjecting the recipient to the ERISA Section 502(l) penalty. This strategy should be discussed with legal counsel.

It may be necessary to hire outside help. Thorough preparation for the actual investigation may substantially minimize the possibility of surprises later. If the plan sponsor discovers an outstanding violation that it cannot handle alone, retaining outside professional assistance should be considered. Similarly, if the investment, operation, or fiduciary issues are complex or obscure, professional assistance may be warranted to assist in preparing documentation and structuring responses that avoid or minimize the imposition of fines and sanctions. Of course, the plan sponsor should be complete and honest in providing such professionals with all of the information necessary to protect the interests of the plan and fiduciaries because their ability to represent a plan is only as good as the information and cooperation presented to them.

669. May the expenses of a compliance audit be charged to a plan?

Maybe. The DOL provided guidance to this question in a July 28, 1998, information letter in which it indicated that the payment of an expense associated with a compliance audit by a multiemployer pension plan may be an appropriate expenditure of plan assets if the plan fiduciaries consider all of the relevant facts and circumstances of a given case. Although this guidance addresses the issue within the context of multiemployer pension plans, the information letter's rationale warrants its extension to single-employer employee benefit pension plans.

Compliance audits examine whether a plan is being operated in accordance with its governing documents, ERISA, and the Internal Revenue Code. Compliance audits include, but are not necessarily limited to, an examination of the administrative aspects of a plan's routine operations, including the plan's collection of contributions, payment of benefits, and investment of assets, as well as its compliance with the qualification provisions of the Internal Revenue Code.

According to the DOL, the fiduciaries must first examine the language of the plan documents in evaluating the payment of compliance audit expenses by a plan. If the expense would be permitted under the terms of the plan documents, then the fiduciaries must determine whether such payment would be consistent with Title I of ERISA. This initial inquiry is consistent with ERISA Section 404(a)(1)(D), which requires plan fiduciaries to discharge their duties in accordance with the documents and instruments governing the plan insofar as such documents and instruments are consistent with the provisions of Title I of ERISA (see Q 298).

Second, the plan's fiduciaries must consider the standards of conduct set forth in Sections 403(c)(1) (see Q 16) and 404(a)(1)(A) of ERISA (see Q 223). With respect to these sections, it is the view of the DOL that, generally, reasonable expenses of administering a plan include direct expenses properly and actually incurred in the performance of a fiduciary's duties to the plan. Consequently, if the trustees of a plan determine that periodic compliance audits are a helpful and prudent means of carrying out their fiduciary duties, including the duty to operate the plan in accordance with its terms, then the use of plan assets to procure compliance audits would not, in and of itself, violate Sections 403 and 404 of ERISA. In support of its conclusion, the DOL referenced the regulatory provision that permits fiduciaries to rely upon information, data, statistics or analysis furnished by persons performing ministerial functions for the plan, provided that they have exercised prudence in the selection and retention of such persons. See Labor Reg. §2509.75-8 (Q-11).

Thirdly, because compliance audits may confer a benefit upon the employer sponsoring plan, the plan fiduciaries have a duty to ensure that the plan's payment of an audit's expenses is reasonable in light of the benefit conferred upon the plan. Moreover, to the extent that the payments are made for the benefit of parties other than the plan's participants or beneficiaries, or involve services for which a plan sponsor or other entity could reasonably be expected to bear the cost in the normal course of such entity's business, the use of plan assets to make such payments would not be a reasonable expense of administering the plan. (See Letter to David Alter and Mark Hess from Bette Briggs (September 10, 1996); See Letter to Kirk F. Maldonado from Elliot I. Daniels (March 2, 1987). See also DOL Adv. Op. 97-03A (January 23, 1997).)

Finally, the DOL reiterated, in an information letter, its view that the payment of sanctions or penalties in connection with the settlement of disqualification matters with the IRS may or may not constitute a reasonable administrative expense of the plan under Title I of ERISA. The payment of such penalties will not constitute a reasonable expense of administering the plan for purposes of ERISA Sections 403 and 404 to the extent that they are a personal liability of someone other than the plan (e.g., penalties under Internal Revenue Code Section 6652 imposed on a plan administrator as a personal liability.) See Letter to Mark Sokolsky from John J. Canary (February 23, 1996). In contrast, if a plan-disqualifying defect is not caused by a breach of fiduciary duty, the plan can pay for any resulting sanctions or penalties only to the extent that such payment will constitute a reasonable expense of the plan. See DOL Adv. Op. 97-03A (January 23, 1997). See Information Letter to Gary E. Henderson from Susan G. Lahne (July 28, 1998).

670. What actions should a plan sponsor take during the course of the initial on-site DOL investigation?

Initial on-site investigations are typically scheduled for no more than three days if the target is a single plan or a single plan sponsor. Service provider investigations are more detailed and usually take one or more weeks, with follow-up on-site visits scheduled as needed.

An official liaison should be ready to meet the DOL investigator/auditor upon their arrival. The liaison should be responsible for working with the investigator/auditor during the on-site investigation. Lower-level employees may assist with the preparation for the investigation, but it is strongly suggested that the plan sponsor should be represented by upper-level management, the key retirement plan administrator, or outside counsel in most dealings with the DOL.

After the initial greeting, the investigator/auditor may make a brief presentation as to how the investigation will proceed. He may have preliminary questions regarding office policies and protocol and may also want to schedule interviews with key personnel in advance. This is an appropriate time for the liaison to ask any general questions regarding the investigation and the DOL. After this initial session, the investigator/auditor may proceed to review the documents that were requested in advance. When the investigator/auditor is escorted to the area prepared for the investigation, he should be assured that the liaison will be available as necessary.

The investigator/auditor may want to make copies of documents relating to the investigation. It is strongly suggested that the target entity make any copies that the investigator/auditor requests, rather than providing unlimited access to a copier. This may prevent the unnecessary copying of documents that do little to prove or disprove an alleged violation of ERISA.

After completing the initial on-site investigation, the investigator/auditor may likely conduct a brief exit interview with the liaison. Responsible parties may attend this meeting so that they may ask any questions or discuss any issues of concern to them.

PRACTITIONER'S POINTER

The documents that the investigator requests for copying may likely be used to substantiate an alleged violation of ERISA. Having a clerk make an additional copy of all documents requested may be useful in gaining insight into the potential issues or possible violations of concern to the investigator/auditor.

No one interviewed during the investigation should provide unrequested information. Only those records that the investigator/auditor requests should be made available, and individuals should be prepared to cooperate and to respond to requests for records and explanations. However, if the investigator does not request specific information, no information should be volunteered. In many cases, plan sponsor personnel have revealed unsolicited information to the DOL that disclosed violations that were not readily apparent during the investigation.

At the exit meeting, or at any time during the investigation, it may be appropriate to ask the investigator/auditor for his opinion as to the status of the plan with respect to its compliance with ERISA. Quite often the investigator may provide insight as to the potential violations being investigated and whether they have been found to exist. The investigator/auditor may even encourage the plan sponsor to correct the violations in the immediate future before an official notification letter is sent by the DOL.

The motives behind the investigator/auditor's disclosure and encouragement may be purely self-serving. DOL investigators and auditors are formally judged and appraised on their ability to detect violations of ERISA. Informally, but just as important in the performance appraisal process, is the fact that investigators and auditors are judged on the number of cases that were closed, the number of cases in which voluntary compliance was achieved, the number of cases that were referred for litigation, and the dollar amounts that were recovered (although DOL managers and directors would adamantly deny this). In this context, obtaining voluntary compliance relatively early in the investigative process may be seen as reducing the paperwork necessary to bring the case to closure and may further eliminate the paperwork associated with the assessment of an ERISA Section 502(l) penalty. Moreover, the investigator is credited with a closed case with voluntary compliance achieved relatively early in the standard investigative time frame.

INVESTIGATIVE INQUIRIES

671. What are the areas of initial inquiry during a Department of Labor audit?

The initial stages of Department of Labor field audits are intended to inform the auditor/investigator concerning the background of the subject plan. After establishing this foundation of fundamental knowledge, the auditor/investigator may then go forward with the investigation and focus on those areas that had been initially targeted for review. The following is a brief outline of the initial areas of inquiry normally undertaken during the initial on-site investigation of an employee benefit plan. Although it is an informal outline, it is routinely relied upon by field auditors and investigators. (This outline is covered in more detail in Q 672 through Q 681.) In addition to all of the necessary background information, it was designed to identify indicators of potential violations which would then be reviewed in detail.

The general areas of initial inquiry during a field audit are:

1.   The background of the plan sponsor and key employees;

2.   The background of the plan (type, benefits offered, participants, fiduciaries, etc.);

3.   The related parties to the subject plan;

4.   The reporting and disclosure obligations;

5.   The investment of plan assets;

6.   The plan service providers;

7.   The receipts, expenses and disbursements;

8.   The non-income producing assets;

9.   The accounting records and annual review; and

10. Bonding and insurance.

The areas of initial inquiry are not representative of a complete DOL investigation. It is merely a review of the initial steps taken when a plan has been targeted for an audit. Once all of the above areas have been reviewed by the auditor/investigator, close attention should be paid to the remaining areas of inquiry. More often than not, these are the areas of interest which have been identified for review. All DOL investigative reports are required to review bonding, reporting, and disclosure procedures of a plan. Inquiries into these areas are routine and, most likely, are not the reason the plan has been targeted for an audit.

PRACTITIONER'S POINTER

These queries would be an excellent place to begin a due diligence audit or a "pre-audit" prior to the date of an initial on-site visit from a Department of Labor representative. If any "red flags" have been identified through the application of the inquiries (see Q 672 through Q 681), plan counsel should conduct a thorough investigation into problem areas prior to the initial on-site investigation. This would allow for sufficient time to prepare documentation, explanations, and if necessary, correction of violations or an adequate defense.

If a blatant prohibited transaction is identified for which there is no adequate explanation, plan counsel should consider reversing the transaction prior to the receipt of official notification from the Department of Labor. The Department of Labor will not impose ERISA Section 502(l) penalties on a reversed prohibited transaction unless the reversal was the result of a Department of Labor "official notification" of an outstanding violation that the subject plan has been ordered to correct (usually through voluntary compliance).

672. What are some of the background areas of initial inquiry during an initial on-site investigation by the Department of Labor?

The first areas of plan information to be reviewed during an initial on-site investigation by a Department of Labor auditor/investigator are likely to be those detailed below:

1.   Background information, including:

a) the name or title of the person interviewed,

b) the business address and background of the subject (to establish a foundation of competence), and

c) the name or background of the plan sponsor.

2.   Plan information, including:

a) the name and type of plan (i.e., defined benefit, defined contribution, health and welfare),

b) the basic benefits offered under the plan,

c) the number of participants, total assets and annual contributions,

d) the plan administrator (both currently and over the past five years),

e) named fiduciaries (both currently and over the past five years),

f) a list of other plans sponsored,

g) any functioning committees and the method in which members are selected, and

h) current investments of the plan.

3.   Information regarding related parties, including:

a) unions connected with the plan, if any,

b) the names of all stockholders who own a 10% or more share of the sponsor,

c) the names of any principal officers or employees who own 10% or more of any business with which the plan does business, and

d) any pending legal proceedings which involve the plan or plan fiduciaries.

This information is intended to provide the auditor/investigator with a detailed overview of the plan, its sponsor and any related parties who may be involved in the issues under investigation.

673. What are the initial DOL inquiries regarding Summary Plan Descriptions, Summary of Material Modifications and Summary Annual Reports?

When beginning a review of the subject plan's reporting and disclosure obligations under ERISA, the auditor/investigator will review the following questions regarding the plan's Summary Plan Description, Summary of Material Modifications and Summary Annual Reports:

1.   Is the plan exempt from reporting requirements? If so, why?

2.   Does the SPD meet the style, format and content requirements of the DOL? (Labor Regs. §§2520.102-2, 2520.102-3.)

3. Has the SPD been provided to participants and beneficiaries receiving benefits within 120 days after the plan is subject to ERISA or 90 days after new participants become eligible to participate in the plan? (Labor Reg. §2520.104b-2.)

4. Is the SPD more than five years old? (Labor Reg. §2520.104b-2.)

5. If material modifications have occurred, has a Summary of Material Modifications been filed with the DOL and disclosed to participants and beneficiaries within 210 days after the end of the plan year in which the change was made? (Note that for plan years beginning after August 6, 1997, plans are no longer required to provide the Department of Labor with copies of the Summary of Material Modifications.) (Labor Reg. §2520.104a-7.)

6. Has the Summary Annual Report ("SAR") been disclosed to participants and beneficiaries within nine months after the close of the plan year? (Labor Reg. §2520.104b-10.)

674. What are the initial DOL inquiries regarding Annual Report Forms 5500 and PBGC forms?

When continuing a review of a subject plan's reporting and disclosure obligations under ERISA, the auditor/investigator will review the following items to determine if the plan has satisfied the applicable requirements:

1. Have Annual Report Forms 5500 been filed with the DOL or IRS within 270 days after the close of the plan year? (Labor Reg. §2520.104a-5.)

2. If applicable, have Schedule A (Insurance Information), Schedule B (Actuarial Information), an Opinion of Qualified Public Accountant, an Actuarial Statement, or Financial Statements been included with the Annual Report Forms 5500? (Labor Reg. §2520.103-1.)

3. If applicable, has Form 5310 (Application for Determination upon Termination; Notice of Merger, Consolidation or Transfer of Plan Assets or Liabilities; Notice of Intent to Terminate) been filed with the IRS or the PBGC?

4. If applicable, has a "Final AR 5500" been filed with the IRS upon complete distribution of assets?

5. If applicable, has the PBGC been notified of a merger, transfer of

assets or liabilities or the termination of a multiemployer plan covered by the PBGC Insurance Program?

6.   For defined benefit plans, has Form PBGC-1 been filed?

675. What are the initial DOL inquiries regarding participant disclosure requirements?

ERISA mandates that plans must disclose certain materials to plan participants under certain circumstances. The following questions were designed to assist field auditors/investigators in determining whether a plan subject to an investigation has satisfied those participant disclosure requirements:

1.   Are copies of the plan, Summary Plan Description, latest annual report and governing documents (under which the plan was established and is operating) made available to plan participants at the principal office of the administrator? (Labor Reg. §2520.104b-1.)

2.   For plans that make a charge for documents, is the charge reasonable (generally, up to 15 cents per page)? (Labor Reg. §2520.104b-30.)

3.   Does the plan respond to written disclosure requests within 30 days? (ERISA Sec. 502(c).)

4.   For those plans to which vesting standards apply, has a statement concerning the nature, amount, and form of deferred vested benefits been provided to those participants that have terminated employment or had a 1-year break in service? (ERISA Sec. 105(c).)

5.   For those applicable plans, has a written explanation been provided to participants before the annuity starting date of the terms and conditions of any joint and survivor annuity and the effect of electing against such options? (Treas. Reg §1.401(a)-(11)(c)(3).)

6.   For participants or beneficiaries with claim denials, does the plan provide notice of denial within 90 days? (Labor Reg. §2560.503-1(e).)

676. What are the initial DOL inquiries regarding plan investments?

In an initial on-site investigation, the auditor/investigator will review the following questions in order to identify the plan's basic asset investment holdings, procedures, philosophies and objectives:

1.   Does the plan now hold for investment, or has it held for invest-
        ment in the last six years, any of the following: (a) participant loans;
        (b) diamonds; (c) gold or other non-income producing assets; (d)
        mortgages; (e) loans other than mortgages; (f) limited partnership
        interests; (g) employer stocks or securities; or (h) stock of a closely
        held corporation?

2.   Who makes the decisions on plan investments, and what criteria
        are used?

3.   What outside advice is obtained to help in investment decisions,
        and how often is it relied upon?

4.   If and when stocks are purchased, who makes the decision and
        through whom is the transaction executed?

5.   What criteria are used in making this decision?

6.   Are commissions negotiated, and how?

7.   What are the plan's basic investment philosophies and objectives?

677. What are the initial DOL inquiries regarding persons or entities providing services to a subject plan?

In reviewing the background information of a plan under investigation, the
auditor/investigator will review the following items to identify the service
providers who are involved in the ongoing administration of the plan and the
management of the plan's assets. The review will require that the name, functions
performed, and contracts of the following service providers be furnished:

*   accountants;

*   attorneys;

*   administrators;

*   actuaries;

*   trustees;

*   insurance agents;

*   investment advisors;

*   broker-dealers;

- banks; and

- all other service providers not identified above.

678. What are the initial DOL inquiries regarding plan receipts, expenses and disbursements?

In an initial on-site investigation, the DOL auditor/investigator will want to ascertain the following information regarding plan receipts, expenses and disbursements in an effort to establish the protocol utilized by the plan and the persons responsible for these tasks.

    1.   Regarding receipts, the auditor/investigator will ask:

        a) Who makes the decision regarding the amount of contributions and when they are made?

        b) What are the plan document's basic funding requirements (within the knowledge of the interviewee)?

        c) How often are contributions received?

        d) If receipts are received by mail, what procedures are used for processing mail receipts?

        e) What is the percentage of receipts received through the mail?

        f) Are contributions received in cash? If so, who handles cash contributions, and how is the accounting for such contributions handled?

        g) What procedures are used to collect delinquent contributions?

        h) Are receipt books used and, if so, are they pre-numbered?

        i) Does the plan maintain a petty cash fund? If so, on what basis is it maintained?

        j) Are all receipts deposited intact? Who makes these deposits?

    2.   Regarding expenses and disbursements, the auditor/investigator will ask:

a) What expenses, other than benefits, are paid by the plan?

b) What are the basic procedures for making disbursements on service provider invoices?

c) Are all invoice disbursements made by check? How many signatures are required? Who can sign checks? Are the plan checks ever pre-signed?

d) What is the basic procedure used to process and approve benefit disbursements?

e) Are any salaries paid from the plan assets?

f) If so, who determines salaries, and how is basic payroll accounting set up?

679. What are the initial DOL inquiries regarding non-income producing assets that may be held by the plan?

During the initial on-site investigation, the DOL auditor/investigator is likely to inquire whether the subject plan holds any of the following non-income producing assets as plan investments, and what procedures are involved in making such investments. The auditor/investigator may ask the following questions:

1.   What equipment (e.g., cars, office furniture, fixtures, buildings, etc.) is owned by the plan?

2.   What controls are set up to maintain proper safeguards of the assets and to prevent their misuse?

3.   Who approves purchases of any capital item (i.e., purchases over $100 with a useful life in excess of one year); and

4.   Are bids sought on major purchases in order to obtain the best price?

680. What are the initial DOL inquiries regarding the accounting records of a subject plan?

During the initial on-site investigation, the DOL auditor/investigator will want to determine what accounting records are maintained by the subject plan, who maintains them and who, if anyone, is charged with reviewing them on an annual basis. In order to make this determination, the auditor/investigator may ask the following questions:

1.   Are any of the following accounting records maintained, and who maintains them?

       a) bank accounts,

       b) receipts and disbursements journals,

       c) vouchers, vendors and invoices,

       d) broker confirmations,

       e) receipt books,

       f) investment acquisition and disposition records, and

       g) Annual Report Forms 5500.

2.   How often and by whom are these records reviewed or audited (internally and externally)?

681. What are the initial DOL inquiries regarding the bonding and insurance coverage of a subject plan?

During the initial on-site investigation, the DOL auditor/investigator will conduct an extensive review of the subject plan's bonding and insurance coverage. This is because the final investigative report that the auditor/investigator will prepare and submit on the case must provide a detailed analysis of these items. Consequently, the auditor/investigator may ask the following questions:

1.   Does a separate trust fund exist?

2.   Are there insurance or annuity contracts?

3.   Are there separate accounts in the books of the employer or do separate funds or other properties exist in the name of the plan? (Note: If the answer to items (1) or (3) is "yes," bonding is usually required. It should be determined whether insurance dividends belong to the plan or the plan sponsor. If they belong to the plan, bonding is required. If cash surrender values exist and the plan can obtain those values, bonding is required. See Chapter VIII for additional bonding rules.)

4.   Are benefits paid from the general assets of the plan sponsor?

5.   Is there any segregation of the plan funds?

6.   Are there separate accounts on the books or are there separate books of account for the plan? (Note: If item (4) is answered "yes" and items (5) and (6) are answered "no," the Plan is unfunded and no bonding is required.)

7.   Do any trustees or plan employees have:

a) physical possession of plan assets?

b) power to obtain physical possession of plan assets?

c) power to transfer assets?

d) authority to disburse plan funds directly or indirectly?

e) authority to sign or endorse checks and/or the authority to make investments?

(Note: If any of the items under (7) are answered "yes," handling of plan funds is indicated and bonding is required for each individual who has such authority. If a corporate trustee holds the plan assets, but the plan trustees can direct the payment of benefits by the corporate trustee or direct the investments to be made by the corporate trustee, the plan trustees are "handling" funds and bonding is required.)

8.   Does the bond provide for payment to the plan in the event of loss? (The plan must be named as an "insured" and the payover rider must be attached unless the plan is the sole insured under the bond. The definition of "employee" in the bond must cover all persons who "handle" funds.)

9.   How many plans are covered by the bond?

10. How many non-plan entities are covered by the bond?

11. Is the bonding company listed in the Department of the Treasury Circular 570 as an approved surety provider? (The auditor/investigator will require the name and the policy lapse date.)

12. Is the plan named as the insured?

13. If there is more than one plan, or the plan and the plan sponsor are covered, is a pay-over rider attached?

14.   If the bond contains a deductible, is an elimination of the deductible rider attached with respect to the plan?

15.   Does the bond protect against fraud and dishonesty?

16.   Does the bond have a 1-year discovery period?

17.   Does the bond provide coverage of 10% of the funds handled with a maximum amount of $500,000?

18.   If the plan or plan sponsor maintains fiduciary liability insurance coverage, what is the name of the company and the amount of coverage?

In its semiannual agenda of regulations issued in November, 2000, the PWBA announced that it is undertaking a review of the temporary bonding regulations under ERISA Sec. 412 for the purpose of developing a regulation that exempts certain investment advisors and broker-dealers from the definition of "plan officials" required to be bonded under ERISA Section 412(a). 65 Fed. Reg. 74071 (11-30-2000).

INVESTIGATIVE FINDINGS AND COMPLIANCE

682. What can a plan sponsor expect after the DOL has completed its investigation?

Once the DOL has completed its investigation of the target plan, it may issue a notice to the fiduciaries, sponsor, or service provider in one of four formats.

1.   *No Violation Letter.* This is a brief, one-page closing letter advising that the DOL has completed its investigation and no further action is contemplated with regard to the case. This letter is issued in cases in which no violations are detected. The letter closes by thanking the recipient for its cooperation during the investigation.

2.   *Cautionary Letter — No Action Warranted; Compliance Achieved.* This closing letter is issued when the DOL has discovered violations of ERISA that have been reversed or rectified prior to official notification by the DOL. It is also issued as a caution to fiduciaries, plan sponsors and service providers for outstanding de minimis violations, or if there are no actual or potential monetary damages to the plan (e.g., bonding, reporting, and disclosure issues). This letter cautions the subject of the investigation to exercise prudence in avoiding such violations in the future. Although this letter is used in circumstances that do not appear to justify the commitment of DOL

resources, the plan may be notified that the matter will be referred to the IRS for possible imposition of excise taxes.

3.   *Voluntary Compliance Notice Letter.* A voluntary compliance notice ("VC") letter notifies plan fiduciaries or others of ERISA violations and requests corrective action. VC letters advise fiduciaries of the DOL's findings and invite the recipient of the letter to discuss with the DOL how the violations may be corrected and any losses restored to the plan. Although the VC letter does not threaten litigation, it informs the recipient that failure to take corrective action may result in referral of the matter to the Office of the Solicitor of Labor for possible legal action. Additionally, the letter advises that if proper corrective action is taken, the DOL will not bring a lawsuit with regard to the issues. However, the assessment of the ERISA Section 502(l) penalty is applicable. The recipient is given 10 days from the date of the VC letter to advise the DOL, in writing, as to what action it intends to take to correct the violations.

4.   *Demand or Litigation Notice.* This notice is usually reserved for the most egregious civil violations under ERISA or cases identified as significant under the DOL enforcement strategy. It is mailed from the Plan Benefits Security Division ("PBSD") in Washington, D.C., or one of the regional solicitors' offices. This is an official notification to the investigatory target that it has transgressed ERISA to the point that the DOL has deemed that litigation may be warranted. A litigation notice may also be sent in cases of outstanding prohibited transactions that are of sufficient seriousness to warrant judicial action. The DOL may make every attempt to resolve prohibited transactions through the VC letter, but if there is a clear indication that the plan sponsor has no intent to reverse a prohibited transaction and the DOL feels that negotiations would have no success, a case may be referred for litigation. If PBSD or the regional solicitor agrees with the assessment of the PWBA field office, either may issue a notice demanding corrective action, or litigation may result.

PRACTITIONER'S POINTER

Quality legal counsel or other professional assistance competent in ERISA-related matters should be retained upon receipt of a VC, demand, or litigation notice.

683. What techniques does the Pension and Welfare Benefits Administration use to correct ERISA violations?

In accordance with its policy of promoting voluntary compliance with ERISA, in many situations, PWBA actively pursues voluntary resolution to correct violations of ERISA. The objective of voluntary correction is to restore the status quo ante. The regional director responsible for the investigation determines whether to pursue corrective action through voluntary compliance in accordance with PWBA national office policy.

If it is decided that correction of the apparent violations should be pursued through voluntary compliance, the PWBA regional office issues a notice letter to plan officials advising them of the results of the investigation. In part, the notice letter describes the ERISA violations and details the PWBA's position on acceptable corrective actions. In some cases, violations of a serious nature are corrected through judicial enforcement decrees at the insistence of the PWBA. PWBA publicly discloses the results obtained through these situations to inform the employee benefit plan community of the enforcement program and of the issues and legal positions of concern to PWBA. In other cases, some violations, by their nature, may jeopardize plan assets or participants rights. In these cases, PWBA may bypass voluntary correction efforts and instead, pursue immediate court action without discussing the matter with plan officials. ERISA Sec. 502(a)(2); *ERISA Enforcement Strategy Implementation Plan*, Sept. 1990, pp. 3, 28.

684. Which types of cases involving ERISA violations are appropriate for voluntary compliance?

PWBA regional offices actively seek to achieve voluntary resolution of all violations of ERISA, because the PWBA considers most issues suitable for voluntary compliance. According to the PWBA, cases most acceptable for voluntary compliance resolution involve benefit disputes, bonding, reporting, and disclosure issues. PWBA may attempt to resolve these types of issues during the course of an investigation. *PWBA Enforcement Manual*, Ch. 34, p. 2.

685. Which types of cases involving ERISA violations may not be suitable for voluntary compliance?

Although many cases are suitable for resolution through voluntary compliance, the PWBA is not bound to seek voluntary compliance in all cases. According to the PWBA, voluntary correction of ERISA violations may not be suitable in cases involving issues identified as significant under the PWBA enforcement strategy, or cases involving novel or interpretive legal issues, such as: (1) when recovery from one who is not a fiduciary can be legally supported; and (2) whether there is a covered plan protected by ERISA. *PWBA Enforcement Manual*, Ch. 34, p. 2.

686. Are any cases involving ERISA violations not suitable for voluntary compliance?

According to PWBA, certain types of cases are not considered appropriate for voluntary compliance, either because of the seriousness of the violation or the individual or entities involved. Generally, these cases include:

1.   Prudence violations of ERISA Section 404(a) with losses in excess of $500,000 (exclusive of interest on the losses);

2.   Prohibited transaction violations of ERISA Section 406 with losses in excess of $500,000;

3.   Cases in which the time for proposed correction of violations will exceed a 1-year period;

4.   Violations involving potential fraud or criminal misconduct with respect to dealings with a plan unless a United States Attorney has agreed to a voluntary compliance settlement;

5.   Situations warranting the removal of a fiduciary or a related entity; or

6.   Cases that involve individuals who have previously violated ERISA or other federal statutes.

Thus, PWBA may insist on judicially enforceable decrees in the above situations, or may initiate court action without offering plan officials the opportunity to voluntarily correct the ERISA violations. ERISA Sec. 502(a)(2); *PWBA Enforcement Manual*, Ch. 34, pp. 2-3; *ERISA Enforcement Strategy Implementation Plan*, Sept. 1990, p. 28.

687. How are plan fiduciaries or others notified of the opportunity for voluntary compliance?

Although PWBA has adopted the policy of not informing plan officials or others as to the basis or source of its investigation, plan fiduciaries or others are typically notified of the opportunity to voluntarily correct violations of ERISA during the course of an investigation or at its conclusion. During the course of an investigation, investigators/auditors may discuss their personal views of the investigative findings with plan officials. These findings are subject to review by PWBA officials and are generally confirmed in writing by PWBA. The investigator/auditor also may attempt to solicit the position and intentions of the plan officials regarding the actions they might voluntarily take to correct the violations. In addition, the investigator/auditor may attempt to determine the financial condition of the fiduciaries and/or related parties, as well as whether the fiduciaries have fiduciary liability insurance (the latter as a potential source of recovery of monetary loss to the plan).

Officially, the investigator/auditor is generally prohibited from proposing corrective actions or discussing tentative settlement terms without the prior consent of the regional director. If given this consent, the investigator/auditor may discuss proposed corrective actions and the civil penalty process with plan officials at the conclusion of the investigation. The investigator/auditor, however, may not officially discuss specific dollar amounts related to the proposed corrective action or any civil penalty that might be assessed as a result thereof. All discussions with plan officials that relate to findings or proposed corrections may likely be put in writing by the investigator/auditor. In the absence of, or subsequent to, the discussions with plan officials concerning corrective action, plan officials may be notified of the opportunity for voluntary corrective action at the conclusion of an investigation, through the receipt of a voluntary compliance notice letter (see Q 688). *PWBA Enforcement Manual*, Ch. 34, pp. 1-2.

688. What is a voluntary compliance notice letter?

A voluntary compliance notice ("VC") letter is issued by the investigating regional office and advises plan fiduciaries or others of the results of an investigation. A VC letter identifies any violations of ERISA, and requests corrective action. The VC letter grants fiduciaries or others an opportunity to comment or discuss with the PWBA how to correct the violations and restore any losses to the plan before the PWBA determines whether to take action, if any.

Although the VC letter does not threaten litigation, it does state that the matter may be referred to the DOL's Office of the Solicitor for possible legal action should the fiduciaries or others fail to take the prescribed corrective action. In addition, the VC letter advises that the PWBA may furnish information to "any person... actually affected by any matter which is the subject" of an ERISA investigation and that the fiduciaries and others remain subject to suit by other parties including plan fiduciaries and plan participants or their beneficiaries. *PWBA Enforcement Manual*, Ch. 34, p. 3.

689. How long will the PWBA conduct voluntary compliance negotiations?

In an effort to achieve voluntary corrections of ERISA violations, PWBA generally will conduct voluntary compliance negotiations. The period of time devoted to these negotiations varies according to the circumstances of the particular investigation and the parties involved. However, PWBA avoids negotiations with undue delay between the initiation of the voluntary compliance efforts and the conclusion of any negotiations regarding compliance (although the corrective action may occur over a more extended period), especially in instances where the investigation is likely to be referred for litigation should the voluntary compliance process prove unsuccessful. *PWBA Enforcement Manual*, Ch. 34, p. 7.

690. What settlement terms are acceptable under voluntary correction?

Generally, PWBA insists on full recovery to the plan under the terms of a voluntary correction agreement. Recovery includes amounts paid to the plan that represent losses incurred by the plan, disgorged profits, and amounts necessary to achieve correction. Other terms may include, where appropriate, the rescission of prohibited transactions, the removal of fiduciaries, the appointment of a receiver, and the indemnification of the plan against future losses. The amount of the recovery is determined as a part of the "settlement agreement" with the party. Full repayment of losses to the plan must be made over a period of no longer than one year. In instances in which the statute of limitations will toll before the terms of the settlement agreement are completed, PWBA may attempt to obtain a tolling agreement that expires six months after the repayment period terminates. In addition, the settlement agreement should provide that interest on repayments be at appropriate rates, and all notes supporting the payment be adequately secured. Moreover, PWBA will demand proof that payment of the recovery amount is actually made to the plan. *PWBA Enforcement Manual*, Ch. 34, p. 4; Ch. 48.

691. What actions are taken by PWBA when voluntary compliance attempts are unsuccessful?

In all cases where voluntary compliance attempts prove unsuccessful, in whole or in part, the PWBA regional office will consider all possible courses of action within its delegated authority for resolving or closing the case, including referral for litigation, referral to the Department of Justice, and referral to the IRS for the imposition of an excise tax under Internal Revenue Code Section 4975. In addition, the PWBA may assess the ERISA Section 502(i) civil penalty, if appropriate. In cases where partial compliance is achieved and the ERISA Section 502(l) civil penalty is applicable, the PWBA will assess the penalty on the applicable recovery amount. In other situations, where voluntary compliance is not achieved, PWBA may close the case.

In the course of closing a case in which voluntary compliance is not achieved, the PWBA may disclose the results of the investigation to affected parties (e.g., by sending them a copy of the closing letter). Disclosure also may be made to a plan participant, beneficiary or fiduciary in the event the investigation arose as a result of such person's complaint. A disclosure will not be made to these individuals if the information to be disclosed was obtained pursuant to: (1) Rule 6(e) of the Federal Rules of Criminal Procedure; (2) IRC Section 6103; (3) the DOL's agreement with the Federal Financial Institution Regulatory Agencies; or (4) from some other source requiring confidentiality. *PWBA Enforcement Manual*, Ch. 34, p. 7.

692. What is a closing letter?

In instances where it is determined that no further action will be taken, the investigating regional office of PWBA issues a closing letter at the conclusion of an investigation. The closing letter informs plan fiduciaries or others of the results of an investigation, including which sections of ERISA have been violated, if any, and that no further action by the DOL is currently contemplated with respect to the issues described in the letter. In addition, any unresolved reporting issues and their referral to PWBA's Office of the Chief Accountant (OCA) are reflected in the closing letter. (The responsibility for the acceptance or rejection of the Annual Report (Form 5500) or any part thereof is delegated to the OCA.)

A closing letter may be issued in various forms, depending on the situation of the case. For example, a "Pattern Closing Letter" is issued in all cases in which no ERISA violations are detected during the course of the investigation. The letter is typically one page in length and will thank the recipient for its cooperation in the investigation, if appropriate.

In some instances, PWBA issues a closing letter other than the pattern closing letter, even if violations are present. This "No Action Warranted Closing Letter" is issued in instances only if there is no evidence of willful misconduct and (1) the violations are de minimis in nature, or (2) there are no actual or potential monetary damages to the plan. For example, PWBA considers it appropriate to use this letter in instances where an investigation disclosed a small prohibited transaction that had been reversed with no harm to the plan, or where a plan failed to submit an accountant's opinion for a particular year, but submitted one for all subsequent years.

A "Compliance Achieved Closing Letter" is issued in instances where corrective action is confirmed and either applicable penalties were paid or the payment period has expired. This letter follows a voluntary compliance notice letter. A modification of this letter is also used in situations where violations were discussed and confirmed with plan officials at the conclusion of an investigation and these violations were or will be corrected by the plan officials pursuant to the discussions with PWBA. The modified compliance achieved closing letter details the violations as well as the specific corrective actions agreed to by the plan officials, including ERISA Section 502(l) and ERISA Section 502(i) matters.

PWBA issues a "Compliance Not Achieved Closing Letter" in instances where a voluntary compliance notice letter has been sent to plan fiduciaries and the fiduciaries: (1) deny the facts disclosed in the investigation; (2) admit to the facts but deny the facts constitute a violation of ERISA; or (3) otherwise fail to comply with the terms of the VC notice letter. The use of this letter is limited to situations in which no enforcement action is contemplated by PWBA after it has considered all possible courses of action, including referral of the case for possible litigation.

In certain situations where no voluntary compliance was attempted, and when the facts and issues do not appear to justify the commitment of PWBA resources, the PWBA may refer the case to the IRS for possible imposition of excise taxes under Internal Revenue Code Section 4975. In these instances, PWBA issues a "Referral to the IRS Closing Letter" to the plan, which notifies it of this action. *PWBA Enforcement Manual*, Ch. 34, pp. 6-7.

693. What action should be taken when fiduciaries agree with the DOL's official findings in an investigation?

If the DOL places a target plan on official notice of outstanding violations of ERISA and plan fiduciaries agree, fiduciaries should follow the instructions for submitting an official response to the DOL office issuing the notice. The plan's response should be tailored to the DOL's notice letter. Each violation should be listed, the fiduciary's agreement stated, and the proposed or completed corrections detailed. The plan sponsor has discretion in the manner of correcting the violations as long as the chosen method does not lead to further violations and plan participants remain unharmed.

In negotiating a settlement with the DOL, the plan sponsor will receive a notice of assessment, issued by the regional office, concerning any penalties assessed under ERISA Section 502(l). The notice will contain a brief description of the violation, the identity of the person being assessed, the amount of the assessment, and the basis for assessing that particular person and that particular penalty amount. If the plan sponsor believes that the 502(l) penalty is unwarranted or extreme, the plan sponsor may, at any time during the 60-day payment period, petition the Secretary of Labor (through the regional director) to waive or reduce the assessed penalty. This petition must be made on the basis that:

1.   Unless such a waiver or reduction is granted, the petitioner will not be able to restore all losses to the plan or any of its participants or beneficiaries without severe financial hardship; and

2.   The petitioner acted in good faith in engaging in the breach or violation.

Additionally, the petitioner is entitled to a conference with the Secretary of Labor regarding a petition for waiver or reduction of the civil penalty. (See Q 694.)

Once the plan sponsor has documented compliance with the DOL order to correct outstanding violations and has reached a settlement with respect to any ERISA Section 502(l) penalties, the DOL will issue a case-closing letter confirming its acceptance of the plan's corrective actions. The plan sponsor should retain this case closing letter in the official plan records file. In the past, the DOL has opened new investigations on previous targets. The case-closing letter serves as protection against the possibility that the DOL will cite the plan again for the same violations.

694. What action should be taken when fiduciaries disagree with the DOL's official findings in an investigation?

If the plan sponsor has received a VC letter from the DOL and plan fiduciaries disagree with some or all of the violations cited, the plan has the right to request a voluntary compliance conference with the DOL. The DOL field office issuing the notice of violations may schedule this conference at its office. Attending the conference on behalf of the DOL may be the investigator/auditor who conducted the investigation and his direct supervisor. If the case is sufficiently complicated, or involves a substantial amount of money, the regional deputy director (or his or her equivalent) or the regional director may also be involved. Given the nature of the conference, it is recommended that both the plan and any service provider involved in the contested violation be represented by legal counsel.

The DOL may be reasonable in discussing mitigating facts and circumstances during voluntary compliance conferences. If the plan sponsor's position is reasonable and provides a reasonable alternative to any DOL demands, the DOL may consider it. If plan representatives firmly believe that an action for which the plan has been cited is not a violation of ERISA, this conference is an opportunity to state the plan's case and to convince the DOL to change its position.

In negotiating a settlement, the DOL considers some factors that are unrelated to the facts and circumstances of the violations, such as: (1) the likelihood that the DOL solicitor is willing to litigate the case as originally cited; (2) the seriousness of the violations cited; (3) the case load of the office and the investigator; (4) the working relationship of the regional office with the Pension Benefits Security Division ("PBSD") or the regional solicitors; and (5) the likelihood that compliance will not be achieved without a negotiated settlement. For these reasons, voluntary compliance conferences can result in a reduction or elimination of the contested violation.

Alternatively, the plan sponsor may refuse to comply with the DOL's requests for voluntary compliance. This involves a risk, but the risk is much lower if the alledged violation: (1) has a strong defensible position; (2) is not flagrant; (3) has few victims; (4) is technically complex; or (5) involves limited losses to the plan. The DOL field office may respond to the plan sponsor's refusal with a threat of litigation. This may be an intimidation tactic, considering the relatively high rate of rejection of such cases by the PBSD and the regional solicitors.

The regional solicitor offices and the PBSD are most inclined to litigate cases that involve many victims, potentially large recoveries, or unique issues of a timely and newsworthy nature. Although they may be well versed in ERISA, some of these attorneys do not have a strong background in finance, accounting or investments. With such shortcomings, they may only accept a case for litigation if they understand the underlying technical theories and premises and their relationship to the alleged violations as well as believing it is likely that the case will be won or a favorable settlement reached. These factors should be discussed with plan legal counsel in any decision to refuse the DOL's request for voluntary compliance.

The DOL regional office may even bypass the voluntary compliance step and submit a request for litigation on a case without even offering an opportunity to settle (indeed, the regional office is "credited" when it refers a case for litigation, even if the case is ultimately rejected for litigation by the PBSD or the regional solicitor's office). If the litigation request is rejected, the DOL may attempt voluntary compliance or may close the investigation and leave the target plan "in violation," even though the DOL contemplates no legal action at that time. However, the target plan is still subject to suits by other parties, including plan fiduciaries and plan participants or their beneficiaries. Additionally, the excise tax on disqualified persons under Internal Revenue Code Section 4975 may be applicable. Because of these risks, plan fiduciaries should review any refusal option with the plan's legal counsel.

695. What is the "Interagency Referral Agreement"?

ERISA Section 506 contains the statutory provisions relating to the coordination and responsibility of agencies for enforcing ERISA and related federal laws. ERISA Section 506(a) states that:

> In order to avoid unnecessary expense and duplication of functions among Government agencies, the Secretary may make such arrangements or agreements for cooperation or mutual assistance in the performance of his functions under this title and the functions of any such agency as he may find to be practicable and consistent with the law. The Secretary may utilize, on a reimbursable or other basis, the facilities or services of any department, agency, or establishment of the United States or of any State or political subdivision of a State, including the services of any of its employees, with the lawful consent of such department, agency or establishment, and each department, agency, or establishment of the United States is authorized and directed to cooperate with the Secretary and, to the extent permitted by law, to provide such information and facilities as he may request for his assistance in the performance of his functions under this title. The Attorney General or his representative shall receive from the Secretary for appropriate action such evidence developed in the performance of his functions under this title as may be found to warrant consideration for criminal prosecution under the provisions of this title or other Federal law.

Due to an interagency referral agreement between the IRS and the PWBA, each field office of the DOL will make arrangements with the Employee Plans Division of the IRS field office within the appropriate jurisdiction to exchange referrals of evidence and reports indicating potential violations of the other agency's statutory jurisdiction that have been identified in the course of routine investigations. Most DOL field offices have made arrangements to meet with the IRS Employee Plans Division within its jurisdiction on a monthly basis for the purpose of discussing and exchanging referrals for consideration of investigation.

This interagency referral agreement is in accordance with the provisions of ERISA Section 506(b), which provides that "[t]he Secretary shall have the responsibility and authority to detect and investigate and refer, where appropriate, civil and criminal violations related to the provisions of this title and other related Federal laws."

DOL CIVIL ACTIONS

696. What types of civil actions may be brought by the DOL?

ERISA Section 502 permits the DOL to file the following civil actions:

1. Suits to enforce Title I of ERISA (Protection of Employee Benefit Rights);

2. Suits to require disclosure of individual benefit statements, in accordance with ERISA Section 105(c);

3. Suits to enforce the fiduciary provisions of ERISA and to make the plan whole for any losses resulting from a breach of fiduciary duty; and

4. Suits to collect civil penalties for:

    a) the failure or refusal to file an Annual Report;

    b) a violation of the prohibited transaction provisions; and

    c) situations in which a breaching fiduciary or a person who knowingly participates in a fiduciary breach is required to make restitution to the plan.

The Fifth Circuit Court of Appeals has held that the DOL's interest in bringing an ERISA action is to safeguard the integrity of the pension system. *Donovan v. Cunningham*, 716 F.2d 1455 (5th Cir. 1983).

ERISA Section 502(j) provides that in all civil actions brought by the DOL, attorneys appointed by the Secretary of Labor may represent him or her. The exception to this general rule is cases presented to the Supreme Court, which will be subject to the direction and control of the Attorney General.

Actions brought by the DOL are subject to the civil procedure rules regarding: (1) standing to sue; (2) jurisdiction over the claim by the court hearing the proceedings; (3) the proper venue of the suit; and (4) under certain circumstances, the seeking of equitable relief, injunctive relief and/ or attorney's fees.

697. Can the DOL intervene in an existing ERISA-related civil action?

A copy of all complaints filed in civil actions brought by a participant, beneficiary or a fiduciary regarding alleged violations of ERISA must be served upon the Secretary of Labor.

As a result of an Eleventh Circuit decision, the Secretary of Labor may sue a plan fiduciary for money damages even though an identical claim by a class of plan participants against the same fiduciary was the subject of a final judgment or court-approved settlement. (See Q 448.) *Herman v South Carolina National Bank*, 140 F.3d 1413 (11th Cir. 1998), *cert. denied*, 119 S.Ct. 1030 (1999).

The Secretary of Labor shall have the right, in his discretion, to intervene in any action, with the exception of suits brought under Title IV (Plan Termination Insurance). ERISA Sec. 502(h).

ERISA PREEMPTION

698. What is the scope of ERISA preemption?

ERISA Section 514(a) says that the provisions of ERISA "shall supersede any and all State laws insofar as they may now or hereafter relate to any employee benefit plan." The objective of this preemption clause is to provide a uniform remedy for the participants and beneficiaries of ERISA covered employee benefit plans.

An employee benefit plan is one that is established or maintained by an employer or employee organization. ERISA Secs. 3(1), 3(2). This does not include individual retirement accounts. Labor Reg. §2510.3-2(d).

ERISA Section 514(c)(1) defines a state law as all laws, decisions, rules, regulations or other state action having effect of law. Any attempt by a state to alter or limit the scope of preemption under ERISA Section 514(a), through legislation, regulatory action, or otherwise, would itself be preempted by ERISA. DOL Adv. Op. 93-04A. For these purposes, a "state" includes any political subdivisions, agencies or instrumentalities of the state. ERISA Sec. 514(c)(2).

The United States Supreme Court, as well as United States District Courts and state courts have held, in more than 300 cases, that state laws and actions have been preempted by ERISA's broad reach.

The United States Supreme Court has held that a state law relates to an employee benefit plan "if it has any connection with or reference to such a plan." *Shaw v. Delta Airlines*, 463 U.S. 85 (1983); *Ingersoll-Rand Co. v. McClendon*, 498 U.S. 133 (1990). In other words, if a claim under state law requires a review of, or reference to the plan, it would be subject to the preemption provisions of ERISA. This is particularly true where a state law has been specifically designed to have an effect upon employee benefit plans, or if the rights or restrictions it creates are based upon the existence of an employee benefit plan. *United Wire Welfare Fund v. Morristown Memorial Hospital*, 995 F.2d 1179 (3rd Cir. 1993). However, the Third Circuit has ruled that ERISA preemption only applies to claims that an HMO (under the provision of health benefits through an employee welfare benefit plan) failed to provide benefits under the plan through the authorization of medical treatment. It does not prevent a claim under state law regarding the quality of treatment received once it has been authorized by the HMO as a benefit under the employee welfare benefit plan. *In re: U.S. Healthcare, Inc.*, 193 F.3d 151 (3rd Cir. 1999). ERISA preempts state laws invalidating beneficiary designations pursuant to divorce. *Egelhoff v. Egelhoff*, 532 U.S. 141 (2001), *reversing*, 989 P.2d 80 (Wash. 1999).

ERISA preempts state laws only. It will not preempt other federal laws or regulations. Specifically, ERISA will not be interpreted in such a way as to alter, amend, modify, invalidate, impair or supersede federal laws and regulations. ERISA Sec. 514(d).

As an affirmative defense, ERISA preemption will be waived if not timely asserted.

699. What are the exceptions to the broad reach of ERISA preemption?

State laws that do not directly relate to an employee benefit plan will not be subject to the preemption provisions of ERISA. In addition to state laws that do not directly relate to an employee benefit plan, the following situations are not preempted by ERISA:

1.   Any state law that regulates insurance, banking or securities (ERISA Sec. 514(b)(3)(A));

2.   Any generally applicable criminal law of a state (ERISA Sec. 514(b)(3));

3.   The Hawaii Prepaid Health Care Act (ERISA Sec. 514(b)(5)(A));

4.   Certain multiple employer welfare arrangements (ERISA Sec. 514(b)(6)(A));

5.   Qualified domestic relations orders and qualified medical child support orders (ERISA Sec. 514(b)(7)); and

6.   Any state cause of action for the recoupment of Medicaid payments.

Further, there have been more than 200 federal and state court cases where the preemption provisions of ERISA have been ruled inapplicable to the state laws at issue. There have also been numerous cases denying ERISA preemption on the grounds that the state law at issue had only a "tenuous" relation to an ERISA covered plan. Some examples of these cases include the application of state tort laws, fraud laws, breach of contract laws, severance pay laws, prevailing wage laws, malpractice laws, escheat laws, and insurance laws. In addition, the United States Supreme Court has ruled that ERISA does not preempt state garnishment laws. *Mackey v. Lanier Collection Agency & Service, Inc.*, 486 U.S. 825 (1988); *Retirement Fund Tr. of the Plumbing, Heating & Piping Indus. of S. Cal. v. Franchise Tax Bd.*, 909 F.2d 1266 (9th Cir. 1990).

ERISA does not preempt state workers' compensation laws. ERISA Sec. 4(b)(3).

The United States Supreme Court has ruled that state laws that regulate insurance and are directed specifically towards the insurance industry are not preempted by ERISA. *Pilot Life Ins. Co. v. Dedeaux*, 481 U.S. 41 (1987). Citing the *Dedeaux* case, the Supreme Court has ruled that state level insurance "notice-prejudice" laws (which state that an insurer cannot avoid liability for an untimely claim unless the insurer can show that it suffered actual prejudice from the delay) are not preempted by ERISA. *Unum Life Inc. Co. of America v. Ward*, 135 F.3d 1276 (1999).

PENSION BENEFIT GUARANTY CORPORATION

700. What is Title IV of ERISA?

Title IV of ERISA established the plan termination insurance program that guarantees the benefits of participants and beneficiaries involved in certain defined benefit plans that, upon plan termination, do not have sufficient assets to cover the actuarially determined benefits that the plan is obligated to pay. In addition, Title IV established the rules applicable to defined benefit plan terminations.

ERISA Section 4002 established the Pension Benefit Guaranty Corporation ("PBGC") to administer the plan termination insurance program and to administer and enforce the defined benefit plan termination rules. As a self-financing federal government corporation, the PBGC protects the retirement incomes of approximately 42 million American workers (one out of every three working persons) in approximately 45,000 defined benefit plans. PBGC is financed through premiums collected from companies that sponsor insured pension plans, investment returns on PBGC assets, and recoveries from employers responsible for underfunded terminated plans. PBGC's Board of Directors consists of the Secretaries of Labor, Treasury, and Commerce with the Secretary of Labor serving as Chair. PBGC is aided by a seven-member Advisory Committee appointed by the President to represent the interests of labor, management and the general public. PBGC is headed by an Executive Director.

The PBGC's operations involve premium revenues of approximately $1.1 billion, assets of nearly $16 billion, benefit payments of more than $820 million, and benefit obligations to more than 465,000 workers and retirees in more than 2,500 pension plans.

The plan termination insurance program is a self-funded program in which covered defined benefit plans participating in the program fund it through premium payments based upon the number of plan participants.

701. What are the investigative powers and authority of the PBGC and which plans do they cover?

ERISA Section 4003(a) provides that the PBGC "may make such investigations as it deems necessary to enforce any provision of this title (Title IV, Termination Insurance Program) or any rule or regulation thereunder, and may require or permit any person to file with it a statement in writing, under oath or otherwise as the corporation shall determine, as to all the facts and circumstances concerning the matter to be investigated."

ERISA Section 4003(b) permits any member of PBGC's Board of Directors or any officer designated by the chairman to conduct investigations, subpoena witnesses, and require the production of books, papers, correspondence, memoranda and other records related to an investigation.

ERISA Section 4021(a) provides that the termination insurance program administered by the PBGC applies to any defined benefit plan, which, for a given plan year:

1.   Is an employee pension benefit plan established or maintained:

       a) by an employer engaged in commerce or in any industry or activity affecting commerce; or

       b) by any employee organization, or organization representing employees, engaged in commerce or in any industry or activity affecting commerce; or

       c) both (a) and (b); *and*

2.   Has been a qualified pension plan, or has been operated as a qualified pension plan for the five plan years prior to the year in which the plan terminates.

702. What ERISA covered plans are exempt from PBGC coverage?

ERISA Section 4021(b) exempts the following plans from PBGC coverage:

1.   All individual account (defined contribution) plans;

2.   All government plans, including those established pursuant to the Railroad Retirement Act;

3.   Any church plan (unless that plan has made an election under Internal Revenue Code Section 410(d), and has notified the PBGC that it wishes to be subject to PBGC coverage);

4.   Any plan maintained outside of the United States primarily for the benefit of nonresident aliens;

5.   Any plan that is unfunded and maintained by an employer prima-
        rily for the purpose of providing deferred compensation to a select
        group of management or highly compensated employees;

6.   Any plan that is established and maintained exclusively for sub-
        stantial owners (sole owner of a trade or business or a greater than
        10% owner of shares or a greater than 10% partner); and

7.   Any plan that is established and maintained by a professional
        service employer that at no time has more than 25 active partici-
        pants.

Further, there are certain nonqualified plans detailed under ERISA Section
4021(b) that are also excluded from the coverage of the PBGC.

703. What is the PBGC premium program?

The primary reason for the establishment of the Pension Benefit Guaranty
Corporation ("PBGC") is to provide an insurance program that guarantees the
provision of pension benefits (within certain limitations) to plan participants and
beneficiaries of terminated defined benefit plans. The PBGC program will
provide these benefits when a covered plan terminates with insufficient trust
assets to cover the actuarially determined vested benefits of participants and
beneficiaries.

ERISA Section 4006(a)(3)(A) establishes premium rates for PBGC covered single employer plans at $19 for each plan participant during the plan year.
Multiemployer plans are required to submit premium payments at an annual rate
of $2.60 per participant. PBGC Regs. §§4006.3(a)(1), 4006.3(a)(2). In the case
of underfunded plans, an additional premium is required, which is equal to $9 for
each $1,000 of a single-employer plan's unfunded vested benefits divided by the
number of participants for whom PBGC coverage premiums were being paid as
of the close of the prior plan year. PBGC Reg. §4006.3(b). Beginning with the
2001 plan year, plan administrators have the option of paying prorated premiums
for short plan years instead of paying the premium on a full year and requesting
a refund at a later date. PBGC Reg. §4006.5, as amended, 65 Fed. Reg. 75160
(2-01-2000).

Participants, for purposes of assessing premium charges, are defined as:

1.   Any individual who is currently in employment covered by the plan
        and who is earning or retaining credited service; this does not
        include individuals who are earning or retaining credited service if,
        on the "snapshot" date (see below), they have no accrued benefits
        (and the plan does not have any other benefit liabilities with respect
        to them).

2.   Any non-vested individual who is not currently in employment covered by the plan, but who is earning or retaining credited service under the plan (excluding any nonvested former employees who: have experienced a 1-year break in service; are deemed to be cashed out under the terms of the plan; or have died);

3.   Any individual who is retired or separated from employment covered by the plan and who is receiving benefits under the plan;

4.   Any individual who is retired or separated from service covered by the plan and who is entitled to begin receiving benefits under the plan in the future;

5.   Any deceased individual who has one or more beneficiaries who are receiving or entitled to receive benefits under the plan; and

6.   All other individuals identified as participants under the terms of the plan. PBGC Reg. §4006.2., as amended, 65 Fed. Reg. 75160 (12-1-2000).

The participant count is made as of the last day of the prior plan year, or for a new defined benefit plan, on the date that it becomes subject to PBGC jurisdiction.

ERISA Section 4007(b) imposes a penalty of up to 100% of the amount due as a late payment charge on unpaid premiums. The late payment penalty charge is based upon the number of months from the due date to the date when payment is made. For any premium payment year beginning after 1995, the penalty rate is 1% per month on any amount of unpaid premium paid on or before the date when the PBGC issues a written notice of the premium delinquency, and 5% per month on any amount of unpaid premium paid after that date. The penalty rate for pre-1996 premium payment years is 5% per month for all months on any amount of unpaid premium. PBGC Reg. §4007.8, as amended, 64 Fed. Reg. 66383 (11-26-99).

The PBGC has expanded its safe-harbor relief from late payment penalty charges effective for all PBGC determinations issued on or after December 27, 1999 with respect to premiums for plans years beginning before 1999, as well as PBGC determinations with respect to premiums for 1999 and later plan years. Under the safe harbor, a plan administrator must do two things to qualify and avoid late payment penalty charges:

1.   By February 28th of the premium payment year, the plan administrator must pay the lesser of: (1) 90% of the flat-rate premium due for the premium payment year; or (2) 100% of the flat-rate premium that would be due for the premium payment year, if that

amount were determined by multiplying the actual participant count for the prior year by the flat-rate premium for the premium payment year; and

2. By October 15th of the premium payment year, the plan administrator must pay any remaining portion of the flat rate premium for the premium payment year. PBGC Reg. §4007.8, as amended, 64 Fed. Reg. 66383 (11-26-99).

ERISA Section 4011 requires plans that are obligated to pay the variable premium as a result of insufficient funding to provide notice to plan participants and beneficiaries of the plan's funding status and the limit on the PBGC's coverage should the plan terminate while underfunded. If a plan administrator fails to provide a participant with notice of the plan's funding status within the specified time limit or omits material information from such notice, the PBGC may assess a penalty of up to $1,100 a day for each day that the failure continues. PBGC Reg. §4011.3(c). The plan administrator must issue the notice no later than two months after the deadline (including extensions) for the filing of the annual report for the previous plan year (i.e., seven months after the close of the plan year). Labor Reg. §2520.104a-5(a)(2).

Defined benefit plans that meet the requirements of Internal Revenue Code Section 412(i) (plans funded exclusively by the purchase of individual insurance contracts), are exempted from the variable rate premium requirements if the plan fits the description of an Internal Revenue Code Section 412(i) plan on a predetermined "snap-shot" date in the previous plan year (which in most cases, the PBGC advises, is the last day of the preceding plan year). PBGC Reg. §4006.5(a)(3), as amended, 65 Fed. Reg. 75160 (12-1-2000). This is a change from the prior requirement that the elements of Internal Revenue Code Section 412(i) be met on every day of the preceding plan year.

Beginning with the 2001 plan year, single employer plans that are exempt from the variable premium payment arrangements will be required to submit their final premium filing for the year on a simplified Premium Form 1-EZ instead of Form 1 and Schedule A. Nonexempt single employer plans are still required to file Form 1 and Schedule A. Multiemployer plans are required to file Form 1 only. PBGC Technical Update 00-6, December 20, 2000. New and existing Form 1 and schedules may be downloaded from the PBGC website at: http://www.pbgc.gov.

The PBGC has extended the premium filing deadline for most plans to nine and one-half months after the beginning of the premium payment year beginning in 1999 (October 15th for calendar year plans).

704. What are the reportable events that must be directed to the attention of the PBGC?

2002 ERISA Facts

Within 30 days after the plan administrator or the contributing sponsor knows or has reason to know that a reportable event has occurred, he will notify the PBGC. ERISA Sec. 4043(a). This 30-day notice is required if any of the following reportable events has occurred:

1.   The plan has been disqualified by the IRS, or the DOL has notified the plan that it is not in compliance with the regulatory provisions of ERISA (PBGC Reg. §4043.21);

2.   There has been a plan amendment that would result in a decrease in benefits to any participant payable from employer contributions (PBGC Reg. §4043.22);

3.   Active participation drops below 80% of those participating at the beginning of the plan year, or to fewer than 75% of those participating at the beginning of the previous plan year (PBGC Reg. §4043.23);

4.   A termination or partial termination has occurred, as defined under Internal Revenue Code Section 411(d)(3) (PBGC Reg. §4043.24);

5.   The plan has been unable to pay vested accrued benefits when they become due (PBGC Reg. §4043.26);

6.   The plan has failed to make the required minimum funding payment (PBGC Reg. §4043.25);

7.   Bankruptcy, liquidation, or dissolution of the plan sponsor, or any member of the plan's controlled group has occurred (PBGC Regs. §§4043.35, 4043.30)

8.   Any distribution has been made to a substantial owner of a contributing sponsor (PBGC Reg. §4043.27);

9.   Plans have been merged or consolidated, or assets or liabilities have been transferred (PBGC Reg. §4043.28);

10.   Any transaction has occurred that resulted in a change in the contributing sponsor or in persons discontinuing membership in the controlled group where the plan had less than $1,000,000 in unfunded benefits or no unfunded vested benefits (PBGC Reg. §4043.29);

11. Any declaration of an extraordinary dividend or stock redemption above stated levels has been made by any member of the plan's controlled group (PBGC Reg. §4043.31);

12. Any transfer has been made within a 12-month period (ending on the date of the transfer) of an aggregate of 3% or more of the plan's total benefit liabilities to any person or to a plan maintained by a person who is not a member of the contributing sponsor's controlled group (PBGC Reg. §4043.32);

13. Any application for a minimum funding waiver has been submitted (PBGC Reg. §4043.33);

14. Any default on a loan has occurred with an outstanding balance of $10,000,000 or more by a member of the plan's controlled group (PBGC Reg. §4043.34); or

15. Any other event detailed in the regulations has occurred that indicates a need to terminate the plan (PBGC Reg. §4043.35).

Any failure to make minimum quarterly contributions by small employers (generally, those with fewer than 100 plan participants, although, in some cases, as many as 500 participants) need not be reported to the PBGC if the employer makes the payments within 30 days of the due date. PBGC Technical Update 97-4.

ERISA Section 4010 requires the following information to be included in any 30-day notice submitted to the PBGC:

1. The name of the plan;

2. The name, address and telephone number of the plan sponsor;

3. The name, address and telephone number of the plan administrator;

4. The plan sponsor identification number (EIN), and the plan number (PN);

5. A brief statement of the facts relating to the reportable event;

6. A copy of the current plan document;

7. A copy of the plan's most recent actuarial statement and opinion; and

8. A statement of any material change in the assets or liabilities of the plan that has occurred after the date of the most recent actuarial statement and opinion relating to the plan.

The PBGC has established PBGC Form 10 and PBGC Form 10-Advance for use in filing a notice of a reportable event. PBGC Form 10 is to be used by plan sponsors or administrators of single employer defined benefit plans to notify the PBGC within 30 days of the occurrence of a reportable event (replacing Form 10-SP). PBGC Form-10 Advance is to be filed by single employer defined benefit plans when they are required to provide the PBGC an advance notice of any reportable event.

The PBGC has made available from their web site (www.pbgc.gov/repevents.htp) the following reportable event forms, which plan sponsors and administrators may fill out and e-mail to the PBGC: Form 10, Form 10-Advance and Form 200. PBGC News Release 98-20.

Any failure to file a required notice or to include any required information may be subject to a penalty of up to $1,100 per day. This is assessed separately against each individual who is required to provide the PBGC with any notice. ERISA Sec. 4071; PBGC Reg. §4043.3(e).

PBGC's Early Warning Program

The PBGC, in July, 2000, issued a model participant notice to plans covered by the termination insurance program that provides details on the PBGC "Early Warning Program." The program is designed to assist the PBGC in avoiding the institution of plan termination proceedings under ERISA Section 4042(a)(4) by identifying plan sponsors in need of protection before business decisions or business transactions significantly increase the risk of loss to the corporate sponsored retirement plan covered by the termination insurance program. The PBGC will screen plans covered by the termination insurance program by focusing on two types of companies:

1.   Financially troubled companies; and

2.   Companies with pension plans that are underfunded on a current liability basis.

Financially troubled companies will be identified by a below investment grade bond rating under the most recent ratings published by the major rating agencies (i.e., Moody's and A.M. Best).

Companies with pension plans that have current liability in excess of $25 million and that have an unfunded current liability in excess of $5 million will be identified through data reported to the PBGC on the most recent Form 5500, Schedule B. Such plans, once identified, will be targeted for PBGC intervention under the Early Warning Program.

Those plans identified under the Early Warning Program as being "at risk" will be contacted by the PBGC with a request for further information. This information will assist the PBGC in accurately assessing whether a transaction or financial situation poses a legitimate risk to the underlying pension plan. If, in the estimation of the PBGC, there is a substantial risk to the plan, the PBGC will negotiate with the plan sponsor to obtain protections for the pension insurance program in lieu of terminating the plan. PBGC Technical Update 00-3 (July 24, 2000). Details on the Early Warning Program, such as a review of those business transactions that are of concern to the PBGC, are available in the text of the model participant notice, which is available on the Internet at: http://www.pbgc.gov/legal_info/tech_updates/tech00-3.htm.

PLAN TERMINATIONS

705. What is a "standard termination"?

Under a standard termination, the defined benefit plan is voluntarily terminated by the plan sponsor after it has been determined that, as of the effective date of the termination, the plan has sufficient assets to satisfy the actuarially determined benefits it is obligated to pay to plan participants and beneficiaries.

A standard termination of a single employer defined benefit plan occurs when:

1.   The plan administrator provides the 60-day advance notice of intent to terminate (see Q 706) to affected parties;

2.   The plan administrator has completed and issued a notice to the PBGC that contains detailed information and a certification prepared by an enrolled actuary (see Q 707);

3.   A notice of benefit commitments to be paid is provided to participants and beneficiaries; and

4.   The PBGC has not issued a notice of noncompliance to the plan administrator advising the plan that the PBGC has determined that the plan does not have sufficient assets for benefit liabilities, and/or that the PBGC determines that there is reason to believe that the requirements of a standard termination have not been met. ERISA Sec. 4041(b).

ERISA Section 4001(a)(16) provides that benefit liabilities are "the benefits of their (the plan sponsor's) employees and their beneficiaries under the plan" (within the meaning of IRC Section 401(a)(2)).

PRACTITIONER'S POINTER

ERISA Section 4041(b)(3)(B) requires that, within 30 days *of the final distribution of plan assets*, the plan administrator must send notice to the PBGC that the assets of the plan have been distributed in accordance with the standard termination provisions of ERISA. If the actuary has determined that the plan's trust assets are insufficient to satisfy the plan's benefit obligations, the provisions of ERISA Section 4041(b)(3)(B) allow the plan sponsor to execute a standard termination by contributing the plan's shortfall amount prior to the date of final distribution of plan assets.

706. Who must receive notice when a plan sponsor intends to terminate a defined benefit plan, and what information must such individuals receive?

ERISA Section 4041(a)(2) requires that "not less than 60 days before the proposed termination date of a standard termination...the plan administrator shall provide each affected party a written notice of intent to terminate stating that such termination is intended and the proposed termination date." This is commonly referred to as the "60-Day Notice of Intent to Terminate," and it may not be provided more than 90 days before the proposed termination date, although the PBGC may consider the notice to be timely filed if it was early by a de minimis number of days and the PBGC finds that the early issuance was the result of an administrative error. If, after the proposed termination date, an individual becomes the beneficiary of a deceased participant or an alternate payee under a QDRO, the notice must also be provided to that individual. The notice must include a statement indicating how the participant or beneficiary can obtain a copy of the plan's summary plan description. PBGC Regs. §§4041.3(b)(1), 4041.21(a).

Affected parties are defined as:

1.　Each participant in the plan;

2.　Each beneficiary of a deceased participant;

3.　Each alternate payee under an applicable qualified domestic relations order;

4.　Each employee organization that currently represents any group of participants;

5.　The employee organization that last represented a group of currently unrepresented employees within the 5-year period preceding the issuance of the notice of intent to terminate; and

6.　The PBGC.

The plan administrator shall issue the 60-day notice of intent to terminate to the affected parties by hand delivery or first class mail or courier service to the last known address of the affected parties. PBGC Reg. §4041.21. The following information must be included in the 60-day notice:

1.   The name of the plan and the contributing sponsor;

2.   The employer identification number ("EIN") and the plan number ("PN");

3.   The name, address and telephone number of the person whom an affected party may contact with questions concerning the plan termination;

4.   A statement that the plan administrator expects to terminate the plan in a standard termination on a proposed termination date that is either a specific date set forth in the notice or a date that is to be determined upon the occurrence of some future event;

5.   The nature of the future event, if the termination date is dependent upon (1) when that event is expected to occur and (2) when the termination will occur in relation to the event;

6.   A statement that benefit and service accruals will continue until the termination date or, if applicable, that benefit accruals have been frozen as of a specific date in accordance with ERISA Section 204(h);

7.   A statement that, in order to terminate in a standard termination, plan assets must be sufficient to provide all benefit liabilities under the plan with respect to each participant and each beneficiary of a deceased participant;

8.   A statement that, after plan assets have been distributed to provide all benefit liabilities with respect to a participant or a beneficiary of a deceased participant, either by the purchase of an irrevocable commitment or commitments from an insurer to provide benefits, or by an alternative form of distribution provided for under the plan, the PBGC's guarantee with respect to that participant's or beneficiary's benefit ends;

9.   If distribution of benefits under the plan may be wholly or partially satisfied by the purchase of irrevocable commitments from an insurer:

        a) the name and address of the insurer(s) from whom the plan administrator intends to purchase the irrevocable commitments; or

        b) if the plan administrator has not identified an insurer or insurers at the time the notice of intent to terminate is issued, a statement that: (i) irrevocable commitments may be purchased from an insurer to provide some or all of the benefits under the plan; (ii) the insurer(s) have not yet been identified; and (iii) affected parties will be notified at a later date (no later than 45 days prior to the distribution date) of the name and address of the insurer(s) from whom the plan administrator intends to purchase the irrevocable commitments;

10.   A statement that if the termination does not occur, the plan administrator will notify the affected parties in writing of that fact;

11.   A statement that each affected party, other than the PBGC or any employee organization, will receive a written notification of the benefits that the person will receive; and

12.   For retirees only, a statement that their monthly (or other periodic) benefit amounts will not be affected by the plan's termination. PBGC Reg. §4041.21(d).

Any non-vested or partially vested participant who has been cashed out under the provisions of Internal Revenue Code Section 411(a)(7) and Treasury Regulation §1.411(a)-7(d) is not a participant who must receive a notice of plan benefits. This includes any 0% vested participant who is "deemed" to have been cashed out under the terms of the plan.

707. What other notice requirements are required in a defined benefit plan termination?

The plan administrator must provide a notice to each affected person (as of the proposed termination date) that details the amount of the individual's plan benefits as of the proposed termination date. The notice must include:

1.   The age of the participant or beneficiary;

2.   The length of service to be credited at termination;

3.   Actuarial assumptions used in calculating benefits (including the applicable interest rate);

4.   The wages at the time of termination; and

5.   Any other information that the PBGC may require.

This notice must be provided no later than the date on which the 60-day notice of intent to terminate has been provided to the PBGC. ERISA Sec. 4041(b)(2)(A); PBGC Reg. §4041.22.

In addition, ERISA Section 4041(b)(2)(A) requires the plan administrator to file PBGC Form 500, "Standard Termination Notice Single-Employer Plan Termination," no later than 180 days after the proposed date of termination. Form 500 must be filed with the PBGC. In addition, an enrolled actuary must certify: (1) the projected amount of assets of the plan; (2) the actuarial present value of the benefit liabilities; and (3) that the plan is projected to be sufficient (as of the proposed date of final distribution) for such benefit liabilities. The enrolled actuary must submit this information on Schedule EA-S, "Standard Termination Certification of Sufficiency," which is attached to Form 500. The Notice is considered filed with the PBGC as of the date of the mailing, provided that there is evidence of a postmark. If the notice is made through a private delivery service, the date of filing is generally the date of deposit with the delivery service so long as the PBCG receives it within two business days. If the filing is done electronically, the date of filing is generally the date of the electronic transmission to the PBGC. Any information deemed received on a weekend, federal holiday or after 5:00 p.m. on a business day, is considered filed on the next regular business day. PBGC Reg. §4041.24.

708. What is a distress termination?

A distress termination occurs when a defined benefit plan does not have sufficient assets to satisfy the benefit obligations owed to participants and beneficiaries. To voluntarily terminate a defined benefit plan under a distress termination, one of the following conditions must be satisfied:

1.   The plan sponsor is in liquidation or bankruptcy proceedings due to insolvency;

2.   The plan sponsor is undergoing reorganization in bankruptcy or insolvency proceedings;

3.   Termination of the defined benefit plan is required in order to allow the plan sponsor to service the payment of debts while staying in business; or

4.   Termination of the defined benefit plan is required in order to allow the plan sponsor to avoid unreasonably burdensome pension costs caused by a declining workforce. ERISA Sec. 4041(c)(2)(B).

Under a distress termination of a single employer plan, the plan administrator must provide a 60-day notice of intent to terminate to all affected parties, which includes the proposed termination date. ERISA Sec. 4041(a)(2). In addition, the plan administrator must provide to the PBGC the following information from a certified enrolled actuary:

1.   The amount of the current value of plan assets;

2. The actuarial present value of the benefit liabilities under the plan; and

3. The actuarial present value of benefits under the plan that are guaranteed by the PBGC. ERISA Sec. 4041(c)(2)(A)(ii).

When the determination has been made that plan assets are not sufficient to satisfy benefit obligations, the PBGC must be provided with:

1. The name and address of each participant and beneficiary under the plan;

2. Any additional information required by the PBGC in order for them to make guaranteed payments to participants and beneficiaries; and

3. Certification by the plan administrator that the information on which the enrolled actuary based his certifications is accurate and complete, and all other information provided to the PBGC is accurate and complete. ERISA Secs. 4041(c)(2)(A)(iii), 4041(c)(2)(A)(iv).

709. What must a plan sponsor do if the plan does not satisfy the requirements of a distress termination?

If a plan does not satisfy the statutory requirements for a distress termination and there are insufficient assets to satisfy the plan's benefit obligations, the plan sponsor cannot terminate the plan. In order to terminate an underfunded plan, the plan sponsor must provide sufficient assets that would enable the plan to go forward with a standard termination. Otherwise, the plan sponsor must continue the plan. PBGC Regs. §§4041.41, 4041.47.

If the plan sponsor must continue the operation of the plan, the plan may be amended to freeze benefit accruals for current participants and to prohibit the addition of new participants. A frozen plan must continue to be maintained in accordance with current law, including any statutorily required amendments.

710. What benefits are guaranteed by the PBGC?

With certain limitations, the PBGC guarantees the payment of all nonforfeitable benefits under a terminated single employer plan. The limitations restrict the amount of benefits that have been increased through a plan amendment within five years of the termination date. ERISA Secs. 4022(a), 4022(b).

The guaranteed benefits payable by the PBGC are defined as the amount, as of the date of termination, of a benefit provided under a plan, to the extent that:

1.   The benefit is a nonforfeitable benefit;

2.   The benefit qualifies as a pension benefit; and

3.   The participant is entitled to the benefit. PBGC Reg. §4022.3.

Qualified pre-retirement survivor annuities "with respect to a participant under a terminated single-employer plan shall not be treated as forfeitable solely because the participant has not died as of the termination date." ERISA Sec. 4022(e).

Under ERISA Section 4022(b)(3), the amount of monthly benefits guaranteed by the PBGC shall not have an actuarial value that exceeds the actuarial value of a monthly benefit in the form of a life annuity commencing at age 65. This amount will be adjusted on an annual basis to reflect the cost of living. PBGC Reg. §4022.23.

The PBGC has issued a regulation that increases the maximum value of benefits payable by the PBGC as a lump-sum distribution from $3,500 to $5,000. This rule has been drafted to reflect the recent amendment of ERISA Section 203(e), which specifies the maximum amount that a plan may pay in a single installment without the participant's consent, and which has been raised from $3,500 to $5,000. PBGC Reg. §4022.7(b)(1)(i).

If the guaranteed benefit is payable at an age earlier than age 65, the maximum guaranteed benefit will be actuarially reduced based upon the earlier commencement of benefits. PBGC Reg. §4022.23.

The PBGC will recoup an overpayment in a PBGC trusteed plan if, at any time:

1.   PBGC determines that net benefits paid with respect to any participant in a PBGC trusteed plan exceeded the total amount to which the participant (and any beneficiary) was entitled up to that time, and

2.   The participant (or beneficiary) is, as of the termination date entitled to receive future benefit payments (PBGC Reg. §4022.81(a)).

For a participant who dies after the termination date, the PBGC will generally not seek recoupment of overpayments from the participant's estate (Preamble to PBGC Reg. §4022).

The PBGC will issue a news release on an annual basis that provides the cost-of-living adjustment.

PBGC currently pays monthly retirement benefits to approximately 465,000 retirees in 2,665 terminated plans. Another 260,000 people will be paid when they reach retirement age. The amount of the monthly benefit guaranteed by PBGC is determined by provisions of ERISA. For single-employer plans terminated in 2001, the maximum guarantee is $40,704.60 yearly ($3,392.05 monthly) for a single-life annuity beginning at age 65. If the benefit starts before age 65, or if there are survivor benefits, the maximum guarantee is less. In some instances, a retiree may receive more than the maximum, such as when the plan has sufficient assets to pay non-guaranteed benefits or when portions of funds are recovered from companies on behalf of trusteed plans.

The PBGC provides insurance for more than 1,800 defined benefit multiemployer plans. These multiemployer plans provide retirement benefits to more than nine million workers and retirees. Under the multiemployer plan program, the PBGC provides financial assistance to plans that become insolvent. A multiemployer plan is considered insolvent if the plan is unable to pay benefits at least equal to the PBGC guaranteed limits when due.

The Consolidated Appropriations Act, 2001, signed into law December 21, 2000, more than doubled the monthly PBGC multiemployer guarantee under Title IV of ERISA. For multiemployer plans, the monthly PBGC guarantee for plans that have not received PBGC financial assistance within a 1-year period ending on December 21, 2000 is 100% of the first $11 of the monthly benefit accrual rate and 75% of the next $33 for each year of service. For example, a worker with 30 years of service and a benefit accrual rate of $23 per month, the maximum guarantee will be $600 per month, or $7,200 per year. PBGC Technical Update 00-7 (Dec. 26, 2000). Prior to the amendment, the monthly guarantee equaled a participant's years of service multiplied by 100% of the first $5 of the monthly benefit accrual rate and 75% of the next $15. The prior limit had been in effect since 1980.

711. Will the PBGC guarantee benefits in a plan that the IRS has disqualified?

ERISA Section 4022(b)(6) states that "no benefits accrued under a plan after the date on which the Secretary of the Treasury (the IRS) issues notice that he has determined that any trust which is a part of a plan does not meet the requirements of IRC Section 401(a), or that the plan does not meet the requirements of IRC Section 404(a)(2), are guaranteed under this section unless such determination is erroneous."

Benefits accrued under a plan after the date on which the IRS has disqualified a plan, or after the date of the adoption of an amendment that causes the plan to be disqualified will not be guaranteed by the PBGC. PBGC Reg. §4022.27.

712. How will a plan amendment affect the PBGC guarantee upon a plan's termination?

ERISA Section 4022(b)(7) provides for a 5-year phase-in of benefits that have been increased through a plan amendment within five years of a defined benefit plan's termination. The formula applied to the phase-in rule is spelled out as follows:

Benefits will be guaranteed to the extent of the greater of:

1.   20% of the amount guaranteed; or

2. $20 per month;

multiplied by the number of years (not to exceed five) during which the plan amendment has been in effect.

Benefit increases are defined as "any benefit arising from the adoption of a new plan or an increase in the value of benefits payable arising from an amendment to an existing plan. Such increases include, but are not limited to, a scheduled increase in benefits under a plan or plan amendment, such as a cost of living increase, and any change in plan provisions that advances a participant's or beneficiary's entitlement to a benefit, such as liberalized participation requirements or vesting schedules, reductions in the normal or early retirement age under a plan, and changes in the form of benefit payments." PBGC Reg. §4022.2.

The definition of years under the phase-in period is each complete 12-month period prior to the plan's termination date. PBGC Reg. §4022.25(c).

Any amendments that benefit a substantial owner will be subject to a 30-year phase-in rule. ERISA Sec. 4022(b)(5)(B); PBGC Reg. §4022.25. A substantial owner is defined as: (1) any individual who owns the entire interest in an unincorporated trade or business; (2) in the case of a partnership, a partner who owns, directly or indirectly, more than 10% of either the capital interest or the profits interest in such partnership; or (3) in the case of a corporation, owns, directly or indirectly, more than 10% of either the voting stock or all stock of that corporation. ERISA Sec. 4022(b)(5)(A).

713. Who are "affected parties" in a defined benefit plan termination?

Affected parties are those individuals who must receive the various notices that must be provided in the defined benefit plan termination process. An affected party is defined as:

1.   Each participant in the plan;

2.   Each beneficiary under the plan who is the beneficiary of a deceased participant;

3.   Each beneficiary who is an alternate payee under a qualified domestic relations order;

4.   Each employee organization currently representing participants in the plan;

5.   The Pension Benefits Guaranty Corporation;

6.   The employee organization that last represented such a group of participants within the 5-year period preceding the issuance of the Notice of Intent to Terminate; and

7.   Any individual identified in writing to receive notice on behalf of an affected party. ERISA Sec. 4001(a)(21); PBGC Reg. §4001.2.

714. What is the importance of a defined benefit plan's termination date?

The termination date of a plan is to be determined by the plan sponsor or by the PBGC, depending upon which of the two is terminating the plan. ERISA Sec. 4048; H.R. Conf. Rep. No. 93-1280, 93rd Cong. 2nd Sess., 323 (1974)(ERISA Conference Report). The importance of the plan's termination date is that it is upon that date that certain determinations are made. Such determinations include:

1.   Which rights accrue to which participants;

2.   When the plan sponsor's funding obligation ends (*Audio Fidelity Corp. v. PBGC*, 624 F.2d 513 (4th Cir. 1980));

3.   The PBGC's obligation for guaranteed benefits; and

4.   The plan sponsor's liability for underfunding.

In situations where the plan sponsor has initiated termination proceedings, the notice of intent to terminate must be provided to affected parties at least 60 days before the intended termination date. ERISA Sec. 4041(a)(2).

715. When will the PBGC initiate a plan termination?

The PBGC may institute proceedings under ERISA Section 4042(a) to terminate a defined benefit plan whenever it has determined that:

1.   The plan has not satisfied the minimum funding standards;

2.   The plan will be unable to pay benefits when due;

3.   A distribution of more than $10,000 was made to a substantial owner in any 24-month period for reasons other than death and, subsequent to such distribution, there remain unfunded vested liabilities; or

4.   The possible long-run loss of the corporation with respect to the plan may reasonably be expected to unreasonably increase if the plan is not terminated.

The PBGC will institute termination proceedings in federal court "as soon as practicable" to terminate a single employer plan whenever the PBGC determines that the plan does not have sufficient assets available to pay benefits that are currently due under the terms of the plan. ERISA Sec. 4002(a).

The PBGC may reinstitute a plan against which it has begun termination proceedings and return the plan to its pre-termination status if the PBGC determines that circumstances have changed. *PBGC v. LTV Corp.*, 496 U.S. 633 (1990). The *LTV* case prompted the establishment of ERISA Section 4047, which expressly grants the authority of restoration to the PBGC. In the *LTV* case, the plan sponsor terminated three underfunded defined benefit plans, covered by the PBGC. After termination proceedings were instituted by the PBGC, the plan sponsor established new defined benefit plans that were to provide the benefits lost as a result of the PBGC's termination of the initial three plans. In effect, the plan sponsor was attempting to provide the entire amount of guaranteed benefits under the first three plans by shifting the burden for the minimum PBGC guaranteed benefits onto the PBGC and picking up the difference through the subsequent plans. The PBGC protested and attempted to reinstitute the initial three plans to their pre-termination status, thereby leaving the full funding obligation to the plan sponsor. The plan sponsor protested, but the United States Supreme Court sided with the PBGC.

716. What is involved in the final distribution of assets in a defined benefit plan standard termination?

In a standard termination, the PBGC has 60 days within which to issue a notice of non-compliance. The final distribution of assets in a defined benefit plan termination must occur no later than 180 days after the expiration of this 60-day period (assuming the plan has not received a notice of non-compliance). ERISA Sec. 4041(b)(2)(D). The PBGC and the plan sponsor may jointly extend the 60-day noncompliance notice period by a jointly executed written agreement. ERISA Sec. 4041(b)(2)(C). Such an extension may be necessary in order for the plan to establish, to the satisfaction of the PBGC, that the plan has sufficient assets to meet benefit obligations and has followed the procedural requirements of a standard termination.

The plan is entitled to an automatic extension of the 180-day distribution period if the plan sponsor:

1. Submits a complete request for a determination letter to the IRS with respect to the plan termination on or before the date when the plan files the standard termination notice (on PBGC Form 500) with the PBGC;

2. Does not receive a determination letter at least 60 days before the expiration of the 180-day period; and

3. On or before the expiration of the 180-day period, notifies the PBGC in writing that an extension of the distribution deadline is required and certifies that the conditions in (1) and (2) have been met. PBGC Reg. §4041.27(e).

The PBGC may grant a discretionary extension of the 180-day period if the plan administrator is unable to complete the distribution of plan assets within that time frame. The PBGC will grant a discretionary extension if it is satisfied that the delay in issuing the final distribution of plan assets is not due to the inaction or action of the plan administrator or the plan sponsor, and that the final distribution can be completed by the date requested. PBGC Reg. §4041.27(f).

ERISA Section 4041(b)(3) provides that in the final distribution of assets through a standard termination, the plan administrator will:

1. Purchase irrevocable commitments from an issuer to provide all benefit liabilities under the plan; or

2. In accordance with the plan provisions and applicable PBGC regulations, otherwise fully provide all benefit liabilities under the plan, including the transfer of assets for missing participants to the PBGC (see Q 718).

Within 30 days after the final distribution of all assets, the plan administrator shall send notice to the PBGC certifying that the assets of the plan have been distributed in accordance with the provisions of ERISA Section 4041(b)(3)(A). This notice will be provided on PBGC Form 501 "Post Distribution Certification for Standard Termination."

The PBGC may assess a penalty, payable to the PBGC, for a failure to timely file any required notice or other required material information. ERISA Sec. 4071. The amount of this penalty is not to exceed $1,100 for each day for which such failure continues. This has been reduced regarding Form 501 to $25 per day for the first 90 days of delinquency, and $50 per day for each day beyond that. The PBGC may reduce or eliminate the penalty if the plan sponsor demonstrates reasonable cause for the delay. PBGC Statement of Policy, 60 Fed. Reg. 36837 (7-18-95).

PRACTITIONER'S POINTER

In issuing the most recent regulations regarding standard termination procedures, the PBGC advises that they intend to conduct post-distribution audits to determine whether these calculations are being made properly. The PBGC says that it is common for them to find errors in their post-distribution audits. The revised forms and packages issued to conform with these new regulations include detailed guidance on calculating lump-sum distributions. They are available on the PBGC's homepage at: http://www.pbgc.gov.

717. Does the Pension Benefits Guaranty Corporation (PBGC) retain any responsibility for the provision of benefits after the purchase of annuities by a terminating pension plan?

No, PBGC Opinion Letter 91-1 provides that the purchase of an irrevocable annuity contract for the provision of benefits to participants and beneficiaries in connection with the termination of a pension plan ends the PBGC's obligation to guarantee any of the plan's obligations. Therefore, if the insurance company is unable to provide all of the benefits guaranteed under the annuity contract, the PBGC will not assume the obligation to make up the difference. Furthermore, the PBGC has indicated, in Opinion Letter 91-4, that the plan sponsor is not required to make up such difference if it acted in accordance with the provisions of the plan and in accordance with applicable regulations. They further advise that the plan sponsor has an obligation under the fiduciary provisions of Title I of ERISA to act prudently in the selection of the annuity provider.

718. How are the assets of missing participants handled when a defined benefit plan terminates?

In the termination of a defined benefit plan, the plan sponsor is required to complete a "diligent search" to locate all missing participants. ERISA Sec. 4050(b)(1). A *diligent search* is one that:

1. Begins not more than six months before notices of intent to terminate are issued and is carried on in such a manner that, if the individual is found, distribution to the individual can reasonably be expected to be made on or before the deemed distribution date (or, in the case of a recently missing participant, on or before the 90th day after the deemed distribution date);

2. Includes an inquiry of plan beneficiaries of the missing participant; and

3. Includes the use of a commercial locator service (without charge to the missing participant, or a reduction of their benefit). PBGC Reg. §4050.4.

If a diligent search yields no result, the plan administrator may request the assistance of the IRS in attempting to locate the missing participants. The IRS will forward a letter to the missing participant's last known address on file with the IRS. The IRS will not levy a charge against the plan if there are fewer than 50 participants in the request for them to forward letters. Rev. Proc. 94-22, 1994-1 CB 608.

Under the PBGC's "Missing Participants Program," for standard terminations, if all attempts to locate a missing participant have failed, the sponsor of the terminating plan is to provide the missing participant's benefits through the purchase of an irrevocable commitment from an insurance company (annuity), or provide a payment of the benefits to the PBGC along with "such information and certifications" as the PBGC specifies. ERISA Sec. 4050(a). The amount of the designated benefit forwarded to the PBGC shall be determined under the detailed rules of the regulations. PBGC Reg. §4050.5.

The sponsor of a terminating plan with one or more missing participants is required to file Schedule MP with the Post-Distribution Certification and pay over to the PBGC the value of benefits payable to all missing participants for whom the plan did not purchase irrevocable commitments from an insurance company.

Schedule MP includes the information necessary for the PBGC to attempt to identify and locate missing participants and to compute and pay their benefits. The PBGC will attempt to locate any participant whose benefits have been transferred to the PBGC or for whom the terminating defined benefit plan has purchased an irrevocable annuity.

Schedule MP must be filed at the same time as the Post-Distribution Certification. PBGC Reg. §4050.6(a). Relief from this deadline is permitted for "late discovered" or "recently missing participants."

If the PBGC locates the missing participant, the PBGC will inform the participant of the identity of the insurer and the relevant annuity policy number, or the PBGC will pay the benefits in accordance with the actuarial assumptions established by the PBGC at the time when the benefits were transferred from the terminating plan and in accordance with the methods of payment established in the terminated plan.

An additional $300 must be paid "as an adjustment for expenses, for each missing participant whose designated benefit without such adjustment would be greater than $5,000." PBGC Reg. §4050.2.

719. What help is available from the PBGC for former participants attempting to locate vested benefits in plans of former employers?

The PBGC has issued an on-line pamphlet entitled "Finding a Lost Pension" that is designed to assist individuals in tracking down information on pension plans of former employers that might still hold vested benefits on their behalf. The booklet is available for viewing on the Internet at http://www.pbgc.gov/lostpendl.htm.

720. Who has authority to enforce certain plan terminations in a civil action?

ERISA Section 4070(a) provides that "any person who is with respect to a single employer plan a fiduciary, contributing sponsor, member of a contributing sponsor's controlled group, participant, or beneficiary, and is adversely affected by an act or practice of any party" (other than the PBGC) in violation of certain provisions of ERISA, may bring an action: (1) to enjoin such act or practice; or (2) to obtain other appropriate equitable relief to redress such violation or to enforce such provision. In order to bring such an action, the violation must be a violation of: (1) the voluntary termination provisions of ERISA Section 4041; (2) the reporting provisions of ERISA Section 4042; (3) the distress termination provisions of ERISA Section 4062; (4) the controlled group withdrawal liability provisions of ERISA Section 4063 and ERISA Section 4064; or (5) the restriction of transactions to evade liability provisions under ERISA Section 4069.

ERISA Section 4070 does not, however, authorize a civil action against the Secretary of the Treasury (the IRS), the Secretary of Labor, or the PBGC. ERISA Sec. 4301(a). For civil actions against the PBGC, see Q 723.

A single employer plan may be sued as an entity under ERISA Section 4070. Service of summons, subpoena, or other legal process of a court upon a trustee or an administrator of a single employer plan, in his capacity as trustee or administrator, constitutes service upon the plan. If a plan has not designated an agent for the service of process within its summary plan description, service may be made upon any contributing sponsor. ERISA Sec. 4070(b).

Any money judgment in an ERISA Section 4070 action against a single employer plan shall be enforceable only against the plan as an entity and not against any other person, unless liability against such person is established in that individual's capacity. ERISA Sec. 4070(b).

A copy of the complaint or notice of appeal in any action under ERISA Section 4070 shall be served upon the PBGC by certified mail. The PBGC has the right to exercise its discretion to intervene in any action filed under ERISA Section 4070. ERISA Sec. 4070(d).

CIVIL ACTIONS UNDER ERISA

721. What is the appropriate jurisdiction and venue to bring a civil action under ERISA Section 4070?

Federal district courts have exclusive jurisdiction of civil actions under ERISA Section 4070. Such actions may be brought in the district court located where the plan is administered, where the violation took place, or where the defendant resides or may be found. Service of process for such civil actions may be served in any district where a defendant resides or may be found. Such jurisdiction resides in the federal district courts without regard to the amount in controversy or the citizenship of the parties. ERISA Sec. 4070(c).

The federal district court hearing any civil action brought under ERISA Section 4070 may, in its discretion, award all or a portion of the costs and expenses incurred in connection with such action, including reasonable attorney's fees, to any party who prevails or substantially prevails in such action. There is an exemption that prohibits plans from being required to pay any costs and expenses in any action. ERISA Sec. 4070(e).

722. What is the statute of limitations for any civil action brought under ERISA Section 4070?

Any civil action under ERISA Section 4070 must be brought within six years after the date on which the cause of action arose, or three years after the earliest date on which the plaintiff acquired, or should have acquired, actual knowledge of the existence of such cause of action. ERISA Sec. 4070(f)(1).

In the case of a fiduciary plaintiff who brings the action in the exercise of his fiduciary duties, the statute of limitations for bringing an action is the date on which the plaintiff became a fiduciary with respect to the plan if such date is later than six years after the date on which the cause of action arose, or three years after the earliest date on which the plaintiff acquired, or should have acquired, actual knowledge of the existence of such cause of action. ERISA Sec. 4070(f)(2).

In the case of fraud or concealment, the statute of limitations is six years, instead of three years. ERISA Sec. 4070(f)(3).

723. Who may bring a civil action against the PBGC?

ERISA Section 4003(f)(1) states that, except with respect to withdrawal liability disputes with multiemployer plans, "any person who is a fiduciary, employer, contributing sponsor, member of a contributing sponsor's controlled group, participant or beneficiary, and is adversely affected by any action of the corporation [PBGC] with respect to a plan in which such person has an interest, or who is an employee organization representing such a participant or beneficiary so adversely affected for purposes of collective bargaining with respect to such plan, may bring a civil action against the corporation for appropriate equitable relief in the appropriate form."

The court may award all or a portion of the costs and expenses incurred in connection with a civil action brought against the PBGC to any party who prevails or substantially prevails in such action. ERISA Sec. 4003(f)(3).

724. What is the appropriate jurisdiction and venue in which to bring a civil action against the PBGC?

The provisions of ERISA Section 4003(f)(1) are the exclusive means for bringing civil actions against the PBGC under the plan termination provisions of ERISA, including actions against the PBGC in its capacity as a trustee. ERISA Sec. 4003(f)(4).

The district courts of the United States have exclusive jurisdiction over civil actions brought against the PBGC, without regard to the amount in controversy. ERISA Sec. 4003(f)(6).

The appropriate court for bringing such actions is the federal district court before which the termination proceedings are being conducted. If no such termination proceedings are being conducted, the appropriate court is the federal district court for the judicial district in which the plan has its principal office, or the federal district court for the District of Columbia. ERISA Secs. 4003(f)(2)(A), 4003(f)(2)(B), 4003(f)(2)(C).

In any suit, action or proceeding in which the PBGC is a party or intervenes in any state action, the PBGC may, without bond or security, remove such suit, action or proceeding from the state court to the federal court for the district or division in which such suit, action, or proceeding is pending. ERISA Sec. 4003(f)(7).

725. What is the statute of limitations on civil actions brought against the PBGC?

Civil actions may not be brought against the PBGC after the later of:

1. Six years after the date on which the cause of action arose; or

2. Three years after the date on which the plaintiff acquired, or should have acquired, actual knowledge of the existence of his cause of action. ERISA Secs. 4003(f)(5)(A), 4003(f)(1)(B).

In the case of a fiduciary plaintiff who brings the action in the exercise of his fiduciary duties, the 3-year statute of limitations begins to run on the date on which the plaintiff became a fiduciary with respect to the plan, if such date is later than the date on which the plaintiff acquired, or should have acquired, actual knowledge of the existence of such cause of action. ERISA Sec. 4003(f)(5)(B)(ii).

In the case of fraud or concealment, the period for the statute of limitations is extended from three years to six years. ERISA Sec. 4003(f)(6).

726. When may the PBGC bring a civil action?

The PBGC may sue in a federal district court to enforce the termination insurance provisions of ERISA or to seek appropriate equitable or legal relief. ERISA Sec. 4003(e)(1).

The PBGC may intervene in an action brought for a declaratory judgment that has been instituted by an employee, employer or plan administrator (in accordance with IRC Section 7476). The PBGC is also permitted to file a petition for declaratory judgment to appeal an IRS ruling relating to plan qualification, plan amendments and terminations. ERISA Sec. 3001(c); IRC Sec. 7476.

727. What is the appropriate jurisdiction and venue in which the PBGC may bring civil actions?

The district courts of the United States have exclusive jurisdiction over civil actions brought under the multiemployer plan provisions; however, state courts of competent jurisdiction have concurrent jurisdiction over an action brought by a plan fiduciary to collect a withdrawal liability. ERISA Sec. 4301(c).

ERISA Section 4301(d) establishes jurisdiction in the district court where the plan is administered or where a defendant resides or does business in any civil action under the multiemployer plan provisions. Service of process may be made in any district where a defendant resides, conducts business, or may be found.

The PBGC may remove any state suit, action or proceeding under the multiemployer plan provisions in which it is a party, or has intervened, to a federal district court. ERISA Sec. 4003(f)(7).

A copy of the complaint in any civil action under the multiemployer plan provisions must be served upon the PBGC by certified mail. The PBGC may intervene in any such action. ERISA Sec. 4301(g).

728. What is the statute of limitations for civil actions brought by the PBGC?

The PBGC is held to similar statutes of limitations for civil actions to enforce the termination provisions of ERISA and for other civil actions brought by the PBGC. ERISA Section 4003(e)(6)(A) provides that a civil action brought by the PBGC may not be brought later than:

1.   Six years after the date on which the cause of action arose; or

2.   Three years after the earliest date on which the PBGC acquired, or should have acquired, actual knowledge of the existence of the cause of action.

If the PBGC brings the action as trustee, the applicable statute of limitations begins to run on the date on which the PBGC became a trustee, if this date is later than the date on which the PBGC acquired, or should have acquired, actual knowledge of the existence of the cause of action. ERISA Sec. 4003(e)(6)(B).

In the case of fraud or concealment, the statute of limitations on civil actions brought by the PBGC is extended to six years after the earliest date on which the PBGC acquired, or should have acquired, actual knowledge of the existence of the cause of action. ERISA Sec. 4003(e)(6)(C).

729. Does the PBGC encourage alternative dispute resolution?

In 1999, the PBGC announced the institution of its policy to use alternative dispute resolution for resolving appropriate disputes in a timely and cost-efficient manner. In announcing the new policy, the PBGC stated that "in appropriate circumstances, there may be more effective methods to resolve issues that would otherwise be resolved through adversarial administrative or judicial processes. Although there is never an entitlement to alternative dispute resolution, the voluntary use of alternative dispute resolution, such as mediation, fact-finding, neutral evaluation, and arbitration, often can provide faster, less expensive, and more effective resolution of disputes that arise with employees, contractors, the regulated community and others with whom the agency does business." 64 Fed. Reg. 17696 (4-12-99).

For further information on the PBGC policy regarding alternative dispute resolution, contact:

> PBGC Office of the General Counsel
> Pension Benefit Guaranty Corporation
> 1200 K Street, NW
> Washington, DC 20005-4026

CHAPTER XIII

CRIMINAL ENFORCEMENT

730. What is the Department of Labor's criminal enforcement program?

The Department of Labor (DOL), through the Pension and Welfare Benefits Administration (PWBA), has statutory authority to conduct investigations. ERISA Sec. 504. ERISA Section 506(b) expressly confers upon the Secretary of Labor shared responsibility and authority to detect, investigate and refer, where appropriate, criminal violations of ERISA as well as other related federal laws, including Title 18 of the United States Code.

On February 5, 1975, the DOL and the Department of Justice (DOJ) executed a Memorandum of Understanding which provided for a specific case by case delegation from the DOJ regarding criminal investigations of criminal matters relating to employee benefit plans. In addition, the Comprehensive Crime Control Act of 1984 (P.L. 98-473) amended ERISA by expressly conferring upon the Secretary of Labor direct responsibility and authority to detect, investigate and refer, where appropriate, criminal violations of ERISA as well as other related federal laws, including Title 18 of the United States Code. This amendment is contained in ERISA Section 506.

With the passage of the Comprehensive Crime Control Act, the DOL's statutory authority to investigate criminal matters relating to employee benefit plans is now expressly stated. Accordingly, the DOL is no longer required to obtain delegation on a case-by-case basis; however, PWBA investigators and auditors contact the appropriate United State's Attorney's Office (USAO) after evidence is developed in an investigation that may warrant consideration and interest by the USAO to initiate criminal proceedings under either ERISA or Title 18 of the U.S. Code. The USAO is contacted at the earliest possible stage of the investigation for coordination purposes to determine whether the DOJ is interested in pursuing the matter, and thus avoid the expenditure of DOL resources on a matter that may not be of interest to the DOJ. When interest in pursuing the investigation is expressed by the DOJ, the PWBA continues with the investigation. If the USAO declines pursuing the case, the PWBA may either close the investigation, refer it to another agency, or pursue the case with a local or state enforcement agency for prosecution under state criminal laws.

A critical part of PWBA's enforcement program under its Strategic Enforcement Program is the prosecution of criminal acts relating to employee benefit plans. The criminal enforcement aspects of PWBA's enforcement strategy are integral to PWBA's broader goal of protecting employee benefit plan assets by detecting abuses and deterring future violations. PWBA's policy is to seek the appropriate enforcement remedy under the facts and circumstances as they develop in each investigation. In certain instances, potential improper conduct will be investigated pursuant to a civil investigation and if appropriate, the case will then be referred to the USAO for criminal prosecution. In some instances, a civil and a criminal investigation will be conducted at the same time using separate investigators and supervisory oversight. In other instances, the investigation may be conducted as a criminal investigation only. *Strategic Enforcement Plan*, 65 Fed. Reg. 18208 (April 6, 2000).

731. How is the PWBA criminal enforcement program operated?

The Pension and Welfare Benefits Administration (PWBA) conducts its criminal enforcement program by decentralizing to the extent possible to its regional offices the decision making and conduct of criminal investigations. Regional Office personnel consult with the local U.S. Attorney prior to or at the initiation of any criminal investigation both to obtain a delegation of authority to conduct the investigation and to receive any specific directions as may be necessary. In a number of instances, the PWBA conducts joint investigations with other agencies such as the Office of Labor Racketeering, the Office of Labor Management Standards, the Federal Bureau of Investigation, the U.S. Postal Inspectors, the U.S. Department of the Treasury, and other local, state and federal law enforcement agencies. This team approach brings together the abilities and backgrounds that may be particularly necessary for any individual investigation. *Strategic Enforcement Plan*, 65 Fed. Reg. 18208 (April 6, 2000).

As part of its criminal strategy, the PWBA has established a position of Criminal Coordinator within its Office of Enforcement that is held by an individual with extensive criminal investigative experience in the area of complex financial crimes. The Coordinator oversees the implementation of PWBA's criminal enforcement activities and coordinates with other agencies within and without the Department of Labor, including the Federal Bureau of Investigation, the Department of Justice, and various U.S. Attorneys. The Coordinator also provides guidance to Regional Office investigators for criminal case referrals, ensures that appropriate criminal investigative training is provided to enforcement staff, and considers whether the criminal enforcement actions are initiated as appropriate based upon the facts obtained in civil investigations. *Strategic Enforcement Plan*, 65 Fed. Reg. 18208 (April 6, 2000).

732. Where does the PWBA obtain its leads to pursue a criminal investigation?

The Pension and Welfare Benefits Administration (PWBA) obtains investigative leads for criminal investigations from a variety of sources, including the review of a plan's Form 5500, civil investigations, contacts with other law enforcement agencies including U.S. Attorneys, informants, media, etc. The PWBA's enforcement strategy involves considering whether there are possible criminal aspects to any of its civil investigations and, if so, to pursue criminal investigative authority from the appropriate U.S. Attorney and seek criminal indictments and convictions where the facts indicate. In this regard, PWBA develops and maintains close contacts and coordination with other law enforcement agencies, and seeks to enhance the ability of its investigators and auditors to conduct criminal investigations. *Strategic Enforcement Plan*, 65 Fed. Reg. 18208 (April 6, 2000).

733. What criminal provisions does the PWBA investigate?

The Pension and Welfare Benefits Administration (PWBA) criminal investigations predominately involve Title 18 and Title 29 crimes. The case type, known as Program 52 investigations, is used to conduct investigations of allegations involving potential criminal violations of the following statute sections:

1. ERISA Section 411, "Prohibition Against Certain Persons Holding Certain Positions" (when the issues relate to a reduction of time for a bar against serving in a certain position or an exemption pursuant to ERISA Section 411(a), the investigation is conducted as a Program 47);

2. ERISA Section 501, "Willful Violation of Title I, Part 1";

3. ERISA Section 511, "Coercive Interference";

4. 18 U.S.C. Section 664, "Theft or Embezzlement from Employee Benefit Plan";

5. 18 U.S.C. Section 1027, " False Statements and Concealment of Facts in Relation to Documents Required by the Employee Retirement Income Security Act";

6. 18 U.S.C. Section 1954, "Offer, Acceptance or Solicitation Influence Operations of Employee Benefit Plans"; and

7. Other criminal statutes that are violated in connection with employee benefit plan operations; such statutes include 18 U.S.C. Section 1341, "Mail Fraud," 18 U.S.C. Section 1343, "Wire Fraud," and 18 U.S.C. Section 371, "Conspiracy."

734. Are PWBA investigators and auditors trained in criminal enforcement matters?

Yes. The Pension and Welfare Benefits Administration (PWBA) has increased its criminal enforcement through increased training for its investigators and auditors on criminal investigative techniques and substantive provisions of applicable criminal laws. The PWBA's program for training enforcement investigators includes a segment in its basic training course on criminal investigation and an investigative course devoted solely to criminal investigative techniques and issues. PWBA investigators also may participate in a White Collar Crime Training Program at the Federal Law Enforcement Training Center located in Glynco, Georgia.

735. Does the PWBA disclose the nature and basis of a criminal investigation?

No. It is the policy of the Pension and Welfare Benefits Administration (PWBA) not to inform plan officials or others as to the source of its investigation. However, the PWBA will state the purpose of the investigation, by clearly identifying the criminal basis of the investigation and the joint interest in the matter by the PWBA and the Department of Justice. *PWBA Enforcement Manual*, Ch. 52.

736. Does the PWBA utilize administrative subpoenas in the course of a criminal investigation?

No. In light of the fact that the Pension and Welfare Benefits Administration (PWBA) conducts both civil and criminal investigations, the PWBA does not use its administrative subpoena power when conducting criminal investigations. This is to avoid potential accusations of improperly using the civil process to obtain information for a criminal case. *PWBA Enforcement Manual*, Ch. 52.

737. Does the PWBA conduct searches and seizures?

Yes. Pension and Welfare Benefits Administration (PWBA) investigators and auditors conduct and participate in search and seizure actions. Although PWBA investigators and auditors may prepare an affidavit as support for a search and seizure, the application or request for a warrant is likely to be made by the United States Attorneys Office, or agents from other law enforcement agencies, who are authorized to apply for a warrant. A PWBA investigator or auditor may serve the warrant; however, on-site search and seizure actions are usually coordinated with the law enforcement agencies applying for the warrant or with the U.S. Marshall's office. *PWBA Enforcement Manual*, Ch. 52.

738. What are the criminal provisions of ERISA?

The criminal provisions of ERISA address the prohibition of certain persons holding certain positions with respect to a plan, willful violations of the reporting and disclosure requirements of ERISA, and coercive interference with the rights of participants and beneficiaries. ERISA Secs. 411, 501, 511. A violation of the prohibition of certain persons holding certain positions is a felony. Violations of the reporting and disclosure requirements and the prohibition of coercive interference with the rights of participants and beneficiaries are misdemeanors.

739. What is the prohibition against certain persons holding certain positions under ERISA Section 411?

ERISA establishes a bar against any person who has been convicted of a broad range of crimes from serving as a fiduciary or service provider of an employee benefit plan. ERISA automatically disqualifies individuals by its terms and subjects those persons to prosecution for violating its provisions. Also, persons who knowingly permit a disqualified person to serve in a prohibited capacity are subject to prosecution. Any person who intentionally violates the statute may be fined up to $10,000, or imprisoned for not more than five years, or both. ERISA Sec. 411. Section 504 of the Labor Management Reporting and Disclosure Act served as a model for the statute. See 29 U.S.C. Section 504. However, the list of crimes in ERISA Section 411 was expanded by Congress. *Presser v. Brennan*, 389 F. Supp. 808 (N.D. Ohio 1975).

The legislative history indicates that Congress considered the prohibitions of the statute necessary because of the large amount of funds involved and the attendant risk of a loss affecting a large number of persons. Without such a provision persons barred from serving as union officers might take positions with employee benefit plans. S. Rep. No. 93-127, 93d Cong., 2d Sess., *reprinted in* 1974 U.S. Code Cong. & Admin. News 4838 (1974); *Greenberg v. Brennan*, 1 EBC 2006 (E.D. NY 1975). As a result of amendments made by the Comprehensive Crime Control Act of 1984, a violation of ERISA Section 411 became a felony for convictions occurring after October 12, 1984. That legislation also expanded the class of prohibited persons and lengthened the time in which they are prohibited from serving as a fiduciary or service provider to a plan. See S. Rep. No. 98-83, 98th Cong., 1st Sess. (1983) and S. Rep. 98-225, 98th Cong., 1st Sess. (1983), *reprinted in* 1984 U.S. Code Cong. and Admin. News 3477.

740. What persons are banned from service as fiduciaries?

A person is prohibited from serving as a fiduciary if he has been convicted of, or imprisoned as a result of, the following offenses:

1.   Robbery, bribery, extortion, embezzlement, fraud, grand larceny, burglary, arson, murder, rape, kidnaping, perjury, or assault with intent to kill;

2.   A felony violation of a federal or state law involving certain "controlled substances" defined in 21 U.S.C. Section 802(6) (Comprehensive Drug Abuse Prevention and Control Act of 1970);

3.   Any crime described in 15 U.S.C. Section 80a-9(a)(1) (Investment Company Act of 1940);

4.   Any crime described in ERISA Section 411, ERISA Section 501, and ERISA Section 511 (see Q 738);

5.   A violation of 29 U.S.C. Section 186 (prohibited payments to labor unions, labor union officials, and employee representatives);

6.   A violation of Chapter 63 of Title 18, U.S. Code (18 U.S.C. Section 1341, et seq.; e.g., mail fraud, wire fraud, etc.);

7.   A violation of 18 U.S.C. Sections 874, 1027, 1503, 1505, 1506, 1510, 1951, or 1954;

8.   A violation of 29 U.S.C. Section 401 (Labor-Management Reporting and Disclosure Act of 1959);

9.   Any felony involving abuse or misuse of a person's position or employment in a labor organization or employee benefit plan to seek or obtain an illegal gain at the expense of the members of the labor organization or the beneficiaries of the employee benefit plan;

10.   Conspiracy or attempt to commit any crime described above; and

11.   Any crime in which any of the crimes described above is an element.

In addition, a person may not knowingly hire, retain, employ, or otherwise place any of the prohibited persons in any of the capacities prohibited by ERISA Section 411. However, a corporation or partnership will not be precluded from acting as an administrator, fiduciary, officer, trustee, custodian, counsel, agent, or employee of an employee benefit plan or as a consultant to an employee benefit plan without a notice, hearing, and determination by a court that the proposed service is inconsistent with the intention of ERISA Section 411. ERISA Sec. 411(a).

741. What positions are subject to the prohibition against holding certain positions?

A person convicted of one of the crimes described in Q 740 is banned from serving as a fiduciary in the following positions:

1.   As an administrator, fiduciary, officer, trustee, custodian, counsel, agent, employee, or representative in any capacity of an employee benefit plan;

2.   As a consultant or advisor to an employee benefit plan, including, but not limited to, any entity whose activities are in whole or substantial part devoted to providing goods or services to an employee benefit plan; or

3.   In any capacity that involves decision making authority or custody or control of the money, funds, assets, or property of an employee benefit plan. ERISA Sec. 411(a).

742. How may a prohibited person have the ability to serve as a fiduciary restored?

For convictions after October 12, 1984, the prohibited person may obtain relief from the prohibition under one of the following situations:

1. By making an application for an exemption from the prohibition against service or employment in a particular prohibited position;

2. By making an application to a court for a reduction of the length of the prohibition (the length of prohibition may not be less than three years); or

3. By having fully restored any citizenship rights that were revoked as a result of the disqualifying conviction. ERISA Sec. 411.

Prior to making any determination under (2), above, the court must hold a hearing and give notice to the proceeding by certified mail to the Secretary of Labor and to state, county, and federal prosecuting officials in the jurisdiction or jurisdictions where the person was convicted. The court's determination in the proceeding is final. ERISA Sec. 411(a).

743. What are the penalties for violating ERISA Section 411?

Any person who intentionally violates ERISA Section 411 may be fined up to $10,000, imprisoned for up to five years, or both. ERISA Sec. 411(b).

744. When is a person considered to be convicted?

A person is considered convicted and under the disability of a conviction from the date of the judgment of the trial court, regardless of whether the judgment is on appeal. ERISA Sec. 411(c)(1).

745. What is a consultant?

The term "consultant" means any person who, for compensation, advises or represents an employee benefit plan, or who provides other assistance to the plan concerning the establishment or operation of the plan. ERISA Sec. 411(c)(2).

746. Is a period of parole or supervised release considered part of the period of imprisonment?

No. A period of parole or supervised release is not considered part of a period of imprisonment. ERISA Sec. 411(c)(3).

747. Is there any provision concerning the salary of a person that appeals his conviction?

Yes. A person who is barred from office or other position in an employee benefit plan as a result of a conviction and who has appealed that conviction has any salary that would otherwise be due the person by virtue of the office or position placed in escrow by the individual or organization responsible for payment of the salary. Payment of the salary into escrow must continue for the duration of the appeal or for the period of time during which the salary would be otherwise due, whichever period is shorter. Upon the final reversal of the person's conviction on appeal, the amount in escrow must be paid to the person. Upon the final sustaining of the person's conviction on appeal, the amount in escrow is returned to the individual or organization responsible for payment of that amount. Upon final reversal of a person's conviction, the person is no longer barred from assuming any position from which the person was previously barred. ERISA Sec. 411(d).

748. What is the disability period for a disqualified person?

A disqualified person is prohibited from serving employee benefit plans for a period of 13 years from the entry of judgment of the trial court or the end of imprisonment resulting from the disqualifying conviction, whichever is later. A court may, under appropriate circumstances, reduce the period of prohibition to not less than three years or determine that service in one of the prohibited capacities would not be contrary to the purposes of ERISA. ERISA Sec. 411.

By the terms of ERISA Section 411, the disability is effective despite any appeal of the disqualifying conviction. For disqualifying convictions on or before October 12, 1984, the period of disability was five years following judgment of conviction, the final sustaining of the judgment on appeal, or end of imprisonment, whichever was later. Congress indicated that the length of the disqualification period is a critical component of the statutory scheme to rid employee benefit plans of corruption. See S. Rep. No. 98-225, 98th Cong., 1st. Sess., 227 (1983), *reprinted in* 1984 U.S. Code Cong. & Admin. News 3477.

749. What are the procedures for seeking an application for a certificate of exemption?

ERISA Section 411 establishes the procedures for seeking an exemption from the statutory prohibitions. For a disqualifying crime committed before November 1, 1987, an Application for Exemption must be directed to the United States Board of Parole. The procedures governing the application are found at 28 C.F.R. Part 4. For a disqualifying crime committed on or after November 1, 1987, the Petition for Exemption is directed to the federal sentencing court, or if the conviction is a state offense, the petition is directed to the U.S. District Court for the district where the disqualifying state offense was committed. A Petition for Reduction of the Length of Disability for disqualifying judgments of conviction entered after October 12, 1994 may be made to the state or federal sentencing judge. No such relief was available prior to October 12, 1994. *PWBA Enforcement Manual*, Ch. 47.

Prior to making a determination on the application, the Department of Labor and the prosecuting officials in the jurisdiction where the person was convicted are notified by the applicable court. ERISA Sec. 411. The Department of Labor is authorized to conduct investigations when the issues relate to a reduction of the bar or an exemption. The investigation is for the purpose of providing information to the court or Board of Parole, rather than to prove a violation of ERISA. *PWBA Enforcement Manual*, Chs. 47, 52.

750. What factors are considered in determining whether a Certificate of Exemption should be granted under ERISA Section 411?

In determining whether a Certificate of Exemption should be granted under ERISA Section 411, the U.S. Board of Parole stated that it was necessary to consider the following factors:

1.   The character and gravity of the disqualifying offense;

2.   The nature of the position for which the applicant is seeking an exemption; and

3.   The extent to which the applicant has been rehabilitated to meet the standards of responsibility required (this is higher than the standard required for release on parole, but the degree of difference depends upon the requirements of the position and any influence the position has on others). *In re Viverito*, 1 EBC 1102 (US BdPar 1975).

The Board in *Viverito* noted that motives and surrounding circumstances may be taken into consideration as mitigating factors under the circumstances. The applicant's motive in *Viverito* appeared to be misplaced loyalty to, and dependence upon, his superior officer who was a main perpetrator and beneficiary of a scheme to embezzle funds. In addition, the applicant received no personal enrichment from his participation in the scheme. Moreover, the position for which the exemption was sought had little influence on the employing organization or other employees or beneficiaries of the plan, the applicant would have no access to plan funds, no authority or responsibility which could create a substantial risk of loss to the plan, and the record reflected evidence of rehabilitation.

751. What is a Debarment Notice?

A Debarment Notice is a letter sent to a person convicted of one of the enumerated crimes listed in ERISA Section 411. It puts the person on notice that he is prohibited from occupying a position related to employee benefit plan administration, and that the intentional violation of this prohibition is a criminal violation subject to prosecution. A Debarment Notice is generally sent to the convicted person after sentencing, and if appropriate, a similar letter may be sent to plan officials or service providers. *PWBA Enforcement Manual*, Ch. 47.

752. What is the prohibition against a violation of the reporting and disclosure provisions of ERISA under ERISA Section 501?

ERISA Section 101 through ERISA Section 111 impose elaborate reporting and disclosure requirements on plan administrators. ERISA Section 501 authorizes criminal penalties for willful violations of these reporting and disclosure provisions. By adopting ERISA Section 501, Congress indicated its preference for criminal sanctions, rather than punitive damages, as a deterrent to willful violations of ERISA. *Whitaker v. Texaco, Inc.*, 566 F. Supp. 745 (N.D. Ga. 1983).

ERISA Section 501 reads as follows:

> Any person who willfully violates any portion of part 1 of this subtitle [Reporting and Disclosure], or any regulation or order issued under any such provision, shall upon conviction be fined not more than $5,000 or imprisoned not more than one year, or both; except that in the case of such violation by a person not an individual, the fine imposed upon such person shall be a fine not exceeding $100,000.

753. What is the meaning of the term "willfully" as used in ERISA Section 501?

Anyone who willfully violates the reporting and disclosure requirements of ERISA or a regulation or order issued under those requirements is subject to criminal liability. ERISA Sec. 501. An act is done "willfully" if it is done with reckless disregard for the requirements of the law. The Eleventh Circuit upheld a trial court's instruction to a jury that it could find a defendant guilty if he had "knowingly and intentionally committed the acts which [violate Part 1 of Title I of ERISA] and . . . [the acts] were not committed accidentally or by some mistake." The court also upheld the trial court's instruction that ERISA Section 501 requires only a general intent and knowledge of one's acts. *U.S. v. Phillips*, 19 F.3d 1565 (11th Cir. 1994).

754. What are examples of violations of the reporting and disclosure requirements?

Examples of violations of the reporting and disclosure obligations include:

1.   Omission or refusal to file an annual financial report (5500 series), terminal and supplementary report, or to furnish a summary plan description, or modifications and changes to the plan, to a participant or beneficiary as required by ERISA Section 104(a);

2.   Omission or refusal to publish a summary plan description and provide annual reports to participants and beneficiaries as required by ERISA Section 104(b);

3.   Omission or refusal to furnish certain information concerning benefits to pension plan participants as required by ERISA Section 105; and

4.   Failure to maintain records from which reports and other required documents can be verified and checked as required by ERISA Section 107.

755. Is there a good faith defense to a prosecution for reporting and disclosure violations?

Yes. A statutory defense to an ERISA Section 501 reporting and disclosure violation is codified in ERISA Section 108. Under ERISA Section 108, no person is subject to liability or punishment under ERISA Section 501 on account of a failure to:

1.   Comply with the reporting and disclosure requirements, or the bonding requirements of ERISA Section 412, if he pleads and proves that the act or omission complained of was in good faith, in conformity with, and in reliance on any regulation or written ruling of the Department of Labor; or

2.   Publish and file any information required by any provision of the reporting and disclosure requirements of ERISA if he pleads and proves that he published and filed the information in good faith, and in conformity with any regulation or written ruling of the Department of Labor issued under those reporting and disclosure requirements regarding the filing of the reports.

If the good faith (reliance) defense is established, it will prevent a conviction under ERISA Section 501, even if:

1.   After the act or omission, the interpretation or opinion is modified or rescinded or is determined by judicial authority to be invalid or of no legal effect; or

2.   After publishing or filing annual reports and other required reports, the publication or filing is determined by judicial authority not to be in conformity with the requirements of ERISA. ERISA Sec. 108.

756. What is the prohibition against coercive interference under ERISA Section 511?

It is a criminal offense to interfere coercively with exercise of the rights of a participant or beneficiary that are protected by ERISA. ERISA Sec. 511. The essence of the offense is the actual or attempted interference with the exercise of the protected rights of a participant or beneficiary of an employee benefit plan by means of the willful use of actual or threatened force, violence, or fraud.

ERISA Section 511 is one of two provisions in ERISA that prohibit interference with protected rights. The other is ERISA Section 510 which makes it unlawful to interfere with the attainment of any right to which a participant or beneficiary may become entitled. The statute's legislative history reveals that ERISA Section 510 and ERISA Section 511 are companion provisions. As ERISA Section 510 prohibits interference with protected rights; ERISA Section 511 provides criminal penalties where that interference is coercive. The legislative history reveals that the prohibitions were aimed primarily at preventing unscrupulous employers from discharging or harassing their employees in order to keep them from obtaining vested pension rights. These provisions were enacted by Congress in the face of evidence that in some plans a worker's pension rights or the expectations of those rights were interfered with by the use of economic sanctions or violent reprisals. *West v. Butler*, 621 F.2d 240 (6th Cir. 1980). The intent of Congress was to make ERISA Section 511 coercive interference a subcategory of ERISA Section 510 interference with protected rights.

The interaction of these two sections was expressed by the Sixth Circuit as follows:

> Every employee is to have the right, enforceable by the Secretary of Labor, to be free from interference with his pension benefits. This means that he cannot be discharged, fined, suspended, expelled or otherwise interfered with in order to prevent him from receiving pension benefits or attaining eligibility for pension benefits. There are stiff criminal penalties if this type of interference takes the form of force, fraud or violence or threats of this nature. *West v. Butler*, 621 F.2d 240 (6th Cir. 1980).

The text of ERISA Section 511 reads:

> It shall be unlawful for any person through the use of fraud, force, violence, or threat of the use of force or violence, to restrain, coerce, intimidate, or attempt to restrain, coerce, or intimidate any participant or beneficiary for the purpose of interfering with or preventing the exercise of any right to which he is or may become entitled under the plan, this subchapter, section 1201 of this title, or the Welfare and Pension Plans Disclosure Act (29 U.S.C. 301 et seq.). Any person who willfully violates this section shall be fined $10,000 or imprisoned for not more than one year, or both.

Unlike ERISA Section 510, which is a civil prohibition, ERISA Section 511 provides criminal penalties for violators. The component that separates the criminal provision of ERISA Section 511 from the civil provision of ERISA Section 510 is the willful use of actual or threatened force, violence, intimidation, restraint, coercion or fraud. Under ERISA Section 510, the participant or beneficiary may bring a civil action against any person who interferes with those rights protected under ERISA. By contrast, ERISA Section 511 contains prohibitory language and a criminal penalty provision; it makes no reference to civil enforcement. Thus, ERISA Section 511 punishes coercive forms of conduct that violate ERISA Section 510. As ERISA Section 511 is a criminal provision, its enforcement is the exclusive prerogative of the U.S. Attorney General.

UNITED STATES CRIMINAL CODE PROVISIONS

757. What are the criminal provisions of Title 18 of the United States Code that are applicable to employee benefit plans?

While ERISA provides for a system of administrative penalties, civil actions, and criminal sanctions, the United States Criminal Code (Title 18 of the United States Code) has a number of provisions under which violators can be prosecuted for certain activities involving employee benefit plans. For example, the United States Criminal Code has prohibitions against: (1) theft or embezzlement from employee benefit plans under 18 U.S.C. Section 664; (2) the making of false statements and concealment of facts in relation to documents required by ERISA under 18 U.S.C. Section 1027; and (3) the offer, acceptance or solicitation of funds to influence the operation of employee benefit plans under 18 U.S.C. Section 1954.

These three sections of Title 18 were enacted in 1962 as part of the Welfare and Pension Plans Disclosure Act Amendments of 1962 in an effort to strengthen the Welfare and Pension Plans Disclosure Act of 1958. P.L. 87-420. In these enactments Congress intended to provide the "enforcement teeth . . . lacking in the existing law." H. Rep. No. 87-998, 87th Cong., 2d Sess., *reprinted in* 1962 U.S. Code Cong. & Admin. News 1532, 1537.

In addition, prohibitions in other criminal statutes may be violated in connection with employee benefit plan operations. Such statutes include: 18 U.S.C. Section 1341 concerning mail fraud; 18 U.S.C. Section 1343 concerning wire fraud; and 18 U.S.C. Section 371 concerning conspiracy.

758. What is the Criminal Code provision for theft or embezzlement from an employee benefit plan?

Any person who embezzles, steals, or unlawfully and willfully abstracts or converts to his own use or to the use of another, any money, funds, securities, premiums, credits, property, or other assets of an employee welfare benefit plan or employee pension benefit plan, or of any connected fund, may be fined, or imprisoned for up to five years, or both. The term "any employee welfare benefit plan or employee pension benefit plan" means any employee benefit plan subject to any provision of Title I of ERISA. 18 U.S.C. Sec. 664.

18 U.S.C. Section 664 was added in 1962 as an amendment to the Welfare and Pension Plans Disclosure Act (former 29 U.S.C. Sections 301 to 309), ERISA's predecessor. P.L. 87-420. Upon the enactment of ERISA in 1974, this section was amended to include the language "ERISA covered plan." It applies to thefts from ERISA covered plans committed after January 1, 1975.

The legislative history indicates that the purpose of 18 U.S.C. Section 664 is to "preserve the designated funds for those entitled to their benefits." *U.S. v. Andreen*, 628 F.2d 1236 (9th Cir. 1980); H.R. Rep. No. 87-998, 87th Cong., 2d Sess., *reprinted in* 1962 U.S. Code Cong. & Admin. News 1532. As the court explained in *Andreen*, "[by] enacting [18 U.S.C.] section 664, Congress made it a federal crime to embezzle, steal, and unlawfully convert or abstract assets of an employee benefit plan and to preserve such funds for the protection of those entitled to their benefits." The statute contains no attempt provision and reimbursement of loss by civil action, insurance, or restitution is no defense. *U.S. v. Daley*, 454 F.2d 505 (1st Cir. 1972). Furthermore, a good faith intent to return embezzled funds does not negate a showing that the defendant acted with the requisite criminal intent to embezzle the funds in the first instance. *U.S. v. Shackleford*, 777 F.2d 1141 (6th Cir. 1985), *cert. denied*, 476 U.S. 1119 (1986).

Cases interpreting 18 U.S.C. Section 664 are few; however, a number of opinions have addressed the meaning of a similar statute that prohibits embezzlement from union funds. 18 U.S.C. Section 664 parallels the language of 29 U.S.C. Section 501(c) which is part of the Labor Management Reporting and Disclosure Act. 29 U.S.C. Section 501(c) provides:

> Any person who embezzles, steals, or unlawfully and willfully abstracts or converts to his own use, or the use of another, any of the moneys, funds, securities, property, or other assets of a labor organization of which he is an officer, or by which he is employed, directly or indirectly, shall be fined not more than $10,000 or imprisoned for not more than five years, or both.

Although in enacting 18 U.S.C. Section 664, Congress provided broader language than 29 U.S.C. Section 501(c), the court in *Andreen* stated that the statutes contain "[p]arallel language" and that "Congress passed the two statutes for a similar purpose: to preserve the designated funds for those entitled to their benefits." The court concluded, "the prohibitory language of both statutes should be given similar interpretation and be applied to similar types of conduct." Further, "our discussion of [29 U.S.C.] Section 501(c) cases . . . applies equally to 18 U.S.C. [Section] 664."

759. What is the meaning of the term "embezzlement" under 18 U.S.C. Section 664?

As used in 18 U.S.C. Section 664, the term "embezzlement" is a traditional term that "encompasses the fraudulent appropriation of the property of another by one in lawful possession thereof. The essence of the crime is theft and in the context of union funds or pension funds the offense includes a taking or appropriation that is unauthorized, if accomplished with specific criminal intent." *U.S. v. Andreen*, 628 F.2d 1236 (9th Cir. 1980). Embezzlement occurs when a person who has lawfully received funds willfully diverts them to his own unauthorized use. *U.S. v. Marquardt*, 786 F.2d 7710 (7th Cir. 1986).

760. Must a person be in a fiduciary relationship to be convicted under 18 U.S.C. Section 664?

No. Criminal culpability under 18 U.S.C. Section 664 does not require that the defendant hold any particular status in relation to an employee benefit plan or fund connected with a plan, or that he act as a fiduciary with respect to an employee welfare benefit plan transaction. In fact, the Seventh Circuit has held that proof of lawful possession or lawful access to property at the time of appropriation is not required to demonstrate conversion in violation of 18 U.S.C. Section 664. *U.S. v. Goodstein*, 883 F.2d 1362 (7th Cir. 1989), *cert. denied*, 494 U.S. 1007 (1990). The Eleventh Circuit affirmed a conviction pursuant to 18 U.S.C. Section 664 predicated on the disbursement of loan proceeds from a plan, where the loan resulted from the borrower's fraudulent overvaluation of the collateral pledged for the loan. *U.S. v. Wuagneux*, 683 F.2d 1343 (11th Cir. 1982), *cert. denied*, 464 U.S. 814 (1983).

761. Who can be convicted in an action under 18 U.S.C. Section 664?

18 U.S.C. Section 664, by its terms, applies to "any person." In stating that "[c]riminal culpability under [18 U.S.C.] section 664 does not require that a defendant hold any particular status in relation to an employee benefit plan or fund connected with a plan . . . Congress intended the statute to be read broadly to include any person who misuses or misappropriates contributions intended for deposit in an employee welfare benefit plan." *U.S. v. Goodstein*, 883 F.2d 1362 (7th Cir. 1989), *cert. denied*, 494 U.S. 1007 (1990). Thus, "any person" under 18 U.S.C. Section 664 is not limited to an officer, administrator, trustee or other fiduciary of the plan but may be, for example, a beneficiary, borrower, employer, trustee, or service provider. The language "any person" in 18 U.S.C. Section 664 includes, but is not limited to, the following groups:

1. *Employers who convert plan funds to their own use.* An employer who withheld welfare benefit plan contributions from employees' paychecks and failed to deliver contributions to the plan was convicted under 18 U.S.C. Section 664. *U.S. v. Grizzle*, 933 F.2d 943 (11th Cir. 1991). The conversion of profit sharing funds by an employer to pay personal and corporate debts of the plan sponsor resulted in a conviction. *U.S. v. Goodstein*, 883 F.2d 1362 (7th Cir. 1989), *cert. denied*, 494 U.S. 1007 (1990). The same result occurred when an employer converted entrusted monies to its own use. *U.S. v. Panepinto*, 818 F. Supp. 48 (E.D. NY 1993), *aff'd*, 28 F.3d 103 (2nd Cir. 1994).

2. *Borrowers.* The Eleventh Circuit affirmed a conviction under 18 U.S.C. Section 664 where loan proceeds were disbursed from a plan based on the borrower's fraudulent overvaluation of the collateral (land) pledged for the loan. *U.S. v. Wuagneux*, 683 F.2d 1343 (11th Cir. 1982), *cert. denied*, 464 U.S. 814 (1983).

3. *Operators of Multiple Employer Welfare Arrangements.* An individual was convicted under 18 U.S.C. Section 664 when he

operated a fraudulent health insurance scheme where he misman-
aged the operation and converted plan assets and, as a result, left
many subscribers to the plan with unpaid medical bills. *U.S. v.
Rowe*, 999 F.2d 14 (1st Cir. 1993).

4.   *Union officials and trustees who embezzle funds from local pension and
      welfare funds*. See *U.S. v. Busacca*, 863 F.2d 433 (6th Cir. 1988);
      U.S. v. Snyder, 572 F.2d 894 (2nd Cir. 1982).

762. Is restitution, or lack of personal gain, a defense to a charge under 18 U.S.C. Section 664?

No. The mere fact that the plan recovers the money or property which was
unlawfully taken is not a defense under 18 U.S.C. Section 664. *U.S. v. Daley*, 454
F.2d 505 (1st Cir. 1972). Neither is a lack of personal financial gain on the part
of the accused. *U.S. v. Santiago*, 528 F.2d 1130 (2nd Cir. 1976), *cert. denied*, 425
U.S. 972 (1976). In addition, a good faith intent to return embezzled funds does
not negate a showing that the defendant acted with the requisite criminal intent
to embezzle the funds in the first instance. *U.S. v. Shackleford*, 777 F.2d 1141 (6th
Cir. 1985), *cert. denied*, 476 U.S. 1119 (1986).

763. What assets are protected by 18 U.S.C. Section 664?

By its terms, 18 U.S.C. Section 664 contains a broad list of assets that are
protected. Embezzlement under 18 U.S.C. Section 664 may be accomplished by
unlawfully depriving the plan of the beneficial use of money, funds, securities,
premiums, credits, property, or other assets. The statute does not define these
terms.

In addition, 18 U.S.C. Section 664 is not limited to those who misappropri-
ate assets directly from a plan, but also includes those who divert assets from
reaching the plan. "[T]he language of the statute, by its terms, does not limit its
reach to protecting only wealth already transferred to a welfare benefit plan or its
administrators." *U.S. v. Panepinto*, 818 F. Supp. 48 (E.D. NY 1993), *aff'd*, 28
F.3d 103 (2nd Cir. 1994). The employer in *Panepinto* converted to its own use the
required contributions that were held as "credits, property, and other assets" of the
plan. Referencing the terms of the collective bargaining agreement, the court in
Panepinto held that the employer willfully failed to remit funds representing its
own contributions to the plan because under the Plan Agreement, the employer
surrendered all legal and equitable rights to the contributions due to the plan.
Likewise, the term "premiums" include insurance and other premiums. The Fifth
Circuit upheld an 18 U.S.C. Section 664 conviction for the conversion of
insurance premiums that were refunded to an employee benefit plan. The plan's
employer sponsor retained and used the refunded insurance premiums. *U.S. v.
Moore*, 427 F.2d 38 (5th Cir. 1970).

764. What is a connected fund in 18 U.S.C. Section 664?

The language of 18 U.S.C. Section 664 provides for punishment in the case of an embezzlement or theft from "any employee welfare benefit plan or employee pension benefit plan, or of any fund connected therewith." The meaning of the term "fund connected" has not been judicially settled. However, a few cases have applied that term.

One court held that the embezzled proceeds of a first mortgage obtained for the purpose of paying certain plan debts did not constitute property of the pension fund and therefore were not "connected funds" for purposes of the statute. The plan sold its property pursuant to a contract that provided for the purchase price to be payable in notes or bonds, secured by subordinated mortgages on the property. The defendant was to obtain a first mortgage on the property and use the proceeds to discharge the debts previously incurred by the plan in the property's construction and management. Although no provision in the contract gave the plan the right to receive any part of the proceeds, the alleged misappropriation did not constitute property of the plan or "of a fund connected therewith." *U.S. v. Delillo*, 421 F. Supp. 1012 (E.D. NY 1976), *aff'd*, 620 F.2d 939 (2nd Cir. 1980).

More recently, the Eleventh Circuit addressed the "fund connected with" language and held that it applies only to ERISA plans. In an embezzlement case, the co-defendants administered a welfare and pension fund that provided health and retirement benefits in addition to a fund that provided supplemental income that was distributed at the end of each taxable year. The welfare and pension fund, but not the supplemental income fund, was covered by ERISA. Although both plans had common beneficiaries and administrators, the court held that, without more, it would not consider the funds connected for purposes of 18 U.S.C. Section 664. *U.S. v. Bell*, 22 F.3d 274 (11th Cir. 1994).

765. Must the principal taker act willfully to be convicted under 18 U.S.C. Section 664?

Yes. In a prosecution under 18 U.S.C. Section 664, it must be established that the defendant intended to deprive the employee benefit plan of the use of its assets. In such a case, sufficient proof must be gathered to establish that the defendant willfully deprived the plan of its property. Courts have referred to 18 U.S.C. Section 664 as a generic theft statute. *U.S. v. Busacca*, 863 F.2d 433 (6th Cir. 1988), *cert. denied*, 490 U.S. 1005 (1989). As one court stated, "[t]he essence of the crime is theft and in the context of . . . pension plans the offense includes a taking or appropriation that is unauthorized, if accomplished with specific criminal intent [to steal]," the essential mental state required for conviction. *U.S. v. Andreen*, 628 F.2d 1236 (9th Cir. 1980). In order to have specific criminal intent, "the criminal act must have been willful, which means an act done with fraudulent intent or a bad purpose or an evil motive." *Young v. West Coast Indus. Relations Ass'n*, 763 F. Supp. 64 (DC Del. 1991).

A knowing and intentional violation of ERISA's prohibited transaction rules was held to be the basis for the criminal mental state requirement. The defendant, as trustee of a plan, knowingly converted plan funds to his own use and arranged for a loan between the pension fund and a company incorporated by his daughter. The transactions were knowing and intentional violations of the prohibited transaction rules in light of the fact that the defendant received legal admonitions regarding their unlawfulness. *U.S. v. Freel*, 681 F. Supp. 766 (M.D. Fla. 1988), *aff'd without opinion*, 868 F.2d 1274 (11th Cir. 1989).

766. What are the rules regarding false statements and concealment of facts in relation to documents required by ERISA?

Whoever, in any document required by ERISA to be published or kept as part of the records of any employee welfare benefit plan or employee pension benefit plan, or certified to the administrator of any such plan, makes any false statement or representation of fact, knowing it to be false, or knowingly conceals, covers up, or fails to disclose any fact the disclosure of which is required by ERISA or is necessary to verify, explain, clarify or check for accuracy and completeness any report required by ERISA to be published or any information required by ERISA to be certified, may be fined, or imprisoned for up to five years, or both. 18 U.S.C. Sec. 1027.

18 U.S.C. Section 1027 prohibits any knowingly made false statements or representations of fact, as well as certain knowingly concealed, covered-up, or undisclosed facts. In order to be convicted under the statute, a false statement or representation of fact must be made in a document required by ERISA to be either (1) published by an employee welfare benefit plan or employee pension benefit plan, (2) kept as part of the records of such a plan, or (3) certified to the administrator of such a plan.

18 U.S.C. Section 1027 also encompasses documents kept as part of the records of an employee welfare benefit plan or employee pension benefit plan. Thus, a concealment, cover-up, or failure to disclose likewise could occur in a similar document, but it also must relate to a fact the disclosure of which is required by ERISA or is necessary to verify, explain, or check for accuracy and completeness any information required by ERISA to be published. *U.S. v. Sarault*, 840 F.2d 1479 (9th Cir. 1988). No regulations have been promulgated interpreting 18 U.S.C. Section 1027.

767. Is any person subject to conviction under 18 U.S.C. Section 1027?

Yes. 18 U.S.C. Section 1027 provides in broad language, unequivocally and without limitation, that the term "whoever" applies to any person who violates its provisions. For example, "whoever" clearly is sufficiently broad to include criminal prosecutions of fiduciaries, such as a trustee of a union pension fund. *U.S. v. Tolkow*, 532 F.2d 853 (2nd Cir. 1976). The term also included the president of a local chapter of the AFL-CIO, who was also the trustee of the union welfare fund. *U.S. v. Santiago*, 528 F.2d 1130 (2nd Cir. 1976), *cert. denied*, 425 U.S. 972 (1976). It also included a defendant who was the salaried supervisor for two employee benefit funds. *U.S. v. McCrae*, 344 F. Supp. 942 (E.D. Pa. 1972).

"Whoever" also includes employers. *U.S. v. S & Vee Cartage Co., Inc.*, 704 F.2d 914 (6th Cir. 1983), *cert. denied*, 464 U.S. 935 (1983); *Central States, Southeast & Southwest Areas Pension Fund v. CRST, Inc.*, 641 F.2d 616 (8th Cir. 1981). Similarly, the term "whoever" was sufficiently broad enough to include medical services providers who filed a false "utilization report." *U.S. v. Martorano*, 596 F. Supp. 621 (E.D. Pa. 1984) *aff'd*, 767 F.2d 63 (3rd Cir. 1985), *cert. denied*, 474 U.S. 949 (1985). Potential defendants under 18 U.S.C. Section 1027 also may include attorneys or bank trust officers. *U.S. v. Furst*, 886 F.2d 558 (3rd Cir. 1989), *cert. denied*, 493 U.S. 1062 (1990); *U.S. v. Sarault*, 840 F.2d 1479 (9th Cir. 1988). Plan participants or beneficiaries can also be convicted under 18 U.S.C. Section 1027. An individual who filed a false hospital invoice for medical services and a false coordination of benefits form was convicted under 18 U.S.C. Section 1027. *U.S. v. Bartkus*, 816 F.2d 255 (6th Cir. 1987).

The Ninth Circuit, in reviewing 18 U.S.C. Section 1027, held that it is not unconstitutionally vague regarding the criminalization of false statements made on required ERISA forms. The Court said that the statute is clear as to what fiduciaries must do - "truthfully fill out the ERISA form according to the instructions." The defendant had accurately reported the value of promissory notes issued on loans made from the plan, but answered "no" to the question of party-in-interest transactions when the promissory notes evidenced extensions of credits from the plan to the fiduciary and certain fiduciary controlled entities. *U.S. v. Harris*, 185 F.3d 999 (9th Cir. 1999).

768. What does the term "knowingly" mean for purposes of 18 U.S.C. Section 1027?

It is a violation of 18 U.S.C. Section 1027 to knowingly make a false statement, representation, or concealment of fact. An act or failure to act is done knowingly if it is done voluntarily and intentionally, and not because of a mistake or accident. Proof of specific intent is not required to establish a violation of 18 U.S.C. Section 1027. The term "knowingly" requires "proof of a voluntary conscious failure to disclose without ground for believing that such non-disclosure is lawful, or with reckless disregard for whether or not it is lawful." *U.S. v. S & Vee Cartage Co., Inc.*, 704 F.2d 914 (6th Cir. 1983), *cert. denied*, 464 U.S. 935 (1983). A conviction was upheld for "knowingly failing to disclose facts" in a required document. *U.S. v. Tolkow*, 532 F.2d 853 (2nd Cir. 1976).

An act (or an omission or failure to act) is done "knowingly" if it is done voluntarily and intentionally, and not because of a mistake or accident or some other innocent reason. The purpose of adding the word "knowingly" to the statute was to ensure that no one would be convicted of an omission or failure to act due to a mistake, accident, or some other innocent reason. A statement or representation is "false" within the meaning of the statute, if it was not true when it was made and the person making it or causing it to be made knew it to be untrue, or if it was made with reckless indifference as to its truth or falsity or with a conscious purpose to avoid learning the truth. *U.S. v. S & Vee Cartage Co., Inc.*, 704 F.2d 914 (6th Cir. 1983), *cert. denied*, 464 U.S. 935 (1983).

It is not necessary to establish that the defendant was aware of any legal duties imposed upon him by ERISA, or that he was aware of the plan's reporting requirements under ERISA, or that he intended to violate any law. *U.S. v. Tolkow*, 532 F.2d 532 (2nd Cir. 1976). As 18 U.S.C. Section 1027 makes no mention of "fraudulent concealment," it does not require proof of fraud or actual reliance upon any false statement of fact. The statute only requires the false statement or representation be made knowingly. *U.S. v. Martorano*, 596 F. Supp. 621 (E.D. Pa. 1984), *aff'd*, 767 F.2d 63 (3rd Cir. 1985).

769. What documents are covered under the provisions of 18 U.S.C. Section 1027?

A violation of 18 U.S.C. Section 1027 occurs when a false statement or false representation of fact is made in a document required by Title I of ERISA to be published, kept as part of the records of an employee welfare benefit plan, or certified to the administrator of such a plan. The only relevant limitation found in 18 U.S.C. Section 1027 deals with the type of documents containing false statements.

Any concealment, cover-up, or failure to disclose must be of a fact the disclosure of which is required by ERISA, or is necessary to verify, explain, clarify, or check for accuracy and completeness any report required by ERISA to be certified. Thus, a knowing false statement of fact falls within the proscription of 18 U.S.C. Section 1027 if it is made in a document required by ERISA to be (1) published, (2) kept as part of the records of an employee welfare benefit plan, or (3) certified to the administrator of such a plan. *U.S. v. Martorano*, 596 F. Supp. 621 (E.D. Pa. 1984), *aff'd*, 767 F.2d 63 (3rd Cir. 1985), *cert. denied*, 474 U.S. 949 (1985).

770. What documents are "published" for purposes of 18 U.S.C. Section 1027?

The documents required to be published are dependent on the type of plan, number of participants, and the use of service providers. ERISA Section 103 and ERISA Section 104 require that an annual report be published by an employee benefit plan subject to ERISA and filed with the Secretary of Labor. The annual report is submitted on Form 5500 and its attached schedules. Labor Reg. §2520.103-1. Thus, the Form 5500 annual report and its supporting schedules are documents required to be "published" within the meaning of 18 U.S.C. Section 1027 and any knowingly made false statement of fact or representation of fact in Form 5500 or an attached schedule is proscribed by 18 U.S.C. Section 1027. *U.S. v. Martorano*, 596 F. Supp. 621 (E.D. Pa. 1984), *aff'd*, 767 F.2d 63 (3rd Cir. 1985), *cert. denied*, 474 U.S. 949 (1985).

The supporting schedules of Form 5500 include:

1. *Schedule A* (Insurance Information). Schedule A is required to be filed by a plan if benefits under the plan are provided by an insurance company, insurance service, or other similar organization; it is certified by the insurer.

2. *Schedule B* (Actuarial Information). Schedule B is required to be filed by defined benefit plans subject to the minimum funding standards; it is certified by an actuary.

3. *Schedule C* (Service Provider and Trustee Information). Schedule C is required to be filed by Form 5500 filers when one or more service providers receive $5,000 or more in compensation for all services rendered to the plan during the plan year, to report trustee information, and to report the termination of certain service providers.

4. *Schedule E* (ESOP Annual Information). Schedule E is required to be filed by every employer sponsoring a pension benefit plan that contains an ESOP benefit; the Schedule E must be filed if required as an attachment to Forms 5500, 5500-C/R or 5500-EZ.

5. *Schedule SSA* (Annual Registration Statement Identifying Separated Participants with Deferred Vested Benefits). Schedule SSA is required to be filed by pension plans that have separated participants.

In addition to Form 5500, other documents that are required to be published include:

1. A financial statement for plans with over 100 participants;

2. An actuarial statement for defined benefit plans; and

3. Stock valuations for ESOPs.

771. What documents are "kept" for purposes of 18 U.S.C. Section 1027?

In addition to documents that are published, 18 U.S.C. Section 1027 also applies to supporting documentation, that is, documents required to be kept as part of plan records. These documents may involve (at least in part) non-financial information that need not be included on Form 5500, but is helpful to verify and check the information that must be included. Examples of these documents include:

1. Plan documents;

2. Trust agreements;

3. Checking account statements with canceled checks;

4. Debit and credit memorandum;

5. Investment account statements;

6. Mortgage notes;

7. Loan agreements with supporting documents;

8. General ledgers, cash disbursement and cash receipts journals;

9. Service provider agreements and reports, including documents containing information from insurance carriers or other similar organizations; see *U.S. v. Martorano*, 596 F. Supp. 621 (E.D. Pa. 1984), *aff'd*, 767 F.2d 63 (3rd Cir. 1985), *cert. denied*, 474 U.S. 949 (1985);

10. Remittance sheets for collectively bargained plans; see *U.S. v. S & Vee Cartage Co., Inc.*, 704 F.2d 914 (6th Cir. 1983), *cert. denied*, 464 U.S. 935 (1983), where documents misstating the number of eligible employees, the names of employees covered, and the contributions the employer owed were the primary source of that information and necessary to verify ERISA Section 1027 reports; see also *U.S. v. Odom*, 736 F.2d 150 (5th Cir. 1984);

11. Claim documents;

12. Hospital invoices for medical services and Coordination of Benefits forms; see *U.S. v. Bartkus*, 816 F.2d 255 (6th Cir. 1987), where the court held that a hospital invoice for medical services qualifies as a "receipt" within the meaning of 18 U.S.C. Section 1027, requiring retention of both the Coordination of Insurance Benefits form that verified the eligibility to receive fund payments and the hospital invoice;

13. Employer payroll records verifying contributions to the plan; see *Combs v. King*, 764 F.2d 818 (11th Cir. 1985), where it was held that 18 U.S.C. Section 1027 provides a duty to maintain records of hours worked by employees so that trustees can determine the accuracy of an employer's contributions; and

14.   Documents submitted to a plan; see *U.S. v. Sarault*, 840 F.2d 1479 (9th Cir. 1988), where statements made by an attorney representing an assetless insurance company to the trustees of a pension plan who were considering the purchase of fiduciary liability insurance falsely stated the company's assets.

772. What documents are "certified by the plan administrator" for purposes of 18 U.S.C. Section 1027?

These are documents or information that are provided to the plan administrator to complete Form 5500 (Annual Report), filed as an attachment to Form 5500, or maintained as records in support of Form 5500. Certain information provided to a plan administrator is required to be certified as to its accuracy. ERISA Sec. 103(a)(2). Examples of certifications include:

1.   *Schedule A* (Insurance Information);

2.   *Schedule B* (Actuarial Information);

3.   Actuarial Report in support of Schedule B that is maintained with the plan records;

4.   ESOP valuations (an appraisal of a privately held company that is certified by a valuation company and maintained with the plan records); and

5.   Asset Valuation Reports (stock broker reports, investment manager reports, bank trust reports, etc. that are certified by a broker, manager, or bank that are used to complete Form 5500 and maintained with the records of the plan).

773. What is an offer, acceptance, or solicitation to influence operations of an employee benefit plan?

18 U.S.C. Section 1954 prohibits the receipt, solicitation, giving, offer, or promise to offer of a fee, kickback, commission, gift, loan, money, or thing of value with respect to an employee benefit plan. Violators of the statute may be fined, imprisoned for up to three years, or both.

The text of 18 U.S.C. Section 1954 reads:

Whoever being

(1)   an administrator, officer, trustee, custodian, counsel, agent, or employee of any employee welfare benefit plan or employee pension benefit plan; or

(2)   an officer, counsel, agent, or employee of an employer or an employer any of whose employees are covered by such plan; or

(3) an officer, counsel, agent, or employee of an employee organization any of whose members are covered by such plan; or

(4) a person who, or an officer, counsel, agent, or employee of an organization which, provides benefit plan services to such plan

receives or agrees to receive or solicits any fee, kickback, commission, gift, loan, money, or thing of value because of or with intent to be influenced with respect to, any of the actions, decisions, or other duties relating to any question or matter concerning such plan or any person who directly or indirectly gives or offers, or promises to give or offer, any fee, kickback, commission, gift, loan, money, or thing of value prohibited by this section, shall be fined under this title or imprisoned not more than three years, or both: Provided, [t]hat this section shall not prohibit the payment to or acceptance by any person of bona fide salary, compensation, or other payments made for goods or facilities actually furnished or for services actually performed in the regular course of his duties as such person, administrator, officer, trustee, custodian, counsel, agent, or employee of such plan, employer, employee organization, or organization providing benefit plan services to such plan.

As used in this section, the term (a) "any employee welfare benefit plan" or "employee pension benefit plan" means any employee welfare benefit plan or employee pension benefit plan, respectively, subject to any provision of Title I of [ERISA], and (b) "employee organization" and "administrator" as defined respectively in [ERISA Section 3(4) and ERISA Section 3(16)]. 18 U.S.C. Sec. 1954.

18 U.S.C. Section 1954 was enacted as part of the Welfare and Pension Plans Disclosure Amendment Act of 1962. In enacting 18 U.S.C. Section 1954, Congress intended to strictly regulate the administration and operation of employee benefit plans and to provide the "enforcement teeth which [was] lacking in the [Welfare and Pension Plans Disclosure Law of 1958]." H.R. Rep. No. 87-998, 87th Cong., 2d Sess., *reprinted in* 1962 U.S. Code Cong. & Admin. News 1532, 1532-36.

The statute is designed to protect the financial interests of participants in employee benefit plans and their beneficiaries from dishonest or unfaithful fiduciaries, and is intended to reach a broad class of persons who are connected with the operation of employee benefit plans by encompassing almost every conceivable person who could deal with or administer an employee benefit plan. The statute itself has been construed to reach all persons with the capacity to influence, directly or indirectly, the use of employee benefit plan funds, as well as all fiduciaries who profit as a result of their decisions to invest employee benefit funds. *U.S. v. Robilotto*, 828 F.2d 940 (2nd Cir. 1987); *U.S. v. Romano*, 684 F.2d 1057 (2nd Cir.1982); *U.S. v. Friedland*, 660 F.2d 919 (3rd Cir. 1981).

The statute prohibits the receipt of any fee, kickback, commission, gift, loan, money, or thing of value either "because of" (i.e., a graft provision proscribing the payment or receipt of gratuities), or with "the intent to be influenced" (i.e., a bribery provision proscribing the corrupt payment or receipt of things of value as the primary motivation for the recipient's actions, duties, or decisions with respect to an employee benefit plan matter). Thus, Congress was not only concerned with corrupt transactions as indicated with the "intent to influence" language, it also was concerned with fiduciaries of benefit plans taking advantage of their position in any way. The statute also bans all conflict of interest payments by requiring all fiduciaries of benefit plans to be honest and straight-forward when handling employee benefit funds. This requires fiduciaries to disclose the financial activities involved in administering plan funds. *U.S. v. Romano*, 684 F.2d 1057 (2nd Cir. 1982).

774. Who is a recipient for purposes of 18 U.S.C. Section 1954?

In order to demonstrate a violation of 18 U.S.C. Section 1954, the receiver must have served in one of the positions specified in the statute. A person with recipient status must receive, agree to receive, or solicit a thing of value because of, or with the intent to be influenced with respect to any of his actions, decisions, or other duties relating to any question or matter concerning the plan. *U.S. v. Palmeri*, 630 F.2d 192 (3rd Cir. 1980), *cert. denied*, 450 U.S. 967 (1981). A receiver may be in one of the following categories.

Category 1 — Employee Benefit Plan Personnel

This category includes a plan administrator, officer, trustee, custodian, counsel, agent, or employee of an employee welfare benefit plan or employee pension benefit plan. A trustee of a pension plan was convicted for soliciting and accepting kickbacks, fees, and commissions from borrowers of plan assets in order to influence an employee benefit fund. *U.S. v. Pieper*, 854 F.2d 1020 (7th Cir. 1988). An administrator of a jointly-trusteed pension plan was convicted for receiving television sets as gifts for new depositors from a bank, when the administrator directed the deposit of plan money into savings accounts at the bank. *U.S. v. Romano*, 684 F.2d 1027 (2nd Cir. 1982), *cert. denied*, 459 U.S. 1016 (1982). Attorneys who served as general counsel to a pension plan and who trustees consulted at meetings were convicted for soliciting and receiving payments from a prospective borrower in return for obtaining assistance in obtaining a loan from the plan. *U.S. v. Friedland*, 660 F.2d 919 (3rd Cir. 1981).

Category 2 — Personnel of an Employer

This category includes an officer, counsel, agent, or employee of an employer, or an employer who has employees covered by a plan. For example, an employer's employee and a representative of the employer trustees were convicted for receiving compensation from a service provider seeking a contract with the plan. *U.S. v. Fernandez*, 892 F.2d 976 (11th Cir. 1989).

Category 3 — Personnel of an Employee Organization

This category includes an officer, counsel, agent, or employee of an employee organization any of whose members are covered by the plan. The executive director of a union sponsored welfare benefit plan was convicted of soliciting and receiving kickbacks (commissions) from a third party medical laboratory in return for influencing the fund to select the medical laboratory as a service provider. *U.S. v. Wiedyk*, 71 F.3d 602 (6th Cir. 1995). A union president was convicted under 18 U.S.C. Section 1954 for soliciting cash from an employer in exchange for the union president's efforts to not impose a lien on the business of the employer for failing to remit contributions to the plan. *U.S. v. Soures*, 736 F.2d 87 (3rd Cir. 1984). Business agents and employees of the employee organization (union) were convicted for accepting personal bank loans in exchange for their efforts in depositing union benefit plan funds into the bank. *U.S. v. Palmeri*, 630 F.2d 192 (3rd Cir. 1980).

Category 4 — Personnel of Benefit Service Providers

This category includes a person who provides benefit plan services to the plan. It also includes an officer, counsel, agent, or employee of an organization that provides benefit plan services to the plan. An example is a brokerage firm officer who helped a pension plan manager substantially reduce his personal federal income tax liability by selling to the manager highly illiquid bonds, which the manager sold back to the firm one week later at a loss. *U.S. v. Rosenthal*, 9 F.3d 1016 (2nd Cir. 1993). The legislative history makes it clear that 18 U.S.C. Section 1954 applies to, among others, an investment broker who provides services to an employee benefit plan. *U.S. v. Schwimmer*, 700 F. Supp. 104 (E.D. NY 1988); see S. Rep. No. 87-908, 87th Cong., 1st Sess., 11 (1961).

775. Who is a "giver" under 18 U.S.C. Section 1954?

A "giver" is any person who gives, or offers or promises to give, directly or indirectly, a thing of value because of or with the intent to influence a prohibited recipient's actions, decisions or other duties relating to any question or matter concerning the plan. Thus, a giver may be any person, and as such, is not required to hold a position affiliated with the plan. 18 U.S.C. Sec. 1954.

776. Must the "receiver" directly receive a payment to be prosecuted under 18 U.S.C. Section 1954?

No. It is not necessary to prove that a defendant in an action under 18 U.S.C. Section 1954 directly received payment of the fee, kickback, commission, gift, money or thing of value. If the defendant caused someone other than the plan to receive the fee, kickback, commission, gift, money or thing of value, then the defendant has also received a thing of value within the meaning of the statute. In other words, being able to control the disposition of the payment is considered a thing of value. *U.S. v. Robilotto*, 828 F.2d 940 (2nd. Cir. 1987); *U.S. v. Schwartz*, 785 F.2d 673 (9th Cir. 1986); *U.S. v. Romano*, 684 F.2d 1057 (2nd Cir. 1982), *cert denied*, 459 U.S. 1016 (1982) *U.S. v. Palmeri*, 630 F.2d 192 (3rd Cir. 1980), *cert. denied*, 450 U.S. 967 (1981).

777. Must the defendant receive a kickback both "because of" and "with the intent to be influenced" to be convicted under 18 U.S.C. Section 1954?

No. A defendant may be convicted of receiving a kickback (1) "because of" *or* (2) "with intent to be influenced with respect to" any actions or decisions relating to the plan involved. The "because of" language of the statute refers to graft and the "with the intent to be influenced" language refers to bribery. Bribery requires that the payment be the motivating factor for the recipient's actions in relation to a plan matter. 18 U.S.C. Sec. 1954. In contrast, the graft provision does not require that the thing of value paid or received be the primary motivation for the action in connection with a related plan matter. *U.S. v. Friedland*, 660 F.2d 919 (3rd Cir. 1981). 18 U.S.C. Section 1954 provides for punishment for both graft and bribery because Congress was not only concerned with corrupt transactions as indicated with the "intent to influence" language, it also was concerned with fiduciaries of benefit plans taking advantage of their position in any way. As one court explained, "[i]f only corrupt transactions were intended to be covered, Congress would not have added the `because of' clause, but would have limited the statute to those possessing the intent to be influenced." Thus, the broad language of the statute reflects the intent of Congress to reach all fiduciaries who profit as a result of their decisions to invest union funds. *U.S. v. Romano*, 684 F.2d 1057 (2nd Cir. 1982).

778. Must the defendant have the actual ability to control the decisions of a benefit plan to be convicted under 18 U.S.C. Section 1954?

No. Under 18 U.S.C. Section 1954, it is not necessary to prove that a defendant had actual ability to control the decisions of a benefit plan, so long as, because of his status, he had apparent power over decisions regarding the plan. For example, the attorneys who served as the general counsel to a pension plan and whom trustees consulted at meetings and on an ad hoc basis but who had no actual authority over the plan's investments were within the ambit of 18 U.S.C. Section 1954. Thus, it is sufficient that the defendant in a prosecution under 18 U.S.C. Section 1954 was in a position to give evaluation, advice, and recommendation, which though not controlling in the final sense, could have some influence on the operations of a plan. *U.S. v. Pieper*, 854 F.2d 1020 (7th Cir. 1988); *U.S. v. Romano*, 684 F.2d 1057 (2nd Cir. 1982), *cert. denied*, 459 U.S. 1016 (1982); *U.S. v. Palmeri*, 630 F.2d 192 (3rd Cir. 1980), *cert. denied*, 450 U.S. 967 (1981).

779. Must the person who paid the kickback know of the recipient's position with respect to a plan in order to be convicted under 18 U.S.C. Section 1954?

No. The state of mind of the person paying the kickback is irrelevant. Rather than focusing on the knowledge of the "giver," it must be established that the defendant received kickbacks "because of" his status, which gave him at least ostensible authority to exercise influence over the decisions of the plan or select the people who did. To accept a contrary position would "create a loophole in the statute by which illegal acts would become decriminalized through delegations and subterfuge." *U.S. v. Pieper*, 854 F.2d 1020 (7th Cir. 1988). Such a result would fly in the face of Congress' clearly expressed legislative intent "to reach all fiduciaries who profit (other than by regular compensation) as a result of their decisions to invest union pension funds." *U.S. v. Romano*, 684 F.2d 1057 (2nd Cir. 1982); see S. Rep. No. 87-908, 87th Cong., 1st Sess., 4-5, 11 (1961).

780. Is a benefit or lack of injury to the plan a valid defense to a prosecution under 18 U.S.C. Section 1954?

No. It is no defense that a kickback, fee, gift, money or thing of value was solicited, agreed to be received or received by a defendant because of actions or decisions that were themselves lawful, beneficial, or not injurious to a plan. The purpose of 18 U.S.C. Section 1954 is to protect the plan from conflict-of-interest payments that may affect the judgment and integrity of persons who exercise direct or indirect control or influence over the operation of the plan. *U.S. v. Pieper*, 854 F.2d 1020 (7th Cir. 1988); *U.S. v. Soures*, 736 F.2d 87 (3rd Cir. 1984); *U.S. v. Palmeri*, 630 F.2d 192 (3rd Cir. 1980), *cert. denied*, 450 U.S. 967 (1981). 18 U.S.C. Section 1954 is not limited to actual misuse of pension funds. For example, a defendant could be convicted for soliciting payments in exchange for refraining from reimposing a lien. *U.S. v. Soures*, 736 F.2d 87 (3rd Cir. 1984), *cert. denied*, 469 U.S. 1161 (1985).

781. What is a "thing of value" for purposes of 18 U.S.C. Section 1954?

It is unlawful for a person to directly or indirectly give, offer, or promise to give or offer any fee, kickback, commission, gift, loan, money, or thing of value to an administrator, officer, trustee, custodian, counsel, agent, or employee of an employee pension plan. 18 U.S.C. Sec. 1954. A "thing of value" is not limited to tangible items with identifiable commercial value, but may include certain intangibles as well, such as providing assistance in arranging for a merger of unions and other services. *U.S. v. Schwartz*, 785 F.2d 673 (9th Cir. 1986), *cert. denied*, 479 U.S. 890 (1986); see also, *U.S. v. Robilotto*, 828 F.2d 940 (2nd Cir. 1987), *cert. denied*, 484 U.S. 1011 (1988). In addition, the "thing of value" need not be illegal itself for the transaction to violate 18 U.S.C. Section 1954. Television sets given away by a bank in return for opening accounts on behalf of pension funds constituted a prohibited "thing of value." *U.S. v. Romano*, 684 F.2d 1057 (2nd Cir. 1982), *cert. denied*, 459 U.S. 1016 (1982). An item is characterized as a "thing of value" if the recipient believed that the item had value, such as when worthless shares of stock nonetheless were considered a "thing of value" because the recipient expected the shares to have substantial worth. *U.S. v. Rosenthal*, 9 F.3d 1016 (2nd Cir. 1993), *cert. denied*, 464 U.S. 1007 (1993). The opportunity to purchase stock warrants was also held to be a "thing of value." *U.S. v. Ostrander*, 999 F.2d 27 (2nd Cir. 1993).

782. What payments are not prohibited under 18 U.S.C. Section 1954?

The payment to or acceptance by a person of a bona fide salary, compensation, or other payments made for goods or facilities actually furnished or for services actually performed in the regular course of one's duties is permitted. 18 U.S.C. Sec. 1954.

783. How is "bona fide" defined for purposes of 18 U.S.C. Section 1954?

18 U.S.C. Section 1954, which prohibits the receipt of fees to influence employee benefit plan operations, contains an exception allowing bona fide salary, compensation, or other payments made for goods or facilities actually furnished or for services actually performed. The term "bona fide" is not restricted to any technical meaning but is used in the statute according to its common and ordinary meaning, which is synonymous with (1) in good faith, (2) without dishonesty, fraud, or deceit, (3) genuine or authentic, and (4) without subterfuge. "Bona fide" is defined as "in good faith, exclusive of fraud or deceit." It contemplates proof of a subjective element that the payment or compensation was given or received in good faith. For example, one who receives a commission from a financial institution for placing employee benefit plan funds, without disclosing to the plan the actual commissions received, is not acting in good faith. Thus, a reasonable construction of bona fide is to require disclosure. *U.S. v. Schwimmer*, 700 F. Supp. 104 (E.D. NY 1988). In order for beneficiaries to decide whether compensation paid to a fiduciary who handles the investment of union funds is bona fide, the beneficiaries must be told the amount of the compensation. It would be wholly inconsistent with ERISA if a fiduciary could unilaterally decide for himself what is bona fide compensation. This is a decision reserved for the plan beneficiaries.

The phrase "bona fide" also contemplates proof of an objective element that the compensation or payments be received for services actually performed (or for goods actually delivered) in the regular course of the recipient's duties. Thus, if a defendant agreed to receive or received salary, compensation, or other payments that he knew were not for services actually performed, or within the regular course of his duties, then the payments are not "bona fide" and do not fall within the exception to the statute. With respect to the term "regular course of duties," the solicitation, agreement to receive, or receipt of compensation, salary or other payments must comport with the defendant's obligations of his position to the employee benefit plan. *U.S. v. Soures*, 736 F.2d 87 (3rd Cir. 1984).

In addition, subject to the limitations of ERISA Section 408(d), ERISA Section 408(b)(2) exempts from the prohibited transaction provisions of ERISA Section 406(a) any contract or reasonable arrangement with a party in interest, including a fiduciary, for office space or legal, accounting, or other services necessary for the establishment or operation of a plan, if no more than reasonable compensation is paid. Regulations clarify the terms "necessary service," "reasonable contract or arrangement," and "reasonable compensation" as used in ERISA Section 408(b)(2). Labor Reg. §2550.408b-2. What constitutes a "necessary service" in a particular case, however, can only be resolved by taking into account the relevant facts and circumstances. Thus, the fiduciaries of a plan must review all services provided to determine whether the services are "necessary services" for which payment would be lawful.

784. Do the criminal provisions of ERISA supersede local criminal laws?

No. ERISA does not supersede generally applicable local criminal laws. ERISA exempts generally applicable criminal laws of a state from the scope of ERISA's preemption. ERISA Sec. 514(b)(4). With this exception for state criminal laws, it is irrelevant as to whether a plan is an ERISA covered plan or if the funds misappropriated are "plan assets" under ERISA. Therefore, a criminal proceeding under state theft statutes may apply with respect to misappropriation of employee benefit funds.

MODEL NOTICES

HIPAA MODEL NOTICE

IMPORTANT NOTICE OF YOUR RIGHT TO DOCUMENTATION OF HEALTH COVERAGE

Recent changes in Federal law may affect your health coverage if you are enrolled or become eligible to enroll in health coverage that excludes coverage for preexisting medical conditions.

The Health Insurance Portability and Accountability Act of 1996 (HIPAA) limits the circumstances under which coverage may be excluded for medical conditions present before you enroll. Under the law, a preexisting condition exclusion generally may not be imposed for more than 12 months (18 months for a late enrollee). The 12-month (or 18-month) exclusion period is reduced by your prior health coverage. You are entitled to a certificate that will show evidence of your prior health coverage. If you buy health insurance other than through an employer group health plan, a certificate of prior coverage may help you obtain coverage without a preexisting condition exclusion. Contact your State insurance department for further information.

For employer group health plans, these changes generally take effect at the beginning of the first plan year starting after June 30, 1997. For example, if your employer's plan year begins on January 1, 1998, the plan is not required to give you credit for your prior coverage until January 1, 1998.

You have the right to receive a certificate of prior health coverage since July 1, 1996. You may need to provide other documentation for earlier periods of health care coverage. Check with your new plan administrator to see if your new plan excludes coverage for preexisting conditions and if you need to provide a certificate or other documentation of your previous coverage.

To get a certificate, complete the attached form and return it to:

    Entity:
    Address:
    For additional information contact:

The certificate must be provided to you promptly. Keep a copy of this completed form. You may also request certificates for any of your dependents (including your spouse) who were enrolled under your health coverage.

****

REQUEST FOR CERTIFICATE OF HEALTH COVERAGE

Name of Participant: _____ Date: _____

Address: _____

Telephone Number: _____

Name and relationship of any dependents for whom certificate are requested (and their address if different from above):

_____

_____

INFORMATION ON CATEGORIES OF BENEFITS

1. Date of original certificate: _____

2. Name of group health plan providing the coverage:

   _____

3. Name of participant: _____

4. Identification number of participant: _____

5. Name of individual(s) to whom this information applies:

   _____

6. The following information applies to the coverage in the certificate that was provided to the individual(s) identified above:

   a. MENTAL HEALTH: _____

   b. SUBSTANCE ABUSE TREATMENT: _____

   c. PRESCRIPTION DRUGS: _____

   d. DENTAL CARE: _____

   e. VISION CARE: _____

For each category above, enter "N/A" if the individual had no coverage within the category and either (i) enter both the date that the individual's coverage within the category began and the date that the individual's coverage within the category ended (or indicate if continuing), or (ii) enter "same" on the line if the beginning and ending dates for coverage within the category are the same as the beginning and ending dates for the coverage in the certificate.

HIPAA MODEL CERTIFICATE

CERTIFICATE OF GROUP HEALTH PLAN COVERAGE

*IMPORTANT - This certificate provides evidence of your prior health coverage. You may need to furnish this certificate if you become eligible under a group health plan that excludes coverage for certain medical conditions that you have before you enroll. This certificate may need to be provided if medical advice, diagnosis, care, or treatment was recommended or received for the condition within the 6-month period prior to your enrollment in the new plan. If you become covered under another group health plan, check with the plan administrator to see if you need to provide this certificate. You may also need this certificate to buy, for yourself or your family, an insurance policy that does not exclude coverage for medical conditions that are present before you enroll.

1. Date of this certificate: _____

2. Name of group health plan: _____

3. Name of participant: _____

4. Identification number of participant: _____

5. Name of any dependents to whom this certificate applies:

    _____

6. Name, address, and telephone number of plan administrator or issuer responsible for providing this certificate:

    _____

    _____

    _____

7. For further information, call: _____

8. If the individual(s) identified in line 3 and line 5 has at least 18 months of creditable coverage (disregarding periods of coverage before a 63-day break), check here _____ and skip lines 9 and 10.

9. Date waiting period or affiliation period (if any) began: _____

10. Date coverage began: _____

11. Date coverage ended: _____ (or check if coverage is continuing as of the date of this certificate: _____).

Note: Separate certificates will be furnished if information is not identical for the participant and each beneficiary.

MODEL DESCRIPTION

If you are declining enrollment for yourself or your dependents (including your spouse) because of other health insurance coverage, you may in the future be able to enroll yourself or your dependents in this plan, provided that you request enrollment within 30 days after your other coverage ends. In addition, if you have a new dependent as a result of marriage, birth, adoption, or placement for adoption, you may be able to enroll yourself and your dependents, provided that you request enrollment within 30 days after the marriage, birth adoption, or placement for adoption.

MODEL PARTICIPANT NOTICE

Model Participant Notice

The Retirement Protection Act of 1994 requires certain underfunded plans to notify participants and beneficiaries annually of the plan's funding status and the limits of PBGC's guarantee. (See Section 4011 of ERISA and 29 CFR Part 4011.) The regulation includes a model notice that plans can use to meet this requirement.

For the convenience of plan administrators, this Technical Update republishes the Model Participant Notice, updated to reflect the 2000 maximum guaranteed benefits.

Participant Notice Worksheet

This Technical Update also includes a worksheet to help plan administrators determine whether they must issue a Participant Notice. Generally, the requirement to issue a Participant Notice applies to the plan administrator of any single-employer plan that pays a variable rate premium for the plan year. However, no notice is required if the plan meets certain funding requirements for the plan year, as explained in the worksheet.

Due Dates

The Participant Notice is due two months after the due date (including extensions) for the previous year's Form 5500. The following table shows the common filing due dates for calendar year plans:

Form 5500	Participant Notice
July 31, 20xx	October 1, 20xx
September 15, 20xx	November 15, 20xx
October 15, 20xx	December 15, 20xx

(Due dates that fall on a weekend or Federal holiday are extended to the next business day.)

Model Participant Notice

The following is an example of a Participant Notice that satisfies the requirements of section 4011.10 when the required information is filled in.

Notice to Participants of [Plan Name]

The law requires that you receive information on the funding level of your defined benefit pension plan and the benefits guaranteed by the Pension Benefit Guaranty Corporation (PBGC), a federal insurance agency.

YOUR PLAN'S FUNDING

As of [DATE], your plan had [INSERT NOTICE FUNDING PERCENTAGE DETERMINED IN ACCORDANCE WITH SECTION 4011.10(c)] percent of the money needed to pay benefits promised to employees and retirees.

To pay pension benefits, your employer is required to contribute money to the pension plan over a period of years. A plan's funding percentage does not take into consideration the financial strength of the employer. Your employer, by law, must pay for all pension benefits, but your benefits may be at risk if your employer faces a severe financial crisis or is in bankruptcy.

[INCLUDE THE FOLLOWING PARAGRAPH ONLY IF, FOR ANY OF THE PREVIOUS FIVE PLAN YEARS, THE PLAN HAS BEEN GRANTED AND HAS NOT FULLY REPAID A FUNDING WAIVER.]

Your plan received a funding waiver for [LIST ANY OF THE FIVE PREVIOUS PLAN YEARS FOR WHICH A FUNDING WAIVER WAS GRANTED AND HAS NOT BEEN FULLY REPAID]. If a company is experiencing temporary financial hardship, the Internal Revenue Service may grant a funding waiver that permits the company to delay contributions that fund the pension plan.

[INCLUDE THE FOLLOWING WITH RESPECT TO ANY UNPAID OR LATE PAYMENT THAT MUST BE DISCLOSED UNDER SECTION 4011.10(b)(6):]

Your plan was required to receive a payment from the employer on [LIST APPLICABLE DUE DATE(S)]. That payment [has not been made] [was made on [LIST APPLICABLE PAYMENT DATE(S)]].

PBGC GUARANTEES

When a pension plan ends without enough money to pay all benefits, the PBGC steps in to pay pension benefits. The PBGC pays most people all pension benefits, but some people may lose certain benefits that are not guaranteed.

The PBGC pays pension benefits up to certain maximum limits.

- The maximum guaranteed benefit is $3,221.59 per month or $38,659.08 per year for a 65-year-old person in a plan that terminates in 2000.

- The maximum benefit may be reduced for an individual who is younger than age 65. For example, it is $1,449.72 per month or $17,396.64 per year for an individual who starts receiving benefits at age 55.

  [IN LIEU OF AGE 55, YOU MAY ADD OR SUBSTITUTE ANY AGE(S) RELEVANT UNDER THE PLAN. FOR EXAMPLE, YOU MAY ADD OR SUBSTITUTE THE MAXIMUM BENEFIT FOR AGES 62 OR 60. THE MAXIMUM BENEFIT IS $2,545.06 PER MONTH OR $30,540.72 PER YEAR AT AGE 62; IT IS $2,094.03 PER MONTH OR $25,128.36 PER YEAR AT AGE 60. IF THE PLAN PROVIDES FOR NORMAL RETIREMENT BEFORE AGE 65, YOU MUST INCLUDE THE NORMAL RETIREMENT AGE.]

  [IF THE PLAN DOES NOT PROVIDE FOR COMMENCEMENT OF BENEFITS BEFORE AGE 65, YOU MAY OMIT THIS PARAGRAPH.]

- The maximum benefit will also be reduced when a benefit is provided for a survivor.

The PBGC does not guarantee certain types of benefits. [INCLUDE THE FOLLOWING GUARANTEE LIMITS THAT APPLY TO THE BENEFITS AVAILABLE UNDER YOUR PLAN.]

- The PBGC does not guarantee benefits for which you do not have a vested right when a plan ends, usually because you have not worked enough years for the company.

- The PBGC does not guarantee benefits for which you have not met all age, service, or other requirements at the time the plan ends.

- Benefit increases and new benefits that have been in place for less than a year are not guaranteed. Those that have been in place for less than 5 years are only partly guaranteed.

2002 ERISA Facts

- Early retirement payments that are greater than payments at normal retirement age may not be guaranteed. For example, a supplemental benefit that stops when you become eligible for Social Security may not be guaranteed.

- Benefits other than pension benefits, such as health insurance, life insurance, death benefits, vacation pay, or severance pay, are not guaranteed.

- The PBGC generally does not pay lump sums exceeding $5,000.

WHERE TO GET MORE INFORMATION

Your plan, [EIN-PN], is sponsored by [CONTRIBUTING SPONSOR(S)]. If you would like more information about the funding of your plan, contact [INSERT NAME, TITLE, BUSINESS ADDRESS AND PHONE NUMBER OF INDIVIDUAL OR ENTITY].

For more information about the PBGC and the benefits it guarantees, you may request a free copy of "Your Guaranteed Pension" by writing to Consumer Information Center, Dept. YGP, Pueblo, Colorado 81009. [THE FOLLOWING SENTENCE MAY BE INCLUDED:] "Your Guaranteed Pension" is also available from the PBGC Homepage on the World Wide Web at http://www.pbgc.gov/ygp.htp.

Issued: [INSERT AT LEAST MONTH AND YEAR]

NATIONAL MEDICAL SUPPORT NOTICE

Part A

Notice to Withhold for Health Care Coverage

This Notice is issued under section 466(a)(19) of the Social Security Act, section 609(a)(5)(C) of the Employee Retirement Income Security Act of 1974 (ERISA), and for State and local government and church plans, sections 401(e) and (f) of the Child Support Performance and Incentive Act of 1998.

Issuing Agency: _____	Court or Administrative Authority: _____
Issuing Agency Address: _____	Date of Support Order: _____
_____	Support Order Number: _____
Date of Notice: _____	
Case Number: _____	
Telephone Number: _____	
FAX Number: _____	

_____)   RE: _____
Employer/Withholder's Federal EIN Number   Employee's Name (Last, First, MI)

_____)
Employer/Withholder's Name   Employee's Social Security Number

_____)
Employer/Withholder's Address   Employee's Mailing Address

_____)
Custodial Parent's Name (Last, First, MI)

_____)
Custodial Parent's Mailing Address   Substituted Official/Agency Name and Address

_____)
Child(ren)'s Mailing Address
(if different from Custodial Parent's)
_____)
_____)
_____)
Name, Mailing Address, and Telephone
Number of a Representative of the Child(ren)

Child(ren)'s Name(s)	DOB	SSN	Child(ren)'s Name(s)	DOB	SSN
_____	___	___	_____	___	___
_____	___	___	_____	___	___

The order requires the child(ren) to be enrolled in [ ] any health coverages available; or [ ] only the following coverage(s): __Medical; __Dental; __Vision; __Prescription drug; __Mental health; __Other (specify): __

THE PAPERWORK REDUCTION ACT OF 1995 (P.L. 104-13) Public reporting burden for this collection of information is estimated to average 10 minutes per response, including the time reviewing instructions, gathering and maintaining the data needed, and reviewing the collection of information. An agency may not conduct or sponsor, and a person is not required to respond to, a collection of information unless it displays a currently valid OMB control number. OMB control number: 0970-0222 Expiration Date: 12/31/2003.

Employer Response

If either 1, 2, or 3 below applies, check the appropriate box and return this Part A to the Issuing Agency within 20 business days after the date of the Notice, or sooner if reasonable. NO OTHER ACTION IS NECESSARY. If neither 1, 2, nor 3 applies, forward Part B to the appropriate plan administrator(s) within 20 business days after the date of the Notice, or sooner if reasonable. Check number 4 and return this Part A to the Issuing Agency if the Plan Administrator informs you that the child(ren) is/are enrolled in an option under the plan for which you have determined that the employee contribution exceeds the amount that may be withheld from the employee's income due to State or Federal withholding limitations and/or prioritization.

❑ 1. Employer does not maintain or contribute to plans providing dependent or family health care coverage.

❑ 2. The employee is among a class of employees (for example, part-time or non-union) that are not eligible for family health coverage under any group health plan maintained by the employer or to which the employer contributes.

❑ 3. Health care coverage is not available because employee is no longer employed by the employer:

Date of termination: _____

Last known address: _____

Last known telephone number: _____

New employer (if known): _____

New employer address: _____

New employer telephone number: _____

❑ 4. State or Federal withholding limitations and/or prioritization prevent the withholding from the employee's income of the amount required to obtain coverage under the terms of the plan.

Employer Representative:

Name: _____ Telephone Number: _____

Title: _____ Date: _____

EIN (if not provided by Issuing Agency on Notice to Withhold for Health Care Coverage): _____

Instructions to Employer

This document serves as notice that the employee identified on this National Medical Support Notice is obligated by a court or administrative child support order to provide health care coverage for the child(ren) identified on this Notice. This National Medical Support Notice replaces any Medical Support Notice that the Issuing Agency has previously served on you with respect to the employee and the children listed on this Notice.

The document consists of **Part A - Notice to Withhold for Health Care Coverage** for the employer to withhold any employee contributions required by the group health plan(s) in which the child(ren) is/are enrolled; and **Part B - Medical Support Notice to the Plan Administrator,** which must be forwarded to the administrator of each group health plan identified by the employer to enroll the eligible child(ren).

EMPLOYER RESPONSIBILITIES

1. If the individual named above is not your employee, or if family health care coverage is not available, please complete item 1, 2, or 3 of the Employer Response as appropriate, and return it to the Issuing Agency. NO FURTHER ACTION IS NECESSARY.

2. If family health care coverage is available for which the child(ren) identified above may be eligible, you are required to:

    a. Transfer, not later than 20 business days after the date of this Notice, a copy of **Part B - Medical Support Notice to the Plan Administrator** to the administrator of each appropriate group health plan for which the child(ren) may be eligible, and

    b. Upon notification from the plan administrator(s) that the child(ren) is/are enrolled, either

        1) withhold from the employee's income any employee contributions required under each group health plan, in accordance with the applicable law of the employee's principal place of employment and transfer employee contributions to the appropriate plan(s), or

        2) complete item 4 of the Employer Response to notify the Issuing Agency that enrollment cannot be completed because of prioritization or limitations on withholding.

    c. If the plan administrator notifies you that the employee is subject to a waiting period that expires more than 90 days from the date of its receipt of **Part B of** this Notice, or whose duration is determined by a measure other than the passage of time (for example, the completion of a certain number of hours worked), notify the plan administrator when the employee is eligible to enroll in the plan and that this Notice requires the enrollment of the child(ren) named in the Notice in the plan.

LIMITATIONS ON WITHHOLDING

The total amount withheld for both cash and medical support cannot exceed ___% of the employee's aggregate disposable weekly earnings. The employer may not withhold more under this National Medical Support Notice than the lesser of:

1. The amounts allowed by the Federal Consumer Credit Protection Act (15 U.S.C., section 1673(b));

2. The amounts allowed by the State of the employee's principal place of employment; or

3. The amounts allowed for health insurance premiums by the child support order, as indicated here: _____

The Federal limit applies to the aggregate disposable weekly earnings (ADWE). ADWE is the net income left after making mandatory deductions such as State, Federal, local taxes; Social Security taxes; and Medicare taxes.

PRIORITY OF WITHHOLDING

If withholding is required for employee contributions to one or more plans under this notice and for a support obligation under a separate notice and available funds are insufficient for withholding for both cash and medical support contributions, the employer must withhold amounts for purposes of cash support and medical support contributions in accordance with the law, if any, of the State of the employee's principal place of employment requiring prioritization between cash and medical support, as described here: _____

_____

DURATION OF WITHHOLDING

The child(ren) shall be treated as dependents under the terms of the plan. Coverage of a child as a dependent will end when similarly situated dependents are no longer eligible for coverage under the terms of the plan. However, the continuation coverage provisions of ERISA may entitle the child to continuation coverage under the plan. The employer must continue to withhold employee contributions and may not disenroll (or eliminate coverage for) the child(ren) unless:

    1.   The employer is provided satisfactory written evidence that:

        a. The court or administrative child support order referred to above is not longer in effect; or

        b. The child(ren) is or will be enrolled in comparable coverage which will take effect no later than the effective date of disenrollment from the plan; or

    2.   The employer eliminates family health coverage for all of its employees.

POSSIBLE SANCTIONS

An employer may be subject to sanctions or penalties imposed under State law and/or ERISA for discharging an employee from employment, refusing to employ, or taking disciplinary action against any employee because of medical child support withholding, or for failing to withhold income, or transmit such withheld amounts to the applicable plan(s) as the Notice directs.

NOTICE OF TERMINATION OF EMPLOYMENT

In any case in which the above employee's employment terminates, the employer must promptly notify the Issuing Agency listed above of such termination. This requirement may be satisfied by sending to the Issuing Agency a copy of any notice the employer is required to provide under the continuation coverage provisions of ERISA or the Health Insurance Portability and Accountability Act.

EMPLOYEE LIABILITY FOR CONTRIBUTION TO PLAN

The employee is liable for any employee contributions that are required under the plan(s) for enrollment of the child(ren) and is subject to appropriate enforcement. The employee may contest the withholding under this Notice based on a mistake of fact (such as the identity of the obligor). Should an employee contest the withholding under this Notice, the employer must proceed to comply with the employer responsibilities in this Notice until notified by the Issuing Agency to discontinue withholding. To contest the withholding under this Notice, the employee should contact the Issuing Agency at the address and telephone number listed on the Notice. With respect to plans subject to ERISA, it is the view of the Department of Labor that Federal Courts have jurisdiction if the employee challenges a determination that the Notice constitutes a Qualified Medical Child Support Order.

CONTACT FOR QUESTIONS

If you have any questions regarding this Notice, you may contract the Issuing Agency at the address and telephone number listed above.

NATIONAL MEDICAL SUPPORT NOTICE

Part B

Medical Support Notice to Plan Administrator

This Notice is issued under section 466(a)(19) of the Social Security Act, section 609(a)(5)(C) of the Employee Retirement Income Security Act of 1974, and for State and local government and church plans, sections 401(e) and (f) of the Child Support Performance and Incentive Act of 1998. Receipt of this Notice from the Issuing Agency constitutes receipt of a Medical Child Support Order under applicable law. The rights of the parties and the duties of the plan administrator under this Notice are in addition to the existing rights and duties established under such law.

Issuing Agency: _____

Issuing Agency Address: _____

_____

Date of Notice: _____

Case Number: _____

Telephone Number: _____

FAX Number: _____

Court or Administrative Authority: _____

Date of Support Order: _____

Support Order Number: _____

_____) RE: _____
Employer/Withholder's Federal EIN Number   Employee's Name (Last, First, MI)

_____)   _____
Employer/Withholder's Name   Employee's Social Security Number

_____)   _____
Employer/Withholder's Address   Employee's Mailing Address

_____)
Custodial Parent's Name (Last, First, MI)

_____)
Custodial Parent's Mailing Address   Substituted Official/Agency Name and Address

_____)
Child(ren)'s Mailing Address
(if different from Custodial Parent's)

_____)
_____)
_____)
Name, Mailing Address, and Telephone
Number of a Representative of the Child(ren)

Child(ren)'s Name(s)	DOB	SSN	Child(ren)'s Name(s)	DOB	SSN
_____	____	____	_____	____	____
_____	____	____	_____	____	____

The order requires the child(ren) to be enrolled in [ ] any health coverages available; or [ ] only the following coverage(s): __Medical; __Dental; __Vision; __Prescription drug; __Mental health; __Other (specify): __

2002 ERISA Facts

Plan Administrator Response

(To be completed and returned to the Issuing Agency within 40 business days after the date of the Notice, or sooner if reasonable)

This Notice was received by the plan administrator on _____.

❏ 1. This Notice was determined to be a "qualified medical child support order," on _____. Complete **Response 2 or 3, and 4,** if applicable.

❏ 2. The participant (employee) and alternate recipient(s) (child(ren)) are to be enrolled in the following family coverage.

    a.   The child(ren) is/are currently enrolled in the plan as a dependent of the participant.

    b.   There is only one type of coverage provided under the plan. The child(ren) is/are included as dependents of the participant under the plan.

    c.   The participant is enrolled in an option that is providing dependent coverage and the child(ren) will be enrolled in the same option.

    d.   The participant is enrolled in an option that permits dependent coverage that has not been elected; dependent coverage will be provided.

Coverage is effective as of __/__/____ (includes waiting period of less than 90 days from date of receipt of this Notice). The child(ren) has/have been enrolled in the following option: _____. Any necessary withholding should commence if the employer determines that it is permitted under State and Federal withholding and/or prioritization limitations.

❏ 3. There is more than one option available under the plan the and participant is not enrolled. The Issuing Agency must select from the available options. Each child is to be included as a dependent under one of the available options that provide family coverage. If the Issuing Agency does not reply within 20 business days of the date this Response is returned, the child(ren), and the participant if necessary, will be enrolled in the plan's default option, if any: _____.

❏ 4. The participant is subject to a waiting period that expires __/__/____ (more than 90 days from the date of receipt of this Notice), or has not completed a waiting period which is determined by some measure other than the passage of time, such as the completion of a certain number of hours worked (describe here: _____). At the completion of the waiting period, the plan administrator will process the enrollment.

❏ 5. This Notice does not constitute a "qualified medical child support order" because:

    ❏ The name of the ❏ child(ren) or ❏ participant is unavailable.

    ❏ The mailing address of the ❏ child(ren) (or a substituted official) or ❏ participant is unavailable.

    ❏ The following child(ren) is/are at or above the age at which dependents are no longer eligible for coverage under the plan _____ (insert name(s) of child(ren)).

Plan Administrator or Representative:

Name: _____ Telephone Number: _____

Title: _____ Date: _____

Address: _____

Instructions to Plan Administrator

This Notice has been forwarded from the employer identified above to you as the plan administrator of a group health plan maintained by the employer (or a group health plan to which the employer contributes) and in which the noncustodial parent/participant identified above is enrolled or is eligible for enrollment.

This Notice serves to inform you that the noncustodial parent/participant is obligated by an order issued by the court or agency identified above to provide health care coverage for the child(ren) under the group health plan(s) as described on **Part B**.

(A) If the participant and child(ren) and their mailing addresses (or that of a Substituted Official or Agency) are identified above, and if coverage for the child(ren) is or ill become available, this Notice constitutes a "qualified medical child support order" (QMCSO) under ERISA or CSPIA, as applicable. (If any mailing address is not present, but it is reasonable accessible, this Notice will not fail to be a QMCSO on that basis.) You must, within 40 business days of the date of this Notice, or sooner if reasonable:

    (1)   Complete Part B - Plan Administrator Response - and send it to the Issuing Agency;

    (a)   if you checked Response 2:

        (i) notify the noncustodial parent/participant named above, each named child, and the custodial parent that coverage of the child(ren) is or will become available (notification of the custodial parent will be deemed notification of the child(ren) if they reside at the same address);

        (ii) furnish the custodial parent a description of the coverage available and the effective date of the coverage, including, if not already provided, a summary plan description and any forms, documents, or information necessary to effectuate such coverage, as well as information necessary to submit claims for benefits;

    (b)   if you checked Response 3:

        (i) if you have not already done so, provide to the Issuing Agency copies of applicable summary plan descriptions or other documents that describe available coverage including the additional participant contribution necessary to obtain coverage for the child(ren) under each option and whether there is a limited service area for any option;

        (ii) if the plan has a default option, you are to enroll the child(ren) in the default option if you have not received an election from the Issuing Agency within 20 business days of the date you returned the Response. If the plan does not have a default option, you are to enroll the child(ren) in the option selected by the Issuing Agency.

    (c)   if the participant is subject to a waiting period that expires more than 90 days from the date of receipt of this Notice, or has not completed a waiting period whose duration is determined by a measure other than the passage of time (for example, the completion of a certain number of hours worked), complete Response 4 on the Plan Administrator Response and return to the employer and the Issuing Agency, and notify the participant and the custodial parent; and upon satisfaction of the period or requirement, complete enrollment under Response 2 or 3, and

    (d)   upon completion of the enrollment, transfer the applicable information on Part B - Plan Administrator Response to the employer for a determination that the necessary employee contributions are available. Inform the employer that the enrollment is pursuant to a National Medical Support Notice.

(B) If within 40 business days of the date of this Notice, or sooner if reasonable, you determine that this Notice does not constitute a QMCSO, you must complete Response 5 of Part B - Plan Administrator Response and send it to the Issuing Agency, and inform the noncustodial parent/participant, custodial parent, and child(ren) of the specific reasons for your determination.

(C) Any required notification of the custodial parent, child(ren) and/or participant that is required may be satisfied by sending the party a copy of the Plan Administrator Response, if appropriate.

UNLAWFUL REFUSAL TO ENROLL

Enrollment of a child may not be denied on the ground that: (1) the child was born out of wedlock; (2) the child is not claimed as a dependent on the participant's Federal income tax return; (3) the child does not reside with the participant or in the plan's service area; or (4) because the child is receiving benefits or is eligible to receive benefits under the State Medicaid plan. If the plan requires that the participant be enrolled in order for the child(ren) to be enrolled, and the participant is not currently enrolled, you must enroll both the participant and the child(ren). All enrollments are to be made without regard to open season restrictions.

PAYMENT OF CLAIMS

A child covered by a QMCSO, or the child's custodial parent, legal guardian, or the provider of services to the child, or a State agency to the extent assigned the child's rights, may file claims and the plan shall make payment for covered benefits or reimbursement directly to such party.

PERIOD OF COVERAGE

The alternate recipient(s) shall be treated as dependents under the terms of the plan. Coverage of an alternate recipient as a dependent will end when similarly situated dependents are not longer eligible for coverage under the terms of the plan. However, the continuation coverage provisions of ERISA or other applicable law may entitle the alternate recipient to continue coverage under the plan. Once a child is enrolled in the plan as directed above, the alternate recipient may not be disenrolled unless:

(1) The plan administrator is provided satisfactory written evidence that either:

(a) the court or administrative child support order referred to above is not longer in effect, or

(b) the alternate recipient is or will be enrolled in comparable coverage which will take effect no later than the effective date of disenrollment from the plan;

(2) The employer eliminates family health coverage for all of its employees; or

(3) Any available continuation coverage is not elected, or the period of such coverage expires.

CONTACT FOR QUESTIONS

If you have any questions regarding this Notice, you may contact the Issuing Agency at the address and telephone number listed above.

Paperwork Reduction Act Notice

The Issuing Agency asks for the information on this form to carry out the law as specified in the Employee Retirement Income Security Act or the Child Support Performance and Incentive Act, as applicable. You are required to give the Issuing Agency the information. You are not required to respond to this collection of information unless it displays a currently valid OMB control number. The Issuing Agency needs the information to determine whether health care coverage is provided in accordance with the underlying child support order. The Average time needed to complete and file the form is estimated below. These times will vary depending on the individual circumstances.

	Learning about the law of the form	....	Preparing the form
First Notice	1 hr.___		1 hr., 45 min.
Subsequent Notices	——		35 min.

VFC PROGRAM CHECKLIST AND SAMPLE VFC PROGRAM NO ACTION LETTER

The checklist and sample VFC Program No Action letter are taken from Appendices B and A, respectively, of the notice announcing the adoption of the permanent Voluntary Fiduciary Correction Program (VFC), which allows plan officials to identify and correct certain prohibited transactions through pre-approved correction methods. The DOL advises that it will take no corrective action against eligible parties who use the VFC program and are able to document their correction of the specified transaction.

CHECKLIST

Use this checklist to ensure that you are submitting a complete application. The applicant must sign and date the checklist and include it with the application. Indicate "Yes," "No," or "N/A" next to each item. A "No" answer or the failure to include a completed checklist will delay review of the application until all required items are received.

❑   1.   Have you reviewed the eligibility, definitions, transaction and correction, and documentation sections of the VFC Program?

❑   2.   Have you included the name, address and telephone number of a contact person familiar with the contents of the application?

❑   3.   Have you provided the EIN # and address of the plan sponsor and plan administrator?

❑   4.   Have you provided the date that the most recent Form 5500 was filed by the plan?

❑   5.   Have you enclosed a signed and dated certification under penalty of perjury for each applicant and the applicant's representative, if any?

❑   6.   Have you enclosed relevant portions of the plan document, and any other pertinent documents (such as the adoption agreement, trust agreement, or insurance contract) with the relevant sections identified?

❑   7.   Have you enclosed a statement identifying the current fidelity bond for the plan?

❑   8.   Where applicable, have you enclosed a copy of an appraiser's report?

❑ 9.   Have you enclosed other documents as specified by the individual transactions and corrections?

❑   a.   a detailed narrative of the Breach, including the date it occurred;

❑   b.   documentation that supports the narrative description of the transaction;

❑   c.   an explanation of how the Breach was corrected, by whom and when, with supporting documentation;

❑   d.   a list of all persons materially involved in the Breach and its correction (e.g., fiduciaries, service providers, borrowers, lenders);

❑   e.   documentation establishing the return on the plan's other investments during the time period the plan engaged in the transaction described in the VFC Program application;

❑   f.   specific calculations demonstrating how Principal Amount and Lost Earnings or Restoration of Profits were computed; and

❑   g.   proof of payment of Principal Amount and Lost Earnings or Restoration of Profits.

❑ 10.   If you are an eligible applicant and wish to avail yourself of excise tax relief under the Proposed Class Exemption, have you made proper arrangements to provide within 60 calendar days following the date of this application a copy of the Class Exemption's required notice to all interested persons and to the PWBA regional office to which the application is filed?

❑ 11.   Where applicable, have you enclosed a description demonstrating proof of payment to participants and beneficiaries whose current location is known to the plan and/or applicant, and for participants who need to be located, have you described how adequate funds have been segregated to pay missing participants and commenced the process of locating the missing participants using either the IRS and Social Security Administration locator services, or other comparable means?

❑ 12.   Has the plan implemented measures to ensure that the transactions specified in the application do not recur? (Do not include this with the application. The Department will not opine on the adequacy of these measures.)

Applicant (Plan Official)
Address

Dear Applicant (Plan Official):

Re: VFC Program Application No. xx-xxxxxx

The Department of Labor, Pension and Welfare Benefits Administration (PWBA), has responsibility for administration and enforcement of Title I of the Employee Retirement Income Security Act of 1974, as amended (ERISA). PWBA has established a Voluntary Fiduciary Correction Program to encourage the correction of breaches of fiduciary responsibility and the restoration of losses to the plan participants and beneficiaries.

In accordance with the requirements of the VFC Program, you have identified the following transactions as breaches, or potential breaches, of Part 4 of Title I of ERISA, and you have submitted documentation to PWBA that demonstrates that you have taken the corrective action indicated.

[The letter briefly recaps the violation and correction. Example: Failure to deposit participant contributions to the XYZ Corp. 401(k) plan within the time frames required by ERISA, from (date) to (date). All participant contributions were deposited by (date) and lost earnings on the delinquent contributions were deposited and allocated to participants' plan accounts on (date).]

Because you have taken the above-described corrective action, which is consistent with the requirements of the VFC Program, PWBA will take no civil enforcement action against you with respect to this breach. Specifically, PWBA will not recommend that the Solicitor of Labor initiate legal action against you, and PWBA will not impose the penalty in section 502(l) of ERISA on the amount you have repaid to the plan.

PWBA's decision to take no further action is conditioned on the completeness and accuracy of the representations made in your application. You should note that this decision will not preclude PWBA from conducting an investigation of any potential violations of criminal law in connection with the transaction identified in the application or investigating the transaction identified in the application with a view toward seeking appropriate relief from any other person. [If the transaction is a prohibited transaction, the following language also appears: Please also be advised that pursuant to section 3003(c) of ERISA, 29 U.S.C. section 1203(c), the Secretary of Labor is required to transmit to the Secretary of the Treasury information indicating that a prohibited transaction has occurred. Accordingly, this matter will be referred to the Internal Revenue Service.]

In addition, you are cautioned that PWBA's decision to take no further action is binding on PWBA only. Any other governmental agency, and participants and beneficiaries, remain free to take whatever action they deem necessary.

If you have any questions about this letter, you may contact the Regional VFC Program Coordinator at applicable address and telephone number.

DIRECTORY LISTINGS

ERISA ADVISORY COUNCIL MEMBERS

The 2001-2002 Council Members* are:

Employee Organizations: Robert B. Patrician, research economist, Communications Workers of America of Washington, DC.

Employer Organizations: Thomas McMahon, senior vice president, Finance and Administration, Pacific Maritime Association of San Francisco.

Investment Management: Catherine L. Heron, assistant general counsel of Capital Research and Management, Inc. of Los Angeles.

Actuarial: Ronnie Susan Thierman, senior consultant, William Mercer Inc. San Francisco.

Employee Organizations: James S. Ray, The Law Office of James S. Ray, Alexandria, VA.

General Public: Evelyn Adams, IBM Business Continuity and Recovery Services of Washington, DC.

Employers: Timothy J. Mahota, general counsel, Integral Development, Inc. of Mountain View CA.

Corporate Trust: Carl T. Camden, president of Kelly Services, Inc. in Troy, MI.

General Public: Norman Stein, law professor, University of Alabama at Tuscaloosa.

Employers: David L. Wray, president of the Profit Sharing and 401(k) Council since 1987.

Employee Organizations: John J. Szczur, director of investments for the Central Pension Fund of the International Union of Operating Engineers and Participating Employers.

Accounting: Michele M. Weldon, director in the Financial Services Industry Practice group of PricewaterhouseCoopers, LLP's Audit and Business Advisory Services.

Insurance: Judy E. Weiss, vice president in charge of retirement and savings business matters for Metropolitan Life Insurance Co.

General Public: Dana M. Muir, associate professor of business law at the University of Michigan Business School.

Shlomo Benartzi of the University of California at Los Angeles recently stepped down from the Council because of health concerns. A vacancy announcement for the investment-counseling field will be printed in the Federal Register soon.

*   See OPA News Release dated 3/15/2002.

DIRECTORY OF REGIONAL AND DISTRICT OFFICES OF
PENSION AND WELFARE BENEFITS ADMINISTRATION

PWBA Atlanta Regional Office
61 Forsyth Street, SW, Suite 7B54
Atlanta, GA 30303
Howard Marsh, Regional Director
Phone: 404/562-2156
Fax: 404/562-2168

PWBA Miami District Office
8040 Peters Road, Bldg. H, Suite 104
Plantation, FL 33324
Jesse Day, District Supervisor
Phone: 954/424-4022
Fax: 954/424-0548
Jurisdiction: Tennessee, North Carolina, South Carolina, Georgia Alabama, Puerto Rico, Mississippi, Florida

PWBA Boston Regional Office
J.F.K. Building, Room 575
Boston, MA 02203
James Benages, Regional Director
Phone: 617/565-9600
Fax: 617/565-9666

PWBA Chicago Regional Office
200 West Adams Street, Suite 1600
Chicago, IL 60606
Kenneth Bazar, Regional Director
Phone: 312/353-0900
Fax: 312/353-1023
Jurisdiction: Rhode Island, Vermont, Maine, New Hampshire, most of Connecticut, Massachusetts, Central and Western New York

PWBA Cincinnati Regional Office
1885 Dixie Highway, Suite 210
Ft. Wright, KY 41011-2664
Joseph Menez, Regional Director
Phone: 859/578-4680
Fax: 859/578-4688

PWBA Detroit District Office
211 West Fort Street, Suite 1310
Detroit, MI 48226-3211
Robert Jogan, District Supervisor
Phone: 313/226-7450
Fax: 313/226-4257
Jurisdiction: Michigan, Kentucky, Ohio, Southern Indiana

PWBA Dallas Regional Office
525 South Griffin Street, Rm. 707
Dallas, TX 75202-5025
Bruce Ruud, Regional Director
Phone: 214/767-6831
Fax: 214/767-1055
Jurisdiction: Arkansas, Louisiana, New Mexico, Oklahoma, Texas

PWBA Kansas City Regional Office
City Center Square
1100 Main, Suite 1200
Kansas City, MO 64105-5148
Gregory Egan, Regional Director
Phone: 816/426-5131
Fax: 816/426-5511

PWBA St. Louis District Office
Robert A. Young Federal Bldg.
1222 Spruce Street, Room 6310
St. Louis, MO 63103
Gary Newman, District Supervisor
Phone: 314/539-2693
Fax: 314/539-2697
Jurisdiction: Colorado, Southern Illinois, Iowa, Kansas, Minnesota, Missouri, Montana, Nebraska, North Dakota, South Dakota, Wyoming

PWBA Los Angeles Regional Office
1055 East Colorado Blvd.
Suite 200
Pasadena, CA 91106-2341
Billy Beaver, Regional Director
Phone: 626/229-1000
Fax: 626/229-1098
Jurisdiction: American Samoa, Arizona, Guam, Hawaii, Southern California, Wake Island

PWBA New York Regional Office
201 Varick Street
New York, NY 10014
Phone: 212/337-2228
(Calls are being received in a voice mailbox and will be returned as quickly as possible.)
Jurisdiction: Eastern New York, Southern Connecticut, Northern New Jersey

PWBA Philadelphia Regional Office
The Curtis Center
170 S. Independence Mall West
Suite 870 West
Philadelphia, PA 19106-3317
Mabel Capolongo, Regional Director
Phone: 215/861-5300
Fax: 215/861-5348

PWBA Washington District Office
S1335 East-West Highway, Suite 200
Silver Spring, MD 20910
Caroline Sullivan, District Supervisor
Phone: 301/713-2000
Fax: 301/713-2008
Jurisdiction: Delaware, Washington, D.C., Maryland, Southern New Jersey, Pennsylvania, Virginia, West Virginia

PWBA San Francisco Regional Office
71 Stevenson St., Suite 915
P.O. Box 190250
San Francisco, CA 94119-0250
Bette Briggs, Regional Director
Phone: 415/975-4600
Fax: 415/975-4588

PWBA Seattle District Office
1111 Third Avenue, Suite 860
MIDCOM Tower
Seattle, WA 98101-3212
John Scanlon, District Supervisor
Phone: 206/553-4244
Fax: 206/553-0913
Jurisdiction: Alaska, Northern California, Idaho, Nevada, Oregon, Utah, Washington

Pension and Welfare Benefits Administration
U.S. Department of Labor
200 Constitution Ave., N.W.
(Insert appropriate room number - see below)
Washington, DC 20210-1111

Public Disclosure Room
Room N-1513
Phone: 202/693-8673

Office of Enforcement
Room N-5702
Phone: 202/693-8440

Assists in searching and retrieving these pension documents: Form 5500s and Summary Plan Descriptions of employer benefit pensions

Division of Technical Assistance and Inquiries
Room N-5625
Phone: 202/219-8776

Request for interpretation and other ruling should be sent to:

Office of Regulations and Interpretations
Room N-5669
Phone: 202/693-8500

Applications for exemptions should be mailed to:

Office of Exemption Determinations
Room N-5649
Phone: 202/693-8540

Toll-Free Publications Hotline
Phone: 1-800-998-7542

Assists members of the public with technical questions relating to pension, health or other benefits offered by employers and protected by ERISA (the Employment Retirement Income and Security Act of 1974), COBRA (the Consolidated Omnibus Budget Reconciliation Act of 1986) and HIPAA, (the Health Insurance Portability and Accountability Act of 1996).

Division of Plan Benefits Security
Office of the Solicitor
Associate Solicitor: Timothy D. Hauser
Deputy Associate Solicitor: Karen L. Handorf
Phone: 202/693-5600

PWBA OFFICES AND DIRECTORS

Ann L. Combs
Assistant Secretary for
Pension and Welfare Benefits
Administration
Room S-2524
Telephone: 202/693-8300
Fax: 202/219-5526

Paul R. Zuraski
Deputy Assistant Secretary for Policy
Room S-2524
Telephone: 202/693-8300

Alan D. Lebowitz
Deputy Assistant Secretary
for Program Operations
Room N-5677
Telephone: 202/693-8315
Fax: 202/219-6531

Morton Klevan
Senior Policy Advisor
Room N-5677
Telephone: 202/693-8315

Ivan Strasfeld
Director of Exemption Determinations
Room N-5645
Telephone: 202/693-8540
Fax: 202/219-7291

Virginia C. Smith
Director of Enforcement
Room N-5702
Telephone: 202/693-8440
Fax: 202/219-6339

Richard Hinz
Director of Policy & Research
Room N-5718
Telephone: 202/693-8410
Fax: 202/219-5333

Daniel J. Maguire
Office of Health Plans Standards
and Compliance Assistance
Suite N-5677
Telephone: 202/693-8335
Fax: 202/219-1942

Robert J. Doyle
Director of Regulations
and Interpretations
Room N-5669
Telephone: 202/693-8500
Fax: 202/219-7291

Ian Dingwall
Chief Accountant, Office of
the Chief Accountant
Room N-5510
Telephone: 202/693-8360
Fax: 202/219-4997

John Helms
Office of Technology and
Information Services
Suite N-5459
Telephone: 202/693-8600
Fax: 202/219-4672

Sharon S. Watson
Director of Participant Assistance
and Communications
Room N-5625
Telephone: 202/693-8630
Fax: 202/219-8141

Brian C. McDonnell
Office of Program Planning, Evaluation and Management
Room N-5668
Telephone: 202/693-8480
Fax: 202/501-6942

Pension Benefit Guaranty Corporation
Technical Assistance Branch
1200 K Street NW, Suite 930
Washington, DC 20005-4026
Telephone: 1-800-736-2444 (or local at 202-326-4242)

Premium Payments and Forms

PBGC
P.O. Box 64880
Baltimore, MD 21264-4880
Telephone: 1-800-736-2444 or 202-326-4242

If a delivery service is used that does not deliver to a post office box, the address
for hand-delivery is:

ALLFIRST Bank
110 South Paca Street
Mail Code: 109-320/Lockbox #64880
Baltimore, MD 21201

Premium Correspondence

PBGC
P.O. Box 64916
Baltimore, MD 21264-4916
Telephone: 1-800-736-2444 or 202-326-4242
E-mail: premiums@pbgc.gov

Coverage Requests and Standard Terminations

PBGC
Technical Assistance Branch
1200 K Street NW, Suite 930
Washington, DC 20005-4026
Telephone: 1-800-736-2444 or 202-326-4242
E-mail: standard@pbgc.gov

Missing Participant Payment Vouchers and Payments

PBGC
P.O. Box 64523
Baltimore, MD 21264-4523
Telephone: 1-800-736-2444 or 202-326-4242
E-mail: standard@pbgc.gov

If a delivery service is used that does not deliver to a post office box, the address for hand-delivery is:

ALLFIRST Bank
110 South Paca Street
Mail Code: 109-320/Lockbox #64523
Baltimore, MD 21201

Distress Terminations

Distress Terminations
Pre-Termination Processing Division/IOD
PBGC
1200 K Street, N.W., Suite 870
Washington, DC 20005-4026
Telephone: 1-800-736-2444, Ext. 4100, or 202-326-4242
E-mail: distress.term@pbgc.gov

Early Warning Program

Early Earning Program
Corporate Finance & Negotiations Department
PBGC
1200 K Street, N.W., Suite 270
Washington, DC 20005-4026
Telephone: 1-800-736-2444, Ext. 4070, or 202-326-4242
E-mail: advance.report@pbgc.gov

Reporting under ERISA Section 4010

(Controlled groups with $50 million underfunding)
ERISA Sec. 4010 Reporting
Corporate Finance & Negotiations Department
PBGC
1200 K Street, N.W., Suite 270
Washington, DC 20005-4026
Telephone: 1-800-736-2444, Ext. 4070, or 202-326-4242
E-mail: ERISA.4010@pbgc.gov

Reportable Events

Reportable Events
Pre-Termination Processing Division/IOD
PBGC
1200 K Street, N.W., Suite 870
Washington, DC 20005-4026
Telephone: 1-800-736-2444, Ext. 4100, or 202-326-4242
E-mail: post-event.report@pbgc.gov

2002 ERISA Facts

General Inquiry Attorney

Office of the General Counsel
PBGC
1200 K Street, N.W., Suite 310
Washington, DC 20005-4026
Telephone: 1-800-736-2444, Ext. 4020, or 202-326-4242
E-mail: AskOGC@pbgc.gov

Further Assistance or Service Complaints

PBGC
Problem Resolution Officer (Practitioners)
1200 K Street, N.W., Suite 670
Washington, DC 20005-4026
Telephone: 202-326-4136
E-mail: premiums.pro@pbgc.gov

Problem Resolution Officer

(Plan Sponsors, Administrators and Advisors)
Problem Resolution Officer (Practitioners)
PBGC
1200 K Street, N.W., Suite 670
Washington, DC 20005-4026
Telephone: 1-800-736-2444, Ext. 4136, or 202-326-4242
E-mail: practitioner.pro@pbgc.gov

TABLE OF CASES

659

2002 ERISA Facts

2002 ERISA Facts

2002 ERISA Facts

2002 ERISA Facts

2002 ERISA Facts

TABLE OF ERISA SECTIONS TO
USC SECTIONS

ERISA Section	USC Section	ERISA Section	USC Section
2	1001	503	1133
3	1002	504	1134
4	1003	505	1135
101	1021	506	1136
102	1022	507	1137
103	1023	508	1138
104	1024	509	1139
105	1025	510	1140
106	1026	511	1141
107	1027	512	1142
108	1028	513	1143
109	1029	514	1144
110	1030	515	1145
111	1031	516	1146
201	1051	517	1147
202	1052	601	1161
203	1053	602	1162
204	1054	603	1163
205	1055	604	1164
206	1056	605	1165
207	1057	606	1166
208	1058	607	1167
209	1059	608	1168
210	1060	609	1169
211	1061	701	1171
301	1081	702	1172
302	1082	703	1173
303	1083	711	1181
304	1084	712	1182
305	1085	713	1183
306	1085a	731	1191
307	1085b	732	1192
308	1086	733	1193
401	1101	734	1194
402	1102	3001	1201
403	1103	3002	1202
404	1104	3003	1203
405	1105	3004	1204
406	1106	3021	1221
407	1107	3022	1222
408	1108	3031	1231
409	1109	3032	1232
410	1110	3041	1241
411	1111	3042	1242
412	1112	4001	1301
413	1113	4002	1302
414	1114	4003	1303
501	1131	4004	1304
502	1132	4005	1305

ERISA Section	USC Section	ERISA Section	USC Section
4006	1306	4206	1386
4007	1307	4207	1387
4008	1308	4208	1388
4009	1309	4209	1389
4010	1310	4210	1390
4011	1311	4211	1391
4021	1321	4212	1392
4022	1322	4213	1393
4022A	1322A	4214	1394
4022B	1322B	4215	1395
4023	1323	4216	1396
4041	1341	4217	1397
4041A	1341A	4218	1398
4042	1342	4219	1399
4043	1343	4220	1400
4044	1344	4221	1401
4045	1345	4222	1402
4046	1346	4223	1403
4047	1347	4224	1404
4048	1348	4225	1405
4050	1350	4231	1411
4061	1361	4232	1412
4062	1362	4233	1413
4063	1363	4234	1414
4064	1364	4235	1415
4065	1365	4241	1421
4066	1366	4242	1422
4067	1367	4243	1423
4068	1368	4244	1424
4069	1369	4244A	1425
4070	1370	4245	1426
4071	1371	4261	1431
4201	1381	4281	1441
4202	1382	4301	1451
4203	1383	4302	1452
4204	1384	4303	1453
4205	1385	4402	1461

TABLE OF ERISA SECTIONS TO IRC SECTIONS

ERISA Section	IRC Section	ERISA Section	IRC Section
3(3)	4975(e)(1)	204(g)	411(d)(6)
3(14)	4975(e)(2)	204(h)(2)	411(d)(6)(B)
3(16)(A)	414(g)	205	401(a)(11)
3(21)	4975(e)(3)	205(b)(2)	401(a)(11)
3(22)	411(a)(9)	205(c)	417(a)
3(23)	411(a)(7)	205(c)(4)	417(a)(4)
3(24)	411(a)(8)	205(d)	417(b)
3(32)	414(d)	205(e)	417(c)
3(33)	414(e)	205(e)(3)	417(c)(3)
3(34)	414(i)	205(g)	417(e)
3(35)	414(j)	205(g)(3)	417(e)(3)
3(37)	414(f)	205(h)(2)	417(f)(2)
3(40)(b)	414(b)-414(c)	205(j)	417(f)(5)
103(a)	6059	206	457(d)
103(a)(4)(C)	7701(a)(35)	206(b)	401(a)(15)
103(d)	6059	206(c)	401(a)(19)
201	401(a)(11), 410(c), 411(e)	206(d)	401(a)(13)
202	401(a)(3), 410(a)	206(d)(3)	414(p)
202(a)(1)	410(a)(1)	206(d)(3)(N)	401(n), 414(p)(12)
202(a)(2)	410(a)(2)	208	401(a)(12), 414(l)
202(a)(3)	410(a)(3)	210(a)(1)	413(b)(1)
202(a)(4)	410(a)(4)	210(a)(2)	413(c)(3)
202(b)	410(a)(5)	210(a)(3)	413(b)(5)-413(b)(6)
202(b)(4)	410(a)(5)(D)	210(b)	413(c), 414(a)
202(b)(5)	410(a)(5)	210(c)	414(b)
203	401(a)(7)	210(d)	414(c)
203(a)(1)	411(a)(1)	301	412(h)
203(a)(2)	411(a)(2), 413(b)(4)	301(a)(8)	412(h)(1)
203(a)(3)	411(a)(3), 411(a)(3)(B),	301(b)	412(i)
	411(a)(3)(D), 411(a)(6)	301(c)	412(j)
203(a)(3)(B)	411(a)(3)(B)	301(d)	412(k)
203(a)(3)(C)	411(a)(3)(C)	302(a)	412(a)
203(a)(3)(D)	411(a)(3)(D)	302(a)(3)	412(a)
203(a)(3)(E)	411(a)(3)	302(b)	412(b)
203(a)(3)(F)	411(a)(3)(G)	302(b)(2)	412(b)(2)(C)
203(b)(1)	411(a)(4), 411(a)(4)(G)	302(b)(2)(A)	412(b)(2)(A)
203(b)(2)	411(a)(5)	302(b)(3)	412(b)(3)(C)
203(b)(3)	411(a)(6)	302(b)(5)	412(b)(5)
203(c)(1)	411(a)(10)	302(b)(6)	412(b)(6)
203(c)(2)	411(d)(2)	302(b)(7)	412(b)(7)
203(e)	411(a)(11)	302(b)(7)(C)	412(b)(7)(C)
203(e)(2)	411(a)(11), 411(a)(11)(B)	302(b)(7)(D)	412(b)(7)(D)
204	411(b)	302(c)(1)	412(c)(1)
204(b)(1)(H)	411(b)(1)(H)	302(c)(2)	412(c)(2)
204(b)(3)	411(b)(4)	302(c)(3)	412(c)(3)
204(b)(4)	411(b)(4)	302(c)(4)	412(c)(4)
204(c)(2)	411(c)(2), 411(c)(2)(C)	302(c)(6)	412(c)(6)
204(c)(4)	411(d)(5)	302(c)(7)	412(c)(7)
204(d)	411(a)(7)(B)	302(c)(8)	412(c)(8)
204(e)	411(a)(7)(B)	302(c)(9)	412(c)(9)

ERISA Section	IRC Section	ERISA Section	IRC Section
302(c)(10)	412(c)(10)	408(b)(3)	4975(d)(3)
302(c)(11)	412(c)(11)	408(b)(4)	4975(d)(4)
302(c)(12)	412(c)(12)	408(b)(5)	4975(d)(5)
302(d)(2)	412(l)(2)	408(b)(6)	4975(d)(6)
302(d)(3)	412(l)(3)	408(b)(7)	4975(d)(7)
302(d)(4)	412(l)(4)	408(b)(8)	4975(d)(8)
302(d)(5)	412(l)(5)	408(b)(9)	4975(d)(12)
302(d)(7)	412(l)(7)	408(b)(10)	4975(d)(14)
302(d)(7)(B)	412(l)(7)(B)	408(b)(11)	4975(d)(15)
302(d)(8)	412(l)(8)	408(b)(12)	4975(d)(13)
302(d)(8)(A)	412(l)(8)(A)	408(b)(13)	4975(d)(13)
302(d)(10)	412(l)(10)	408(c)(1)	4975(d)(9)
302(e)	412(m)	408(c)(2)	4975(d)(10)
302(e)(3)	412(m)(3)	408(c)(3)	4975(d)(11)
302(e)(5)	412(m)(5)	408(d)	4975(d)
302(f)	412(c)(11), 412(n)	408(e)	4975(d)(13)
302(f)(1)	412(n)(1)	408(e)(2)	408
302(f)(4)	412(n)(4)	502(c)(1)(B)	6690
302(f)(4)(A)	412(n)(4)(A)	601	4980B(d)
302(f)(6)(B)	412(n)(6)(B)	601(b)	4980B(d)(3)
303	412(d)	602(1)	4980B(f)(2)(A)
303(a)(1)	412(d)(1)	602(2)	4980B(f)(2)(B)
303(c)	412(d)(3)	602(2)(A)	4980B(f)(2),
303(d)(1)	412(d)(4)		4980B(f)(2)(B)
303(d)(2)	412(d)(5)	602(2)(A)(iii)	4980B(f)(2)(B)
303(e)	412(f)(4)	602(3)	4980B(f)(2)(C),
304	412(e)		4980B(f)(3)
304(b)	412(f)	602(4)	4980B(f)(2)(D)
305	412(g)	602(5)	4980B(f)(2)(E)
306	412(f)(3)	603	4980B(f)(3)
307	401(a)(29)	603(1)	4980B(f)(3)
401	4975(g)	603(2)	4980B(f)(3)
403(a)	401(a)	603(3)	4980B(f)(3)(C)
403(b)(3)	401(f), 408(h)	603(4)	4980B(f)(3)(D)
403(b)(3)(i)	401(f)	603(5)	4980B(f)(3)
403(c)	401(a)(2)	603(6)	4980B(f)(3), 4980B(f)(3)(F)
403(c)(2)	401(a)(2)	604	4980B(f)(4)
403(c)(3)	401(a)(2)	605	4980B(f)(5)
404(a)(1)	401(a)(2)	606	4980B(f)(6)
404(d)	4980(d)	606(a)(2)	4980B(f)(6)(B)
404(d)(1)	4980(d)	606(a)(3)	4980B(f)(6)(C)
406	4975(e)	606(b)	4980B(f)(6)(D)
406(a)(1)	4975(c)(1)	606(c)	4980B(f)(6)(D)
406(b)	4975(c)(1)	607(1)	5000(b)(1)
406(c)	4975(f)(3)	607(2)	4980B(f)(7)
407(b)(2)(C)	401(m)(4)	607(3)	4980B(g)(1)
407(c)(6)	4975(e)(7)	607(3)(C)	4980B(g)(1)
407(d)(1)	409(l), 409(l)(4)	607(5)	4980B(f)(8)
407(d)(5)	4975(e)(8)	609(d)	4980B(f)(1)
408(a)	4975(c)(2)	701	9801
408(b)(1)	4975(d)(1)	702	9802
408(b)(2)	4975(d)(2)	703	9803

TABLE OF ERISA SECTIONS TO IRC SECTIONS

ERISA Section	IRC Section	ERISA Section	IRC Section
711	9811	4044(d)	401(a)(2)
712	9812	4062(e)	411(d)(3)
733	9832	4241	418
734	9806	4242	418A
2006(b)	401(k)(6)	4243	418B
3001	7476	4244	418C
4001(a)(1)	4980B(g)(3)	4244(g)	418C(g)
4001(a)(9)	418(b)	4244A	418D
4001(a)(12)	418(b)(7)(E)	4245(f)	418E(f)
4001(a)(14)	4062	4303	414(f)(5)

TABLE OF IRC SECTIONS TO ERISA SECTIONS

IRC Section	ERISA Section	IRC Section	ERISA Section
401(a)	403(a)	411(d)(6)	204(g)
401(a)(2)	403(c), 403(c)(2),	411(d)(6)(B)	204(h)(2)
	403(c)(3), 404(a)(1), 4044(d)	411(e)	201
401(a)(3)	202	412(a)	302(a), 302(a)(3)
401(a)(7)	203	412(b)	302(b)
401(a)(11)	201, 205, 205(b)(2)	412(b)(2)(A)	302(b)(2)(A)
401(a)(13)	206(d)	412(b)(2)(C)	302(b)(2)
401(a)(15)	206(b)	412(b)(3)(C)	302(b)(3)
401(a)(19)	206(c)	412(b)(5)	302(b)(5)
401(a)(29)	307	412(b)(6)	302(b)(6)
401(c)	201	412(b)(7)	302(b)(7)
401(f)	403(b)(3), 403(b)(3)(i)	412(b)(7)(C)	302(b)(7)(C)
401(k)(6)	2006(b)	412(b)(7)(D)	302(b)(7)(D)
401(m)(4)	407(b)(2)(C)	412(c)(1)	302(c)(1)
401(n)	206(d)(3)(N)	412(c)(2)	302(c)(2)
408	408(e)(2)	412(c)(3)	302(c)(3)
408(h)	403(b)(3)	412(c)(4)	302(c)(4)
409(l)	407(d)(1)	412(c)(6)	302(c)(6)
409(l)(4)	407(d)(1)	412(c)(7)	302(c)(7)
410(a)	202	412(c)(8)	302(c)(8)
410(a)(1)	202(a)(1)	412(c)(9)	302(c)(9)
410(a)(2)	202(a)(2)	412(c)(10)	302(c)(10)
410(a)(3)	202(a)(3)	412(c)(11)	302(c)(11), 302(f)
410(a)(4)	202(a)(4)	412(c)(12)	302(c)(12)
410(a)(5)	202(b), 202(b)(5)	412(d)	303
410(a)(5)(D)	202(b)(4)	412(d)(1)	303(a)(1)
411(a)(1)	203(a)(1)	412(d)(3)	303(c)
411(a)(2)	203(a)(2)	412(d)(4)	303(d)(1)
411(a)(3)	203(a)(3), 203(a)(3)(E)	412(d)(5)	303(d)(2)
411(a)(3)(B)	203(a)(3), 203(a)(3)(B)	412(e)	304
411(a)(3)(C)	203(a)(3)(C)	412(f)	304(b)
411(a)(3)(D)	203(a)(3), 203(a)(3)(D)	412(f)(3)	306
411(a)(3)(G)	203(a)(3)(F)	412(f)(4)	303(e)
411(a)(4)	203(b)(1)	412(g)	305
411(a)(4)(G)	203(b)(1)	412(h)	301
411(a)(5)	203(b)(2)	412(h)(1)	301(a)(8)
411(a)(6)	203(a)(3), 203(b)(3)	412(i)	301(b)
411(a)(7)	3(23)	412(j)	301(c)
411(a)(7)(B)	204(d), 204(e)	412(k)	301(d)
411(a)(8)	3(24)	412(l)(2)	302(d)(2)
411(a)(9)	3(22)	412(l)(3)	302(d)(3)
411(a)(10)	203(c)(1)	412(l)(4)	302(d)(4)
411(a)(11)	203(e), 203(e)(2)	412(l)(5)	302(d)(5)
411(a)(11)(B)	203(e)(2)	412(l)(7)	302(d)(7)
411(b)	204	412(l)(7)(B)	302(d)(7)(B)
411(b)(1)(H)	204(b)(1)(H)	412(l)(8)	302(d)(8)
411(b)(4)	204(b)(3), 204(b)(4)	412(l)(8)(A)	302(d)(8)(A)
411(c)(2)	204(c)(2)	412(l)(10)	302(d)(10)
411(c)(2)(C)	204(c)(2)	412(m)	302(e)
411(d)(2)	203(c)(2)	412(m)(3)	302(e)(3)
411(d)(3)	4062(e)	412(m)(5)	302(e)(5)
411(d)(5)	204(c)(4)	412(n)	302(f)

675

2002 ERISA Facts

IRC Section	ERISA Section	IRC Section	ERISA Section
412(n)(1)	302(f)(1)	4975(d)(9)	408(c)(1)
412(n)(4)	302(f)(4)	4975(d)(10)	408(c)(2)
412(n)(4)(A)	302(f)(4)(A)	4975(d)(11)	408(c)(3)
412(n)(6)(B)	302(f)(6)(B)	4975(d)(12)	408(b)(9)
413(b)(1)	210(a)(1)	4975(d)(13)	408(b)(12), 408(b)(13),
413(b)(4)	203(a)(2)		408(e)
413(b)(5)	210(a)(3)	4975(d)(14)	408(b)(10)
413(b)(6)	210(a)(3)	4975(d)(15)	408(b)(11)
413(c)	210(b)	4975(e)	406
413(c)(3)	210(a)(2)	4975(e)(1)	3(3)
414(a)	210(b)	4975(e)(2)	3(14)
414(b)	3(40)(b), 210(c)	4975(e)(3)	3(21)
414(c)	3(40)(b), 210(d)	4975(e)(7)	407(c)(6)
414(d)	3(32)	4975(e)(8)	407(d)(5)
414(e)	3(33)	4975(f)(3)	406(c)
414(f)	3(37)	4975(g)	401
414(f)(5)	4303	4980(d)	404(d), 404(d)(1)
414(g)	3(16)(A)	4980B(d)	601
414(i)	3(34)	4980B(d)(3)	601(b)
414(j)	3(35)	4980B(f)(1)	609(d)
414(l)	208	4980B(f)(2)	602(2)(A)
414(p)	206(d)(3)	4980B(f)(2)(A)	602(1)
414(p)(12)	206(d)(3)(N)	4980B(f)(2)(B)	602(2), 602(2)(A),
417(a)	205(c)		602(2)(A)(iii)
417(a)(4)	205(c)(4)	4980B(f)(2)(C)	602(3)
417(b)	205(d)	4980B(f)(2)(D)	602(4)
417(c)	205(e)	4980B(f)(2)(E)	602(5)
417(c)(3)	205(e)(3)	4980B(f)(3)	602(3), 603, 603(1),
417(e)	205(g)		603(2), 603(5), 603(6)
417(e)(3)	205(g)(3)	4980B(f)(3)(C)	603(3)
417(f)(2)	205(h)(2)	4980B(f)(3)(D)	603(4)
417(f)(5)	205(j)	4980B(f)(3)(F)	603(6)
418	4241	4980B(f)(4)	604
418(b)	4001(a)(9)	4980B(f)(5)	605
418(b)(7)(E)	4001(a)(12)	4980B(f)(6)	606
418A	4242	4980B(f)(6)(B)	606(a)(2)
418B	4243	4980B(f)(6)(C)	606(a)(3)
418C	4244	4980B(f)(6)(D)	606(b), 606(c)
418C(g)	4244(g)	4980B(f)(7)	607(2)
418D	4244A	4980B(f)(8)	607(5)
418E(f)	4245(f)	4980B(g)(1)	607(3), 607(3)(C)
457(d)	206	4980B(g)(3)	4001(a)(1)
4062	4001(a)(14)	5000(b)(1)	607(1)
4975(c)(1)	406(a)(1), 406(b)	6059	103(a), 103(d)
4975(c)(2)	408(a)	6690	502(c)(1)(B)
4975(d)	408(d)	7476	3001
4975(d)(1)	408(b)(1)	7701(a)(35)	103(a)(4)(C)
4975(d)(2)	408(b)(2)	9801	701
4975(d)(3)	408(b)(3)	9802	702
4975(d)(4)	408(b)(4)	9803	703
4975(d)(5)	408(b)(5)	9806	734
4975(d)(6)	408(b)(6)	9811	711
4975(d)(7)	408(b)(7)	9812	712
4975(d)(8)	408(b)(8)	9832	733

2002 ERISA Facts

TABLE OF ERISA SECTIONS CITED

ERISA Section	Q	ERISA Section	Q
203(a)(3)(B)	39	206(d)(3)(G)	133
203(a)(3)(D)	39	206(d)(3)(G)(i)(II)	127, 131
203(a)(3)(D)(ii)	39	206(d)(3)(G)(ii)	128
203(b)	60	206(d)(3)(H)	132
203(b)(1)	19	206(d)(3)(I)	130
203(b)(2)	60	206(d)(3)(K)	122
203(b)(2)(A)	33	206(d)(4)	41, 447
203(b)(3)(A)	34	208	339
203(b)(3)(B)	34	209	60
203(b)(3)(C)	34	209(a)	114
203(b)(3)(D)	29, 34	210(c)	22
203(b)(3)(D)(iii)	34	210(d)	22
203(b)(3)(E)	38	267(c)(4)	401
203(b)(3)(E)(i)	38	301(a)	48
203(b)(3)(E)(ii)	38	301(a)(2)	32
203(c)(1)(A)	25	301(b)	32
203(d)(3)(J)	134	302	47, 56
203(e)	710	302(a)	557
204(b)(1)	32	302(a)(1)	49
204(b)(1)(F)	32	302(b)	557
204(b)(1)(H)	30	302(b)(1)	49
204(b)(1)(H)(ii)	30	302(b)(5)(B)	53, 56
204(b)(1)(H)(iii)	30	302(b)(5)(B)(ii)(II)	53
204(b)(2)(A)	30	302(b)(5)(B)(iii)	53
204(b)(3)(B)	31	302(c)(1)	50
204(b)(4)	29	302(c)(3)	50
204(b)(4)(C)	29	302(c)(3)(A)	50
204(c)(2)(A)	31	302(c)(3)(B)	50
204(c)(3)	32	302(c)(4)	56
204(g)	135	302(c)(7)	53
204(g)(1)	18, 26, 27, 39	302(c)(8)	39
204(g)(2)	27	302(c)(8)(C)	97
204(h)	28, 706	302(c)(9)	56
205	110	302(d)(7)	53
205(a)(2)	40	303(c)	49
205(c)(2)	60	304(a)	56
205(c)(3)	60, 109	305(a)(1)	51
205(c)(3)(B)	110	305(b)(1)	51
205(c)(5)(A)	109, 110	305(b)(2)	51
205(d)(1)	60	305(c)	51
205(e)(1)	60	401(a)	225, 226, 336
206(d)(1)	42	401(a)(1)	13
206(d)(3)	129	401(a)(2)	13
206(d)(3)(A)	120, 135, 136	401(b)(2)(B)	527
206(d)(3)(B)	120	402(a)	2, 194
206(d)(3)(B)(ii)	60, 121	402(a)(1)	1, 191, 308
206(d)(3)(C)	123, 130	402(a)(2)	191, 195, 504
206(d)(3)(C)(iv)	126	402(b)	2, 3
206(d)(3)(D)	124, 138	402(b)(1)	516
206(d)(3)(E)	138	402(b)(4)	16
206(d)(3)(E)(i)(III)	124	402(c)(1)	3, 201
206(d)(3)(E)(ii)	139	402(c)(2)	3, 309

ERISA Section	Q	ERISA Section	Q
402(c)(3)	3, 4, 217, 218, 308, 309, 504, 518	406(a)(1)(C)	341, 381, 387
403	4, 263, 551, 669	406(a)(1)(D)	342, 387, 529, 532
403(a)	208, 308, 518	406(a)(1)(E)	343, 380, 381, 382, 393
403(a)(1)	278, 510	406(a)(2)	380, 382, 393
403(a)(2)	278, 309	406(b)	233, 344, 385, 388, 393, 396, 397, 420, 424
403(b)	4, 519	406(b)(1)	345, 346, 380
403(b)(3)	347, 543	406(B)(1)	381
403(c)	263	406(b)(1)	382, 392, 398, 400, 406, 512, 532, 534, 543, 552
403(c)(1)	16, 135, 224, 232, 235, 536	406(b)(2)	346, 380, 383, 400, 543, 596
403(c)(3)	589	406(b)(3)	347, 361, 368, 380, 381, 382, 384, 398, 400, 406, 532, 543
403(d)	136	407	224, 337, 343, 381, 543, 656
404	223, 224, 228, 241, 263, 264, 268, 316, 335, 379, 393, 398, 455, 529, 543, 544, 556	407(a)	380, 382, 393, 412, 413, 539, 544
404(a)	129, 224, 226, 227, 246, 325, 388, 508, 686	407(a)(2)	539
404(a)(1)	231, 233, 453, 499, 512, 550	407(a)(2)(A)	296
404(a)(1)(A)	16, 231, 235, 550	407(b)	296
404(a)(1)(B)	239, 240, 259, 270, 282, 297, 298, 453, 458, 502, 503, 544, 550	407(b)(1)	539
404(a)(1)(C)	282, 284, 287, 289, 294, 449, 538	407(b)(2)(A)	539
404(a)(1)(D)	269, 298, 299, 300, 301, 502	407(d)	401
404(a)(1)(d)	510	407(d)(1)	113, 537
404(a)(1)(D)	510, 547, 669	407(d)(2)	538
404(a)(2)	294	407(d)(3)	294
404(b)	302	407(d)(3)(A)	539
404(c)	101, 315, 317, 318, 319, 320, 321, 322, 323, 324, 325, 326, 327, 328, 329, 330, 331, 332, 333	407(d)(3)(B)	539
404(c)(1)	338	407(d)(4)	538
405	267, 326	407(d)(5)	397, 537
405(a)	198, 216, 306, 307, 310, 453	407(d)(6)	397, 540, 541
405(a)(2)	453	407(e)	537
405(a)(3)	453	407(f)(1)	537
405(b)(1)	456	407(f)(1)(A)	539
405(c)(1)	3, 305, 306, 309	407(f)(1)(B)	539
405(c)(2)	198	408	224, 329, 362, 394, 407, 412, 645
405(c)(2)(A)	267	408(a)	362, 407, 413
405(c)(3)	3	408(b)	401
405(d)	267, 453, 456	408(b)(1)	113, 394, 395
406	224, 326, 335, 337, 339, 342, 357, 361, 377, 379, 412, 413, 430, 449, 455, 538, 543, 544, 686	408(b)(2)	15, 16, 341, 383, 394, 396, 400, 783
406(a)	15, 340, 342, 344, 383, 392, 393, 398, 543, 596, 783	408(b)(3)	394, 397, 543, 551
406(a)(1)	335, 337, 346	408(b)(4)	394, 398
406(a)(1)(A)	339, 387, 393	408(b)(5)	394, 399
406(a)(1)(B)	340, 387, 395	408(b)(6)	394, 400
		408(b)(7)	402
		408(b)(8)	394, 403
		408(b)(10)	394, 405
		408(b)(11)	394, 406
		408(c)	16, 209, 401
		408(c)(2)	16, 268
		408(c)(3)	233
		408(d)	394, 401, 783
		408(e)	401, 543, 544, 552

ERISA Section	Q	ERISA Section	Q
409	316, 335, 428, 454	502(l) 349, 428, 430, 433, 434, 435, 436,	
409(a)	428, 447, 450		437, 438, 439, 440, 449, 668,
409(b)	428		670, 671, 682, 691, 692, 693
410(a)	456, 499	502(l)(2)	431, 433
410(b)	456, 499, 500	502(l)(4)	430
410(b)(2)	500	503(1)	44
410(b)(3)	501	503(2)	46
411	221, 412, 593, 643, 733,	504	316, 361, 730
	738, 739, 740, 742, 743,	504(a)	350, 637, 648
	748, 749, 750, 751	504(a)(1)	637
411(a)	643, 733, 740, 741, 742	504(a)(2)	637
411(b)	743	504(b)	637
411(c)(1)	744	504(c)	637, 638
411(c)(2)	745	505	316
411(c)(3)	746	506	316, 695, 730
411(d)	747	506(a)	695
412	113, 196, 471, 472, 473,	506(b)	695, 730
	475, 479, 480, 488, 489,	510	441, 442, 443, 444,
	491, 493, 497, 681, 755		445, 452, 463, 756
412(a)	472, 475, 480,	511	441, 446, 733, 738, 740, 756
	482, 490, 493, 681	512	633, 635
412(a)(1)	473	512(a)	633, 634
412(a)(2)	474	512(b)	633
412(a)(2)(D)	481, 493	512(c)	635
412(b)	472	514(a)	621, 698
412(c)	491	514(b)	621
412(e)	498	514(b)(2)	621
413	458, 459	514(b)(2)(B)	617
413(a)(2)	458	514(b)(3)	699
441	413	514(b)(3)(A)	699
501	733, 738, 752, 753, 755	514(b)(4)	784
502	316, 452, 665, 696	514(b)(5)(A)	699
502(a)(1)	185	514(b)(6)	618, 621
502(a)(2)	316, 428, 434, 683, 686	514(b)(6)(A)	617, 619, 621, 699
502(a)(3)	428, 445, 454, 455	514(b)(6)(A)(i)	617
502(a)(5)	316, 335, 434	514(b)(6)(D)	618
502(a)(9)	277, 428	514(b)(7)	699
502(c)	675	514(c)(1)	698
502(c)(1)	103, 118, 185	514(c)(2)	698
502(c)(2)	72, 73, 81, 92	514(d)	698
502(c)(6)	95	515	470, 604
502(g)	467, 470	601	173
502(g)(1)	185, 465, 466, 468	602(1)	178
502(g)(2)	470, 604	602(2)	180
502(g)(2)(B)	470	602(2)(A)(i)	180
502(g)(2)(C)	470	602(2)(A)(ii)	180
502(g)(2)(D)	470	602(2)(A)(iv)	180
502(g)(2)(E)	604	602(2)(C)	181
502(h)	448, 697	602(3)	181
502(i)	357, 358, 359, 360,	602(4)	178
	430, 438, 691, 692	603	175
502(j)	696	605(1)	177

ERISA Section	Q	ERISA Section	Q
606(a)(1)	177	4022(b)(3)	710
606(a)(2)	177	4022(b)(5)(A)	712
606(a)(3)	177	4022(b)(5)(B)	712
606(a)(4)	177	4022(b)(6)	711
607(1)	173	4022(b)(7)	712
607(2)	175	4022(e)	710
607(3)(A)	175	4022A	603
609(a)	140	4031(a)(2)	607
609(a)(2)	140	4041	412, 720
609(a)(5)	140	4041(a)(2)	706, 708, 714
702(a)(1)	657	4041(b)	705
702(b)(1)	657	4041(b)(2)(A)	707
703	657	4041(b)(2)(C)	716
711(d)	107	4041(b)(2)(D)	716
1027	771	4041(b)(3)	716
3001(c)	726	4041(b)(3)(A)	716
3003(a)	352	4041(b)(3)(B)	705
3003(b)	348	4041(c)(2)(A)(ii)	708
3003(c)	348	4041(c)(2)(A)(iii)	708
4001(a)(2)	371, 382	4041(c)(2)(A)(iv)	708
4001(a)(3)	554	4041(c)(2)(B)	708
4001(a)(16)	705	4041A(a)(1)	558
4001(a)(21)	713	4041A(a)(2)	558, 579, 595, 597
4001(b)	611	4041A(a)(3)	558
4001(b)(1)	559	4041A(b)(2)	558, 579
4002	700	4042	558, 720
4002(a)	715	4042(a)	715
4003(a)	701	4042(a)(4)	704
4003(b)	701	4043	412
4003(e)(1)	726	4043(a)	704
4003(e)(6)(A)	728	4047	715
4003(e)(6)(B)	728	4048	714
4003(e)(6)(C)	728	4050(a)	718
4003(f)(1)	723, 724	4050(b)(1)	718
4003(f)(1)(B)	725	4062	720
4003(f)(2)(A)	724	4063	720
4003(f)(2)(B)	724	4064	720
4003(f)(2)(C)	724	4069	720
4003(f)(3)	723	4070	720, 721, 722
4003(f)(4)	724	4070(a)	720
4003(f)(5)(A)	725	4070(b)	720
4003(f)(5)(B)(ii)	725	4070(c)	721
4003(f)(6)	724, 725	4070(d)	720
4003(f)(7)	724, 727	4070(e)	721
4006(a)(3)(A)	703	4070(f)(1)	722
4007(b)	703	4070(f)(2)	722
4010	704	4070(f)(3)	722
4011	117, 703	4071	704, 716
4021(a)	701	4201	559
4021(b)	702	4202	568
4022(a)	710	4203(a)	560
4022(b)	710	4203(b)	560

2002 ERISA Facts

ERISA Section	Q	ERISA Section	Q
4203(c)	560	4220(b)	590
4203(d)	560	4220(c)	590
4204	569	4221	585
4204(a)(1)	569	4221(a)(1)	585
4204(a)(2)	569	4221(a)(3)	584
4204(a)(3)	569	4221(b)(2)	588
4205(a)	560	4221(c)	588
4205(b)(1)(A)	560	4225	563
4205(b)(1)(B)	560	4225(a)	592
4205(b)(2)(A)	560	4225(a)(2)	592
4205(b)(2)(B)	560	4225(b)	591
4206(a)(2)	567	4225(d)(1)	591
4206(a)(2)(B)	567	4225(d)(2)	591
4207	606	4225(e)	591, 592
4209	563	4231	406, 593, 596, 600
4209(a)	571	4231(c)	596
4209(b)	571	4232(b)	598
4210(a)	572	4232(c)(1)	598
4210(b)	572	4232(c)(2)	598
4210(b)(1)	572	4232(c)(3)	598
4211	563, 594	4232(c)(4)	598
4211(b)(2)(B)	563	4233(a)	603
4211(b)(2)(C)	563	4233(b)(1)	603
4211(b)(3)	563	4233(c)	603
4211(b)(4)(B)	563	4233(d)	603
4211(b)(4)(C)	563	4233(e)	603
4211(b)(4)(D)	563	4233(f)	603
4211(c)	564	4234	597, 600
4211(c)(2)	564	4234(a)	597
4211(c)(3)	565	4234(c)	597
4211(c)(4)	566	4234(e)(1)	600
4211(c)(5)(A)	590	4234(e)(2)	600
4211(f)	594	4235(a)	600
4218(1)	569	4235(b)	600
4218(2)	570	4235(b)(3)	600
4219	563	4235(b)(3)(A)	600
4219(b)(1)	573	4235(f)	600
4219(b)(2)(A)	573	4235(f)(2)	601
4219(b)(2)(B)	574	4244A	99
4219(c)(1)	575	4244A(b)(1)(A)	99
4219(c)(1)(B)	563, 579	4245(b)(3)	582
4219(c)(1)(C)(i)	575	4245(e)(1)	99
4219(c)(1)(D)	579	4261(b)(2)	582
4219(c)(2)	575	4301(a)	470, 720
4219(c)(3)	575, 577	4301(a)(1)	607
4219(c)(4)	575	4301(c)	727
4219(c)(5)	576	4301(d)	727
4219(c)(5)(A)	576	4301(f)	470, 608
4219(c)(5)(B)	576	4301(g)	727
4219(c)(6)	577, 589	4302	583

TABLE OF IRC SECTIONS CITED

IRC Section	Q	IRC Section	Q
45E	15	409(o)(1)(B)	547
72(p)	395	409(o)(1)(C)	547
401	20, 329, 413	409(o)(2)	547
401(a)	42, 355, 412, 543, 711	409(o)(C)	547
401(a)(2)	705	409(p)	542
401(a)(7)	20	410	33, 336
401(a)(11)	40	410(a)(1)(A)	60
401(a)(13)(B)	135	410(a)(3)(A)	60
401(a)(14)	60, 547	410(a)(3)(C)	33
401(a)(28)(B)	546	410(a)(5)	29, 60
401(a)(28)(B)(ii)	546	410(b)	66
401(a)(28)(C)	544, 546	410(d)	7, 21, 64, 226
401(c)(1)	4, 559	410(d)(4)	33
401(k)(11)	327	411	20, 23
401(m)(2)	333	411(a)	39, 41
401(m)(3)	333	411(a)(1)	31
401(m)(4)(A)	18	411(a)(2)(A)	18
402(d)	111	411(a)(2)(B)	18
402(e)	111	411(a)(2)(C)	24
402(f)	111	411(a)(3)(A)	40
403(a)	42, 54	411(a)(3)(B)	39
403(b)	4, 12, 42	411(a)(3)(D)	39
404	578	411(a)(3)(D)(ii)	39
404(a)	52	411(a)(3)(E)	572
404(a)(1)(A)	52, 56	411(a)(4)	19, 60
404(a)(1)(A)(i)	52	411(a)(5)	33, 60
404(a)(1)(A)(iii)	55	411(a)(6)(A)	34
404(a)(1)(B)	52	411(a)(6)(B)	34
404(a)(1)(D)	52	411(a)(6)(C)	34
404(a)(1)(E)	52	411(a)(6)(D)	29, 34
404(a)(2)	711	411(a)(6)(D)(iii)	34
404(a)(3)(A)	540	411(a)(6)(E)	38
404(a)(9)	540	411(a)(6)(E)(i)	38
404(g)(1)	578	411(a)(6)(E)(ii)	38
408	4, 64, 333	411(a)(7)	32
408(a)	10	411(a)(7)(A)(I)	18
408(b)	10	411(a)(7)(A)(i)	27
408(c)	401	411(a)(7)(A)(ii)	18, 27, 31
408(m)	333	411(a)(8)	32
408(p)	327	411(a)(10)(A)	25
408(p)(5)(A)(i)	514	411(a)(10)(B)	25
409(e)(2)	545	411(b)(1)	32
409(e)(3)	545	411(b)(1)(F)	32
409(e)(5)	545	411(b)(1)(H)	30
409(h)(1)(A)	547	411(b)(1)(H)(ii)	30
409(h)(1)(B)	547	411(b)(1)(H)(iii)	30
409(h)(2)(B)	542, 547	411(b)(2)	30
409(h)(3)	548	411(b)(3)(B)	31
409(o)(1)(A)	547	411(b)(4)	29

IRC Section	Q	IRC Section	Q
411(b)(4)(C)	29	414(p)(7)	132
411(c)(2)(A)	31	414(p)(8)	122
411(c)(3)	32	414(u)	37
411(d)(6)	18, 26, 27, 39, 135	414(u)(2)	37
411(d)(6)(B)	27	414(u)(4)	37
411(e)(1)(A)	21	414(u)(8)	37
411(e)(1)(B)	21	414(v)	327
411(e)(1)(D)	21	415	7, 21, 60
412	66	417(a)(2)	60
412(a)	557	417(a)(3)	60
412(b)	49	417(a)(3)(A)	109
412(b)(5)(B)	53	417(a)(3)(B)(i)	110
412(b)(5)(B)(ii)(II)	53	417(a)(3)(B)(ii)	110
412(b)(5)(B)(iii)	53	417(a)(5)(A)	109, 110
412(c)(1)	50	417(b)	60
412(c)(3)	50	417(c)	60
412(c)(3)(A)	50	419A(f)(5)	557
412(c)(3)(B)	50	501	21
412(c)(4)	56	501(a)	557, 616
412(c)(7)	53	501(c)(2)	519
412(c)(8)	39	501(c)(3)	5
412(c)(9)	56	501(c)(4)	616
412(e)	56	501(c)(6)	616
412(f)(4)(A)	56	501(c)(8)	21
412(g)(1)	51	501(c)(9)	21, 557
412(g)(2)(A)	51	503(b)	412, 413
412(g)(2)(B)	51	736	13, 21, 226, 336
412(g)(3)	51	1361(a)	542
412(h)(2)	32	1563(a)	22
412(i)	32, 54	3121	56
412(l)	52	4941	352
412(l)(7)	53	4961(a)	352
413(c)(4)	557	4961(b)	355
414(c)	611	4961(c)	355
414(d)	175	4963(e)	352
414(g)	395	4975	335, 336, 348, 352, 354,
414(m)(1)	23		355, 356, 357, 358, 361,
414(m)(2)	23		413, 430, 438, 551
414(m)(3)	23	4975(a)	348, 352, 354, 377, 412, 413
414(n)(1)	175	4975(b)	348, 352, 353, 354, 355, 412
414(n)(3)(C)	175	4975(c)(1)	337
414(p)	120	4975(c)(1)(E)	344, 420
414(p)(1)(A)	120	4975(c)(1)(F)	344, 361
414(p)(1)(B)	60, 121	4975(c)(2)	407, 412, 413
414(p)(2)	123, 130	4975(d)(2)	391
414(p)(2)(D)	126	4975(d)(3)	541, 543
414(p)(3)	124, 138	4975(d)(9)	394, 404
414(p)(4)(A)(iii)	124	4975(d)(10)	404
414(p)(4)(B)	139	4975(e)(2)	362
414(p)(6)	128, 133	4975(e)(7)	541, 545
414(p)(6)(A)(ii)	127, 131	4975(f)(1)	354

IRC Section	Q	IRC Section	Q
4975(f)(2)	352	4980B(f)(6)(D)	177
4975(f)(4)	352, 358	4980B(f)(7)	175
4975(f)(4)(B)	352	4980B(g)(1)(A)	175
4975(f)(5)	353, 412, 413	4980B(g)(1)(C)	175
4975(f)(6)(B)	542	4980B(g)(2)	173
4975(h)	352	6057(a)	66
4980B(b)	185	6057(b)	65
4980B(c)(1)	185	6103	691
4980B(c)(2)	185	6212	352
4980B(c)(3)(B)	185	6213(a)	352
4980B(c)(4)(A)(i)	185	6501(a)	355
4980B(e)(1)(A)	185	6501(e)(3)	355
4980B(f)	173	6621	604
4980B(f)(2)	178, 180	6621(a)(2)	351
4980B(f)(2)(A)	178	7422(g)	352
4980B(f)(2)(B)(i)	161, 180	7476	726
4980B(f)(2)(B)(ii)	180	7704(b)	330
4980B(f)(2)(B)(iii)	181	9801(a)	143
4980B(f)(2)(C)	181	9801(a)(1)	144
4980B(f)(3)	175	9801(c)(1)	149
4980B(f)(4)(C)	181	9801(c)(2)(A)	147
4980B(f)(5)(A)	177	9801(d)	145, 158
4980B(f)(6)(A)	177	9801(d)(3)	145
4980B(f)(6)(B)	177	9802(a)(1)	157
4980B(f)(6)(C)	177	9802(b)(1)	157

INDEX

Q

2002 ERISA Facts

Q

Q

Q

Q

2002 ERISA Facts

Q

Q

Q

Q

Q

Q

2002 ERISA Facts

2002 ERISA Facts

Q

Q

2002 ERISA Facts

Q

Q

2002 ERISA Facts

2002 ERISA Facts

Q

Trustee

V

Vesting

Q

Veterans
Voluntary compliance
Voluntary employee contributions
Voluntary fiduciary correction

W

Welfare Benefit Plan
Women's Health and Cancer Right Act of 1998

To order, call **1-800-543-0874** and ask for operator BB,
or fax your order to **1-800-874-1916**.
Or, visit our online catalog at **www.nationalunderwriter.com/nucatalog**

Payment Information

Add shipping & handling charges to all orders as indicated.
If your order exceeds total amount listed in chart, call
1-800-543-0874 for shipping & handling charge.
Unconditional 30 day guarantee. Prices subject to change.

SALES TAX (Additional)

Sales tax is required for residents of the following states: CA, DC, FL, GA, IL, KY, NJ, NY, OH, PA, WA.

Shipping & Handling (Additional)

Order Total	Shipping & Handling
$0.00 to $9.99	$3.00
10.00 to 19.99	5.00
20.00 to 39.99	6.00
40.00 to 59.99	7.00
60.00 to 79.99	9.00
80.00 to 109.99	10.00
110.00 to 149.99	12.00
150.00 to 199.99	13.00
200.00 to 249.99	15.50

Shipping and handling rates for the continental U.S. only. Call 1-800-543-0874 for overseas shipping information.

The NATIONAL UNDERWRITER Company
PROFESSIONAL PUBLISHING GROUP

The National Underwriter Company • Customer Service Dept #2-BB
P.O. Box 14448 • Cincinnati, Ohio 45250-9786

2-BB

_____ Copies of *2002 ERISA Facts*
❏ Print (#1170002) $31.90
❏ CD-ROM (#1179002) $70.00
❏ 12-month Internet subscription (#1179101) $70.00

_____ Copies of *2002-2003 Benefits Facts*
❏ Print (#6020003) $50.00
❏ CD-ROM (#6029003) $70.00
❏ 12-month Internet subscription (#6029101) $70.00

❏ Check enclosed*   ❏ Charge my VISA/MC/AmEx (circle one)

*Make check payable to The National Underwriter Company.
**Please include the appropriate shipping & handling charges and any applicable sales tax. (See charts above.)

Card # _____ Exp. Date _____
Name _____ Title _____
Signature _____
Company _____
Street Address _____
City _____ State _____ Zip+4 _____
Business Phone (____) _____ Fax (____) _____ email _____
❏ May we e-mail you?

The NATIONAL UNDERWRITER Company
PROFESSIONAL PUBLISHING GROUP

The National Underwriter Company • Customer Service Dept #2-BB
P.O. Box 14448 • Cincinnati, Ohio 45250-9786

2-BB

_____ Copies of *2002 ERISA Facts*
❏ Print (#1170002) $31.90
❏ CD-ROM (#1179002) $70.00
❏ 12-month Internet subscription (#1179101) $70.00

_____ Copies of *2002-2003 Benefits Facts*
❏ Print (#6020003) $50.00
❏ CD-ROM (#6029003) $70.00
❏ 12-month Internet subscription (#6029101) $70.00

❏ Check enclosed*   ❏ Charge my VISA/MC/AmEx (circle one)

*Make check payable to The National Underwriter Company.
**Please include the appropriate shipping & handling charges and any applicable sales tax. (See charts above.)

Card # _____ Exp. Date _____
Name _____ Title _____
Signature _____
Company _____
Street Address _____
City _____ State _____ Zip+4 _____
Business Phone (____) _____ Fax (____) _____ email _____
❏ May we e-mail you?

NO POSTAGE
NECESSARY
IF MAILED
IN THE
UNITED STATES

BUSINESS REPLY MAIL
FIRST-CLASS MAIL   PERMIT NO. 68   CINCINNATI, OH

POSTAGE WILL BE PAID BY ADDRESSEE

ORDERS DEPARTMENT #2-BB
THE NATIONAL UNDERWRITER CO.
P.O. BOX 14448
CINCINNATI, OH 45250-9786

NO POSTAGE
NECESSARY
IF MAILED
IN THE
UNITED STATES

BUSINESS REPLY MAIL
FIRST-CLASS MAIL   PERMIT NO. 68   CINCINNATI, OH

POSTAGE WILL BE PAID BY ADDRESSEE

ORDERS DEPARTMENT #2-BB
THE NATIONAL UNDERWRITER CO.
P.O. BOX 14448
CINCINNATI, OH 45250-9786